Global 1979

The Iranian Revolution of 1979 not only had an impact on regional and international affairs, but was made possible by the world and time in which it unfolded. This multidisciplinary volume presents this revolution within its transnational and global contexts. Moving deftly from the personal to the global and from the provincial to the national, it draws attention to the multiplicity of spaces of the revolution such as streets, schools, prisons, personal lives, and histories such as the Cold War and Global 1960s and 1970s. With a broad range of approaches, *Global 1979* conceives of the Iranian Revolution not as exceptional or anachronistic, but as an uprising constituted by multiple, interwoven geographies and histories, which disrupt static and bounded notions of the local, national, regional, and global.

ARANG KESHAVARZIAN is Associate Professor of Middle Eastern and Islamic Studies at New York University. He is the author of *Bazaar and State in Iran: The Politics of the Tehran Marketplace* (2007). His articles have been published in journals including *Politics and Society*, the *International Journal of Middle East Studies*, *Geopolitics*, *Economy and Society*, and the *International Journal of Urban and Regional Research*. He is currently a member of the editorial committee of *Middle East Report* (MERIP).

ALI MIRSEPASSI is Albert Gallatin Research Excellence Professor of Middle Eastern and Islamic Studies and Director of the Iranian Studies Initiative at New York University. From 2007 to 2009, he was a Carnegie Scholar. He is the co-editor, with Arshin Adib-Moghaddam, of The Global Middle East, a book series published by Cambridge University Press. His most recent publication is *Iran's Quiet Revolution: The Downfall of the Pahlavi State* (2019).

The Global Middle East

General Editors

Arshin Adib-Moghaddam, *SOAS, University of London*
Ali Mirsepassi, *New York University*

Editorial Advisory Board

Faisal Devji, *University of Oxford*
John Hobson, *University of Sheffield*
Firoozeh Kashani-Sabet, *University of Pennsylvania*
Madawi Al-Rasheed, *London School of Economics and Political Science*
David Ryan, *University College Cork, Ireland*

The Global Middle East series seeks to broaden and deconstruct the geographical boundaries of the "Middle East" as a concept to include North Africa, Central and South Asia, and diaspora communities in Western Europe and North America. The series features fresh scholarship that employs theoretically rigorous and innovative methodological frameworks resonating across relevant disciplines in the humanities and the social sciences. In particular, the general editors welcome approaches that focus on mobility, the erosion of nation-state structures, travelling ideas and theories, transcendental techno-politics, the decentralization of grand narratives, and the dislocation of ideologies inspired by popular movements. The series will also consider translations of works by authors in these regions whose ideas are salient to global scholarly trends but have yet to be introduced to the Anglophone academy.

Other Books in the Series

Global 1979

Geographies and Histories of the Iranian Revolution

Edited by

ARANG KESHAVARZIAN
New York University

ALI MIRSEPASSI
New York University

CAMBRIDGE
UNIVERSITY PRESS

CAMBRIDGE
UNIVERSITY PRESS

University Printing House, Cambridge CB2 8BS, United Kingdom

One Liberty Plaza, 20th Floor, New York, NY 10006, USA

477 Williamstown Road, Port Melbourne, VIC 3207, Australia

314–321, 3rd Floor, Plot 3, Splendor Forum, Jasola District Centre,
New Delhi – 110025, India

103 Penang Road, #05–06/07, Visioncrest Commercial, Singapore 238467

Cambridge University Press is part of the University of Cambridge.

It furthers the University's mission by disseminating knowledge in the pursuit of
education, learning, and research at the highest international levels of excellence.

www.cambridge.org
Information on this title: www.cambridge.org/9781108839075
DOI: 10.1017/9781108979658

© Arang Keshavarzian and Ali Mirsepassi 2021

First published 2021

A catalogue record for this publication is available from the British Library.

ISBN 978-1-108-83907-5 Hardback
ISBN 978-1-108-96974-1 Paperback

For Sahar, Shadi, Leo, and Minu

Contents

Figures

Tables

Contributors

MARYAM ALEMZADEH is Postdoctoral Research Associate at the Sharmin and Bijan Mossavar-Rahmani Center for Iran and Persian Gulf Studies at Princeton University. She holds a PhD in sociology from the University of Chicago (2018), and has previously worked as a junior fellow at the Crown Center for Middle East Studies, Brandeis University. Her research is focused on the formation of the Islamic Revolutionary Guards Corps after the Iranian Revolution. She has published academic and policy papers in the *British Journal of Middle Eastern Studies* and *Foreign Affairs* magazine, among other places.

ARASH DAVARI is Assistant Professor of Politics at Whitman College. He holds a PhD in political science from the University of California, Los Angeles. His research and teaching interests include modern political theory; history and theory; aesthetics and politics; postcolonial political theory; and state formation and social change in the Middle East, with a focus on modern Iran. In 2013, he cofounded *Blta'arof*, a print journal for Iranian arts and writings. His work is forthcoming or has appeared in *Comparative Studies of South Asia, Africa and the Middle East*, *Political Theory*, the *International Journal of Middle East Studies*, and *Comparative Islamic Studies*, among other venues.

CHRISTOPHER DIETRICH is Associate Professor of History and Director of American Studies at Fordham University. He specializes in US diplomatic history, the history of twentieth-century American political thought, and the history of international politics, including the oil industry. His first book is *Oil Revolution* (Cambridge University Press, 2017). He has published several essays on globalization, the war on terror, the 1970s energy crisis, anti-colonialism, oil, the Middle East, and US foreign relations in journals such as *Diplomacy*

& Statecraft, The International History Review, Itinerario, Humanity, and *Diplomatic History.*

RASMUS CHRISTIAN ELLING is Associate Professor at the University of Copenhagen, Denmark, where he teaches Middle Eastern studies and global urban studies. He is the author of *Minorities in Iran: Ethnicity and Nationalism after Khomeini* (Palgrave Macmillan, 2013) and, in Danish, *Modern History of Iran* (Gyldendal, 2019). His current research focuses on the modern histories of Abadan and Tehran.

HOSSEIN KAMALY holds the Imam Ali Chair in Shia Studies and Dialog among Islamic Schools of Thought at the Hartford Seminary. Before obtaining his PhD in history from Columbia University, he earned an MSc in mathematics from New York University. Kamaly is interested in the history and philosophy of science, mathematics, and technology. Between 2000 and 2017, he taught in various capacities at the City University of New York, Columbia University, and Barnard College. He is the author of *God and Man in Tehran: Contending Visions of the Divine from the Qajars to the Islamic Republic* (Columbia University Press, 2018) and *A History of Islam in 21 Women* (Oneworld, 2020), and currently working on several projects, including a monograph entitled *Giving Voice to Scripture: Tafsir in the Imami Shia Tradition.*

ARANG KESHAVARZIAN is Associate Professor of Middle Eastern and Islamic Studies at New York University. He is the author of *Bazaar and State in Iran: The Politics of the Tehran Marketplace* (Cambridge University Press, 2007). He has published articles on the political economy and history of Iran, the Persian Gulf, and the broader Middle East in journals including *Politics and Society,* the *International Journal of Middle East Studies, Geopolitics, Economy and Society,* and the *International Journal of Urban and Regional Research.* He is currently a member of the editorial committee of *Middle East Report* (MERIP).

ALI MIRSEPASSI is Albert Gallatin Research Excellence Professor of Middle Eastern and Islamic Studies and Director of the Iranian Studies Initiative at New York University. Mirsepassi was a 2007–2009

Carnegie Scholar and is the coeditor, with Arshin Adib-Moghaddam, of The Global Middle East, a book series published by Cambridge University Press. He is the author of, among others, *Transnationalism in Iranian Political Thought: The Life and Thought of Ahmad Fardid* (Cambridge University Press, 2017), *Iran's Troubled Modernity: Debating Ahmad Fardid's Legacy* (Cambridge University Press, 2018), and *Iran's Quiet Revolution: The Downfall of the Pahlavi State* (Cambridge University Press, 2019).

MANIJEH MORADIAN is Assistant Professor of Women's, Gender, and Sexuality Studies at Barnard College, Columbia University. She received her PhD in American studies from NYU and her MFA in creative nonfiction from Hunter College, City University of New York. She is the former codirector of the Association of Iranian American Writers. Her first book, *This Flame Within: Iranian Revolutionaries in the United States*, is forthcoming from Duke University Press. Her essays and articles have appeared in *The Routledge Handbook of the Global Sixties*, *Scholar and Feminist Online*, *Women's Studies Quarterly*, *Comparative Studies of South Asian, Africa, and the Middle East*, *Social Text Online*, jadaliyya .com, and *Callaloo*. She is a founding member of the Raha Iranian Feminist Collective.

NEGAR MOTTAHEDEH teaches media studies in the Program in Literature at Duke University. Her research on film, social media, and social movements in the Middle East has been published by Stanford University Press, Syracuse University Press, Palgrave, and Duke University Press, as well as in *WIRED* magazine, salon.com, *The Hill*, and *The Observer*. Her work on the global culture of memes and selfies has been featured at the Victoria and Albert Museum in London, at the Museum of the Moving Image in New York, and at TEDx. Her most recent book is entitled *Whisper Tapes: Kate Millett in Iran* (Stanford University Press, 2019). Mottahedeh holds a PhD in comparative studies in discourse and society from the University of Minnesota.

GOLNAR NIKPOUR is Assistant Professor of History at Dartmouth College, and holds a PhD from Columbia University's Department of Middle Eastern, South Asian, and African Studies. From 2015 to 2017,

Nikpour was A. W. Mellon Postdoctoral Fellow at the Center for the Humanities at the University of Wisconsin, Madison, and in 2017–2018, she served as Neubauer Junior Research Fellow at the Crown Center for Middle East Studies, Brandeis University. Her research has been supported by the Social Science Research Council, the A. W. Mellon Foundation, and the Giles Whiting Foundation. She is currently finishing her first book, *The Incarcerated Modern: Prisons and Public Life in Iran*, a study of prisons and punishment in nineteenth-to-twenty-first-century Iran that situates the expansion of Iran's modern prison system in the context of the global expansion of incarceration. Nikpour serves on the editorial collective of the journal *Radical History Review* and on the editorial boards for the *Jadaliyya Iran Page* and the Radical Histories of the Middle East series on Oneworld Press. She is also cofounder and coeditor of *B|ta'arof*, a journal for Iranian arts and writing.

NAGHMEH SOHRABI is the Charles (Corky) Goodman Professor of Middle East History and Director for Research at the Crown Center for Middle East Studies, Brandeis University. She is the author of *Taken for Wonder: Nineteenth-Century Travel Accounts from Iran to Europe* (Oxford University Press, 2012) and articles in the *International Journal of Middle East Studies* and *History Compass*. For her second book on the Iranian Revolution, she has been a recipient of the A. W. Mellon New Directions Fellowship, the American Council for Learned Society Fellowship, the Berlin Prize Fellowship from the American Academy in Berlin, and a corecipient of a Mellon-Sawyer Seminar in Comparative Revolutions. She is the President of the Association for Iranian Studies, 2020–2022.

HAMED YOUSEFI is a filmmaker and PhD candidate in art history at Northwestern University. He researches interactions between modern art, Islam, and 'erfan (Iranian-Islamic mysticism) in the late twentieth century. His writings have appeared in numerous publications in English and Persian including *e-flux* and *Herfeh: Honarmand*, and in exhibition catalogs by the Metropolitan Museum of Art, Grey Art Gallery (NYU), and MAXXI (Rome), among others. As a filmmaker, he has made a series of essay-films on the aesthetic history of the Islamic Republic and, most recently, a feature-length documentary called *The Fabulous Life and Thought of Ahmad Fardid* (with Ali Mirsepassi).

Acknowledgments

This volume is the product of two workshops we organized in 2019 for the fortieth anniversary of the Iranian Revolution. The first was held at New York University in May 2019, and the second at Columbia University in December 2019. These two-day events were generously supported by a number of institutions at both universities that we would like to recognize. At NYU we thank the Gallatin School for Individualized Study, the Iranian Studies Initiative, Center for the Humanities, Kevorkian Center for Near Eastern Studies, Global Research Initiatives of the Office of the Provost, and the Department of Middle Eastern and Islamic Studies. The second workshop and conference was made possible by contributions from Columbia University's Middle East Institute, Institute for Religion, Culture, and Public Life, and the Ehsan Yarshater Center for Iranian Studies. We also appreciate funding from the Persian Heritage Foundation. We are grateful for the support and assistance of Atefeh Akbari Shahmirzadi, Hamid Dabashi, Carolyn Dinshaw, Lynette Hacopian, Fidel Harfouche, Allison Jungkurth, Marion Katz, Brinkley Messick, Manijeh Moradian, Marianna Pecoraro, James Ryan, Greta Scharnweber, Tandi Singh, and Helga Tawil-Souri.

Discussions at these workshops not only informed the individual chapters in this collection, but were invaluable in calibrating the intellectual compass of our project and the opportunities and limitations in approaching the 1979 revolution from a global perspective. We were fortunate to have the active participation and feedback of colleagues and students who attended one or both of the workshops. We acknowledge with much gratitude Ervand Abrahamian, Roham Alvandi, Arash Azizi, Hamid Dabashi, Mehdi Faraji, Yalda Hamidi, Firoozeh Kashani-Sabet, Setrag Manoukian, Bita Mousavi, Brian Plungis, Leila Pourtavaf, Saira Rafiee, Nasrin Rahimieh, Golbarg Rekabtalaei, Saharnaz Samaeinejad, Atefeh Akbari Shahmirzadi, Shahla Talebi, and Omid Tofighian.

At Cambridge University Press, Maria Marsh expressed enthusiastic interest in the book from the outset and offered professional and diligent support throughout the publishing process. Atifa Jiwa, Muhammad Ridwaan, and Natasha Whelan seamlessly shepherded the manuscript through the production stages.

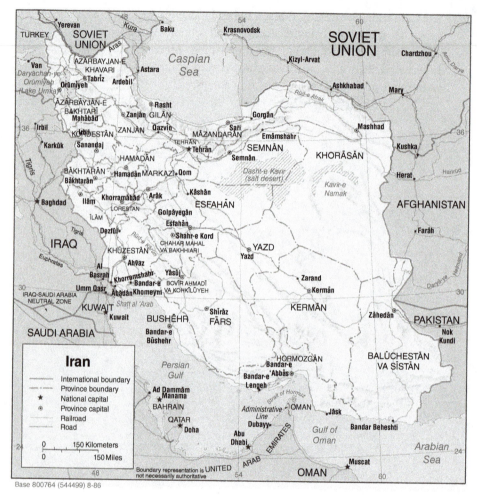

Figure 0.1 Map of Iran.

Source: Adapted from a map courtesy of the General Libraries, The University of Texas at Austin.

Orientations

Introduction

ARANG KESHAVARZIAN AND
ALI MIRSEPASSI

In that unbounded moment, I saw millions of delightful and horrible acts; none amazed me as the fact that all occupied the same point, without superposition and without transparency. What my eyes saw was *simultaneous*; what I shall write is *successive*, because language is successive. Something of it, though, I will capture.

Jorge Luis Borges, *The Alpeh*[1]

The men and women that made the 1979 Iranian Revolution were of their time and place. We could not expect them to be otherwise, short of certain arguments that they were "guided by the eternal." As researchers, we face a similar predicament of spatial and temporal specificity. Yet, neither time nor space are isolated; they become meaningful analytical categories when "made" in relation to larger social processes interconnecting times and places.

Despite being drawn from diverse disciplinary backgrounds and theoretical persuasions, the contributors to this volume all share one condition; they live and write about Iran's revolution and the founding of the Islamic Republic with over four decades of reflection, hindsight, and reappraisal of causes and consequences. This expanding time horizon distances us from the events and emotions leading to the fall of the Pahlavi monarchy and founding of the Islamic Republic. Such separation may enable deeper appraisal. It may permit examining a wider array of archives and a broader recovery of the forces involved in mobilizing people for mass rallies, coordinating strikes and bazaar closures, and articulating political demands in party pamphlets and public statements. This additional time, however, does not necessarily

---

[1] Jorge Luis Borges, *The Aleph and Other Stories: 1933–1969*, trans. and ed. Norman Thomas Di Giovanni (New York: Bantam Books 1970), 13.

3

guarantee either certainty or consensus. Yet, the creeping doubts and speculations can "contribute to the possibility of understanding."[2]

This volume, too, is a product of its intellectual time and place. It therefore must contend with the challenges of synthesizing our contemporary concerns with those of the people and places integral to making the revolution possible. We write about the making of 1979 at our own specific historical conjuncture. To begin with, draconian US sanctions make the everyday lives of Iranians arduous and erect barriers to the circulation of people, commodities, and ideas. Secondly, the Islamic Republic's ideological filters shaping its foreign policy together with the securitization of domestic politics have mediated Iran's place in international society in ways that deter exchange and collaboration. In academia, the social sciences and humanities have gone through more than a quarter century of being deeply marked with popular and intellectual interest in globalization, cosmopolitanism, and transnational connectivity and mobility.[3] In the process, methodological debates and initiatives have grappled with the task of writing global history, designing multi-sited ethnographies, and defining the relationship between the local and the global, the particular and the universal, or the authentic native and external other. The thrust has been to decenter nationalist historiography, if not to move against "methodological nationalism."[4] With this context in mind, we envision the making of the Iranian Revolution not as a byproduct of globalization,

---

[2] Albert O. Hirschman, "The Search for Paradigms as a Hindrance to Understanding," *World Politics* 22:3 (1970): 333.

[3] See, inter alia, Luis Eduardo Guarnizo and Michael Peter Smith, "Locations of Transnationalism," in Michael Peter Smith and Luis Eduardo Guarnizo, eds., *Transnationalism from Below* (New Brunswick, NJ: Transaction Publishers, 1998), 3–34; Anna Tsing, "The Global Situation," *Cultural Anthropology* 15:3 (August 2000): 327–360; Frederick Cooper, *Colonialism in Question: Theory, Knowledge, History* (Berkeley, CA: University of California Press, 2005), 91–112; James Ferguson, *Global Shadows* (Durham, NC: Duke University Press, 2006); C. A. Bayly, Sven Beckert, Matthew Connelly, Isabel Hofmeyr, Wendy Kozol, and Patricia Seed, "*AHR* Conversation: On Transnational History," *The American Historical Review* 111:5 (December 2006): 1441–1464; Samuel Moyn and Andrew Sartori, eds., *Global Intellectual History* (New York: Columbia University Press, 2013); Engseng Ho, "Inter-Asian Concepts for Mobile Societies," *The Journal of Asian Studies* 76:4 (November 2017): 907–928; Neil Brenner, "Beyond State-Centerism? Space, Territoriality, and Geographical Scale in Globalization Studies," *Theory and Society* 28:1 (February 1999): 39–78.

[4] Andreas Wimmer and Nina Glick Schiller, "Methodological Nationalism and Beyond," *Global Networks* 2:4 (2002): 301–334.

nor merely a local or national phenomenon, but as an expression of the wide interconnectedness shaping a radically unequal and disjointed, yet inextricably interrelated world of simultaneities.

What happens if we begin to consider Iran's revolutionary processes and situation as simultaneously part of a global phenomenon? As we enter the fifth decade of the Islamic Republic, this volume sets this as its task, to treat the global as neither preceding nor succeeding the revolution. This requires consideration of how those political movements, which targeted the Pahlavi monarchy and mobilized the nation, intersected with and even coproduced different versions of world society, be it *jahan*, *dunya*, or *bayn ol-mellali* in Persian, or the international, universal, postcolonial, the Third World, planetary, and more. In doing so, this collection of essays poses new questions, revisits archives, and articulates new chronologies and temporalities. Our energies are less focused on understanding the revolution in terms of causes and outcomes, something that the existing literature has done with much vigor. Instead, the collection is centered on examining the revolution as an intricate process filled with contingencies, dialogical interplays, and foreclosed pathways. This is an emergent approach that maintains that "the revolution as simultaneously multiple things, all of which contained multiple contingencies, and thus as a contingency-filled phenomenon, its post-revolutionary future was not easily borne out of its revolutionary present – highlighting aspects of the history that are marginalized, ignored, or remain unwritten."[5]

* * *

The scholarship conducted in proximity to the 1979 revolution was the product of the academic and intellectual life of the 1970s and 1980s in two senses. On the one hand, much of the English-language scholarship on the revolution to come out in the immediate aftermath of the uprising was written by young faculty and graduate students working on Iran in the US or UK prior to the revolution. These were research projects written in parallel or close proximity to the events themselves. These books and articles, published between 1979 and 1990, were primarily inspired by approaches, methodologies, and questions of the English-speaking scholarly community and strong convictions about

---

[5] Naghmeh Sohrabi, "The 'Problem Space' of the Historiography of the 1979 Iranian Revolution," *History Compass* 16:11 (2018): 1.

what were the indispensable rudiments for good theory. Much of the scholarly works published immediately following the revolution were guided by and framed within two principal scholarly traditions defining the time: the social scientific tradition and the humanistic approach.

The *social scientific tradition* of the late 1970s was composed of assorted academic disciplines and worldviews which shared an elective affinity through their commitment to positivist methodology to decipher societies and people. These studies included modernization theory, dependency theory, and political economy approaches. These notable scholarly traditions were deployed in Iranian studies as much as scholarship on other parts of the Middle East, South Asia, Latin American, and elsewhere. They were the defining trends in European and American academic environments. Modernization theory was very much concerned with measuring the degree of accommodation and resistance to "Westernization" by "traditional societies," while Marxist-influenced works adopted capitalism as the benchmark to evaluate Iran's "feudal society."[6] This social scientific tradition labored to demonstrate how modern institutions (capitalism, representative government) and ideas (labor movements, liberalism, communism, etc.) had already been established and rooted through social development.[7]

The political economy approach defining the Marxist framework provided analysis of class interests and the nature of the state, as well as the formation of social movements.[8] Some of these works on class also theorized global capitalism and imperialism in innovative and sophisticated ways. Other works were influenced by important academic debates about modernization, such as the criticisms advanced by

[6] Abbas Vali, *Pre-capitalist Iran: A Theoretical History* (London: I.B. Tauris, 1993).

[7] Amin Banani, *The Modernization of Iran, 1921–1941* (Stanford, CA: Stanford University Press, 1961); Marvin Zonis, *The Political Elite of Iran* (Princeton, NJ: Princeton University Press, 1971); Leonard Binder, *Iran: Political Development in a Changing Society* (Berkeley, CA: University of California Press, 1964); George Lenczowski, ed., *Iran under the Pahlavis* (Stanford, CA: Hoover Institution Press, 1978).

[8] Fred Haliday, *Iran: Dictator and Development* (Harmondsworth: Penguin, 1979); Nikki R. Keddie, *Iran: Roots of Revolution* (New Haven, CT: Yale University Press, 1981); Ervand Abrahamian, *Iran between Two Revolutions* (Princeton, NJ: Princeton University Press, 1982); Hossein Bashiriyeh, *The State and Revolution in Iran, 1962–1982* (New York: St. Martin's Press, 1984).

dependency theory.[9] An important debate ensued among sociologists and others centered on Theda Skocpol's work on the nature of rentier state and the vulnerability of the Pahlavi regime. Skocpol's intervention occurred in the aftermath of the publication of her seminal work, *States and Social Revolutions*, in the same year as Iran's revolution.[10] In her examination of the Iranian Revolution she sought to argue that her structuralist approach, that revolutions are not "made," but "happened," applied to the Iranian case because the Pahlavi state's dependence on oil revenue made it institutionally vulnerable and because Shia Islam as "a world-view and a set of social practices long in place can sustain a deliberate revolutionary movement."[11]

This emphasis on the role of Shia Islam in the revolution echoed the second approach to the revolution among this first generation of scholarship, that is, the *humanistic scholarship* on Iran and Islam. The time-honored tradition of scholarship on Iranian "classical" culture (religions, literature, and philosophy) enjoyed a much longer history in the Western academy. Unsurprisingly, it received generous support from the Iranian government. The scholars of "humanity" at this time worked within the scholarly discourse pioneered in Western European societies that had built colonial empires. It was a scholarly tradition that is currently regarded – often disdainfully – as "Orientalist."[12] This convention was predisposed to privileging the study of canonical texts, while taking an interest in questions already raised and framed by European scholars. It gave almost sole attention to the premodern period while remaining dismissive toward studies of the modern history and culture of Iran.[13] This is not to suggest that the

---

[9] John Foran, *Fragile Resistance: Social Transformation in Iran from 1500 to the Revolution* (Boulder, CO: Westview Press, 1993), and *Taking Power: On the Origins of Third World Revolutions* (Cambridge: Cambridge University Press, 2005).

[10] Theda Skocpol, *States and Social Revolutions: A Comparative Analysis of France, Russia, and China* (Cambridge: Cambridge University Press, 1979).

[11] Theda Skocpol, "Rentier State and Shi'a Islam in the Iranian Revolution," *Theory and Society* 11:3 (May 1982): 276.

[12] Interestingly, Edward Said's now classic critique of this scholarly tradition was published at the same time as the Iranian Revolution: Edward Said, *Orientalism* (New York: Vintage Books, 1978). Said applied this line of analysis to media coverage of the Iranian Revolution in *Covering Islam: How the Media and the Experts Determine How We See the Rest of the World* (New York: Pantheon Books, 1981).

[13] Henri Corban and Hossein Nasr are two well-known scholars.

scholars of Iranian "classics" were a homogeneous group. Although their approaches and questions were often alike, they clashed on certain issues. Some insisted on an epistemic endurance in Iranian history and culture, stemming from the ancient (pre-Islamic) to the post-Islamic period. They also imagined Iranian culture as an embodiment of the Zoroastrian and Islamic traditions, contending that Iranian culture had substantially contributed to the formation of Islamic civilization. Others fashioned a rather harsh way of thinking about Islam and its relations to Iranian history and culture. They deemed Islam an alien influence upon Iranian culture, critiquing it as almost a colonizer's burden and imposition. They therefore studied the search for the "recovery" of the genuine Iranian culture, untainted by Islam.[14]

Against such established conventions, however, the 1979 revolution suddenly exploded many accepted assumptions. The revolution perhaps marked the starting point for a major transformation of what had been known as Iranian studies until 1979. The "classicists" and social scientific scholars of Iran all at once realized that theory could no longer support their "disciplinary territories." The securely mapped academic boundaries began to unfurl and throw open an unfamiliar epistemic terrain. What had seemed so clear, stable, and routinely taken for granted, now became yesterday's scattered debris. The social scientists were forced to study ideas and institutions of a reality they had "normally" considered of a different time and even world in "modernizing" Iran.[15] Similarly, the Orientalist scholars, perhaps more willingly, started to think and write about what appeared to them as a contemporary reincarnation of "medieval" Iranian Islam.[16]

Many of the symbolic representations of the revolution, including Shia rituals and ulama rhetoric, were familiar to classicist scholars of

[14] A notable example is Aramesh Doustdar's writings: *Emtena' e tafakkor dar farhang dini* [The impossibility of religious thinking] (Paris: Khavaran Publication, 1994) and *Derakhshesh hay-e tire* [Dark sparkles] (Cologne, Germany: Andishe Azad Publication, 1993).

[15] Michael M. J. Fischer, *Iran: From Religious Dispute to Revolution* (Cambridge, MA: Harvard University Press, 1980).

[16] One early reaction to the rise of political Islam was an attempt to see it as a delusional or even "made-up" dream presented as reality; see Daryush Shayegan, *Qu'est-ce qu'une révolution religieuse?* (Paris: Albin Michel, 1991), and *Le regard mutilé, Schizophrénie culturelle: pays traditionnels face à la modernité* (Paris: Albin Michel, 1982), translated as Daryush Shayegan, *Cultural Schizophrenia: Islamic Societies Confronting the West* (Syracuse, NY: Syracuse University Press, 1997).

Iran and Shia Islam. However, the idea that Islam (either in its doctrinal Sharia or mystical variety) could become an agent of radical change and political transformation was unthinkable for them. Henri Corbin was perhaps a prophetic Orientalist scholar who dreamed of such a revolutionary event. He died on October 7, 1978, thereby leaving us without his thoughts on the revolutionary unfolding. Nevertheless, one of the most interesting cultural explanations of the 1979 revolution was written by a historian of early Islam, Roy Mottahedeh. He has authored only a single book on modern Iran;[17] however, it is a fascinating narrative on several dualities intersecting in modern Iranian society. He suggested that sharp dualities had become familiar and rooted in the cultural, moral, and political experience of Iranians. These would sooner or later replace the superficially modern state. The Iranian masses, Mottahedeh argued, had never really felt that Pahlavi modernity welcomed them. It had no harmonious relationship with their everyday world. On the whole, the humanist studies of Iran focused on unearthing the "Idea of Iran" as they understood it. They either evaded attention to serious study of modern Iran, or they presented contemporary Iranian society as "a lost nation" in search of the vanished cultural identity.

The earlier scholarly literature on Iran primarily considered its history and culture as insular. The social scientific studies paid some attention to Iran's links to other regions and histories as a means to substantiate a universal model, but the humanist scholarship either treated Iran as a distinctive cultural unit or deemed it as part of a larger civilizational formation, such as Shiism or Islam. The scholars whose contributions are contained in this volume have been fortunate to study with and learn from many of the pioneering scholars of postrevolutionary Iranian studies. This volume presents a conversation with the scholarly productions passed down by this crucial generation as well as others.

* * *

We began this project with a conference in which the participants were asked to reflect upon the Iranian Revolution as "the Global 1979." The global was not an answer but a question; it was not a destination,

---

[17] Roy Mottahedeh, *The Mantle of the Prophet: Religion and Politics in Iran* (New York: Simon and Schuster, 1985).

but a pathway. It was an invitation to think through the disparate and intricate events that culminated in radical social transformation by locating it within what is often now referred to as "the global." These events, however, were conceived quite differently in the years preceding the fall of the monarchy and the building of the Islamic Republic.

The responses we received to this provocation and our subsequent discussions constitute the substance of this book. Using different methods, theoretical tools, and archives, the authors have explored both more commonly studied topics, including US-Iran relations, leftist politics, and the women's movement, as well as often forgotten moments or ignored spaces. These include the death of a popular wrestler, politicization in provincial towns, and struggles over the meaning of guerrilla warfare before and after the revolution. They plumb the depths of these and other topics to draw previously hidden geographies and temporalities integral to creating the conditions for the fall of the Pahlavi monarchy and the founding of the Islamic Republic. What is at stake is not a theory of the revolution, but rather articulating a narrative of the revolution that centers on multiplicity and simultaneity of social relations and spaces that coexisted in the contingent-filled messiness of the revolution, or what Borges describes as witnessing the simultaneity of the "unbounded moment."

Similarly, the collection does not insist on a single conception of the global as either a place, a contemporary era, a model, or a yearning. The global is conceived, instead, as drawing together new relationships between spaces and events. These chapters insist on historicizing the revolution in ways that are contemporaneous with a series of other struggles and transformations. Thinking globally does not mean that the national, local, and fragment are demoted or even erased. Globality, on the contrary, heightens the specificities of certain places ranging from prisons and science labs to borderlands and US congressional committees, as will be illustrated in the subsequent chapters. Meanwhile, thinking about the global in this concrete manner has encouraged the authors to reconsider standard periodizations of history, unearth hidden or unthought historical episodes, and blur distinctions between regime and opposition or Islamist and secular. The authors reconceptualize geographic scales, transnational mobilities, or cosmopolitan sensibilities. This makes sense because, if one recalls that "the global" is a concept associated in recent years with the American academy,[18] we must account for alternative formations of political, social, cultural, ethical, or religious solidarity articulated at the time of the revolution. These world-making projects are only recoverable if we are attuned to the geographies and moments that remain excluded from standard accounts of the revolution.

***

Multiplicity and simultaneity are not just the theme in our discussions or the diverse perspectives inherent to any edited volume. They inform our approach to collaboration. For over a decade, we have led the Iranian Studies Initiative at New York University in organizing both public programming and intensive workshops. In these many projects we have remained committed to three principles. We have insisted on giving space to research and debates on modern Iran that strive to de-exceptionalize its history and society through engagement with theory, relational history, or comparative frameworks. Often this has taken place by bringing scholars from outside of the "Iranian studies" field to denaturalize the categories and stories we tell about Iran and the world. This does not mean that we believe in sacrificing careful engagement with specificities of Iranian history, culture, religion, and language; that would be a false choice. Secondly, we have emphasized multi- and interdisciplinarity by inviting scholars who have worked with these objectives. We have also asked our speakers to engage in conversations with discussants drawn from different fields. Finally, we have consciously created an environment in which researchers from multiple generations exchange their research. Given the challenges in the academic job market, we have sought to design concrete opportunities in which junior colleagues and graduate students can interact with each other as well as engage interlocutors who are their seniors. Having overcome challenges and moments of tension, our ongoing endeavor is to open channels of communication and collaboration across generations. This has been wanting in the field of Iranian studies due to the vicissitudes of revolution, displacement, institutional fickleness, and the academic penchant for adopting the latest approach. An example of our explicit attempt to implement these objectives was the

[18] Isaac Kamola, "Why Global? Diagnosing the Globalization Literature within a Political Economy of Higher Education," *International Political Sociology* 7:1 (2013): 41–58.

convening of a two-day junior scholars workshop in 2013. This brought together a dozen newly minted doctoral recipients and students in the final stages of their dissertation writing.[19] Not only was this an opportunity for these researchers, drawn from different disciplines and scholarly traditions on modern Iran, to present their work to each other at various stages of development, but also to share it with and receive feedback from faculty drawn from a number of local institutions.

It is with these objectives, experiences, and sensibilities that we convened the workshops that laid the foundations for this volume. As such, the authors are drawn from history, American studies, political science, art history, sociology, and interdisciplinary programs. Yet, they also represent different strands of what we conceive of as capacious understanding of writing a global history of the Iranian Revolution. While much of the scholarship on Iran that informs these chapters has been written by an older generation of researchers, a number of whom were either intimately involved in the revolutionary fomenting or proximate eyewitnesses to it, many authors are from younger generations with less immediate relations to the Pahlavi and revolutionary history. They also have had different relations with postrevolutionary Iran, the US academy, and processes that we conceive as globalism. The two of us, also, approach the question from different intellectual traditions and personal trajectories. The intellectual stakes and challenges of returning to 1979 and trans-nationalizing Iran have different valance for us. Although Keshavarzian's engagement with conducting research in and writing about Iran stretches back to the mid-1990s, he was a child during the revolution and raised predominantly outside of Iran. Mirsepassi, as he recounts in Chapter 3, is from the generation of youth who participated in the events of 1977–1979, as well as being active in Iranian politics in the late 1960s and 1970s.

Rather than hammering out a nebulous consensus or compromise in the form of a single introduction and orienting chapter, we have elected to each articulate our conceptualizations of "Global 1979" independently through two opening chapters. This allows readers to explicitly

[19] This workshop was restructured into an interuniversity initiative between New York University, Princeton University, and the University of Pennsylvania and led to two additional meetings.

see the points of convergence and departure as well as the issues that we each foreground or treat in a more cursory fashion. Readers may see how our interpretations of relevant literature and the volume's chapters differ and overlap. This introductory part will therefore move from this opening joint statement to two single-authored explanations of motivations for and insights drawn from *Global 1979*. These twinned introductions appear and will be read in succession even if they were conceived simultaneously. In this way, the remaining ten chapters in the volume are synthesized into an intellectual whole. This multiauthored volume provides an innovative platform for expanding our understandings of revolution-making and world-making.

1 | *A Quiet Revolution:*
In the Shadow of the Cold War

ALI MIRSEPASSI

The Thought and Unthought on the 1979 Revolution

Raymond Williams's approach to the complexity of "culture," focused on the interactive modes of ideas and traditions with social structures and political power, can revealingly explore the multidimensional reality of the 1979 Iranian Revolution. This chapter draws on Williams's theory of "cultural materialism" to explore the revolution through a new frame. Williams's theory of culture may help us interpret the 1979 revolution as comprising multiple visions, diverse local and national spaces, and manifold regional and global connections. Williams's concepts of "residual" and the "emergent" encompass "culture" as multiple interconnected histories and institutions.[1] While defending modern scientific progress, Williams decries confusing abstract concepts for concrete realities. This contrasts with romantic assertions that the "scientific worldview" intrinsically does violence to everyday reality. Williams's method is based on Marxist theory. It explains the relationship between culture and society, and, specifically, between literary traditions and political power. I believe revisiting Williams's idea of culture as a lived reality can provide a novel perspective on the 1979 revolution.[2]

Williams's theory of culture centers on "elements," comprising the *emergent* as the immanent moment of ceaseless and untraceable transformation. This methodical concept contrasts with obsessively *defining* the Iranian Revolution, as has characterized much work over the last several decades. Williams's "emergent" is "new meanings and values, new practices, new relationships and kinds of relationship [that] are

---

[1] Raymond Williams, *Marxism and Literature* (Oxford: Oxford University Press, 1977).
[2] I am grateful to Negar Mottahedeh for reading an earlier draft of this chapter and for suggesting Raymond Williams's approach as a suitable way to framing my overall argument.

continually being created."[3] The transnational is composed of *elements*, not totality, specific in unreproducible time and variable in assemblage, rather than an encompassing "universal" space. The "purity" of Aristotelian "definitions" contrasts with the heteroclite impurity of everyday social realities. "Elements" are relational and based on differences, not essences. Williams writes:

In authentic historical analysis it is necessary at every point to recognize the complex interrelations between movements and tendencies both within and beyond a specific and effective dominance.[4]

This short maxim usefully theorizes Iranian revolutionary complexity. Not only are events internally heterogeneous, but intrinsically linked to other events occurring elsewhere in time and space. This vision of the Iranian revolutionary "event" thematically unites this edited volume. Williams identifies two types of theories. First, there are usefully abstract fictions, as exemplified in "epochal" analysis, "feudal or bourgeois culture," emphasizing "definitive lineaments." Secondly, there is immanent analysis of cultural events through "immediate historical and internally comparative differentiation." Through the second type, "hegemony" is analyzable without constricting definition through the "differentiation of the 'residual' and the 'emergent.'" The "residual" and the "emergent" are irreducible to one definition. An elective affinity exists, for example, between culture and class as "emergent" forces, but neither are reducible to the other. Williams therefore identifies "two sources of the emergent – the class and the excluded social (human) area." The theory of "residuality," meanwhile, invokes a nonlinear theory of historical time. Williams's theory of the "residual," especially in the Iranian revolutionary context, offers a pathbreaking understanding of the role of Islam or religion. Williams contrasts the "archaic" with the "residual":

The residual, by definition, has been effectively formed in the past, but it is still active in the cultural process, not only and often not at all as an element of the past, but as an effective element of the present.[5]

Williams's insight captures the quintessence of the twisted relation between the Pahlavi dictatorship and the Islamic Republic. It also helps to explain these in relation to prior Iranian social formations through a

---

[3] Williams, *Marxism and Literature*, 123.   [4] Ibid., 121.   [5] Ibid., 122.

complex circulatory exchange of "elements." He sees organized religion having a double function, like all "residual cultural elements." It is both conservative and revolutionary. This epitomizes the Iranian experience. Islam could lend itself to upholding traditional power hierarchies, while urging the revolutionary overthrow of existing ones. Islamist political discourse was internally contradictory in terms of its diverse power functions, plural agents, and multiple ends. Iranian experience similarly confirmed Williams's thesis on the "rural community" as "residual." The Pahlavi elites and Islamists celebrated the "rural community" as a utopia to be retrieved from Western modernity. Williams recognized how, in "limited respects," the "rural community" is "alternative or oppositional to urban industrial capitalism." He concluded, however, that "for the most part it is incorporated, as idealization or fantasy, or as an exotic – residential or escape – leisure function of the dominant order itself." Williams, with Britain in mind, cites monarchy integrated into capitalist democracy as a further example of "residual cultural element." Williams's analysis of religion therefore throws important light on the 1979 Iranian Revolution:

organized religion is predominantly residual, but within this there is a significant difference between some practically alternative and oppositional meanings and values (absolute brotherhood, service to others without reward) and a larger body of incorporated meanings and values (official morality, or the social order of which the other-worldly is a separated neutralizing or ratifying component).[6]

The "residual" is distant from power, yet paradoxically also a part of it, a surrogate version of it. This not only captures how Islamism was an underground self of the Pahlavi state, but also how both operate through a logic of excluding and defining public identity and being. Williams's theory of the "emergent" and the "residual" permits us to better conceptualize the thinkable/unthought in the Iranian revolutionary "event":

there is always other social being and consciousness which is neglected and excluded: alternative perceptions of others, in immediate relationships; new perceptions and practices of the material world.[7]

The circulatory principle of the "emergent/residual" excludes total explanation: "no mode of production and therefore no dominant

[6] Ibid.   [7] Ibid., 126.

social order and therefore no dominant culture ever in reality includes or exhausts all human practice, human energy, and human intention."[8] This is because "the modes of domination ... select from and consequently exclude the full range of human practice." They exclude "the personal or the private, or the natural or even the metaphysical," while "what the dominant has effectively seized is indeed the ruling definition of the social." Williams's discussion of the "residual" therefore uses a materialist analysis (of class/social formations, and technology/mode of production) to explain how previous regimes revive as either oppositional or supporting forces for any subsequent regime. He writes that: "Any culture includes available elements of its past, but their place in the contemporary cultural process is profoundly variable."[9] Williams's core argument is deeply Marxist, based on a "mode of production," the fundamentally "relational" nature of nonessential social reality, and a certain dialectics in which the regime is its own gravedigger. Yet, Williams has subtly transformed these Marxist concepts into a radical theory which envisions a certain autonomy for culture from class, without romanticizing it as a "supernatural" force eluding the material realities of societies.

Williams's theory contrasts with those sociologists and political scientists who have almost endlessly searched for the one appropriate way, within the disciplinary limits of the social sciences, to "understand" the Iranian Revolution in a definitely final but "special" way – perhaps because of the role of religion and what has been regularly imagined as an anti-modern or postmodern "surprise." An approach to the 1979 Iranian Revolution based on Williams's materialist theory of culture may be helpful.

The obsession with a unifying "definition" to solve the "mystery" of the 1979 Iranian Revolution has been noted by Charles Kurzman, who acknowledges how much theorization of 1979 has been constructed upon thin air:

More than fifty books, and more than 100 academic articles, have appeared in English alone dealing in significant part with the Iranian revolutionary movement. This impressive output, published in just 15 years, does not reflect a similarly copious wealth of source materials. In fact, the study of the Iranian revolutionary movement is largely, one might argue, sound and fury, a lot of grand theorizing lacking a solid empirical basis.[10]

---

[8] Ibid., 125.   [9] Ibid., 122.
[10] Charles Kurzman, "Historiography of the Iranian Revolutionary Movement, 1977–79," *Iranian Studies* 28:1–2 (Winter–Spring 1995): 25.

In the spirit of Williams's theory, the following are my reflections on the Iranian Revolution of 1979 and the works in this edited volume. The discussion of the various contributions made by scholars on this subject are defined by a unified problematic, while also offering a diversity of perspectives in this methodologically rich collection of writings on the prerevolutionary decades. The contributions engage what Edward Said called "the crisis in the history of Western thought about dealings with the Orient," while also going beyond this "Western crisis" to rethink contemporary *transnational* landscapes marked by histories of empire and resistance.[11] The West is no longer the center. We accordingly pursue the following question: How can one write a local history of a major event, while considering trans-national ideas and forces, and thereby also undertaking a global his-tory? The challenge is in telling the "local" or "national" stories in a meaningful way, while also reflecting global dynamics in local experi-ences. In the 1979 Iranian Revolution, this task requires study of the lived experiences of those participants who struggled for and eventu-ally made the revolution. Initially, the global should not be imagined as a self-contained universe, embodying all historical occurrences within a unifying totality. We cannot assume a meta-history that creates the local by a cold logic from above. On the contrary, the local or national may indeed shape and transform the global. We might, therefore, understand the global as the space where the local engages catalytically in intellectual exchange and institutional processes, making possible the passage between multiple places. The result is, fascinatingly, nei-ther purely local nor trans-local. It may be more helpful to think of the global as a "third space" of complex connections and exchanges. What really matters, then, is the relative power configurations defining these multiple relationships.

Iran in the 1960s and 1970s, as a social reality, was open to the global flows of ideas. Meanwhile, it also remained the site of a quiet but profound revolution. This "quiet revolution" transpired in relative occlusion from the outside world, while paradoxically interacting with its major forces. This overlooked revolution was rooted in Iran's own political history, while constructing meaning through transnational exchanges of people and ideas. The Iranian "quiet revolution" evolved in the Cold War shadow. To fully understand and appreciate the

---

[11] Edward Said, *Orientalism* (New York: Vintage, 1994), 104.

global aspects of the 1979 Iranian Revolution, we must first critically study the characteristics of the "quiet revolution" in its intimate connections under the pressures of the Cold War.[12]

Initially, we should distinguish between the wider Global 1979 phenomenon and the revolution as a global event. I argue that the revolutionary event was not a global one, in the sense of being universal or the product of globalization. Nor was the revolution necessarily a new template for rest of the world. Those who participated, in their inspirations and aims, were diverse. Among them were nativists, liberal nationalists, Islamists, and socialists. In nearly all cases, participants were rooted in the Iranian national history of recent decades, while also inspired by various ideas and social movements partaking of the global 1960s and 1970s. These included Third Worldism, anti-imperialism, communism, and Islamic identity, all of which emerged in the Cold War environment. It may therefore be more appropriate to describe the 1979 revolution as "emergent" in relation to the Cold War global exchange of ideas, people, and political aspirations. It created something new that drew deeply from multiple "residual cultural elements," in a circulatory interaction of secular revolutionary currents, religious traditions, and global pressures.

Most scholars, we should remember, have looked at the Iranian Revolution as exemplifying Iranian exceptionalism. Either the revolution was very specific to Iran's recent political history (US intervention in 1953, Pahlavi authoritarian modernization), or it expressed a uniquely Iranian Shia tradition. Over the past four decades, analysis of the revolution has been constricted to the national frame. Scholars have mapped opposition actors or the Pahlavi apparatus, while considering institutional strength or weakness ("the rentier state," "mosque networks," or leftist parties). Even approaches seeking to foreground Islamism as a discursive tradition have slipped into Iranian exceptionalism: Shia Islamic peculiarities, clerical leadership, and Ruhollah Khomeini as a charismatic figure. In other instances, Islamic ideas were woven into fashionable postmodern conceptions of native authenticity. For the structuralist tradition, Iran's place was

---

[12] For a detailed study of Iranian cultural politics in the 1960s and 1970s, see Ali Mirsepassi, *The Quiet Revolution: Downfall of the Pahlavi State* (Cambridge: Cambridge University Press, 2019).

traced within the international capitalist matrix or US regional hegemony. Even here, Iran is treated as a single "national" unit.

Many scholars, either intentionally or implicitly, have deployed the
Iranian exceptionalist framework: linking the rise of the Islamic
Republic to Iranian Islam (Shiism), or indicating a unique continuity
joining pre-Islamic elements to the Islamic period and modern Iran.[13]
Others, in a social scientific framing, have reproduced a mysterious
version of Iranian exceptionalism in declaring the revolution "unthinkable," or impervious to "rational explanation or understanding."[14]
Even the prominent thinker Michel Foucault has clearly hinted at
Iranian exceptionalism. Foucault and his many followers excitedly
present the 1979 revolution as a grand new experiment for the "postmodern" age, a "spiritual" or "mystical" phenomenon. By this
account, it is a mysterious social event only possible within the
unique Iranian situation. It is a passing miracle that we must remember
and revere.[15]

Framing the 1979 Revolution

The existing scholarly literature on the Iranian Revolution falls short of
fully appreciating the *contemporaneity* of the revolution as an experience for the Iranians. That is, the Iranian Revolution as a "transnational" social and political event, as experienced by Iranians. The
contemporaneity and transnational quality of the experience embed
the revolution in the preceding two decades of widespread cultural
transfiguration at every social level, in the "quiet revolution." The
"quiet revolution" itself cannot be understood except in terms of a
circulatory system of flows of people and ideas between Iran, the West,
the Middle East, and Asia, and other countries like the Soviet Union
and those in Latin America.

---

[13] The idea was coined by Henry Corbin and now has become popularized by
some Islamic intellectuals and political figures associated with former president
Mahmoud Ahmadinejad.
[14] Behrooz Ghamari-Tabrizi, *Foucault in Iran: Islamic Revolution after the
Enlightenment* (Minneapolis, MN: University of Minnesota Press, 2016), 2–16.
[15] Ali Mirsepassi, *Transnationalism in Iranian Political Thought: The Life and
Thought of Ahmad Fardid* (Cambridge: Cambridge University Press, 2017),
chapter 6.

Three tendencies predominate in "framing" the 1979 revolution:

(1) *The circular argument*: all that happened prior to the rise of the Islamic Republic is read as an inevitable passage to its establishment by the Shia clerics. This approach "disremembers" the distinct everyday life textures, or the lifeworld that provides the possibility for understanding the revolution as a phenomenon of human meaning. This teleological argument invokes supra-objective stages. Cruder versions of Marxism sometimes fall within the same trap.

(2) *The social scientific heights*: a universal key is sought to explain all revolutions, which will reveal pristine causes, transcending the local, and permitting a scientific power to prophesy future revolutions. This approach also relegates everyday meanings to the domain of the trivial. These sophisticated perspectives tend to quarrel among one another, each asserting the other has missed a crucial – or *the* crucial – piece of a mind-boggling puzzle.

(3) *Revolutionary spirits as method*: this is the scholarly error that Francois Furet warned us about regarding the French Revolution.[16] If we simply accept the revolutionary ideology, expressed by leaders amidst the turmoil, as the real account, we are trapped in a hopelessly shallow and false interpretation. This is usually adopted by scholars sympathetic to Islamism, or scholars hungry for a radically "incommensurable" revolution (the seeming source of Foucault's excitement). God took over the reins of history, and little more need be said.[17]

The *circular*, *heights*, and *spirits* arguments, firstly, share the conviction that the Iranian Revolution exploded all social scientific conventions. Either a new scientific paradigm or total relinquishment of the scientific vocation are in order. Secondly, these three tendencies embrace a comparative optic. The Iranian Revolution is only intelligible when juxtaposed with other "great" revolutions: the Russian, Chinese, and so forth. Its difference from the leftist paradigm defines its

---

[16] François Furet, *Interpreting the French Revolution* (Cambridge: Cambridge University Press, 1981), presented a double argument. Mansoor Moaddel seems deeply influenced by one aspect: "discourse" has an autonomy and explains the actions of revolutionary agents.

[17] Bruce Lawrence, *Defenders of God: The Fundamentalist Revolt against the Modern Age* (Columbia, SC: University of South Carolina Press, 1995).

unique and special aura. There is no question that the Iranian
Revolution was a transnational revolution. However, it was – to use
a cliché often employed by English apologists for empire to explain
Churchillian racism – a "product of its time." It was a product of Cold
War geopolitics as much as a slow sea change in the "quiet revolution." The Iranian Revolution was not – as Foucault "dreamed" – a
unique and pure rupture with "modern history."[18] It was a product of
the swinging 1960s and 1970s as much as Michelangelo Antonioni's
1966 *Blow Up*, Andy Warhol's Factory, or the Italian Red Guard
abduction of the children of rubber industry barons. We cannot get
close to the Iranian Revolution without getting close to the confusions
and struggles of its people – while keeping the transnational optic
which renders intelligible their ideas and actions as crystallized ideologies and movements.

The Mistaken Revolution?

Once we closely examine everyday life in prerevolutionary Iran, we
immediately see the linkages between the proliferation of carceral institutions imprisoning millions, the new sociological knowledge of
"crime" permeating the university discourses, both features of the
"quiet revolution," and the US military industrial complex hungrily
selling its deadly wares to Saudi Arabia and Iran in the world chess
game of the Cold War. Leading scholars, remaining unsatisfied with
existing scholarly work on revolutions, continue to speak primarily
among themselves above the heads of the banal daily realities. They
imply the inadequacy of their peers as scholars of revolution.
Sometimes the time is too early, or the reality too complex for any
judgment or sound understanding of revolutions. The following
examples show how many scholars each claim that the other has
"overlooked" the kernel of the Iranian Revolution, while they have
"isolated" the core logic. The core epiphany explains the revolution
either as a "unique" destruction of the social science paradigm, or,
alternately, an occasion for "fundamentally" rethinking it. Bakhsh, for
example, surveys the various representations of the Iranian Revolution
by professional colleagues:

[18] For a critical discussion of Foucault's writing on the Iranian Revolution, see
Mirsepassi, *Transnationalism*, chapter 6.

Lambton treated the Shi'i view that all states are essentially usurpatory as facilitating opposition to the government in times of political crisis. In Algar's hands, this concept became central in defining the essential, conscious attitude of the religious leaders and community of believers to the state. This interpretation has been challenged by Said Arjoman.[19]

John Foran depicts a massive conquest of new causes to explain a highly unfamiliar event:

The mass upheaval that swept Iran in the course of 1978 startled almost all observers, from journalists and diplomats to Iran scholars and theorists of Third World social change. ... Now, more than a decade later, the literature on the causes and nature of the Iranian revolution has achieved sizable proportions, although a number of controversial issues remain unsettled and the theoretical implications of the case of Iran for social theorizing about revolution have yet to be fully drawn.[20]

Clearly, the Cold War itself figured fundamentally in framing the expectations that made the Iranian Revolution such a shock to so many spectators. Would the apple of the shaken Pahlavi tree fall into the Soviet garden or that of the self-described "free world"? Neither, it turned out. The conventional frame was thrown into pandemonium. In the ensuing hysteria over rescuing (or jettisoning) the "foundations" of the venerable old theoretical architecture, scholars neglected to simply look at the Iranian "quiet revolution" in its fatal entanglement with the Cold War. Thus, Misagh Parsa also sought to relocate the frame of debate:

Most analyses of the collective actions that led to the Iranian revolution rest upon one of two classical models: social breakdown or social movement ... Conflicts of interest, capacity for mobilization, coalition formation, and the structure of opportunities that shaped the collective actions of various groups and classes are ignored or downplayed.[21]

Mansoor Moaddel crashes through to a whole new reality in examining discourse, seemingly influenced by François Furet's writings on the French Revolution:

[19] Shaul Bakhash, "Iran," *The American Historical Review* 96:5 (December 1991): 1481.
[20] John Foran, "The Iranian Revolution of 1977–79: A Challenge for Social Theory," in John Foran, ed., *A Century of Revolution: Social Movements in Iran* (Minneapolis, MN: University of Minnesota Press, 1994), 160.
[21] Misagh Parsa, "Theories of Collective Action and the Iranian Revolution," *Sociological Forum* 3:1 (Winter 1988): 4.

Sociological research on ideology and revolution has been guided by three models. the subjectivist model … the organizational model … and the Marxian model … I argue for a fourth model, one that treats ideology as an episodic discourse, consisting of a general principles, concepts, symbols, and rituals that shape human actions in a particular historical period, and considers revolutionary phenomenon as a particular mode of historical action constituted by revolutionary ideology. The Iranian Revolution is examined to demonstrate the fruitfulness of the episodic discourse model.[22]

Nikki Keddie starkly explains how the Iranian Revolution presented a brainteaser, not merely to scholars, but to the entirety of civil society in countries everywhere:

The Iranian Revolution of 1978–79 shocked the world and set in motion a search for causes. Most of the resulting analyses tend to locate the origins of the revolution in the errors of the shah and of various Americans, although some scholarly works assay socioeconomic explanations for the upheaval. Enough time has now passed to permit a greater range of investigations, and one written from the comparative perspective ought to be revealing.[23]

We propose that these scholars, by adopting too abstractly lofty a vista, seek the revolution in a mistaken place. Many scholars are known for being overly eager in predicting revolutions. Many feel the lack of revolutions painfully. The idea of revolutions is far more present and integral to our lives than the relatively rare reality of social or political revolutions. Revolutions occur very infrequently. To fully understand them, we must also consider the great imaginary surplus that spills over into everyday life everywhere. This imaginary surplus explains the hunger among scholars to plummet to fresh depths of interpretative analysis of the rare revolutionary events.

Keddie also voices the excitement conjured up by a revolution that seemingly breaks from the mold, perhaps unveiling new possibilities:

Iran's two major twentieth-century revolutions, and especially the second, appear so aberrant. They do not fit very closely widespread ideas of what modern revolutions should be like. Yet there is no doubt that the Islamic revolution in 1978–79 provided a thoroughgoing overthrow of the old

---

[22] Mansoor Moaddel, "Ideology as Episodic Discourse: The Case of the Iranian Revolution," *American Sociological Review* 57:3 (June 1992): 353.
[23] Nikki R. Keddie, "Iranian Revolutions in Comparative Perspective," *The American Historical Review* 88:3 (June 1983): 579.

political, social, and ideological order, although what will replace it is not yet clear.[24]

Halliday similarly voices this enthusiasm, raising the Iranian Revolution to the level of an enigma that – pregnant with unfathomable meaning – might occupy scholarly inquiry over untold generations in a new mystery of world history:

It will be some years before it becomes possible to provide a comprehensive account of the Iranian revolution of 1978–9. One reason is the complexity and the many levels of the process one has to separate out – the urban and the rural, the court and the bazaar, the Iranian and the American, the left and the right, the secular and the religious, the material and the ideological. Intractable theoretical problems have been posed by these events. Another reason is that some of the components of this story are still hidden from us: The evolution of US policy is still obscure. The development of Khomeini's strategy – how he saw the situation at different phases, what he was trying to achieve at each of these points – may always remain a bit hazy. The Shah's memoirs are unlikely to tell us very much since, on the evidence of what has already been published in England (Now! December 7, 14, 1979), they seem to be written in the same bland, apologetic and dishonest vein as his previously published works.[25]

The scholarly debate on the Iranian Revolution, even to this day, somehow misplaces the subject of its own study. The literature seems more interested in challenging what other scholars have written and think about the revolution. It often fails or forgets to write about the revolution itself. Those who publish regarding the revolution should write more about the history of the event, and less the history of writing about it.

Revolution in a Time of "Prosperity"?

The desire to produce a general theory of revolution, or to situate an event within a preexisting theory of revolution, has obstructed full understanding of the Iranian case. The structural approach – especially the argument that Iran was experiencing economic crisis – is exemplary. It denies that Iran was economically doing better than any time

---

[24] Ibid., 580.
[25] Fred Halliday, "Testimonies of Revolution," *MERIP Reports* 87 (May 1980): 27.

prior to the 1960s. One may argue that Iranians had good reason to condemn the ruling elite, where economic resources were distributed unfairly, comprising one principal catalyst for the revolutionary events of 1978. The question remains, however, as to which social group endured the most serious grievances. To effectively explore the revolutionary course, two preliminary questions occur:

(1) Why do people reach a point at which they become conscious of a desire for revolution, something they have neither seen nor experienced in their lives? Is a revolution about a total and absolute rejection of the power relationship as it exists? Is it necessarily motivated by an "ideal" imagining of the future?

(2) For an event which has happened so rarely, can one, as a scholar or political person, offer any reasonable explanation? And, if this is possible, is this a "general theory" of all revolutions? Or, rather, are all revolutions unique, each requiring specific study, the articulation of a story, and so on?

This study proposes an exploration of these two questions. That is, firstly, on how those Iranian scholars and experts on revolution explain the 1979 event. For example, Said Amir Arjomand, in 1986, proposed a comparative optic, showing the similitude between Islamist populist ideology and the blood and soil ideologies of European fascism in the category of anti-modern "authenticity." Homa Katouzian, in 1988, encouraged a structural-demographic analysis of the revolution, against modernization theory (i.e. Samuel Huntington) and conjunctural structuralism (the multi-causality of Theda Skocpol or Charles Tilly). Misagh Parsa, in 1988, urged a theory of collective action to transcend the limits of "breakdown" and "social movement" theories. Mansoor Moaddel, in 1992, rethought revolution in terms of ideology as episodic discourse, that is, the autonomy of discursive ensembles based on regime/revolution antinomy. Charles Kurzman, in 1996, promoted a theory of revolution as structural and perceived opportunity. We will briefly explore such accounts of the revolution, and why they offer important insights while falling short based on a bid to explain the event holistically.

If the shah's regime collapsed despite his army remaining intact, and in the absence of military defeat, while the Pahlavi state was spared the dangers of either financial crisis or peasant insurrection, how do the usual generalizations about revolutions stand? They fall. War has been called the midwife of revolution, and peasant insurrections are considered indispensable in many currently fashionable theories of revolution.[26] Consider the following passage in an important analysis by Abrahamian:

> The present crisis in Iran is a classic example of a political revolution caused by society's superstructure, especially the state, failing to reflect, represent, and keep up with changes in a society's infrastructure, namely its class formations. The roots of the crisis reach back not to 1963, when Ayatollah Khomeini first raised his voice, nor to 1953, when the CIA deposed Premier Mosaddeq, but to 1949 when the Shah began the long process of creating an autocratic state that would stifle all opposition, including aristocratic and bourgeois opposition, and would attempt to remold society in his own image – or rather, in the image of his dictatorial father.[27]

Abrahamian's paragraph exemplifies exceeding abstraction in Iranian revolutionary scholarship. An accuracy of analysis is built upon a broadness of interpretation that obscures the textures of the pre-1978 decades, as a story-structured experience rooted in local conditions and a transnational passage of time. His analysis of state dynamics underpinned by changing relations (i.e. peasant and industrial labor) and forces (i.e. technological revolutions) of production is essentially correct. Yet the abstract pattern Abrahamian invokes could encompass any number of Third World countries seeking modernization to avoid imperial entrapment. It remains remote from the collective experiences that moved people, which might be captured as an image in the 1978 Cinema Rex fire, where 420 individuals were incinerated.[28] The public were watching Masoud Kimiai's film *The Deer*, an emotionally wrenching Iranian New Wave film. *The Deer* depicted addiction, poverty, and depleted public values, while making a call for heroic public action against the forces of oppression. If we watch Iranian New Wave cinema today, it is hard to miss the visceral aesthetic portrayal of passion to live, crushed hopes, fear, and claustrophobia. The performances depict everyday angels with dirty faces

[26] Said Amir Arjomand, "Iran's Islamic Revolution in Comparative Perspective," *World Politics* 38:3 (April 1986): 387.

[27] Ervand Abrahamian, "Iran in Revolution: The Opposition Forces," *MERIP Reports* 75/76 (March–April 1979): 3.

[28] The prevalent belief at the time was that the security forces were responsible for the Cinema Rex fire. We now know that the fire may have been planned by a small group of activists with connections to Qum.

seeking public redemption through revolution. Iranian New Wave cinema curiously anticipates later cinematic revolutions concerned with comparable experiences of spatial suffocation and yearning to breathe, such as Mathieu Kassovitz's 1995 controversial French film *La Haine* (*Hate*) about the children of immigrants brutally ghettoized in Parisian suburbia. Revolution is not, in this sense, the mechanical outcome of a universal interplay of cold structures. Its meaning is contained in the existential experience of those who lived through its unpredictable permutations. Abrahamian's main argument is too broad to explain the actual events in Iran. It requires a prior examination of the lifeworlds to become truly meaningful. This analysis of the multiple contingent facets of the lifeworlds is what we call the "emergent" approach to understanding the Iranian Revolution. "Residual" components interact with transnational forces to produce an "emergent" politics, in patterns that characterize material "culture" in struggles over power everywhere.

Emergent Questions

This rich collection of scholarship, primarily from the US and Europe, therefore, furnishes a newly nuanced narrative of the 1979 revolution grounded in the "emergent" principle. The questions reflect the methodologies of the contributing scholars. No questions are "invented" for the sake of their "creative" symbolism. The questions concern everyday realities already pursued as problems by other scholars. This volume, however, proposes innovative scholarly explanations shaped by new histories and concepts. We explain the revolution within the historic context of two crucial decades leading to the demise of the old regime. This juncture reveals diverse global inspirations driving the revolution. We see this transnational spectrum in the lived experiences of Iranian activists who, individually or collectively, spread revolutionary ideas. We examine agency processes in the struggle over public ideological framing, involving individuals, organized groups, and institutions. Closely examining the everyday worlds of these crucial prerevolutionary decades, we analyze the agency structures fomenting resistance and sowing revolutionary seeds. These examinations reveal how the functioning of the dominant political structures either extinguished or – increasingly in the 1970s – empowered their own executioners through misguided political experiments with nativist ideologies. This edited volume contains chapters defined by fresh inquiry into vexing critical questions, pointing to unfamiliar multicultural and transnational solidarities.

The chapters include Negar Mottahedeh's exploration of a transnational women's mobilization at the heart of Iran's 1979 revolution, preserved in a short film loaded with mass activism, public dialogue (including Tehrani schoolgirls), and striking cultural symbolism. Manijeh Moradian also discusses the women's uprising in Tehran in March 1979 as a political inheritance extending to the present, an object lesson and inspiration. Her account proves how deeply modern Iranian politicization has always been embedded in multiple transnational dialogues on the possible meanings of liberation, the nation, and global solidarities. Maryam Alemzadeh, meanwhile, documents the 1960s–1970s revolutionary leftist and Muslim-Marxist guerrilla groups who adopted global ideologies, mobilization strategies, and organization patterns. These movements partook of activism and training across the world. Alemzadeh remakes the orthodox understanding of the Islamic Revolutionary Guards Corps (IRGC). In its early days, it was entangled with global, mostly leftist, armed movements. Its defining activists lived, trained, and fought alongside revolutionaries of diverse national origins, pursuing global emancipation for the wretched. After revolutionary regime change, however, the IRGC transformed from a politics of global insurgency to a state-sponsored entity. Rasmus Christian Elling, too, details how the Iranian People's Fada'i Guerrillas deployed urban organization to channel global forces in the name of universal socialist revolution, inspired by revolutionary experiences of Soviet Russia, China, Vietnam, the Arab Middle East, and, above all, Latin America. Another chapter on the controversial death of Gholamreza Takhti, the Olympic gold medalist wrestler, written by Arash Davari and Naghmeh Sohrabi, analyzes the Iranian national icon's biography as enmeshed in an emergent public politics of contesting dominant power.

Other chapters outline a wider structural globality of the Iranian "quiet revolution" in the prerevolutionary decades. In each, a contingent system of influences becomes discursively enshrined as "inevitability." Christopher Dietrich analyzes the US government response to the growingly instable Pahlavi government, driven by vulnerability anxiety and fearmongering. Dietrich analyzes the uncontrollably expanding global arms market, emphasizing the contingency of decisions today accepted as foregone foreign policy conclusions. These

arbitrary judgments have deeply impacted Iran. The Vietnam War, the
Bretton Woods monetary crisis, the shift from industrial to service
economy, Watergate, and the energy crisis resulted in the bolstering
of authoritarian oil states and Cold War allies, Pahlavi Iran and Saudi
Arabia. Golnar Nikpour, meanwhile, identifies the continuity linking
pre-and postrevolutionary Iran through the "carceral imagination,"
naturalizing the incarceration of millions as inherent to progress and
modernity. Nikpour shows that modern Iranian carceral networks
emerged in tandem with the reformist rule of law in the late Qajar
period, then in the aftermath of 1920s legal centralization. The
Ottoman and Russian empires also influenced the "carceral imagination." The 1920s demanded a "Mussolini who can break the influence of the traditional authorities." Nikpour demonstrates how these
contingent and transnational influences, by the 1970s, had made
modern prisons a natural "inevitability" across the Iranian political
spectrum. The Islamic Republic of Iran thereby became one of the most
heavily carceral states in the contemporary world.

In order to introduce these diverse investigations of the Iranian
Revolution, three questions define the present chapter:

(1) The "emergent" domain of politics in the 1960s–1970s: What is
revealed about the fall of the Pahlavi state by studying Iranian political
life prior to the revolution? The prevailing scholarship presupposes a
clean rupture dividing the pre- and post-1979 periods. This volume
seriously assesses the possibility of a continuity joining elementary
aspects of both periods. The continuity is not based on any "essence"
that might justify Iranian exceptionalism. Rather, multiple contingencies became systemic through national/transnational interactions. Here
are several examples.

Ali Mirsepassi's chapter, "Seeing the World from a Humble
Corner: A Political Memoir," considers the relevance of a quiet but
nevertheless serious struggle of resistance to the Pahlavi state among
many young people in the 1960s and 1970s. Even if not blatantly
political, quiet insurgency focuses on small but meaningful actions in
everyday life, in a small town far away from the capital city of Tehran.
The backdrop is a lively exchange of forbidden literature and cassettes,
circulated and read in secrecy. Sometimes, quiet insurgency is secretly
listening to alternative perspectives through foreign radio stations
broadcasting in other languages. In this sense, even learning foreign

languages constitutes a potential transgression. This cultural battle of ideas enacts resistance through questioning the state's legitimacy in private-cum-public patterns made possible through a wider transnational grid of communication and exchange.

A second example is in Hossein Kamaly's "The Cold War and Education in Science and Engineering in Iran, 1953–1979." This chapter offers a historically grounded mapping of how modern science interacted with power in post-1953 Iran. The chapter highlights an interesting triangle, in *firstly* linking the highly ideological Pahlavi educational/research policy to US influence through the Cold War. This was an alliance shot through with ambiguity, the shah stating: "we like the imperialists, but they bully us." *Secondly*, the chapter links the Pahlavi regime to emergent Islamism in civil society through the same political logic. The argument unearths new historical depth in highlighting the 1960s "cultural shift" as official policy with a specifically anti-left and antidemocratic political agenda. The project of building a national education edifice is an important part of the ideological story of the Pahlavi era. This includes the large number of Iranian students traveling to universities abroad, especially the United States. An "elective affinity" defines the Pahlavi promotion of a certain type of science education and the emergence of a new culturalist politics committed to an Islamist revivalist salvation path.

These two examples already suggest subversion of narrowly "national" frameworks, while nevertheless undermining romantic Iranian exceptionalism. We therefore ask certain well-known questions in a novel way. What explains the ascendency, dominance, and leadership of Khomeini and political "Islam," for example? What forces thrust Islamists to a supreme leadership position after 1979? Many scholars locate the roots of clerical domination in the radicalizing metamorphosis of Shia theology. There is also its ability to creatively absorb other radical ideologies. To reply to this question, this volume carefully studies Iranian political culture through the national and transnational circulation of ideas. These include religious and secular currents, with their influence upon people and events in the revolutionary path. The religious and secular currents are not antinomies. Instead, they mutually interpenetrate and freely borrow from one another.

Here, where nothing is pure, the "emergent" principle becomes manifest. Political life in the two seminal decades requires investigation of multiple contingencies. This is exemplified in Davari and Sohrabi's chapter, "'A Sky Drowning in Stars': Global '68, the Death of Takhti, and the Birth of the Iranian Revolution." It chronicles a series of processes in self-constituting politics, providing insight into the lived experiences of a specific resistance mode. This began in the 1960s and developed through to the 1979 revolution. The chapter chronicles a defining event in prerevolutionary Iranian history, reconstructing Takhti's death as a liminal moment. The event is a crossroad of the "in between": at once personal (suicide, a personality, family matters) and political (assassination, ideas of *senfi/siyasi*, national celebrity, and local/global). The life story of this event unravels its complex relation to other events in Iran, culminating in the revolution. The chapter highlights the *ambiguity* of this event, in its meanings and its impact, illuminating its genealogy. Theoretically, therefore, the chapter is the exploration of a unique form of political action, discussed in its national/global aspects. Its conclusion ties the meaning of Takhti's death to analysis of various political modes for understanding the 1979 revolution.

(2) "Emergent" politics as hybridizing religious and secular politics: Many scholars have described the 1979 revolution as a "nativist" social event. In this volume, we appraise this claim. Several chapters evaluate to what extent the political ideas and forces opposing the Pahlavi state were either secular or religious. Were they national, or inspired by intellectual exchanges with global realities of the 1960s and 1970s? In this context, how did the "secular" and "religious" forces of the prerevolutionary decades interact? More importantly, how did they overlap despite appearances of opposition? What did the fissures within opposing groups reveal about shared underlying identity? In Golpayegan, Marxist teachers talked about the "straight path," as if world revolution were a religious commitment. Religious radicals similarly borrowed the idiom of secular Third Worldism. The curious hybridity of a small provincial town like Golpayegan, upon examination, extends to the heights of the Pahlavi state. This is manifested in how the Pahlavi state constructed its political identity and that of its opposition, betraying opponents who deeply informed one another.

Several chapters study the simultaneously local and global nature of the revolution. Overlaps between religious and secular forces and ideas are explored in Hamed Yousefi's chapter, "Between Illusion and

Aspiration: Morteza Avini's Cinema and Theory of Global Revolution." This chapter examines the complexity of Islamism and the revolution, arguing that two seemingly contradictory currents made the Iranian Revolution and political Islam in Iran. We can observe a nativist and anti-modernist ideology, and a global and even universalist vision in the revolutionary ideology propagated by its leaders and intellectuals. Its nativism was a critical alternative to nationalism. Its universalism opposed the "Western" modernist humanism of the secular vision. Yousefi studies this complex and ambiguous quality of Iranian political Islam, in the life and work of postrevolutionary figure Morteza Avini, a revered artist and revolutionary intellectual.

(3) A gender dynamic driving revolution in the modern world attests to transnationalism: "Planetarity: The Anti-disciplinary Object of Iranian Studies," by Negar Mottahedeh, offers a broad theoretical argument shaped by an important but little-known historical event. The 1979 women's mass mobilization in Tehran, at the height of the Iranian Revolution, radically subverted the dominant narrative of the fledging Islamic Republic. This revolt by thousands of Iranian and some foreign women upon Tehran's streets occurred on the eve of the eclipse of women's freedoms by the new state. Women of all classes and ages participated. This fascinating event was documented as a short film by French and American women of second-wave feminism. Sometimes an event discloses everything that remains silenced beneath a dominant discourse. The oppressed victims of violence, hidden beneath a discourse celebrating the self-affirming myths of power, explode into visibility in a moment of mass activism. Just as often, the organs of dominant power (i.e. the state, the police, and the military) instantly crush the uprising to restore silence and order, the evidence supporting a dominant myth that is really the product of systemic violence. On this occasion, however, the pattern of silence was broken. The 1979 women's mass mobilization in Tehran was filmed in a powerful documentary which continues to circulate today. "Emergent" history overthrows the seamless myth of power.

The compound of the film and the event provide a unique portal for reflection upon transnationalism in the Iranian Revolution. Fascinatingly, the Western feminists frame the meaning of the event in terms of the anti-imperialist Vietnamese Revolution, as an instance

where women collectively broke established frameworks (of local tradition, capitalism, and Eurocentrism) by creatively revolutionizing the
public sphere. It became a space where women make the future in
equal participation with men based on ideals of universal freedom. The
film and the event invite profound reflections upon gender politics,
twentieth-century revolution, anti-colonialism, and strategies for fighting capitalism, as well as the risks to human freedom (i.e. women's
emancipation) from modern oppression and revivalist movements
committed to traditional gender/class, and other, hierarchies.

  Mottahedeh offers a theory of transnationalism and revolution.
Restoring "history" with universal significance, she inflects the
Iranian Revolution with the creative shockwaves of the Vietnamese
Revolution, which in turn deeply molded the experience of May
1968 in France. Mottahedeh's intervention reconstructs revolution to
center gender empowerment as the defining momentum behind all
revolutions. This is salient today as women's rights are rolled back
worldwide by new populist authoritarian states, notably in the recent
Turkish law forcing girls to marry their rapists. Mottahedeh indicates a
larger possible terrain of historical research focused theoretically on
the core gender dynamic in modern revolutions. In her argument, the
Vietnamese Revolution is important because of a revolution in gender
relations. This is a fundamental insight into world revolutions.
Consider, for example, that, in the Indian freedom struggle, more
women participated than in either the Chinese or Russian revolutions,
because nonviolence permitted the participation of the population in
far greater numbers than guerrilla action.[29] There are striking corol-
laries with the long twentieth-century revolutionary tradition in Iran,
which centered the *bastnishini* tradition. The chapter opens this often-
neglected discussion of how gender figured centrally in twentieth-
century revolutions. Vietnamese women had shed their traditional
roles as mothers and caregivers to support the "gentle revolution."
The germinal force in planetary transformation was women's participation in the social struggles of oppressed underclasses.
A transnational solidarity was ignited within the movement by the
courage and passion of the Iranian women in March 1979, only weeks
after the return to Iran of the "undisputed leader of the revolution,"

[29] Tadd Fernée, *Enlightenment and Violence: Modernity and Nation-Making*
   (New Delhi: Sage, 2014), 185.

Ayatollah Ruhollah Khomeini, from his French exile in Neauphle-le-Château.

The theme of transnationalism and revolution is continued in Mirsepassi's chapter. Small towns like Golpayegan in the late 1960s and 1970s underwent an intense intellectual and political awakening, centered in high schools, bookshops, and other public places. Activists drew inspiration from ideals arriving in Iran from all around the world. Nehru's India and the Palestinian struggle provided ideals for the Iranian nation. These vehement convictions daily undermined the official and forced rituals celebrating the Pahlavi state and modernization program. Activists in small towns like Golpayegan had a growing "cosmopolitan" consciousness which partook of wider global interactions. Providing a corrective to narrow Tehran-centrism, the world experience of Golpayegan also opens a new perspective on exchanges and circulations occurring in twentieth-century politics and intellectual life. This forms the everyday landscape for articulating an "emergent" theorization of the prerevolutionary decades.

"Emergent" Iranian nationalism was the cohabitation of multiple small worlds. Golpayegan had a "humble" but vibrant cultural and educational life. Ebn-e Sina and Ferdowsi high schools were centers of cultural and political life. Our high school teachers were involved in cultural, political, and religious activities. The literature teacher was a very effective and caring teacher and mentor, and a puritanically religious man. He resembled a personality out of religious books: ideal in all qualities. Other small worlds thrived within the same social space. Two younger teachers from Tehran were Marxists. They would discuss Samad Behrangi, Maxim Gorky, Latin American revolutionaries, and so on. Audio tapes informed students about critical political ideas articulated in Islamic discourse, notably tape recordings in literature class by the well-known cleric Mohamad Taqi Falsafi. The modernist Iranian novel *Chashmhayash* (*Her Eyes*, 1952), by Bozorg Alavi, was deeply infused with the early Tudeh Marxism, which fired the imaginations and discussions of young Iranians struggling to make political sense of everyday life.

2 Globalizing the Iranian Revolution: A Multiscalar History

ARANG KESHAVARZIAN *

It is a testament to the extent to which Iran was enmeshed in global networks that the fall of the shah in 1979 generated many works besides those written by Iranians themselves. A diverse array of writers tried to make sense of the unexpected fall of the Pahlavi dynasty and the founding of an Islamic republic. A major French social theorist, a prominent Egyptian journalist, an internationally recognized Polish reporter, and less famous figures were moved to narrate their discoveries, often after traveling to Iran in the midst of the revolutionary turmoil and its aftermath.[1] In doing so they pieced together the meaning of the revolution for Iran and beyond, for politics and social theory, and for conceptions of modernity and tradition. In the months and immediate years after the revolution there was also a raft of social scientists that applied and challenged one theory or another with their interpretations of Iran's insurrection, while establishing the cornerstones of what would become the established chronologies, critical junctures, revolutionary repertoires, and alliance blocs of the revolutionary story. A significant portion of this scholarship was written by Iranian graduate students and junior faculty studying and teaching outside of Iran in the 1970s and 1980s.[2] In these early years, this

* In addition to discussions with the authors in this volume during the two workshops generating this book, I want to acknowledge comments and suggestions by Ismail Alatas, Arash Davari, Mona El-Ghobashy, Naghmeh Sohrabi, and Hamed Youssefi. I thank them for their generosity and take responsibility for any shortcomings.
1 Janet Afary and Kevin Anderson, *Foucault and the Iranian Revolution: Gender and the Seductions of Islamism* (Chicago, IL: University of Chicago Press, 2010); Mohammad Haykal, *Iran: The Untold Story – An Insider's Account of America's Iranian Adventure and Its Consequences for the Future* (New York: Pantheon Books, 1982); Ryszard Kapuscinski, *The Shah of Shahs*, trans. William R. Brand and Katarzyna Mroczkowska-Brand (New York: Vintage, 1992 [1985]).
2 Matthew K. Shannon, "Reading Iran: American Academics and the Last Shah," *Iranian Studies* 51:2 (2018): 289–316; Thomas M. Ricks, "Letters to the Editor," *Iranian Studies* 51:6 (2018): 987–990.

scholarship was animated by the resurgence in the study of revolutions in the Anglo-American world; a literature that was labeled as "the third generation" of theories of revolution by one leader in the field.[3] This act of writing and understanding was mediated by the growing sentiment among both Iranian and non-Iranians that something had gone awry after the shah was toppled, the revolution was "stolen," there was a "reversal of history," or Iran was regressing and even "lost."[4] In Tehran, Washington, and elsewhere, factions formed as blame was distributed and the revolution's narrative turned from triumph to tragedy.

However much these rich accounts depended on transnational circulations, they tend to draw a stark line between Iran's political upheaval and the world. The international interest and sense of stakes did not translate into narratives of the revolution that foreground the role of international factors or the world-historical context. Either the focus was on the unique vulnerabilities of the Pahlavi monarchy or the exceptional powers of the revolutionary movement. For the former group, a litany of characteristics ranging from the more structural condition of Iran's political economy (i.e. rentier state, clientelism, or dependent development) or the shah's inconsistent and erratic decision-making (e.g. personal psychology) were evoked to show the Iranian state was afflicted with particular weakness. Even if it was ensnared by "international forces," the regime was repeatedly deemed as autonomous and a singular case. For the latter group, the presence of a religious hierarchy leading the revolution and a Shia Islamic idiom in the claims-making rendered 1979 as distinct, if not peculiar, and the revolution uniquely Shia.

This volume returns to 1979 as both a historical moment and a revolutionary uprising, constituting multiple, interwoven geographies and scales. The notion of "Global 1979" orients us to chart the Iranian Revolution by examining the complex interplay of space and time. The

---

[3] Jack A. Goldstone, "Theories of Revolution: The Third Generation," *World Politics* 32 (1980): 425–453; see also his "Toward a Fourth Generation of Revolutionary Theory," *Annual Review of Political Science* 4 (2001): 139–187.

[4] Regret and melancholy is not unique to the 1979 revolution and a trope in discussing many revolutionary episodes. Branches of historiography on the Constitutional Revolution were similarly animated by an urge to examine what went wrong; see Afsaneh Najmabadi, "'Is Our Name Remembered?' Writing the History of Iranian Constitutionalism as if Women and Gender Mattered," *Iranian Studies* 29:1–2 (1996): 85–109.

very term fuses a spatial form with a temporal interval, while the notion of itineraries evokes a multitude of pathways and junctures – a plurality of paths and possibilities. This collection of essays insists on looking at different aspects of the revolution through optics that situate "the global" in relation to what is often subsumed under the guise of "the local." Rather than treating the global, national, or local as natural, preexisting, or opposed to one another, we begin by assuming that they are coproduced in specific historical contexts.[5] If we scrutinize space in this relational manner rather than as absolute objects, then we let ourselves notice the movements across borders as well as the shifting and overlapping meanings of boundaries. In doing so we offer new histories of the Pahlavi state and the making of revolutionary Iran, while new conceptions of the global, national, local, provincial, urban, and regional are contested, imagined, and deployed politically. In "a world of overlapping and interpenetrating orientations,"[6] what is at stake is not a retelling of the story of the revolution, although that is a valuable endeavor, but an insistence on polyphony and using methods to attune us to what has often been elided or relegated as prehistory or realm of the all too familiar. Globalizing the Iranian Revolution in this manner is an enterprise to recover the histories of the revolution non-teleologically. Forty years after the revolution we have an opportunity to ask questions that have been either too obvious or uncomfortable to be articulated when the stakes of the revolution were proximate and self-criticism was a matter of life and death.

Global 1979 is a resolute attempt to work with the unthinkability of the revolution, rather than solving it as a riddle. For as Albert Sachs famously remarked, "All revolutions are impossible until they happen. Then they become inevitable."[7] Investigating different archives, charting new territories, asking new questions, plotting different chronologies, and engaging disparate fields of study, the chapters in this volume coalesce around arguments about how the revolution was

[5] Anna Tsing, "The Global Situation," *Cultural Anthropology* 15:3 (August 2000): 327–360; Doreen Massey, *For Space* (London: Sage, 2005).

[6] Charles Sabel and Jonathan Zeitlin, "Stories, Strategies, Structures: Rethinking Historical Alternatives to Mass Production," in Charles Sabel and Jonathan Zeitlin, eds., *World of Possibilities: Flexibility and Mass Production in Western Industrialization* (Cambridge: Cambridge University Press, 1997), 31.

[7] Albie Sachs, "Towards a Bill of Rights for a Democratic South Africa," *Journal of African Law* 35 (1991): 21; see also Michel-Rolf Trioullot, *Silencing the Past: Power and the Production of History* (Boston, MA: Beacon Press, 1995).

in fact thinkable and planned for, even if it was peppered with unintended consequences and dashed hopes. We demonstrate that people contemplated and labored to radicalize, mobilize, and liberate themselves, their immediate communities, and the wider world. Their political consciousness was the manifestation of concrete forms of organization and different practices of politics that were spatialized. While these goals, tactics, and spaces were not always realized nor left more than mere traces in the postrevolutionary polity, that is not a reason for them being absent from the historiography of the revolution.

The Global as Theory and Variable

"The global" has preoccupied many scholars for over a quarter century, but it means different things to different researchers, in particular to those who have written about the 1979 Iranian Revolution. This is in part because of disciplinary practices and debates, but also because of implicit and explicit conceptions of space, time, and the role of theory. While different understandings of the global are not mutually exclusive, and in fact the most generative works engage with more than one of them, they are distinct in that they authorize their own theoretical and methodological proclivities, archival requisites, and offer their own challenges and possibilities for researchers.

This rich scholarship written by scholars primarily in the US and Europe has focused on one set of questions: why the Pahlavi regime fell, why Khomeini and its associates were able to position themselves as leaders after 1979, or why other factions of and political strands of the coalition of insurgents were sidelined or submerged within the first couple years after the founding of the Islamic Republic.[8] This corpus, dominated by social scientists, has sought to rise "above the contingency and messiness of everyday life to find the lawful regularities that actually govern the whole."[9] Instead, they often devise a sort of

---

[8] For thoughtful discussions of the historiography in English versus Persian works published in Iran and the different questions, archives, and stakes involved in them, see Naghmeh Sohrabi, "The 'Problem Space' of the Historiography of the 1979 Iranian Revolution," *History Compass* 16 (2018): 1–10; and her "Remembering the Palestine Group: Global Activism, Friendship, and the Iranian Revolution," *International Journal of Middle East Studies* 51:2 (2019): 281–300.

[9] William Sewell Jr., *Logics of History* (Chicago, IL: University of Chicago Press, 2010), 8.

checklist of factors or variables to be tested – measurements and proxies for economic grievances, weakness of state institutions, class positions of parties and individual participants, and the circulation and traction of particular discourses and rhetorical framing.

Within this mix, explicitly international variables were less central. The most common way that scholarship on the 1979 revolution has thought about Iran in relation to the rest of the world has been through comparative analysis – or specifically *explaining* how the fall of the shah and the fashioning of a radically new social and political order is compatible with, or divergent from, other revolutions, or more accurately theories of revolutions. For some revolutionaries as well as scholars, relevant comparisons are to the histories and theories of "great revolutions" – the October Revolution, the French Revolution, or the Chinese Revolution.[10] For other researchers it was the Third World, postcolonial, or more contemporaneous revolutions and ruptures such as those in Cuba, Algeria, Vietnam, Nicaragua, and the Philippines that are the appropriate universe of cases.[11] In these studies, which continue to be published until this day and often now include the Arab uprisings after 2011 as part of the comparative set, "the global" is understood as a set of variables and processes that operate universally.[12] These factors come together in various places and times to make revolution more or less likely and even dictate stages of action and reaction. Social scientists seek to discover causal laws

[10] I mention revolutionaries because the imprints of revolutions from other places and pasts were so strong that even the internecine conflicts on the left after 1979 adopted the nomenclature of Bolshavik-Menshevik, that is, *aksariat-aqaliyat* or majority and minority.

[11] Inter alia, Farideh Farhi, *States and Urban-Based Revolutions: Iran and Nicaragua* (Urbana, IL: University of Illinois Press, 1990); Misagh Parsa, *States, Ideologies, and Social Revolutions: Comparative Analysis of Iran, Nicaragua, and the Philippines* (Cambridge: Cambridge University Press, 2000); John Foran, *Taking Power: The Origins of Third World Revolutions* (Cambridge: Cambridge University Press, 2005); Edmund Burke III and Paul Lubeck, "Explaining Social Movements in Two Oil-Exporting States: Divergent Outcomes in Nigeria and Iran," *Comparative Studies in Society and History* 29 (October 1987): 643–665; Asef Bayat, "Revolution without Movement, Movement without Revolution: Comparing Islamic Activism in Iran and Egypt," *Comparative Studies in Society and History* 40:1 (1998): 136–169.

[12] See the Roundtable "Echoes: Iranian Uprisings and the Arab Spring," *International Journal of Middle East Studies* 44 (2012): 147–155; Asef Bayat, *Revolution without Revolutionaries: Making Sense of the Arab Spring* (Stanford, CA: Stanford University Press, 2017).

that are independent of time and space, or at least for a defined category of cases. The challenge of this scholarship from the 1980s and 1990s is to calibrate the Iranian experience in order to confirm or reject prevailing theories and build a more "unified" or "robust" model of and for revolution. It is in this sense that this approach is both useful for social scientists wanting to "explain," "predict," or forestall revolution or revolutionaries who want to make them. From this perspective "the global" stands in for a social scientific theory that is, or at least should be, transhistorical and international in scope. Theory functions as the universalizing force that helps decipher the Iranian Revolution, like any other.

A related subset are works that examine the international as entailing a bundle of consequences associated with Iran's insurrection. These academic and more policy-oriented works focus on understanding the significance of the 1979 revolution as a regional or even international rupture that had deep and long-lasting effects beyond Iran's borders.[13] The fall of the shah and rise of the Islamic Republic therefore was consequential for regional alliances, oil markets, conceptions of security threats by the US, the Soviet Union, and other countries, as well as religious and cultural solidarities and schisms among Muslims and other communities. Some writers explore how the US security architecture in the Middle East was attenuated by "the loss of the shah," who was a pivotal ally or policeman.[14] For others, global energy markets and attendant financial instruments were at least momentarily in turmoil due to the revolution and second oil shock. These "shocks" implied and worked with subsequent structural changes to the geopolitical and geoeconomic structures in the 1980s and 1990s (e.g. financialization, the rise and regionalization of capital from the Arabian Peninsula).[15]

---

[13] David W. Lesch, *1979: The Year That Shaped the Modern Middle East* (Boulder, CO: Westview Press, 2001).

[14] R. K. Ramazani, *Revolutionary Iran: Challenge and Response in the Middle East* (Baltimore, MD: Johns Hopkins University Press, 1986); James Bill, *The Eagle and the Lion: The Tragedy of American-Iranian Relations* (New Haven, CT: Yale University Press, 1988); Arshin Adib-Moghaddam, *The International Politics of the Persian Gulf: A Cultural Genealogy* (London: Routledge, 2006); Mohammad Ayatollahi Tabaar, *Religious Statecraft: The Politics of Islam in Iran* (New York: Columbia University Press, 2018).

[15] Duccio Basosi, Giulano Garavini, and Massimiliano Trentin, eds., *Countershock: The Oil Counter-revolution of the 1980s* (London: Bloomsbury, 2018);

The 1979 revolution has also been understood as an inspiration for others seeking to confront despotic power, in particular monarchies. Authors have asked if the revolution was the start of global Islamism or a model for Islamists in Egypt, Turkey, Saudi Arabia, and elsewhere.[16] For Islamists and some philologically minded scholars, the Iranian experience was consistent with and part of a broader return to an "authentic Islam" or "fundamentalism."[17] For most researchers, however, the answer was far more equivocal since political Islam or Islamism is certainly more varied than this question implies and not tied to some core essence in Islamic or Shia doctrine or Muslim societies.[18] It has been suggested that the revolution also has had an effect on social thought – whether this is in the form of a challenge to secularization theory, understandings of modernity, and critiques of modernism, or a direct consequence for thinkers such as Michel Foucault and Kate Millet, who traveled to Iran and grappled with events "there" and what it portended for the world (see Chapter 12).[19] In social movement theory, the Iranian Revolution

Adam Hanieh, *Money, Markets, and Monarchies: The Gulf Cooperation Council and the Political Economy of the Contemporary Middle East* (Cambridge: Cambridge University Press, 2018); Matthew Huber, *Lifeblood: Oil, Freedom, and the Forces of Capital* (Minneapolis, MN: University of Minnesota, 2013); Mazen Labban, "Oil in Parallax: Scarcity, Markets, and the Financialization of Accumulation," *Geoforum* 41:4 (2010): 541–552.

[16] John Esposito, ed., *The Iranian Revolution: Its Global Impact* (Miami, FL: University of Florida, 1990); Oliver Roy, *The Failure of Political Islam* (Cambridge, MA: Harvard University Press, 1994).

[17] Bernard Lewis, *Political Language of Political Islam* (Chicago, IL: University of Chicago Press, 1988).

[18] Inter alia, Sami Zubaida, *Islam, the People and the State: Essays on Political Ideas and Movements in the Middle East* (London: Routledge, 1989); Nikki R. Keddie, *Iran: Roots of Revolution* (New Haven, CT: Yale University Press, 1981); Ervand Abrahamian, *Khomeinism: Essays on the Islamic Republic* (Berkeley, CA: University of California Press, 1993); Ira Lapidus and Edmund Burke III, eds., *Islam, Politics, and Social Movements* (Berkeley, CA: University of California Press, 1988); Asef Bayat, *Making Islam Democratic: Social Movements and the Post-Islamist Turn* (Stanford, CA: Stanford University Press, 2007). Note Ernest Gellner's rather awkward term to differentiate the Iranian case of political Islam from other cases – "Che Khomeinism," which meant to describe "non-hierarchical and popular Islam." Ernest Gellner, *Muslim Society* (Cambridge: Cambridge University Press, 1981), 67.

[19] On Millet's visit to Iran, see Negar Mottahedeh, *Whisper Tapes: Kate Millet in Iran* (Stanford, CA: Stanford University Press, 2019); On Foucault's visit to Iran, see Afary and Anderson, *Foucault and the Iranian Revolution*; Behrooz Ghamari-Tabrizi, *Foucault in Iran: Islamic Revolution after the Enlightenment*

helped encourage a new generation of "culturalist" studies of revolution, which focused on perceptions, ideology, and performativity as essential components of effective mobilization.[20] This work both reinterpreted histories of revolutions by adopting the linguistic turn and referenced post-1968 protests to speak of "new" or "identity-based" social movements as a hallmark of late capitalism and the postcolonial condition. These analyses were a direct critique of structuralist theories of revolution that distinguished the 1960s and 1970s.

A more epochal version of this line of causal analysis is to insist on revolutions as part of world historical eras that transcend the borders of any given revolutionary polity. People speak about the Age of Revolution in the Atlantic World running from 1789 to 1843 and extending to the French, Haitian, Irish, and Latin American wars of independence.[21] Iran, as well as the neighboring Russian and Ottoman empires, participated in a wave of constitutional revolutions in the early twentieth century.[22] Historians have offered us several proliferating lenses through which to think about the post–World War II era –

(Minneapolis, MN: University of Minnesota Press, 2018); Ali Mirsepassi, *Transnationalism in Iranian Political Thought: The Life and Thought of Ahmad Fardid* (Cambridge: Cambridge University Press, 2017).

[20] Theda Skocpol, "Rentier State and Shi'a Islam in the Iranian Revolution," *Theory and Society* 11:3 (May 1982): 265–283; Charles Kurzman, "Structural Opportunities and Perceived Opportunities in Social Movement Theory: Evidence from the Iranian Revolution of 1979," *American Sociological Review* 61 (1996): 153–170; William A. Gamson and David S. Meyer, "Framing Political Opportunity," in Doug McAdam, John D. McCarthy, and Mayer N. Zald, eds., *Comparative Perspectives on Social Movements: Opportunities, Mobilizing Structures, and Cultural Framings* (New York: Cambridge University Press, 1996), 275–290; Mansoor Moaddel, *Class, Politics, and Ideology in the Iranian Revolution* (New York: Columbia University Press, 1992).

[21] Eric Hobsbawm, *Age of Revolution: 1875–1914* (New York: Vintage Books, 1989). For Hobsbawm this was a double revolution – economic and political or industrial and republican – that emanated outward from Europe. For a critical discussion of this formulation, see David Armitage and Sanjay Subrahmanyam, eds., *The Age of Revolutions in Global Context, c. 1760–1840* (Basingstoke: Palgrave Macmillan, 2010).

[22] Nader Sohrabi, "Historicizing Revolutions: Constitutional Revolutions in the Ottoman Empire, Iran, and Russia, 1905–1908," *The American Journal of Sociology* 100:6 (1995): 1383–1447; Charles Kurzman, *Democracy Denied, 1905–1915: Intellectuals and the Fate of Democracy* (Cambridge, MA: Harvard University Press, 2008); Houri Berberian, *Roving Revolutionaries: Armenians and the Connected Revolutions in the Russian, Iranian, and Ottoman Worlds* (Berkeley, CA: University of California Press, 2019).

Cold War, postcolonialism, Keynesianism and state-led development, second-wave feminism, or simply the global 1960s or global 1970s.[23] The mid-1970s were also a moment in which the "Third Wave of Democracy" is said to have begun and one study calculates that of the sixty-seven authoritarian regimes dismantled between 1972 and 2002, over 70 percent were the result of nonviolent uprisings.[24] As such Iran's 1979 revolution can be grouped with different types and waves of protest movements. Therefore, the question is, what can be gleaned from different genealogies and temporalities?

Despite their differences these approaches too often share the common feature of treating the global as a ready-made stage, which is located outside of Iran. Understood as imperialism, global hegemony, the world capitalist system, or dependent development, these "forces" impose themselves on Iranian rulers, activate potential revolutionaries, or are impacted or shocked by events radiating out from Tehran as a sort of progenitor of a new age.[25] Iran, as part of the "peripheral formations,"[26] and the global are implicitly kept at arms distance until the events of 1979 bring them into collision. From this perspective "the global" tends to position Iran as a "case" appended to the rest of the world through theory or, for scholars thinking in terms of "waves" and "ages" of revolution, Iran is integrated by world historical time. As George Lawson concludes, much of the scholarship on revolutions results in "an analytical bifurcation between international and domestic in which the former served as the backdrop to the latter's causal agency."[27] Notably the domestic or the local is typically rendered as discrete nation-state units; this approach does not necessarily have to lead to "methodological nationalism," wherein

[23] See "Forgotten Dreams and Misplaced Revolutions: Contextualizing Twentieth Century Revolutions in the Middle East, Latin America, and the Caribbean," Sawyer Seminar, 2017–18, www.brandeis.edu/misplaced-revolutions/index.html.
[24] George Lawson, "A Global Historical Sociology of Revolution," in Julian Go and George Lawson, eds., *Global Historical Sociology* (Cambridge: Cambridge University Press, 2017), 92.
[25] Fred Halliday's analyses of Iran and the Third World in the 1970s and 1980s is exemplary in centering imperialism and international oppression in analyses of revolution. See his *Arabia without Sultans* (London: Saqi Books, 2020 [1974]); *Iran: Dictatorship and Development* (Hamondsworth: Penguin, 1979); and his many essays in *Middle East Report* (*MERIP*) in the 1970s and 1980s.
[26] Farhi, *States and Urban-Based Revolutions*.
[27] Lawson, "A Global Historical Sociology," 76.

the state is considered a unified bordered whole, but in many treatments, it often does.[28]

Extending Spatial Scope and Temporal Range

What is lost in this drive for predictive explanations and theoretical parsimony is grappling with histories of Iranians living in, moving through, and defining the world with varying degrees of efficacy. If globalizing the Iranian Revolution is a method to recover these histories of the revolution in a non-teleological and multi-spatial manner, we present them around five specific propositions: (1) *geographic and archival margins are a powerful means to decenter political struggles*; (2) *global guerrilla tactics politicized space before and after the revolution*; (3) *tracing genealogies allows us to think simultaneously, rather than linearly, about causation*; (4) *the circulation of expertise left divisive imprints on society*; (5) *part of what gave the revolution meaning was imagining the world*. Each theme extends across several chapters with authors weaving more than a single thread into their approach; yet, we have elected to group only two chapters under each heading, or part, with additional themes simultaneously running through the collection.

Although not articulating a unified narrative of the revolution, an edited volume is a useful instrument to tackle the messy pluralism and the confusing and amazing changes of a revolutionary situation.[29] Just as the revolution was a broad and (not always coherent) alliance of social classes and political agendas, a global approach to the revolutionary will have to be plural and nimble to address the set of questions, archives, and struggles that come into view as we adopt this Global 1979 sensibility. This volume's edited form, therefore, is itself a manifestation of this argument for multiplicity. In curating the parts of the volume, we consciously juxtapose a series of accounts and invite our readers to contemplate side by side features submerged by a desire for a unified explanation: university campuses in northern California and a provincial town in central Iran, Islamist and Marxist guerrilla fighters, scientific knowledge and experts in prison management, the

---

[28] Andreas Wimmer and Nina Glick Schiller, "Methodological Nationalism and Beyond," *Global Networks* 2:4 (2002): 301–334.

[29] Mona El-Ghobashy, *Bread and Freedom: Egypt's Revolutionary Situation* (Standford, CA: Stanford University Press, 2021).

1968 generation and US congressional committees, and an Islamist filmmaker and collective of French feminists. Unlike works on the revolution published in close temporal proximity to the struggle, the emphasis here is on fine-grained social accounts that do not assume that lived experiences are self-evident or background material.

One strand of this approach traces how people, organizations, and objects traveled and ideas echoed across long distances and cultural and political borders to ricochet through social relations. As several of the contributions to this volume illustrate, how people and ideas circulate to and from Iran in the 1960s and 1970s generates the conditions of possibility for politicization and organizations for struggles of various sorts. It is through these entanglements that people are radicalized, develop identities and strategies, and articulate political projects to preserve the Pahlavi monarchy or topple it and subsequently preserve the revolution (see Chapters 6, 11, and 12). Student activism in North America and Europe, most of it centered on the left-oriented groups, makes up the bulk of the existing scholarship.[30] These accounts illustrate how revolutionary discourse was composed abroad and in relationship to political struggles and projects held by organizers who were not exclusively Iranian or concerned solely by Pahlavi dictatorship. A target of their opposition was everything from imperialism, capitalism, traditionalism, and, as Manijeh Moradian's contribution to this volume illustrates, patriarchy. We have less work on the circuits through which clerics and lay Islamists traveled in the 1950s–1970s, but these religious thinkers and agitators were clearly involved in translocal processes not only because Shia education and political thought was by definition not bound up by nation-state boundaries, but also because Khomeini was in exile and many thinkers studied and lived beyond Iran's borderers – the most obvious examples being Ali Shariati, Beheshti, Bani Sadr, and Chamran, who spent time in Europe, the US, and the Middle East as well as diasporic communities in all these places (see Chapters 3 and 6).[31]

---

[30] Afshin Matin-Asgari, *Iranian Student Opposition to the Shah* (Costa Mesa, CA: Mazda Publishers, 2002); Manijeh Moradian, *Neither Washington, Nor Tehran: Iranian Internationalism in the United States* (Durham, NC: Duke University Press, forthcoming).

[31] In addition to Chapters 3 and 6, see Laurence Louër, *Transnational Shia Politics: Religious and Political Networks in the Gulf* (New York: Columbia University Press, 2008); Elvire Corboz, *Guardians of Shi'ism: Sacred Authority*

Part I, "Global Shadows," brings together two chapters that unearth translocal entanglements by recentering "marginal" places and moments in order to explore the ways in which Iranians were politicized and defined the loci of struggle. For Ali Mirsepassi, it is the acquired knowledge and interpersonal relations of a high school student in a provincial town in the late 1960s that orients us to emergent forms of politics and worldliness. For Manijeh Moradian, it is a leftist pamphlet written by unknown university students in California that shows how striking against gender-based oppression was folded into national liberation and transnational feminism. As both authors uncover these forgotten episodes, they reveal how radicalism was defined in terms of positions taken in debates, interpretations of novels, everyday interactions, and ideologies of their time, but also across geographic and political boundaries between Islamists and Marxists or feminists and anti-colonial movements. Notions of radicalism and gender consciousness emerged out of lived experiences of women and men in concrete circumstances and sometimes violent altercations. Operating under global shadows these histories have been unseen or ignored, but can be recovered for political "possibilities" in the future and conceived as a multifaceted inheritance.

Therefore, struggles over space go beyond capturing the nation-state, the Islamic world, or the Middle East region. What is being mapped out in this approach is less "globalism" as a fully-formed, all-encompassing systemic matrix or a distinct geographic scale, and more a close examination of relational histories that rework the meaning of places. Therefore, the categories of local, national, and global interpenetrate one another and are not necessarily ordered hierarchically or sequentially. The local or the national therefore is not superseded by the global. Neither is the global a unified whole, coherent system, or abstract two-dimensional space, and instead mapping transnationalism illustrates the well-worn channels made by migration, shared experience, technology, and historical precedent, but also reminds us of the places and peoples that are left out of these

and Transnational Family Networks (Edinburgh: Edinburgh University Press, 2015); Fariba Adelkhah, *The Thousand and One Borders of Iran: Travel and Identity*, trans. Andrew Brown (New York: Routledge, 2016); "Farzand-e Enqelab: Zendegi va Marg-e Saeq Qotbzadeh," BBC Persian Documentary, 2020, www.bbc.com/persian/iran-51438370.

networks – or at least left out of our archives.[32] We must contend with the unevenness and plasticity of the global, the national, and the local. Like James Ferguson, this is why I prefer to think of translocal movements as hopping and skipping, rather than as flows.[33] We can more carefully detect the jagged edges if we locate our research in a place and set of social relationships, rather than on a spaceship looking down upon the planet, which is what happens in much of the discussion about "globalization." Places that at first glance may seem highly localized or marginal – provincial towns, prison cells, congressional hearings, and university dorms – become opportunities to reread international relations and universalist claims.

Social production of space is the theme of Part II, "Militarized Cartographies," examining the movements, representations, and tactics of "guerrillas" as making new terrains of politics. Although ultimately examining very different political organizations, Rasmus Christian Elling and Maryam Alemzadeh return to the 1970s to trace the paths through which Iranian opposition groups engaged with debates around armed resistance. The leftists that Elling studies began to consider "the urban," and not the village or "the forest," as the main front for opposition to the shah. Drawing inspiration from Latin American theorists, the Marxist Fada'i Guerrillas conducted research on cities and trained recruits in urban guerrilla tactics, which transformed the urban space and "urban toiler" into a resource for revolutionary action. It is the urban that becomes the pivot between local-specific conditions and Third World revolutionary Marxism. Alemzadeh considers this same era from the vantage point of Iranians who traveled to Syria and Lebanon to acquire military training. While little of this instruction was central in disarming the shah's troops, some of the men (and a few women) found themselves ironically deploying their training to protect the state, once it had

---

[32] Henri Lefebvre, *Production of Space* (Oxford: Blackwell, 1991); Edward W. Soja, "The Socio-spatial Dialectic," *Annals of the Association of American Geographers* 70:2 (1980): 207–225; Jon Bird, Barry Curtis, Tim Putnam, George Robertson, and Lisa Tickner, eds., *Mapping Futures: Local Cultures, Global Change* (London: Routledge 1993); David Harvey, "Space as a Key Word," in Noel Castree and Derek Gregory, eds., *David Harvey: A Critical Reader* (Oxford: Blackwell Publishing, 2006), 270–293; Massey, *For Space*.

[33] James Ferguson, *Global Shadows* (Durham, NC: Duke University Press, 2006); see also Waleed Hazbun and Arang Keshavarzian, "Re-mapping Transnational Connections in the Middle East," *Geopolitics* 15:2 (2010): 203–209.

become a revolutionary one. As the Islamic Revolutionary Guard Corps was founded as an informal, volunteer organization, it claimed the internationally recognized moniker of "guerrilla" and battled "anti-revolutionaries" in Iran's periphery, specifically suppressing Kurdish and Turkmen dissidents. Simultaneously, their actions and selective appropriation of guerrilla tactics left them open to criticism from those who were detached from the emerging Khomeinist state apparatus, but who participated in the same military training in the Arab world and made claims to being authentic "guerrillas."

The global releases us from national histories, but also unhampers us from revolutionary lineages allowing us to see histories of the 1960s and 1970s as far more open-ended and multistranded than totalizing approaches to the revolution. The decades before 1979 were not simply a "slide to revolution,"[34] but a friction-laden terrain of political struggle on many fronts. By beginning with the assumption that Iranians are participants in and originators of different worlds (or "worlding"[35]), we open ourselves to a sense of globalism that is variegated and malleable. Historicizing the global also avoids either extreme of treating Iran's revolution as a hyper-exceptional case or merely yet another manifestation of a revolutionary formula or epochal "wave." We are sensitive to the different speeds through which complex changes manifest into revolution, ranging from long-drawn processes associated with urbanization, mechanization of farming, organizational formation and decay, or developments in intellectual thought and political ideals to the more rapid twists and turns of boom-and-bust cycles in the economy, election campaigns and congressional hearings in the US, or volatile swings in tactical decisions made by the shah and opposition leaders. They all laid the conditions for vanquishing the monarchy. Yet, we are not dealing with a neat chain of events, but layers of trajectories intersecting, intertwining, and sedimenting. This is an understanding of the situatedness of politics or rootedness that does not imply a single or essential root. We avoid treating events as "dress rehearsals" and "precursors" of subsequent episodes and telescoping of single incidents as ruptures. By treating

---

[34] Michael Axworthy, *Revolutionary Iran: A History of the Islamic Republic* (Oxford: Oxford University Press, 2013), 76.

[35] Ananya Roy and Aihwa Ong, eds., *Worlding Cities: Asian Experiments and the Art of Being Global* (Malden, MA: Wiley-Blackwell, 2011).

continuity and change as coupled, one guards against forgetting or *remembering certain episodes.

Hence, when prompted to consider 1979 as global, several of the authors elected to reconsider the historiography, periodizations, and archives to write new histories of the revolution. Our next two chapters, under Part III, "Hidden Geneologies," consider historical moments that challenge overly ends-oriented accounts. The "much narrated tale of outrage and grievance,"[36] which Afsaneh Najmabadi describes as "stories" of revolution, homes in on 1977–1979. Our authors widen this temporal scope along with the spatial. It is 1967 and 1968 and the activism of students, nationalists, and seminarians around the death of the iconic Iranian wrestler Gholamreza Takhti that Arash Davari and Naghmeh Sohrabi assemble to explore Iran's parallel 1968 moment. As a conjunction between the global *New Left* patterns of student politics, on the one hand, and the local circumstances that generated the "*sinfi-siyasi*," or corporatist student-labor activism, on the other, Iran's 1968 is rendered neither a replica of its contemporary uprisings nor an antecedent to the national-centered politics that would be mobilized a decade later to bring down the shah. Christopher Dietrich, similarly, unmoors our accepted narrative. US-Iran relations have standard points of departure and pivots – 1953, the Nixon administration, or the Carter breeze of "human rights outreach." By investigating congressional records and debates in the mid-1970s, we appreciate the ways that US-Iran relations were being written anew as Congress intervened in a tumultuous phase of American global power as the US economy began to be redirected away "from factory to finance" by way of arms of sales in the name of "global economic health" and the preservation of the "Free World Economy." Even before the fall of the shah, US-Iran relations were being transfigured with components generated that would be picked up in remaking US-Saudi relations and US presence in the Persian Gulf. Through examining different sources and expanding our understanding of political struggles, both chapters unsettle stories about how alliances were made and remade by revolution. These moments before 1979 were not preludes, dress rehearsals, or the start of a "slide" that can be skimmed over in order to turn to their revolutionary denouement.

---

[36] Najmabadi, "'Is Our Name Remembered?'" 86.

If temporal disruptions and scale-making are themes of globalizing the revolution, thinking about the global relationally allows us to also break up the state/opposition dichotomy. The Pahlavi regime, or the institutions of the state, also participated in both nostalgia for lost tradition as well as situating Iran internationally through a series of networks composed of contractors, experts, ministers, international organizations, and discourses of modernism.[37] This may have not been an "Age of Aryamehr" and we may be cautious not to slide from romanticizing revolutionaries to the longing for the ancien régime, but Pahlavi internationalism sustained as well as attenuated monarchical rule. For the shah and the cadre of elites around him not only understood that Iran was intimately enmeshed in international circuits of capital and consultants, but by the 1970s perceived themselves as players in fashioning a new world order. Through skyrocketing oil revenues and positions in the mushrooming of international organizations in the emerging postcolonial era of the 1960s and 1970s, Pahlavi Iran's state officials traveled to conferences attended by a diverse set of leaders engaging in world-making anew.[38] Along with other recent publication this volume takes an initial step in weaving the threads of oppositional politics and regime agendas together. Pahlavi self-conceptions operated in conjunction with dissident discourses of their

[37] In addition to Chapters 9 and 10, see Bill, *The Eagle and the Lion*; Grace E. Goodell, *The Elementary Structures of Political Life: Rural Development in Pahlavi Iran* (New York: Oxford University Press, 1986); Talinn Grigor, *Building Iran: Modernism, Architecture, and National Heritage under the Pahlavi Monarchs* (New York: Periscope, 2009); Cyrus Schayegh, "Iran's Karaj Dam Affair: Emerging Mass Consumerism, the Politics of Promise and the Cold War in the Early Post-war Third World," *Comparative Studies in Society and History* 54:3 (2012): 612–643; Arang Keshavarzian, "Geopolitics and the Genealogy of Free Trade Zones in the Persian Gulf," *Geopolitics* 15:2 (2010): 263–289; Alex Boodrookas and Arang Keshavarzian, "The Forever Frontier of Urbanism: Historicizing Persian Gulf Cities," *International Journal of Urban and Regional Research* 43:1 (2019): 14–29; Roham Alvandi, ed., *The Age of Aryamehr: Late Pahlavi Iran and Its Global Entanglements* (London: Gingko Library, 2018); Gregory Brew, "'What They Need Is Management': American NGOs, the Second Seven Year Plan and Economic Development in Iran, 1954–1963," *The International History Review* 41:1 (2019): 1–22.

[38] Adom Getachew, *Worldmaking after Empire: The Rise and Fall of Self-determination* (Princeton, NJ: Princeton University Press, 2019). See also Arash Davari's essay on Getachew's analysis in relation to Pahlavi Iran: "On Inexactitude in Decolonization," *Comparative Studies of South Asia, Africa, and the Middle East* 40:3 (2020): 627–635.

time – human rights, effective sovereignty, nonalignment, and cultural authenticity.[39] While at moments they may have been operating as two ships passing in the night, intersections in such places as Beirut, Dubai, Hamburg, Dhofar, Washington, DC, and Paris as well as unlikely sets of bedfellows have been lost in the postrevolutionary sorting of people into the binaries of "regime" and "opposition" or "secular" and "religious."

These currents are detected in Part IV, "Circulating Knowledge," which examines the circulation of ideas and people claiming expertise. Golnar Nikpour's experts are self-proclaimed reformers and modernizers of the prison system, while Hossein Kamaly examines the role of science education as a means to explore how the Pahlavi era adopted it to depoliticize education in the context of its delegitimization in the years after the 1953 coup. Meanwhile, the natural and physical sciences, especially from Soviet institutions, became part of the political critique of the monarchy among dissidents. In both the context of criminology and sciences, the international circulation of ideas and the institutional mechanism to gain credentials became a vehicle to produce "cosmopolitan" elites and internationally recognized ways of being. But these globally circulating bundles of knowledge also differentiate between political projects and populations – prisoners or scientists – at the scale of the nation or the Cold War. Nikpour illustrates that "carceral modernity" was fashioned by Pahlavi reformers within global networks of criminologists and prison designers seeking civilizational progress. While torture and prison populations in Pahlavi Iran was a lightning rod for revolutionaries and critics of the shah, the category of "ordinary" and "political" prisoners remained hermetically sealed from one another for both revolutionaries and statesmen before and even after 1979. The vast majority of the prison population, the so-called nonpolitical inmates, were elided from discussions of progress, justice, and emancipation.

As mentioned in the Introduction, the notion of "the global" indexes our own historically conditioned way of thinking about the world. Yet, many of the people discussed in this volume thought in terms of Third

---

[39] Christopher Dietrich, *Oil Revolution: Anticolonial Elites, Sovereign Rights, and the Economic Culture of Decolonization* (Cambridge: Cambridge University Press, 2017); Arash Davari, "Indeterminate Governmentality: Neoliberal Politics in Revolutionary Iran, 1968–1979" (PhD diss., University of California, 2016).

World, *umma*, the international, "Westoxification," or interdepend-
ence for many reasons including to stress inequalities and borders that
carve up the world and buttress hierarchies within societies or between
states. It was because of this that many in the 1960s and 1970s
advocated for a new round of world-making that would be distinct
from earlier forms defined by empire, capitalism, national self-
determination, patriarchy, or the Cold War. The evoking of *dunya* or
jahan with their multiple meanings by Pahlavi loyalists or opponents
echoes distinct desire to escape the past and geographical destiny (see
Chapters 3 and 11). The Iranian Revolution, like other political movements, was bound up with aspirational cartographies and universalisms. Prevailing approaches fixated on explaining outcomes of 1979 do
not capture these unrealized universalisms, or if they do, they are often
treated as parochial, local, or nativist. If social space, including the
global or the universal, is produced through struggle, then all such
projects are susceptible to floundering and being defeated by expedi-
ency and unequal power – universalisms may not entail universality.[40]

What interests us is less the exclusions of dominant universalisms, be
they liberalism, capitalism, or communism, than the manifold declarations in the name of humanity. Part V, "Aspirational Universalisms,"
concludes the volume by examining two such political projects, one by
an Iranian filmmaker and one by a collective of French feminists
(Mouvement de Libération des Femmes). Hamed Yousefi outlines the
radical critique of modernity and revolutionary hopes of Morteza
Avini, a documentary filmmaker closely associated with "propagandistic" or "messianic" coverage of the Iran-Iraq War. In this chapter,
Yousefi instead explores Avini's prerevolutionary career and early
revolutionary writing and films focused on the plight of rural Iran to
articulate a universalism tethered to aesthetic cosmopolitan forms of
avant-garde cinema and anti-modernist philosophy. For Avini, Islam
was as a revolutionary religion and a negation of modernity, something that both brought him close to Khomeini's project, but generated
tensions with more developmentalist trends embedded in the postrevolutionary synthesis. Negar Mottahedeh grapples with the tensions
in translating between the revolution's internal conflicts and inter-
nationalizing and universalizing forces seeing it as a transhistorical

[40] Darryl Li, *The Universal Enemy: Jihad, Empire, and the Challenge of Solidarity* (Stanford, CA: Stanford University Press, 2020).

and multiscalar project. By mining the thinking, ruminations, and films of a group of French feminist activists, she reveals how they unearth "the seeds of planetary transformation" as they project their "fleshy feminism" upon Third Worldist struggles of the time. For Antoinette Fouque, the main theoretician of this circle, Iranian women's participation in the revolution that toppled the shah articulated a critique of contemporary feminisms and post-1968 Marxist politics in France. The discourse of nature, ecology, and planet collided awkwardly with the struggles of Iranian women and men as postrevolutionary leaders attempted to narrowly define women's public roles by deploying a conception of female biology and the essential nurturing characteristics of women. While the founders of the revolution succeeded in both expelling the feminist film crew and regulating women's bodies and social roles, feminism was imagined as a universalism that could be a bridge between Paris and Tehran, much as Avini's revolutionary universalism was a method to reverse the modernist model of salvation that subjected rural people as mere recipients of aid from a distant metropolitan core in Tehran and what after the fall of the Soviet Union becomes the Global North.

Conclusion

In gathering these essays into this volume, we orient readers toward many open avenues for future research on how the particulars of modern Iran and the varieties of global play out. The rich bibliographies and diverse sources of each of our chapters demonstrate the potential globalism of Iranian historiography as well as a need to think of global history as multidirectional, rather than emanating out from an epicenter or moving down from the global to the local scale. The volume's criss-crossing geographies resist the the polarizing notion of West vs. East that motivated some Iranians, including the shah and Khomeini, and significant swaths of punditry about the revolution and its aftermath. The analysis in the chapters tacks back and forth across different places in Iran and beyond its borders as well as back and forth between concrete social relations and aspirational imaginaries that brought people together and held them apart. While connectivity and mobility between space are foregrounded neither is the global assumed nor frictionless. Collectively and individually, the chapters disrupt familiar stories and interrupt hackneyed historical sequences by making us attuned to configurations of space and time obfuscated by a penchant to explain outcomes, assign responsibility, and second-guess decisions. As such the goal of writing the history of revolution should not be to draw "lessons" for the future and avoid mistakes of the past, but to conceive of the past as a "resource" and become aware of its resonances with our present and possible futures.[41]

[41] Kristin Ross, *Communal Luxury: The Political Imaginary of the Paris Commune* (London: Verso, 2015), 2–4.

PART I

Global Shadows

3 | *Seeing the World from a Humble Corner:*
A Political Memoir

ALI MIRSEPASSI[*]

Figure 3.1 Ali Mirsepassi, three years old, Malayer.

A one-day event, in the fall of 1978, indelibly marked my life as a revolution roared in the background. It robbed me of all that had inspired me and my hope for realizing a life of my own making.

[*] Christopher Dietrich, Naghmeh Sohrabi, Hossein Kamaly, and Arang Keshavarzian have kindly reviewed an earlier draft of this chapter and their valuable comments helped me revise and finalize it. Many other colleagues and friends also reviewed a very early and expanded version and kindly shared their comments (Hamid Dabashi, Saharnaz Samainejad, Arash Azizi, Hamed Yousefi, and Mehdi Faraji). I am grateful for their thoughtful and generous input. Tadd Fernée has been very helpful in editing this chapter and I would like to acknowledge his assistance and contribution. Bita Mousavi reviewed the final version and I would like to express my gratitude for her thoughtful edits.

Forty years later, the ghost of that event continues to haunt me. Today, as I write these words, sitting in the early morning light in a coffeeshop in New York City, the unforeseen and harrowing trauma I experienced forty years ago still remains very fresh. It buzzes in my mind, and, its picture, dark and painful to glance, forces itself before my eyes. This is not, for me, a usual way of remembering my past in tragic terms. I have never shared this sad event with my family or friends. Only very recently, and after nearly four decades, have I done so. I am now amazed to have taken so long to have come to terms with the nefarious side of my political life. It now seems to me that, by burying the ugly face of politics, no hope could flourish. Neither goodness nor peace could find inspiration in my mind where this darkness remained undisturbed by reflection. It may be time to let the "unthought" speak for itself by allowing the uncomfortable truth to surface at last, whatever the risks.

I had never intended to veil this horrible event. My fear was that any account of this powerful ordeal may unfairly overshadow the otherwise precious, if turbulent, experiences of my early youth. After all, this event transpired just as I optimistically prepared for the sweet realization of my dreams. I could literally see them materializing, everything I hoped for was just around the corner. Only then did I learn, violently and very sadly, how life may be the story of competing "plans" that you and others simultaneously strive to give birth to. Often, I learned, one becomes the victim of dreams nurtured and executed by the more powerful. How sad, and what a humbling experience.

It was a fall day in 1978, during the Iranian Revolution. After another full day of political organizing, my return trip home began with a walk to my car (an old white Paykan, Iranian-made) to drive home. Although tired, I was also delighted and honored by what I had just achieved. I had addressed hundreds of fellow university students at the National University in Tehran. My talk was very well received, and I had convinced students to proceed with the ongoing university strikes. The debate whether to strike or not and my talk in support of the latter action were precipitated by an announcement by Ayatollah Khomeini, the grand revolutionary leader, ordering a break in the nation-wide strikes and the resumption of normal university operations. I was nominated by the left faction of student activists to make the case on their behalf, perhaps because I had experience as a student activist from my Tehran University years. I accepted this grave responsibility with considerable anxiety, so it was a great relief to have carried it out successfully.

After everyone had vacated the campus, a vast emptiness and powerful silence settled over the space. I slowly walked in the direction of my car, parked outside of campus in a vacant lot. After about fifteen minutes of walking, the car was safely in sight. The Paykan was the only presence in an otherwise stripped landscape extending to the horizon. With it in my field of vision, I quickened my pace, extracting the car key from my pocket to unlock the car. Exactly at that moment, however, I felt the entire world crash down on my head. Then there was nothing. When I opened my eyes – many hours after the fact, I discovered – I found myself lying down in what appeared to be a garbage dump grown atop a hollow ditch. Looking up, I saw a few young kids and perhaps three adults looking down at me. Upon seeing my eyes open, they yelled out, "he is not dead!" I may not have been dead, but, unable to stand up or move my neck enough to peer around, I was uncomfortably aware of the limited control I had over my body in that moment. Overcome with confusion, I was unable to understand what had happened, or why I was in a deep ditch. However, an ambulance soon arrived to transport me to a hospital.

What followed the ambulance's merciful arrival remains hazy, and I very likely lapsed in and out of consciousness during the drive to the hospital. Once there, I remember waking up again, this time conscious enough to grasp that I was in the hospital at nighttime. The nurse and later a doctor came to tell me that God must have liked me. Luck, they made sure to emphasize, had been the deciding factor in my survival. Some kids had seen a car stop at a garbage dump in a village on the outskirts of Tehran. A few men emerged from the car, opened the trunk, and extracted from it a body. They tossed the body into a ditch before quickly driving away. The kids informed their parents of what they had witnessed, and their parents immediately called emergency services. An ambulance delivered me to the hospital, where doctors counted a total of twenty-one stab wounds. Some were superficial, others more serious, and a great deal of blood had been lost. None of the knife wounds were in sensitive areas. I was released from the hospital that night. This ended the revolution for me two or three months earlier than for most others.

The terrible extremity of that unforgettable day can only be made meaningful by setting it against the wider horizon of the everyday, the forgotten and quieter flow of ordinary time. My early life in Golpayegan offers a suitable vista for better understanding the revolution and its aftermath, as well as the shocking violence of that day. The Golpayegan experience opens a window onto Iranian political and intellectual life during the 1960s and 1970s, a period seldom studied outside the narrow confines of Tehran, the capital. Approaching this era from the vantage point of Golpayegan raises the tarpaulin that conceals those "local" meanings beneath the "official" state narratives that fail to explain either the revolution or the violence of that terrible day. The story used to correct these tendencies is simple enough on the surface. A provincial young man leaves his small town for Tehran, then spends two years in the UK. He returns to Tehran to play a role in the 1978 revolution. This simple narrative conceals the dynamics to remold our understanding of what the Iranian Revolution was. The story, upon examination, reveals how Iran was greatly more dynamic – engaged as it was in circulatory movements of people and ideas – than conventional Tehrani narratives allow us to see. The following reflections therefore occur against the backdrop of my political and intellectual biography. My own story is a small part of a much wider struggle to understand the minds and hearts of the many Iranians of my generation who participated in the 1978 Iranian Revolution.

The word *golpayegan* means "land of tulips," and the city, located northwest of Isfahan, lives up to the pastoral intonations of its name, producing heaps of wheat, cotton, barley, apricots, cherries, and cucumbers each year. In addition to its agricultural plenty, Golpayegan is known for its history of animal husbandry and carpet-weaving and wood-carving traditions. Bordered by mountains and cut through by the Ghebla River, Golpayegan is also home to roaming jackals, foxes, and wolves.

My experience of living in a small town like Golpayegan is, to a large extend, representative of the experience of many Iranians in the 1960s and 1970s. Golpayegan was a more religious-leaning place than many other small towns I know. My father worked for the Finance Ministry. His position obliged us to move from one city to another throughout my elementary to high school years. We were a typical civil servant family, spending our time with family friends among the government officials of the small towns in the western and central parts of Iran where we lived. Places like Golpayegan, neither fully rural nor urban, most likely comprised the vast bulk of Iran's national population at the time. Golpayegan's population in the late 1960s was around 35,000 with 40 per cent living in the town and the rest in nearby villages. Yet such towns received almost no attention in discussions about the revolution. This is perhaps because they affirm neither the urban nor peasant templates of modern theories of social change. While Golpayegan perhaps lacked the circumstances most conducive to radical political activities, the fervor of 1967–1968 and of the youth movement in Paris, the anti-war movement in New York, and of our own radical groups in Tehran, Tabriz, Mashhad, and Shiraz did not escape us in Golpayegan. Through this landscape of the collective mind, even our humble town joined the radical 1960s. I am inclined to think it did, which should provoke new thought about the circulation of ideas and what local and global may mean.

In small towns like Golpayegan an intense intellectual and political awakening was underway in the late 1960s and 1970s. In high school classrooms, bookshops, and other public places of intellectual production and consumption, activists of my generation gathered to debate and draw inspiration from ideas articulated around the world, from Nehru's independent India to the Palestinian struggle for dignity in autonomy. Our ideal of the Iranian nation resembled such distant examples more than the enforced official rituals celebrating the Pahlavi state and its modernization program. This "cosmopolitan" consciousness wedded to an impassioned political activism highlights how a local intellectual and political efflorescence partook of wider global interactions, and an investigation of this experience may offer a corrective to the narrow Tehran-centrism dominating scholarship on the revolution. The world experienced from a small town like Golpayegan provides a new perspective on how exchanges and circulations of ideas and politics coincided to forge one of the most important events of the twentieth century.

In an ironic way, my family was the product of the Pahlavi modernization project, and we felt rather comfortable with this fact. My father was a staunchly pro-Pahlavi figure. He was an Iranian nationalist who reserved special admiration for the originary efforts of the first Pahlavi monarch, Reza Shah. Although he divulged to me little about his impressions of the 1950s oil nationalization struggle, I was aware that my father had sided with the royalists and opposed Mossadegh. He developed a very strong anti-Tudeh Party stand. My father repeatedly told me: "I and everything I believe in are the result of Reza Shah's

Figure 3.2 Ali Mirsepassi, thirteen years old, Nahavand.

labors." He regarded the Shia clerics as embodying the opposite of what he stood for – modernization and the defense of national interests and government – and I remember the wariness he frequently expressed over growing clerical influence in Iranian cultural and political life. Yet my father was also a man of faith, with a deep emotional attachment to Shia Islam and his own nationalistic interpretation of its meaning. He did not become involved in politics, declining to join any pro-shah political party. My father simply admired the shah's modernization vision for Iran.

For the most part, I shared my father's positive view of Iranian modernization, while remaining sympathetic to Shiism. I felt uncomfortable, however, with the elitism of my father's cadre of government official acquaintances, with their open contempt for other Iranians (non-Tehranis in particular). Even as a very young boy, I early on perceived the condescension that characterized the Pahlavi state's outlook on the Iranian masses. As a child in Golpayegan, many of my friends were rooted in the local town and occasionally in nearby villages. My family did not refrain from voicing their discomfort with the way I socialized with, in their view, "provincial" or *dahati* kids. As I grew older and developed the confidence needed to express my own views, I tried to challenge my father's notion of nationalism. I would ask him, "Why is it that in your nationalism most regular Iranians have no place?" Never liking this, he would respond: "Regular people don't know what is good for them ... I admire our leaders, who know what is good for the country and make it happen." My father's rationale was curt but effective. Within it, solutions to the world's problems were reducible to a simple historical comparison. Our nation had declined, losing its sovereignty and prestige under feeble Qajar rule, but had regained all that it had lost due to the strong and visionary leadership of Reza Shah. He lacked time or enthusiasm for discussing any other contemporary political issues. He loved, however, to tell me stories about Iran's past victories and miseries. In his telling, Iran's national history was that of a people tragically victimized by lesser peoples.

Although I shared my father's respect for our country, I had little interest in recounting Iran's fabled greatness. Nor did I share my father's harsh attitude toward Arabs, Turks, and others who had encountered Iran throughout its historic past. In my view, all nations and ethnic groups mistreated each other, so it made no sense to grieve over historic injustices supposedly perpetrated against Iran as we also had occasionally unkindly treated Indians and others. Nor was I interested in the many stories I heard from my father, teachers, and state radio broadcasters about the Qajar rulers and their total ineptitude. Despite the little knowledge I had about eighteenth- and nineteenth-century Persia, I personally concluded that it had been a time of material privation I was not interested in revisiting. "Our country" had simply been unable to overcome the great powers. It was unhelpful to constantly mourn the events of those times.

At the same time, I developed a genuine love for "regular" people. My admiration was inflected by yearning for their communitarian way of life. I was drawn especially to the way they spoke about their community, and, what seemed to me, their deeply fulfilling social relations with one another. The depth of connectedness I perceived among them was perhaps important to me because, outside of my immediate family, I felt no genuine or natural connections with any group of people. I felt furious at my situation, where, in every town we relocated to, the "locals" always designated me an outsider. While a sense of community and belonging evaded my early adolescence, solidarity was provided by the small intellectual world to which I belonged, and consequently the path of political activism I followed.

The intellectual roamers I counted as my tribe represented a generation of Iranians, many of whom would participate in the revolution, who still aspired to the democratic ideals of the Mashruteh (Constitutional) project, which peaked in the initial years of the twentieth century. We understood this project to mean the realization of a modern Iran that embraced its citizens as active participants in the country's affairs. Sadly, this is a part of the story of the revolution that is gradually being forgotten by many of us. It is the dream that I had in mind on the terrible day in the vacant lot, as I quickened my pace to reach the car. The reality of a collective push toward the Mashruteh horizon is perhaps eclipsed by an academic emphasis on structural explanations for the causal factors of the revolution, a frame disinterested in human will, and the triumphalist narratives of Islamist victory consolidated in the aftermath of the clerical seizure of power in 1979.

This autobiographical account thus helps to recover the Mashruteh project not as a discrete moment in time ending in 1911 but a long-standing struggle for a democratic Iran, while refuting pervasive myths of the "local" as a "pure" cultural unit bounded and untainted by the force of the global. I recount the experience of the prerevolutionary period from a small town in Iran. From there and countless other small towns and villages like it, millions of Iranians participated in the revolution. These millions lived and experienced politics not merely from a limited "local" view. Instead, young high school students marshalled a far richer assortment of evidence in the process of politicizing self and others as they passionately interacted with multiple events occurring beyond their small city, in the capital Tehran, but also in the West and across the diverse countries of the Third World.

Islam and Marxism in Our Town

Golpayegan was not a typical small town of 1960s and 1970s Iran. At the time of my adolescence, in the late 1960s, the external markers of what we now call rapid modernization were hardly discernible. The town did not have a movie theater, alcoholic beverages were not permitted for sale or consumption, men (including students at the two all-male high schools) were expected to grow their beards, and hardly any women appeared in public without a *chador* (hijab was not mandatory for the one all-female high school in the town). We would escape to the neighboring smaller towns of Khansar and Khomein, which boasted new hotels and a movie theater, to have fun. In Golpayegan almost everyone was involved in agriculture, caring for livestock, and performing religious rituals. Perhaps this was an ideal place for anthropologists to conduct fieldwork. It was not, however, a very cool place for a teenage boy, especially one new to the town. The religiosity of its citizens was ingrained and found outlet daily in mundane proprieties and intimacies of everyday lives. The situation was markedly different from the current state of affairs in Iran, where religiosity is an official ideology enforced onto the minds and bodies of Iranians from on high and practiced skin deep. A visitor from the outside world would have immediately and clearly observed the town's affections for land, cattle, and God.

The process of authoritarian modernization perhaps affected Iranian youth more than any other segment of the population. Flush with the vigor of youth, I was ready and eager to embrace new ways of being and living. I felt, however, that some of these changes were in fact overwhelming Iranian society and left absolutely no space for young people to creatively participate in and claim ownership of these transformations. Neither our thoughts nor our initiatives could have guided a modernization process that treated most Iranians with such brutal indifference. It was this separation between design and implementation, I thought, that rendered modernization such a violent and frightening process, devoid of liberatory potential, for so many. At a personal level, I had the yearning to "belong." This hunger for community was widespread among people my age, and the state of "alienation" endured by me and my generation helps explains our intense involvement in both religious and radical leftist politics. We found our "belonging" in a shared sense of solidarity and a shared imaginary of the Iran of tomorrow.

During my last four years of high school, which coincided with my years in Golpayegan, I developed a budding interest in radical politics and intellectual ideas. As I said earlier, Golpayegan was a deeply religious town. Even a family friend visiting from Qom, a famous center of Shiite learning and learning, expressed surprise at the deep religiosity of the little town. The city was a very humble place, both in its unassuming appearance and in the studied modesty of its people and their attitudes and behaviors. Despite my radical turn, I remained fond of how kind and caring they were, even if at times they annoyed me with their relentless religiosity.

How do we explain the political trajectory, witnessed in Golpayegan and across Iran, from a public ethics of piety to modern state and movement ideologies calling for a "return to the sources" or "the self"? This distinction cannot merely be explained in terms of grand pre-modern traditions corrupted by modernity, as if there were a simple dichotomy. The relation seems instead dialectical. This small town was also connected to the larger world outside. This gives further substance to the idea that perhaps knowing the "world" is genealogically prior to the imagining of the national. To better apprehend this relationship, we ought to look at grassroots or "emergent nationalism," not "official nationalism" forced on populations from above.

What is initially striking is that the unofficial "emergent" Iranian nationalism involved the cohabitation of multiple small worlds. This seemingly tame town had a robust cultural and educational life of its own. The two all-male high schools in town, Ebn-e Sina (named after Avicenna) and Pahlavi, were centers of the town's cultural and, to an extent, political life.[1] Most of our high school teachers were involved in cultural and (mostly, though not exclusively, religious) political activities. I took as a model of inspiration our literature teacher. To me, he was dazzlingly smart, unbelievably learned, and an exemplary person. He was an effective teacher, a caring mentor, and an intensely religious man. Although I thought he approached perfection, I could not identify with his lifestyle or even contemplate friendship with him. He resembled a personality out of our religious books: ideal in all qualities, but too "good" to be real and relatable. Why did I feel this way? Perhaps it was the antihero, whose imperfection at least made him multidimensional, to whom I really gravitated. Or perhaps I simply desired a more open and diverse lifestyle, since to me the literature teacher lived a rather one-dimensional life.

There were other small worlds orbiting around the same social space. I was also drawn to two younger teachers, both new to the town. They came from Tehran, whereas almost all other teachers were either natives of Golpayegan or from Isfahan. These two younger teachers were Marxists who had yet to learn to code their speech with

---

[1] There was one all-female high school in Golpayegan, but boys were not allowed to go to events there. Based on my sister's reports, they planned regular cultural activities and she felt the high school was a more open space for women's activities. As far as I can remember, all "public" events in Golpayegan were only attended by men.

the euphemisms common among political activists at the time. Instead, their Marxism announced itself as soon as you talked to them. They assumed that all political students were sympathetic to Marxism, as they bulldozed ahead with their references to Samad Behrangi, Maxim Gorky, Latin American revolutionaries, and taboo others. Their forth-right and plain political language was interesting because, during this time, we mostly read literary works, like Bozorg Alavi's *Chashmhayash* (*Her Eyes*, 1952), if we wanted to learn about Marxism and revolution-ary ideas. For exposure to critical and political readings of Islam, we turned to audio tapes, such as a tape recording by a well-known cleric, Mohammad Taqi Falsafi. The tapes were mostly lectures on cultural corruptions and decline of traditional values in Iran.

In my view, Iran was a society in transition, experiencing radical social change. Like many other very young people, we were steeped in the immediacy of local cultural and the daily intimacies of family life, but we were connected to wider national happenings. We faithfully imbibed the literature and politics of worlds beyond ours. So keen were we to learn about the broader world that we even looked to American detective stories for instruction.

The late 1960s witnessed the birth of a new social consciousness among the younger population of Golpayegan. Although we were bound by the bonds of home and family to Golpayegan, this conscious-ness occurred within a nonempirical "imaginary" and across multiple transnational linkages. For us, the late 1960s and the 1970s was a "place," and the whole world was present there. Evidence of the synchronous change was everywhere: in the youth movement in Europe, the unfolding events in Vietnam and the Third World, the Palestinian cause, the dramatic changes state radio reported about the Arab world, and even in the world of music. The Beatles championed to pop melodies a new vision of cosmopolitan humanism and change. We came to feel certain that a worldwide movement for change was transpiring around us, and this feeling opened new ways for Iranians to engage hitherto vague worlds over the course of several dramatic decades. Books, schools, cinema, and radio defined a new informa-tional space. Translations from European and Arabic languages were a critical information source, since the available Persian books were mostly either literary studies, novels, short stories, histories, or reli-gious books. Within Iran, very little was on offer concerning politics after the post-Mashruteh era. Even world politics were muted. This absence reveals the workings of state censorship. We dreamed within an informational world of translations and traces. Despite this gap, we avidly read Iranian magazines and newspapers, and I was especially fond of the weekly *Ferdowsi*.

Imagining Iran

As a prelude to discussing how fellow students and activists imagined Iran, I will recall two distinct political-intellectual encounters with the "idea of the Iranian nation." These images of Iran recurred in my thoughts and actions, and very likely in those of my friends.

On one level, we experienced the idea of Iran promoted by the Pahlavi state. We listened to Radio Iran. The political party that controlled both the parliament and the cabinet was, not coincidentally, also a state-sanctioned one: the Iran Novin Party (New Iran Party). For routine celebrations of the shah's birthday on October 27, students from all parts of Iran were forced to present themselves to their city's main sport stadium. There, under obligation, we were compelled to celebrate the shah as God's gift to the nation. The shah's speeches proclaimed him the embodiment of the Iranian nation. Foreign dignitaries and Iranian state officials alike addressed the shah as the very personification of Iran.

This "official" – or national – representation of Iran felt distant from my own imagining of the country. The "official" version was burdened with tedious rituals demonstrating nothing other than the shah's power. I reluctantly participated in these rituals under duress. Given the compulsion involved, the displays of kingly grandeur stirred nothing in my heart. I saw only a giant bureaucratic machine owned by the shah. Without him, it could not survive. The regime's narrative about the Iranian nation conflated Iran with the monarchy, reaffirming our view that the existing Iran was not ours but someone else's. In a recent study on nationalism in Iran, Ali Ansari confirms my then intuitive view about how Iran was imagined during this period. Ansari notes that Mohammad Reza Shah, over time, expunged the familiar notion of nationhood inherited from the epic poem *Shahnameh* from the Iranian body politic, while fashioning his own image as the true embodiment of the Iranian nation.[2]

---

[2] Ali Ansari, *The Politics of Nationalism in Modern Iran* (New York: Cambridge University Press, 2012), 176–178.

Therefore, despite the propaganda saturating our everyday lives that identified the Pahlavi state with the Iranian nation, our eyes remained fastened on a completely different Iran. As I remember it now, we had perhaps a more political and even emotional affinity with faraway places such as Vietnam, Palestine, Cuba, and India than Iran. We were expected to acquaint ourselves with works like Jawaharlal Nehru's *Discovery of India*. While I was saddened to see my country dominated by Western imperialism, especially in the form of outsized US influence over Iran and its affairs, I recognized that the Pahlavi state, rather than defend Iranian independence, was happily party to this game of geopolitics. Many political discussions among students and politicized older people focused on US involvement in the 1953 coup d'état. I felt that everything wrong in Iran was the outcome of this foreign involvement in Iranian affairs. Through this my interest in the struggles of other countries, such as Vietnam, became enlivened. The question is, why this emotional affinity? What was the commonality that drew us to identify with the national experience of Cuba more than with contemporary Pahlavi Iran? What made us envision our ideal Iran in terms of international experiences? The Tudeh Party, which emerged in 1941, helped realize considerable "national" achievements. It was crushed, however, after the 1953 coup by the autocratic Pahlavi state. The Marxism we embraced in 1960s Golpayegan had been systematically stripped of its organizational potential and was a ghost of this wave of mass Iranian activism. Nonetheless, we continued reading and learning about the radical and national liberation movements in Vietnam, Cuba, China, Palestine, and elsewhere. Their notion of the nation as a politico-ethical ideal yet to be realized resonated with me much more than did the Pahlavi presentation of Iran through daily rituals of allegiance and brazen whitewashing of the historical past.

The community we cared for was absent in these official imaginings of Iran. We perhaps thought of this "absence" as *our* Iran. This historically formed cultural "space" (since absences too occupy space) encompassed a tangle of histories and ideas. Along the manifold horizon of "Iranian absence," we imagined Iran as an "emerging" idea. This "emergence" was a mirror reflection of India, Japan, Central Asia, Europe, or the Soviet Union. On a cultural level, however, Iran embodied the endogenous literary traditions of Hafez, Saadi, Rumi; the philosophy of Farabi, Avicenna, and Suhrawardi; the political legacy of Mashruteh figures (Sattar Khan, Bagher Khan, Dehkhoda,

Mosaddegh, etc.); and the innovation of free verse poets (Ahmad Shamlu, Akhavan Sales, and Forough Farrokhzad). In one respect, Iran was a project for the future tentatively held in our mind which partly resembled Nehru's India, Castro's Cuba, Lenin's Soviet Union, and the country the Iranian Constitutionalist revolutionaries had envisioned and articulated. This last idea was advocated by our Marxist teachers (more on which later). Thus, while we admired Japanese and European achievements, we still considered ourselves to be citizens of a distinct cultural world. This sense of cultural difference did not vitiate the fact that, as Iranians, we were committed to the transnational mobilization of impoverished countries.

In view of these considerations, we might argue that "nationalism" involves an altered temporality. Its three interconnected sections form a unified structure. And the piecing together of this structure is perhaps part of the "unthought" I have been seeking through these recollections. First, there is the past: the latent consciousness of the youth of Golpayegan of "a historically formed cultural space." Second, there is the present: Iran as I hoped and desired it to be. An "emerging" idea, very much in relation to, or as mirror image of, India, Japan, Central Asia, Europe, or the Soviet Union. From this perspective, we notice a striking and counterintuitive detail: the act of imagining the world precedes nationalism genealogically. Third, there is the future: the future we envisioned in our mind partly looked like Nehru's India, Castro's Cuba, Lenin's Soviet Union, and the country of the Iranian Constitutionalists.

This future was highly imaginative and of course contradictory. For example, the simultaneous idealization of the Soviet Union and Nehru's India appeared to us as two harmonious instances of mass struggle for justice for the poor. Yet their similarity was only nominal. These two regimes had conflicting political and economic logics, the dire consequences of which cannot be dispelled by any amount of utopian enthusiasm. But we are describing an emergent mass consciousness among youth in a country facing the turmoil of an uncertain future. The contradictions should therefore scarcely surprise us.

We might typically think of the "transnational" as the domain of a privileged, cosmopolitan jet-setter. Yet here, "transnational" is an imaginative experience compelled by a mix of institutional pressures, technological possibilities (i.e. radio, print media, etc.), and the dreams of a desperate population facing neocolonial oppression, imminent

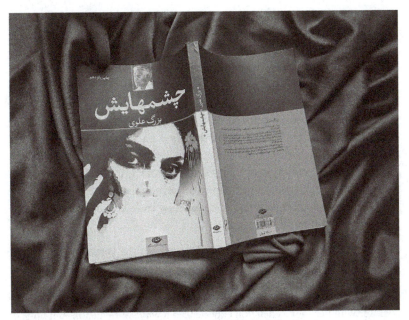

Figure 3.3 Cover of Bozorg Alavi, *Chashmhayash* (*Her Eyes*).

state-collapse, and revolution. It undercuts the notion of the indigenous as "pure," unmediated by the "outside," a kind of subaltern trope. On the contrary: the outside inhabited the inside from the beginning, as the national germinated in the imaginary space of the transnational.

Chashmhayash (Her Eyes)

At this time, 1968–1969, I had regular arguments with my two Marxist teachers over their annoyance at my reading habits, and our heated differences of opinion about contemporary Persian literature. I had just completed reading Bozorg Alavi's splendid novel, *Chashmhayash* (*Her Eyes*).[3] This work of fiction was the most inspiring and true-to-life piece of political literature I had ever chanced to read. Although only sixteen years old, I had become an avid reader.

---

[3] Bozorg Alavi, *Chashmhayash* [Her eyes] (Tehran: Amir Kabir, 1357/1978). The book has been translated into English: Bozorg Alavi, *Her Eyes*, trans. John O'Kane (Lanham, MD: University Press of America, 1989).

I deemed it an honor to have access to *Chashmhayash* and read it, a novel banned at the time and unavailable at bookstores. To me, *Chashmhayash* was a dazzling piece of literature and a must-read for anyone concerned with Iran and its people.

Chashmhayash spins a web of concentric circles, beginning with a painting at its center, then extending outward to show Iranian society as reflecting the same pattern of terror and turmoil contained in the eyes of the painting's subject. Ostensibly a narrative about the painter Ostad Makan, the text builds atop him successive domes of meaning. A single image contains myriad contradictory impulses, and the enigmatic eyes of the woman in the portrait evade fixed interpretation. We can never trust what we see, for it varies by moment and seems to have nothing solid behind it:

The woman was very beautiful but what amazed the beholder was not the beauty of her face. It was rather the riddle and mystery of the eyes themselves ... At times you looked at the painting and were moved to tears. Other times, on the contrary, you imagined a woman who was torturing the painter with her look. Then you experienced a wave of revulsion. But none of the painter's friends or relatives believed a woman had ever played an important role in his life.[4]

The concentric circles widen and contract as the eyes of the painted woman at their core of the narrative represent the mental condition of a society ensnared in conflicting information circuits. The mystery is not just in the woman's eyes, but in Iranian society:

Journalists brought forth incredible incidents from their repertoire of lies and deceit ... Fortunately, these stories have subsided little by little and now the moment is drawing near when someone might take a deeper look into the career of Ostad during the period of the dictatorship, and clean up the mystery that shrouds his life.[5]

The writer's quest recounted in the novel is itself the unveiling of this mystery, an elaborate aesthetic encasing, driving the revelation of events that transport the reader to the heart of Pahlavi society:

The events do not form an unbroken sequence, and yet, there seems to be a mysterious thread running through them ... From the first day that the idea occurred to write the history of Iran's great painter, I realized that if I didn't

---

[4] Alavi, *Her Eyes*, 11.   [5] Ibid., 14.

find the unknown woman whose eyes appear in the painting, all I could write was what had been published in the newspapers. I'd read the police documents too. But there were no clues in them either.[6]

We too must venture beyond the official Iran of state-controlled newspapers and police records to another Iran to reach the national spirit of Iran nurtured by the lives of ordinary people. Without the subtle tension and ultimate impact built into this aesthetic stratagem, it is difficult to imagine the powerful epiphany that the novel subtly provokes within the reader.

I was keen to share this reading experience with the two Marxist teachers. They were always very tactful in sharing their criticisms with me. On this occasion, however, they softly but forthrightly told me that I was misguided concerning the political worth and literary quality of *Chashmhayash*. They said that it was too romantic, lacking a proper representation of Iran's class structure under Reza Shah's reign. Alavi's writing was crude and the book's narrative style passé. It would not, they charged, reach the rank of important literary work bestowed on other Iranian political novels. They urged me to read what they considered the more important literary works, pointing me to writers like the celebrated dramatist Gholamhossein Sa'edi and others I no longer recall.

Upset with their comments, I replied that their judgment was unfair and one-sided concerning this wonderful novel. I had to admit, however, that I lacked their literary expertise, and that, as my teachers, I respected their views. I decided that I would reflect further on my reaction to the book and write a response to them explaining my love for it. By defending it, I hoped to change their minds. They both expressed approval of my attitude, however misguided they thought it to be, and looked forward to reading my defense. They too hoped to change my mind, helping me "find the straight path" (*beh rah-ye rast biya'id*). The *straight* path (*rah-ye mustaqim*), I replied, coincided with *the true path to Islam*, a favorite religious expression of my literature teacher, and as Marxists they had already erred in choosing not the right but the "left" path to truth. We all laughed, but I felt a burden on my shoulders: defending a book I adored to the learned men I held in equal esteem.

[6] Ibid., 21.

معلمان قدیمی گلپایگان - ۱۳۴۵

Figure 3.4 High school teachers, Golpayegan, 1966.

Today, only a cloudy impression remains of what I wrote to them. My present recollections may suggest a clearer and brighter defense than what I really mounted, since the substance of my defense is not as clear as are the strangely vivid memories I retain of the feelings swelling in me as I debated my two teachers. I cannot explain why this exchange has remained alive in my mind, their faces still appearing vividly.

Perhaps it is because of the acute awareness of my limitations with which I entered the defense. I was a teenage student full of admiration and gratitude for those who, like my teachers, took my opinions seriously. While they were kind to engage me on issues I thought important, I knew they were better versed in the matters under discussion. I explained to them how hard it was to debate them together, as they routinely and seamlessly finished each other's thoughts. I asked them to bear these disadvantages in mind. In the past, I had almost always hesitated to challenge them, either changing the subject, staying silent, or stopping the conversation. On this occasion, however, I chose to speak truthfully, because I truly felt they had failed to recognize what was clearly good.

Figure 3.5 Bozorg Alavi.

And so I openly confessed my frustration and bewilderment at their refusal to accept that this was a treasured novel written by a distinguished writer (Figure 3.5). I explained that my admiration for *Chashmhayash* was on solid ground from both a literary and political perspective. I reminded them that Bozorg Alavi belonged to the Tudeh Party, that he had spent time in jail as part of the "group of fifty-three," during Reza Shah's 1930s dictatorship, and was now living in East Germany.[7] Alavi had also written other important books, many of them political: *Chamedan* (*The Suitcase*, 1934), *Varaq Pareh-ha-ye Zendan* (*Scrap Papers from Prison*, 1941), *Panjah-o Seh Nafar* (*Fifty-Three Persons*, 1942), *Nameh-ha va Dastan-ha-ye Digar* (*Letters and Other Stories*, 1952). Given the sheer scale of his output, how could they fail to consider Alavi a pioneer and leading Iranian writer? I did my best to argue that *Chashmhayash* was a powerful and inspiring novel, even apart from the political affiliation of its author. It

[7] A group of fifty-three allegedly communist activists were arrested in 1937. All of them were charged with organizing a communist cell and promoting "collectivist ideology," outlawed by Reza Shah's national security law. The group included some of the most prominent intellectuals and political figures of the time, including Taqi Arani and Bozorg Alavi.

was perhaps the best novel recently written among well-known Iranian writers from leftist backgrounds.[8] Even as a mere piece of literary work, *Chashmhayash* was brilliant:

The painting *Her Eyes* was no more than the simple face of a woman, the elongated face of a woman whose hair flowed down over her shoulders like molten pitch. Everything in the face appeared subdued. The nose, mouth, cheeks and forehead were indicated in dark colors. It seemed what the artist wanted to say was that the owner of the face no longer existed in the external world and only the eyes had left a lasting impression in his memory.[9]

I should pause to present a short analysis of some important themes in *Chashmhayash* to underline its structural complexity.

(1) On the most obvious level, the novel, which is also a police detective story, analyzes the *abuse of power*, reconstructing from fragments Iranian public and political memory. Dread for the police state, the paranoia engendered by neighbors ubiquitously spying on one another, and the secrecy of 1930s transnational political networks pervade the emotional frame of the novel.

(2) *Chashmhayash* is also an *existential* novel dealing with the opacity of inner motivation: the narrator ("Farangis," whose name is a veil for hidden realities) is constantly uncertain about her own motivations and identity.

(3) This existential theme suggests a *sociological* analysis. Farangis's confession, her sense of ambivalence, testifies to the complexity of a modern complex wherein incommensurable worldviews and conflicting interests conceal the consequences of actions done to us, and of our actions done to others.

(4) Finally, it is a *Marxist* analysis of class dynamics. The novel recounts Farangis's painful discovery of the *meaning of her class privilege*, which, she learns, rests upon violence against the Iranian masses. This realization sets in during her encounter with Iranians exiled in Paris, including with a politically committed gardener's

---

[8] I may have mentioned my view that only Sadeq Hedayat was a superior writer to Alavi. I was more familiar with Hedayat's work, having read many of his books earlier when we lived in Nahavand. They included *Zendeh be gur* [Buried alive] (Tehran: Ferusi Publisher, 1309/1930, a collection of short stories), *Seh ghatreh khun* [Three drops of blood] (Tehran: Amir Kabir, 1311/1932), and, of course, *Buf-e kur* [The blind owl] (Bombay: 1315/1936).

[9] Alavi, *Her Eyes*, 10.

son who is lifted by the revolutionary and spiritual leadership of Ostad, but doomed to an early death because poverty had crushed his health from the outset. Inexplicable mental anguish haunts Farangis as she contemplates her lifetime of material ease and unlimited possibilities.

Examining these four points, it becomes clear that *Chashmhayash* is not a work of cold social realism, nor a condemnation of certain classes, but an intimate exploration of interactions between different social classes who had hitherto lived together – but apart – within a single modern society. These observations would not have occurred to me at the time, and I explained to my teachers how the novel exposed me to the desolation of the Reza Shah period with passages like the following:

A death-like silence reigned over the whole country. Everybody made believe he was content. The newspapers published nothing but eulogies on behalf of the dictator. People were starved for new and secretly circulated fantastic lies. Who would dare say publicly that anything was wrong? Was it possible anything could be wrong in the land of the King of Kings?[10]

I could empathize with the novel. Alavi depicted our experience in a creative, yet simple way. He described a society filled with potential, where many individuals driven by positive ideas endeavored to inspire and do good, while feeling victimized by the ruling class.

Ostad Makan was a great painter and was certain that through the art of painting he could fight against injustice and oppression. Ostad was more than just a painter; he was a great artist because as a human being he felt compassion for the suffering of others. For him painting was a means of combating tyranny; his pursuit of art had a social and humanitarian dimension. Ostad wanted to render service to his fellow man. This is what painting meant to him and for precisely that reason his art moved people.[11]

I told my teachers that Makan, a character in the novel, represented to me the well-known Iranian painter Kamalolmolk (1848–1940), who was born Mohammad Ghaffari (Figure 3.7).[12] I spoke of my own love

---

[10] Ibid., 7. [11] Ibid., 28.

[12] At this time in my life, I was seriously interested in painting and was planning to pursue it both academically and professionally. I was hoping to go to the Faculty of Art at Tehran University. My father strongly opposed this decision, wanting me to attend medical school. However, after many arguments, as a compromise, I agreed to apply to law school. Sadly, I did not apply to the art school.

Figure 3.6 High school teachers, Golpayegan, late 1966.

Figure 3.7 Portrait of Kamalolmolk.

of painting to them, explaining how Kamalolmolk was an almost mythical figure in my eyes: "Crowds of people turned up to see their own selves. For in Ostad's paintings of clear color and solid form what they found portrayed was themselves. In particular they stood with fixed gaze before the painting which had written below it in his own hand: *Her Eyes.*"[13]

Kamalolmolk was a distinguished artist who traveled to Europe and acquired a deep knowledge of both the Iranian and European artistic traditions. He also had a political career: He participated in the Constitutional Revolution, and despite Reza Shah's attempt to lure him into his circle as an ally, he refused the temptation. Critical of Reza Shah's tyrannical rule, Kamalolmolk resigned as director of his own art school, leaving Tehran in 1928 to live in exile in Nishapur until his death in 1940. The year Kamalolmolk died, Alavi was released from prison following Reza Shah's forced abdication and exile.

The passion felt by my generation for this painter explains why *Chashmhayash* so deeply impacted us. It invited us to find our distinctive path in modern Iran, a call paralleled by the narrator's own investigative quest to unravel the mystery of Ostad's well-concealed life, leading to his exile and death in the provinces. He spends many years tracking a mysterious woman who was the subject of Ostad's painting, *Her Eyes*, thinking she holds the key to explaining his life. With the secrets of Ostad's life discovered, the narrator hopes to provide narrative order and meaning to a fractured Iranian nation. The incompleteness of Ostad's known life has left Iran haunted by an enigma. The narrator thus concocts a convoluted plan for extracting a confession from the "unknown woman" of the painting.

Rather than advance this existential rationale, I attempted my best argument for why *Chashmhayash* was a good political novel. In my view, Makan was an exemplary radical, someone I felt inspired to emulate. An accomplished person dedicated to his people and nation, yet open to knowledge of other places and ideas, he retained enough integrity to reject the allure of power and wealth. Makan resisted them because of belief, a solid character, and heightened sense of honor. Perhaps all teenage activists idealized radicals this way. At the time, this was my image of Kamalolmolk, in the simple, realistic, and powerful prose by Alavi. Alavi's Makan had reached an almost perfect balance between strong-mindedness in his early encounter with Firangis and his gentle composure elsewhere.

Alavi, I continued, brilliantly described Firangis as a woman strong enough to rise above a complex of personal and political circumstance

---

[13] Alavi, *Her Eyes*, 10.

to follow her own desires. Makan and Firangis shared a rare personal quality: Each had faith in their beliefs so as to never confuse the good for the convenient. This explains why Makan refused a life of wealth and prestige out of political conviction, while Firangis, in Europe, left a comfortable life and went to Iran to pursue her love. These were characters in *Chashmhayash* whom I loved and admired. Alavi's message, I explained, should be taken to heart, for it provided a powerful counter-narrative to the "good old days" image of the first Pahlavi ruler. It told readers that the "modernizing" shah was perhaps a "modern ruler," but certainly not one fit for a progressive Iran. He was power hungry and tyrannical, inhibiting the abilities of genuinely progressive Iranians, such as Makan, to contribute to the development of Iran and its people. I referred them to the first paragraph of the book and how brilliantly Alavi sketched the political situation of Iran under Reza Shah:

Tehran is suffocating. Nobody is breathing. Everybody is afraid of another person. Families are afraid of each other. Children fear their teachers; the teacher fears the janitor and the janitor fears the hairdresser. Everybody is afraid of himself and his shadow. The people can see the shadow of the government thugs everywhere: in their house, in the mosque, behind the shop counter, in the school, in the university and in the bathhouse. When the royal anthem is played in the cinema the people watch their neighbors lest a crazy fellow should forget to rise and create problems for the audience. A deadly silence prevails all over the country. Everybody pretends to be happy. The papers had nothing to write but to praise the dictator.[14]

I concluded my defense of Alavi by affirming before the two brother teachers that I unabashedly identified with Alavi's political views and emotional sensibilities about 1930s Iran. It was too convenient for them to oppose and reject everything. It is more radical to fight on behalf of what is good and useful. This is what *Chashmhayash* stands for. I cannot remember if my conclusion was quite as absolute as this, but I was very upset and certain of my own view. Upon finishing my comments, I handed them (or one of them, to be precise, though I now feel as if the two teachers shared the same face) my notes. After a few days, they asked me to visit them during lunchtime (after lunch, I regularly used to play volleyball, which I skipped that day). To my absolute surprise, they were not convinced at all, telling me in less than

[14] Ibid., 1.

Figure 3.8 High school teachers, Golpayegan, late 1960s.

diplomatic language that I was behaving like a "child" (*bacheh*) and was merely captivated by Alavi's simplistically romantic storytelling skills. I found them cold and their treatment of me arrogant. In my thinking, it was as Kamalolmolk was treated by Reza Shah. I had never imagined I would be in a similar place.

They urged me to overcome my fascination with the aesthetic dimensions of *Chashmhayash*, so that I might see the trivial substance lurking beneath the prose. I was frustrated that two Marxist teachers so loathed *Chashmhayash* and disappointed with myself for failing to convince them of its worth. At this point, my teachers became exasperated, their comments turning harsher and uncharacteristically dismissive. With their patience for a stubborn student having run out, they insisted that Alavi's literary style in *Chashmhayash* was influenced by the romantic upper-class (*ashrafi*, or aristocratic, was the word they used) genre of 1940s Iran. They compared him to Mohammad Hejazi's novel, telling me to read *Homa* or other cheap novels to see how similar *Chashmhayash* is.[15] They also named Hosseingholi Mosta'an and perhaps Javad Fazel[16] as novelists with similar styles to Alavi.[17] I did not respond, fearing I had already crossed them to warrant such severity. They did not realize that I had already read all of Hejazi's novels, about which I felt wholly indifferent. Many characters in Hejazi's novels reminded me of "upper-class" people I knew and had always resented.

My silence and perhaps my sad face too led to a happier ending in my debate with the two teachers. One amiably asked if I would care to read a small book of their choice. Relieved and delighted not to lose their friendship, I enthusiastically agreed. Handing me a book covered with blank brownish paper, they asked that I hide it in my jacket. They advised me not to share or mention it to anyone. They also commented that I needed to start reading classical texts, so that I might acquire a toolkit outside literature for analyzing social relations. I thanked them and left for my afternoon class, as it was getting late.

I was highly eager to read this mysterious book. Those hours remaining till I finished class and left home at 4:40 in the afternoon seemed to stretch interminably . As soon as school ended, I did not stay to talk to friends, but bolted home. I was carrying a banned book and had a secret to discover. I removed the book from my pocket and slipped off its plain paper jacket. I discovered beneath its cover two lines of text: a three-word title and the author's name, nothing else. My first impression was ambivalent. I did not like the amateurish and plain cover, although the fact that it differed so starkly from other books made it special.

The book was entitled *Dowlat va Enqelab* (*State and Revolution*). Having never heard of it before, I did not find the title attractive. It was written by Vladimir Lenin, a name I knew perhaps from listening to

---

[15] Mohammad Hejazi (1900–1974) was an Iranian novelist, translator, and a member of the senate before the revolution. He was well known in Iran for writing romantic novels about upper-class life. He was a senator for many years during the second Pahlavi regime.

[16] Javad Fazel (1914–1961) was a popular serial writer known for his religious-oriented stories.

[17] Hosseingholi Mosta'an (1904–1983) was a popular novelist and journalist. He was known as a writer of historical and romantic novels. He was also a translator of European literary texts. His translation of Victor Hugo's *Les Misérables* (*Binavayan*) was one book I liked very much. Most students of my generation read and valued it.

Radio Berlin. This resonance, however, piqued my interest, and I decided to learn more. What I read, however, was nothing like what I had expected my two teachers to share with me. I was expecting and perhaps even led to believe that they would recommend their own favorite Iranian novel. I was nevertheless happy at the opportunity to read a real Marxist book for the first time in my life. I think I had read *Mother*, by Maxim Gorky, and several other Russian texts, but, never one by a Marxist revolutionary, such as Lenin himself.

I spent that night and perhaps another ten occasions trying to understand *State and Revolution* and absolutely failed. The writing, in my view, verged on the indecipherable – it was technical and tough – and impossible to connect to, as it seemed Lenin was debating a roomful of Russians I did not know and did not care to know. Yet, I somehow liked Lenin's polemical style. His verbal spars were calculated but energetic, and I imagined he left his detractors absolutely intimidated and confounded. This model of interaction, however, made me feel it was hard for me to learn from Lenin, since my interlocutors, the religious literature teacher and the two Marxist teachers, were not my enemies, but my mentors. It is hard to do as Lenin does to his adversaries, when you want the other side only to affirm you. I respectfully decided that Lenin and I have different personalities.

I also reckoned that those radicals, such as Lenin, who were engaged in the practice of politics, were much tougher and less forgiving than a person like me. Still, I was happy to learn how a radical revolutionary makes his case. Most of what I learned from Lenin concerned rhetoric and modes of argumentation. I finally decided to return the book. I told my teachers that, just as Firangis is a bourgeois unable to do much about this regrettable reality than grow out of it, I am a teenager who consumes a beautiful novel like *Chashmhayash* in one night, but is unable to read Lenin even if it makes my teachers happy.

If debate is the destruction of an enemy's view, then even demagoguery and disinformation can be marshaled to serve that purpose. This view, however, takes for granted that one side possesses the truth, while other sides trade in falsehoods and must therefore be eliminated. Bullying and personal attack within this logic are scarcely out of the question. Looking back and comparing Alavi's views to the polemical stance in Lenin's *State and Revolution*, which professes a certain pathos of inevitability, *Chashmhayash* clearly proposes a different understanding of what dialogue means in modern societies.

In hindsight, the two teachers' understanding of Marxism seems to me unforgivingly dogmatic. Their attitude toward Iranian literature was highly sociological. The merit of the author's class analysis and of the book's aesthetic value were, for them, one and the same. They therefore disliked Jalal Al-e Ahmad and other novelists we students liked, including the dearly beloved Sadeq Hedayat. In conversations, they reminded me that "culture" and "ethics" should not guide analysis. Instead, class should override every other optic. Al-e Ahmad's analytical abilities, they reasoned, were diminished as the defeatism of the previous generation seeped into his writing. They urged students to think and act as progressives, forbearing the present while feeling optimistic for the future. Although we often argued with them, I was personally drawn to them and found their worldview refreshing. I found them more real than our religious literature teacher, although in a way not that familiar to me. In contrast to the literature teacher, I saw them as part of my generation and was eager to befriend them. They were agents of the future, so even their hesitations about Al-e Ahmad and Hedayat were permissible to me.

Al-e Ahmad, of course, was a Marxist and radicalism suffused his writings. It was his disillusionment with the Soviet Union and the Iran left under the Tudeh Party that pushed him to seek an alternative to institutionalized leftism in a "return to our roots" ideology. Examining Al-e Ahmad's writings, the transition from organic feelings of religious solidarity, which were even then slowly dissolving among younger, internationalist generations, to a future state politics of official religion begins to make sense. Al-e Ahmad idealized the harmony of religious life and projected it onto a modern ideology of popular mobilization. It is a difficult trajectory to trace, but something goes tragically astray in the process. In a way, and as I think of it now, the Marxist teachers were right: Al-e Ahmad did express a kind of defeatism. A personal defeat for him and a broader national mistaken vision for the nation. What they failed to see, though, was that Al-e Ahmad was redrawing the boundaries of politics to accommodate a middle ground for the new Iranian middle class who no longer fully believed in the religious rituals of old, but yearned to take action in defense of their traditional homeland against Western exploitation.

Both the religious literature teacher and the two Marxist teachers were, in my mind, radical mentors and anti-government activists. Their views explain the everyday social roots of *gharbzadegi*. While our experiences are real, the theoretical conclusions we draw from them are sometimes mistaken. They all spoke about Iran and its dire situation in a nonpolitical manner. Their critiques were heavily cultural and morally based. The literature teacher powerfully articulated the corruption and arrogance eating away at Iran's political system. He explained why we were so alienated from our own history and ethical traditions. He was particularly convincing in pointing out the hazards of materialist consumerism in Iranian society, a trend concentrated among the elites of Tehran. In his mind, Tehran was the embodiment of all that was wrong. The notion that ethics and good conduct were most stifled precisely where alien and Western lifestyles had taken root seemed both shocking and sensical to me. My conclusion as a teenage activist was that this was all the fault of the shah. He was debasing our culture and ruining our country, turning Iran into a hell. This gives some clear insight into the growing appeal of the ideas of Al-e Ahmad, and how he might have unknowingly provided a highway from the organic unselfconsciousness of a traditional town like Golpayegan to a theocratic state promising to export the Islamist ideology to cure the planet of modernity's scourge. This, too, reflects the unthought: for it is unlikely that Al-e Ahmad envisioned or intended such a state.[18] Nor did most of the population of Golpayegan.[19]

We thought of ourselves as radicals and futurists. I now sadly realize a reactionary worship of the past characterized Iranian cultural currents. We sincerely desired a prosperous future for our country which we might be proud of, but our thinking was steeped in the past. We did not know how to implement the futures we imagined for Iran. Although I increasingly suspected this, as activists, our main concern was doing politics and not thinking too much about the consequences

[18] Our thought works as a discursive universe and it is already enclosed in such a way that it licenses certain sets of ideas about ourselves and how we have lived our lives. It precludes us from seeing our past experiences and ideas outside of our own conventional framing of our life narrative (unthought). The unthought is a part of our lives that is sadly concealed from us and becomes unreachable. The idea of "discursive universe," in religious traditions, is a reference to revelation as an account of total reality that explains the meaning of life and the universe, prior to empirical experience. This suggest that all human experiences, within the limits of the "unthought/thought," are somehow also framed discursively.

[19] It is like the famous line at the end of the Wan Kar-Wei film *In the Mood for Love*: "In the beginning I wanted to understand how everything began. Now I know. Things happen without us realizing."

of our actions. "Consequentialism" is still lacking in leftist thought, and this is a complex problem going back to "dialectics" among other things. As a religious youth, I was also more concerned with belonging to the community than with how life in heaven would transpire. The mere fact of belonging, or wanting to belong, explains many things in politics, including some of the worst. On the crucial question of the ideal society worth fighting for, my teachers strongly disagreed with each other.

My literature teacher mined the wisdom of Persian poets and historians to learn what a virtuous person, community, and society should look like. He never tired of sharing with us his synthetic yet culturally coherent vision of morality, adorned as it was with the beautiful, picturesque images of Rudaki's poetry,[20] of everyday life, of Rumi's abstract and almost universalistic musings on life's mysteries, and of Imam Hossein's passion for justice and good. Poetry, Sufism, and messianic romance were a complete and appealing story to fight for or, even, die for to achieve. His vision informed my understanding of radical politics at that time.

My literature teacher, however, was not necessarily a nationalist. He was quick to recommend exemplary works from Arab and Islamic societies of the past and present. He had traveled to the Arab Middle East and would tell us about the inspiration that filled him as a pilgrim in Mecca, the undeterrable courage of the Palestinian resistance (in coded language), and he even spoke positively of Iraq. He had a library of materials on Palestine, and I remember him playing audio recordings about Palestine for us. I was very much moved by the intellectual dedication and passion that sustained the Palestinian cause, and I admired Palestinians' willingness to fight for liberation.

I was so inspired by my teacher's discussions of Palestine and Mecca that I decided to switch from studying English to Arabic with great seriousness. I let the sounds of Arabic Radio fill the house. This was not hard to do in Iran then, since Arabic Radio had much clearer reception than Iranian radio stations. My brothers and sister were annoyed with my new radio habit and drilled me on my newfound interest in Arabic. This change, however, led them to ponder why they found spoken

---

[20] Rudaki was a tenth-century Persian poet, considered one of the pioneering classical poets, who composed poems in Persian in post-Islamic Iran.

Arabic harsh, but singing in Arabic to be very pleasant and joyful. This was the extent of our family conversations on "transnationalism."

As the disparity of my various teachers' political perspectives, as well as the diversity of their interests, suggests, Golpayegan was a hive of discussion about events transpiring around the world. The variety of intellectual perspectives that characterized these informal debates were in no way reducible to the trite confines of Pahlavi official discourse.

In view of this scenario, the world was being imaginatively made and remade with some rapidity at multiple centers across Iran in the 1960s and 1970s. Provinces – and not just Tehran – offered competing conceptions of *jahan*, or the "new world" through multiple ideological optics. This was also part of the revolution. Local voices in Golpayegan therefore – however covertly – challenged the Pahlavi regime for being out of step with the world, directly undermining Pahlavi claims to universalism, while proposing alternate roads for making Iran an international nation. In this light, Tehran-centrism is its own form of provincialism, since activism was proliferating at multiple centers throughout Iran. Golpayegan shows one example of many.

"God in Our Classroom"

In my last two years of high school, our literature teacher developed a new strictness in his teaching and class organization. We began to view him as a disciplinarian. At the same time that he underwent a pedagogical change of heart, my literature teacher started bringing the tape-recorded speeches of a well-known Tehrani cleric to class. I felt confused by this highly unusual and unanticipated act. I was also pleased, however. Perhaps, I thought, the teacher had realized that there's more to learning than memorizing classical Persian poetry, learning Arabic grammar, and studying Iranian history. I was unaccustomed to see this well-respected teacher venture into troublemaking. Nor was it in his character to explain to us his teaching rationale, but he did so with the taped speeches. He conducted the class as seriously as any other academic class.

We only listened to a recording of one man, but devoted perhaps twenty to thirty classes to it over almost two years. The man was Mohammad Taqi Falsafi (1908–1998), a well-known Shiite cleric (Figure 3.9). I was acquainted with his name and reputation thanks

Figure 3.9 Taqi Falsafi.

to my political-leaning friends. I knew him as a fearless cleric.[21]
Despite being barred from public preaching or speaking, he continued,
at the invitation of patrons, to preach in private homes and religious
ceremonies attended by hundreds of people. Falsafi used these occasions to criticize the Pahlavi state and Shia policies. I had also heard
that he traveled outside of Iran extensively, making his opposition
known to Muslims in Pakistan, the Persian Gulf, and across the Arab
world. He was a kind of transnational Shia preacher.

Even in provincial Golpayegan, the plurality of political discourse
there made it clear that there were multiple understandings of Iranian
nationhood. Falsafi voiced yet another nationalist imagining, one distinct from the idea of Iran I debated bitterly with my Marxist teachers.

---

[21] Falsafi had a history of rabble-rousing. In June 1951, he was identified as "one
of Iran's most influential younger mullahs" whose lectures against the UK, US,
and USSR led to riots. In May 1952, he was involved in disorders in the Tehran
bazaar. Also, he was sponsored by a CIA operation called BEDAMN as an
alternative to Kashani during the oil crisis (US State Department telegram 3453,
788.00/27JUN51, RG-59, Box 4107; Mashad Consulate telegrams 2 and 4,
788.00/2AUG51; Shahrough Akhavi, *Religion and Politics in Contemporary
Iran: Clergy-State Relations in the Pahlavi Period* (Albany, NY: SUNY Press,
1980), 64; Mark Gasiorowski, *U.S. Foreign Policy and the Shah: Building a
Client State in Iran* (Ithaca, NY: Cornell University Press, 1991), 70). On
Falsafi's relations with the government, see Willem M. Floor, "The
Revolutionary Character of the Ulama: Wishful Thinking or Reality?" in Nikki
R. Keddie, ed., *Religion and Politics in Iran: Shi'ism from Quietism to
Revolution* (New Haven, CT: Yale Univeristy Press, 1983), 76.

I listened to Falsafi's recorded speeches with utmost interest. This was a rare experience for me and, I imagine, for other students in the class. This was the first time that we, as a group of about thirty students, listened collectively and publicly to a well-known oppositional figure. It was made possible by our teacher, who was otherwise a rather prudent man. I should note that our teacher never made any comments about the recorded speeches by Falsafi. He never asked any questions about them. We, of course, extensively discussed our view of Falsafi's ideas outside of class. The electrifying power of Falsafi's speeches, whether we agreed with his message or not, testifies that anti-Pahlavi radicalism was not the exclusive domain of the left. Islamists too had critiques of their own to add to a chorus of radical dissent.

The excitement of being witness to collective political action – even if this action was merely listening – was exhilarating. Initially, I did not really think about the content of the speeches. I was thrilled by the experience, indeed, by Falsafi's enchanting voice and rhetorical power. Being in Falsafi's presence and listening to him in public was a dizzying experience. Most of my "protest" acts, such as reading banned books or listening to opposition radio, I had performed individually. And I was acutely aware of their solitary nature. I always dreamed of sharing my political sentiments with students, family members, or others generally. I was very grateful that our literature teacher had made this possible.

As a high school student, I was fond of performance – acting, painting, and writing all captured my attention. Yet my friends and I always found ourselves participating in government-sponsored rituals we disliked. Listening to Falsafi was my first act of public rebellion against the state. I felt older and wiser because of it. Perhaps my teacher was aware of the maturing effect it would have and chose for this reason to stop regularly teaching and instead to simply play us Falsafi's sermons.

However, after several weeks of careful listening to the taped speeches, I saw beyond Falsafi's captivating voice and elegant speaking style. As the novelty wore off, I ascertained that he belonged to my father's generation and had little to offer me. I no longer recall his precise words. Falsafi spoke much of the Iranian youth and moral issues, while connecting all social ills to the Iranian government. His moralizing made clear that we had opposite aspirations for Iran. I felt that the Iranian youth were neither immoral nor deviant, but good-natured and well-behaved. Cultural constraints and political oppression were the web limiting our existential possibilities. Falsafi seemed troubled by the government's permissive moral and cultural policies and their corrupting influence on younger generations. The Iranian youth, he believed, no longer cared about Islam, family norms and customs, or other moral values. I differed, feeling we were constantly told what to do, while never being given the freedom to express our thoughts or aspirations.

I questioned friends and teachers outside of class about Falsafi and his politics. I learned that he was a virulently anti-Baha'i cleric, and a powerful one at that, with links to Ayatollah Khomeini. I was displeased that he was anti-Baha'i and apprehensive about his connection to Khomeini. Several messages by Khomeini from Radio Baghdad had left me unimpressed. I admired the man's courage for standing up to the shah in 1963, but not his words.

The following year was my last year of high school. I lost my tolerance for Falsafi's speeches in class. Becoming resentful, I developed a kind of "nostalgia" for our teacher's dry lectures. Still, I admired my teacher and did not want to upset him by making negative comments in class. For some time, I struggled, wanting neither to stay silent, nor to speak. Eventually I hit upon a plan. One day after class I approached the teacher and politely whispered in his ear, "I have some private thoughts which I would like to write down in order to ask you a few questions. Do you mind if I give them to you, so that you might kindly read them and give me your reflections?" My literature teacher gave me a gentle but very serious look, before replying, "Yes, of course, I am your teacher ... that is what I do, in or outside of class."

That night was a real test and a struggle for me. Writing the questions, which were more expressions of disappointment to a teacher I admired, was a difficult emotional task. I rewrote the questions repeatedly, discarded them, then started again. I was unable to ask the questions without preemptively fearing his anger at my indiscretion. I finally decided to write my questions in a straightforward, essay style, expressing measured dissatisfaction with how his views had grown increasingly inconsistent with his insistence on valuing knowledge and science, logical reflection, and independence of mind.

The letter opened by declaring how much I valued him and his mentorship. I went so far as to write: "I know I am not from

Golpayegan but a *gharibeh* [a stranger in this town] and my father is the head of the finance office, therefore being considered a high official in the city. I am very sorry for this. I hope you understand that we do not choose the family we are from. I have tried to follow your advice and be a good person. I hope this essay will not change your view of me." I then raised three crucial inconsistencies, asking the teacher to clarify them for me:

(1) Why did he constantly tell us to be fearful of God while also telling us to study hard, learn as much as possible, and value independence of mind? If we ought to study hard to learn to think independently, then how could fearing God be a valuable motivation? If our love of God is to fear his wrath, then why learn about Islam or the Prophet? Furthermore, I considered myself a good Muslim in trying to be an ethical person and performing religious rituals. Yet, I had difficulty agreeing with certain abstract ideas in Islam, such as the afterlife and heaven. The accounts of afterlife seemed to me like a children's story. He seemed to so firmly believe in these dogmas that I dared not ask him questions about our Holy Qur'an. Yet I humbly implored him to encourage students to ask such questions.

(2) I also asked him if he viewed Islam as the only source of ethical instruction, or whether other nonreligious sources were legitimate and helpful in building character. If there are nonreligious areas, why did he never talk about them or share views on these important aspects of life?

I indicated my deep involvement in theater, painting, and sports, which I took with equal seriousness to my religious studies. Yet, how could I advance academically in these important parts of my life when I heard only his negative comments about artists and athletes? I requested that he clarify these points and explain these important issues. I noted how I personally believed Islamic civilization owed much to Muslim artists, poets, architects, and other cultural pioneers. Limiting Islamic history and way of life to the teachings of preachers and jurists denied the civilization its broader horizons.

(3) Finally, I asked my genuine political question. I stated my disappointment at seeing him select Mr. Falsafi as a thinker worth emulating. I argued that Falsafi's thoughts are limited to moral tropes, while his understanding of modern Iran is outdated and

something with which young Iranians cannot identify. Falsafi seemingly only speaks from the perspective of the ulama and would like to see all Iranians rearrange their lives to the satisfaction of clerics. I asked him to kindly explain the rationale for using class time for listening to Falsafi.

It is difficult to remember everything I wrote. It was a thirty- or thirty-five-page piece full of detail and reference to Falsafi's ideas that I especially disliked. For me, this was a monumental task and I was happy yet anxious with the achievement. Concerned that the teacher may interpret the first two questions as a sign of me losing faith in God, I worried about his reaction. In truth, at that time, I was undecided about believing in God. Yet, this was not an especially important issue for me.

I presented my questions to the teacher the following day, then waited one week before he asked to see me after class. I followed him to the teacher's room. He asked me to sit next to him, before kindly telling me that he appreciated my questions. He joked that it was almost a book, when he had expected a one-page list of questions. However, he was pleased that one of his students had the courage to raise these important issues. He removed an envelope from his jacket and handed me his response to my questions. Thanking him, I left the office, then headed to the schoolyard to read his response.

His reply was brief, perhaps three or four pages, but he addressed nearly every issue I had raised:

(1) Responding to my first set of questions, he wrote, "I remind you that this world's existence is not an accident of nature. Our life and being, resulting from Divine Creation, exists for a sacred purpose. We must strive to live a purposeful life according to God's teachings and our faith. But we achieve our own principle of life and right action by using our hearts and minds. We therefore need two different kinds of knowledge: (1) *'elm-e dini*, faith; and (2) *'elm-e in-jahani*, the sciences." He saw no tension between having absolute faith and also devoting one's life to the pursuit of worldly knowledge. "Achieving worldly knowledge," he wrote, "gratifies God and abides by the wise path of the Prophet. However, worldly knowledge is always partial in reach and substance. Sciences are neutral on matters of life's ultimate meaning and even other matters where much is unknown. Where we do not or cannot

know, we must depend on faith." He concluded the section by saying, "If something in your studies is not in accordance with religious teachings, do not lose your faith or love of science. Find others with whom to discuss the issues. One must remain open to discussions and debates." He reminded me of "a long and rich history of debate in religious seminaries" saying we needed "more of this today."

I very much liked his line of reasoning and felt liberated knowing his arguments were rational rather than dogmatic. My respect for him grew and he gave me much to think about. I felt bolder after reading his letter and regretted not having raised specific points where I perceived science undermining religious teachings.

(2) His response to my second question was brief. I was wrong, he said, in my mistakenly limited view of Islam, which resembled a Christian view of religion. He indicated that Muslims who write, practice art, or design magnificent buildings are part of Islamic tradition and not outside of it. He ended this section by saying that Islam values the arts and philosophy, but, if some artists or philosophers do not care for Islam, their problem is as for any other person.

(3) On my criticism of Falsafi, he was adamant that I was mistaken, politically inexperienced, and perhaps even misguided. He briefly explained that Falsafi was a respected religious leader and a learned man, the kind of man whom Iranians should be proud of. I needed to listen to him more carefully and complain less.

My memories of this teacher remain fond. Despite our many differences, I owe who I am partly to him and his devotion to teaching. After graduating from high school and moving to Tehran, I had no further contact with him. I have been trying to find out what happened to him following the revolution and where he is now. While writing this I reached out to several people who I thought might know about him. So far, I have obtained little information. The only news I have is that a person from Golpayegan with the same name as my literature teacher (Jafar Tavakoli) was elected to the First Majlis after the revolution (1980). However, his election became controversial and his credentials were not approved, preventing him from sitting as a member of the parliament. I have also read some brief reports in local newspapers. His picture reminds me of him and I am almost certain the man in the newspaper report is my literature teacher. The report also mentioned his name as visiting the war fronts during the Iran-Iraq War, providing comfort and assistance to soldiers from Golpayegan.

Small Town, Grand World (*Donya*)

The earlier allusion to *donya* and *jahan*, or a "new world" of populist possibility, becomes more distinct when we closely examine the layers of everyday life in Golpayegan. Our differing notions of Iran's place in the modern world were all imagined within a transnational conceptual space. For many of my friends and me, ideas such as "transnational" or global did not directly surface in our political or intellectual discussions. Nonetheless, we clearly and intentionally defined ourselves as intellectuals and activists with great interest in and curiosity about events, past and present, occurring outside of Iran. It may now seem strange, but in this period we had more access to world news and international intellectual and political ideas than we had to events in Iran. The state was more generous in the access it afforded Iranians to world affairs, while it severely restricted information about recent and contemporary Iran. Mainstream newspapers and magazines published descriptive and analytical reports of political conflicts, revolutionary movements and ideas, and social movements worldwide. State censorship was also far less strict when it came to the publication of books and other materials in translation. Thanks to this counterintuitive ease of access, I read a considerable number of books and articles about the Arab, African, and Latin American revolutionaries and movements of that time.

It is hard to explain how we imagined and conceptualized the "national" or "global." We used two words, often interchangeably, to articulate our perspectives or interests in the world: *donya* and sometimes *jahan*. Both words mean "the world" in English. Yet, they embody more than it seems. *Donya* projects the idea of an integrated and interrelated world. It also has a normative quality, usually referring to this world and the material world. Whereas *jahan* more closely approximates the idea of the global or the cosmopolitan. The use and meanings of the two words are imprecise, so their uses differ in varying contexts. But, for those of us sympathetic to Marxism, we preferred *donya*. I clearly remember many of us speaking about our interest in *donya-ye gharb* (the Western world) or *donya-ye communist* (the communist world). More religious-leaning friends, including our literature teacher, seemed to prefer *jahan*. They would say: "An intellectual will see Persian literature in the context of *adabiyat-e jahani* [world literature]." They would talk about *jahan-e 'arab* (the Arab world). We all, of course, used the term *jahan-e sevvom* (the Third World). Our Marxist teachers proudly informed us that the first real intellectual journal published in Iran was *Donya*, the brainchild of a German-educated Iranian, Taqi Arani. The journal *Jahan-e Islam* was a popular religious publication read by everyone in our town. Yet, there was not a clear distinction between the two words.

We showed our interest in the broader world by listening to English, Arabic, and Persian foreign radio stations based in East Berlin, Baghdad, and Peking. We also listened to the BBC and were highly interested in acquiring copies of *Time Magazine* and *Newsweek*. It required hard work for us, because we had to get the American magazines from a friend or teacher from Tehran. One of our English teachers was very helpful in facilitating our access to English magazines. We suspected that he had pro-Western sentiments and obtained American magazines to sway our politics. I imagined Golpayegan must have been a lonely place for him at times, but he was a farmer content with working the land.

We also made sure to put ample time and effort into learning foreign languages, meeting non-Iranians if possible, and reading books in English and Arabic. My friends and I were not very successful in improving our English. We could only read a Golpayegan atlas with the help of our English teacher. Arabic, however, was a different story. There was a vibrant culture of Arabic teaching and learning in Golpayegan at the time. It was quite normal for some of my high school classmates to read Arabic literature, poems, religious scholarship, and newspapers. I personally excelled in learning Arabic and was able to read some Arabic books or journals about contemporary politics and religious and historical matters.

My contact with non-Iranians was very limited in Golpayegan. The only chance I had was time spent with a young American couple. I became very close to this couple, who were in town as part of the Peace Corps. I liked them very much. Strangely, they insisted on teaching me carpentry, setting up a workshop at our school. I did what they wanted because I did not want to lose their friendship. I saw them as important sources of learning about the US and improving my

English. However, the most important craft in Golpayegan was wood-working, which, to my mind, was a higher form of carpentry. There were hundreds of woodworking shops in town. Still, the Americans felt it their duty to teach us basic carpentry skills. Was this a sort of transnationalism in reverse? Of course, eager as I was to learn of different people and places, just talking to them in English and learning about the US was the precious fruit of my friendship with them. Doing carpentry was the cost I willingly paid. I was keen to hear what young Americans had to say about US culture and politics, but they were very reticent to talk about themselves or their country. I think they lived a rather isolated life in Golpayegan, refraining from mixing more than necessary with the "locals."

In Golpayegan, I formed what I believed at the time to be an intellectually sophisticated view of myself and the world. I identified two worldviews as mirror images of what I felt was unacceptable: anti-intellectualism or *bifarhangi*, and provincialism or *mahaligera'i*. I (and perhaps most of my friends) set up these rather vague categories to distinguish myself from others I viewed as reactionaries. I disliked the uncultured and pitied the nativists. One perhaps may blame our mod-ernizing impulses for our resistance to "localism." We did not, how-ever, consider ourselves nationalists or even *tajaddodgera* (modernizers). These were ideas we considered part of the "regime's" ideology, outdated and meaningless. I felt more at home embracing a new and broader world (*donya*). To me, this was a rather forward-looking window onto the world.

My rejection of provincialism (*mahaligera'i*) was related to the nativist ideology I considered undesirable. Yet I did not scorn the pride that Golpayeganis felt for their town, or their tendency to reminisce about their lives. I always treasured these moments of generational exchange and was eager to learn about local cultures and lifestyles. If anything, I had little tolerance for those, mainly from Tehran, who visited our town without showing interest in its people and culture. The Tehran-centrist attitude, to me, was culturally debasing our way of life. For so many Tehranis, beyond Iran's capital lay nothing of interest but the "simplicity" and "innocence" of provincials. To me, Tehran-centrism and *mahaligera'i* were two sides of the same ideological dogmatism. These two cultural modes of seeing the world were too narrow to glance beyond their own immediate surroundings. Tehran-centrism, it follows, was another form of provincialism.

I imagined that my religious literature teacher would have agreed with me. For me, "localism" was not the same as "traditionalism." In a way, perhaps, I was at least partly a traditionalist, but not a provincialist (*mahaligera*). I was very much interested in Iranian history, culture, and religion. For me, the idea of *farhang* (culture) was the key to defining myself and my world. Yet, I did not think in the dichotomous terms of modern/traditional *farhang*. Perhaps, in my mind, there was "good" and "bad" *farhang*, but certainly not modern and traditional. I was taught to embrace the views of those interested in reading, knowing, and having a broadly open view of the world. I named this condition of intellectual openness "*bafarhang*" (cultured). Those who were only interested in the received habits and customs of Golpayegan we called "*bifarhang*" (uncultured).

Interestingly, we thought of Iran as a political nation (the Pahlavi state) that was neither part of *donya* nor *jahan*. I now think that, for me, *donya* was part of my own imaginative remaking of the world. In other words, I imagined myself as part of *donya* and I wanted Iran to also join it. *Jahan*, by contrast, seems a more "neutral" world "out there," only capable of being observed. In this respect, Iran at that time was not part of *donya* but an odd part of *jahan*. Conversely, the Pahlavi state in the late 1960s and 1970s sought to make Iran of central importance to regional and world affairs. In the shah's mind, "his" Iran was isolated from the wider world while, at the same time, existing at its very center. In other words, the shah's attitude was rather hostile to the modern world. He viewed "his" Iran as a superior alternative to what already existed.

In my imagination, Iran as it then existed was outdated and obsolete. It had insulated itself both from the larger world and, in my view, of what Iran had been in the past and should be in the future. This situation was a dangerous one. I did not feel myself a citizen of the country. Therefore, I neither demanded much from the state, nor felt much responsibility for its affairs. For me and perhaps most others, politics were a much larger issue. We were focused on politics at the international and national levels. This, of course, was also what the government desired: that young Iranians remain uninvolved in the affairs of the country, acting only as pliant cheerleaders for the shah's activities.

In this complex and confusing situation, I felt liberated to think of my idea of Iran as a mirror image of the *donya* I had invented, a complex of transnational, intellectual, and cultural exchanges. I certainly thought of my own ideas and vision of Iran as a space for circulating Iranian and world cultures. This does not indicate any absence of ideas specifically rooted in Iranian culture or history, or that world affairs have priority over national ones. I think that, for me, as an activist and intellectual, there was a critical struggle to define and craft our national consciousness. We participated in making the national through this imaginative and collective process, preferring to think of Iran as the crown jewel in this world (*donya*).

We might, then, reflect anew upon Iranian small-town life in the 1960s–1970s. The Golpayegan experience presents a window onto understanding the hopes and horizons of "local" Iranians during "global" decades. It is only one example, but most Iranians of my generation lived not in Tehran but in places similar to Golpayegan. The Golpayegan example exposes the nature of "local" meanings beyond "official" state narratives. It is a corrective to those activists and intellectuals who see everything in this story from Tehran's gaze. The local is not "pure" or simple. Although small, it is as complex as life gets. It is engaged in deeply interwoven evolutions in Tehran, Iran, and the world. The emergence of political Islam or new forms of Marxism were the fruits of complex national and transnational processes. These did not in the least fit a universal/local dichotomy. How, then, are we to better understand this global/local and national relationship? Iran was dynamized by the circulatory movements of people and ideas. It is important to appreciate this, especially given the popularity of depicting Islamist politics as a type of retrograde or static embrace of antiquated political forms. This exposes the new theoretical terrain required to seriously understand the 1978–1979 revolution. We must go beyond the formulas that adopt the very discursive claims of the Islamist leadership, as if their self-interpretation provides the fullest and most accurate explanation.

Banality of Evil?

My relationship with my literature teacher grew distant and cloudy by the end of my high school studies. I continued to respect him as a teacher, but my disappointment created an emotional barrier between us. Confused and lonely, I had the opportunity to connect with another religious teacher in Golpayegan. This time it was a purely accidental encounter. I was on the bus headed to Tehran in the November of my senior high school year. I noticed that a science teacher from the other high school in Golpayegan was sitting next to me. We started a conversation, and he asked if I was involved in any extracurricular activities. There was a group of students and teachers with whom I practiced painting and sports. Yet, in such a religious town, I still felt isolated from the community. He asked if I was seriously interested in religious activities, and I answered that I was interested in meeting any and all politically oriented people critical of the regime. Smiling, he proposed to introduce me to a person whom I would appreciate. Giving me a name, he asked me to tell them that he recommended I join the Anjoman (association or society).

Upon returning from Tehran to Golpayegan, I contacted the person, the owner of a stationery shop in town who helped me join the Anjoman. The Anjoman operated like an underground group, usually meeting like a class where an older man talked to us about Islam and particularly about the Baha'i faith. Very soon I realized they were anti-Baha'i crusaders. They were also critical of the shah, but practiced more caution here when expressing their views.

After about two months, one of the Anjoman leaders asked to speak to me privately. When we met he complimented me and said I was a very "special" person. Because of my father, he said, it was safe to involve me in important tasks without fearing for my safety. He then asked me if I were willing to be part of an important religious mission. Flattered, I told him I was. Overcome with excitement and anxiety about my new role, I forgot to ask about the nature of the mission.

As it happened, the man organizing the mission requested that we meet the following day after school. We met in a house – perhaps his. Upon entering, I encountered four other students and an older man who was perhaps in his late twenties. He appeared slightly worried and restless, talking in a low voice, informing us that we were entrusted with an important and sensitive undertaking. A long lecture followed on the importance of confidentiality and absolute allegiance to the Anjoman. He listed the best ways to disavow involvement should we be called for questioning by high school officials or the police. After his monologue, anxiety gnawed at me. I suddenly and forcefully realized I disliked and distrusted him. That an older man should entrust high school students with so dangerous a mission struck me as callous and reckless. This tension, however, was part of the mysterious allure of political activism. It is empowering. One feels a new sense of agency in actively engaging and even endangering one's life. Yet becoming part of collective action and a secret operation, one also feels powerless and carried helplessly by a larger current. This issue became even more significant for me later in my life when I grew more seriously engaged in politics, both during the Iranian Revolution and in the US working with the Confederation of Iranian Students.

My misgivings were confirmed when the man told us that late one night the following week, we would be sent to "disrupt" a Baha'i home and terrify the family into leaving Golpayegan voluntarily. He then "comforted" us, insisting the plan was very safe and no one would be hurt. Nor would anyone find out about it. Even if the police discovered our involvement, they would look away, since they too were worried about the influence of Baha'is in Golpayegan. He concluded by saying that the homeowner was a high school teacher (at that time, he did not give us a name or address). If others found out about our deed, we should say the fellow had been pressuring us to abandon our Islamic faith and convert to Bahaism. Everything had been planned and accounted for, he proudly concluded.

The news sent shockwaves throughout my body, devastating me and my thought process. I tried to look at the man, who appeared to me like Norman Bates from Alfred Hitchcock's *Psycho*. He was creepy, but too domineering for me to dare stand up to him. We were five high school students, but I was so unsettled that they faded from my vision. I cannot remember what they said or how they reacted. I felt I was alone with the older man and at a complete loss. I was too caught in my own thoughts and dreams, completely flustered by this unexpected situation. I suddenly started sobbing violently, as if it were my only choice. I lacked the nerve to tell this man he was a monster, or that his plans were deeply wrong, even worse than SAVAK. The older man grew furious, his hand gesture showing me the door, as he yelled at me, "You are too weak-willed, go home and never return to the Anjoman." I told him how sorry I was, leaving the house. His name-calling did not bother me. I felt I had courageously done the right thing. I was saddened and wounded for other reasons, however. In searching for an alternative religious model, I chose the Anjoman and rejected my kind literature teacher, who I felt was not for political actions. I was mistaken to think the Anjoman was more of a scholarly association. Later that night I felt furious at myself. I kept asking, why did I apologize to that man?

I always wanted to know more about the Anjoman-e Hojjatieh, as the furtive group was known, but never had the chance to research them. After I left Golpayegan and entered Tehran University, I did not hear a word about them until after the revolution. We now know that the Anjoman is a conservative anti-Baha'i and anti-Marxist religious group with a major presence in the security forces of the Islamic Republic. It is a cruel irony that, searching for a utopia and a kinder humanity, I was recruited into this appalling organization. Now I am tainted with a two- or three-month history as a member of the Anjoman. Our life, as we have lived it, sometimes appears "unreal" more often than we are willing to disclose. Today, as I write these words, I find myself still lost in a void with respect to these early life events. They are so estranged that it feels I am telling the story of another person's life. Is this me, as I have known myself for all these years? And then I think of the "unthought," our failure to recall parts of our life we lack the audacity to either retell or even remember.

Remembering what I have tried to forget, however, makes understanding how well-intentioned and "ordinary" people can in certain situations become embroiled in deadly and "evil" political acts more sensible. At the most general level, my own experience with the Anjoman in Golpayegan approaches what Hannah Arendt called "the banality of evil." While I am taking some liberty in applying her idea to a situation unlike what she describes, it seems to me that in organized political mobilization, as in bureaucratized political persecution, ordinary people are lured, perhaps because of the risks of resistance and ostracization in the face of collective action, into compliance that makes violence, often against the most marginalized, permissible if not palatable. I am a living testimony to this as are the other poor students who actually participated in the act.

4 Iranian Diasporic Possibilities:
Tracing Transnational Feminist Genealogies from the Revolutionary Margins

MANIJEH MORADIAN

In New York City in the summer of 2009, when diasporic activism in support of the democratic uprising in Iran was in full swing, an ad hoc network of Iranian American women and one Iranian immigrant woman decided to form the Raha Iranian Feminist Collective.[1] Iranians all over the world were galvanized by the mass demonstrations in Iran, which became known as the "Green Movement." These demonstrations, the largest since the revolution in 1978–1979, began as a rejection of a fraudulent presidential election, and then expanded to encompass broader demands against dictatorship. Rather than simply repeating the slogans from the streets of Tehran on the streets of New York City, the women who came together to launch Raha were committed to a transnational feminist practice attentive to multiple sources of oppression and multiple sites of struggle (Iran, the US, and the Iranian diaspora itself) at the same time. This approach required thinking critically about what it meant to condemn dictatorship in Iran while standing in the heart of US empire. Raha members were intent on standing in solidarity with the millions of Iranians who were protesting the actions of their own government, but were also concerned that a singular focus on the lack of democracy and human rights in Iran would dovetail with a right-wing US agenda of sanctions and war. Feminists in Iran, as well as Raha members in New York, were also concerned that issues of gender and sexual inequality would be marginalized by the mainstream of the Green Movement or, worse, used as a pretext for US intervention, as was the case in Afghanistan and Iraq.[2] With signs decrying human rights abuses by both the US and the Iranian governments, and a banner that read "Liberation comes from

---

[1] See www.rahafeministcollective.org/.
[2] See Manijeh Nasrabadi, "Letter from Tehran," www.jadaliyya.com/Details/24067/Letter-from-Tehran.

below," Raha members, including myself, joined the rallies outside the United Nations and elsewhere in an effort to oppose imperialism *and* dictatorship and to uplift a transnational feminist vision of the meaning of solidarity.

Although we were self-conscious of our location outside Iran, we were also engaged with Iranian feminist legacies emanating from the Iranian revolutionary movement thirty years earlier. The women's uprising in Tehran in March 1979 was our inheritance, our object lesson, and our inspiration.[3] In the midst of the transition to a post-shah era, those Iranian women who came before us had fought to secure equal citizenship and basic democratic rights as primary, and not secondary, issues on the revolutionary agenda. They had, if briefly, launched a mass movement that opposed imperialism and gender oppression at the same time and challenged the notion that women's rights represented a foreign threat to national unity. We needed to learn their story and find within it an orientation that could help us make sense of our current predicament, in which Iranian diasporic denunciations of the lack of democracy and women's and human rights in Iran could easily fan the flames of Islamophobia and bolster threats of war. We organized a public screening of the French documentary about the March 1979 uprising, *Liberation Movement of Iranian Women, Year Zero*, on International Women's Day in 2010 for a packed audience in downtown Manhattan.[4] That night it became clear that we were not only claiming this event as part of a genealogy of transnational feminism, but we were also recuperating an all-but-lost history of Iranian women's revolutionary activity, passing it on to a new generation of feminist and queer diasporic activists, Iranian and otherwise. This diasporic perspective, and the ongoing need for an anti-imperialist politics of gender and sexual liberation, informs the following exploration of Iranian women's organizing in the US in years before the revolution.

---

[3] For a detailed account of the March 1979 women's uprising in Tehran, see Negar Mottahedeh, *Whisper Tapes: Kate Millet in Iran* (Stanford, CA: Stanford University Press, 2019). For a critique of the role played by French, Canadian, and American feminists in Tehran during the protests, and of the difficulties of transnational feminist solidarity, see Nima Naghibi, *Rethinking Global Sisterhood: Western Feminism and Iran* (Minneapolis, MN: University of Minnesota Press, 2007), 74–107.

[4] www.youtube.com/watch?v=odmlfa986mk.

Rethinking the Narrative of the Global Iranian Left

In fact, there is a longer (even less acknowledged) transnational genealogy of Iranian women's activism that precedes 1979 and that endeavored to place gender equality squarely on the organizing agenda of one of the largest anti-shah groups, the Confederation of Iranian Students (National Union) or CISNU. This coalition was a transnational phenomenon in and of itself, organizing Iranian foreign students concentrated in Western Europe and North America, with smaller chapters in Turkey and India. The majority of Iranian foreign students went to the US, which hosted over 82,000 of these young scholars between 1960 and 1977.[5] There were 50,000 Iranian students in the US on the eve of the revolution.[6] From 1962 through 1979, thousands of students participated in CISNU cultural events, rallies, and other forms of protest designed to highlight the injustices of the shah's regime and the complicity of Western powers. As an opposition force located in the West, the CISNU would largely reject both Western liberalism and Iranian nativism, and instead become part of radical student milieus that were organizing against capitalism and colonization.

By the mid-1960s, most of the chapters were dominated by the political influence of a handful of underground leftist organizations that marked a break with the pro-Soviet Tudeh Party (Iranian Communist Party) of the previous era. Broadly speaking, these Iranian "Third Worldist" groups had Marxist-Leninist tendencies akin to those popular among other student leftist movements of their day; they looked to countries such as China, Cuba, Vietnam, Algeria, Albania, and also to the Palestinian liberation movement for political models and inspiration.[7] By 1975, the CISNU split as a result of

---

[5] Mohsen Mobasher, *Iranians in Texas* (Austin, TX: University of Texas Press, 2012), 26.

[6] Matthew K. Shannon, *Losing Hearts and Minds: American-Iranian Relations and International Education during the Cold War* (Ithaca, NY: Cornell University Press, 2017), 3.

[7] Many scholars have noted that the Iranian left of the late 1960s and 1970s took the "Maoist turn" along with other leftists in Western and non-Western countries. For example, see Stephanie Cronin, "The Left in Iran: Illusion and Disillusion," *Middle Eastern Studies* 36:3 (July 2000): 237; and Parvin Paidar, *Women and the Political Process in Twentieth-Century Iran* (Cambridge: Cambridge University Press, 1995), 170.

disagreements over the influence of these leftist groups; however, the different sections continued to attract new students and the Iranian student movement as a whole continued to grow until the shah was overthrown.[8]

The history of the Iranian left's relationship to the broader anticolonial moment has generally been told as a male-centered narrative, one that charts the influence of transnationally circulating revolutionary ideas and movements on Iranian male leftists.[9] This male-centered story ignores masculinity as an analytical category through which revolutionary ideas and subjectivities were forged and through which norms and hierarchies within these movements were established. By incorporating this version of Iranian leftist history into global histories of Tri-continentalism and the Bandung era, scholars reproduce the "hegemonic comparative analysis [that] help[ed] to constitute fraternal politics across race, ethnicity, and nation" and suppress heterogeneities and hierarchies among the colonized.[10] In centering gender, and not just the presence of women, this chapter contributes to feminist reappraisals of the era of Third World internationalism as a critical intervention into the project of recovering a marginalized leftist past that challenges masculinist and male-dominated narratives.[11] I focus on the CISNU's largest affiliate, the Iranian Students Association (ISA)

---

[8] Afshin Matin-Asgari, *Iranian Student Opposition to the Shah* (Costa Mesa, CA: Mazda Publishers, 2002), 13.

[9] For male-centered historiographies of the Iranian left, see Ervand Abrahamian, *Iran between Two Revolutions* (Princeton, NJ: Princeton University Press, 1982); Maziar Behrooz, *Rebels with a Cause: The Failure of the Left in Iran* (New York: I.B. Tauris, 1999); Afshin Matin-Asgari, *Both Eastern and Western: An Intellectual History of Iranian Modernity* (Cambridge: Cambridge University Press, 2018); and Eskandar Sadeghi-Boroujerdi, "The Origins of Communist Unity: Anticolonialism and Revolution in Iran's Tri-continental moment," *British Journal of Middle Eastern Studies* 45 (2017): 796–822. This body of work has been foundational for situating the Iranian opposition within Third World revolutionary networks of ideas and movements. However, by writing this history as a narrative of the ideas and actions of men, it also limits our full understanding of the politics of the era and its many legacies.

[10] Grace Kyungwon Hong and Roderick Ferguson, "Introduction," in Grace Kyungwon Hong and Roderick Ferguson, eds., *Strange Affinities: The Gender and Sexual Politics of Comparative Racialization* (Durham, NC: Duke University Press, 2011), 8.

[11] For an example of this recent feminist historiography, see Elizabeth Armstrong, "Before Bandung: The Anti-imperialist Women's Movement in Asia and the Women's International Democratic Federation," *Signs: Journal of Women in Culture and Society* 41:2 (Winter 2016): 305–332.

in the US, which initiated women's committees in the late 1960s and early 1970s in order to address the problem of "male chauvinism" and to promote women's leadership in the movement. Based on interviews with former members of the Northern California ISA women's committee, the first of its kind and the trendsetter for the other chapters, and on a close reading of a pamphlet produced by that committee and circulated throughout the ISA, this chapter examines the explicit and implicit transnational influences that attended the emergence of "gender consciousness" within the Iranian leftist student opposition.[12] These transnational influences, described in detail below, were generated by a global anti-imperialist upsurge, and anti-shah students, in Iran and abroad, understood themselves to be a part of this broader, epochal shift underway.

The ISA aimed to recruit and mobilize as many Iranian students as possible, including women, to play a very specific part in this historic push toward freedom: to end US popular and governmental support for the shah. The desire to sustain high levels of activist participation provided the initial impetus for the organization to grapple with the entrenched sexism that permeated social relations as well as political ideas and practices – within the ISA and on the left in general. In the process of trying to address the barriers to the recruitment of women and the development of women leaders, ideas began to emerge that are recognizable today as part of transnational feminist frameworks.

I approach this history with what I call a "methodology of possibility," a reading practice attentive to those revolutionary roads not taken, to the potential power latent within revolutionary ideas and practices that might have resulted in other/alternative futures, and that might contribute to a transnational feminist approach to Iranian women's oppression today.[13] This methodology builds on queer and

---

[12] Haideh Moghissi uses the term "gender consciousness" to describe an awareness among women of the need for women's liberation. See her *Populism and Feminism in Iran: Women's Struggle in a Male-Defined Revolutionary Movement* (New York: St. Martin's Press, 1996), 30–31.

[13] My formulation of a "methodology of possibility" shares a deep affinity with José Muñoz's interpretation of "hope as a critical methodology ... best described as a backward glance that enacts a future vision." See José Muñoz, *Cruising Utopia: The Then and There of Queer Futurity* (New York: New York University Press, 2009), 4; and José Muñoz and Lisa Duggan, "Hope and Hopelessness: A Dialogue," *Women & Performance: A Journal of Feminist Theory* 19:2 (2009): 275–283, in which the notion of "concrete hope" is offered

feminist scholarship that theorizes from the margins of history and initiates new engagements with affective and political orientations often disqualified in their own time. As Gayatri Gopinath wrote in her queer critique of the pan-Third Worldist era of which the ISA was a part, "engagement with the pitfalls and dangers of both dominant and anticolonial nationalist projects ... suggests that the memory of these apparently failed, ephemeral movements, marked as out of time and out of place, may still have a powerfully transformative effect on the present."[14] In this vein, a methodology of possibility describes a way of opening up an exploration of the complex lived experience of such movements and works against the political foreclosure implied by the notion of "failure." More than just a history from below or a move against what Walter Benjamin called historicism, a methodology of possibility avows its present social justice concerns and traces new genealogies of resistance that respond to our current moment. It offers a way of engaging with what Naghmeh Sohrabi, building on David Scott, has called the "problem space" of the historiography of the Iranian Revolution.[15] Sohrabi describes a new wave of scholarship that reconsiders the "horizon of identifiable ... stakes" that have previously been attached to the revolution.[16] A methodology of possibility seizes on the opportunity to raise "new sets of questions arising out of the historical conditions of our own time."[17] Furthermore, as I argue below, a methodology of possibility dwells in this open relationship between past and present, allowing us to inhabit a temporality in which what might have been and what might yet be can coexist.[18]

---

as "the primary way we bring ourselves to take the risk of breaking out of the constraints of present conditions" (281).

[14] Gayatri Gopinath, "Archive, Affect, and the Everyday: Queer Diasporic Revisions," in Janet Staiger, Ann Cvetkovich, and Ann Reynolds, eds., *Political Emotions: New Agendas in Communication* (New York: Routledge, 2010), 168.

[15] "Problem space" is David Scott's term, which Sohrabi employs to rethink approaches to writing the history of the Iranian Revolution. According to Scott, a "problem space" is "an ensemble of questions and answers around which a horizon of identifiable stakes (conceptual as well as ideological-political stakes) hangs." Quoted in Naghmeh Sohrabi, "The 'Problem Space' of the Historiography of the 1979 Iranian Revolution," *History Compass* 16 (2018): 2.

[16] Scott, quoted in ibid.   [17] Ibid.

[18] David Eng and David Kazanjian, "Introduction: Mourning Remains," in David Eng and David Kazanjian, eds., *Loss: the Politics of Mourning* (Durham, NC: Duke University Press, 2003), 4.

A Possible Genealogy of Transnational Feminism

In reading through the documents of the ISA women's committees, I recognize tenuous efforts to reconceptualize the relationship between women's liberation and anti-imperialism that have implications for the fraught terrain of transnational feminism today. Rather than arguing, as Iranian (and other) Marxists typically did, that women's liberation could only come about after the revolution and that women who joined the left were already treated as equals, the ISA showed that "male chauvinism" was systematic in society *and* in the movement, and argued that it had to be fought consistently and immediately. This marginalized history reveals another possible framework for understanding the relationship between feminism, the left, and the struggle against imperialism. Crucially, it centers the space of diaspora, and specifically the milieu of student activism on and around college campuses, as a site of multiple exchanges between revolutionary movements. Iranian student leftists abroad were embedded in a series of transnational dialogues about the future of the Third World and about the role of women within the project of decolonization.

The temporary dispersal of Iranian students predominantly across Europe and North America occurred during a time when anti-colonial revolutions were understood to be the vanguard of a global revolutionary upsurge, not only by students across Asia, Africa, and Latin America, but also by large sections of the student left in the West. The idealization of these revolutions extended to the figure of the female guerrilla fighter, in places like Vietnam, Algeria, and Palestine, and thus a model of female empowerment, through participation in the anti-imperialist revolution, circulated widely during this time. Men and women in the ISA were influenced by these ideas, images, and figures, even before the Iranian guerrilla movement offered Ashraf Dehghani as the Iranian equivalent to Djamila Bouhired and Leila Khaled. Annual ISA celebrations of International Women's Day often featured tributes to revolutionary women leaders from around the world, and the poster in Figure 4.1 illustrates these internationalist affiliations among Iranian women activists. The visible role of Third World women in revolutionary movements also had a significant impact on the activist milieu in which ISA members lived and organized, becoming a catalyst for American women, of different racial backgrounds, to develop a Third World-oriented revolutionary feminism in the US. Thus, the

Figure 4.1 The Iranian Students Association celebrates March 8 – International Women's Day.
Source: The Black Mountain Press Iranian Poster Collection as published in *In Search of Lost Causes: Fragmented Allegories of an Iranian Revolution*, by Hamid Dabashi.

formation of women's committees within the ISA must be understood as a local, diasporic, and transnational expression of debates over gender and sexuality unfolding in Third World and Western countries in the context of revolutionary movements and the radical student organizing inspired by those movements.

The ISA Northern California Women's Committee pamphlet, "University Women Are Getting Organized" (pub. c. 1968), a piece of movement ephemera tucked away and forgotten in an archive, constitutes a partial and tentative articulation of political ideas that would, almost a decade later, ring out in the chants and slogans of thousands of Iranian women who took to the streets of Tehran in March 1979.[19] While feminist scholars such as Haideh Moghissi have decried the "absence of gender-consciousness" among leftists in Iran, there was an organized effort to

---

[19] I came across this pamphlet in May 2015, in the Hoover Institute Archives on the Iranian left at Stanford University.

critique and alter existing gender relations by Iranian leftists in the US.[20]
Using a methodology of possibility, I argue that the ISA's attempts to
apply a gender analysis to conditions inside Iran exceeded Marxist orthodoxies[21] and contained within them elements that would later be foundational to socialist feminist and transnational feminist frameworks, despite
the fact that ISA members could not apprehend them as such at the time.
These kernels of other possible versions of Iranian revolutionary politics
existed alongside more typical renderings of the exploitation of women
under feudalism and capitalism, revealing tensions between Marxism and
feminism that were constitutive of the Third Worldist left of the Cold War
era. It is thus a useful document for tracking discursive and political shifts
in debates that have left an indelible mark on progressive politics today.

The pamphlet also contributes to feminist historiography in the US.
Recent scholarship has challenged the "wave" analogy, in which the
"second wave" of the 1960s and 1970s is represented as a white,
middle-class, liberal movement.[22] "Third World" women, "postcolonial"
women, and women of color only enter this narrative as part of a subsequent "third wave" in the 1980s. As I will discuss further, the presence of
Iranian foreign students organizing against imperialism and "male chauvinism" within the US in the late 1960s was made possible by the fact that
the "second wave" was initiated not only by liberals, but by women
involved in anti-imperialist, anti-capitalist movements who wanted to
incorporate struggles against patriarchy into these larger leftist projects.[23]

---

[20] Moghissi, *Populism and Feminism*, 182.

[21] According to Paidar, the "Marxist-Leninist analysis of women" developed by
groups in Iran described poor women as the victims of imperialism and regime
oppression, while upper-class women "were considered accomplices in this
imperialist conspiracy." See Paidar, *Women and the Political Process*, 170–171.

[22] See Kimberley Springer, *Living for the Revolution: Black Feminist
Organizations, 1968–1980* (Durham, NC: Duke University Press, 2005), 7–10.

[23] See Keeanga-Yamahtta Taylor's discussion of the emergence of Black radical
feminism as an effort to "extend Marxist analysis" rather than abandon it in
How We Get Free: Black Feminism and the Combahee River Collective
(Chicago, IL: Haymarket Books, 2017), 7. Nancy Fraser asserts that "most
second-wave feminists – with the notable exception of liberal feminists –
concurred that overcoming women's oppression required radical transformation
of the deep structures of social totality. This shared commitment to systemic
transformation betokened the movement's origins in the broader emancipatory
ferment of the times." See Nancy Fraser, "Feminism, Capitalism and the
Cunning of History," *NLR* 56 (March–April 2009), https://newleftreview-org
.ezproxy.cul.columbia.edu/issues/II56/articles/nancy-fraser-feminism-
capitalism-and-the-cunning-of-history.

Therefore, feminism in the West was not a monolithic entity, but a space of contentious debate, in which proponents of socialist feminism and Third World feminism centered the critical revolutionary role of women in colonized and formerly colonized nations. By offering a window into the multiple influences shaping the ISA's analysis of gender inequality, this pamphlet illustrates the extent to which the Iranian student opposition to the shah was part of this global constellation of Third World and Third Worldist revolutionary ideas and movements that seemed to offer – even to many activists in the West – the best hope for human liberation.[24]

The Formation and Impact of ISA Women's Committees

The Northern California ISA branch, based in Berkeley, brought together campus ISA chapters as far south as San Jose and as far north as Richmond and exerted a major influence over the development of the ISA in the US. According to several former ISA members I interviewed, the idea for a women's committee first emerged in 1967 in response to concerns about the low numbers of women involved in the movement in the Bay Area. While the numbers of Iranian women studying abroad were increasing by the end of the 1960s, the ISA was not successfully recruiting or retaining women members. Jaleh Behroozi, a Jewish woman who was a UC Berkeley student and an ISA activist, recalled that the gender imbalance in the chapter was extreme. "Out of fifty to seventy active members, there were three or four women," she said.[25] In 1967, Hamid Kowsari, who was part of the chapter's local elected leadership and served as the organizational affairs secretary, decided to do something about this problem. He proposed a "Committee to Struggle against Male Chauvinism," which Behroozi joined along with a few other women and men. As more women joined, the committee changed its name to the Women's Committee and a regular program of Sunday morning

---

[24] I use "Third Worldist" to refer to the political orientation of grassroots movements located in the US and Europe that looked to anti-colonial movements in the Third World as sites of solidarity, inspiration, and influence. For an account of how this political tendency developed in the US, see Max Elbaum, *Revolution in the Air: Sixties Radicals Turn to Lenin, Mao and Che* (New York: Verso Books, 2002).

[25] All quotations from former ISA members are from phone interviews with author conducted in May and June of 2019.

meetings, research, study, and debate ensued. "I am pretty sure one of the first books they read was Simone De Beauvoir's *The Second Sex*," Kowsari recalled. "They read it in English. We had no access to Persian translations." While there is no clear evidence of a sustained engagement with French feminism by ISA members, the effort by a group of Iranian students to read this canonical feminist text – and in English no less – gives some indication of the sincerity and dedication with which members approached the committee's mandate.

Members from Northern California actively promoted the formation of women's committees in chapters around the US. "A lot of chapters were smaller," said Jaleh Pirnazar, another Jewish ISA activist studying at Berkeley. "They looked to the Northern California chapter as their mecca and would follow us. When they had a chance, a summer break, they would get in their cars and drive out here to join our committee ... Northern California inspired many of these young women" who went back to their campus branches and started local women's committees. Written materials produced by the Northern California Women's Committee, including the Persian-language "University Women Are Getting Organized" *(Zanan-e Daneshjoo Motashakel Meshavand)*, were copied and distributed throughout the ISA chapters and for sale at below cost on literature tables at ISA conventions and public events.

We "really expanded the role of women in the entire organization," Behroozi said, looking back on what the women's committees had accomplished. "We even thought we were superior to the European chapters because we were more organized and more women were involved," she recalled. While the women's committees, "started discussing [Freidrich] Engels at a very theoretical level in the beginning," Behroozi said, referring to the canonical Marxist text *The Origins of the Family, Private, Property and the State*, they also tried to figure out how to apply these ideas in their own lives. As Behroozi explained, they wanted to know "what does it mean in practice, how men should look at the role of women, and how women should be taking leadership positions. So this resulted in the flourishing of a lot of young women who had secondary roles to become more active and take on leadership." For example, Behroozi became part of the elected committee in charge of the entire Northern California ISA, first as secretary of publications and then as secretary of culture. This latter position "meant we had to organize all the speeches and cultural activities which were mostly of course political." Pirnazar was elected to the national ISA leadership body as the secretary of publications, and was sent to represent the ISA at the annual CISNU congress in Frankfurt, Germany, in 1972. Indeed, because of the work of ISA women's committees, gender quotas were established to ensure that women held two out of the five seats on the formal, elected leadership bodies of local chapters and of the national organization.[26]

Kowsari explained how he first got the idea to initiate work around gender inequality in the ISA:

I was not only involved in the ISA, but very active in the movement in the US, mostly in SDS [Students for a Democratic Society] against the war [in Vietnam] and also in the civil rights movement. My [American] girlfriend was very active both in SDS and also in the women's liberation movement. So I learned a lot from the American women's liberation movement. I became myself aware of male chauvinism and I thought we should introduce [this term] into our movement.

While Kowsari was one of a handful of ISA members who were also members of American student organizations, the ISA as a whole was part of a broader political milieu that, by 1967, was swirling with debates about sexism and revolution. This milieu, and not only the concentration of large numbers of Iranians in an area with many colleges and universities, enabled the Northern California ISA to function as a kind of political vanguard for the ISA as a whole, what Pirnazar called a "mecca." Oakland, Berkeley, and San Francisco formed the epicenter of some of the most dynamic, innovative, and militant student movements in the entire country. The free speech movement, SDS, the Black Panther Party for Self-Defense, Black Student Unions, the Third World Liberation Front, and mass student strikes at San Francisco State and at UC Berkeley against racism and war created a vibrant political and social sphere which shaped the ISA. When SDS split in 1969, the ISA worked closely with Maoist organizations like the Revolution Union (later the Revolutionary Communist Party) and the Progressive Labor Party. The ISA was part of the anti-imperialist left in the US and this provided the overall context in which the ISA women's committee was formulating its ideas about the causes

---

[26] Manijeh Nasrabadi, "'Women Can Do Anything Men Can Do': Gender and the Affects of Solidarity in the U.S. Iranian Student Movement, 1961–1979," *Women's Studies Quarterly* 42:3 and 4 (Fall–Winter 2014): 134.

of and solutions to gender inequality. Women leftists in many other Bay Area (and nationwide) movements were raising the issue of "male chauvinism" openly and with mixed results, and ISA members were aware of, and sometimes directly involved in, these discussions.

The Northern California ISA had especially close connections with SDS. There is ample archival evidence of jointly organized meetings and demonstrations in Berkeley and San Francisco around a range of issues from opposition to the US war in Vietnam to US support for the shah to solidarity with the Palestinian freedom struggle. "We were reading SDS literature," Behroozi remembered. In fact, both she and Jaleh Pirnazar said that the term "male chauvinism" entered the ISA lexicon via SDS, which published a resolution against male chauvinism in its periodical *New Left Notes* in 1967.[27] The resolution calls on men to confront "male chauvinism" and calls on women to "demand full participation in all aspects of movement work, from licking stamps to assuming leadership positions."[28] This resolution is cited in the ISA women's committee pamphlet produced by the Northern California ISA chapter.[29] In addition, interviews with former ISA members of this chapter revealed strong personal and political ties with individual members of SDS. "They were fellow activists," Pirnazar said. "We would participate in their events and they showed up to our demonstrations and our activities. They provided help with typing [English-language ISA publications such as *Resistance* and] *Iran Report*, and with Xerox machines. Some SDS members would reprint our articles." The connections were intimate as well. Several Iranian men, including Hamid, were dating or married to white American women active in SDS and its splinter groups who became part of the ISA's social circle. "I can think of at least four," Pirnazar recalled. "We sat around together in the evenings. We would go camping and sit around the fire and sing SDS songs and they would be singing the Iranian revolutionary songs. We were a very close, tight-knit circle of friends, boyfriends, and girlfriends."[30] These face-to-face interactions were crucial for

---

[27] *New Left Notes* (July 10, 1967), 4.   [28] Ibid.

[29] Iranian Students Association, Northern California Women's Committee, "University Women Are Getting Organized" (Shokat Collection, Hoover Archives, Stanford University, c. 1968), 15.

[30] I found no evidence of Iranian women dating American men in Northern California, the reasons for which are beyond the scope of this study.

making ideas circulating on the US left accessible to those Iranians who had difficulty reading in English.

It would be ahistorical to read the influence of white American women on the emergent gender consciousness of Iranian women through an Orientalist lens as evidence of a hierarchical relationship between American women and Iranian women activists at the time. As Behroozi noted of the American women activists who were around the ISA and sometimes involved in its activities, "They were a lot more influenced by the Iranian movement than vice versa," due to the radicalizing political education about the US role in the Middle East they received from Iranian student activists. In the late 1960s and early 1970s, American women leftists were just as likely "to see Third World women liberation fighters as models of revolutionary womanhood" as to imagine themselves as saviors of their less fortunate "sisters."[31] For example, Vivian Rothstein, a leading member of the Chicago Women's Liberation Union, traveled to North Vietnam and said of her meeting there with Vietnamese women revolutionaries, "That was my most clear women's liberation experience." The feminist historian Sara Evens argues that revolutionary movements of racialized and colonized peoples profoundly influenced the efforts of white American women in SDS to articulate and theorize their own oppression:

Any activist knew that third world peoples – the Vietnamese, blacks in Africa and in the United States, Chicanos, American Indians – were oppressed. Their struggles constituted guideposts for the movement ... In a sense, therefore, the women were saying to SDS in the strongest language they could find, "We are oppressed as women, and our oppression is as real, as legitimate, as necessary to fight against as that of blacks, Chicanos or the Vietnamese."[32]

A cynical reading would view this simply as evidence of white women co-opting the movements of colonized and formerly colonized people by way of an analogy to their own oppression. Such a reading would also make it impossible to reckon with a period in which Third World peoples held political and moral leadership among significant sections

---

[31] Judy Tzu-Chun Wu, *Radicals on the Road: Internationalism, Orientalism, and Feminism during the Vietnam Era* (Ithaca, NY: Cornell University Press, 2013), 7.

[32] Sara Margaret Evans, *Personal Politics: The Roots of Women's Liberation in the Civil Rights Movement* (New York: Knopf, 1979), 190.

of the Western left.[33] A more generous reading allows us to consider the lived experiences of those who confronted sexism, racism, and imperialism in a moment in which anti-colonial revolutions had transformed the political horizons of activists around the world and made it possible for new generations of Americans to imagine a future beyond patriarchy, capitalism, and empire.

In order to avoid naturalizing a racial hierarchy among women, it is important to remember that, in the 1960s and 1970s, the notion that American women were already liberated was far from the common operating assumption it would become a few decades later. This is not to minimize the racism of white women, but rather to emphasize that across anti-war and anti-racist organizations, women from different racial and class backgrounds were in the thick of confronting the deep impact of sexism on their lives and on their position within progressive and leftist movements. It was a painful process that unfolded differently depending on the organization and on the historical character of the oppression targeting distinct groups of women. The dominant response American women faced, even within radical movements, was that their oppression was deemed trivial and/or biologically justified, and the fact that they raised it at all was often attacked as an irresponsible diversion from the more important struggles against racism, capitalism, and imperialism. When white women in SDS first began to address the issue of "male chauvinism" within the movement, they were shouted down, mocked, and ridiculed.[34] Even when they did succeed in passing the resolution cited by the ISA Women's Committee pamphlet, it was published alongside an infantilizing caricature of a woman throwing a tantrum.[35] This kind of misogyny would eventually lead many women to embrace feminism and to conclude that they needed to organize separately from men.[36]

Women in the ISA had a negative assessment of this approach. As Behroozi summarized:

---

[33] See Elbaum, *Revolution in the Air*.

[34] This phenomenon has been widely documented. See, for example, Jo Freeman, *The Politics of Women's Liberation: A Case Study of an Emerging Movement and Its Relation to the Policy Process* (Lincoln, NE: iUniverse.com Inc., 2000), 57–58.

[35] *New Left Notes* (July 10, 1967), 4.

[36] See Evans, "The Dam Breaks," in *Personal Politics*, 193–211.

Feminism at that time for us ... because we knew about other organizations, they interpreted feminism as women being separate from men, and they have to be organizing themselves without men. It was like an antagonistic relationship with men. Our thinking wasn't like that. Women are part of the movement. They have to bring awareness to men about male chauvinism and they have to be together in the struggle. The term "feminism" wasn't kosher.

Both Behroozi and Pirnazar remember men in the ISA treating them with respect and taking the work of the Women's Committee seriously. "There was general acceptance of the Women's Committee. Men would participate, they would come and listen," Behroozi said. "It was just as important to educate men. Otherwise we couldn't have so many women getting involved and becoming leaders of the organization." Pirnazar recalled that "if men tried to stay away or ridicule [the committee], that was shunned."

Kowsari could not recall any open resistance from men to the contributions of the Women's Committee to the ISA. "I'm not saying the members were not chauvinist," he quickly added, but he recalled that enthusiasm generally greeted the Women's Committee's reports to the chapter as a whole. Then he recounted this memory:

One day, one [male] member came to me and said, "I'm really glad you formed this committee. It had a really good effect on me. To be honest with you, when our female members were talking, I didn't listen to them. Now I am listening to them and I am learning from them." Chauvinism was that bad that you don't think it was worth it to even listen to a woman speak.

This anecdote reveals both the depth of the problem and the small, yet significant, changes that occurred as a result of an organized effort to forge more egalitarian gender relations within the ISA.

When Ali Hojat moved to Northern California to attend San Jose State College in the spring semester of 1970, he joined the ISA chapter and the Women's Committee. He recalled that he "was the only man" among between five and seven women at that time. He would get up early every Sunday to drive from San Jose to Berkeley to attend committee meetings. "I was a very radical person," he said by way of explaining his participation.

I thought, how can we have progress without half of the population and what prevents them to join. I encouraged other men to join, but they brushed it away and laughed a little bit. They thought it was something that women should work on. But that wasn't my opinion. This is for women but probably more so for men because they need to be educated. We should all work on it. Of course, women should be at the forefront.

This idea, that challenging male chauvinism was the work of women and men, with women in the leadership, was seen as an alternative to a feminist-separatist strategy at the time. Looking back at the pamphlet, written just before he moved to the area, Hojat assessed the descriptions of women's oppression contained within it as "very correct. [Those sections] were factual and to the point in discussing the real issues of women. Now, with the later terminology, they [committee members] were feminists and I consider myself to be a feminist at that time." This retroactive claiming of feminism speaks volumes about the political changes that have happened in Iran since the revolution, a point to which I will return in the Conclusion.

The political work of the Women's Committee also led to real changes in the gendered division of labor when it came to cooking and other support tasks for ISA events.[37] Behroozi recalled earnest, and in her opinion sometimes overbearing, efforts to "put these ideas in to practice" by demanding that men share the tasks of social reproduction in the home as well:

I remember my brother-in-law had come from Iran with his wife and a little baby. He was a young man going to school all day and his wife was staying at home cooking. Every night he would come home and we would roast him. "You have to do work in the kitchen and [your wife] shouldn't have to do all this." We were so harsh in our criticism toward all the imbalances that existed. To the extreme!

These efforts, whether extreme or not, were part of an uneven process of attempting to create new forms of gender relations.[38] And they appear to have triggered a backlash in some sections of the movement. In 1976, in a special issue of a periodical in honor of International Women's Day, the West German chapter of the Confederation denounced the kinds of transformations in gender roles which the ISA was trying to implement: "Those who are concerned with their own individual liberation are no more than bourgeois and daydreaming intellectuals ... Anyone demanding women to give up domestic responsibilities, or perform them partially and sharing them

[37] Nasrabadi, "'Women Can Do Anything Men Can Do,'" 135.   [38] Ibid., 141.

with men should know that this will not lead to the mobilisation of the masses."[39]

It proved difficult indeed to spread the ideas and practices developed by the Northern California ISA to the Confederation as a whole. Pirnazar remembered being sent as an elected representative from the ISA's national secretariat to the Confederation's annual international congress in Frankfurt "with the specific mission of raising awareness of women's committees because the American experience was so good." She went on to describe a scene reminiscent of what women experienced at SDS conventions when they tried to raise similar issues:

I was there at the podium discussing male chauvinism and the man who was chairing began semi ridiculing, "*chi chi mard, khanum*" [male what what, miss?] and the whole hall erupted in laughter. "Do we have a committee *mardan* [a men's committee]?" one man shouted. I remember that clearly. I was so embarrassed. I blushed. Total ridicule. And then the laughter. It was miserable. So it wasn't all that accepted within the rest of that movement.

According to Pirnazar, the congress attacked the women's committees as "divisive" and they were "accused of secessionism." Even without the use of the term feminism, modest efforts to talk about gender inequality met with the charge of "separatism." This was a powerful way of shutting down the conversation because Iranian women in the ISA believed in the need for a united movement against the shah and Western imperialism just as much as did the men.

Simply having women involved, even in high-level positions, as the Confederation eventually did, is not in and of itself evidence of gender equality. I have written elsewhere about the rigid gendered terms on which Iranian women were incorporated into the ISA and the underground left groups active within it.[40] While conditions varied from chapter to chapter, and among the different leftist organizations, overall, women were supposed to cut their hair short and dress androgynously in order to conform to dominant notions of proper revolutionary subjectivity. This mode of revolutionary belonging associated anything deemed "feminine" with counterrevolutionary forces (Western imperialism and the bourgeoisie) and maintained the primary legitimacy of a masculine revolutionary subject. Parvin Paidar calls this

[39] Confederation of Iranian Students Abroad (1976), 6, quoted in Paidar, *Women and the Political Process*, 172.
[40] See Nasrabadi, "'Women Can Do Anything Men Can Do.'"

a process of "masculinization," practiced among underground Marxist guerrillas in Iran as well.[41] As Minoo Moallem has argued, Iranian women activists found themselves in an ambivalent relationship to the masculinist norms of the movement, which could be a liberating alternative to hyper-sexualization and a future circumscribed by the roles of wife and mother.[42] The opportunity to be valued, and to value oneself, based on one's political commitments, rather than attractiveness or marriageability, was often compelling enough that women put aside any discomfort with the rigid demands of anti-feminine revolutionary gender norms.[43] And yet, this did not result in the complete subordination of women's issues. The pamphlet "University Women Are Getting Organized" reveals a much more uneven process in which the desire to incorporate more women into the movement, even on these masculinized terms, created an opportunity to write openly about women's oppression in ways that, however unwittingly, exceeded leftist orthodoxies.

The rejection of feminism based on defining it, as some feminists did, as separatism was also a common response among African American, Asian American, Latina, and indigenous women leftists in the US who felt the need to build united movements of women and men against racism, settler colonialism, and imperialism. While some "Third World US women" would redefine and embrace feminism as a powerful political framework for analyzing the dynamics of overlapping systems of oppression and the particular conditions of racialized women, women in the ISA seem to have remained unaware of these specific political developments (such as the Third World Women's Alliance formed in 1968).[44] Iranian student activists also seem to have been unaware of explicit efforts to meld Marxism and feminism into a socialist feminist ideology that were happening at the same time that the ISA was crafting its gender analysis. Instead of engaging with non-separatist and/or explicitly leftist forms of feminism, the Confederation, like the Iranian left as a whole, focused on the question of whether addressing "male chauvinism" systematically would

---

[41] Paidar, *Women and the Political Process*, 171.
[42] Minoo Moallem, *Between Warrior Brother and Veiled Sister: Islamic Fundamentalism and the Politics of Patriarchy in Iran* (Berkeley, CA: University of California Press, 2005), 78.
[43] See Nasrabadi, "'Women Can Do Anything Men Can Do.'"
[44] Springer, *Living for the Revolution*, 47–50.

strengthen the movement or undermine it. It is in light of the broader tensions between Marxism and feminism that the work of the ISA women's committees must be assessed.

Socialist Feminist Gestures, Transnational Feminist Concerns

"University Women Are Getting Organized" developed out of collect-ive study, research, and discussion and reflected ideas generated col-laboratively.[45] The pamphlet opens with the assertion that "women's emancipation from the shackles of patriarchy (male chauvinism) and the feudal system ... has been forgotten and is not being addressed" by the Iranian people's movement and the Iranian student movement.[46] In order to correct this, it states, "female students are taking the first steps," presumably by offering the analysis, proposals, and slogans that follow. The very next paragraph, however, launches into a recur-ring and scathing critique of the shah's top-down approach to women's rights that were part of his White Revolution reform package.[47] Using language charged with anger and disdain, the authors hoped to discredit the regime's initiatives as a precondition for linking women's liberation to the broader opposition movement. "By holding a mask to his ugly chauvinist visage," they wrote of the shah, "he pretends that he supports Iranian women's freedom, and thus keeps them from the main fight, which is fighting against his anti-civic regime and imperialism and feudalism." This formulation appears to reproduce the very hierarchy of oppression that led to the "forgetting" of patriarchy in the first place, positioning the struggle against dictatorship, imperialism, and feudalism as the "main fight" and women's oppression as something less important. An abrupt switching back and forth, between a hierarchical leftist framework

[45] This pamphlet was translated into English by Atefeh Akbari, to whom I am exceedingly grateful.

[46] The placement of "male chauvinism" in parentheses next to "patriarchy" implies that the authors saw the two terms as interchangeable. From this point on, the pamphlet only uses "male chauvinism," the term borrowed from the US context.

[47] The shah's "White Revolution" was a six-point policy program initiated in 1963, which granted women voting rights. For a discussion of the social and political forces leading to the enfranchisement of Iranian women, see Eliz Sanasarian, *Women's Rights Movement in Iran: Mutiny, Appeasement, and Repression from 1900 to Khomeini* (New York: Praeger, 1982), 82.

and an effort to place women's oppression at the heart of the workings of economic and political power, characterizes the pamphlet as a whole. This dynamic illustrates the authors' intention to remain within an already well-established left discourse *and* the difficulty in doing so.[48]

What stands out to this reader are the places where the pamphlet discusses the plight of women, not only in relation to production and economic exploitation, but also in relation to social reproduction, intimate relationships, culture, and even how men and women are socialized to feel about each other and about themselves. This is one key place from which another possible feminist gender politics might have emerged. For example, a detailed discussion of the economic exploitation of women workers in factories, traditional workshops, and in agriculture – complete with data on the gender pay gap across all economic sectors – is followed by the question "Who benefits from this situation?" The answer to this question begins, predictably enough, with the following list: "Landowners and feudalists, and other wealthy village men on the one hand, and the big owners of industries and workshops, imperialist and capitalist brokers and other wealthy men of the cities on the other hand." This formulation maintains the economistic Marxist view that women's oppression is essentially a strategy the ruling classes use in order to increase their wealth through the hyper-exploitation of women for lower pay. However, this view is immediately complicated by the next sentence, in which a definition of male chauvinism appears for the first time in the text:

Male chauvinism means the ideological representation of the unequal and exploitative relationship between men and women in society and this ideological representation appears in all of our society's moral, psychological and political relationships, and in this manner, men's feeling of superiority over women emerges.

Suddenly the explanation for gender inequality is not reducible to crude logics of economic profit in the productive sphere; it is expansive, applying to "all of our society" and to "men" in general, rather than only wealthy men. The main goal of the pamphlet was, after all, to challenge sexism among men within the Confederation, who were

---

[48] Both Pirnazar and Behroozi reported that they were immersed within a leftist analysis and that the Women's Committee was extremely critical of religiously informed anti-imperialism of figures such as Ali Shariati. Interviews with author.

neither bosses nor landlords. In this vein, the definition of male chauvinism covers ideology, morality, psychology, politics, relationships, and even feelings! It is here that the pamphlet begins to trespass, however unwittingly, on the terrain of feminist politics, a tendency that continues throughout the remainder of the text.

The feminist economist Heidi Hartmann, in her 1979 essay "The Unhappy Marriage of Marxism and Feminism: Towards a More Progressive Union," argues that "the 'woman question' has never been the 'feminist question'":

> The feminist question is directed at the causes of sexual inequality between women and men, of male dominance over women. Most Marxist analyses of women's position take as their question the relationship of women to the economic system, rather than that of women to men, apparently assuming the latter will be explained in their discussion of the former.[49]

Almost a decade before Hartmann wrote these lines, the ISA's pamphlet on women addressed this "feminist question" through an analysis of women's oppression in the family that crossed class lines and the rural-urban divide.

The "slave-like exploitation of women in villages and cities" is combined with "internal colonization in the household by the 'husband's power,'" the pamphlet argues, adapting the language of the anti-colonial left to the condition of women in the domestic sphere. The use of the concept of "internal colonization" may also be indebted to the framework dominant among many US anti-racist organizations, which stipulated that African Americans were an internal colony sharing a common struggle with those resisting colonialism in the Third World. In 1967, white women in SDS argued on the convention floor that "women are in a colonial relationship to men and we recognize ourselves as part of the Third World."[50] The ISA's use of this term renders the domestic sphere of intimate relations and social reproduction as a necessary, legitimate, and explicit site of political critique and struggle, a move central to feminist politics. "The family in Iran ... is a prison with hundreds of chains for the daughters and women of Iran," the text continues, "whether in her husband's home or her father's home." Arranged marriages, financial dependence on

---

[49] Heidi Hartmann, "The Unhappy Marriage of Marxism and Feminism: Toward A More Progressive Union," *Capital and Class* 3:2 (Summer 1979): 2.
[50] Quoted in Evans, *Personal Politics*, 190.

men, and unpaid domestic labor turn the home into a place of "numerous hardships" from which most women "do not see a way out." In the home, a woman "is exactly like an exploited farmer and laborer who does not . . . own anything." In making this analogy with exploitation in the productive sphere, the pamphlet seems to adhere to the discourse of Marxism-Leninism inside Iran. According to Paidar, this leftist literature sympathetically described "the experiences of deprived groups such as working-class women, rural women and urban prostitutes" and "affluent women were condemned as sex-objects, accomplices of the Shah and oppressors of lower-class women."[51] Yet, in the ISA pamphlet, the woman exploited and imprisoned in the home can come from any class background. As an example of how "the relations and culture governing our families exacerbate exploitation of the woman by man," we read that "women give up studying in scientific majors" because these are deemed irrelevant to their future as wives and homemakers. "Women are thus forced to learn skills such as embroidery, floral design, and cooking, and in this manner a future is made for these women in which they only rear children and take care of the husband's house and property." Rather than issue a blanket condemnation of economically privileged women, there is heartfelt concern for the stunted condition of the educated, bourgeois housewife, a future from which women ISA activists had escaped. Not only is the family the subject of sustained critique throughout this pamphlet, but it also figures into the vision of "women's freedom" described in the final section, in the demand for "the fundamental transformation of the feudal family as well as the half-feudal, half-imperial family." While this description of the family as "half-feudal, half-imperial" reproduced the leftist characterization of Iranian society at the time, these terms are used to render the family, in *all* of its existing forms, the target of a revolutionary demand.

This emphasis on the family as a foundational institution of male domination over women owes much to Engels's classic description of the fall in the status of women as a consequence of the transition from communal societies to societies based on private property.[52] However, because of the combined and uneven development of the Iranian

---

[51] Paidar, *Women and the Political Process*, 171.

[52] Frederick Engels, *The Origin of the Family, Private Property and the State* (New York: International Publishers, 1972).

economy, the pamphlet does not draw the same conclusions as Engels about how to liberate women. As Hartmann summarizes,

For Engels then, women's participation in the labor force was the key to their emancipation. Capitalism would abolish sex differences and treat all workers equally. Women would become economically independent of men and would participate on equal footing with men in bringing about the proletarian revolution.[53]

Through descriptions of enduring patriarchy in capitalist industries, the pamphlet's opening paragraphs dispense with the notion that the entrance of Iranian women into factory labor led to their equality as workers. The lengthy opening section of the pamphlet ends with a proclamation that positions women's oppression at the center of leftist critique: "In the fight against chauvinism and all its representations, the women of Iran challenge unequal rights, and fight against imperialism and feudalism, so the path can be paved through the freedom of women and their equal rights." While it was a leftist axiom to assert, as this pamphlet does elsewhere, that "[w]ithout overthrowing the system of colonialism and exploitation, Iranian women cannot become free," it was quite unusual to reverse this logic. In the previous sentence, there is a rare glimpse of the idea that the fight against imperialism and feudalism can only proceed "through the freedom of women and their equal rights." Again, preempting Hartmann's analysis at the end of the 1970s, the pamphlet gestures toward the "more progressive union of Marxism and feminism" that she advocates when she writes that "alliance must replace dominance and subordination in leftist politics." The Northern California Women's Committee may not have forged this "more progressive union," but it certainly challenged a dominant form of leftist politics that subordinated, when it did not diminish or postpone, the problem of gender inequality.

This analysis, combined with the attack on the family in all of its existing forms, illustrates that patriarchy is integral to the economic and social logics that shape Iranian society across classes *and* that it has a logic of its own not reducible to any one economic mode – both key insights of socialist feminism. For example, several years later, in 1972, the Hyde Park Chapter of the Chicago Women's Liberation Movement issued a manifesto titled "Socialist Feminism: A Strategy

[53] Hartmann, "Unhappy Marriage," 3.

for the Women's Movement" in which it fused structural critiques of capitalism with feminist analysis and attention to the specific problems faced by women into a call for mass organizing.[54] The ISA pamphlet also provides evidence for an argument crucial to the development of transnational feminist politics in the 1990s: women's oppression has multiple, overlapping causes that must be investigated in their geographic and historical specificity.[55] These causes always include the impact of global forces such as capitalism and imperialism and cannot be reduced simply to a static notion of culture or religion.[56] These elements of the ISA Women's Committee's pamphlet are all the more remarkable when measured against the tendency of the secular left in Iran to apply abstract Marxist ideas without much attention to the particular conditions and history of Iranian society, especially when it came to "the woman question." In her discussion of Marxist-Leninist groups in Iran, Paidar argues, "What was said about the historical development of women's position in Iran could be said about any other society equally."[57] In contrast, the Northern California ISA Women's Committee set out to engage specifically with the Iranian context.

Under the section heading "The Women's Condition in History," the pamphlet provides a sweeping overview of the status of women on the land that became Iran from the Medes period (678–549 BC) all the way to the Constitutional Revolution (1905–1911). This limited and cursory account is most interesting as an attempt to generate an historical materialist analysis of Iranian women's oppression, as opposed to simply reproducing a Western Marxist schema. While the Northern California ISA Women's Committee read texts by Marx, Engels, Lenin, and Kruspskaya, as well SDS and other contemporary US leftist literature, "this was the Western context," Pirnazar said. "For Iran, which was semicolonial, we had to do our own research." She remembered taking advantage of her job at the UC Berkeley library

---

[54] Heather Booth, Day Creamer, Susan Davis, et al., "Socialist Feminism: A Strategy for the Women's Movement," Hyde Park Chapter, Chicago Women's Liberation Union, 1972, www.historyisaweapon.org/defcon1/chisocfem.html.

[55] See Chandra Talpade Mohanty, "'Under Western Eyes' Revisited: Feminist Solidarity through Anticapitalist Struggles," *Signs* 28:2 (Winter 2003): 499–535.

[56] Ibid.   [57] Paidar, *Women and the Political Process*, 170.

to conduct research on the condition of women in Iran in ancient and modern times. "We used a three-volume book, *Tarikh-e Ejtemaiye Iran (A Social History of Iran)*, by Morteza Ravandi," she recalled, without having yet had the opportunity to look at the pamphlet again after so many decades. This source does indeed appear in the endnotes.[58]

In the summary of each historical era, the pamphlet is attentive to whether or not women were allowed to participate in public life, whether they worked outside the home, when hijab was mandatory vs. voluntary and for which classes of women, when seclusion was practiced, and the relative rights of women regarding marriage and divorce. What emerges is a dynamic and changing picture of women's roles and status in different historical periods. With the arrival of Islam in the seventh century, "woman's social position and therefore her position in the family were degraded even more and it was presented as a natural order," the pamphlet argues. While certain specific aspects of Islamic law are criticized, such as inheritance rights for men that are twice those of women and gender segregation, the hostility to Islam quickly becomes synonymous with hostility to feudalism: "Generally, it can be said that during this era – that is, feudalism – women were considered men's sexual objects and economic slaves, and ... their rights were completely abused." The pamphlet then laments the fact that this state of affairs was not fundamentally altered by the Constitutional Revolution of 1905–1911. Even though the Constitution's eighth article stated "all of the country's people possess equal rights," parliament would later "clarify that no rights were considered for women in the family and all the previous feudal-patriarchal relations were strengthened and became law." The Constitutional Revolution, the pamphlet argues, inaugurated an era in which women have struggled almost continuously for their rights against entrenched "feudal-patriarchal relations inside the family."

The following section, "Women's Fight for Freedom," does the important work of crafting a narrative of women's participation in political struggle, resonant with the kind of feminist historiography that writes women into the male-dominated histories from which they

---

[58] For a summary of Morteza Ravandi's work, see Ali Mirsepassi, *Intellectual Discourse and the Politics of Modernization: Negotiating Modernity in Iran* (Cambridge: Cambridge University Press, 2000), 57.

had been erased. Women are praised for demonstrating "sacrifice and heroism at the same time" and, thus, are shown to possess revolutionary agency. The list of examples given is too long to reproduce here, but it is worth noting that women are often depicted as more resolute and militant than men. For example, the pamphlet describes an incident in 1911 when the Iranian parliament was about to surrender to a Russian tsarist occupation of several cities: "But suddenly, 300 fighter women who had hid knives, pistols, and daggers in their clothes, appeared in the parliament." When their demands to participate in the session underway were rebuffed, "these brave-hearted women threateningly displayed their pistols, took off their masks and threw them away." One of the women spoke and said, "If parliament legislators hesitate in their responsibility to protect the Iranian nation and preserve its dignity, we will kill our men and children and will throw their bodies right here." These threats proved effective, the pamphlet explains, and the tsar recalled his troops. "Without a doubt," the paragraph concludes, "such an organized group could not have been disconnected from underground organizations."[59]

The text then launches into almost five pages cataloging Iranian women's organizations and publications in the 1920s and 1940s, including those linked to the Tudeh Party. It argues that the shah's 1935 decree banning hijab was "the result of consistent fights of women" in organizations such as "Messenger for Prosperity" (Peyk-e Sa'adat) and the "Women's Awakening" (Bidari-e Nesvan).[60] Rather than praise the removal of hijab as progressive for women, the pamphlet argues that the ban "sprayed water on the fire that was the real revolution of women," implying that the actual liberation of women was not accomplished through this imposition of state power.[61] Based largely on Tudeh Party literature, which circulated from the Tudeh central committee in exile in East Germany throughout the various Confederation branches, this section also describes women's participation in the oil nationalization movement of the early 1950s. It brings the reader into the present by pointing out that women played a role in protests by teachers, students, and Kurdish revolutionaries against the shah throughout the 1960s. In this way, a genealogy of Iranian women's political struggle on behalf of the nation is established. In

---

[59] This incident is also described by Paidar, *Women and the Political Process*, 58.
[60] "University Women Are Getting Organized," 11.   [61] Ibid.

and of itself, this can be read as a nationalist history and not a distinctly feminist one. Within the structure of the pamphlet, however, it is offered as a necessary starting point for the argument that women and women's rights should be taken seriously as an intrinsic and long-standing part of the Iranian opposition to imperialism and dictatorship.

In the pamphlet's final section, "Women's Fight in the Student Movement," women are not asked to heroically sacrifice themselves in the present for a free Iran in the future; instead the struggle for gender equality, including particular demands for the liberation of women, are placed on the current organizing agenda. It is here, more than anywhere else, that the pamphlet exhibits its feminist possibilities and addresses issues that today appear central to a transnational feminist praxis. First, the problem is diagnosed: "the participation of female students in the movement ... is not only important, but also necessary" and yet "no effective measures have been made ... to include women, especially in challenging male chauvinism." The current gender relations inside the ISA are heavily criticized for being dismissive of women and for allowing the "feudal and semi-imperial habits of men" to discourage women from speaking up and taking on leadership. Second, the objectives of the Women's Committee are enumerated. These include "a deep understanding and knowledge of the roots of the phenomenon of male chauvinism" as it relates to Iranian social, political, and economic relations. They also include an active fight against male domination in the everyday life of the group by changing "incorrect values and also creating knowledges so that currently healthy relationships can be created in the association." In order to take this on, the authors argue, "we must find the representation of this phenomenon in our own relationships with others and resolve this issue with persistent endeavors." This call for changing gendered social relations in the here and now inside the ISA is a far cry from the leftist dogma that women's equality could only be achieved under socialism. The committee wanted more women to participate in the ISA, yes, but also wanted to "increase ... their knowledge about the phenomenon of male chauvinism, and subsequently to understand their situation in the family (father's house, husband's house), the educational environment, and the work environment." In other words, women active in the ISA would also be taught about the pervasive, structural role of male domination across the private and public spheres of Iranian society. This education was deemed necessary for women to become consistently involved at all levels of the organization.

The location of foreign students outside Iran was also part of the discussion about what it would take to welcome and promote women leaders in the ISA. On the one hand, the "weakening of patriarchal and feudal family relations ... creates the conditions for increased thought away from the country" and the opportunity to "encounter international issues and develop a more expansive view," which the cross-pollination of student movements in Northern California and elsewhere certainly facilitated. On the other hand, "distance results in national issues becoming more inaccessible to us." The location of diaspora, it seems, could be radicalizing or depoliticizing for women students. It could also be disorienting. It was possible that "unsuitable conditions that would not allow a correct understanding of issues would lead to an appreciation of false freedoms in Western societies, and to consider it as a way of living for themselves, without understanding that in these capitalist societies there are also severe conditions of male chauvinism." The main example of this severity given is the gender wage gap in the US. This example, while still true today, evinces the economism that plagued the left. However, the authors pointed out the "severe conditions of male chauvinism" in the US in order to prevent Iranian women from being lulled into "an appreciation of false freedoms." Also, as noted above, ISA members were aware of and influenced by the efforts of leftist American women to challenge intense sexism in social movements and in the broader society. Refusing to idealize or emulate either American women or "advanced" Western society, the young Iranian activists who produced this pamphlet laid the groundwork for a transnational feminist politics that rejected an Orientalist hierarchy between the US and Iran and, instead, positioned both as locations in which women must actively struggle for their own liberation.

The concluding paragraph of "University Women Are Getting Organized" humbly admits that the Northern California Women's Committee is "young" and has "plenty of problems." Despite these weaknesses, "the women of the committee unanimously believe in the necessity of this committee and see it as the first step for creating solidarity between themselves and the majority of Iran's oppressed women ... and we believe in the necessity of ... the creation of such committees in other student associations in the U.S. as well." This introduces a new element into the argumentation for why these committees should spread and continue the work of fighting male chauvinism: as an act of solidarity with women in Iran. With this assertion, the prose shifts into a list of emotionally charged slogans, illustrating the affective attachments these young women had to the women they had left behind and to the idea of "creating solidarity" with "the majority of Iran's oppressed women":

Let us not forget the pain and suffering of our mothers and sisters who were used and abused for years simply because they were women, and were even deprived of basic human rights.

Let us not forget the suffering of female farmers who were exploited for years on end both by their husbands and the landowners and were forced to work like slaves.

Let us not forget the premature death of women and girls who labor as carpet makers in dark and dusty workshops.

Let us not forget our own mothers who have been abused like a servant in their own homes.

Let us remember how our sisters were forced to sell their bodies in order to afford their basic life necessities and threw themselves in cruel and corrupt houses; and let us topple these corrupt houses and their perpetrators with the help of our organizations and alongside the fighting men.

Let's destroy imperialism and feudalism.

Let's topple patriarchal feudal relations.

Let's fight male chauvinism.

Female students, unite and organize under the banner of the Confederation.

These slogans, taken together, constitute a capacious call for women's liberation across all classes and sectors of Iranian society – from the city to the countryside, from "our own mothers" in the middle and upper class to "our sisters" working in the sex industry, from the productive spheres of farms and workshops to the domains of social reproduction in the brothel and the home. Patriarchy is not simply a tool used to enhance profits, but rather a broader set of "relations" that justify and maintain a state of affairs in which women, "simply because they were women ... were denied basic human rights." In the final call to action, the fight to "destroy imperialism," "patriarchal feudal relations," and "male chauvinism" issues a mandate for nothing less than a gender conscious student opposition movement. While the ISA did not systematically implement this mandate, or even interpret it to the fullest extent, as I am here, the ideas in this pamphlet veer from an economistic Marxist conception of the "woman question" toward a socialist feminist analysis based on a complex understanding of how the economic, the social, the intimate, the political, the cultural, and even the psychological dynamics of male domination over women function in different times and places.

It was possible, therefore, based on the available ideas and experiences of the time, to begin to formulate a feminist approach to anti-imperialist revolutionary politics. As Hojat noted, "The point is that they don't postpone their demands for women's equality for after achieving socialism. They didn't postpone the demands to an unknown future. Looking back, I think that was feminist." The significance of refusing to postpone such demands would only become apparent in Iran immediately after the revolution, when women protesting for basic democratic freedoms and legal equality were told by Marxists, liberal nationalists, and Islamists that raising these "secondary" issues only weakened the revolution and strengthened Iran's imperial enemies.[62] All the more remarkable that they were written down in a pamphlet in California more than a decade earlier.

Conclusion

"Gender consciousness" tended to emerge out of the lived experiences of women and men within revolutionary movements, in the Third World and in the West. The need for women's participation may have been instrumental at first – an effort to increase the raw numbers of activists and to reach wide sectors of an oppressed population. However, as the case of the ISA's Northern California chapter shows, for significant numbers of women to stick around and become committed leaders, attitudes and practices toward them would have to change. ISA members who joined women's committees wanted to understand where patriarchy came from, how it evolved and changed over time across the history of Iran, and how it manifested among

---

[62] For an account of how these disparate political forces worked to undermine the women's uprising, see "The Reign of Terror, Women's Issues, and Feminist Politics," in Behrooz Ghamari-Tabrizi, *Foucault in Iran: Islamic Revolution after Enlightenment* (Minneapolis, MN: University of Minnesota Press, 2016), 113–158.

different classes at the intersection of imperialism, feudalism, capitalism, and dictatorship. They wanted to access a history of Iranian women's organizing and they endeavored to make the work of undoing "male chauvinism" into an urgent and legitimate priority for the anti-shah movement.

Yet, they did not go so far as to articulate a strategy for women's liberation, not because of a uniform lack of gender consciousness, but because they were unable to fully realize the implications of ideas that were veering well beyond the boundaries of leftist engagements with the "woman question." This inability was more than just a sign of the times, although it was replicated across many different leftist movements and contexts in the 1960s and 1970s. The perception that feminism was always and only about separatism was certainly common among the revolutionary left, but the particular history of Western-backed modernization in Iran had done special damage, resulting in an association between women's rights, the shah's top-down reforms, and Iran's subordination to the West.[63] This confluence, and the political confusion it created, severely limited Iranian student activists' engagement with actually existing feminist organizations, especially among other racialized and/or colonized populations.

The fact that certain rights for women were imposed from above by an authoritarian police state, in the words of Moghissi, "distorted the women's movement, and fragmented women's rights activists."[64] During the 1960s and 1970s, the Iranian left, including the ISA, denounced the shah's reform policies, known as the White Revolution. While the Confederation supported voting rights for women in theory, the organization dismissed the shah's enfranchisement of women as meaningless in a country without free elections. The shah's Family Protection Laws of 1967 and 1975, which expanded women's rights when it came to marriage, divorce, custody, and limited polygamy, was also met with searing critique. The ISA argued that, since the implementation of these rights was left to the courts to interpret and often went unenforced, they had no positive impact on the majority of Iranian women.[65] Behroozi was emphatic in her change of heart on this issue:

[63] For a discussion of "state-sponsored Pahlavi feminism," see "Global Sisters in Revolutionary Iran," in Naghibi, *Rethinking Global Sisterhood*, 74–107.
[64] Moghissi, *Populism and Feminism*, 21.
[65] See Sanasarian, *Women's Rights Movement*, 94–97.

We were deeply, deeply wrong about the shah's White Revolution. Later on, when Khomeini took over and they abandoned the family laws and they abandoned a lot of rights for women, we started realizing that those reforms were important for women. [Before the revolution,] we sided with Khomeini rather than realizing those were important steps. Shah was a dictator! No doubt about it! The political repression was the problem. But the reforms they did were progressive with regard to women ... Those were all important moves forward that we didn't recognize. We said all of those were conspiracies of imperialism. We were so bookish and stupid in that regard! No left organization has ever come out and said we were wrong!

Behroozi's comments pose a distinction between "progressive" reforms that were "moves forward" for women and the repressive character of the government that carried them out. Her expressions of regret and self-critique of the left emerge from the experiences of a generation of leftist students studying abroad who returned home to participate in a revolution that turned against them, forcing many, including those interviewed for this chapter, to flee into exile. I want to acknowledge these reactions to the pamphlet and the particular traumatic history that informs them. At the same time, the pamphlet is no longer attached to a movement or to the individuals who wrote it. At least two of its authors are dead, one executed by the Islamic Republic, while others are scattered in different parts of the global Iranian diaspora. Two are living in Iran. The pamphlet sits in an archive in California, available for new generations to pick up and interpret through new sets of experiences and concerns.

By using a methodology of possibility to analyze the work of the ISA's women's committees and the pamphlet, "University Women Are Getting Organized," this chapter has made available gestures toward a politics that center the fight against women's oppression as an immediate and necessary task for building a successful anti-imperialist opposition. Such a politics would manifest with far greater clarity and urgency in days of mass protest on the streets of Tehran in March 1979. As Negar Mottahedeh has written, "Men and women, both, had sacrificed their lives for a freedom that was suddenly elusive."[66] It was only then, when the new revolutionary government moved to regulate women's clothing, overturn existing family laws, and take away other democratic rights, that the possibilities for an anti-imperialist feminist politics became imaginable as an alternative

---

[66] Mottahedeh, *Whisper Tapes*, 176.

direction for the revolution as a whole.[67] It was only then that equality for women could be explicitly put forward as something intrinsic to the meaning of freedom.

The marches and sit-ins that unfolded over several days in Tehran were overwhelmingly organized and attended by Iranian women who had not been abroad. The ISA women's committees had no direct impact on these events and there is no evidence that women in Iran read the pamphlet on male chauvinism written in Berkeley. Returning Confederation members had different attitudes toward the March uprising. Many men and women toed the leftist line of their organizations, either opposing or remaining neutral toward the women's demands, while others joined in. Kowsari was part of group of leftist men who linked arms to defend the women marchers from right-wing vigilantes, and Behroozi was an active organizer, working with Iranian women who had not been abroad to build a new women's organization, the Society of Women's Awakening (Jamiyat-e Bidari-ye Zan). Iranian feminist and participant in the March actions, Azar Tabari, notes that many of the women who organized women's groups in the immediate aftermath of the revolution "had spent some time as students in Europe and the United States in the late 1960s and early 1970s. Invariably they had been affected, in some cases quite deeply, by the rise of women's movements in these countries."[68] If we understand the US as a diasporic site of multiple revolutionary struggles, rather than only of Western domination and assimilation, then we can understand the development of revolutionary "gender consciousness" among women activists in Iran and in the Confederation as iterations of a transnational phenomenon – demands for women's equality – unfolding on the contested terrain of anti-imperialist movements around the world.[69] This perspective offers an alternative to the ideologically

---

[67] As Naghibi points out, this was an incredibly precarious position to hold in the ideological and political space of the revolution and women were "forced to abandon it" when they were denounced for being pro-Western. See Naghibi, *Rethinking Global Sisterhood*, 99.

[68] Azar Tabari, "Islam and the Struggle for Emancipation of Iranian Women," in Azar Tabari and Nahid Yeganeh, eds., *In the Shadow of Islam: The Women's Movement in Iran* (London: Zed Press, 1982), 9.

[69] As Stuart Hall writes, "the New World ... has to be understood as the place of many, continuous displacements: of the original pre-Columbian inhabitants, the Arawaks, Caribs and Amerindians, permanently displaced from their homelands and decimated; of other peoples displaced in different ways from Africa, Asia and Europe." Stuart Hall, *Theorizing Diaspora: A Reader*, ed. Jana Evans Braziel and Anita Mannur (Malden, MA: Blackwell Publishing, 2003), 234.

polarizing notion of West vs. East, which constrained the Iranian left overall in its approach to questions of gender and sexual oppression and liberation.

In the space provided by the Raha film screening of *Liberation Movement of Iranian Women, Year Zero*, the faces and voices of Iranian women in Tehran in 1979, their aspirations, disappointments, and demands, could mingle with the hopes and fears of a multiracial, multinational gathering of feminists in New York City in 2010. From one International Women's Day to another, more than thirty years apart, the possibility of a future without imperialism or dictatorship still felt urgent and resonant. This chapter traces this genealogy back even further to the fledgling efforts of Iranian students in the US in the late 1960s and 1970s to center gender oppression within the matrix of the economic and political forces they opposed. Their refusal to counterpose US and Iranian societies as polar opposites when it came to the treatment and status of women, their conceptualization of both nations as deeply patriarchal, and the insistence on linking both nations as complicit in the oppression of Iranian women are remarkable and instructive. Today, rigid and destructive binaries between the West and Islam position Iranian women's rights as an agenda in sync with US demonization of Islam and of Iran. In this context, "a methodology of possibility" reads the incipient feminist analysis of Iranian student activists in the US more than fifty years ago as a "useable tradition," one that can assist in the project of reimagining the gender and sexual politics of transnational solidarity.[70]

[70] Hong and Ferguson, "Introduction," 18.

PART II

Militarized Cartographies

5 | "In a Forest of Humans":

The Urban Cartographies of Theory and Action in 1970s Iranian Revolutionary Socialism

RASMUS CHRISTIAN ELLING*

Historical analyses tend to agree that the Iranian Revolution was an overwhelmingly "urban" revolution. But how did the revolutionaries themselves see "the urban," that is, the material, social, and ideological phenomena entangled with the processes of urbanization? In this chapter, I will explore how the arguably most prominent revolutionary Iranian socialist organization prior to the Iranian Revolution in 1979, the Organization of the Iranian People's Fada'i Guerrillas (henceforth the Fada'i/s), engaged "the urban." I examine a range of Fada'i materials from the end of the 1960s to the end of the 1970s that reflect the organization's theory and action through four analytical points related to "the urban," namely: (1) as a central feature of the organization's historical context and profile; (2) as elements in the organization's revolutionary theory and strategy; (3) as a setting and resource for its armed action; and (4) as a site for detection of revolutionary potential.

I contend that *the urban* was used by the guerrillas to work through *the global,* that is, the universalistic pretentions of Marxist ideology and of Third Worldist revolutionary theory, toward an *Iran-specific* praxis. "The urban" became an abstract *and* concrete link, I will argue, connecting a transnational space of ideas to a particular, localized

* I would like to thank Peyman Vahabzadeh, Siavash Randjbar-Daemi, and of course Arang Keshavarzian, Ali Mirsepassi, and all participants in the NYU workshop on this volume for feedback and support. I would also like to thank Mahfarid Mansoorian for kindly sharing a hard-to-find document; and the people behind Iranian Opposition Documents Archive in Berlin for all the valuable materials they have made available and without which the research behind this chapter would have been impossible.

141

struggle for national liberation and thus, in short, to anchor theory in practice.

Hence, I look at how key urban aspects of Fada'i thinking and practice developed with inspiration from historical experiences and revolutionary theories from Russia, East Asia, the Middle East, and, above all, Latin America – but never at the expense of the Fada'is' analysis of Iran's historical and sociological particularities. This process took the Fada'is from student activism in the late 1960s[1] to urban guerrilla warfare in the early 1970s and then on to clandestine activism in Tehran's shantytowns before eventually being overtaken by the actual revolution in 1979.

With this chapter I will contribute to a recent blossoming in analyses and histories of the Fada'is[2] while also deepening our understanding of the Iranian Revolution by adding a global urban history[3] of revolutionary socialism. By a global urban history, I mean the systematic analytical attention to "the urban" as a connection between different scales and spaces and between micro- and macro-level history. Such a methodology allows me to explore what was *urban* about the quintessential *urban guerrilla* in the decade leading up to the revolution.

---

[1] See also Chapter 7.

[2] T. Atabaki and N. Mohajer, eds., *Rahi digar: Ravayet-ha'i dar bud-o-bash-e charik-ha-ye fada'i-ye khalq-e iran* [The road not taken: Narratives on the life and times of the Iranian Fada'i Guerrillas], 2 vols. (Cedex, France: Noghteh, 2018); Ali Rahnema, *Call to Arms: Iran's Marxist Revolutionaries* (London: Oneworld Publications, 2021); A. Salehi, *Esm-e shab: Siahkal (Jonbesh-e Cherik-ha-ye Fada'i-ye Khalq az aghaz ta esfand 1349)* [The name of the night: Siakhal (The People's Fadayan Guerrilla Movement from the beginning until March 1349 [1971])] (Spånga, Sweden: Baran, 2016); Peyman Vahabzadeh, *A Guerrilla Odyssey: Modernization, Secularism, Democracy, and the Fadai Period of National Liberation in Iran, 1971–1979* (Syracuse, NY: Syracuse University Press, 2010). Other important works dealing with the Iranian left and socialist guerrillas of the period covered in the present chapter include Ervand Abrahamian, *Radical Islam: The Iranian Mojahedin* (London: I.B. Tauris, 1989); Maziar Behrooz, *Rebels with a Cause: The Failure of the Left in Iran* (New York: I.B. Tauris, 1999); Maziar Behrooz, "The Iranian Revolution and the Legacy of the Guerrilla Movement," in Stephanie Cronin, ed., *Reformers and Revolutionaries in Modern Iran: New Perspectives on the Iranian Left* (London: Routledge, 2004), 189–205; Peyman Vahabzadeh, *A Rebel's Journey: Mostafa Sho'aiyan and Revolutionary Theory in Iran* (London: Oneworld Publications, 2019).

[3] For a manifesto for this exciting, budding field of research, see Carl Nightingale, "The Global Urban History Project," *Planning Perspectives* 33 (2018): 135–138.

Between the Mountain, the City, and the World

> From the green trails
> men are descending
> with love on their bodies
> inescapable, like moss on a rock
> and wounds on their chests[4]

So wrote Ahmad Shamlu, arguably Iran's most important modern poet, in 1980 (Figure 5.1) to commemorate the attack on a rural gendarmerie station on the lush, green hills of Siahkal in the northern province of Gilan on 19 February 1971 – an event considered the genesis not just of the Fada'is but of the broader militant anti-shah movement that culminated in the revolution of 1979.

The Siahkal attack, known as a *rastakhiz* or "resurrection," was embedded in a heavily naturalistic aesthetics through a broad range of cultural products including the so-called *jangal* ("forest") poetry written by countless supporters, the Cubist/surrealist paintings of key theoretician Bizhan Jazani, abundant sympathetic allusions in pop songs and in blockbuster movies, as well as in Fada'i auto-panegyrics and martyr eulogies. In this mythology, the Siahkal epic associated the guerrilla campaign of the 1970s with *kuh*, "the Mountain(s)," with *jangal*, "the Forest(s)," and even with particular animals and flowers. The symbolism of *cherik* or guerrilla portrayed these new political hero figures as the historical extension of the 1910s and 1920s Jangali Communist movement in the forests of northern Iran as well as the local manifestation of fabled Latin American guerrillas.

It is easy to forget that the rural imaginary sharply contrasted with the largely urban reality of the Fada'i movement. The individual guerrillas did not, generally, come from "the green hills." Almost all the key thinkers and leaders were either born in Tehran, or in provincial cities and then migrated to Tehran with families or for continuing studies; or they were born and educated in Iran's second and third largest cities at the time, Mashhad and Tabriz. Only a handful came from smaller cities or towns and even fewer from villages or farms.

At the height of the organization's activism, from 1971 to 1979, the Fada'i cadres were young and generally from the intelligentsia with a

---

[4] Extract of Ahmad Shamlu's poem "Ziyafat" [Banquet] published in *Ketab-e jom'eh* 1:27 (Esfand 2, 1358/February 21, 1980): 143.

Figure 5.1 Illustration from the "Siahkal, 1971" theme in *Ketab-e jom'eh* weekly that carried Ahmad Shamlu's poem. The trees are an obvious reference to the forests of northern Iran.

Source: Scan of original, public domain.

significant majority of college students.[5] Rather than in the mountains or forests, most of the Fada'is' formative experiences with political activism in the 1950s and 1960s took place in urban space: universities and high schools; youth organizations and student journals; demonstrations and rallies in squares and stadiums; street riots. Indeed, it can be argued, that the Siahkal attack was the exception to a prerevolutionary history of largely urban activity.[6]

A case in point was the abovementioned key theoretician. Born to rural migrants in Tehran in 1938, Jazani had joined the Tudeh Youth Organization at the age of ten, but after the tumultuous events of the 1953 coup in Tehran, and after spending time in prison in 1954–1955, he became disillusioned with Tudeh. Jazani then spent a couple of years as a Tehran University student activist in the Second National Front, but like many of his peers, he too lost faith in this political force even before 1963, when the National Front was unable to counter violent state repression of all opposition following a clergy-led popular unrest in June of that year. Indeed, 1963 represented a turning point for many radicals, including the circle in Tehran that would later develop into Group One under Jazani.[7]

Activists who would later become Fada'i cadres carried out urban guerrilla operations as early as in the spring of 1968 when they bombed a power station and "expropriated" bank deposits from a bank in southern Tehran.[8] Even the Siahkal operation in 1971 was at least partially funded by bank robberies carried out in Tehran in 1970. Those two years generally witnessed significant urban unrest with demonstrations and strikes among university and high school students,

---

[5] For a breakdown of occupations and age of guerrillas, including the Fada'is, see Ervand Abrahamian, *Iran between Two Revolutions* (Princeton, NJ: Princeton University Press, 1982), 480–481.

[6] Arguably another exception (that merits its own study) is the case of Dr. Hushang A'zami from Lorestan who advocated for rural insurrection by indigenous people. I thank Shima Houshyar for raising this point. Furthermore, there is an important chapter to the history of Fada'i rural activism *after* the revolution – namely, in the Kurdish- and Turkmen-inhabited regions of western and northeastern Iran, respectively. That, unfortunately, is a topic outside the scope of the present chapter.

[7] On this period, see Afshin Matin-Asgari, *Iranian Student Opposition to the Shah* (Costa Mesa, CA: Mazda Publishers, 2002); Salehi, *Esm-e shab*; Chapter 7.

[8] Mohammad Majid Kianzad, quoted in Atabaki and Mohajer, eds., *Rahi digar*, 22.

industrial factory workers, and teachers in Tehran, as well as mass protests against price hikes on bus fares.

Iran underwent significant urbanization in this period. Between 1956 and 1976, the urban population tripled in size; by the time of the revolution, almost half of all Iranians lived in cities, with close to five million in Greater Tehran alone. The capital's spectacular growth in the 1960s and 1970s was connected to uneven land reforms, rapid industrialization, and the resulting waves of rural-to-city migration. With urban development unable to keep pace with the incoming flood of rural migrants, shantytowns mushroomed around Tehran.[9] In films, novels, and newspapers of the late 1960s and 1970s, Tehran appears as an overcrowded, underserviced, nerve-wracking place marked by glaring inequalities, crime, and insecurity.

It was in such an urban setting that Fada'i theory and praxis took shape. The foundational thinkers generally had a background in either the communist pro-Soviet Tudeh Party or in leftist youth and student organizations associated with the National Front, and several had been arrested during either the unrest surrounding the 1953 coup against Prime Minister Mohammad Mosaddeq or the June 1963 demonstrations against the Pahlavi regime.[10] The Fada'is framed their activism as a continuation of the struggle for national liberation and democracy heralded by the 1905 Constitutional Revolution as well as an independent path to socialism distinct from the Moscow- and Beijing-aligned groups and parties.

The Fada'is expressly identified with a global struggle, symbolized in their logo, which shows a hand holding an AK-47 machine-gun from within a map of Iran set on top of a globe and framed by hammer and sickle. The Fada'is studied and discussed communist revolutions and resistance in Russia, China, Cuba, Bolivia, and Vietnam. In terms of principles for armed struggle, they critiqued, in turn, the Leninist, Maoist, and then Latin American models for revolution – while taking direct inspiration from what was seen as anti-imperialist liberation struggles in Algeria and Palestine. In the case of Palestine, some Fada'is even obtained personal experience with armed resistance.[11]

---

[9] This topic is covered in the seminal Asef Bayat, *Street Politics: Poor People's Movements in Iran* (New York: Columbia University Press, 1997).

[10] See Atabaki and Mohajer, eds., *Rahi digar*; Salehi, *Esm-e shab*.

[11] See Naghmeh Sohrabi, "Remembering the Palestine Group: Global Activism, Friendship, and the Iranian Revolution," *International Journal of Middle East Studies* 51:2 (2019): 281–300.

Notably, the Fada'is engaged with the *foco* model formulated by the French Marxist Régis Debray[12] on the basis of the experiences with revolutionary guerrilla warfare in Latin America under Che Guevara and Fidel Castro. From there, attention turned toward the unfolding urban rebellions of the Tupamaros in Uruguay, Montoneros in Argentine, and the MIR in Chile. Around 1970, the Fada'is obtained – from Iranian activists based in other Middle Eastern countries – Persian translations of Castro and Guevara's works and, perhaps most importantly, of the *Minimanual of the Urban Guerrilla* by Brazilian revolutionary theorist Carlos Marighella.[13] As we shall see below, Marighella's work – and the critique of Debray's *foco* theorization by the Brazilian sociologist Clea Silva – would have significant impact on Fada'i thinking.

However, despite subscribing to a global discourse of Marxism-Leninism and despite significant inspiration from thinkers and events in other countries, the Fada'is were careful to anchor their theory and practice in Iranian realities by "linking," in the words of Peyman Vahabzadeh, "the particularity of the Iranian dependent capitalism to the assumed universality of the Marxian model of dialectical analysis." In fact, "indigenous" approaches were constantly proclaimed to take precedence over what the second-most important Fada'i theoretician, Masud Ahmadzadeh, disapprovingly called "borrowed political theory."[14]

It was thus in a rapidly urbanizing setting and on the background of a globalized ideological terrain that the Fada'is launched their armed

[12] Régis Debray (b. 1940) was a professor of philosophy at the University of Havana in postrevolutionary Cuba, where he became acquainted with leading communists. He was captured together with Che Guevara in 1967 during an attempted guerrilla uprising in Bolivia. The same year his book *Revolution in the Revolution?* was published and became important inspiration for leftist rebellions across the world.

[13] Carlos Marighella (1911–1969) was a Brazilian politician and guerrilla leader who theorized the importance of cities for Marxist-Leninist revolutions. On the translation of his work, see Eskandar Sadeghi-Boroujerdi, "The Origins of Communist Unity: Anticolonialism and Revolution in Iran's Tri-continental Moment," *British Journal of Middle Eastern Studies* 45 (2017): 813; Vahabzadeh, *Guerrilla Odyssey*, 158.

[14] M. Ahmadzadeh, *Mobâreze-ye mosallahâneh. Ham esterâtezhi, ham tâktik* [Armed struggle: Both strategy and tactic] (n.p.: 1970; republished by Fada'is on 19 Bahman 1359 / 8 February 1981; republished online www.iran-archive.com), p. 42.

revolutionary struggle against the Iranian monarchy. Next, we will see how this context shaped the urban analysis of key Fada'i thinkers.

Double Encirclement

At the center of attention in much of Jazani's work – and of Ahmadzadeh's *Armed Struggle: Both a Strategy and a Tactic* – were the land reforms launched by the Pahlavi state in 1961 and boosted through the top-down "White Revolution" enacted in 1963. These reforms, Jazani argued, acted as a catalyst for the structural transformation from feudalism to dependent capitalism. The resulting social-political formation was defined by repressive development: modernization and industrialization to the benefit of the aristocratic elite and a comprador bourgeoisie aligned with Western imperialism. The dependency of the shah's autocracy on a neocolonialist USA, argued Jazani, integrated Iran into global capitalism as a peripheralized zone and caused significant changes across Iranian society.

In Fada'i analyses, these changes were at least implicitly associated with the process of urbanization. As the land reforms by the mid-1960s had displaced feudalism in the countryside, Jazani argued, the peasants came under indirect exploitation by "urban bourgeoisie or petite bourgeoisie" through taxation, forward buying, usury, and exploitative commercial contracts.[15] This situation complicated what Jazani understood as a previously straightforward contradiction between peasant and feudalist:

[C]onsidering the backwardness of the peasants, it has become more difficult for them to understand the contradiction. They (i.e. the new smallholders [brought about by reforms]) see that they now have their own land and that landlords are no longer breathing down their necks; but also that they nonetheless remain poor and hungry. And as a result of the abolition of feudalism, followed by the penetration of capital and the influence of urban culture in rural areas, the peasants' needs and expectations have increased in the face of a wide gap between their income and their requirements. Finally, the regime's administrative setup and system of control has effectively filled

---

[15] B. Jazani, *Vaqaye'-e si-saleh-ye akhir-e Iran* [Events of the recent thirty years in Iran] (n.p.: 1976), 86. This is a collection of various texts that were published at different times during Jazani's final years and after his death. It is available at https://iran-archive.com/sites/default/files/sanad/jazanifvaghayee-si-saale.pdf.

the vacuum left behind by the feudal system, thus putting the rural areas to a large extent under the control of a police system like that in urban areas.[16]

"The urban" is in this quote simultaneously cultural, social, economic, and ideological: it is the process that accompanies and/or facilitates the penetration of capital into the last remaining precapitalist parts of society; it is the practices that stand in contrast to a traditional agrarian lifestyle and worldview; and it is the condition associated with a police state – while at the same time also the site of at least a *mirage* of progress and welfare.

This multilayered understanding of "the urban" seeps through Jazani's analytical oeuvre. The peasants have "lost their class unity," Jazani explained, and those who had not already lost their livelihood and left village life "to join the reserve army of labor" in the cities would eventually succumb to the urbanizing onslaught of repressive development and consumerism. However, at the same time, urbanization also brought literacy, social awareness, political consciousness, and thus the ability to organize and express demands.[17] Indeed, Jazani noted that there was now "a new generation in the rural areas" who experienced "no barrier between themselves and the urban world as there had been for their fathers in the shape of serfdom to the feudalists," and through "a constant relationship with urban areas," these young agrarians refused to accept "any eternal or everlasting law condemning them to destitution."[18] Thus, in this urban-centric, developmentalist understanding of cultural, social, and political progress, Jazani and his comrades subscribed to the idea that (only?) through urbanization would the rural masses realize their revolutionary potential.

Like Jazani, Ahmadzadeh argued that the regime's main objective with land reforms was "the expansion of the economic, political, and cultural domination of bureaucratic comprador capitalism in the rural areas"[19] – allowing the comprador bourgeoisie to extend capital accumulation beyond the cities and into the countryside (what David Harvey would call a "spatial fix"[20]). Ahmadzadeh described how "the weight of debts and the pressure of finance capitalism, the

---

[16] Ibid.   [17] Ibid., 166.   [18] Ibid., 175–176.
[19] Ahmadzadeh, *Mobareze*, 24.
[20] See David Harvey, *The Urbanization of Capital: Studies in the History and Theory of Capitalist Urbanization* (Baltimore, MD: Johns Hopkins University Press, 1985).

Ministry of Land Reform, and the cooperative and joint stock companies" was putting the "rural masses" under inhumane pressure.[21] By intensifying the contradiction between peasants and capitalists, however, this process also brought about a "closer relationship between the peasantry and the proletariat" in cities,[22] where, in turn, "the brutal rule of comprador capital" had brought the proletariat closer together with its erstwhile enemy, the national bourgeoisie and the petite bourgeoisie.[23]

Thus, in both Jazani's and Ahmadzadeh's analyses urbanization was simultaneously repressive *and* potentially emancipatory. In a remarkable passage, Jazani dissected part of this complexity:

Due to the evolution of the present system, the ever-increasing migration of deprived peasants to towns has gained momentum. The dependent status of the economy and industry, which is not geared to absorb these deprived migratory forces into commerce, industry, and other occupations, will gradually create layers of extremely deprived people in the towns and surrounding areas where these deprived people will encircle the system of dependent capitalism [*chun halqe'i sistem-e sarmaye-dari-ye va-basteh-ra dar miyan mi-girad*].[24]

In this analysis, there is a realization that the forces unleashed by land reforms were changing everything, giving way to a sort of double encirclement: on the one hand, capital and urbanization penetrated and transformed the countryside, uprooted traditional agrarian life, and displaced thousands of peasants from their villages; on the other hand, this massive migration from the hinterland laid siege to that bastion of capital, the city, threatening its rulers with the new solidarities and revolutionary potential engendered by the urbanization of consciousness.

Roars in a Forest of Humans

Victory to the unity of struggling peasants and city-dwellers! proclaimed the manifesto distributed under the Siahkal attack in 1971. For years prior to the attack, Fada'i activists had used hiking as a smokescreen for mapping the hills of northern Iran and planning the first major guerrilla strike against the Pahlavi regime. Even if the

[21] Ahmadzadeh, *Mobareze*, 19.   [22] Ibid., 28.   [23] Ibid.
[24] Jazani, *Vaqaye'*, 185–186.

گروه شهر
تئوری و زندگینامهٔ ۹ چریک

امیر پرویز پویان
مسعود احمد زاده
عباس مفتاحی
حسن نوروزی
عباس جمشیدی رودباری
علیرضا نابدل
مهرنوش ابراهیمی
بهروز دهقانی
احمد زیبرم
و .....

Figure 5.2 *The City Team: The Theory and Biography of Nine Guerrillas*, a Fada'i underground publication from 1976 about the Ahmadzadeh-led group. Source: www.iran-archive.com

purpose of the attack was limited to dispelling the illusion of regime invulnerability, it did, as the launch of armed insurgency, make pertinent the question *where should the revolution start?*

Nonetheless, already in the mid-1960s – well before they had read and employed Marighella's work on the urban guerrilla to dismiss the

Cuban blueprint of the rural guerrilla as befitting for the case of Iran –
the Fada'i thinkers had decided that the revolution could *not* start in
the Iranian countryside.[25] By making feudalism obsolete, the land
reforms had simply eviscerated the key target of a *foco*-style uprising,
that is, the feudalist (see Chapter 11). Time was needed before the rural
masses could recognize and target their new enemy. For now – as a
1969 text by another key member, Ali-Akbar Safai-Farahani, stated –
the rural masses would have to be "spectators" and receive a necessary
"awakening jolt" by the urban guerrillas before they would eventually
pick up arms.[26] Or, as Jazani put it, "the village" would only be
"awakened from its pacification and despondency" when "a political
atmosphere in the city" came into being.[27]

Instead of moving into the actual forests, "the principle of *big cities
are forests of humans* took hold in the group," Jazani wrote.[28] After
his group met and joined forces with Ahmadzadeh's group in August
1970, the latter – who, under the influence of the Brazilian guerrilla
doctrine of urban insurgency, were exclusively focused on cities –
reluctantly accepted that the first major attack, as an exception, would
be rural.[29] Although the Fada'i leaders continued to insist in propaganda that there should be rural guerrilla cells (even when it was
obvious that these were unfeasible[30]), the practical focus settled on
the city as the key to all other stages of the revolutionary struggle
(Figure 5.2). Jazani believed that "the political environment of the city
will be in the exclusive [*darbast*] hands of that revolutionary force,

---

[25] It should be noted that the idea of the Cuban *foco* model as a completely rural
phenomenon is itself a propagandistic construction that downplays the
significant role of urban cadres in the Cuban Revolution. See Julia E. Sweig,
Inside the Cuban Revolution: Fidel Castro and the Urban Underground
(Cambridge, MA: Harvard University Press, 2002).

[26] A.-A. Safai-Farahani, *An che yek enqelabi bayad bedanad* [What a
revolutionary should know] (n.p.: 1349/1970; online version republished by The
Organization for the Unity of the People's Fada'iyan of Iran, Mordad 1381/
July–August 2004), 19.

[27] B. Jazani, *Che kesani be marksism-leninism khiyanat mi-konand?* [Who betrays
Marxism-Leninism?] (n.p.: Entesharat-e 19-e Bahman, n.d.), 27.

[28] Members of the Group, "Goruh-e Jazani-Zarifi, pishtaz-e jonbesh-e
mosallahaneh-ye Iran" ["The Jazani-Zarifi Group, pioneers of the armed
movement in Iran"], pamphlet published in *19-e Bahman Te'orik*, no. 4 (Tir
1374/June–July 1975): 21 (emphasis added).

[29] See H. Ashraf, *Jam'bandi-ye se-saleh* [A three-year summary] (Tehran:
Entesharat-e Negah, 1358/1979), 10.

[30] See ibid., chapter 2.

which initiates the overthrow operation against the regime."[31]
Assuming the role of vanguard, in other words, depended on taking
a lead in the city.

Yet the tension over tactical and strategic differences between the
group under Jazani and the more "practice-oriented" generation around
Ahmadzadeh continued.[32] Ahmadzadeh came to realize it was a "theoretical error" to dismiss the Cuban experience and Debray's work out
of hand.[33] In particular, Ahmadzadeh clung to the Guevarian idea of the
guerrilla as a "small motor" that could ignite a larger "motor" in society
and thus popularize or "massify" (*tude'i kardan*) the revolutionary
struggle. In contrast to the Jazani group, Ahmadzadeh insisted that the
"objective conditions" in Iran were in fact ripe for revolution, that this
could be witnessed by "sporadic outbursts of the popular movement,"[34]
and that with armed insurrection by the vanguard, "the roaring torrent
of mass struggle" could be "unleashed."[35] As we shall see later, Jazani
did not view Iran as ready for revolution and preferred to supplement
guerrilla action with non-armed activities.

Such deliberations would take the Fada'is through different stages,
but in 1971, an overwhelming focus on armed insurrection prevailed.
Just two months after the Siahkal attack, on April 3, 1971, the Fada'is
executed their first armed operation in an urban setting when
Ahmadzadeh's team attacked a police station in Qolhak on the northern outskirts of Tehran.[36] Over the following three years, the Fada'is
engaged in a broad range of armed attacks framed as the practice of
"armed propaganda" (*tabligh-e mosallahane*). The idea was that with
each violent act carried out by the guerrilla, the pessimism, defeatism,
apathy, and suspicion among ordinary people would lessen and their
"self-confidence" would be boosted. As Jazani explained:

---

[31] B. Jazani and H. Zarifi, *Masa'el-e jonbesh-e zedd-e este'mari va azadi-bakhsh-e khalq-e Iran va 'omdeh-tarin vazayef-e komunist-ha-ye Iran dar sharayet-e konuni* [Issues for the anti-imperialist and emancipatory people's movement of Iran and the biggest duties of Iran's communists under present circumstances] (n. p.: 1346/1967; online version republished by The Organization for the Unity of the People's Fada'iyan of Iran, 1382/2003), 15.

[32] Vahabzadeh, *Guerrilla Odyssey*, 45, 133–155.

[33] Ahmadzadeh, *Mobareze*, 31. [34] Ibid., 34–35. [35] Ibid., 37.

[36] Organization of the Iranian People's Fada'i Guerrillas (OIPFG), *Pare'i az tajrobiyat-e jang-e chariki-ye shahri dar Iran* [Some experiences with urban guerrilla warfare in Iran] (n.p.: 1973; republished by Payam-e Fada'i: Organ of the People's Fada'i Guerrillas of Iran (n.p.: 2017)), 14.

The people stop seeing each other as "police" and agents. They begin to trust each other. And in a situation where every day the sound of the machine-gun roars and bomb explosions rock the city, the people find the courage to talk with each other, to show solidarity with one another, and eventually to cooperate with each other.[37]

In other words, the shock therapy of armed attacks would empower citizens of an urban society riddled with fear and apathy. Beyond that immediate result, there was also an underlying idea that armed action could be more straightforwardly emancipatory. It was never clearly spelled out, but in both Ahmadzadeh's and Jazani's writings, there are allusions to establishing "liberated zones."[38] Ahmadzadeh argued that

As soon as a guerilla force is established and can create revolutionary support bases, or liberate some zones, all kinds of possibilities for political education of the masses, training of cadres, and political propaganda, etc., are conceivable.[39]

In another striking passage, Jazani laid out a vision for the (near?) future of a guerrilla-led total uprising, where the goal of armed struggle was explained as

the establishment of a kind of revolutionary sovereignty *beneath* the enemy's sovereignty and *within* his field of action . . . Even before attaining a liberated zone, the guerrilla exercises sovereignty. Even in the city can such a situation, with its own characteristics, be predicted. This dual sovereignty will be established in a situation where the urban guerrilla is approaching the height of its power and the city is engulfed in waves of popular protest. This is the beginning of the massification of the armed struggle.[40]

In other words, the very act of the guerrilla attack was in more than one sense liberating and might even lead to the establishment of actually liberated spaces. It constituted an exercise of sovereignty right in the middle of what was otherwise thought to be spheres under the sole jurisdiction of the state – the spatial manifestation of revolutionary defiance.

---

[37] B. Jazani, *Cheguneh mobareze-ye mosallahaneh tudeh'i mi-shavad* [How to "massify" armed struggle] (n.p.: 1973; republished in *19-e Bahman Te'orik*, no. 2 (Tir 1355/July 1976)), 28.

[38] The notion of "liberated zones" appears to be as old as guerrilla warfare itself. It is, however, plausible that the Fada'is drew on the concept as used by Che Guevara in his *Guerrilla Warfare*.

[39] Ahmadzadeh, *Mobareze*, 50.   [40] Jazani, *Cheguneh*, 42 (emphasis added).

This is also why the key concept of *qahr*, as Vahabzadeh explains, cannot be fully captured by the English word "violence"[41] but rather denoted "a mode of political articulation" that drew a line between "the people and its enemies."[42] Every armed operation, Vahabzadeh underlines, had a "metonymic significance."[43] Operations became epic transgressions through which the myth of state supremacy was punctured and one could catch the glimmer of a possible future emancipation.

Theater of Action

With armed propaganda, "the urban" became a stage for the performance of revolutionary action. To better understand this aspect of Fada'i revolutionary struggle, one work is of particular interest: the recently republished *Selected Experiences with Urban Guerrilla Warfare in Iran*, a collection of detailed field reports from armed operations in the period 1971–1972 that were circulated among the Fada'is and their supporters at the time.[44]

The accounts treat bank robberies, assassinations, sabotage bombings, street shoot-outs, safehouses under siege, and escapes from police and intelligence agents. The text blends spectacular reenactments of the deed with dry self-criticism and practical evaluation for future Fada'is to learn from failures and build on successes. Some accounts read almost like action thrillers with blow-by-blow narratives under headlines such as "About fighting and fleeing in the plains outside southwestern Tehran" or "Fistfight with the enemy's venal police in the vicinity of the intersection of Amiri and Baba'iyan streets." Fiascos are also mentioned: a gun that jams; a car that will not start; a dynamite accident that kills a Fada'i in a safehouse.

One of the early defining acts in Fada'i guerrilla warfare was the assassination of Lieutenant General Zia'-od-Din Farsiu, who had presided over the military court proceedings that led to the execution of thirteen Fada'is over the Siahkal attack. "Brimming with feelings of revenge, resolve, and beyond the point of no return," the account goes,

---

[41] Vahabzadeh, *Guerrilla Odyssey*, 100.   [42] Ibid., 96.   [43] Ibid., 100.
[44] OIPFG, *Pare'i*; for a complete overview of Fada'i armed actions, see
H. Nowzari, "Kam-o-keyf-e 'amaliyat-e nezami-ye cherik-ha" ["The quality of the guerrillas' military operations"], in Atabaki and Mohajer, eds., *Rahi digar*, 293–325.

a team constituted itself as an "execution squad" working on behalf of a "people's tribunal."[45] On April 5, 1971, following reconnaissance and stakeout, the team attacked Farsiu while he was in a car with his son and their driver, throwing Molotov cocktails, firing machine-guns, and shooting Farsiu in the head (from which he died later that day) – but only after having assured a taxi driver, whose car the team "expropriated" as a getaway, that he, being a poor toiler, would get his car back.

The Farsiu assassination was a type of operation that aimed at pure power display: to give the enemy the impression that nowhere in the "forest of humans" were they safe from the guerrilla's wrath. A variation on this, where the Fada'is claimed to take revenge on behalf of "the people," was when two female guerrillas detonated a string of bombs at traffic police stations across Tehran in protest against "the unbridled pressure on and fining of taxi and van drivers."[46]

Another type of operation was extractive: it aimed to appropriate resources from the city's fortified spaces. The abovementioned attack on the Qolhak police station was aimed at "expropriating" a machine-gun. Other examples include several bank robberies such as that against a branch of the Bank Melli on Eisenhower St. in Tehran.

---

[45] OIPFG, *Pare'i*, 26.

[46] Ibid., 103. This is just one of several examples that women – despite all the sexist and gendered limitations on their participation and status within the organization – played an active role. Vahabzadeh, relying on Fada'i accounts, gives clues to how women often played a "covering role" (*naqsh-e pusheshi*), using their presence to divert attention away from operations and activities or to use their relative invisibility to perform various missions such as reconnaissance. This intersection of gender, urban space, and revolutionary activism is a topic that deserves more attention. On women Fada'is, see e.g. V. Hadjebi-Tabrizi, *Dad-e bidad: Femmes politiques emprisonées 1971–1979*, vol. 1 (Cologne: BM-Druckservice, 2003); V. Hadjebi-Tabrizi, *Dad-e bidad: Femmes politiques emprisonées 1971–1979*, vol. 2 (Cologne: BM-Druckservice, 2004); Haideh Moghissi, *Populism and Feminism in Iran: Women's Struggle in a Male-Defined Revolutionary Movement* (New York: St. Martin's Press, 1996), 107–138; Hammed Shahidian, 'The Iranian Left and the 'Woman Question' in the Revolution of 1978–79," *International Journal of Middle East Studies* 26 (1994): 223–247; Hammed Shahidian, "Women and Clandestine Politics in Iran, 1970–1985," *Feminist Studies* 23 (1997): 7–42. See also N. Qajar, "Sazman-e mahbub-e man" ["My beloved organization"] and R. Daneshgar, "Zanan-e fada'i dar zendan" ["Fada'i women in prison"], both in Atabaki and Mohajer, eds., *Rahi digar*, which contains several entries authored by female Fada'is.

However, even acts of stealing were designed with propaganda in mind. The team later described a scene from the bank:

A comrade told [the employees and bank customers]: "Gentlemen, we don't have any problems with you, and only if you don't listen to our demands will you face violence – you decide." The comrades gathered all employees and customers together in the middle of the bank ... At that moment, Comrade No. 5 started a speech, and after his speech – which was about the bitter realities of Iranian society – Comrade No. 5 pulled down from the wall a picture of the dirty, sell-out hireling shah, which was then trampled to pieces with full hatred under the feet of the People's Fada'i Guerrillas, while fourteen examples of the guerrillas' statement were distributed among fourteen employees and eighteen customers in the bank.[47]

In this case, one of the hostages complained about the poor quality of the printed statements; the Fada'i promised to use some of the money stolen from the bank to purchase better printing facilities![48]

Yet another type of attack would use the city's position as infrastructural node to target services needed by the regime for special occasions. Most notably, the Fada'is bombed transmission towers, power grids, and gas pipelines to cause a blackout on October 16, 1971, the final day of the Pahlavi regime's festivities for the 2,500-year celebration of the Persian Empire when the shah inaugurated the Shahyad Tower (later Azadi Tower) in Tehran. While one team succeeded, another realized that they needed first to attain more technical know-how about power infrastructure.

Many of the more dramatic accounts – and others like them in journals such as *Nabard-e Khalq* – came with hand-drawn maps that located the events geographically and thus also made it clear just how close to sites of Pahlavi power and prestige these brazen attacks came. One example from *Nabard-e Khalq* (Figure 5.3) depicts the shah's court, royal palaces, and the prime minister's palace right around the corner from where the Fada'is carried out a "revolutionary execution" in broad daylight.

Another visual aid were hand-drawings of scenes of action. In a *Nabard-e Khalq* article, "The Execution of One of the Torture Agents of the Intelligence Services," a drawing (Figure 5.4) shows a

[47] OIPFG, *Pare'i*, 40.
[48] On the Fada'i underground press, see M. Tohidast, "Chapkhane-ye makhfi" ["Secret printing house"], in Atabaki and Mohajer, eds., *Rahi digar*, 257–291.

Figure 5.3 Map printed in *Nabard-e Khalq*, no. 5, to situate a description of a guerrilla attack in Tehran.
Source: Author's photo.

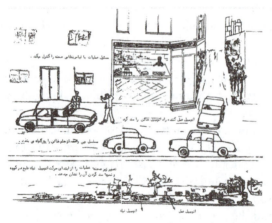

Figure 5.4 Hand-drawn scene of action from *Nabard-e Khalq*, no. 5.
Source: Author's photo.

street scenery where the attackers' car has blocked the target's car; a guerrilla is holding up the target at gunpoint on the sidewalk while a bystander is staring through a window from inside a shop. The drawing is simplistic, almost childish; that, however, only adds to the impression that this is raw eyewitness documentation.

From the guerrilla operation accounts we can see that the urban was more than a random setting: the urban landscape was seen as a materialization of the forces of capitalism, imperialism, and authoritarianism, and by pinpointing and then striking symbols of these forces – a police station, a SAVAK infiltrator, the American Club, the Western oil company offices, a hotel, the director of a large factory, and so on – the guerrilla humiliated, taunted, and exposed the enemy. In planning, executing, and then chronicling and even visualizing armed insurrection in urban space, the Fada'is were not just "performing" on a stage to expose regime vulnerability; they were also exposing a militarized understanding of society and self.

Seeing the City like a Fighter

Many political dissidents experienced Iran in the 1970s as a hellish police state with an increasingly sophisticated intelligence service trained by imperialist powers to sniff out and clamp down on any dissent. To understand the Fada'i perception of and response to the regime's emerging technologies of repression, surveillance, and counterterrorism, we can explore their urban guerrilla warfare manuals and internal security documents.

In the 1974 pamphlet *Lessons for Guerrilla Warfare in Cities*,[49] anonymous Fada'i authors outline a so-called guerilla urbanology (*shahr-shenasi-ye cheriki*) based on their preliminary experiences with armed operations. "The question of security and protection is a matter of life and death for guerrillas," the manual begins: "Urban guerrillas are active in zones of enemy power, influence, and posting, and are therefore always in danger of coming under siege."[50] Guerrilla activity in the city, the reader is told, is much more dangerous than its rural counterpart, which is why urban comrades needed to be "fastidious and precise."[51]

Indeed, in the 1970s, the Fada'is were dealing with an urban society quite different than that of the late 1960s: the increased disciplining, bureaucratization, and securitization of urban life, including new rules for registration of tenants, zoning, gated communities, and so on, went

---

[49] Organization of the Iranian People's Fada'i Guerrillas (OIPFG), *Amuzesh-ha'i bara-ye jang-e chariki dar shahr* [Lessons for guerrilla warfare in cities] (n. p.: 1974).
[50] Ibid., 1.   [51] Ibid., 11.

hand in hand with constantly updated counterterrorism and policing methods such as phone tapping, new torture devices, the use of infiltrators and informers, and so on.[52] Hence, the manual was an attempt, in a quasi-scientific language, to systematize Fada'i knowledge about security, insurgency, and the city.

Over fifty pages, the manual gives relatively detailed and technical guidance on urban mapping, reconnaissance, intelligence-gathering, safehouse logistics, encoding of intra-cadre communication, evasion, shadowing, and other practical matters, as well as on questions of organization, chain of command, morale, physical training, disguise, and so on.

The information in the manual is delivered in concise imperatives: "The sooner you begin to train your running, the better"; "The best place for keeping notes is in your heart"; "Never be caught alive." The detached, practical tone is only interrupted when the authors invite the reader to celebrate Fada'i martyrs for their boundless bravery in resisting torture or committing suicide rather than being apprehended.

This tone, the overall style of the manual, and some of the information contained within it bear close resemblance to Marighella's classic *Minimanual of the Urban Guerrilla* (1969). Marighella is also mentioned. In exhorting the potential guerrilla to never, even under torture, disclose information about rendezvous with other guerrillas, a footnote adds:

The experiences of other revolutionary combatants support this premise. Carlos Marighella was killed at the rendezvous with a priest who had revealed the location under torture. Khosrow Ruzbeh too was captured at a rendezvous.[53]

The Fada'i authors thus sought to convey the impression that Marighella, the Tudeh revolutionary Ruzbeh, and all the Fada'i martyrs belonged to the same pantheon, so to speak – sharing a perilous fate as guerrillas.

In the chapter "Urbanology," the manual calls on guerrillas to obtain and memorize detailed information about the city's street-grids, roads, and alleys, as well as about enemy positions across the city (e.g. traffic control stops and police stations). The guerrilla is told to obtain the following necessary equipment for his or her survey: (1) a city map

---

[52] Vahabzadeh, *Guerrilla Odyssey*, 51.   [53] OIPFG, *Amuzesh-ha'i*, 3n1.

(recommends 1/10,000 based on aerial photography from the Organization of Mapping but gives alternatives); (2) a vehicle of transportation (recommends a bicycle since a car or motorcycle moves too quickly for the guerrilla to notice and record key points in the surrounding environment); and (3) a city guidebook (that also includes bus lines and other information).[54]

The guerrilla is then told to work from the following procedure: divide the map into sections and traverse each section systematically, beginning with the general – the main arteries and junctions – and then finishing with the particularities of each area, the alleys, and back-alleys. The guerrilla should then "compare specific information with overall knowledge."[55]

To give an example, the manual outlines a "Plan for reconnaissance in Tehran."[56] Beginning with central Tehran (delimited by specific points) and then zooming into twenty-two different sectors (*mahalleh,* "neighborhood," and with reference to an appendix with a hand-drawn sector-divided map, Figure 5.5), respectively – and finally moving out to the suburbs. The guerrilla is told to focus on the sectors they do not already know well. Some sectors can be surveyed in one day, the manual explains, while others require several days.

Then, after reconnoitering the city, the guerrilla is told to survey the urban periphery: villages, suburbs, and townships such as Shemiranat and Shahr-e Rey. Here, the urbanology moves into peri-urban and then rural areas as the guerrilla is told to map out watercourses and streams, trails, lines of communications, and transport connections. "As you can see, Tehran is bigger than you may think, and even old Tehranis do not know the city in its entirety."[57]

With such exercises, guerrilla urbanology expressed a particular way of seeing the city. This view, framed by security concerns and saturated with the existential issues of being a guerrilla at war, mirrored a new understanding of everyday life and subjectivity. The manual stated that despite the usefulness of other Fada'is' experiences, "the most important factor in any kind of urban guerilla activity is the individual, personal innovations"[58] – a call, in other words, for the need to study and gain firsthand experience and knowledge of the city as a battleground.

---

[54] Ibid., 18–20.   [55] Ibid., 21.   [56] Ibid., 22–25.   [57] Ibid., 19.
[58] Ibid., 18.

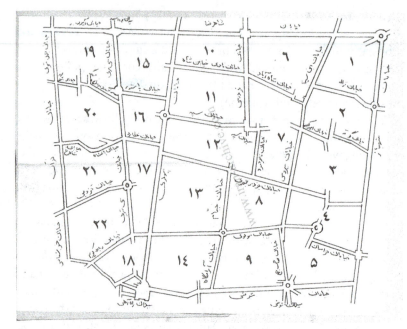

Figure 5.5 Sector-divided map of Tehran for Fada'i "urbanonology." From *Amuzesh-ha'i bara-ye jang-e chariki dar shahr* (*Lessons for Guerrilla Warfare in Cities*).

Source: www.iran-archive.com.

However, it is interesting to note that the focus in this kind of literature seems to be mostly on the built environment and not demography, density, social spaces, lived patterns, or even traffic flows; in other words, an abstract conception of space instead of a relational understanding. The latter, however, would become important in one of the final stages of Fada'i activism prior to the revolution.

Discovering the Toiler

After a period with numerous urban guerrilla operations in the early 1970s, the Fada'is went through a phase that historian Nasser Mohajer describes as characterized by both setbacks and growth. While the urban guerrilla cause generally and the Fada'is specifically attracted tremendous support from left-leaning students, intellectuals, artists, and activists, the Fada'i organization was also marred by arrests, executions, and deaths in street battles or under torture that drastically decimated leadership and cadres.[59] On top of this, there was incessant infighting, fragmentation, expulsions, and disciplining.

By the mid-1970s, the organization as a whole underwent a shift from the "strategic armed struggle"-line championed by Ahmadzadeh toward Jazani's "political struggle"-line of establishing a broader political organization to lead a popular movement. This shift of focus from the momentary and spectacular politics of armed attacks to the broad-spectrum politics of everyday resistance brought to the fore the issue of *tudeh'i-shodan* or "massifying" the struggle.

As opposed to Ahmadzadeh, Jazani had argued that armed struggle, at least in its first phase, could not, in its very nature, be a mass phenomenon.[60] Jazani took issue with those Fada'is who "still" believed "that people in the cities are close to joining existing guerrilla organizations in urban guerrilla resistance": the masses, even the urban masses, were simply not technically skilled or trained enough. Even more importantly, the city itself had limited capacity for guerrilla warfare, which required room for maneuver, concealment, compartmentalization, and secrecy. Hence, in contrast to a rural guerrilla, a rapid expansion of the urban guerrilla would be directly counterproductive.[61] Instead, Jazani mentioned the many forms of non-armed resistance exercised by the urban masses.[62]

Crucially, Jazani was developing a more nuanced understanding of the working class. With historical, social, and cultural analysis that did not reduce the different classes to their position in the relations of production,[63] Jazani came to reject the abstract, objectivist, and unnuanced notion of the worker, and – as Vahabzadeh notes[64] – added the crucial category of *qeshr* or "stratum" to the analysis. This led Jazani to argue that

with respect to the particular characteristics of the working class in Iran under the present circumstances we must replace the singular concept of the working class with the broader and more realistic concept of *the urban toiler* [*zahmatkesh-e shahri*]; and we stress that within that broad stratum [*qeshr*] of the toiler, the working class is the most organized and most advanced class and power.[65]

[59] Atabaki and Mohajer, eds., *Rahi digar*, 70–71.   [60] Jazani, *Cheguneh*, 18.
[61] Ibid., 33–34.   [62] Ibid., 33.   [63] E.g. Jazani, *Vaqaye'*, 167.
[64] Vahabzadeh, *Guerrilla Odyssey*, 88.   [65] Jazani, *Che kesani*, 15.

Having thus replaced a fetichized, singular category with the at once broader *and* more specific category of *urban toiler*, Jazani could now identify a revolutionary potential: a historical agent of change brought about by urbanization under dependent capitalism.

This revolutionary subject had in fact already been located on the outskirts of the city when Jazani and Zarifi in 1967 wrote about the suffering of urban toilers "under the immense pressure of poverty, destitution, disease, and unemployment, as well as intense, cruel oppression." They argued that this social stratum, in contrast to peasants and the middle classes, had "not forgiven the regime for the [1953] coup."[66] In 1969, Safai-Farahani wrote about how "a force of several millions" among "the workers and the toiling and destitute class of the cities," influenced by "revolutionary events in the world," were in fact "the most promising power in the beginning of a revolution."[67] Later, Jazani gave more substance to the urban toiler concept:

This highly accumulated force, lacking any skill, capital, and education, faces continuous unemployment and horrific deprivation. Standards of sanitation and nutrition and their conditions will decline to such an extent that they will not be comparable to any urban or rural society. This reserve army of unemployed [*zakhire-ye ordu-ye kar*] has, due to a tremendous drop in their standard of living, to live in far worse conditions than the workers. This is what qualifies it as "sub-proletariat."[68]

With reference to the Marxist concepts of "reserve army of labor" and "sub-proletariat," Jazani was talking about a segment of society that in Persian were known as *zagheh-neshinan* ("slum-dwellers") and *hashiyeh-neshinan* ("margin-dwellers") who inhabited the *mahalat-e siyah* ("dark neighborhoods") and the *halabi-abad* ("tin-city," i.e. shantytowns) as *alunak-neshin* (hut- or shed-dweller) or even as *chador-neshin* (tent-dweller).[69] In Tehran and other major cities, these informal dwellings were shooting up at a dramatic pace in the areas just outside of the city limits, known in Persian as *kharej-az-mahdudeh* ("outskirts/perimeter").

[66] Jazani and Zarifi, *Masa'el*, 10.   [67] Safai-Farahani, *An che*, 20.
[68] Jazani, *Vaqaye'*, 186.
[69] See Bayat, *Street Politics*; A. Banuazizi, "Alunak-neshinan-e khiyaban-e profesor Brown" ["Hut-Dwellers of Professor Brown Avenue"], *Ketab-e Alefba*, no. 3 (July 1983): 53–64; Farhad Kazemi, "Urban Migrants and the Revolution," *Iranian Studies* 10 (1980): 257–277.

While the urban sub-proletariat remained relatively under-theorized in Jazani's work, he nonetheless predicted that this segment of society, hitherto generally overlooked by the opposition, were on the verge of revolt:

The horrific deprivation and the feeling of gaping inequality when comparing themselves with the bourgeoisie and the comfortable petite bourgeoisie does, occasionally, during economic and social crises, push these people into a state of explosion culminating in spontaneous and bloody riots. At the stage of general mobilization of the masses, the working-class movement will be able to take these sections into account, as is done by the non-proletarian movement.[70]

This "discovery" of the urban toiler, in turn, enabled the Fada'i theorist to broaden the key concept of *khalq* or "people," as we shall see below. Thus, when repression brought guerrilla warfare to a halt in the second half of the 1970s, it was only natural for the Fada'is to look to the shantytowns for new energy for the popular movement. "For communists," Jazani and Zarifi had written already in 1967,

unity is never achieved in rooms behind closed doors or by signing manifestos of unity. Communists achieve unity through revolutionary action in the alleys and bazaars together with the masses.[71]

Praxis in the Alleys

In this section, I will explore how a group of unnamed Fada'is went into the city to seek unity with, or at least a deeper understanding of, the masses. I will do this through an analysis of fieldwork-based accounts of slums and shantytowns, a particular genre with which the Fada'is, particularly after the crushing repression and near-extinction of the organization in 1976, documented the struggles of the urban toiler.

This "going to the people"[72] was a practical manifestation of the strategic shift toward Jazani's "political struggle." Jazani had earlier

[70] Jazani, *Vaqaye'*, 186.
[71] Jazani-Zarifi Group, "Tez-e goruh-e Jazani" ["The Jazani Group thesis"], *19-e Bahman* (Farvardin 1355/March 1976; originally compiled in fall 1967).
[72] A reference to the Russian Narodnik movement, whose "going to the people" campaign in the 1870s bears some resemblance with what the Fada'is attempted,

argued that the principal contradiction or conflict in Iran was not between labor and capital, but between *the people* and *the anti-people* (*zedd-e khalq*),[73] the latter signifying all the internal enemies of the people that may be propped up by global imperialism but nonetheless constitute a tangible, immediate target inside Iran – in short, the shah's regime.

In terms of method, there was of course an important prior history of field study as Marxist practice. As Naqi Hamidian – a student activist close to the early Fada'is – has explained in his memoirs, several of the later Fada'i cadres spent their time in the so-called Literary Corps (*sepah-e danesh*, i.e. doing civil service in villages) observing and documenting the rapidly evolving role of capitalism in rural communities.[74] In time, this developed into proper studies, including three book-length analyses of agrarian economy and village life compiled by the early Fada'is.[75] However, as Hamidian notes, he and his comrades "never accepted Mao Zedong's theses on going to the villages, establishing rural bases, and surrounding cities from the villages."[76] Again, local analysis trumped the universalist prescriptions.

Indeed, there had been, from the very beginning of proto-Fada'i activity, an imperative to seek to *understand* the worker, the peasant, and the toiler as they "actually" were, rather than how theory supposed them to be. Jazani argued that it was "the historical task of the vanguard proletarian organizations" to obtain a "scientific understanding [*shenakht-e 'elmi*] of the socioeconomic conditions" of not just the working class,[77] but also peasants. "To assess the peasants' true state of mind and their social outlook," Jazani argued, "one has to get in direct contact with this

---

on a much smaller scale and with a somewhat different purpose, in the shantytown fieldwork and similar activities.

[73] Jazani, *Vaqaye'*, 149–150; see also Vahabzadeh, *Guerrilla Odyssey*, 93.

[74] N. Hamidian, *Safar bar bal-ha-ye arezu* [Journey on the wings of hope] (Stockholm: self-pub., 2010), 18, 34–25.

[75] P. Vahabzadeh, "FADĀʾIĀN-E ḴALQ," *Encyclopaedia Iranica*, www.iranicaonline.org/articles/fadaian-e-khalq. This, in turn, paralleled an interest in rural culture among Fada'is such as Behruz Dehqani, who worked in villages and together with the influential radical short story writer and translator, Samad Behrangi, published Azerbaijani folk tales. An interesting urban counterpart to this overwhelmingly rural-focused radical left literature can be found in the Fada'i guerrilla Marziyeh Oskuʻi's *Dokhtaran-e kowli* (1972) about a shantytown in Ahvaz.

[76] Hamidian, *Safar*, 32.   [77] Jazani, *Vaqaye'*, 161.

class and its day-to-day existence."[78] Similarly with the urban proletariat: "We must determine the proletariat's degree of consciousness and their psychological state of mind: Do they understand class unity?" asked Jazani. "Are they conscious of their own power?"[79] The Fada'is should strive to understand the lives and demands of the urban toilers and, by showing solidarity, make them understand the Fada'i way.[80] To give examples of talking points that could illustrate the regime as "anti-people," Jazani mentioned that the Fada'is could raise issues such as privatization of education, tuition fees, quality of education, and so on.[81]

Even before 1976, Vahabzadeh argues, the Fada'is "were no longer optimistic or hopeful about the spontaneous support of the masses" and so attempted to reach out to the working class more directly, among other things by establishing a worker's wing of the organization. In addition, there was a long-standing practice of sending cadres to labor in factories, sometimes as a disciplinary punishment and always as a means to open their eyes to working-class reality. This was what Vahabzadeh calls the "occasional pilgrimages of the intellectuals to the shrine of 'the toiling masses'"[82] and which subsequently turned into a more concerted effort to participate in the workforce in order to establish contact with the proletariat.

It was in direct extension of this work that some Fada'is went to the urban periphery in the second half of the 1970s.

Going to the People

The year 1978 – when the Iranian Revolution broke out – saw the delayed publication of the first systematized and comprehensive attempt by the Fada'is to map the seeds of revolution in the shantytowns.[83] While Fada'i underground publications had brought scattered reports of urban unrest over the years, the *Reports from the Brave Struggles of the People outside City Limits!*[84] was much more

---

[78] Ibid., 170.   [79] Ibid., 163.   [80] Jazani, *Cheguneh*, 39–40.   [81] Ibid., 40.
[82] Vahabzadeh, *Guerrilla Odyssey*, 44.
[83] Importantly, two other radical left opposition groups – Paykar (Organization of Struggle for the Emancipation of the Working Class) and the People's Mojahedin of Iran (PMOI) – also produced shantytown struggle reports.
[84] Organization of the Iranian People's Fada'i Guerrillas (OIPFG), *Gozareshati az mobareze-ye dalirane-ye mardom-e kharej az mahdudeh!* [Reports from the brave struggles of the people outside of city limits!] (n.p.: 1978).

comprehensive in scope. Over 143 pages, it contained 24 accounts of everyday resistance, most of them written during fall 1977.[85] At the center of attention was that key urban issue of the right to housing.

The Fada'is documented how poor people uprooted from the countryside by the land reforms scrambled for a living on the margins of Tehran (with a handful of reports from Karaj, Zanjan, and Qazvin). These migrants would start by building shanties from whatever scrap materials they could find; later they would build actual houses with one or two rooms in order to stake a claim to the ground they were now living on. On top of the squalor, destitution, and lack of sanitation and security, the shantytown-dwellers were subject to constant harassment and repeated waves of demolitions carried out by authorities, generally the municipality, but often backed up by violence from security forces.

Investigating the shantytown-dwellers' reactions to or inaction vis-à-vis this repression, and documenting how they found the power and courage to continue to build and rebuild their homes, the report states as its purpose "to expose the nature of ... mass movement resistance"[86] and to highlight how the urban toilers' social protests "evolve ... from individual to collective, from economic to political, from scattered to organized, from peaceful to violent."[87] The reports contain eyewitness accounts of excessive violence: raids by police, gendarmerie, army, sometimes backed up with helicopters or with support from fire brigades. There is talk of shantytown-dwellers wounded in most of the cases; a few fatalities are also mentioned. This violence is clearly integral to state-led gentrification, which remains under-theorized in Fada'i work generally, but was conveyed as follows by an inhabitant:

Those living outside city limits have no more than two options: those with money must move to the city and live in apartments and those without must go to the villages.[88]

The report does not follow a strict structure but is presented as reproductions of conversations with shantytown-dwellers, or as isolated quotes from shantytown-dwellers. Some reports contain in-depth

---

[85] Many reports are undated but a handful seem to have been gathered as early as 1974 or at least carry direct reference to earlier years.
[86] OIPFG, *Gozareshati*, x.   [87] Ibid., 2.   [88] Ibid., 55.

inquiry into one family's travails but often we are just introduced to "a young man," "an elderly woman," and so on. Many of the reports start in medias res with little or no background information. The language is largely jargon-free and thus different from the convoluted, theory-heavy language of other Fada'i publications. The cadres are often invisible and implicit in the text; only sometimes do they move to the forefront in the first-person singular. We know from the introduction that the cadres worked "both openly and clandestinely" and in some reports, the author briefly mentions if he or she is playing a role to conceal the real objective of their visit; for example, as someone looking to build a house in the area under investigation. However, the volume does not reveal anything else about the involved cadres – including their numbers.

The Fada'is were particularly interested in detecting whether the housing struggles could lead to any of three possible consequences: (1) the development of a political awareness that the shah's regime was oppressive and his project for a "great civilization" an empty gesture; (2) the strengthening of class solidarity, exemplified in how shantytown-dwellers helped each other when houses were demolished; and (3) the elevation of "the spirit of resistance and confrontation" when people discovered their true power during direct confrontation with the authorities.[89] Such developments, the Fada'is predicted or hoped, would eventually lead the urban toiler to *mobareze-ye qahr-amiz* ("forceful" or "violent resistance") against the regime in its totality.

The reports are above all an insight into the Fada'i worldview. While the cadres express sympathy and understanding for the plight of the shantytown-dwellers, there is also a somewhat distant and superior attitude at display. We are told that the shantytown-dwellers' responses to queries differ due to three possible factors: class, level of consciousness, and psychological state. However, in the same text, the authors even negate the first factor, stating that repression has led to fear, despair, and lack of self-confidence to the extent that "class location cannot play a decisive role in shaping their [political] position" (*movze'-giri*).[90] The shantytown-dweller is at once a historical agent of change *and* somehow lacking agency and needing orientation.

Working with Jazani's terminology, the Fada'i social analysis uncovered significant differences within the stratum of "urban toiler,"

[89] Ibid., 6–8.   [90] Ibid., 2.

which they described as ranging from (1) "urban laborers, low-income and disadvantaged petite bourgeoisie, intellectuals (pupils, students, etc.), low-ranking officials at private and public offices" to (2) "petite bourgeoisie with village roots" and on to (3) "urban middle-class petite bourgeoisie" – even including military and municipal officers.

Each of these three substrata are then ascribed particular political capacities. The first group, due to its proximity to industrial production, "urban lifestyle," and "the social spaces of the city," the Fada'is claim, exhibited a relatively high level of class and political consciousness, strong experience with resistance and organizing, as well as a degree of knowledge of capitalism and of the guerrilla's armed struggle. They were generally better prepared to resist the authorities, including with violence.[91]

Again we see how the Fada'i cultural analysis had clearly geographic dimensions: physical proximity to urban centers and culture was associated with progress and awareness while the origin of the second group, the villages, was associated with a "weak spirit" of resistance. This substratum, the Fada'is judged, was less willing to stand up in defense of its collective rights and when targeted with eviction, it tended to "cry and beg" or, at the most, write a petition to the court or to the ruling royalist Rastakhiz Party. They were presented as traditional-minded people who ascribed their problems to "supernatural forces, destiny, and fate."[92]

Indeed, while on the ground the Fada'is used religious language to present themselves as relatable to the shantytown-dwellers, they also left clues, in their reports, of secularist disapproval of the urban poor's strong religious feelings and superstitious beliefs. The reader is left with the impression that Muslim fatalism may lie at root of a mindset of inaction, docility, and servitude. The urban poor see the cruelty of the demolitions or their general destitution in terms of Shiite notions of justice and injustice, some likening the shantytown uprisings to Imam Hussain's epic battle at Karbala or to signs of the messianic return of the Hidden Imam.

When shantytown-dwellers' responses do not fit with the Fada'i view, they are dismissed as under the influence of monarchic propaganda or as gullible illiterates. This is particularly true of the numerous examples of locals who expressed a blind faith in royal benevolence

[91] Ibid., 3.   [92] Ibid., 4–5.

and believed that the shah was opposed to or unaware of the demolitions, that the imperial family, particularly Farah Diba, could be trusted to listen to petitions, or that the court was separate from and morally above the rest of the state apparatus.[93] An example, undoubtedly included to portray the folly of such beliefs, was an elderly lady who hoped the shah would "fly his airplane" over the shantytown, see what was going on, and intervene on her behalf.[94]

Finally, the third substratum – the shantytown "petite bourgeoisie" – is described as placatory if not reactionary. Instead of confronting the authorities, this group of shantytown-dwellers relied on bribery, cronyism, and trickery in order to mitigate threats of eviction: "This reaction is rooted in their [social] stratum's interests and culture," the Fada'is conclude. It is also in this substratum we find the "minor *builder-sellers*" (*besaz-befrush*), which is slang for those who profited from the Tehran building frenzy that started after World War II and accelerated drastically in the 1960s and 1970s. Together with the *bongahs* ("real estate agents") and certain shops that sprang up in the Klondike-like space of the shantytown, the builder-sellers are described as outright class enemies within the urban toiler community, mini-capitalists, as it were, who would co-opt or thwart protests or even collaborate with the regime in order to defend their private material interests. As such, these elements were often at odds with the *alunak-neshinan*, the hut-dwellers, who saw them as greedy profiteers.

Vietnam in Tehran

Throughout the report, one can find scattered ethnographic, demographic, and political information of great value. One example is from observations in Javadiyeh, where fifty houses had been demolished. Locals reported that "Ansari, Alam, Farmanfarmayan, and someone else want to build a township" and have "told folks to bring their land title deeds and get their money, but people didn't accept."[95] When the developers sent an engineer to measure the land, he found that *ghorbati-ha* (travelers or gypsies) – in fact "slum-dwellers from Shush [Square]" in southern Tehran – had settled there. In these brief passages we see that major crony capitalists were known by name; that

---

[93] E.g. ibid., 18–19, 28, 31.   [94] Ibid., 31.   [95] Ibid., 13.

there was a process of dispossession involved in planning and constructing the new townships that were meant to symbolize Pahlavi modernity; and that there were particular ethnic dimensions to the socioeconomic dynamics of urban transformation.

The reports also give an insight into the technologies of domination employed by the Pahlavi state. A typical conversation recorded in the reports mentions the centrality of *the map*:

I ask a couple of workers: "Sir, haven't they given construction permit around here?"
A: "*Vallah*, they've given permit on this side but not on that side; generally, anywhere on the municipality's map has a construction permit."
Q: "Why did they demolish those shops?"
A: "Well, they probably weren't on the map."[96]

Or another exchange:

Here, they have demolished around ten to twelve houses, and I ask a worker standing next to one of the wrecked houses: "Why did they tear down these houses?"
A: "They wanted to. Poor people had spent so much money and they just came and tore them down. Motherfuckers say this is 'outside city limits.'"[97]

The shantytown-dwellers here were clearly under the impression that until their home was etched on the municipality's maps, it was not just outside city limits but also beyond legal bounds and protection. In a very literal sense, the shantytown-dwellers struggled to be seen and have their homes recorded and legalized.[98] Another oppressive aspect of life on the urban margins were the conflicting messages from authorities. On the one hand, permit-less construction outside the city limits was regularly announced as illegal by municipal authorities trying to control Tehran's haphazard expansion. On the other hand, there are numerous examples when shantytown-dwellers thought the shah had legalized all building up until a particular date, and that soon, the shantytown houses would be officially recorded. Together with rampant corruption, arbitrary actions of various local authorities, uncertainty, and abuse of power were fueling discontent.

[96] Ibid., 9.   [97] Ibid., 51.   [98] See Bayat, *Street Politics*.

While the shantytown-dwellers were often able to see their predicament in the context of Iranian national politics – such as the qualitative difference of having Amir-Abbas Hoveyda or Jamshid Amuzegar as prime minister – they also sometimes managed, in the Fada'is' presentation, to place their situation in a comparative, international context. An inhabitant complained:

They ask *why doesn't Iran progress?* In countries abroad, they *first* build houses for people; *then* get them to work. They do that for the people; but here, they nurture singers and dancers! We build our own houses here and then they come and tear them down.[99]

The inhabitant compared Iran to Saudi Arabia, where the government allegedly cared for its inhabitants, and then referred to Shiite mythology:

Yazid tore down 72 tents and 1,300 years later, we're still talking about it. They [the authorities] just demolished 100 houses in one night.[100]

In another particularly violent case from the shantytowns of Shemiranat-e Now on Tehran's northern city limits, an inhabitant reported that local youth were calling their neighborhood Vietnam – with reference to the Vietnam War, which had been a regular newspaper feature in the years leading up to the demolitions.[101] An inhabitant in yet another case, Majidiyeh shantytown, claimed that the regime was using arms it had purchased for war abroad on its own citizens at home.[102] These scattered allusions to global politics were used by the Fada'is to hint at a budding ideological consciousness.

Unsurprisingly, however, it was the Fada'is themselves who most clearly tied the housing struggles in Tehran to a universal struggle:

[The regime forces] leveled [the urban toilers'] houses, in some cases they buried people together with their homes under dirt and bricks; [the regime] answered any popular protest with violence and beatings at the hands of the forces of oppression; and when the people started resisting, their chests became targets for American and Israeli bullets.[103]

In this fashion, the Fada'is sought to connect the local to the global, the particular to the universal, through an investigation into the seeds of revolution.

[99] OIPFG, *Gozareshati*, 15.   [100] Ibid.   [101] Ibid., 64.   [102] Ibid., 54.
[103] Ibid., 10–11.

As a matter of fact, an actual revolution *was* underway, and the housing struggles *did* become entangled in the final stages of that revolution. By then, the Fada'is had exhausted their capabilities and were overtaken by events – and by Islamist forces able to lead the urban masses to a final showdown with the shah. Jazani's analysis thus turned out to be correct: the urban toiler had revolutionary potential – it was just not communist guerrillas but a populist cleric who could finally catalyze that potential and only in the later stages of a revolution that was spearheaded by the middle classes.[104] The revolution led to an Islamic republic that co-opted the housing issue and positioned itself as champion of the urban sub-proletariat through both spectacular expropriations and, in the long term, programs, however incomplete, for public housing, social redistribution, and welfare.

Conclusion

In a recent essay, sociologist Stuart Schrader recreated the intellectual genealogy of a key term in the works of the famous French philosopher Henri Lefebvre.[105] When Lefebvre wrote about *la ville mondiale*, Schrader reminds us, he did so with reference to a Third Worldist conceptualization of "the global urban" found in a Maoist statement from 1965.[106] The Maoist proposition that cities across the Global South were encircled by rural hinterlands teeming with revolutionary

[104] Following Bayat's trailblazing work (*Street Politics*), many historians of Iran tend to argue that the slum-dwellers only joined the revolution very late and played a marginal role in toppling the Pahlavi regime. This is an argument that should be still open to debate; Vahabzadeh, for example, argues that shantytown-dwellers participated "in great numbers as early as late spring/early summer of 1978" (personal exchange, August 2020). In an interesting work, scholar-activist Mohammad Ghaznavian's *Ta'amolati darbare-ye kharej az mahdudeh* [Thoughts about the outside city limits] (Praxies, 2016) – published by the Iranian Marxist online magazine *Praxies* – accuses Bayat of limiting his work on both the urban poor movements and the urban guerrillas to a "romanticization of poverty and the struggle for survival."

[105] Stuart Schraeder, "Henri Lefebvre, Mao Zedong, and the Global Urban Concept," *Global Urban History Blog* (May 1, 2018), https://globalurbanhistory.com/2018/05/01/henri-lefebvre-mao-zedong-and-the-global-urban-concept.

[106] Lin Biao, "Long Live the Victory of People's War! In Commemoration of the 20th Anniversary of Victory in the Chinese People's War of Resistance against Japan," pamphlet written September 3, 1965; republished online: www.marxists.org/reference/archive/lin-biao/1965/09/peoples_war/index.htm.

guerrillas prompted Lefebvre to think about the reverse: that urbanization and urbanism had surpassed and overflown the conceptual confines of "the city," erasing the urban/rural divide and heralding a new historical phase in which "the right to the city" would become "a cry and a demand" across a planet covered with urban tissue.[107]

With this conceptual history, Schrader invites us to unsettle prevalent Eurocentric ideas underpinning the narrative of global urbanization and instead globalize our understanding of the urban condition. As this study has attempted to show, by the time Lefebvre's *La Révolution Urbaine* appeared in print, a key driver of revolutionary action and thinking in Iran had already decided that the urban was spilling into the rural, becoming a "forest of humans" that made urban guerrilla warfare more feasible than the rural counterparts in China and Cuba.

This points to a broader issue of how the revolutionaries saw "the urban." The Fada'is, I have argued, tended to see it simultaneously in abstract, theoretical terms and in concrete, practical, and local-specific ones. The local and the global, as it were, intersected *through* "the urban"; or, put differently, theory and action linked and coproduced the local and global scales.

Often the theoretical work took shape with inspiration from global engagements and entanglements with revolutionary internationalist and Third Worldist socialism; but the analysis always tied the praxis to the specific historical, socio-material conditions in which the Fada'is lived and fought. Thus, rather than being a question merely of which dimension trumped another – the local/particular or the global/universal – it is also a question of temporality. As we have seen, Jazani's group had already identified the urban as a starting point for the revolution long before reading Marighella. Of course, the fact that Marxist guerrilla in Latin America had simultaneously arrived at similar analyses and strategic considerations empowered the Iranian guerrilla, giving their revolutionary line legitimacy and confidence. Yet it is important that the Fada'is had realized that it was not "the peasant," nor even "the working class," but the "urban toiler" – together with intellectuals, students, and the "national bourgeoisie" – that would drive revolution.

---

[107] See Neil Brenner and Christian Schmid, "Towards a New Epistemology of the Urban?" *City: Analysis of Urban Trends, Culture, Theory, Policy, Action* 19 (2015): 151–182.

Such findings should help strengthen our analyses of the global and transnational dimensions in local micro-histories.

So how was the leading urban guerrilla before the Iranian Revolution *urban*? I have argued that the Fada'is' profile was strongly urban: they were largely urbanites with an urban-based history of political activism and an individual and collective experience of a rapidly evolving urban life and culture. This led to an urban-centric understanding of progress – and of revolution. However, while they situated the revolution and therefore emancipatory potentials in the city, the Fada'is also saw how urbanization was closely entwined with capitalism and imperialism.

The Fada'is thus came to see the city as a stage for revolutionary performance. Seeing the city in a different light was part of the project of seeing oneself in a different light: as guerrilla, as vanguard, as revolutionary. It was also about seeing others in the city in a different light, which led to the "discovery," so to speak, of the urban toiler as a revolutionary agent. This discovery, I believe, has been under-studied in the existing literature of the left's role in the revolution. It is true, as Vahabzadeh has argued, that Jazani's class analysis – even as it evolved and became more nuanced – did *not* lead to a solution for his theoretical "aporia"; and that he "ultimately yield[ed] to the essentialism of conferring on certain classes various degrees of revolutionary potential."[108] However, by identifying the urban toiler, the handful of Fada'is who went to the urban margins were in fact on to something concrete, tangible, and useful. While there is a discussion about the extent of urban poor participation in the revolution, there is no doubt that their plight and struggle left a significant imprint on the revolutionary movement.

Hence, the post-guerrilla sought out a different revolutionary destiny for the Fada'is, at the most difficult moment in the organization's history, in the urban margins. The shantytown exploration, I have argued, shows that the Fada'is no longer saw themselves as *already being* the vanguard (embodied in the decision to wage guerrilla warfare), but were instead striving to *become* the vanguard by embedding themselves with the ideal "real people" of the new urban terrain.

This takes us back to the notion of the city as "a forest of humans." What did Jazani and others have in mind when they spoke of this

---

[108] Vahabzadeh, *Guerrilla Odyssey*, 88.

"principle"? Perhaps the sylvan imagery alluded to the multitude of the urban masses within a densely built environment? Or perhaps, in more practical terms, it referred to the way in which being a guerrilla changes one's perception of urban society? If so, the principle can be better understood by reading Ahmadzadeh's words:

If we accept that the struggle is a protracted one and if we accept too that it begins through organization in groups, why should it matter if one of the groups disappears? What is important is that the weapon that drops from the hands of a fighter [*razmandeh*] will be grabbed by another fighter.[109]

Of course, it is also possible that the "forest of humans" was simply an inversion of the earlier romanticizing of the rural guerrilla: the realization that cities were the destined stage for the revolutionary subject. It is nonetheless fair to surmise that the Fada'is will continue to be associated with the green trails and the mountains.

[109] Ahmadzadeh, *Mobareze*, 3.

6 Revolutionaries for Life:
The IRGC and the Global Guerrilla Movement

MARYAM ALEMZADEH

From the 1960s to the late 1970s, revolutionary guerrilla groups rattled the world as the exalted emblem of anti-imperialist resistance. Prerevolutionary Iran was no exception. Leftist and Muslim-Marxist groups followed and appropriated globally adopted ideologies, mobilization strategies, and organization patterns, and found their way to international hotbeds of activism and guerrilla training all across the world. Many of the religious, non-leftist activists in Iran shared the burning desire for taking up arms to overthrow the existing political system as well, and they did: either as individuals or in small, short-lived organizations, they participated in the global guerrilla movement. After the 1979 revolution, some of these guerrillas joined the endeavor to create a state militia, soon to be known as the Islamic Revolutionary Guards Corps (IRGC).

Flash forward to the peak of the Kurdish conflict in Iran, in August 1980: the IRGC participated in the repression campaign, alongside the regular army. Politicians in Tehran were still fighting over the IRGC's raison d'être, the legitimate boundaries of its reach and its overlap with that of the regular army, and the degree of central control and professionalism required for it to function. In addition to political disputes, the IRGC suffered from insufficient training, equipment, and organizational order as well. Both during and after the Kurdish conflict and other ethnic insurgencies, however, IRGC commanders and personnel interpreted those shortcomings as advantages inherent in a guerrilla force. For instance, Hoseyn Ala'i, a first-generation IRGC commander, counted the regular army's lack of knowledge about guerrilla warfare as one of the army's "problems" and the reason behind the IRGC's alleged upper hand in Kurdistan:

The army had two problems during the Kurdistan war. One was that they did not know the principles of guerrilla warfare [*jang-e cheriki*]; they had not

178

even dabbled in it. The other was that their commanders were constantly changing [due to the revolutionary transition].[1]

Contrary to Ala'i's claim and other similar ones, my field and archival research shows that guerrilla organization and training was minimal, if existing at all, in IRGC units across the country.[2] What is depicted post hoc as an intentionally designed irregular structure consisted in fact of inexperienced field commanders who, in the lack of solid military structure, enjoyed a generous deal of authority to fight as they saw fit, and minimally trained volunteers who were to learn about warfare only through trial and error.

What was at stake for the Guards in claiming to be a guerrilla organization, then? What was the nature of the IRGC's claim to guerrilla identity? What did the organization inherit from a few leaders' encounters with insurgent irregular warfare, if not the organization and the practice itself? Is there any sense, in other words, in which the IRGC can be seen as a participant in and a contributor to the global network of guerrilla activities that had changed the face of world politics? To answer these questions, this chapter follows key individuals' life trajectories from guerrilla training camps across the Middle East in the early 1970s to Iran's Kurdish provinces a decade later. Although guerrilla-trained Guards constituted a small number, possibly not even close to 100, the connection they provided to the global guerrilla movement left its mark on the IRGC's identity, as I will demonstrate through their stories.

Upon its formation in April 1979, the IRGC had inherited a sophisticated set of ties with guerrilla organizations in Iran and elsewhere. This chapter begins by illustrating Iranian networks of resistance outside of the country that facilitated guerilla training for "Islamist" activists. By the term Islamist I am referring to devoted followers of Ayatollah Khomeini, cleric or non-cleric, who prioritized Islamic principles and practices in their resistance efforts. In historical reality, boundaries among revolutionary ideologies and practices are blurry, and they were even more so in prerevolutionary years studied in this

---

[1] Transcribed interview with Brigadier General Ala'i, 2005, document no. 14881 (Islamic Revolution Document Center, Tehran, Iran). All excerpts from Farsi sources are translated into English by the author.

[2] Maryam Alemzadeh, "Institutionalization of a Revolutionary Army: The Islamic Revolutionary Guards Corps (1979–82)" (PhD diss., University of Chicago, 2018).

chapter. Indeed, it is the very aim of this study to highlight the forgotten ties among the Guards, known to be devoted Shiites and Khomeinists, and secular leftist guerrillas within global spaces. I use the term somewhat anachronistically, then, only to distinguish the subjects of this narrative – Shia activists who dissociated themselves from Muslim-Marxists, leftists, and liberals and religious-nationalists more strongly only in postrevolutionary years.

In the rest of the chapter I review the encounters of influential Islamist figures with Iranian and transnational guerrilla fighters before the 1979 revolution, and the experience they took away from such encounters. After the fall of the shah, grassroots militias that a few of these individuals had created were summoned to be part of a state militia, the IRGC. As the target regime had already collapsed, the very agenda of the global guerrillas, that is, insurgency against a sovereign state, was no longer in the picture for the IRGC. Nevertheless, IRGC founders and leaders saw preserving organizational flexibility as a way to preserve the revolutionary, insurgent spirit and identity. In the second part of the chapter I narrate the IRGC founders' maneuvers to avoid organizational rigidity and to entrench the organization into a nationwide military force at the same time. The order the Guards gradually institutionalized was one based on a combination of ideological commitment and tolerance for independent, direct action, which they legitimized under the rubric of irregular warfare. The IRGC, in other words, left out the organizational meticulousness that guerrillas needed to practice in order to further their (sometimes transnational) liberation cause, in order to keep the revolutionary identity legible in a postrevolutionary time. Simultaneously, they drifted apart from the radical global agenda of continuing the revolution outside of Iran, which would indeed require the programmatic approach that they saw in contrast to their newly found revolutionary freedom of action.

This account is built upon published memoirs and documents as well as interviews I have conducted with IRGC founders and first-generation members in 2016 and 2017. Exploring the formation of the IRGC in the context of the global wave of militantism by putting together pieces from personal narratives and documents reveals yet another aspect of the Iranian Revolution's role in the making of the global 1970s. In so doing, it challenges prominent clichés about the IRGC's nature at the same time – that it formed as a strictly

Khomeinist organization with no ties to the left-leaning guerrillas in Iran and elsewhere, and developed as a rigid, centrally controlled security apparatus comparable to policing organizations of totalitarian postrevolutionary governments.

Global Guerrillas and Islamist Activists: The Infrastructure

The Algerian War of Independence (1956–1962) and the Cuban Revolution (1959) introduced irregular warfare as a globally attainable pathway toward national liberation in the early 1960s. In the international context of the Cold War, liberation activists around the world took up arms, modeling their efforts after the heroic Algerian fighters and the pioneering guerrilla warriors of Latin America, and building a network that seemed to target not just particular governments, but "the structures of global power."[3] What connected the geographically separate movements, regardless of their success or failure, was an anti-imperialist ideology, localized against incumbent governments, and the aspiration to replicate the success of the *foco* campaign in Cuba – that of creating focal guerrilla groups to jump-start the revolution as opposed to waiting for revolutionary classes to form.[4] Activists from around the world started traveling to the newly transformed countries to live their political dreams, and leaders of the successful revolutions received delegations of revolutionaries and exported their ideological, tactical, and material support for the new movements. In addition to the transnational liberationist awareness, a concrete global network of guerrillas was taking shape. In one way or another, to use Jeffrey Byrne's words, "the desire to escape one's geographical fate was wide-spread."[5]

Similar desires were on the rise in the Middle East, specifically among Palestinian liberation fighters, when the 1967 defeat against Israel dulled the state-centered Arab nationalism led by Egypt's Nasser.

---

[3] Paul T. Chamberlin, *The Global Offensive: The United States, the Palestine Liberation Organization, and the Making of the Post-Cold War Order* (Oxford: Oxford University Press, 2012), 3.

[4] Timothy P. Wickam-Crowley, *Guerrillas and Revolution in Latin America: A Comparative Study of Insurgents and Regimes since 1956* (Princeton, NJ: Princeton University Press, 1992).

[5] Jeffrey J. Byrne, *Mecca of Revolutions: Algeria, Decolonization, and the Third World Order* (Oxford: Oxford University Press, 2016), 5.

Palestinian activists sought the answer in embedding their agenda within the global guerilla network and ideology. By so doing, they gave the armed liberation struggle yet another aspect of globalism, as they started their struggle from a state of statelessness. Foco-style guerrilla warfare was geographically limited in practice, although it was global in its ideology and support network. It was aimed at fighting a country's government on its own soil. Especially if successful, revolutionaries would be more concerned with state-building in their own country, rather than pursuing the revolution globally.[6] Palestinian fighters, however, deployed the international political and underground militant networks with a new set of tactics, such as airplane hijacking, attacking Israeli athletes in the Olympic games, and targeting political leaders around the globe, that brought non-state actors to the foreground of international relations.[7]

Iranian opposition was linked to this global space through two interconnected channels. Similar to other guerrilla organizations across the world, they were, for the most part, avidly consuming Latin American models through ideological writings, warfare manuals, and historical narratives.[8] Iranian activists' actual connection to global guerrillas, however, was mainly through their mediated or direct ties with guerrilla organizations in the Middle East. The Mojahedin-e Khalq Organization (MKO) as well as other leftist guerrilla groups in Iran had established connections to Palestinian guerrilla camps in the region, sending individuals for training starting in the late1960s.[9]

Individuals who were to become influential IRGC associates had multiple direct and indirect ties to organized guerrilla groups in Iran and the Middle East, albeit on a smaller scale. A number of them had gone through guerrilla training in various camps in Lebanon and Syria in the month leading to the Iranian Revolution, and a few like Mohammad Montazeri had become professional guerrillas who

---

[6] See ibid.   [7] Chamberlin, *Global Offensive.*
[8] Peyman Vahabzadeh, *A Guerrilla Odyssey: Modernization, Secularism, Democracy, and the Fadai Period of National Liberation in Iran, 1971–1979* (Syracuse, NY: Syracuse University Press, 2010); Maziar Behrooz, *Rebels with a Cause: The Failure of the Left in Iran* (New York: I.B. Tauris, 1999); Ervand Abrahamian, "The Guerrilla Movement in Iran, 1963–1977," *MERIP Reports* 86 (1980): 3–15; see also Chapter 5.
[9] Naghmeh Sohrabi, "Remembering the Palestine Group: Global Activism, Friendship, and the Iranian Revolution," *International Journal of Middle East Studies* 51:2 (2019): 281–300.

helped train others. Mostafa Chamran, who was never officially a Guard but cooperated with the IRGC closely, was another pivot in Islamist guerrillas' activity. In addition, some Islamist activists who had not left Iran embarked on armed activity across the country, modeling their groups' agenda and structure after that of the MKO. Leaders of these small and short-lived groups were former MKO members who had left after its turn from Islamist-Marxism to a strictly Marxist ideology in 1975. Members of these groups, who later participated in the formation of the IRGC, were exposed to the transnational armed resistance program only indirectly, through the MKO.

These individuals were embedded in several overlapping networks of Iranian activists, operating simultaneously outside of Iran. Analyzed in conjunction, these networks paint a picture of the future Guards' encounters with the global ideology and practice of guerrilla warfare. These included the clerics around Khomeini while he was in exile, especially during the time he resided in Najaf (1965–1978); Chamran and Musa Sadr's network of civil and armed resistance based in Lebanon; and Montazeri's ties with multiple guerrilla groups in the region and Iranian activists he trained.

Below I will introduce these overlapping networks and the context and resources they provided for individuals who later participated in creating the IRGC. Two other expansive clusters of Iranian activists were thriving in the same timeframe – that is, the extraterritorial network of leftist and Muslim-Marxist organizations mentioned above, and that of religious-nationalists connected to the Liberation Movement of Iran. A full discussion of either of these clusters is beyond the scope of this chapter. Instead, I will focus on future Guards' occasional interactions with individuals in these networks. I will then review the particular experience future Guards took from their encounters with guerrilla warfare as a global phenomenon, to then analyze how it was incorporated in the formation of a state militia.

The Transnational Clerical Network

The clerical network around Ayatollah Khomeini was the point of convergence for the group of individuals this chapter is concerned with – that is, Islamist or pro-Islamist activists who chose armed resistance as their revolutionary method. In 1965, Khomeini traveled from Turkey, where he had been in exile slightly short of a year, to Iraq.

Upon arrival in the city of Najaf, he was immediately settled in the transnational network of Shia clergy and seminary students there. Iranian clerics had long lived, studied, taught, and even established seminaries in Najaf, while maintaining a close relationship with their peers in Iran. Even though his radical politics was not embraced by other prominent ulama in Najaf, Khomeini was still at home as a respected cleric: he took up the conventional senior roles of teaching, leading prayers, and paying alms to students, shortly after arrival.[10]

Before addressing this network's connection to guerrillas, it is important to lay out the general structure of resistance within it, as it was partially transported to postrevolutionary entities such as the IRGC. The clerical community and nonclerical individuals connected to it were reluctant to delineate a specific organization around their collectivity. Whereas other political and military opposition groups in the Middle East, such as the Muslim Brotherhood, the Palestine Liberation Organization (PLO), and Fatah, all declared titles, statutes, and relatively clear leadership structures and recruitment patterns, the Iranian clerical network avoided such measures to a large extent. Activists close to Khomeini remember his disapproval of distinguishing activists based on group membership.[11] He was of the opinion that operating under specific flags defeated the purpose of a "true Islamic grassroots movement."[12] A long history of informal collective work in Iranian Shia communities concurred with this approach. For instance, within neighborhood communities, mosques and informal religious groups called *hay'at*s had long served as non-state, grassroots centers for upholding Shia rituals and addressing community needs. With some modifications, such communities were widely deployed during the revolutionary movement to organize resistance.[13]

---

[10] Abdorrahim Abazari, *Dar vadi-ye eshgh: Khaterat-e hojjat-ol-eslam seyyed Taqi Musavi Dorche'i* (Tehran: Oruj, 1389/2010), 164–167; Ali Araghchi, *Partov-e aftab: Khaterat-e hazrat-e ayatollah haj sheykh Ali Araghchi* (Tehran: Oruj, 1389/2010), 274–275.

[11] For instance, see Seyyed Mohammad Kimiafar, *Khaterat-e Habibollah Askarowladi* (Tehran: Markaz-e Asnad-e Enqelab-e Eslami, 1391/2012), 78; and Abdorrazagh Ahvazi, *Emam Khomeini be ravayat-e ayatollah Hashemi Rafsanjani* (Tehran: Oruj, 1385/2006).

[12] Kimiafar, *Askarowladi*.

[13] See Arang Keshavarzian, "Regime Loyalty and Bazari Representations under the Islamic Republic of Iran: Dilemmas of the Society of Islamic Coalition," *International Journal of Middle East Studies* 41 (2009): 225–246.

The clerical hub in Najaf was no exception. A seminary student at the time recalls that the only thing that structured people around Khomeini was their different levels of commitment to revolutionary activism. "Fifteen to twenty people carried most of the burden of resistance activities," he contends, which consisted of "transcribing [Khomeini's lecture] cassettes, and rewriting, editing, printing, and distributing them."[14] He describes these individuals as those who "were already revolutionaries, and met with the Imam and took care of important matters."[15] Others were more reluctant to participate directly, although they supported the cause; and yet others disputed the very idea of a revolutionary movement. Groups emerged *naturally* along these lines – boundaries, missions, and organizational distribution of roles were not explicitly discussed and spelled out.

The clerical network and informal clusters that had emerged out of it were not actively pursuing armed resistance. Khomeini never endorsed armed struggle directly, whether it was pursued by congenial Islamist groups (such as the assassination of the shah's prime minister in 1965, supported by the Islamic Coalition Organization), or the sustained campaigns led by the MKO.[16] A few *individuals* within the clerical network, however, pursued this agenda actively. As I will describe below, the clerical network provided a variety of forms of social capital for such individuals, and occasionally provided financial resources for them as well.

Iranian Islamist Guerrillas Abroad: Montazeri and Chamran

The most prominent individual cleric that pursued guerrilla activism was Mohammad Montazeri. He was a known anti-shah cleric in Iran in the early 1960s and had been imprisoned along with his father, the influential Ayatollah Hosseyn-Ali Montazeri, in the early 1960s. After his release, he was facing immense pressure from the SAVAK (National Organization for Security and Intelligence under the shah) in Iran. He fled to Pakistan in the early 1970s and traveled to Afghanistan, Iraq,

[14] Mo'asseseh-ye Tanzim va Nashr-e Asar-e Emam Khomeini [hereafter, Mo'asseseh], *Khaterat-e hojjat-ol-eslam Mohammad Hasan Akhtari* (Tehran: Oruj, 1392/2013), 37.
[15] Ibid., 36.
[16] For instance, see Hashemi-Rafsanjani's recollections of Khomeini's stance in Ahvazi, *Rafsanjani*, 44–45.

Syria, and Lebanon.[17] During this time, he established ties with seminary students across the region spreading awareness about the resistance movement in Iran.[18] He traveled rather frequently to Europe as well, meeting with "activists and revolutionaries" and "exchanging ideas with them."[19] In fact, this was not Montazeri's first experience in international networking. An activist cleric in Najaf recalls that around 1960, when clerics in Iran were eagerly following Algeria's independence struggle, Montazeri transferred the financial aid procured by influential clerics to Algerian independence fighters.[20] Arriving in Najaf in early 1970s, and after spending a year in prison on the charge of crossing the border illegally, Montazeri presented himself to the clerical network there.[21] Driven by his experience and ambition, he quickly became one of the central figures in organizing armed opposition in support of Khomeini.

His close companions confessed to SAVAK that he had close contacts and cooperated with many resistance organizations – the Liberation Movement of Iran (led by religious-nationalists who adopted a moderate reformist approach), Hezb-e Melal-e Eslami (Islamic Nations Party, a short-lived Islamist organization that pursued armed resistance in Iran), and the MKO before its turn to Marxist ideology.[22] A report written for SAVAK by an agent in Iraq went as far as claiming that Montazeri led all of the Muslim activists who separated from the MKO. The report stated that "about 2,500 individuals" from the strictly Muslim faction of the MKO, who were "caught in a state of aimlessness" after leaving the organization, left the country and contacted Montazeri.[23] It continued to say that "in order to prevent further disintegration of the group," Montazeri "helps them abundantly and orders them to go to other countries ... and stay connected to him to be sent back to Iran when the time comes." It is

---

[17] Javad Mansuri, *Tarikh-e shafahi-ye ta'sis-e sepah-e pasdaran-e enqelab-e eslami* (Tehran: Markaz-e Asnad-e Enqelab-e Eslami, 1393/2014), 45.

[18] Mo'asseseh, *Khaterat-e hojjat-ol-eslam Esma'il Ferdowsipur* (Tehran: Oruj, 1389/2010), 184.

[19] Ibid., 186.   [20] Abazari, *Dar vadi-ye eshgh*, 107.

[21] Mo'asseseh, *Ferdowsipur*, 184.

[22] Markaz-e Barrasi-ye Asnad-e Tarikhi [hereafter, Markaz], *Shahid hojjat-ol-eslam Mohammad Montazeri, Yaran-e Emam be revayat-e asnad-e SAVAK*, jeld-e 37 (Tehran: Markaz-e Barrasi-ye Asnad-e Tarikhi-ye Vezarat-e Ettela'at, 1385/2006), 89, 93.

[23] Ibid., 304.

hard to imagine that Montazeri's leadership was this far-reaching in reality, and there is no other evidence to corroborate this claim. What can be confirmed by a multitude of individual instances is that he did have strong ties with the MKO before the ideological split and with some of its deserters afterward.[24]

In line with the spirit of organized guerrilla groups around the globe, Montazeri was a committed and proactive planner – a characteristic that became the IRGC's breaking point from him and classic guerrilla organizations in general. According to SAVAK records, he was very close to Khomeini and acquired a lot of financial support from the clerical network.[25] His radical independence and his programmatic approach are observable in the liberty he took to disregard Khomeini's recommendations, despite this connection. For instance, in organizing a sit-in in Paris, arranged in collaboration with other activist groups, Montazeri mobilized the Shia network's resources in a way not authorized by Khomeini. One of the goals of the sit-in was to protest the imprisonment of a few clerics – including Ayatollah Montazeri – in Iran. Mohammad Montazeri wanted as many clerics to be there as possible to signal the strength of the clerical community's opposition to the shah. He asked a young cleric in Khomeini's circle to seek his approval for a number of Najaf clerics to travel to Paris. Khomeini disapproved. Montazeri, therefore, activated his plan B: he asked the young cleric to clandestinely procure as many clerical robes and turbans as he could. Montazeri then dressed lay activists at the sit-in as clerics.[26] Marzieh Hadidchi, a guerrilla fighter who worked closely with Montazeri, remembers her surprise at seeing a fellow fighter dressed as a cleric at the sit-in.[27]

Montazeri's work in providing Iranian activists with guerrilla training was largely facilitated in turn by Chamran and Sadr. Chamran is known for holding military offices in postrevolutionary Iran, including the Ministry of Defense and leadership of the Irregular Warfare Unit in the Iran-Iraq War, for the short stretch of time before he was killed in action in 1981. In the preceding decades, he was a revolutionary with a passion for irregular warfare and the goal of assisting repressed Muslim populations in the region. To this end he

[24] For instance, see the case of Hossein Elmi (alias Emla'i) in ibid., 298.
[25] Ibid., 270.   [26] Mo'asseseh, *Ferdowsipur.*
[27] Alieh Shafi'i, *Parvaz ba noor: Do revayat az zendegi-ye khanom-e Marzieh Hadidchi (Dabbagh)* (Tehran: Oruj, 1385/2006), 48.

had established the arguably most extensive involvement with non-Iranian guerrilla organizations. He was attracted to the Liberation Movement of Iran in college in the 1950s, and actively pursued the movement's agenda when he traveled to the US to continue his studies.

A few years after he earned a PhD in physics at UC Berkeley, opposition against the shah reached one of its peaks in Iran and Chamran decided to pursue guerrilla training in support of the movements in Iran and the rest of the Middle East. He traveled to Egypt in 1964 and sought guerrilla training there for two years. According to a Ministry of Intelligence publication the trip was arranged through two prominent revolutionaries and their international contacts: Ali Shariati and his connection with Algerian revolutionaries, and Ayatollah Taleqani and his ties with Gamal Nasser.[28] In 1972 Chamran joined Sadr, the Iranian cleric who led an extensive pro-Shia movement in Lebanon, and became his close ally in expanding the movement, Harakat al-Mahrumin. In 1975, Sadr and Chamran founded the movement's armed wing in Lebanon, Amal.

Chamran's main focus in Lebanon was to train, organize, and command Lebanese military and nonmilitary institutions, but he was also a known point of contact for Iranians who wanted to leave the country for Palestinian camps in the region. He became an independent broker among many Iranian groups and organizations in their pursuit of revolutionary activism. He held his strong affinity with the Liberation Movement, for instance, prominently through his close friendship with Sadr's nephew, Sadeq Tabatabai. The latter, who had familial ties to Khomeini as well, was also Chamran's main point of contact with Khomeini and the clerical circle in Najaf and later Paris. Chamran's correspondences with Tabatabai reveal his "strength as a weak tie" – an individual with connections to multiple groups but with no strong affiliation with any one of them.[29] Chamran occasionally wrote to Tabatabai about the movement in Iran. In one letter, for instance, he shows his concern for and involvement with activists of other circles, such as Ahmad Nafari, a close companion of Montazeri:

---

[28] Markaz, *Shahid-e sarafraz doktor Mostafa Chamran, yaran-e emam be revayat-e asnad-e SAVAK, jeld-e 11* (Tehran: Markaz-e Barrasi-ye Asnad-e Tarikhi-ye Vezarat-e Ettela'at, 1378/1999), 8.

[29] Mark Granovetter, "Strength of Weak Ties," *American Journal of Sociology* 78:6 (1973): 1360–1380.

"Mr. Nafari is now free and in Syria, soon returning to Lebanon. Do not take further action with regard to his case."[30]

Although Chamran was not closely associated with the Islamists, who eventually took over the formation of the IRGC, the apparatus that he and Sadr had established and the connections they maintained with Fatah, although sometimes troubled by the dynamics of the Lebanese Civil War, facilitated Montazeri's activities.[31] SAVAK reports show that Montazeri and Chamran cooperated on multiple levels. One report finds, for instance, that an activist is being trained for printing the movement's declarations and books "following a recommendation from [Montazeri] and under Chamran's supervision."[32] Another report finds that Montazeri and others are "receiving monthly payments from Musa Sadr's establishment."[33] There is also a meaningful overlap of individuals who appear in SAVAK reports documenting the activities of Montazeri and Chamran, separately. The two guerrillas' collaboration was never documented in its full extent, and it is not clear whether Montazeri had direct ties to Fatah independently of Chamran, either.[34] Given the breath of Chamran's engagement in guerrilla training and warfare, the frequency of Montazeri's contacts with him, and the other lines of anti-shah activity that kept Montazeri busy, it is safe to assume that Chamran, Sadr, and Amal laid the groundwork for Montazeri to train individual Iranian activists in international camps. The clerical network that Montazeri was a part of and the Sadrist network it overlapped with also mobilized financial and social capital in support of this endeavor. In addition to providing funds, the network helped facilitate smuggling activists out of Iran, occasionally dealt with Iraqi police, and provided housing

---

[30] Ali Hojjati-Kermani, *Lobnan be revayat-e emam Musa Sadr va doktor Chamran* (Tehran: Ghalam, 1364/1985), 182.

[31] Sadeq Tabatabai's narrative suggests that under the influence of another Iranian guerrilla fighter, Jalaleddin Farsi, Montazeri did not think highly of Sadr and Chamran, seeing them as rivals in Lebanon. Chamran had to spend "hours talking to Montazeri ... to enlighten him" (Sadeq Tabatabai, *Khaterat-e siyasi-ejtema'i-ye doktor Sadeq Tabatabai*, 3 vols. (Tehran: Oruj, 1387/2008), 2:171–172). According to this account, Sadr still strongly supported both Montazeri's and Farsi's efforts.

[32] Markaz, *Mohammad Montazeri*, 276.   [33] Ibid., 227.

[34] Documents procured by SAVAK just before Montazeri fled Iran, for instance, show that he had already been in touch with Fatah (ibid., 290). But it is not clear how the connection was established.

for clerical activists in Najaf seminaries.[35] The result was particular encounters between Islamist activists that were later affiliated with the IRGC and guerrilla organizations within the global network of liberation fighters. The future Guards' transnational relationships not only crossed national boundaries but bridged political fault lines that are often forgotten or denied after the 1979 revolution, as I will discuss below.

Islamists and Global Guerrillas: Ideas and Practices

A core group of activists, including at least one simultaneously affiliated with the MKO, worked around Montazeri in Iraq, Syria, and Lebanon to facilitate the travel and training of others in Iran. According to one of the activists, training consisted of a fifteen-day introductory phase, followed by a "gruesome" three-month period of training, after which trainees were sent to Palestinian front lines in South Lebanon "to gain practical experience by fighting Israeili forces."[36] According to another activist, in Palestinian camps, they underwent an intensive month-long military training. They learned to work with handguns, rifles, and heavier equipment such as rocket launchers, built up their physical strength and agility, practiced reacting to night raids and ambushes, and learned how to make explosive devices.[37]

From the core group around Montazeri, Marzeih Hadidchi and Mohammad Gharazi transitioned to the IRGC, after the 1979 revolution. Hadidchi, perhaps the only well-known female guerrilla within the Islamist organizations, had worked with Montazeri when they were both in Iran,[38] and reconnected with him when she traveled to England to flee SAVAK, in 1972. After undergoing initial training in PLO camps in Lebanon and Syria, she spent more than six months

---

[35] Abazari, *Dar vadi-ye eshgh*; Mo'asseseh, *Gushe'i az khaterat-e hojjat-ol-eslam seyyed Mahmud Doa'i* (Tehran: Oruj, 1387/2008); Majid Najafpur, *Az jonub-e Lobnan ta jonub-e Iran: Khaterat-e sardar seyyed Rahim Safavi* (Tehran: Markaz-e Asnad-e Enqelab-e Eslami, 1383/2004).

[36] Reza Ra'isi, *Khahar Tahereh: Khaterat-e khanom-e Marzieh Hadidchi (Dabbagh)* (Tehran: Oruj, 1392/2013), 86.

[37] Sa'id Fakhrzadeh, *Khaterat-e Ali Jannati* (Tehran: Markaz-e Asnad-e Enqelab-e Eslami, 1381/2002), 102.

[38] Mohsen Kazemi, *Khaterat-e Marzieh Hadidchi (Dabbagh)* (Tehran: Sureh Mehr, 1393/2014), 112.

among Palestinian fighters in southern Lebanon, participating in raids against Israeli forces, and became one of the trainers herself. She was active on the margins of the negotiations leading to the formation of the IRGC, and was appointed as a regional IRGC commander shortly after. Mohammad Gharazi was another future Guard who had worked closely with Montazeri outside of Iran. He participated in the early endeavor for the formation of the IRGC,[39] but later drifted away from military activity and served in several political offices in the Islamic Repulic. According to some of the Iranian activists trained under Montazeri's group, Gharazi was in charge of indoctrinating the trainees.[40]

The most prominent IRGC commander who was trained for guerrilla warfare with Montazeri's help is Major General Yahya (Rahim) Safavi – former IRGC commander in chief (1997–2007) and an influential figure throughout its history. In 1978, he decided to leave Iran to both evade SAVAK scrutiny and train for taking up arms against the Pahlavi government. At the time, the Islamist circles were apprehensive of other branches of activism outside Iran. Safavi went to Ayatollah Meshkini, an established religious figure who had demonstrated allegiance to Khomeini's cause, to acquire his endorsement for his decision:

To embark upon [the departure], I went to Qom to see Ayatollah Meshkini, explained the situation to him, and asked for his advice. He asked, "Where do you plan to go and who is your contact?" I responded that I wanted to go to either Syria or Lebanon and my contact was Mohammad Montazeri. Ayatollah Meshkini approved and said, "If he's your contact point, then go."[41]

With the help of revolutionary activists, Safavi smuggled into Syria through Iraq and, after a month of being stranded in Damascus, was finally approached by Gharazi. He then started training along with a few other Islamist activists who had found their way to Damascus, in "one of the Palestinian camps in Syria."[42]

Living in the international community of guerrillas all training together was a defining experience for Islamist activists. It exposed them to a wide range of ideologies and practices that they were not fully comfortable with. The ideological divide between Islamists, on

---

[39] Mansuri, *Tarikh-e shafahi*.   [40] Fakhrzadeh, *Jannati*; Najafpur, *Safavi*.
[41] Najafpur, *Safavi*, 86.   [42] Ibid., 94.

the one hand, and the internationalists of a leftist persuasion, on the other, was palpable in these training periods, both in daily practices and in explicit discussions. The 1975 ideological break within the MKO had turned a great many of the Islamists against them. Gharazi was once sympathetic to the MKO and was closely working with Do'ayi, a former MKO member, and favorably disposed to them even in 1978. Nevertheless, Safavi recalls that he used the MKO as a prime example of how "diluted" Islam is not to be trusted as a resistance ideology.[43]

Transnational life as a guerrilla presented young Muslim activists with daily practical challenges as well. Commitment to religious rituals and practices, for instance, was an explicit sign of belonging or otherness for the Islamists in the camps. Safavi remembers that the practice of saying daily prayers brought him and his companion closer to a particular trainer in the camp:

Ahmad Faza'eli and I had a very friendly relationship with our instructor during training, and the reason was that the three of us said prayers. . . . in this camp, none of the Lebanese and Syrian guerrillas said prayers; they did not care about it.[44]

When Safavi and Faza'eli joined Fatah during the Lebanese Civil War, they experienced the same disappointment:

None of the Fatah members said prayers; when we confronted them, they responded, "We will say prayers in Jerusalem when we conquer it" . . . in addition, gender segregation was not observed; men would shake hands with women and did not have a problem with it.[45]

This source of friction overlapped with the ideological one and was tightly connected in the Islamists' minds. Safavi recalls their ideological debates with a dozen "Marxist-Leninist" Palestinian fighters in the camp:

No matter how much Ahmad Faza'eli and I debated with them and reasoned based on the Qur'an, that the only path to nations' and peoples' salvation, independence, and dignity, and the only path to emancipating Jerusalem, was to rely on God, the Qur'an, and religious doctrines, it did not make a difference. They never agreed with us and sufficed to their leftist resistance doctrines.[46]

---

[43] Ibid., 94–95.   [44] Ibid., 97.   [45] Ibid., 99–100.   [46] Ibid., 100.

The indoctrination sessions and the ideological and orthopraxical frictions constituted only one part of the Islamists' experience. Another long-lasting influence of the encounter was due to the fact that for many Islamist activists, training in camps and operating as part of a guerrilla network was their first exposure to organized, radical resistance. In addition to the well-programmed and intensive life in camps, the experience of proactive organizational work was new and rather unpleasant to the few Guards-to-be who were exposed to it. For instance, what Hadidchi recalls of her protracted cooperation with Montazeri corroborates what the latter's own actions reveal about his approach to resistance. She remembers Montazeri's activism to have two key characteristics. First, he was a "radical revolutionary" with a global mindset:

His thoughts knew no borders; he thought globally. He worked for the freedom of all subjugated peoples and especially for the dignity of the Islamic *umma*.[47]

Hadidchi also emphasizes that he "strongly believed in systematic, organizational work."[48] Months after Hadidchi had cut her communication with her family in Iran, her husband traveled to Lebanon and found her through Sadr's office. While Sadr's affiliates were still looking for Montazeri to ask if they should give away Hadidchi's location to this man, she learned about the situation and met with her husband. Montazeri, furious that she had risked the group's safety, punished her in the next few days by ordering her to wait in a hotel room in Damascus for a mission. There was no mission awaiting her. Rather, Montazeri abandoned her in the hotel room without sustenance, which led to her passing out from hunger. The rest of the group confronted Montazeri about this radical measure, but, according to Hadidchi, he was of the mindset that "every line of work requires its own sacrifices."

This instance is surely an exaggerated take on following principles of organizational work. But even on a more moderate level, Islamists had a penchant for seeing any programmatic approach and commitment to organizational principles as contradictory to the "natural" order of the circles they were used to. As I will elaborate in the next section, Montazeri's initial involvement and later exclusion from the IRGC,

---

[47] Ibid., 113. [48] Ibid., 112.

as well as Chamran's distanced involvement with it, were partially a result of this mismatch, especially after the revolution eradicated the need for well-planned underground activities.

Through key individuals such as Chamran and Montazeri, and embedded within the transnational clerical network, a few future Guards were exposed to the global scene of armed resistance. They experienced disciplined guerrilla training, struggled with combat ideologies that they felt alienated from, and became weathered in actual irregular warfare during the Lebanese Civil War. The unexpectedly quick tumbling of the Pahlavi apparatus, however, rendered their guerrilla expertise and their revolutionary ethos irrelevant. It had to be transformed and repurposed if it were to be preserved at all.

The Rise of the IRGC as a Revolutionary State Militia

In the initial endeavor to establish a state militia, soon to be named the Islamic Revolutionary Guards Corps, three organizational mindsets clashed – the liberationist, global mindset imported by the likes of Montazeri, the penchant for "natural," and organizationally limited order inherited from the clerical circles, and the provisional government's technocratic agenda of unifying mini-militias that had formed during the revolutionary movement. In particular, the provisional government run by moderate politicians and led by Mehdi Bazargan (a prominent member of the liberal-nationalist Liberation Movement of Iran) pushed for a quick transition from revolutionary chaos to routine governance. Transitional institutions such as the Revolutionary Council, led by clerics close to Khomeini, preserved a degree of authority parallel, and often superior, to that of the provisional government, whereby they occasionally granted legitimacy to revolutionary radicalism. Formation of the IRGC was entangled in this parallelism. The structure that emerged out of the clashes among existing militias, political debates, engagement in urban unrest, and participation in repression of ethnic insurgencies embodied not only the IRGC's connections to global armed resistance, but its divergences from it, and the new directions it took irregular armed resistance.

In the months preceding February 1979, some of the Islamist activists who had gained direct and indirect experience of guerrilla organization and training continued their activities within small militias that mushroomed in Iran. These militias were not immediately dismantled after the revolution. In the demise of the police and the regular army, these groups claimed to be the true "guardians" of the revolution, independently of one another. The abundance of such grassroots formations was one of the reasons the provisional government proposed a state-sponsored guardian corps. As a result, some of these paramilitaries served as the nuclei of the eventual IRGC, becoming a channel for the activists' global encounters and their interpretations to penetrate into the official state militia.

Montazeri was behind one of these militias. Upon returning to Iran after the fall of the shah, he settled a group of the trained activists in a prerevolutionary police station in Tehran and pronounced PASA (acronym for Pasdaran-e Enqelab-e Eslami [Guardians of the Islamic Revolution]) as the militia guarding the revolution. A few army officers, including Kolahduz, who later became the deputy chief in the first IRGC command council, and other non-guerrilla activists such as the IRGC's first commander in chief, Javad Mansuri, joined Montazeri in the effort to organize the paramilitary unit. One of these army officers, who was a defector from the shah's Imperial Guard as well, recalls the process:

The revolution succeeded. Kolahduz and I and other army officers known [for their revolutionary commitment] went to the Joint Staff to purge, rebuild, and reorganize the new army. . . . we had only been there for a few days when Kolahduz told me to go help with establishing a new organization. It must have been February 16 or 17... we went to [a prerevolutionary police station] . . . it had been delegated to Mohammad Montazeri. He had somehow found a few Imperial Guard officers who were trustworthy and gathered them there to help with training new recruits . . . that was the first nucleus of the IRGC's training program.[49]

Some sources contend that this group enjoyed the support of a few prominent Islamist members of the Revolutionary Council such as Ayatollah Beheshti,[50] who were also sympathetic to Montazeri's activities outside of Iran. By the time the provisional government announced the initiation of a transitional militia to restrain order and absorb the various grassroots militias on the ground, Montazeri's guardian group, PASA, had developed far enough to issue IDs, send

---

[49] Interview with author, 2017.
[50] Ahmad Rashidi, *Obur az shatt-e shab: Khaterat-e Alimohammad Besharati* (Tehran: Markaz-e Asnad-e Enqelab-e Eslami, 1383/2004), 227.

individuals on semiofficial missions, and make announcements in the press to make itself known to the public.[51]

Abbas Aghazamani, more commonly recognized with his nom de guerre Abusharif, had erected another such militia. Prior to the revolution he had joined the short-lived Hezb-e Melal-e Eslami, which pursued the goal of taking up arms against the Pahlavi government. After being released from prison in the early 1970s, he traveled to Lebanon and spent one year with Fatah guerrillas – where he adopted his famous alias. Upon his return to Iran close to February 1979, he claimed a prerevolutionary army barrack, recruited members, and trained them in irregular warfare. The group called themselves the "Guardians of the Revolution" (Pasdaran-e Enqelab) and, according to an interview with Abusharif, was active in containing early insurgencies around the country.[52] Many activists, including Abusharif himself and Abbas Duzduzani – who did not have guerrilla training, but was Abusharif's fellow in the Hezb-e Melal-e Eslami – found their way to early IRGC command councils from this group.

The most enduring group that inherited global guerrilla experience and later contributed to the formation of the IRGC was the Mojahedin-e Enqelab Organization (MEO). The MEO was established after the revolution, when a few small Islamist militias joined forces. A few of the devoted Shia members who broke apart from the MKO after the ideological schism had established small armed groups in Iran between 1976 and 1978, and opted for a similar guerrilla structure around a "purely" Islamist ideology. Ommat-e Vahedeh, Falah, Saf, Mansurun, and Movahhedin were among the small formations that imitated the MKO in structure and practice.[53] These militant Islamist groups' recruitment and armed activity remained very limited. In addition to groups initiated by former Mojaheds, a few other Islamist groups and clusters formed with no direct link to the MKO or guerrilla activities in other contexts, but still resembled such organizations' cell-structured militia format. These emerged either from within of existing religious communities such as Shia mourning congregations, or by individuals who worked with student associations outside of Iran.[54]

---

[51] Author's interview with a PASA member, 2017.
[52] Raja News interview with Abusharif, https://bit.ly/31DdcRM.
[53] Jalil Amjadi, *Tarikh-e shafahi-ye goruh-ha-ye mobarez-e haftganeh-ye mosalman* (Tehran: Markaz-e Asnad-e Enqelab-e Eslami, 1383/2004), 60–70.
[54] Ibid.

In both cases, they provided a few individuals in their groups with limited guerrilla training, such as building and planting explosives in urban settings.

Together, these seven groups merged to form the MEO, which was established in March 1979. Mohsen Reza'i, a young revolutionary who would later take the IRGC command during the war with Iraq, was among the leaders of the MEO. He was never a member of the MKO, nor had he been trained for guerilla warfare outside of Iran. He had learned about guerrilla operations from an experienced MKO member and undertook small operations such as bombing a statue of the shah in Ahvaz, within Mansurun (one of the nuclei of the MEO). When other MEO leaders started to prioritize political activity over armed activity against "counterrevolutionaries," Reza'i decided to join the IRGC instead.

It is interesting to note that Chamran did not care to establish an independent militia upon his return to Iran, most likely because he found the ongoing struggle for Palestine and the underprivileged population of South Lebanon to be a more pressing concern, compared to the already achieved goal of regime change in Iran.[55] Chamran recalled that when armed conflict surged a few days before the collapse of the Pahlavi government, he prepared to transport 500 Amal fighters to Iran through Syria. With the unexpectedly rapid success of the revolution, however, the opportunity did not arise "for these fighters, stars in battle and especially in guerrilla battles, to go to Tehran to fight alongside their Iranian brothers,"[56] as Chamran put it. Although Chamran's military expertise was consulted when the Kurdish conflict started, he neither led an organization, nor was officially appointed in the government until the war with Iraq started in September 1980.[57]

Exacerbating the cacophony of revolutionary guardianship were the semi-independent Komitehs: neighborhood-based, lightly armed units

---

[55] From a series of public speeches that Chamran delivered after returning to Iran, it appears that he was still predominantly occupied with the Lebanese war and the transnational aspect of the Iranian Revolution. See Mostafa Chamran, *Lobnan* (Tehran: Bonyad-e Shahid Chamran, 1362/1983), 20.

[56] Markaz, *Chamran*, 16.

[57] With the start of the war, Chamran trained a small group of guerrillas under the Irregular Warfare Headquarters. As the commander of this group he cooperated closely with the IRGC.

that had acquired an aura of legitimacy as revolutionary law enforcement centers. The provisional government embarked on incorporating
these militias and the many Komitehs into a state militia, both to create
a loyal armed unit for the time of transition, and to bring the independent, sometimes rogue units under central control. On February 21,
only ten days after officially assuming power, the provisional government announced its decision to establish a national guard,[58] alterna-
tively called the IRGC. As Bazargan stated in an interview on the same
day, it was proposed as a temporary replacement for the unpopular
and strained police and armed forces only until they were restored and
restaffed with reliable personnel.[59]

A group consisting of liberal-nationalists of the provisional government commenced on February 24 to discuss the foundation of this
guardian corps. Although Islamists of the Revolutionary Council were
aware of this development, they were not invited by the Bazargan-led
government to help establish the militia. Lahooti, a later-disputed
clerical figure, was present in the founding council as Khomeini's
representative, but clerics of the Revolutionary Council believed there
were reasons not to trust him: they believed his connections with the
nationalists and the MKO were too strong, and that they would easily
influence him.

On February 24, prominent religious figures of the Revolutionary
Council who had learned about the government's plan sent a trusted
fellow to the meeting. The unofficial representative, Mohsen
Rafighdust, recalls the rather arbitrary but consequential process of
his involvement:

Ayatollahs Beheshti and Motahari saw me at Refah School that day and said,
"Haj Mohsen, the Imam just gave a decree to Mr. Lahooti to establish a
guards corps under the government's supervision. It'd be good that you be
part of this corps as well." ... Although I preferred to join the Islamic
Republic Party's leadership, I obeyed and went straight to [the meeting
location]. I entered the room and saw a bunch of gentlemen ... I said,
"Greetings; I'm here on the Revolutionary Council's behalf." Then I asked,
"Is the guards corps supposed to be established here?" They said yes. I took a

---

[58] Interview with Keyhan, quoted in Mansuri, *Tarikh-e shafahi*, 47.
[59] March 5, 1979, interview with Resalat, quoted in Sepah-e Pasdaran-e Enqelab-e
Eslami [hereafter, Sepah], *Ruzshomar-e jang-e Iran va Iraq: Peydayesh-e nezam-
e jadid* (Tehran: Markaz-e Motale'at va Tahqiqat-e Jang, 1373/1994), 186.

piece of paper and wrote on it: "In the Name of God. The Islamic Revolutionary Guards Corps is hereby established. Members are as follows: (1) Mohsen Rafighdust." Others added their names afterward.[60]

The IRGC was officially born and announced to the public after this meeting. In various interviews, officials of the provisional government introduced the IRGC as a transitional force in charge of domestic security, which would be absorbing smaller groups as well as unaffiliated volunteers. At the same time, they emphasized the necessity of professionalization by introducing salaries, systematic training, IDs, and uniforms.[61]

An Insurgent State Militia

The first sign of the (eventual) IRGC's reinterpretation of the global encounters appeared in the dispute over central control. The independent militias were unanimously reluctant to forego their autonomy and submit to government control. While the irregularity of the guerrilla organizations is intended to provide them the flexibility to avoid detection and repression and fight on unequal battlefields, the IRGC would not be facing such a problem as a postrevolutionary state militia. Nevertheless, militia leaders were reluctant to submit to bureaucratic authority. Activists of the grassroots militias who had experienced armed revolutionary resistance within a global context were unwilling to give away their revolutionary ethos, even though they were no longer fighting a sovereign government.

Therefore, instead of becoming *the* state militia, the *government's* IRGC became one among many contenders of the title. The independent guardian corps were flourishing under the government's nose. On the same day that the government announced the formation of IRGC, for instance, Montazeri's PASA published an announcement in the press, asking *pasdars* (guards) to *only* submit the acquired weapons and explosives to police stations if an official PASA representative was present.[62] Weeks later, there were still reports in the papers of "some

---

[60] Mohsen Rafighdust, *Baray-e tarikh miguyam: Khaterat-e Mohsen Rafighdust*, 2 vols. (Tehran: Sureh-ye Mehr, 1393/2014), 1:51–52.
[61] Press interviews with Mehdi Bazargan, Abbas Amir-Entezam, and Ebrahim Yazdi, reprinted in Sepah, *Ruzshomar*, 202ff.
[62] Ibid., 178.

guards" active throughout the country who were arresting prerevolutionary politicians and breaking into suspicious houses without
warrants.[63]

It was only the promise that the IRGC would operate under the
Revolutionary Council and not the prime minister that softened independent commanders. Clerics of the Revolutionary Council arranged
multiple protracted meetings among select members of all groups,
including the government's IRGC, urging them to come to terms.[64] It
was finally Rafighdust, the Revolutionary Council's man imposed on
the government's IRGC, who encouraged the other groups to join in,
with the promise it would release itself from the provisional government's supervision. He remembers the odd interaction that led to the
unification as such:

I told [leaders of the other groups] that the people in charge of the Guards
now are not good enough to staff the corps. "Come join [the government's
IRGC] and we'll make a single corps. You are the right people, but don't
have the legitimacy. We have legitimacy, but don't have the right people." It
was taking too long. I had a pistol; I took it out and said jokingly, "If you
don't agree with this plan, I'll shoot you all and then kill myself!"[65]

The preference to move the IRGC to the Revolutionary Council was
not just a matter of political side-taking, but also a preference for the
latter's loose organizational constraints. As with imposing Rafighdust in
the first IRGC meeting as "the Council's Representative," personal and
informal decisions based on clerics' momentary insights could be made
in the name of the Revolutionary Council. The Revolutionary Council,
in other words, was not unlike the informal prerevolutionary circles of
the clerical resistance. Being accountable to the Revolutionary Council
instead of the technocratic government would make it easier for leaders
to reproduce and maintain the same structure in the IRGC itself.

This would be ideal for militia activists in particular, on two different levels. For those closer to the prerevolutionary clerical circles, it
was a chance to replicate the informal modus operandi they were used
to in prerevolutionary circles, as opposed to the military discipline

---

[63] March 15, 1979, report in Keyhan, reprinted in Sepah, *Ruzshomar*, 351.
[64] Ali Akbar Hashemi-Rafsanjani et al., *Hashemi-Rafsanjani: Karnameh va
khaterat-e sal-ha-ye 1357 va 1358, enqelab va piruzi* (Tehran: Dafter-e Nashr-e
Ma'aref-e Enqelab, 1383/2004), 261.
[65] Rafighdust, *Khaterat*, 53.

expected within a regular force. For leaders such as Abusharif and Montazeri who were more concerned with a liberationist agenda in accord with the global guerrilla movement, refraining from top-down control was tantamount to preserving a degree of their ideal revolutionary independence and the chance to pursue their transnational agenda. Even though the claim to revolutionary guerrilla ethos and identity was preserved, the latter group and their preferences were gradually pushed to the margins of the IRGC's universe, as I will explain in the next section.

The promise to put the IRGC under Revolutionary Council supervision was realized shortly after the independent groups agreed to unite under the official IRGC. A command council consisting of members of each of the previously independent militias selected Javad Mansuri as the provisional chief commander.[66] The refurbished IRGC issued its first declaration on April 22, 1979. The command council was thereby introduced, and it was declared that the IRGC would now take orders only from "the Imam" and the Revolutionary Council, not from the provisional government.[67] In this elaborate introductory statement, the IRGC's "goal" was declared as "guarding the Islamic Revolution in Iran and expanding it globally based on authentic Islamic ideology." Nevertheless, it soon became clear that this global agenda was not as seriously pursued as global guerrillas such as Montazeri and Chamran desired.

Global Guerrillas, How?

The second manifestation of the IRGC's unique take on their experience of global guerrillas appeared in Montazeri's approach to the unification and the way others treated his agenda. He had implemented his radical approach to resistance and his methodical commitment to an organized guerrilla force within the militia he led, PASA. Due to this mindset and with support from clerics and individual army officers, PASA was arguably the most organized militia on the ground, and pursued the most ambitiously global goals, as I will explain below.

---

[66] Mansuri, *Tarikh-e shafahi*, 145.
[67] Announcement reprinted in Sepah, *Sepah dar gozar-e enqelab*, 11 vols. (Tehran: IRGC Publications, 1389/2010), 6:205.

Montazeri and PASA were invited to the meetings for the unification of militias.[68] Despite the fact that he had the strongest background in irregular warfare and organizational work,[69] he was not assigned a role in the IRGC's command council. Surprisingly, it is never even suggested in the existing recollections that he was a candidate for taking command. In a later interview with the IRGC's weekly magazine, he was asked why he "stepped aside and did not take up any positions," suggesting that it was his choice not to, to which he vaguely responded that there were enough people to fill leadership positions.[70] Other individuals from PASA, including Mansuri and Kolahduz, started to work with the IRGC on the highest level of command. Montazeri, however, left the negotiations with discontent and continued to command a group of armed activists independently.[71]

There are no detailed records of the intensive talks leading to the formation of the new IRGC. But from Montazeri's subsequent comments it seems that his contempt had two sources, along the very lines of his specific approach to resistance. He believed that the IRGC was not systematically training military personnel,[72] and that the statebuilders in general were ignorant of the *global* revolutionary agenda. In line with the latter critique, Montazeri pursued his extraterritorial agenda independently, causing occasional frictions with the IRGC. In one such incident, Montazeri and a few others went to the verge of an armed confrontation with the IRGC and other state forces: In June 1979, he showed up at Tehran's international airport to leave for London, in his own words, to "meet with religious friends in Europe and elsewhere who had accompanied the Islamic Revolution from the beginning." Airport security stopped them, because two of them did not hold valid passports. Montazeri left and came back with twelve armed men, and ordered them to occupy the runway. They stayed in the airport until the morning after, engaging in heated arguments and fights with IRGC security guards present. Montazeri and his

---

[68] Mansuri, *Tarikh-e shafahi*, 113.
[69] From a strictly technical point of view, Chamran would perhaps be the most qualified person to command the new militia. According to most accounts, however, he did not participate in the negotiations. See note 55.
[70] Pasdar-e Enqelab interview with Montazeri, reprinted in Sepah, *Gozar*, 570.
[71] Author's interview with a retired army officer and member of PASA.
[72] An interview on October 1980 with Pasdar-e Enqelab, reprinted in Sepah, *Gozar*, 569.

companions were eventually allowed to leave, when Abusharif (IRGC chief of staff at the time) and Chamran intervened and guaranteed the validity of Montazeri's cause. After the incident, Montazeri explained:

I believe that this victory [i.e. the Iranian Revolution] belongs to all Muslims of the world and I believe that Islam is now mobilized for *"al-nas"* [the people] and for all the repressed of the world. I therefore do not see the need to hold an Iranian passport and there is no reason for [airport security] to block my departure from one Muslim country to another [*sic*].[73]

After the airport ordeal, the IRGC spokesperson emphasized in a press interview that Montazeri's armed group was not part of the IRGC and it was not responsible for any of his actions.[74]

Montazeri's continuation of the prerevolutionary global agenda was not appealing to the new IRGC men, even though some of them were descendants of the same global guerrilla experience. Two of the early IRGC leaders expressed this dislike in an interview, highlighting the fact that he did not belong to the IRGC:

Montazeri was not there as a part of the Guards ... he had a separate armed group. ... they were mostly concerned with foreign affairs, global revolutions [*enqelab-ha-ye jahani*], toppling reactionary rulers, treacherous countries of the region, and dictators through guerrilla warfare and exporting trained guerrillas, and so on.[75]

The friction between the IRGC and Montazeri points to a twist that the former put on the globally valorized guerrilla organization. Although founders of the IRGC fought to preserve their organizational autonomy from the government (or at least parts of it), they did *not* intend to create a systematically trained and organized guerrilla group either. Montazeri's approach (and later, that of Abusharif and Chamran) to leadership was deemed too programmatic to go with the new spirit of revolutionary freedom that they had acquired. In other words, even though they had preserved the spirit of insurgency and constant movement that was prevalent among guerrilla fighters, they did not need to imitate the organization and discipline that guerrillas deployed to survive. As a result, the IRGC demonstrated extensive tolerance for lack of discipline and local, impromptu orders when the organization started to expand. But what would this mean

[73] An interview in 1958 printed in *Resalat*, quoted in Sepah, *Ruzshomar*, 733.
[74] Interview with Etela'at, quoted in Sepah, *Ruzshomar*. [75] Sepah, *Gozar*, 52.

for an organization that was to grow into a full-scale military, expanding across Iran and, in the long run, the Middle East? And how would the IRGC's transnational agenda today, as manifested in the activities of its extraterritorial Qods Force, relate to the early global aspirations? The next two sections address these questions.

IRGC's Expansion and Preservation of Guerrilla Identity

Attempts to expand the IRGC started immediately after formation. Command council representatives traveled to various cities to either start local branches or incorporate existing local militias into the IRGC. Khorramshahr, the only major city to fall to Iraqi forces during the war (1980–1988), was an example of the latter pattern. Jahanara, later a prominent war commander, had already gathered a small militia in this southern city. A trusted Islamist, he was able to obtain the legal status from Tehran to turn his group into the Khorramshahr branch of the IRGC. Occasionally, a small number of trained Guards were commissioned from Tehran to take responsibility in local branches until trustworthy local Guards were recruited to replace them. A handful of IRGC branches were established in Kurdistan and Kermanshah provinces, for instance, when Hadidchi visited the area with a delegation.[76] Conventions, workshops, and meetings were held occasionally to coordinate local offices with the command council in Tehran. Specialized units and branches were also rapidly growing. In a short period, for instance, the IRGC's intelligence office proved to be an influential agent in repressing opposition.[77]

All this expansion and ordering was not in spite of, but in accordance with, the flexibility that the IRGC leadership had vied for. The creation of the intelligence office, for instance, happened through Reza'i's personal negotiation with commander in chief Mansuri. Although a branch was not envisioned in the statute, Mansuri, who was "very happy with [Reza'i's] decision to join the IRGC, promised to do something about it by talking to 'friends in the Council.'"[78] The presence of "the Imam's representative" office along with a commander in chief, which caused ample conflict and ambiguity,[79] was

---

[76] Shafi'i, *Hadidchi.*
[77] Hoseyn Ardestani, *Rah: Tarikh-e shafahi-ye Doktor Mohsen Reza'i* (Tehran: Markaz-e Asnad va Tahghighat-e Defa'-e Moghaddas, 1394/2015), 243.
[78] Ibid.   [79] Rashidi, *Besharati,* 236–238.

another manifestation of the tendency to preserve organizational loop-
holes, even though the totality of the IRGC was now under Islamists'
control. The new specialized branches were established quite infor-
mally, based mainly on resources available through personal ties.
Small groups farther from the center were trusted and granted official
status if the individuals leading them were trusted by the Islamists'
core; and organizational matters were handled on a personal level.

The structural ambiguity that was being institutionalized in the
IRGC was legalized within the constitution as well. The first draft of
the constitution prepared by the moderate liberal-nationalists did not
include any articles regarding the IRGC – it was assumed that the
IRGC was a transitional force that would be dismantled soon.[80] The
controversial later draft that was submitted to the Assembly of Experts
for the Constitution for detailed discussion, however, included an
article that perpetuated the IRGC as a standing force. To explain this
transformation, a prominent activist at the time claims that IRGC
leaders sensed the necessity of securing the IRGC by inserting it into
the constitution, and negotiated the matter with Beheshti, their
strongest advocate in the Revolutionary Council.[81] The article, which
was passed with a majority vote in the Assembly of Experts after
predominantly favorable remarks, reads as follows:

The Islamic Revolutionary Guards Corps, established in the early days after
the revolution succeeded, will continue to play its role in guarding the
revolution and its achievements. Boundaries of its duties and responsibilities
with this regard are determined by law, according to boundaries of other
armed forces' responsibilities, with a focus on brotherly cooperation
among them. (Islamic Republic of Iran Constitution, Article 150)

During discussions, emphasis was placed on the ambiguous term *"defa'
az maktab* [defending the creed]" as the IRGC's distinctive responsibility. As one member of the IRGC command council at the time
approvingly acknowledged, defending the creed could mean anything:

One day the creed might need you to fight a battle, the other day it might
require someone to sweep the floor. We [the Guards] would step up and
sweep the floor for the sake of the creed.[82]

---

[80] First draft of the constitution, www.iran-amirentezam.com/node/31.
[81] Author's interview with one of the IRGC founders and commanders, 2016.
[82] Interview with author, 2016.

When the refurbished IRGC was introduced on April 22, 1979, urban unrest was already underway in a number of cities, and so were minor and major ethnic uprisings in border provinces. Volunteers who joined the IRGC were thus needed at work around the country even sooner than expected. The recruits had to be trained and dispatched rapidly. An army officer in Montazeri's team remembers that even before the unification, the various training camps that had been set up would train up to 500 volunteers every week, who were then dispatched from Tehran to the provinces where unrest had surged.[83] Some of the activists who were trained as guerrillas were indeed involved in running training camps.[84] Nevertheless, the two-week training program, half of which was dedicated to ideological education, stopped at very basic information and practices, before being stylized into either irregular or regular forms of combat. What it did leave volunteers with was freedom from conventional military discipline. The training period was too short to ingrain discipline. But more importantly, discipline was not the main concern of IRGC commanders in the first place. Even full-time personnel dismissed discipline as unnecessary and against the revolutionary spirit and grassroots order.[85]

At the same time, the guerrillas' presence in the leadership circle and in training camps enabled the Guards to claim that the IRGC was an expert guerrilla force at large. In the summer of 1980, the Kurdish conflict on the western provincial borders reached one of its highest peaks. The IRGC, already engaged in battle with Kurdish fighters alongside the regular army, found a chance to claim legitimacy for the informal, decentralized organization that was in the making. Military structure and chain of command was not introduced to the IRGC yet. Training of the volunteers was still limited to the two-week course. The low intensity and irregular nature of the fight against Kurdish guerrillas served as a perfect setting for validating the IRGC's modus operandi in the name of conventional guerrilla warfare: Small groups of Guards would be sent to the western border from various cities across the country, sometimes without the IRGC command council's knowledge. When on the battle ground, they would do their best to coordinate with other groups of Guards who had arrived

---

[83] Interview with author, 2017.
[84] Author's interviews with activists, 2016–2017.
[85] Author's interview with a retired IRGC officer, 2016.

there earlier and, in turn, were trying to sync their efforts with the army. The small IRGC dispatches were either assigned scattered responsibilities, or independently made themselves useful as best as they could.[86]

The flexibility that the Guards enjoyed due to the lack of central command and discipline was partially advantageous in encountering the irregular style of Kurdish guerrillas. More importantly, however, because of the links that the organization had with the recognized model of guerrilla warfare, it was able to claim a militarily legible structure in its discourse, if not fully in practice. In other words, without giving in to a meticulously organized and preplanned guerrilla organization, the Guards were able to claim military legitimacy under the guerrilla rubric: the nominal guerrilla identity justified the Guards' lack of *conventional* military order and discipline. At the same time, it aligned the IRGC's ethos of revolutionary freedom of action with the globally valorized spirit of ever-insurgent stateless liberation fighters, within a militia run by the state.

Conclusion: Global Militants after the Age of Revolutions

In its early days, the IRGC was much more entangled with global, mostly leftist, armed movements than is imaginable today. Many of the activists who played a defining role in the IRGC had lived, trained, and fought alongside revolutionaries of diverse national origins. Others had cooperated with and learned from Iranian leftist guerrillas, who had in turn established a systematic connection to transnational guerrillas in the Middle East and beyond, in the late 1960s and early 1970s. Through both of these channels, the Guards-to-be had been introduced to the programmatic physical and military training in Palestinian camps across the Middle East, indulged themselves in ideological and orthopraxical debates with fellow guerrillas, pursued armed resistance in Iran aspiring to reach the MKO's level of influence, and shared the global dream of liberating all the wretched of the world.

Born only after regime change, however, the IRGC became a novel addition to the global phenomenon of armed insurgency. It came to being as a legal, state-sponsored entity that, nevertheless, sought to

---

[86] Author's interviews with IRGC veterans of the Kurdistan battle and a participating army officer, 2016–2017.

remain revolutionary. IRGC leaders had learned the global "script"[87] of revolutionary guerrillas – that of fighting imperial exploitation within underground, transnationally connected cells of armed activism, with the aim of toppling corrupt sovereigns who were dependent on superpowers, especially the Western Bloc. As they could no longer define their revolutionary ethos in a fight against the government, they rewrote the global guerrilla script as defying rigid and centralized bureaucracy. With the help of previously tested informal order within clerical circles and under the command of the same circles, the IRGC emerged as a revolutionary organization for postrevolutionary times. Scholars of Iran commonly distinguish the Guards from regular militaries by highlighting their religious dedication and selfless commitment to Khomeini and his leadership, the structuring role of Shia symbolism among its ranks (especially in early postrevolutionary years), and the unconditional financial and political support they keep receiving from the state.[88] Situating the IRGC within the lively global space of guerrilla warfare disrupts this monolithic image. First-generation Guards embodied a great many entanglements with the variety of global trajectories taken by guerrillas in Iran and across the world, and, over time, they created one of their own.

The IRGC was not just an isolated entity added to the global repertoire. From the outset it had set the transnational ambition of exporting the revolution upon itself. The fact that the word "Iran," although included in the constitutional article, is intentionally left out of the de facto organizational title and its logo is telling. The way this goal was pursued, however, left the Islamic Republic and the IRGC's particular mark on global insurgencies. Shortly after the formation of the eventual IRGC in the spring of 1979, the international Liberation Movements branch was also introduced as a chapter. Mehdi Hashemi, a relative of Montazeri who had worked with him in Lebanon, was in charge of this branch. Interestingly, many clerics and IRGC leaders had

[87] Dan Edelstein and Keith Baker, eds., *Scripting Revolution: A Historical Approach to the Comparative Study of Revolutions* (Stanford, CA: Stanford University Press, 2015).
[88] For example, see Afshon Ostovar, *Vanguards of the Imam: Religion, Politics, and Iran's Revolutionary Guards* (New York: Oxford University Press, 2016); and Hesam Forozan and Afshin Shahi, "The Military and the State in Iran: The Economic Rise of the Revolutionary Guards," *The Middle East Journal* 71:1 (2017): 67–86.

the same assessment about his activities that they had about Montazeri's and, to some extent, Chamran's. They deemed direct involvement in insurgent activities in other countries as too radical. The Liberation Movements branch faded with time, and Hashemi was shunned from the leadership circle and eventually executed over controversial murder charges.

A transnational project that has survived time, however, is the IRGC's successful endeavor in creating state-sponsored revolutionary militias just in its own image, in other countries of the Middle East. The Lebanese Hezbollah and the Iraqi Hashd ash-Sha'bi can be seen as harbingers of the IRGC's rerouting of the global guerrilla revolutionaries of the 1970s into militarism that is state-sponsored, yet operates parallel to regular state forces. The IRGC inherited a revolutionary legacy from the global moment of insurgency, and transformed it into the service of an alternative – one could say counterrevolutionary, given its temporal proximity to the age of counterrevolutions – militantism.

PART III

Hidden Genealogies

7 | *"A Sky Drowning in Stars":*

Global '68, the Death of Takhti, and the Birth of the Iranian Revolution

ARASH DAVARI AND NAGHMEH SOHRABI

February '79

Two men who loom large in the hearts and minds of modern day Iranians died within a short span of one another. Mohammad Mossadegh, Iran's popular nationalist prime minister, succumbed to cancer on March 5, 1967, while living under house arrest since his removal from office by a CIA-led coup. There were no public ceremonies to mourn him, leaving a handful of members from the party he founded and led, the National Front, to mark Mossadegh's passing at a small private gathering. One of the attendees, Gholamreza Takhti, Iran's beloved Olympic gold-winning wrestling champion, was found dead in Tehran's Atlantic Hotel nine months later on January 7, 1968. Newspaper headlines announced he had committed suicide apparently by ingesting poison. The headline ran: "In a letter he left behind, Takhti did not blame anyone for his death."[1]

Unlike Mossadegh's funeral, mourning ceremonies for Takhti almost immediately became a political flash point, culminating forty days after his death into full-blown demonstrations organized by university students across the country. The differences between these two moments of mourning cannot be explained by popularity; the men are arguably two, if not *the* two, most popular national figures in modern Iranian history. Nor by repression: the state security apparatus did not appreciably change in the nine months between each death. The difference, we argue in this chapter, was in the singularity of the latter moment, in the ways in which a confluence of factors – from Takhti's reputation to the evolution of student protests in the years preceding his death – created the conditions for what one student activist later called "a political explosion." The aftershocks of that

---

[1] *Ettela'at Newspaper*, Dey 18, 1346/January 8, 1968.

explosion continued into the 1979 revolution that toppled the Pahlavi state.[2]

While student protests were not new, the demonstrations organized around Takhti's fortieth day of mourning (henceforth, fortieth) were one of the first to venture outside the bounds of the university. These mobilizations did not concern tuition or dormitory conditions, but rather a national symbol whose unique figure provided cover for political organizing. In other words, Takhti's fortieth allowed students to forge allegiances beyond their corporatist interests as students. Up to that point, many of them had only been active in small circles of friends and acquaintances. They got their first taste of large-scale political organizing as a result and, for some, of prison, which only expanded their political networks. Two years later, many of the networks behind Takhti's fortieth organized a city-wide strike in Tehran against a planned increase in bus fares. In response, the shah withdrew the announced hike. Participants remembered this victory (even as subsequent historiography forgot it altogether) as one of the few successful public protests of the 1970s prior to the revolution. For those new to activism, Takhti's fortieth was their first protest in the streets, a sensation they would not experience again until 1978.

This chapter is a work of theoretical construction and historical reconstruction, intervening in the historiography of the global 1960s and that of the 1979 revolution in Iran. It begins with a short exposition of two concepts that underlie much of our analysis. The first is *les révoltes logiques*, a concept borrowed from Jacques Rancière's analysis of the May and June 1968 uprisings in France. Characteristic features of events in France, we argue, echoed across student protests in the period, even in the absence of traceable lines of influence. The second concept is *senfi-siyasi*, a widely used term in the student literature of the period. The neologism, we claim, explains the mechanism through which Takhti's fortieth in particular became a defining political moment, one that reverberated through the 1970s.

The sections that follow describe the rumors that swirled around Takhti's death and the tumultuous mourning ceremonies held on his seventh and his fortieth, customary events that morphed into public

---

[2] Mehdi Same', "Seh ruydad: Takhti, Hamid Ashraf va salgard-e Siyahkal" ["Three events: Takhti, Hamid Ashraf, and the anniversary of Siyahkal"], *BBC Persian*, February 3, 2011, www.bbc.com/persian/iran/2011/02/110203_l42_siahkal_part_eight.

protests in which students from universities in Tehran and some provincial cities took center stage. The news of Takhti's suicide and the public disbelief surrounding it inspired an intense cycle of rumors directly connected to his revered status as a man of the people. These rumors, combined with the successful experience of *senfi-siyasi* activities in 1967 that mobilized students to strike on behalf of their corporatist interests, enabled the demonstrations organized on Takhti's fortieth. While unprecedented and unique, the Takhti demonstrations nevertheless drew from a longer historical process.

Our analysis resituates Takhti's fortieth – remembered and memorialized among various segments of society in its time but marginalized in historiography – as a prominent event in modern Iranian history. We place these events in the historiography of the global sixties and the 1979 revolution, two bodies of scholarship where they have been conspicuously absent. Discussions of "global '68," and approaches to global history more broadly construed, must account both for the local specificity and the global echoes signaled by events like the Takhti demonstrations. The account of the demonstrations provided here, moreover, explains a mobilization tactic used to great effect in the lead up to the 1979 revolution: the staging of protests on the fortieth day of mourning after a previous set of protesters had been felled by state forces. Locating this tactic in 1968, before ideological disputes between leftists and Islamists would congeal, casts a spotlight on the indeterminate quality of the revolution as a lived event. The differences between these two moments, 1968 and 1979, shed light on the revolution's non-global characteristics.

Mai '68

For contemporaries and later scholars alike, the words "students," "protests," and "1968" evoke the storied radicalism of May '68 in France. The French uprisings witnessed an unprecedented alliance between university students and industrial workers culminating in a general strike. While professional sociologists dismissed May '68 as an aimless eruption of passing discontent,[3] Jacques Rancière saw "the

---

[3] Kristin Ross, *May '68 and Its Afterlives* (Chicago, IL: University of Chicago Press, 2002), 19–24.

blurring of conventional sociological categories and identifications as the basis for political transformation and reengagement."[4] For Rancière, students did not mobilize for narrow corporatist interests, nor did workers limit their mobilization to the factory floor. Instead, both groups disidentified: they abandoned their given social class positions to manufacture new identities through a conjunction between students *and* workers.[5] From these observations, Rancière coined the phrase *les révoltes logiques* – the idea that revolts, while seemingly spontaneous and thus arbitrary, in fact create a distinct logic of their own.[6]

The events surrounding Takhti's death in January and February of 1968 both affirm and subvert Rancière's concept. A strikingly similar notion appears in the archives of the shah's secret police five months prior to May 1968, in a document discussing the circumstances around the arrest of Bijan Jazani (one of the founders of Iran's guerrilla movement):[7]

---

[4] William Marotti, "Japan 1968: The Performance of Violence and the Theater of Protest," *The American Historical Review* 114:1 (2009): 97. See also Ross, *May '68*, 57.

[5] Ross, *May '68*, 24–25.

[6] English-language scholarship variably translates the phrase (the title of an academic journal Rancière established in the 1970s) as "logics of revolt" and "logical revolts." While "logical revolts" (the translation that occupies the most prominent place in secondary scholarship) best captures the phrase's literal meaning and Rancière's method, early translations of the phrase as "logics of revolt" more directly communicate the phrase's intent. Consistent with Rancière's effort to write theory through archival research, the centrality of France's 1968 uprising in his thought, and the difficulty of translating concepts crafted to capture the specificity of select historical events, we have addressed the problem of translation by maintaining the original French. This choice does not preclude theories seemingly indigenous to one national time and space from bearing global roots, as others note, or, as we argue here, from traveling. For an explanation of the phrase *les révoltes logiques*, see Jacques Rancière, *Staging the People: The Proletarian and His Double*, trans. David Fernbach (London: Verso, 2010), 10. See also Jason Frank, "Logical Revolts: Jacques Rancière and Political Subjectivization," *Political Theory* 43:2 (2015): 249–261.

[7] Jazani was arrested on January 9, 1968 (Dey 19, 1346), one day following the discovery of Takhti's lifeless body. The prolonged silence around his arrest fueled rumors that he had been imprisoned for organizing and leading chants on Takhti's seventh. See Nasser Mohajer and Mehrdad Baba Ali, *Beh zaban-e qanun: Bizhan Jazani va Hassan Zia Zarifi dar dadgah-e nezami* [In the language of law: Bizhan Jazani and Hassan Zia Zarifi in military court] (Creteil, France: Noghteh, 1395/2016), 25–27.

the shape of the actions taken [*nahveh-ye eqdamat*] and the distributed announcements on the part of the students of this faculty [Polytechnic College] in connection to the events of the seventh night of Takhti's death indicate that there are elements in said faculty who have communist thoughts and who are orchestrating the activities of others.[8]

Why would SAVAK highlight the *nahveh-ye eqdamat*, or the shape of the actions taken by students in January 1968? Akin to *les révoltes logiques* that occurred in France later the same year, the phrase signals a change in the reasoning and tactics of those in revolt. In both cases, activists disavowed their given identity as students, converging with workers and chanting slogans traversing local and global concerns at once. Yet events in Iran brought to light a logic unacknowledged in most extant global histories. Student activists deployed a tactic characteristic of strictly student activism to transcend their given identity without abandoning the safety it provided. Rancière's concept suggests a stark difference between commonsense behavior before a revolt occurs and the logic that emerges in the midst of revolt. The events surrounding Takhti's death, however, indicate a measure of continuity.[9]

In contrast to SAVAK's attribution of the difference to communism, students created a new *nahveh-ye eqdamat* by mobilizing already existing *senfi-siyasi* activities. A *senf* technically refers to a guild. In the context of prerevolutionary student activities, the adjective *senfi* also referred to groups in universities organized around shared interests such as film, literature, or hiking that at times acted as a cover for political discussions. Calling these groups *senfi-siyasi* connotes that the gatherings, while political (*siyasi*) in purpose, were *senfi* and hence

[8] *Chap dar Iran beh ravayat-e SAVAK* [The left in Iran according to SAVAK] (Tehran: Markaz-e Barrasi-ye Asnad-i Tarikhi-ye Vezarat-e Ettela'at, 1378/ 1999), 178.

[9] For a critique of Rancière in this vein, focused on what follows a moment of revolt, see Ella Myers, "Presupposing Equality: The Trouble with Rancière's Axiomatic Approach," *Philosophy and Social Criticism* 42:1 (2016): 54–56, 59–62. For a related critique, focused on what not only precedes but also endures in a moment of revolt, see Ayten Göndogdu, "Disagreeing with Rancière: Speech, Violence, and the Ambiguous Subjects of Politics," *Polity* 49:2 (2017): 214–219. For the aspects of Rancière's thinking that encourage these critiques, see Samuel Chambers, "Jacques Rancière and the Problem of Pure Politics," *European Journal of Political Theory* 10:3 (2011): 316–318.

seemingly nonpolitical in form.[10] This concept was not limited to Iran. As William Marotti describes, with reference to 1960s Japan:

> The term [*nonpori*] denoted an individual's status outside standard political classifications. It thus reflected a common view of the "political" as an overly narrow domain of government action, party politics, or hierarchical protest networks marked by firm ideological commitments. During the 1960s, however, *nonpori* came increasingly to designate individuals who were likely to self-mobilize spontaneously. They occupied a kind of "not-yet" position that was of great concern to both committed activists and the state. Rather than a contradiction in terms, however, the possibility of political engagement by the *nonpori* reflected an expansion of the field of the political itself as it came to encompass a much wider range of potential issues, actors, and possibilities ... Categories that previously demarcated some degree of distance from political engagement come instead to identify potentially subversive social agents. It is for this reason that such unexpected and emergent political identifications tend to be read as "spontaneous."[11]

Iranian students' *senfi-siyasi* activities over the course of the 1960s reflected concurrent transformations of the figure of the student in the context of the Cold War. National student organizations from communist countries demanded that international student organizations take a direct political position. Meanwhile student organizations from Western Europe (barring strong left minorities) sought out nonpolitical positions strictly focused on student affairs. Influenced by syndicalism, the International Student Conference (ISC) – formed in 1950 as an alternative to the Soviet-sponsored International Student Union (IUS), which all Western European student movements had abandoned by 1956 – organized nonpolitical activities in the interests of "students as such."[12] For their part, states aligned with the West, like Pahlavi Iran, treated forms of social and political life that were unaligned with the Soviet Union as nonpolitical. By the mid-1960s, the ISC and IUS had increasingly neared one another's positions as efforts to garner legitimacy from students on either side ended up blurring lines between the political and the nonpolitical.[13]

[10] Naghmeh Sohrabi, "Remembering the Palestine Group: Global Activism, Friendship, and the Iranian Revolution," *International Journal of Middle East Studies* 51:2 (2019): 293.
[11] Marotti, "Japan 1968," 98–99.
[12] Philip G. Altbach, "The International Student Movement," *Journal of Contemporary History* 5:1 (1970): 159–164.
[13] Ibid., 168–169, 172.

Through the cover provided by their identity, students in Iran were able to experience the efficacy of "nonpolitical" contention firsthand. Takhti's reported suicide in January 1968 created fertile grounds for the overt politicization of *senfi-siyasi* activities in Iran. A seemingly spontaneous "political explosion" was rooted in years of successful organizing. In other words, the Takhti demonstrations of 1968 provided Iranian students a unique opportunity to expand what they had rehearsed in mobilizations on behalf of "students as such." Along the way, they created a novel form of mobilization, using fortieth-day mourning ceremonies to safely stage protests in public.

Dey '46

Gholamreza Takhti was, and remains to this day, one of the most beloved national figures in Iran. Born in 1930 in the neighborhood of Khani Abad in southern Tehran, Takhti was a wrestler who throughout the 1950s won multiple championships both at home and abroad. But in what seems to be a confluence of his age and state-created obstacles, his athletic success turned to defeat in the 1960s, even as his popularity remained as high as ever. In a passport application for a trip to West Germany in 1965, Takhti identified his current job as "railway employee."[14]

In Iran, the term *pahlavan* (in contrast to *ghahreman*) refers to wrestlers who win a select kind of national competition where wrestlers face off across weight classes. Takhti won three consecutive *pahlavan* competitions between 1957 and 1959.[15] At the same time, beginning with the Olympic games in Melbourne in 1956, Takhti was the first Iranian wrestler to win an international medal.[16] He continued to regularly do so in the Olympic games and other global

---

[14] Seyyed Abbas Fatemi Nevisi, *Zendegi va marg-e Jahan Pahlavan Takhti dar ayeneh-ye asnad* [The life and death of Jahan Pahlavan Takhti in the mirror of documents], part II "Asnad" ["Documents"] (hereafter, Fatemi Nevisi, *Zendegi va marg*, "Asnad") (Tehran: Entesharat-e Jahan Ketab, 1377/1998), 24.

[15] Esma'il Khadkhudazadeh, *Saramadan-e varzesh-i Iran: Moruri bar tarikh-e varzesh-e qahremani-ye Iran: Zendegi nameh-ye saheban-e neshan-hayeh olampik va jahan* [The end of sports in Iran: A survey of the history of championship sports in Iran: Biographies of Olympic and world medal holders] (Tehran: Negareh Pardaz Sabah, 1386/2008), 119.

[16] Houchang E. Chehabi, "Sport and Politics in Iran: The Legend of Gholamreza Takhti," *The International Journal of the History of Sport* 12:3 (1995): 52.

wrestling competitions, casting him in Iranian parlance as a world figure, a *jahan pahlavan*.[17]

Takhti's skills as an athlete alone cannot explain his enduring popularity. As noted by Houchang Chehabi, "other Iranian wrestlers have won more medals." Rather, Takhti's popularity was predicated on stories about his moral exemplarity.[18] Throughout the turbulent 1950s until his death, Takhti became (or came to be seen as) a figure of opposition to the shah and a champion of "the people." In 1963, he was elected to the National Front's high council. Shortly after, when the shah imprisoned Ayatollah Mahmud Taleqani along with several other National Front members, Takhti visited Taleqani's family on a weekly basis, solidifying their relationship.[19]

His reputation in life and the later narrative of his death tell the story of a principled man devoted to "the people" who refused to bow down to the system. For many, nothing better reflected Takhti's virtue than his public efforts to bring relief to the victims of natural disaster. A devastating 7.1 magnitude earthquake struck Bouin Zahra, near Qazvin, on September 1, 1962 [Shahrivar 10, 1341] shortly after a flood in the Tehran neighborhood of Javadiyyeh earlier that spring. The afflicted distrusted the state and viewed its response slow and ineffective. Groups like the National Front stepped into the void to provide volunteer relief services, making sure recipients knew where those services came from. The weekly sports magazine, *Kayhan Varzeshi*, contacted Takhti to lead a relief mission. Four days after the disaster, Takhti published a call for people from "all classes" to donate goods and money. He then marched through the streets of Tehran with "a caravan of lorries" to collect and deliver the aid.[20]

[17] Fariba Adelkhah, *Being Modern in Iran*, trans. Jonathan Derrick (New York: Columbia University Press, 2000), 142–143.
[18] Chehabi, "Sport and Politics," 48.
[19] Rasul Jafarian, *Jaryanha va jonbeshha-ye mazhabi-siyasi-ye Iran: Az ru-ye kar amadan-e Mohammad Reza Shah ta piruzi-ye enqelab-e eslami, salha-ye 1320–1357* [Religio-political currents and movements in Iran: From Mohammad Reza Shah's reign to the Islamic Revolution, the years 1941–1979] (Tehran: Pazhuheshgah-e Farhang Va Andisheh-ye Eslami, 1381/2002), 417.
[20] Chehabi, "Sports and Politics," 54; Neda Sanech, "Nim qarn ba'ad az Boin Zahra, baz in zamin milarzad" ["Half a century after Boin Zahra this land still shakes"], *BBC Persian*, September 1, 2012, www.bbc.com/persian/iran/2012/09/120901_l13_beoin_zahra_earthquake_50_anni.shtml.

In retrospect, it comes as little surprise that the announcement of his suicide on January 7, 1968, in a hotel room no less, was met with a flurry of rumors that rejected the official story.[21] Unwilling to accept the notion that a legend of such grandeur and popularity would take his own life, many believed "they suicided Takhti," a reference to the shah's feared and despised secret service SAVAK.[22] The more newspapers and officials insisted otherwise, the stronger the rumors became.

The day after announcing Takhti's suicide, as if to explain the unfathomable, the daily newspaper *Ettela'at*'s front-page headlines recounted a grim story of family strife. *Ettela'at* printed a photograph of Takhti's lifeless body, his head cradled by two hands at a slight angle, a zigzag line running down his chest. "This is a photo of Takhti's corpse," the caption explains, following an autopsy. Above the gruesome image two photos strangely mirror each other. One is of Shahla, Takhti's young wife, her swollen eyes downcast, her fingers seemingly holding her lower lip. The other is of Babak, their infant son, staring into the camera, the fingers of one hand almost completely submerged in his mouth. The corresponding headline proclaims a new "document" had been discovered showing Takhti contemplated suicide for more than two and a half months. The women's magazine *Zan-e Ruz* raised the issue of family problems as a potential cause leading to Takhti's suicide. They asked Shahla to explain his state of mind for readers before he died.

From the first day I got engaged to him, he said if I ever have the courage, I'll kill myself – even though he was very scared of death. He was sensitive and irritable [*zudranj*] and demanding. He didn't speak much and thought more. He was stuck in the midst of life's chaos and its problems. And he didn't know what he wanted, or why he was dissatisfied.[23]

---

21 Mossadegh's advanced age and documented poor health may have precluded insinuations of state-sanctioned murder. The deaths of younger figures, however, regularly fostered rumors in late Pahlavi Iran. See Brad Hanson, "The 'Westoxification' of Iran: Depictions and Reactions of Behrangi, Āl-e Ahmad, and Shari'ati," *International Journal of Middle East Studies* 15:1 (1983): 3, 20–21. Samad Behrangi's death in August 1967, months before Takhti died, is particularly noteworthy. The most prominent public insinuations that Behrangi had been murdered appeared nearly a year after the Takhti incidents. See *Arash*, no. 18 (Azar 1347/November–December 1968): 3–12. Like Mossadegh, Behrangi's mourning rituals did not occasion political protests.

22 Nima Ahmadpur, "Takhti ra khodkoshi kardand" ["They suicided Takhti"], *Javan Online*, April 11, 2019, https://bit.ly/2Pwx7PR.

23 *Zan-e Ruz* [Modern woman], no. 149 (Dey 23, 1346/January 13, 1968): 4–6.

Ensuing interviews with Shahla similarly painted a picture of a difficult marriage and a despondent man.

Large portions of the public rejected these explanations out of hand, instead circulating creative interpretations of their own.[24] Rumors spread at such an alarming rate that one SAVAK report later regretted the state's policy of not giving the mourning ceremonies greater media coverage.[25] On the day of Takhti's death, an intrepid informant reported from the cafe bakery in the basement of the Plasco building in Tehran. One Musa Shabkhazadigan said the story of Takhti's death could not have been "so simple," for Tahkti was beloved both inside and outside Iran. Shabkhazadigan went on to say "there are rumors of knife wounds behind Takhti's neck and they weren't allowing anyone to see his corpse in the morgue. If Takhti wanted to commit suicide, he could have done it in his home or ran a car off the cliff. It would have been a better and easier way for him to end his life."[26] That the report was stamped "very confidential" points to the seriousness with which the security apparatus took these offhand remarks. The notion that he committed suicide could not readily register as truth.

Popular discourse about Takhti as an ethically decent and political man facilitated the rumors' spread. A SAVAK report from the day after his death notes that a crowd gathered outside the coroner's office consisting of "National Front elements, bazaaris, athletes, and passersby." The informant writes that some in the crowd said, "Takhti has not killed himself, rather he has been killed ... When you put the military in charge of sports in a country this is what happens."

---

[24] There is an important gendered (and class) dimension both in the formulation of the reasons for Takhti's suicide around marital strife and the persistent rejection of those reasons in the minds of the public. While this chapter cannot delve into this aspect of the story, we invite others to explore its gendered and class dimensions in future scholarship.

[25] Seyyed Abbas Fatemi Nevisi, *Zendegi va marg-e Jahan Pahlavan Takhti dar ayeneh-ye asnad* [The life and death of Jahan Pahlavan Takhti in the mirror of documents], part I (hereafter, Fatemi Nevisi, *Zendegi va marg*) (Tehran: Entesharat-e Jahan Ketab, 1377/1998), 181. For an account of a SAVAK agent conceding the power of the rumor, see Abbas Abdi, *Jonbesh-e daneshju-yi politeknik-e Tehran (Daneshgah-e Amir Kabir), 1338–1357* [The student movement at the Tehran polytechnic (Amir Kabir University), 1959–1979] (London: Nashr-e Ney, 2013), 144.

[26] SAVAK document dated Dey 18, 1346/January 8, 1968, in "Dah sanad darbareh-ye gozaresh-e SAVAK az zendegi-ye Gholamreza Takhti" ["Ten documents about SAVAK's report on Gholamreza Takhti's life"], https://psri .ir/?id=36wz1m8d.

Others said, "Takhti wasn't a kid to just kill himself over a tiny matter such as family differences. He was a hero, and if his wife was bad or deviant, he would just divorce her."[27] Five days after his death, the rumors increased in range and detail. One report from the district of Jajrud states that, after being turned down by Takhti to head the country's Wrestling Confederation, Shahpur Gholamreza Pahlavi, the shah's half-brother, invited him "somewhere." When Takhti arrived, the prince and his associates poisoned him. They then took his body to the Atlantic Hotel where it was found. The report ends by saying that the homogeneity of newspaper and magazine reports around Takhti's death (to the degree "that even the sentences are the same") confirms these rumors in people's minds.[28] Secret service documents from the ensuing months show that the idea of Takhti having been killed by the state cut through entire swaths of Iranian society – from Tehran to Abadan, from women on the streets to soldiers in government buildings and military conscripts, and from jewelers in the bazaar to students in universities who decided to weaponize the public's discontent against the shah.[29] In response to the "whispers," authorities decided to "not prevent his memorial services [from being held] so that the propagation of harmful and untruthful [information] can be neutralized."[30]

Several days after Takhti's burial, a hawk-eyed informant noticed that signs had been popping up in Tehran University with "a picture of Takhti and underneath it, the declaration of human rights in relation to individual rights." The signs invited all to take part in Takhti's seventh by marching barefoot from Shush to Ibn Babviyeh cemetery while beating their chests. In one version of this invitation, which importantly was printed and not hand-written – indicating a network of printers and the intention to distribute the pamphlet widely beyond student groups – the students of Tehran University asked "the honorable people of Tehran" to join them in mourning the loss of Takhti, "the symbol of the love of nation and of humanity," by gathering in Shush Square at 1:30 p.m. on Dey 23, seven days after his death.[31]

Not all calls to mourn Takhti on his seventh in Ibn Babviyeh were issued by students, and not all expressed grief in tongue-and-cheek political language. Perhaps the most significant call to attend the

---

[27] Fatemi Nevisi, *Zendegi va marg*, "Asnad," 36.   [28] Ibid., 43.

[29] Security officials were particularly disturbed by military conscripts who, on the day of their conscription on Bahman 1, 1346 (January 21, 1968), held a protest where they chanted in Takhti's memory. Fatemi Nevisi, *Zendegi va marg*, 180.

[30] Ibid., 36–37.   [31] Ibid., 129.

seventh not authored by students came from "the youth of Khani Abad," the neighborhood Takhti called home.[32]

With the utmost grief, we express our condolences to the entirety of the Iranian people [*beh omum-e mellat-e Iran*], in particular its athletes. On the eve of the deceased's seventh, a gathering will assemble on Saturday 23 Dey 1346 in Ibn Babviyeh.

> Regret for Takhti, that valiant hero
> Who became in life wretched and gloomy
>
> He put an end to his life and passed away
> With his death, all became tearful and distressed
>
> Brought he from the fields of wrestling
> Silver medals on behalf of the country
>
> The eyes of our people [*khalq*] lit up
> From the stature of the great champion
>
> Those from Khani Abad in particular
> Wear garments of mourning in grief
>
> God give patience to his family
> Forgive him beside the descendants of Haydar [*al-e haydar*]
>
> Associate him with the descendants of Muhammad (peace be upon him)
> With thy mercy, living arbiter
>
> We collectively ask of you, O God
> To turn a blind eye for him on the Day of Judgment

The poem on the poster describes Takhti's death as a suicide, a sin in Islam, and requests that God pardon him on the Day of Judgment. Despite acknowledging the sin, the poster nevertheless asserts that mourning activities would proceed on the seventh and asks God to associate Takhti with the descendants of the Prophet (the Shia Imams). It expresses no moral judgment.

On the morning of January 13, 1968 [Dey 23, 1346], the day of Takhti's seventh, *Kayhan Varzeshi* published an article by Hossein Fekri insinuating that Takhti's death was not a suicide.[33] It was the

---

[32] Poster from Arash Davari's private collection. For a reproduction of the image, see Arash Davari, "Indeterminate Governmentality: Neoliberal Politics in Revolutionary Iran, 1968–1979" (PhD diss., University of California, Los Angeles, 2016), 290.

[33] Mehdi Haqshenas and Zahra Zar'ei, eds., *Bacheh-ye Khani Abad (Zendegi va zamaneh-ye marhum Jahan Pahlavan Gholamreza Takhti)* [The kid from Khani

first published statement of its kind, giving further credence to rumors circulating among the populace at large. Suggestively titled "The Crown of Our Neighborhood" (*Taj-e sar-e mahhal-e ma*, or figuratively "The Honor of Our Neighborhood"), Fekri's storied article describes an exceptional life in sports disrupted by state interference and political vendetta.[34] On account of perceptions that Takhti was "part of the National Front and politically active," the "lord" (*arbab*, a reference to the shah) prevented Takhti from participating in the Olympic games in the early 1960s. When Takhti was finally permitted to return to the mat, age had taken its toll.[35] From the distance and protection afforded by writing about sports, Fekri publicly suggested that Takhti did not commit suicide and that the state was lying.

The following day, *Ettela'at* described a world in the throes of exceptionally cold weather. In Europe, 200 people died due to subzero temperatures. Packs of wolves attacked the city of Athens. Meanwhile, headlines informed readers that "tens of thousands of people from Tehran and the provinces" participated in ceremonies around Takhti's seventh. The newspaper devoted space to a report on page four, above the fold. A photograph shows throngs of men in the street as far as the eye can see. Some are on rooftops, swallowing an iconic photo of Takhti and his *hejleh*. The article reports a crowd consisting of "athletes, students, guilds [*asnaf*], craftsmen [*pishvaran*], and people from the provinces" who gathered at the cemetery to place flowers and photos on Takhti's grave from "ten in the morning until nighttime" and who, due to the closing of roads by police to "facilitate movement," found themselves stuck in the crowd and forced to find their way in and out through side roads.[36]

The crowd brought more than just flowers and photos to the gravesite; they brought words that were not reflected in the newspaper account of the ceremonies. A student representative intoned: "We do not know if they killed Takhti directly or indirectly, but we agree with

Abad (The life and times of the late Jahan Pahlavan Gholamreza Takhti)] (Tehran: Markaz-e Asnad-e Enqelab-e Eslami, 1390/2011), 147.

[34] Commonly referred to as the "father of football" in Iran, Fekri had grown up alongside Takhti, with whom he had maintained an enduring friendship. See "Mardi az kucheh-ye javanmardha keh pedar-e futbal-e Iran shod" ["A man from the alleyways of chivalry who became the father of football in Iran"], *Khabargozari-ye Fars*, Tir 9, 1392/June 30, 2013.

[35] Haqshenas and Zar'ei, eds., *Bacheh-ye Khani Abad*, 154–155.

[36] *Ettela'at Newspaper*, Dey 24, 1346/January 14, 1968.

all of the people in saying that Takhti was martyred as a champion in the pursuit of freedom ... Takhti did not die. He lives on in the hearts of each and every individual Iranian."[37] A university professor declared:

Takhti could not live in this country, a country that cultivates the unmanly [*na-mard parvar*], a country that kills men [*mardkosh*]. Takhti was no house cat, going to any available spread of food in search of a bite. He was a lion. He could not abide being reduced to a house cat by his surroundings. Takhti was killed because he was from the Truth Front [*jebheh-ye haqq*].[38] Gentlemen, do you know who killed Takhti? The unmanly, the cowards [*na-mardan*] killed him. In my view, Takhti committed two sins. First, he was Iranian by birth. Second, he was free. He was part of the Truth Front and we have the right [*haqq*] today to be as disturbed [*na-rahat*] as we are for him.[39]

Hassan Khorramshahi, a longtime political activist and one of the first people to arrive at the Atlantic Hotel when Takhti's body was discovered,[40] set up speakers to amplify sound in Ibn Baviyeh. Khorramshahi reportedly received permission from Lieutenant General Mohsen Mobasser, head of the country's police force [*shahr-bani*], on the condition that the amplified sound not be used for political purposes. After eulogizing Takhti, one presenter began to praise Takhti's special sense of devotion for the shah, at which point Khorramshahi cut sound from his microphone, saying that political discssions were not allowed at the event in light of his promise to Mobasser. He added that there might be elements outside of the burial grounds for whom a speech in praise of the shah would be disagreeable and who might express their dissatisfaction.[41] While it remains unclear as to whether Khorramshahi's actions were motivated by a genuine effort to comply with Mobasser's edict or a cleverly cloaked effort to block speech about Takhti's earlier career as a darling of the state, the

[37] Fatemi Nevisi, *Zendegi va marg*, 173. For a firsthand account, further confirming this dilemma among student activists, see Abdi, *Jonbesh-e daneshju-yi*, 139–140.

[38] This is a play on "*Jebheh-ye Melli*," or the National Front, which, as noted earlier, Takhti was close to if not a member of.

[39] Fatemi Nevisi, *Zendegi va marg*, 158.

[40] Hasan Khorramshahi, "Ostureh-ye pahlavani-ye Takhti" ["The myth of Takhti as champion"], *Iran Mehr*, nos. 9 and 10 (Dey and Bahman, 1383/2005): 52–53.

[41] Fatemi Nevisi, *Zendegi va marg*, 172–173.

event demonstrated that one could speak as long as the speech was not perceived to be political.

Similar events took place across the country as students took to microphones and transformed Takhti's death into a malleable metaphor. At a mourning ceremony in Isfahan, one student argued that Takhti could not have committed suicide without reason. "In this country, they don't treat people with humanity. There also aren't any [real] men. Even if a real person does exist and wants to do something, they chain him. They humiliate him. Takhti was one of those, one of the people who couldn't tolerate bullying."[42] Another, quoting Freud, argued that Takhti had such a well-developed superego, he understood the reasons for existence. "How can one believe that a man like Takhti committed suicide?" he lamented.[43]

Ettela'at's coverage of Takhti's seventh (however partial it may have been) indicates that these events successfully skirted the line between impermissible political opposition and permissible mourning ceremonies. The "political explosion" that took place on Takhti's fortieth would cross that line, rendering the watershed moment strangely invisible: One finds no newspaper reports either before, on, or after the fortieth day of mourning. In fact, there seems to be no publicly available photograph of Takhti's fortieth anywhere, as if the cycle of grief stopped short or turned private a mere week after he died.

Mai '67

In December 1968, on a trip to the United States, then prime minister Amir Abbas Hoveyda was asked, "Do you have student riots, hippies, racial problems, traffic jams and other modern conveniences, or is Iran still a civilized country?" Hoveyda responded: "We have some hippies but we shouldn't mind them." He went on to explain that Iran had been "spared ... the kind of riotous student demonstrations that have afflicted the United States and many other nations" by giving control to the students in "all matters concerning students including welfare, restaurants and the like."[44]

---

[42] Fatemi Nevisi, *Zendegi va marg*, "Asnad," 29-1.   [43] Ibid., 29-2.
[44] Paul Ward, "Iran Premier Has Riot Plan," *The Baltimore Sun*, December 7, 1968, 6.

Coverage of the country in *The New York Times* supported the prime minister's suggestion that nothing of import was happening. Over the course of 1967 and 1968, the newspaper of record made no reference to protests in Iran. The murder of German student Benno Ohnesorg in the streets of West Berlin during protests against the shah's visit in June 1967 garnered modest attention, but Iranian students were not represented as the primary subjects of that affair.[45] Takhti's death received a one-paragraph mention in passing: on January 22, 1968, *The Times* carried an AP report stating that of eight suicides in the previous two weeks, only two attempted to mimic Takhti.[46]

For the most part, Hoveyda's assessment proved correct. Despite sustained activity over the course of the 1960s, student protest in Iran generally was not "riotous." The 1960s arrived in Iran on the heels of a period of quiet induced by government suppression designed to solidify the gains of the 1953 coup. At the outset of the Persian calendar year 1339 [March 1960], a series of factors opened public space for sanctioned expressions of discontent. After having insisted on the presence of unobstructed and free democratic procedures across the country, the shah acknowledged unmistakable fraud in parliamentary elections. The admission led to resignations that summer, a new round of elections, and significant changes in domestic politics.[47] Later that year, the election of John F. Kennedy to the US presidency, and his insistence on liberal reforms as a Cold War counterweight to communist influence in Iran, furthered the trend. These events gave rise to the public announcement of the Second National Front in Iran and a three-year period of open, semiformal opposition. Demands made during this period were noticeably and deliberately situated "within the realm of the law."[48]

The Second National Front significantly differed from its earlier incarnation. It worked within the parameters set by the shah and

[45] See e.g. David Binder, "A Slaying Unites German Students," *The New York Times*, 10 June 1967, 4. See also Quinn Slobodian, *Foreign Front: Third World Politics in Sixties West Germany* (Durham, NC: Duke University Press, 2013), 122–123, 132–133.

[46] "Iran Disputes Suicide Link," *The New York Times*, January 23, 1968, 11.

[47] Abdi, *Jonbesh-e daneshju-yi*, 51–52.

[48] Houchang E. Chehabi, *Iranian Politics and Religious Modernism: The Liberation Movement of Iran under the Shah and Khomeini* (Ithaca, NY: Cornell University Press, 1990), 150.

where Mossadegh, the deposed prime minister, had refused to compromise or comply. A series of factors absent in the early 1950s conditioned student leadership in the 1960s. The repression of established political figures created a void filled by student activism in an increasingly radicalized global atmosphere. Meanwhile, a sharp increase in the number of university students solidified their presence as a powerful constituency.[49] Between 1960 and 1963, student activists worked through the Second National Front to push the envelope. Where National Front leaders could not sustain a publication, students controlled and communicated the Front's agenda through their permitted publishing organ, *Payam-e daneshju* (*The Student Message*).[50] And yet, however influential and however far to the margins of that envelope they may have pushed, student activism still remained circumscribed, skirting the lines of what Hoveyda would later call "riotous" behavior without crossing it.

Protests against the shah's proposed "White Revolution" in 1963, a series of reforms designed to co-opt revolutionary opposition while further consolidating the Pahlavi state, resulted in the arrests of National Front leaders. Six months later, the Khordad 15 uprising (which originated in the holy city of Qum) resulted in further suppression, arrests, and exiles, most famously of Ayatollah Khomeini. University students did not comprise an appreciable part of this uprising, but seminary students certainly made their presence felt. These events changed the domestic political calculus, after which formal political opposition drastically reduced.

The ensuing period saw a surge in student activism focused on strictly student concerns. The state crackdown on semiformal opposition following the announcement of the White Revolution discouraged student activism beyond their scope. Students responded by increasing activities within the parameters of their identity as students. In January 1963, a *senfi* organization appeared in the Industrial College-Tehran Polytechnic (hereafter, Polytechnic College), one of the main institutions of higher education that furnished many of the activists responsible for igniting Tehran's Takhti protests on his seventh and fortieth. The first article of the organization's bylaws declared that it held "absolutely no political position [*janbeh*] and under no pretense should its existence be used for political activity."[51] Rather, it

---

[49] Abdi, *Jonbesh-e daneshju-yi*, 52.   [50] Ibid., 56.   [51] Ibid., 66.

stringently focused its activities on student housing; financial assistance (for which it formed a cooperative with a robust budget); the management of cafeterias, libraries, and shuttle services; curricular decisions and exam procedures; student safety; and, in what would become the most important issue of all, the administration of tuition fees. While it was led by non-Tudeh affiliated leftists, the organization carefully and deliberately disavowed political sympathies in public so as to avoid repercussions.[52]

If student unrest expressed concerns related to student interests, the state permitted and at times even facilitated their occurrence. It did not matter if the protests left the perimeter of university campuses, the geographic location where student identity should have remained confined, as long as student sloganeering remained within the parameters of their social identity when they did.[53] Student activism thus self-policed accorded with the expectations of the Pahlavi state. Hoveyda would aptly, albeit unintentionally, call the matter "student control."

Self-policing similarly undermined any potential conjunction between (student) activism on behalf of local concerns and (student) activism on behalf of global issues. In the period of semiformal political opposition, students expressed solidarity with Patrice Lumumba and the Algerian struggle for decolonization alongside expressions of support for Mossadegh and the National Front.[54] After 1963, student activists avoided global expressions of solidarity to maintain the integrity of their organization's *senfi* status. The *senfi* organization at the Polytechnic College scuttled a request to cancel classes and instead stage protests in front of the US embassy in solidarity with the Vietnamese under the pretense that the proposed protests contravened their nonpolitical objectives.[55] Where students secured safe passage for their activism by adhering to a strictly local identity, others took cover under the veneer of strictly global preoccupations. Both avoided being seen as local and global at once. During their trial in 1970, the Palestine Group responded to charges that they were members of the

---

[52] Ibid., 117–118.

[53] With the exception of one event where they prevented students from entering campus, the police did not intervene to stop student actions at the Polytechnic College between 1343 and 1347 (c. 1964–1968). Ibid., 138.

[54] Ibid., 89; Roy Mottahedeh, *The Mantle of the Prophet: Religion and Politics in Iran* (Oxford: Oneworld, 2002), 113–115.

[55] Abdi, *Jonbesh-e daneshju-yi*, 131.

Tudeh Party and had attempted to cross into Iraq in order to fight against the shah and endanger Iran's national security by stating that their only goal had been to join the global struggle in defense of Palestine.[56] This was seen as a viable line of defense. In a parallel fashion, student affairs and reading groups about injustice in distant places were *senfi*. The absence of a conjunction between local and global concerns precluded a proper challenge to national power.

Senfi student activism reached its zenith in 1967. Just before final exams in the spring semester of the 1966–1967 academic year, students staged extended strikes and protests in Tehran and Tabriz over tuition. The point of contention was familiar. In the 1962–1963 academic year through the fall of 1963, the state attempted to impose tuition fees. Students at the University of Tehran mobilized in response.[57] At the Polytechnic College, similar protests compelled the newly reappointed dean, Habib Naficy, to remove tuition altogether.[58] On the cusp of a transition from one manner of revolt to another, tuition-based protests intermingled with the formal political demands that sustained student mobilization on behalf of the National Front, raising suspicions among security officials.[59]

When the issue arose again in 1967, any apparent links with formal political demands had disappeared. The first round of protests occurred at the University of Tehran. A new system implemented in 1345–1346/1966–1967 split the academic year into two semesters and deemed those students who had not paid their tuition for the second semester ineligible to take final exams in the month of Khordad.[60] Tuition almost doubled. In late April 1967, the president of the University of Tehran, Jahanshah Saleh, confidentially proposed that students who had not paid tuition fees should not be permitted to sit for final exams. The document leaked, raising students' ire.[61] The

[56] Sohrabi, "Remembering the Palestine Group."
[57] *Asnadi az jonbesh-e daneshju-yi dar Iran* [Documents from the student movement in Iran] (Tehran: Sazman-e Chap va Entesharat, Vezarat-e Farhang va Ershad-e Eslami, 1380/2001), 1:251–252, document 51.3.
[58] Abdi, *Jonbesh-e daneshju-yi*, 121–122.
[59] *Asnadi az jonbesh-e daneshju-yi dar Iran*, 247–248, 249–251, 264–265, documents 51, 51.2, and 51.5.
[60] Ibid., 324, document 75.
[61] Ibid., 283, document 55. Notably this document is dated Farvardin 15, 1346. Two aspects of the document lead us to believe that this date is an error and should instead read Khordad 15, 1346. First, the document lists this date as a

university administration and outside donors attempted to secure the students' reentry. A further administrative error, however, precluded the afflicted students from registering for their final exams.[62] The students raised the issue with Prime Minister Hoveyda and, when they received no response, staged a sit-in in front of the university's central administrative offices on May 3. They were joined by other self-interested students who had paid tuition, but who had not sufficiently prepared for their exams.[63] By May 8, the issue had seemingly been resolved. Empress Farah Pahlavi had intervened with a gift to cover students' tuition expenses and the school had announced a closure to prevent further protest activity on campus. It would reopen on June 3 for final exams.[64]

In the meantime, an altercation at the University of Tabriz sparked a new round of protests that spread back to Tehran. A sixth-year medical student named Hossein Salari fell into dispute with a staff member at the university's hospital. Salari was beaten, leading to an eruption of student protest on May 14–15. On May 16, approximately 300 students gathered in front of the medical school. Later that day, 1,000 students reportedly gathered in front of the technical college (*danesh-kadeh-ye fanni*). Some first-year students understood the protests as a response to Salari's beating. Others understood it as a response to tuition fees. In either case, the protests grew to encompass a broader range of issues concerning student welfare, reminiscent of the demands made in the weeks before in Tehran. Students' official chants demanded the removal of financial burdens from their shoulders.[65]

The Tabriz sit-in and demonstrations were met with a violent response. Nearly 200 students were arrested and at least one was killed. Distressed activists traveled to Tehran to share what had

Monday when in fact Farvardin 15 was a Tuesday. Khordad 15 was a Monday. Second, the document recollects events that could only have taken place by Khordad. For instance, students at the College of Political Science and Law are said to have not attended their final exams. Final exams were not administered until Khordad 13. See ibid., document 57.

[62] Ibid., 286, document 57.
[63] Rahim Nikbakht, *Jonbesh-e daneshju-yi-e Tabriz beh revayat-e asnad va khaterat* [The student movement in Tabriz according to documents and memories] (Tehran: Sureh, 1381/2002), 194; *Asnadi az jonbesh-e daneshju-yi dar Iran*, 286 and 323–325, documents 57 and 75.
[64] *Asnadi az jonbesh-e daneshju-yi dar Iran*, 286 and 323–325, documents 57 and 75.
[65] Nikbakht, *Jonbesh-e daneshju-yi-e Tabriz*, 191–195.

transpired with peers at the University of Tehran and the Polytechnic College.[66] The encounter ignited protests on both campuses with renewed vigor. On June 3, the date when final exams at Tehran University were scheduled to commence, student activists not only staged a strike, refusing to sit for their own exams, they also disrupted exams in general so as to preclude others from taking theirs. After a brief period of quiet on June 4, strikes and protests reemerged with increased intensity on June 5 (Khordad 15), the anniversary of protests that rocked the country in response to Ayatollah Khomeini's arrest in 1963. Between June 5 and 10, fifty-four students were imprisoned in Tehran, fifteen of whom are released on June 18.[67]

Beginning in the spring of 1967 and lasting over the course of the 1967–1968 academic year, university students in eight of Iran's institutions of higher education organized demonstrations "pressing complaints about the educational system." Their demands concerned the administration of their education, including lowering newly instituted tuition fees, raising university budgets, and providing better facilities.[68] The initial Tehran University strike in May ended after three days. The Tabriz University movement lasted thirty-five days, even as students took their final exams.[69] The ensuing University of Tehran strike in solidarity with the students imprisoned in Tabriz in late May lasted the entirety of the month of June, from June 3 when the school reopened until June 24 when most students finally sat for exams.[70] At the Polytechnic College, on June 16, 1967, Prime Minister Hoveyda con-

---

[66] *Asnadi az jonbesh-e daneshju-yi dar Iran*, 287, document 57; Abdi, *Jonbesh-e daneshju-yi*, 137–138.

[67] Ibid., 293–294, document 59. These events coincided with the Six-Day War, in response to which Tunisian students organized protests that would prove pivotal to the events of 1968. On the Tunisian protests and their significance for student protests in March and May 1968 in Tunisia and France, respectively, see Burleigh Hendrickson, "March 1968: Practicing Transnational Activism from Tunis to Paris," *International Journal of Middle East Studies* 44:4 (2012): 759–760.

[68] Memorandum from the Director of the Central Intelligence Agency (Helms) to the President's Assistant for National Security Affairs (Kissinger) from September 2, 1970; U.S. National Archives, Nixon Presidential Materials, NSC Files, Box #1325, NSC Unfiled Material, 1970.

[69] On the length of the "movement," see Nikbakht, *Jonbesh-e daneshju-yi-e Tabriz*, 197. For reports of Tabriz students taking their final exams, see *Asnadi az jonbesh-e daneshju-yi dar Iran*, 305–315, documents 67–73.

[70] *Asnadi az jonbesh-e daneshju-yi dar Iran*, 315, document 73.

ceded and removed all requests for tuition (apart from lab fees).[71]
According to two separate students active at the time, striking students
at Tabriz University controlled and administered the campus for the
duration of the 1967–1968 academic year. "Student control" finally
came to an end when the *senfi* organization's leaders were imprisoned
and sent to military service in the summer of 1968.[72]

The 1967 student protests signaled a breach of the contract established between university students and the state. A commission visited
the universities in Tehran and Tabriz and wrote evaluative reports for
the prime minister. These reports sympathized with the students'
tuition concerns, arguing that increased fees had not amounted to
improved provisions and services in welfare. In Tabriz, a lack of library
services, housing, competent faculty, and dining options contrasted
with the bloated number of staff members hired by the university –
from among whom one engaged in the infamous physical altercation
with a medical student. According to the commission's assessment, the
continued provision of poor services in the face of increased tuition fees
warranted resentment. It was incumbent on the state and the universities to provide better services and administration.[73]

Framing the protests as a breach of contract suggests that they
remained within the purview of student issues. That is, for all of the
upheaval that took place, the events were not "riotous." Protests at the
University of Tabriz even spread off campus and onto city streets
where residents actively assisted students in their endeavor.[74] And
yet, despite this apparent transgression of social identity categories,
protest demands remained focused on issues pertaining to "students as

---

[71] Abdi, *Jonbesh-e daneshju-yi*, 122.

[72] Arash Davari, interviews with two University of Tabriz student activists at the
time, Tehran and Qom, Iran, April–June 2015 (names withheld). For an account
of how the event caught the attention of SAVAK agents, see "Koshtar-e faji'-e
9 Fadai va Mujahed beh dastur-e shah bud" ["The heinous killing of 9 Fadai
and Mujaheds was ordered by the shah"], *Ettela'at Newspaper*, Khordad 31,
1358/June 21, 1979, 9.

[73] The commission that authored the reports included Hushang Nahavandi,
Mohammad Nassiri, and Nasser Yeganeh. See *Asnadi az jonbesh-e daneshju-yi
dar Iran*, 315–322, document 74; Nikbakht, *Jonbesh-e daneshju-yi-e Tabriz*,
199–200.

[74] *Asnadi az jonbesh-e daneshju-yi dar Iran*, 318, document 74; Nikbakht,
Jonbesh-e daneshju-yi-e Tabriz, 194; Arash Davari, interviews with two
University of Tabriz student activists at the time, Tehran and Qom, Iran, April–
June 2015 (names withheld).

such." Student activists would later use the tactics honed in these affairs to arrange revolts in response to Takhti's passing. Security forces responded as they had with the student strikes, seeking to contain them by keeping the affair from becoming a "riot." Events, however, would exceed their grasp.

Bahman '46

All of this came to a head on a cold day on February 15, 1968, forty days after Takhti's death in response to which student activists embarked on a novel enterprise: They used the permission to gather collectively as part of a mourning ritual to organize cross-class political protest. Fortieth-day commemorations had never before been sites of street protest. Inhabiting a practice that was neither clearly religious nor secular, the students expanded the possibilities of communal politics.[75] None of this was inevitable even if it seems so today. When Ayatollah Boroujerdi died in 1961, in the midst of a domestic atmosphere permitting semiformal opposition, some attempted to turn the processions into protests.[76] Two years later, after the events of Khordad 15, 1963, one unheeded call asked for a general strike on the fortieth to commemorate those killed in the uprising. The call was not for a protest, but still nothing happened on the fortieth.[77] When

---

[75] There is a long history of fortieth-day commemorations held as mourning rituals beyond solely religious categorization in Iran and elsewhere. For similar (and clearly non-Islamic) practices in 1960s and 1970s France, see Ross, *May '68*, 42.

[76] Abdi, *Jonbesh-e daneshju-yi*, 54.

[77] Charles Kurzman identifies two newly constructed strategies of political mobilization around fortieth-day commemorations. The first, which is said to have appeared after the June 1963 uprising, involved strikes, withdrawals, and boycotts. The second, which is said to have first occurred in 1977 in response to Mostafa Khomeini's death, involved street demonstrations and protests. See Charles Kurzman, *The Unthinkable Revolution in Iran* (Cambridge, MA: Harvard University Press, 2005), 54–55. Cf. Ali Davani, *Nehzat-e ruhaniyun-e Iran* [Iran's clerical movement] (n.p.: Bonyad-e Farhang-e Imam Reza, n.d.), 4:153–154. There is evidence to suggest that no actual mobilization occurred on the fortieth day after the Khordad 15 uprising in 1963, not even in the form of a general strike. Kurzman's account of 1963 refers to a flyer from an anonymous group that calls itself the "Council of United Muslims" that called for a general strike on the fortieth day of the Khordad 15 uprising. Whereas the fortieth day would have been Tir 25, 1342 (July 15, 1963), the flyer identifies it as Tir 23 (July 13). In either case, no significant protest action is reported until Tir 31 (July 21). On Tir 29 (July 19), all of the clerics who were imprisoned after the uprising

Mossadeq died in March 1967, no street ceremonies marked his passing.

Takhti's death was the first instance when a fortieth-day commemoration occasioned a street protest.[78] The demonstration started from Shush Square in the south of Tehran and continued to Ibn Babviyeh cemetery where Takhti was buried, a distance of roughly eight kilometers. News of the protest spread through leaflets scattered around the city.[79] By one count, a student named Davud Solhdust had printed as many as 200,000 leaflets in an underground print shop announcing the event.[80] According to another, the students of the Polytechnic College planned on printing and distributing 10,000 copies of a signed declaration that began with a famous line of poetry by the leftist poet Siyavash Kasrayi: "Every night they pull a star down and / still this mournful sky is drowning in stars." The declaration went on to insinuate that Takhti had been killed.[81]

Leaflets and posters were not just printed in Tehran. One SAVAK report tells of "discontented" students in Mashhad University who had printed 1,000 copies of a "13-page bulletin" of poetry in praise of Takhti using a photocopying machine owned by an army sergeant. They intended to send these 13,000 pages of paper to a contact in Tehran. SAVAK, the report notes, arrested and detained all of the parties involved in the scheme for engaging in "communist activities."[82] When compared to the poster for the seventh discussed earlier, the language of one of the posters announcing the fortieth ceremonies

---

were released except for ayatollahs Khomeini, Qomi, and Mahalati. The protests that occurred in Tehran, Shiraz, and other provincial cities two days later are reported to have occurred against their continued imprisonment. See Baqer 'Aqeli, *Ruzshomar-e tarikh-e Iran: Az mashruteh ta enqelab-e eslami* [A chronology of the history of Iran: From constitutionalism to the Islamic Revolution] (Tehran: Nashr-e Goftar, 1384/2005), 2:159. In 'Aqeli's account, there is no mention of even these protests occurring in terms of fortieth-day ceremonies, much less of the general strike called for by the "Council of United Muslims." Nasser Mohajer brought this point to Arash Davari's attention.

[78] Davari, "Indeterminate Governmentality," 174–178.

[79] Same', "Seh ruydad."

[80] Hedayat Sultanzadeh, "Yad-e yar-e mehraban" ["Remembering a kind companion"], *Asr-e Now*, Khordad 1, 1383/May 21, 2004, http://asre-nou.net/1383/khordad/5/m-yadeyar.html.

[81] Same', "Seh ruydad."

[82] Fatemi Nevisi, *Zendegi va marg*, "Asnad," 166. The Mashhad bulletin included a poem by Nemat Mirzazadeh titled "An Obituary for Takhti." See Ali Rahnema, *An Islamic Utopian: A Political Biography of Ali Shari'ati* (London: I.B. Tauris, 2014), 210–211.

printed and distributed by students reflects a distinct "confidence" accumulated over a month-long successful campaign. Unlike the seventh, it does not ask the people of Tehran to join the students in mourning. It *tells* them "we are gathering at Takhti's grave on the fortieth day of his absence."[83]

The students had taken a map of Tehran and divided it into neighborhoods, focusing on southern Tehran (through which the demonstration route went) where they would distribute fliers in groups of two or three.[84] These fliers seem to have also been distributed by people living in the neighborhoods. Their participation not only expanded the sectors of society involved in this event; it also created a conjunction between students and nonstudent residents of the city.

Workers appeared alongside student activists. One report indicates that a day before the fortieth a railway employee, a worker from Mehr Iran printers, and an unidentified person got together to discuss the demonstrations and the distribution of announcements, stating, "we will not be silent until we take revenge for Takhti" and "the ulama, the students, and intellectuals will not sit silently."[85] In another report, an employee in the Leland Motor Factory was caught the day after the fortieth trying to distribute 2,000 announcements among his fellow workers. When asked about his activities, he said he had been distributing the students' slogans and that he was "somehow" [*beh vasileh-yi*] acquainted with the students. The report ends by noting that the announcements printed in the name of students and placed on the back of the door of the factory's bathroom was written in this worker's handwriting.[86] Finally, police intelligence records indicate that employees of the railway in Tehran of which Takhti had been an employee stopped working at 10 a.m. to attend Takhti's fortieth. The bare bones report notes that they returned at noon.[87]

Multiple SAVAK documents filed by various informants tell of a large crowd, particularly of students, both men and women, that had amassed by the cemetery gates by early afternoon. On their way into

[83] Fatemi Nevisi, *Zendegi va marg*, "Asnad," 132.
[84] Naghmeh Sohrabi, interview with former student activist, London, 2017 (name withheld).
[85] Fatemi Nevisi, *Zendegi va marg*, "Asnad," 182.   [86] Ibid., 184-1.
[87] "Tehran Police Intelligence Report," Bahman 28, 1346/February 17, 1968. This document was downloaded from www.irdc.ir by Naghmeh Sohrabi but is no longer accessible online.

238 Arash Davari and Naghmeh Sohrabi

the cemetery, the students created a human chain to protect the crowd from the security forces. Once inside, the crowd held a minute of silence at the graves of the "martyrs of 30 Tir" who had been killed in 1952 while protesting Mossadegh's resignation. They then moved on to Takhti's grave where they laid flower wreaths and continued chanting·slogans as they walked back.[88]

From there, the order of things remains unclear. Existing accounts from SAVAK informants and memoirs of participants paint a picture of chaos. Examined more carefully, what seems like a lack of organization (compared, for example, to Takhti's burial and seventh) was more the opening of an unexpected space in which alliances and grievances were vocalized. Students shouted slogans such as "Oh laborers [zahmatkeshan], know that Takhti has been martyred; Oh workers [kargaran], know that Takhti has been martyred; Oh Iranians, know that Takhti has been martyred; and Takhti has been martyred but the movement continues."[89] From a call and response that tied various sectors of Iranian society to Takhti, the slogans expanded to include "Praise to Mossadegh," "Praise to Khomeini," "Death to this Dictator," "Death to the Murderer Johnson," and "A Free Viet Cong Is a Victorious Viet Cong."[90] There were also celebratory references to former leaders of Iran's communist (Tudeh) party, Taqi Arani and Khosrow Ruzbeh, both of whom had been political prisoners, alongside calls to free political prisoners in Greece.[91] The slogans chanted read as a blueprint of the revolution yet to come:

> Free people salute the hero Takhti
> Bazaaris salute the hero Takhti
> Students salute the hero Takhti
> Workers salute the hero Takhti
> Educators salute the hero Takhti.[92]

Various accounts of the day noted that the slogans chanted by the crowd took on a different tone as they left the cemetery and spilled into parts of southern Tehran. There were more sustained chants of "death to this dictator" and more slogans connecting the moment to Khordad

---

[88] Fatemi Nevisi, *Zendegi va marg*, "Asnad," 64 and 193.
[89] *Jebheh melli beh ravayat-e asnad SAVAK* [The National Front according to SAVAK documents] (Tehran: Markaz-e Barresi-ye Asnad-e Tarikhi-ye Vezarat-e Ettela'at, 1379/2000), 1:209–210.
[90] Ibid.   [91] Fatemi Nevisi, *Zendegi va marg*, "Asnad," 60-1.   [92] Ibid., 201-1.

15, to Mossadegh, and to Khomeini. By SAVAK's own account, it was around Shush Square when the procession ran into police who seemed to have had no problems dispersing an already fracturing crowd.[93] Perhaps not surprisingly, Takhti's fortieth is not connected to the arrest of any known or soon-to-be known people. Most arrests occurred weeks later – like those of the members of the Palestine Group, several of whom had been active in organizing and implementing the fortieth, the success of which emboldened them to step up their activities.

Years later, when the lines between the left and Islamists had been drawn in permanent marker, some participants would actively deny that there had been any pro-Khomeini slogans.[94] But at the time, and from the perspective of the participants as well as the security apparatus, there was no qualitative difference between this wide array of slogans. "Sociological classifications and identifications" were in flux. In a postmortem report that laid out actionable items for SAVAK, the director for the third sector requested that "separately, the elements who supported the oppositional clerics and Khomeini, members of National Front and related parties, and the communists who had taken part in these events must be identified."[95] A confluence of chants and groups that could qualify as *both* Islamist *and* secular leftist, a confluence unique to Iran, would reappear in 1978.

Bahman '68

How do the Takhti demonstrations relate to other protest events of the global sixties? How do they compare to the Paris uprisings of May and June 1968, the widely accepted synecdoche for "global '68"? As scholars note, all protests in the period took part in a shared global imaginary of anti-imperialist struggle, with Paris just one node in a "big 1968" or "68 culture."[96] Be they January and February 1968 in Tehran or May and June of the same year in Paris, these protests were conjunctions between local and global concerns. Protests in Paris (and, to a lesser extent, Italy) were also distinctly conjunctions between

---

[93] Ibid., 201-4.   [94] Same', "Seh ruydad."
[95] Fatemi Nevisi, *Zendegi va marg*, "Asnad," 200-2.
[96] Ross, *May '68*, 38; Timothy S. Brown, "'1968' East and West: Divided Germany as a Case Study in Transnational History," *American Historical Review* 114:1 (2009): 71; Salar Mohandesi, "Bringing Vietnam Home: The Vietnam War, Internationalism, and May '68," *French Historical Studies* 41:2 (2018): 221.

students and other sectors of society, workers in particular.[97] May and June in Paris have since come to exemplify the moment, used to explain any iteration of singularity in "1968." As in Paris, so too in Tehran protesters understood their struggle as both global and local. But also as in Paris, in Tehran there were students who disidentified with their social identity as students.

Despite these similarities, Iran's 1968 was neither derivative of events in Paris nor connected to events in Paris through transnational networks. Rather, the Takhti demonstrations relate to the historiography of the global sixties as an "echo." We use scare quotes here with purpose. The January–February protests in Iran occurred at least four months prior to events in Paris. For those intent on writing global history as a story of simultaneity, or of similar events happening in different parts of the world seemingly by chance, this chronology supports claims about "the spirit of '68."[98] For those intent on writing global history as a story of connectivity, or of concrete networks crisscrossing national borders, this chronology might amplify the global roots of May '68. Similar revolts, for instance, were present in the March 1968 demonstrations in Tunisia, where students shared activist networks with their French peers who would repeat tactics first honed in North Africa.[99] There are, however, no demonstrable links between the activists involved in Takhti's fortieth and students or workers in France and Tunisia. The source linking these shared *révoltes logiques* to Iran remains unclear, hence an "echo."

The Takhti demonstrations call instead for a relational approach to global history, focusing on overlaps between local and global concerns as they arise in the lived experience of events.[100] Iranian students could not imagine any form of protest in the late 1960s but ones that looked like and linked to a global mold, evoking faraway places like Palestine and Vietnam to legitimate their demands. The approach to writing global history suggested by the term "echo," however, requires a slightly altered concept of relational history. Here, a narrative of the

[97] Ross, *May '68*, 4.
[98] Gerd-Rainer Horn, *The Spirit of '68: Rebellion in Western Europe and North America, 1956–1976* (Oxford: Oxford University Press, 2007).
[99] Hendrickson, "March 1968," 756–757.
[100] See e.g. Ross, *May '68*, 11, 80–98; Slobodian, *Foreign Front*, 10–12; Brown, "'1968,'" 69–70.

local and the global means that the singularity of an experience in Iran, taken as a whole, reads as a global phenomenon. The Takhti demonstrations were part of global patterns unfolding in real time, a quality we capture through the use of the phrase *les révoltes logiques*. The demonstrations were also specific to their local circumstances, which this chapter communicates through the use of the phrase *senfi-siyasi*. Including the Takhti demonstrations in the historiography of the global sixties, therefore, amounts to revising the significance of "global '68." The year 1968 should not only signify the disruption of categorical boundaries separating the social identities of, say, students and workers or of a national citizen and a global cause. It should also signal the disruption of the boundary separating the *senfi* from the *siyasi*.

This disruption provides another explanation for the different responses to Mossadegh and Takhti's deaths beyond noting state repression. Mossadegh's death occurred before the first student strikes in Tehran and Tabriz – which is to say, before student activists tasted the success of *senfi* activism on behalf of their corporatist interests. Takhti passed away nine months after Mossadegh, the period of time during which student activists experienced effective mobilization under a seemingly nonpolitical cover. Unlike comparable histories in France or Tunisia, *les révoltes logique* in 1968 Iran translated the previous success of *senfi-siyasi* activities into direct political confrontation. Where Mossadegh cut an explicitly political figure, popular associations of Takhti with *senfi* activities furnished a more suitable conduit for activists. A clear enemy of the state – by virtue of his biography, his condition of house arrest, and his positions against the Second National Front – Mossadegh's funeral in March 1967 provided little to no cover. Takthi, by contrast, embodied enough ambiguities to allow effective *senfi-siyasi* mobilization beyond the limits of student identity: Iranians associated their *jahan pahlavan* with sports and charity, both of which evaded the boundary delimiting activities the state deemed politically impermissible.

Over the course of the 1960s, student activists embraced sports, particularly hiking and mountain climbing, as an outlet for *senfi* activism. Yusef Momtahen, a graduate of the Polytechnic College in 1968 and an active participant in the school's *senfi* organization, recalls being chided by a politically active student for playing on the basketball team. The activist later changed his perspective after noticing the impact sporting activities had on strengthening students' sense of solidarity and the increasing stature Momtahen accrued among peers as an athlete.[101] That is, even the most politically minded students came to appreciate the benefits of using sports as an organizing tool, broadening the scope of possible *senfi* activism on offer in their imaginations.

Charity, such as Takhti's public relief mission for the earthquake in Bouin Zahra, provided another route for *senfi* activity at the bounds of what the state identified as politics. Polytechnic students were especially involved in relief efforts because they presented themselves as possessing the requisite technical skills to assist in reconstruction. More significant than any overt political strategy (again, they made it clear that they represented the National Front), the experience of providing aid had an effect on the students themselves. They stood shoulder to shoulder not only with Takhti, but also with the dispossessed.[102] Activist students replicated the experience of flattening their differences with those they dreamt of helping when they marched on Khani Abad for Takhti's seventh, and then again during his fortieth.

Bahman '57

Iran's "1968" explains two aspects of its 1979 revolution: the mobilization of protest used in the first half of 1978 and the status of the event as a global revolution. In the first instance, Takhti's death in January 1968 arrived after students had cut their teeth in collective mobilization around *senfi* issues. A fortieth-day ceremony mourning a popular figure readily associated with *senfi* activities like sports and charity provided a viable reason to gather in public. That is, it provided the occasion and inspiration the students needed to translate their *senfi-siyasi* activities into street protests. This new protest tactic would resurface a decade later during the revolution when thousands of Iranian protesters "did the forty-forty."[103] Beginning in January 1978, fortieth-day mourning ceremonies honored protestors killed in previous demonstrations. More unarmed protesters would fall to state

---

[101] Abdi, *Jonbesh-e daneshju-yi*, 111–112.   [102] Ibid., 97–101.
[103] Kurzman, *Unthinkable Revolution*, 50.

forces, inspiring a further round of fortieth-day ceremonies-turned-protests, a practice that persisted into the summer of 1978. Many histories of the revolution associate this practice with Islamism. Charles Kurzman notably locates the first efforts to organize against state repression on the fortieth day after its occurrence in 1963, bolstering a trend in the historiography of the 1979 revolution that gives pride of place to the Khordad 15 uprising. Kurzman then locates the first use of fortieth-day mourning ceremonies to stage street protests in 1977 and in response to the death of Khomeini's son, Mostafa. These readings do not take 1968 and the Takhti demonstrations into account.

Secondly, by 1978, the "echoes" of global protest that undergird the Takhti demonstrations in 1968 had given way. The networks that made the demonstrations possible remained, albeit hidden under seemingly formal organizations. As the 1970s progressed, organizational activities (in the forms of the guerrilla organizations such as the Mujahedin and Fadayin, or the Liberation Movement of Iran) "overlay but did not replace" *senfi-siyasi* networks. The flexiblity of these networks allows us to "deepen our understanding of the later stages of the revolution when seemingly incongruous currents such as Islamists, religious-nationalists, Islamist-Marxists, secular-nationalists, and secular Marxists came together to form the revolutionary crowds."[104] Looking at the slogans chanted throughout 1978 and into 1979, however, one is struck by the absence of the transnational references that permeated the Takhti protests. Where, one might ask, were slogans of solidarity with Nicaragua, a revolution that unfolded around roughly the same period and of which Iran's revolutionaries were aware? Or take the revolution's most familiar slogan, "Neither East, nor West," whose roots go at least as far back as Kwame Nkrumah's anti-colonial nationalism and the principle of non-alliance in the 1960s: "We face neither East, nor West. We face forward." The slogan, as articulated by Nkrumah in 1960, became the siren call for a new order in a decolonizing world. By 1978 when it was chanted by oceans of Iranians in the streets, its various endings – Islamic Republic, Worker's Government, Islamic Government – had shifted to a demand

[104] Sohrabi, "Remembering the Palestine Group," 293–294.

for changes at the level of the nation-state. The global roots of the revolution, it would seem, had been all but forgotten. Instead, the revolutionary movement's success depended in large part on a national imaginary – even if it still bore global repercussions in the actions and projections of the postrevolutionary state.[105]

[105] For a discussion of postrevolutionary Iran's distinct brand of internationalism, see Timothy Nunan, "'Neither East Nor West,' Neither Liberal Nor Illiberal? Iranian Islamist Internationalism in the 1980s," *Journal of World History* 31:1 (2020): 43–77.

8 "We Must Have a Defense Build-up":
The Iranian Revolution, Regional Security, and American Vulnerability

CHRISTOPHER DIETRICH

At 6:50 a.m. on August 28, 1976, a black Dodge sedan crept through a side street in the Tehran Now neighborhood of Iran's capital. Suddenly, the red Volkswagen ahead slammed on its breaks, and a minibus rammed the car from the rear. Four men – which the Iranian National Bureau of Security and Intelligence, SAVAK, later reported were members of the Mujahidin-e-Khalq group – sprinted up to the Dodge. They yelled at the Iranian chauffeur to get out and lie face down next to the car and then shot to death its other occupants, US citizens Donald Smith, Robert Krongard, and William Cottrell. American ambassador in Tehran Richard Helms, formerly the director of the CIA, reported to the State Department that the three men were Rockwell International employees working on "an electronics research project" for the Imperial Iranian Air Force.[1] Washington Post journalist Bob Woodward revealed months later that they were working "on a secret project of truly Buck Rogers proportions called IBEX" – the code name for a $500 million border surveillance system. As an added detail, a small irony meant to capture what he believed was a larger problem, Woodward reported that one of the guns used in the assassination was a stolen pistol from the US Military Assistance Advisory Group.[2]

Woodward meant for his story to pull back the curtain on the corruption and intrigue that characterized the US arms merchandising program worldwide. But the Rockwell killings are also interesting in the context of American power in the Persian Gulf in the late 1970s and early 1980s. The shape and nature of US power in the region was

---

[1] "Telegram from the Embassy in Iran to the Department of State," in U.S. State Department, *Foreign Relations of the United States* (hereafter, *FRUS*), 1969–1976, *Volume XXVII, Iran; Iraq, 1973–1976*, doc. 186.

[2] Bob Woodward, "IBEX: Deadly Symbol of U.S. Arms Sales Problems," *The Washington Post*, January 2, 1977.

determined in part by "the loss of Iran" in 1979, which was a twofold defeat for the United States. First, Washington lost a stalwart ally in the Cold War. Second, it was that specific ally that the United States had depended upon for "regional security" in the oil-rich Persian Gulf since the early 1970s. Rather than examine the development of the special relationship between Iran and the United States during the Cold War, this chapter closely analyzes the immediate response in the US government to the instability of the Pahlavi government and its fall in 1979 through the lens of the arms sales decisions the United States made immediately before and in the wake of the revolution.[3]

This chapter focuses on the debates over US military sales in the Persian Gulf — Woodward entitled his report "IBEX: Deadly Symbol of U.S. Arms Sales Problems" — in part to remind scholars that it was and still is common to paint US foreign relations in the late 1970s and early 1980s in stark Cold War tones, as twisted and warped by a sense of impending danger resulting from the perceived nadir of US power. It is true that American policymakers and the public emphasized the most drastic potential consequences that could result from the Iranian Revolution. Faced with incontrovertible evidence, we should acknowledge that fear and fear-making played an important role in the formation of policy. But the loss of Iran also occurred within a longer, more nuanced debate about national security and the proper role for US military power in the Middle East. In fact, influential actors in foreign policy often embraced calls for caution and denounced moves by different presidential administrations in the 1970s and 1980s to increase regional arms sales. By turning to the domestic politics of arms sales in the United States, in particular Senate hearings on Iran and Saudi Arabia, scholars can return some of the contingency

---

[3] Many scholars have examined the US relationship with Iran in the second half of the twentieth century. Recently, see Roham Alvandi, *Nixon, Kissinger, and the Shah: The United States and Iran in the Cold War* (New York: Oxford University Press, 2016); Paul T. Chamberlin, *The Cold War's Killing Fields: Rethinking the Long Peace* (New York: Harper, 2018), 393–417; Matthew K. Shannon, *Losing Hearts and Minds: American-Iranian Relations and International Education during the Cold War* (Ithaca, NY: Cornell University Press, 2017); Javier Gil Guerrero, *The Carter Administration and the Fall of Iran's Pahlavi Dynasty: US-Iran Relations on the Brink of the 1979 Revolution* (New York: Palgrave Macmillan, 2016); Claudia Castiglioni, "No Longer a Client, Not Yet a Partner: The US-Iranian Alliance in the Johnson Years," *Cold War History* 15:4 (2015): 491–509.

to decisions made after 1979 that seem now to be foregone conclusions. Nonetheless, the hearings also reveal that the Iranian Revolution reordered discussions toward the militarization of US power in the Middle East in 1979 and after. Both continuity and change are thus crucial to the following story.

Debates over arms sales also provide other insights about US diplomacy in the late Cold War and early stages of contemporary globalization. For one, American diplomacy before and after the Iranian Revolution rested upon an important claim about the link between regional security and what was often referred to as "global economic health": that the United States had the right and even the responsibility to preserve the political stability of the Arabian Peninsula because the region's resources were crucial to the Free World economy. Regional security had long been a Cold War preoccupation of the United States, but it became close to an obsession after the British announced its retreat from East of Suez in 1968 and the price of oil exploded in 1973 and 1974. A close examination of personal papers, declassified government records, corporate lobbying strategies, and Congressional funding debates reveals that calls for a more aggressive foreign policy hardened into a set of policy assumptions in which American military power, extended through arms sales, played a growing role in securing stability. At the same time, American policymakers made a set of three interrelated arguments about economics and national security that extended from the era of the Cold War into that of globalization. First, they held that Middle Eastern oil was crucial to US and global economic well-being. Economic prosperity was a crucial weapon in the global Cold War and a necessary factor of US legitimacy in the 1980s and beyond. Second, they made arguments that arms sales were a domestic economic imperative. Third, they held that arms sales were key to good relations with the ruling monarchies in Iran and then Saudi Arabia.

The burgeoning military sales relationship between the United States and Saudi Arabia in the late 1970s and 1980s, now a hallmark of US-Saudi relations and regional security, arrived through an Iranian workshop. The US experience with Iran in the 1970s provided a ready-made logic for relations with Saudi Arabia after the Iranian Revolution. The above and other related arguments hardened into conventional wisdom rather quickly after 1979 and would help dictate diplomacy toward the Persian Gulf into the twenty-first century. Each, it should be reiterated, rested on a vision of vulnerability shared across the Nixon, Ford, Carter, and Reagan presidential administrations. The debates over arms sales and regional security help reveal how the centrality of military force in American diplomacy toward the Middle East would become a defining characteristic of the new era of contemporary globalization.

National Vulnerability and Regional Security in the 1970s

To understand US foreign relations surrounding the Iranian Revolution, a word about context is necessary. As historians have noted, the 1970s was a period of unprecedented vulnerability for the United States at home and abroad. The Vietnam War, the crisis of the Bretton Woods monetary system, the shift from an industrial to a service economy, Watergate, the investigation of the Church Committee into abuses by the US intelligence community, and the energy crisis acted together to upend the sense of abundant prosperity, political stability, and moral righteousness that had served as the basis for domestic tranquility and Cold War strength since the late 1940s.[4] Experts from urban planning to foreign aid acutely felt American vulnerability, in particular in the new field of "energy security" and in strategic discussions about "oil lifelines" and "global choke points."[5] By the end of the decade, the specter of "Soviet adventurism" in sub-Saharan Africa, the Horn of Africa, South Arabia, Central

---

[4] Thomas Borstelmann, *The 1970s: A New Global History from Civil Rights to Economic Inequality* (Princeton, NJ: Princeton University Press, 2011); Daniel J. Sargent, *A Superpower Transformed: The Remaking of American Foreign Relations in the 1970s* (New York: Oxford University Press, 2014); Daniel T. Rodgers, *Age of Fracture* (Cambridge, MA: Harvard University Press, 2011).

[5] For the changing nature of domestic politics in the United States, see Lizbeth Cohen, *Saving America's Cities: Ed Logue and the Struggle to Renew Urban America in the Suburban Age* (New York: Farrar, Straus and Giroux, 2019); Kim Phillips-Fein, *Fear City: New York's Fiscal Crisis and the Rise of Austerity Politics* (New York: Metropolitan Books, 2017). On the energy crisis, see Victor McFarland, *Oil Powers: A History of the U.S.-Saudi Alliance* (New York: Columbia University Press, 2020); Elisabetta Bini, Giuliano Garavini, and Federico Romero, eds., *Oil Shock: The 1973 Crisis and Its Economic Legacy* (London: Bloomsbury, 2016); Rüdiger Graf, "Between 'National' and 'Human Security': Energy Security in the United States and Western Europe in the 1970s," *Historical Social Research/Historische Sozialforschung* 35:4 (2010): 329–348; Roger J. Stern, "Oil Scarcity Ideology in US Foreign Policy, 1908–97," *Security Studies* 25:2 (2016): 214-257.

America, and Afghanistan added to the sense of impending danger and led most American officials to assume that the Soviet Union sought to take advantage of the nation's unprecedented weakness, especially in the Middle East.[6] All the while, the domestic questions of high oil prices and "energy dependence" drove apprehension about the state of the national political economy, which was already shaky because of a trade deficit, deindustrialization, and stagflation.[7] Instability in Iran, an important ally since the early Cold War and the critical protector of regional security for the Nixon administration and its successors, thus exacerbated a wider perception of ongoing crisis *in* the United States. This was an urgent sentiment shared among many, who in turn believed that any challenge to US power demanded a forceful response.

The complex relationship of national vulnerability to regional security and military power can be seen clearly in Congressional debates over arms sales to Iran and Saudi Arabia in the second half of the 1970s. One characteristic of US politics after the Vietnam War was the rise of foreign policy activism in the legislative branch, with the professed goal of bringing balance to diplomacy that had largely been conducted in the twentieth century by what historian and Kennedy adviser Arthur Schlesinger, Jr., called "the imperial presidency."[8] The passing of the War Powers Act in 1973 is one well-known case of the

---

[6] Nancy Mitchell, *Jimmy Carter in Africa: Race and the Cold War* (Stanford, CA: Stanford University Press, 2016); Elisabeth Leake, "Spooks, Tribes, and Holy Men: The Central Intelligence Agency and the Soviet Invasion of Afghanistan," *Journal of Contemporary History* 53:1 (2018): 240–262; Theresa Keeley, "Reagan's Real Catholics vs. Tip O'Neill's Maryknoll Nuns: Gender, Intra-Catholic Conflict, and the Contras," *Diplomatic History* 40:3 (2015): 530–558; W. Taylor Fain, "Conceiving the 'Arc of Crisis' in the Indian Ocean Region," *Diplomatic History* 42:4 (2017): 694–719.

[7] Meg Jacobs, *Panic at the Pump: The Energy Crisis and the Transformation of American Politics in the 1970s* (New York: Macmillan, 2016); Judith Stein, *Pivotal Decade: How the United States Traded Factories for Finance in the Seventies* (New Haven, CT: Yale University Press, 2010).

[8] Arthur Schlesinger, Jr., *The Imperial Presidency* (New York: Houghton Mifflin, 1973). For discussion of the importance of Congressional activism in US foreign relations regarding the Cold War and human rights, see Sarah Snyder, *From Selma to Moscow: How Human Rights Activists Transformed U.S. Foreign Policy* (New York: Columbia University Press, 2018); Barbara J. Keys, *Reclaiming American Virtue: The Human Rights Revolution of the 1970s* (Cambridge, MA: Harvard University Press, 2014).

new role members of Congress saw for themselves.[9] Hearings on arms sales, especially to oil-rich allies, were another. These were marked by a consistent debate between presidential administrations who proposed arms sales and legislators who urged caution.

A combination of factors – most importantly ballooning oil income, the close relationship between Richard Nixon and Reza Pahlavi, and the British decision to end its military presence East of Suez and grant independence to several states in the Arabian Peninsula – led the Nixon administration to give Iran "a blank military check" in 1972.[10] Afterward, Congressional critics claimed that the Nixon, Ford, and Carter administrations showed a great deal of continuity with each other in terms of arms sales to Iran, despite the presidents' rhetorical differences.[11]

The critics in Congress were at least partially correct. Policy toward Iran in the 1970s was part of a broader shift in US foreign relations as the nation's military gaze shifted from Southeast to Southwest Asia. In particular, the United States began to center its diplomatic efforts in the Middle East on ramping up the courtship of the authoritarian oil states that were its Cold War allies, namely, Iran and Saudi Arabia. The three nations shared important concerns about the regional and global dangers of Soviet and "radical Arab nationalist" influence. Already in the Johnson administration and then with the proclamation of the Nixon Doctrine, the United States had turned to the other two as "Twin Pillars" that would provide regional security in the wake of the British withdrawal from its East of Suez stations, announced in

---

[9] For contemporary analysis by a former secretary of state, see Cyrus R. Vance, "Striking the Balance: Congress and the President under the War Powers Resolution," *University of Pennsylvania Law Review* 133 (1984): 79–96.

[10] James A. Bill, *The Eagle and the Lion: The Tragedy of American Iranian Relations* (New Haven, CT: Yale University Press, 1988), 201. On the link between oil, the British withdrawal, and the Nixon Doctrine, see Jeffrey Kimball, "The Nixon Doctrine: A Saga of Misunderstanding," *Presidential Studies Quarterly* 36:1 (2006): 59–74. On the British decision, see Elizabeth Monroe, *Britain's Moment in the Middle East, 1914–1971* (New York: Vintage, 1981); Shohei Sato, *Britain and the Formation of the Gulf States: Embers of Empire* (Manchester: Manchester University Press, 2016); Simon C. Smith, *Ending Empire in the Middle East: Britain, the United States, and Post-war Decolonization* (New York: Routledge, 2013).

[11] Alvandi, *Nixon, Kissinger, and the Shah*; Cyrus Schayegh, "Iran's Global Long 1970s: An Empire Project, Civilisational Developmentalism, and the Crisis of the Global North," in Roham Alvandi, ed., *The Age of Aryamehr: Late Pahlavi Iran and Its Global Entanglements* (London: Gingko, 2018).

1968 and completed in 1971. Both Iran and Saudi Arabia had long wanted the United States to supply more military equipment and training, and the United States had long used "this military carrot," as one NSC official called it, to help keep them in the capitalist Cold War bloc.[12] In Saudi Arabia, for example, a small US military training mission begun in 1951 had grown by the late 1960s into a 235-soldier garrison, complemented by training for around 100 Saudi military officials in the United States per year, as well as large contracts for the Army Corps of Engineers and corporate arms manufacturers, all part of a Mobility Modernization Agreement signed by Secretary of Defense Robert McNamara and Saudi Defense Minister Prince Sultan.[13]

Iran was the more important of the twin pillars. The American ambassador in Tehran during the Johnson administration, Armin Meyer, wrote to McNamara that sales to Iran were of "considerable political value" in the bilateral relationship because the shah was "one of the best friends we have in the Afro-Asian milieu." In a report for the White House, McNamara made a domestic economic argument for increasing sales to Iran: "Our sales have created about $1.4 million man-years of employment in the U.S. and over $1 billion of profits to American industry in the past five years."[14] In its first briefing to Nixon on the region after he assumed the presidency in January 1969, the State Department reported that military equipment was "the key to our relations with the Shah." If the United States did not remain the nation's main arms supplier, "our interests in Iran, including our ability to maintain our own strategic interests there and to influence the Shah in the direction of constructive foreign and domestic policies,

---

[12] "Memorandum, Komer to McGeorge Bundy, 'Iran Problem,'" June 27, 1964, Box 136 [1 of 2], Folder 4, National Security File, Country File, Middle East, Lyndon Baines Johnson Presidential Library, Austin, Texas (hereafter, LBJL).

[13] "USG Assurances and Actions Vis a Vis Saudi Arabia in Light Current Saudi-UAR Confrontation," April 6, 1967, Box 1, Folder 10, Howard Cottam Papers, LBJL. For a recent analysis, see Laleh Khalili, "The Infrastructural Power of the Military: The Geoeconomic Role of the U.S. Army Corps of Engineers in the Arabian Peninsula," *European Journal of International Relations* 24:4 (2018): 911–933.

[14] Andrew L. Johns, "The Johnson Administration, the Shah of Iran, and the Changing Pattern of U.S.-Iranian Relations, 1965–1967: 'Tired of Being Treated like a Schoolboy,'" *Journal of Cold War Studies* 9:2 (2007): 78–79.

will be seriously weakened."[15] US-approved arms sales had risen consistently since the mid-1960s, but grew precipitously after the secret open-ended commitment made by Nixon to the shah in 1972. "As long as Iran can financially afford both guns and butter, there is no reason for us to lose the market, particularly when viewed over the red ink on our balance of payments ledger," coal-magnate-turned-ambassador Joseph Farland told National Security Adviser Henry Kissinger.[16]

The ability of the United States to project its military power became a basic yardstick by which policymakers measured success, and the scale of arms sales to Iran and Saudi Arabia increased dramatically after the oil price increases of 1973 and 1974. In one example from 1975, despite greater public scrutiny of executive power in the aftermath of Vietnam and Watergate, the Ford administration pressed forward with a multibillion dollar program for the Saudi armed forces, to be managed by private contractors Vinnell, General Electric, and Cadillac Gage.[17] In those years, officials in the State Department and the National Security Council consistently maintained that Iran and Saudi Arabia played a constructive role in the region, and their ability to do so had been enhanced by their acquisition of sophisticated modern weapons. Analysts in the CIA agreed that Iranian and Saudi "self-assertiveness" was made possible by stronger military power and was necessary to prevent Soviet encroachment, as evidenced when the shah "tipped the balance ... in the struggle against Soviet-backed rebels" in Oman.[18]

---

[15] "U.S. Relations with Iran," January 1969, Box 601, Folder 2, National Security File, Country Files – Middle East, Richard Nixon Library, Yorba Linda, California (hereafter, RNL).

[16] Saunders to Kissinger, "Message from Ambassador Farland," July 14, 1972, Box 602, Folder 3, National Security File, Country Files – Middle East, RNL.

[17] Oakley to Scowcroft, "President's Meeting with Prince Abdallah Ibn Abd Al-Aziz Al Saud," July 7, 1976, Box 28, National Security Adviser's Presidential Country Files for the Middle East and South Asia, Gerald Ford Presidential Library (hereafter, GFL).

[18] "CIA, Directorate of Intelligence, Office of Political Research, 'The Soviets in the Persian Gulf/Arabian Peninsula,'" December 1976, NLC-25-87-5-1-3, Jimmy Carter Presidential Library (hereafter, JCL). On Oman, see Geraint Hughes, "A 'Model Campaign' Reappraised: The Counter-insurgency War in Dhofar, Oman, 1965–1975," *Journal of Strategic Studies* 32:2 (2009): 271–305; Marc DeVore, "The United Kingdom's Last Hot War of the Cold War: Oman, 1963–1975," *Cold War History* 11:3 (2011): 441–471.

Substantial evidence existed for policymakers that arms sales to Iran benefited the Cold War interests of the United States. In a meeting with Kissinger in 1974, Helms listed the shah's accomplishments in support of regional security: in addition to military aid to the Sultan of Oman, Iran had transferred aircraft to Pakistan, urged the Sheikh of Bahrain to permit the US to continue its naval presence, and supplied weapons and aid to the Kurdish rebellion inside Iraq. All of this was necessary, Helms and others noted, to counter the advance of Soviet interests in South Yemen and Iraq.[19]

But not everybody in the United States was pleased. While the Nixon and Ford administrations believed that sales responded to legitimate security needs, other political actors in the United States believed that the volume of arms transfers created larger and larger appetites for weapons. Noting an increase in US arms sales abroad from $300 million in 1952 to over $20 billion by 1975, the Senate Foreign Relations Committee gave Kissinger, now secretary of state, "a rough ride" on the extent of the US military sales commitment to the region.[20]

Kissinger promised a systematic review of policy to the Senate, but the US military boot-print in the Middle East would only increase as the nation made its post-Vietnam strategic pivot to the Persian Gulf. Here, the history of the Vinnell Corporation is a particularly revealing example of changes the United States went through in the mid-1970s. Founded in 1931 in Alhambra, California, as a construction company, Vinnell built parts of the Grand Coulee Dam, the Pan-American Highway, and the new Dodger Stadium in Los Angeles. After its first overseas job moving material from US-controlled Guam to Chinese nationalists during the Chinese Civil War in 1946, it became a favorite of the US government and was contracted to build and manage airstrips in Okinawa, Taiwan, Thailand, and Pakistan. The company won $200 million in Defense Department contracts in Vietnam between 1957 and 1974 and employed an estimated 5,000 people there.

---

[19] Kissinger to Ford, "Ambassador Helms Assessment of Situation in Near East and South Asia," September 6, 1974, Box 12, National Security Adviser's Presidential Country Files for the Middle East and South Asia, GFL; Saunders and Applebaum to Kissinger, "Iranian Request for Authorization," April 27, 1973, Box 602, Folder 3, National Security File, Country Files – Middle East, RNL.

[20] R. J. S. Muir to R. Kealey, "US Military Sales to Saudi Arabia," August 27, 1976, FCO 8/2628, National Archives of the United Kingdom, Kew (hereafter, UKNA); R. J. S. Muir to R. M. James, September 8, 1976 FCO 8/262, UKNA.

In January 1975, it shifted gears with a $77 million contract to train
Saudi Arabian troops, set up through the Defense Department. Led by
James D. Holland, a former army colonel who lost an eye in Vietnam,
the company would provide 1,000 Special Forces veterans to train
King Faisal's 26,000-man Royal Palace Guard, commanded by his
son Prince Abdullah, whose primary responsibility had evolved from
serving as royal family bodyguards to the protection of oil installations.[21] (Another important consequence of Vietnam, and what many
in military circles saw as the threat of demobilization, was the rise of
private security contractors. Vinnell claimed its contract was the first
instance in history in which a private American company had been
given the role of forming and training a foreign army.) When the
company advertised jobs in military newspapers at Fort Ord,
California, and Fort Carson, Colorado, hundreds of soldiers lined up
outside their offices in suburban Los Angeles to fill out applications.
They received ten applications for every job available.[22]

The disclosure of the contract to the Senate made Vinnell the center
of a controversy over whether American firms should train foreign
military forces. John Stennis, the Mississippi Democrat who chaired
the Senate Armed Services Committee, was joined by Henry Jackson
and Hubert Humphrey in calling for an official inquiry.[23] Not to be
outdone, Senator Ted Kennedy of Massachusetts called for a six-
month moratorium on arms sales to the Persian Gulf. Senator
Harrison Williams, a Democrat of New Jersey, also announced inquiries into the role of the Lebanese Bank, Banque de Liban et d'Outre
Mer, which was slated to become a major stockholder in Vinnell in its
forthcoming corporate reorganization.[24]

The Ford administration defended the contract. The Vinnell training
mission fulfilled "the basic objectives of U.S. foreign policy to improve
relations with nations of the Middle East and see that their security is

---

[21] Henry Weinstein, "Vinnell, Its Vietnam Work Past, Tries to Rebound in Saudi
Arabia," *The New York Times*, February 25, 1975.

[22] "U.S. Company Will Train Saudi Troops to Guard Oil," *The New York Times*,
February 9, 1975.

[23] "Hearing on Training of Saudis Is Sought," *The New York Times*, February 10,
1975; Letter to Editor: Gilbert Wasserman and Bernard Sanow, *The New York
Times*, March 2, 1975.

[24] "Senator Plans to Investigate Arab Role in U.S. Company," *The New York
Times*, February 16, 1975.

enhanced," Secretary of Defense James R. Schlesinger said.[25] "We are not mercenaries because we are not pulling the triggers," one former army officer told a *New York Times* reporter. "We train people to pull triggers." Another joked, "Maybe that makes us executive mercenaries."[26] The controversy died down by the end of 1975, and the company joined other US contractors in Saudi Arabia, including Lockheed and Raytheon. In the next half-decade, it trained three newly mechanized infantry battalions and an artillery battalion of about 1,000 men each. The contract occurred at a time of increasingly thick connections between the Saudi government and American defense contractors, all with the support of the Department of Defense. A year later, for example, the Saudi government announced a $16 billion, ten-year construction plan for its armed forces under the supervision of the US Army Corps of Engineers. The Ford administration hoped the Vinnell contract would overcome what one Pentagon official described as "that old Merchant of Death stigma."[27] In other words, they believed that training and engineering contracts were fundamentally different than arms sales.

This was a potential miscalculation, especially given the reassertion of Congressional oversight of US war-making, but it also made an important point: Vinnell and other military contractors fit the American assessment of what Saudi Arabia needed. That perception of regional danger and military needs was a fundamental, if little studied, shift in American diplomacy in the Persian Gulf. The financial wealth of Iran, Saudi Arabia, and other oil producers, in conjunction with the uncertain regional environment, meant that the US military would astronomically increase their investment in regional security. In response to the Senate inquiry, the Department of Defense for the first time made public its listing of "technical assistance contracts" with foreign countries. Government and private teams had contracts through the Pentagon in thirty-four countries worth $727 million. The largest numbers of training programs were in Iran and Saudi Arabia, which totaled $676 million. The companies that joined

[25] "Pentagon Chief Defends Training of Saudi Force," *The New York Times*, February 13, 1975.
[26] "U.S. Company Will Train Saudi Troops to Guard Oil," *The New York Times*, February 9, 1975.
[27] Michael C. Jensen, "U.S. Arms Exports Boom, Particularly to the Mideast," *The New York Times*, April 14, 1975.

Vinnell included Bell Helicopter, Northrup, Westinghouse, McDonnell-Douglas, General Electric, and Raytheon, which had a $32.5 million contract to train Iranian personnel in the use of Hawk antiaircraft missiles.[28]

The 1976 F-16 Hearings

Those contracts were parts of a whole. Military sales to Iran increased from $524 million in 1972 to $3.91 billion in 1974. This included contracts for hundreds of fighter aircraft and helicopters, missile systems, ships, radars, guided bombs, anti-tank missiles, and other hardware.[29] The political scientist James Bill has noted one important effect of the unprecedented scope of the US-Iran military relationship: "The seamier side of American capitalism was especially visible to the Iranian people, who suddenly saw thousands upon thousands of American military advisers and commercial adventurers spread throughout their country."[30] There is no doubt that the most influential policymakers in the United States, including Henry Kissinger, largely failed to question the effects of the military relationship in domestic Iranian politics.[31] In the United States, the new degree of military transactions also sparked an institutional response in Congress in the form of the 1975 Nelson Amendment to the Arms Control Export Act, which gave legislators the power to disapprove arms sales. This was followed by a new Arms Export Control Act in 1976, which again called for Congressional oversight.

In that context, the Ford administration's decision to support the sale of 150 F-16 fighter jets to Iran set off an even larger domestic controversy and a new series of arms sales hearings. "This is a whole new ball game," Senator Hubert Humphrey said on the first day of hearings, after complaining that both the Department of Defense and the State Department had stonewalled Congressional requests for

[28] John W. Finney, "U.S. Teams Train Forces in 34 Lands," *The New York Times*, February 25, 1975.
[29] Transfers of Major Weapons, United States to Iran, 1969–1981, Stockholm International Peace Research Institute, Strategic Arms Database, generated May 22, 2020. The values are measured by SIPRI's "trend-indicator value" expressed in US dollars at constant 1990 prices.
[30] Bill, *The Eagle and the Lion*, 210.
[31] Recently, see Shannon, *Losing Hearts and Minds*.

information on Iranian and Saudi threat assessments and military sales.[32] The Senate hearings in 1976 raised issues – of constitutional power, of the definition of national security, and of US policy toward the Middle East – that would come up repeatedly in the following years. On one side were the arguments of the Ford administration, which lined up neatly with critiques of superpower détente that were becoming popular in the CIA, and which were beginning to be deployed publicly by groups like the Committee on the Present Danger and conservative magazines like *Commentary* and *Human Events*, as well as by presidential frontrunners for both parties.[33]

On the other side, dissent against arms sales was deep and wide. Politicians and the public interest groups made a series of interlinked arguments. For one, the United States yielded too much and gained too little. The sales also violated the spirit, if not the letter, of Congress's role in setting limits to US foreign policy. Finally, care and caution in arms sales also implied flexibility in foreign relations – a more rational and pragmatic approach to diplomacy that, in turn, was more likely to secure the national interest.

In August 1976, Humphrey's Senate Foreign Relations subcommittee on foreign assistance published a staff study on US military sales to Iran. On the day the Senate published the report, both *The New York Times* and *The Washington Post* carried front-page headlines about the "uncontrolled" sales of sophisticated armaments to Iran. The White House responded with their now-standard argument that Iran had played a constructive role in the region, and that its ability to do so had been enhanced by the acquisition of modern weapons. Iranian power, according to one NSC official, had allowed the shah to mediate the conflicts between Pakistan and India and between Pakistan and Afghanistan. As importantly, the shah's arms also had countered

---

[32] *Hearings before the Committee on Foreign Relations and the Subcommittee on Foreign Assistance of the Committee on Foreign Relations, on Proposed Sales of Arms to Iran and Saudi Arabia*, United States Senate, 94th Congress, 2nd Session (U.S. Government Printing Office, 1977), 3.

[33] Laurence Jurdem, *Paving the Way for Reagan: The Influence of Conservative Media on U.S. Foreign Policy* (Ithaca, NY: Cornell University Press, 2018); John Rosenberg, "The Quest against Détente: Eugene Rostow, the October War, and the Origins of the Anti-Détente Movement, 1969–1976," *Diplomatic History* 39:4 (2015): 720–744.

"the PFLO terrorist campaign" in Oman.[34] Nonetheless, the Senate
report (and the reporting on it) claimed that the 1972 "blank check"
arrangement with the White House had undermined Congressional,
State Department, and Defense Department reviews of arms sales.
"This Humphrey report was a disaster," Kissinger told the president.
"We have no better friend than the Shah."[35] Three years earlier,
Kissinger had been joined by Pentagon official William Clements in
arguing strongly for using arms sales as a means to maintain positive
relations with Iran. Clements even wanted to grant the shah his request
of personally flying in an F-14. "Not only is he interested in this
weapon, but this is a great image builder for him," he said. "A
demonstration of his virility."[36]

Some within the Ford administration agreed with the general thrust
of the Congressional critique. Secretary of Defense James Schlesinger
told Ford in September 1975 that although it was in the national
interest that Iran remain a strong military power, there was growing
doubt in his office about the "current policy of supporting an apparently open-ended Iranian military buildup." The Department of
Defense believed that Iranian military supply lines were "in shambles."
It also was telling that even the better-organized US military would find
it impossible to grow in the way the shah envisioned.[37] Regional
analysts in the State Department agreed. "In the last year there has
been increasing recognition that Iran's capability to absorb effectively
large numbers of advanced weapons systems is severely limited by the
paucity of trained manpower, long military construction delays, inadequate ports, and internal transportation systems," Assistant Secretary
of State Alfred Atherton reported to Kissinger in 1976, when the shah
first requested a Letter of Offer for the F-16s. To add to the problem in
US domestic politics, the shah's government sought to overcome a hard
currency crisis by negotiating a "barter oil deal" with General
Dynamics, the F-16 manufacturer, and two oil companies, whereby

---

[34] R. C. Samuel to I. T. M. Lucas, "US Arms Sales to Iran," August 2, 1976, FCO
8/2628, UKNA.
[35] Editors' footnote to Action Memorandum, "Sale to Iran of 150 F-16's," July 29,
1976, *FRUS, 1969–1976, Volume XXVII, Iran; Iraq, 1973–1976*, doc. 179.
[36] Minutes of Senior Review Group Meeting, July 20, 1973, *FRUS, 1969–1976,
Volume XXVII, Iran; Iraq, 1973–1976*, doc. 23.
[37] Memorandum from Secretary of Defense Schlesinger to President Ford,
September 2, 1975, *FRUS, 1969–1976, Volume XXVII, Iran; Iraq, 1973–1976*,
doc. 142.

the companies would receive Iranian crude and place their receipts in a special account tied to the purchase of the fighter jets. This would undoubtedly raise questions about Iranian influence in the jittery domestic economy. Nonetheless, Atherton understood that rejecting the shah's request for weapons "would create serious frictions in our relationship." The past was prelude to the present for him: "To sum up, our existing policy and the political/strategic importance of Iran argue in favor of approving the sale and sending the advance notice to Congress."[38] The State Department continued to find the military alliance with Iran valuable in other ways, too. In late 1976, for example, the department began to negotiate the transfer of rehabilitated M-60 tanks from Iran to Zaire.[39]

When Philip Habib, the undersecretary for political affairs at the State Department, went to the Senate Foreign Relations committee to justify the F-16 sale, he knew the reaction would be harsh. As the magnitude of sales increased, the critique became more pointed. In one telling example, Humphrey told him that arms sales were a double-edged sword. "You can never quite be sure who is going to be your ally. We have no guarantee of what the political situation in Iran is going to be," he said. "This is not being said as a cheap shot against the Shah, but these are the facts of life."[40] Habib nonetheless made a strong argument for the sales, basing his testimony on internal documents written by officials in the State Department, Department of Defense, and National Security Council. For him, the repercussions of not selling F-16s to Iran were greater than the risks. In terms of Iran, Congressional activism threatened to undo the trust built "over the administrations of six presidents."[41]

Humphrey shot back: "We have a special responsibility to say, 'Go Slow.'" He called MIT professor Lincoln Palmer Bloomfield to testify, who compared US foreign policymakers to "unwitting sorcerers'

---

[38] Atherton to Kissinger, "Sale to Iran of 150 F-16's," July 29, 1976, Box 13, National Security Adviser's Presidential Country Files for the Middle East and South Asia, GFL.
[39] Plowden to Scowcroft, "Arms for Zaire," October 1, 1976, Box 7, National Security Adviser's Presidential Country Files for Africa, GFL.
[40] *Hearings before the Committee on Foreign Relations and the Subcommittee on Foreign Assistance of the Committee on Foreign Relations, on Proposed Sales of Arms to Iran and Saudi Arabia*, United States Senate, 94th Congress, 2nd Session (U.S. Government Printing Office, 1977), 37.
[41] Ibid., 36.

apprentices" who in following their narrow rationale for military buildup had created a "potentially lethal brew."[42]

In addition to the blowback argument, domestic opponents to arms sales used other rationales. Human rights advocates cited the shah's poor human rights record. Others questioned Iran's ability as a developing nation to manage the responsibility of handling such technologically advanced weaponry. After the 1979 revolution, television coverage of the hostage crisis created a convergence of those two lines of thought into a widespread public discourse – a "captivity narrative" that connected terrorism and Islam as threats to American life. That view of Iran was accompanied by a geographical shift in US discussions from identifying the Middle East as "the Arab world" to the "Islamic world." Whereas the shah once was held up as a Westernized model and moderate force in the region, Khomeini and Iran were discussed using the same iconography that had been reserved for Arab "Cadillac Sheikhs" during the 1973–1974 energy crisis. "Don't Waste Gas, Waste Khomeini" bumper stickers became popular in 1979 and 1980, for example.[43]

But in 1976, the Ford administration successfully protected the sales. The National Security Council captured the overriding rationale in a proposed presidential message on Iran. The bilateral relationship was one of fundamental importance to the United States "and to the interests of the entire free world." Military supply was an important element of that relationship, and it could not be separated out for attack by "topsy-turvy" elements in Congress without calling into question the overall relationship – which was crucial given Iran's border with the Soviet Union and its control over oil that was "so vital to the world's energy needs." Iran was a strong ally and a "force for stability and moderation in the region."[44]

The White House wound the link between regional security, oil for the global economy, and arms sales tighter and tighter. Ford wrote to

---

[42] Ibid., 91, 94.

[43] See Melani McAlister, *Epic Encounters: Culture, Media, and U.S. Interests in the Middle East since 1945* (Berkeley, CA: University of California Press, 2005), 198–234; Salim Yaqub, *Imperfect Strangers: Americans, Arabs, and U.S.-Middle East Relations* (Ithaca, NY: Cornell University Press, 2016), 302–336.

[44] Backchannel Message from Robert B. Oakley of the National Security Council Staff, August 6, 1976, *FRUS, 1969–1976, Volume XXVII, Iran; Iraq, 1973-1976*, doc. 181.

the shah a month after the hearings concluded. He connected his ongoing personal diplomacy on oil prices to military assistance, celebrating his team's "successful resistance" to Congressional attempts to block the F-16 sale. In this case, the global context of high oil prices was crucial. The president was worried that a new price increase by Iran and the other OPEC nations would reverse what he saw as the favorable trends toward increased consumption and economic recovery in the United States and the rest of the noncommunist bloc. "The fragile and uneven nature of the global economic recovery requires that responsible nations avoid action which would endanger it," he wrote. Iranian support for an OPEC price increase, he warned, "would play directly into the hands" of his domestic opponents who attacked the military relationship between the two nations.[45]

Carter, the Free World, and National Interests

The military relationship between Iran and the United States seemed to some to have the unstoppable forces of history behind it, but it was also open to question. On May 19, 1977, new US President Jimmy Carter made a speech on "arms transfers" meant to signal a major policy shift. "The virtually unrestrained spread of conventional weaponry threatens stability in every region of the world," he said. Carter had campaigned on reducing arms sales and already had issued a Presidential Directive that called for restraint. From the Presidential Directive studies, he now concluded that the US government would view weapons sales as "an exceptional foreign policy instrument, to be used only where it can be clearly demonstrated that the transfer contributes to our national security interests."[46] But controversy continued when the Carter administration proposed further sales to Iran and Saudi Arabia, and senators again aired their opinions. Both supporters and detractors of US arms sales saw themselves as the protectors of the national interest and criticized their opponents for undermining it. As is often the case, such categories made for strong

---

[45] SecState to AmEmbassy Tehran, "Letter from President Ford to His Imperial Majesty," October 30, 1976, Box 5, National Security Adviser's International Economic Affairs Staff: Files, GFL.

[46] Jimmy Carter, "Conventional Arms Transfer: Policy Statement by the President," May 19, 1977, American Presidency Project.

domestic political arguments but meant little in terms of actual changes in policy.

Internal documents reveal that in 1977 the Carter administration believed what it said. In preparing his team's response to the new Presidential Directive, Policy Planning Director Anthony Lake wrote Secretary of State Cyrus Vance that the administration would encourage its oil-producing allies Iran and Saudi Arabia to match their weapons acquisitions to their "absorption capacities" – a popular term at the time that questioned how quickly developing economies could grow. For Lake the application of neoliberal development economics to military policy presented a dilemma. How could the Carter administration reconcile its "moral rejection" of arms sales as "the premier instrument of US foreign policy" with its need to accomplish the goals of "peace in the Middle East and access to Persian Gulf oil"? Lake also noted that the Treasury Department believed that limiting sales would hit the domestic defense industry, especially the aerospace industry, "fairly hard."[47]

The administration's understanding of national interest dictated the resolution of Lake's dilemma. Carter, despite his arms restraint speech and campaigning on a popular platform of arms control, decided to continue to increase sales to both Iran and Saudi Arabia. If the presidential decision didn't sit well with certain senators, it did please officials in the Pentagon, many of whom had argued since the 1950 Tripartite Declaration on the Arab-Israeli arms balance that to restrain regional sales was to deny the United States hard currency profits and political leverage.[48] A Carter administration report leaked to *The New York Times* noted the importance of these economic considerations. It estimated that arms sales supported about 700,000 jobs, including employees of large aerospace and arms producers and

[47] Lake to Vance, Talking Points, "Third World Economic Relations," April 15, 1977, Box 2, Record Group 59: Records of the Department of State (hereafter, RG 59), Records of Anthony Lake, 1977–1981, National Archives and Records Administration of the United States, College Park, Maryland (hereafter, NARA). To understand these arguments in their context, see Michael Brenes, *For Might and Right: Cold War Defense Spending and the Remaking of American Democracy* (Amherst, MA: University of Massachusetts Press, 2020); Jennifer Mittelstadt, *The Rise of the Military Welfare State* (Cambridge, MA: Harvard University Press, 2016).

[48] "Action Memorandum, Phillips Talbot to the Secretary of State," July 25, 1964, Box 1, Folder 4, Cottam Papers, LBJL.

their subcontractors. The report also estimated that an immediate 40 percent cut in the volume of orders would displace 132,000 workers, while a gradual reduction would leave 75,000 without jobs by 1983.[49] In this and other ways, the continued rationale for arms sales linked economic and military policy into a holistic understanding of the national interest that naturalized important assumptions. Among them: not only were sales good for the domestic economy and the growing aerospace industry, they also helped maintain access to the Middle Eastern oil that was so crucial to the continuation of the energy intensive development programs that provided the foundation of US economic and ideological power. In the United States, as in the world's other arms manufacturers, economic arguments and industry lobbying would come to play an important role in securing and sustaining production and sales.

An early State Department assessment for the Carter administration revealed the extent of sales to Iran, as well as the justification for them. In 1973 and 1974, for example, weapons transfers to Iran had accounted for between 17 and 24 percent of all US sales, for a total of over $3 billion. Such sales, it was widely agreed, contributed to "our national interests" in several ways: they enabled friends and allies to defend themselves and deter aggression, they "cemented good relations and enhanced our influence," and they provided much-needed foreign exchange. Security assistance in the region was "part of a web of cooperation and mutual confidence, critical to furthering major U.S. national goals in energy, international finance, and the pursuit of Middle East peace."[50]

Secretary of State Vance, who was in charge of the Presidential Review Memorandum process for arms sales, understood this complex of factors and favored what two scholars have described as the continuation of "a permissive arms sales regime" with Iran.[51] Ultimately, Vance worked to shield the shah's previous request for 160 F-16s from

[49] Bernard Weinraub, "The U.S. Policy on Arms Has a Life of Its Own: Rhetoric and Guilt," *The New York Times*, September 18, 1977.

[50] "Response to PRM/NSC-12, Arms Transfer Policy Review," April 9, 1977, Box 2, RG 59, Records of Anthony Lake, 1977–1981, NARA.

[51] For a more detailed analysis, see Stephen McGlinchey and Robert W. Murray, "Jimmy Carter and the Sale of the AWACS to Iran in 1977," *Diplomacy & Statecraft* 28:2 (2017): 254–276. For the longer history, see Stephen McGlinchey, *US Arms Policies towards the Shah's Iran* (New York: Routledge, 2014), 61–120.

renewed scrutiny and, after meeting the shah in Tehran, proposed a $1.2 billion sale of seven E-3 AWACS aircraft to Iran. Although Vance is depicted as a "dove" in terms of Iran, in large part because his opposition to the planned rescue of US hostages in Tehran led to his resignation, he followed the lead of his predecessor Kissinger in the earliest discussions of weapons sales to Iran.

As they had during the Ford administration, many senators balked. Thomas Eagleton, a Democrat from Missouri, and John Culver, a Democrat from Iowa, led the opposition to the AWACS sale in 1977. An AWACS plane was essentially a Boeing 707 loaded with more than $100 million worth of the United States' most "sophisticated and esoteric radar, computer, and communications equipment," Eagleton said at the beginning of the hearings. It was the most expensive aircraft ever developed, and it "represented the state-of-the-art in our electronic arsenal." The senator then recounted AWACS' checkered history of development. It had shifted from being designed for US continental defense, then as a tactical lever in the European theater, and finally as "an instrument of technology aid in the semi-developed but oil-rich country of Iran." Logic dictated skepticism of the sale of such advanced equipment to a "semi-literate country," he said.[52]

Moreover, this was not an "ordinary arms deal," according to Eagleton. It was not born of Carter's election calls for moderation and restraint, rather it was the continuation of the "atmosphere of secret deals" of what Eagleton called the Kissinger years. Of special concern to him and others was the potential for blowback. Echoing Humphrey's arguments to the Ford administration, this perspective contradicted the assumption that the US-Iran military relationship would help bring stability to the regional. Neither the White House nor the Pentagon had thoroughly analyzed the national security risks of the sale, Eagleton charged, including the potential loss of military secrets through espionage. Along similar lines, the senator was also worried about what the Carter administration had misrepresented as the "support personnel" or "American technicians" that would go to Iran as part of the deal. These he characterized bluntly as troops. Their presence created a new foreign policy risk, one that loomed all the

---

[52] *Hearings before the Subcommittee on Foreign Assistance and the Committee on Foreign Relations, Sale of AWACS to Iran*, United States Senate, 95th Congress, 1st Session (U.S. Government Printing Office, 1977), 2–3.

larger because of the defeat in Vietnam. Hostilities in the perennially insecure Middle East would put American lives in jeopardy. "President Carter – or down the road, his successor – might face a disturbing policy decision," he said. "Either to allow Americans to fight a foreign war or withdraw them, thereby assuring the defeat of an ally."[53]

Culver echoed the sentiments. Like Eagleton, he was worried about the stability of the region. "We don't know which way the guns will point if the regime changes overnight," he said. After all, Iran was an autocratic state in "the volatile Middle East." He then emphasized his personal experience discussing AWACS with military brass and the common rank and file. "I have wargamed [*sic*] the system from the simulators," he said. He had seen it at work – at least virtually – and described to the other senators the largest and most advanced airborne computer the world had ever seen, its complex display consoles blessed with the ability to pinpoint distant targets with great accuracy and send planes to bomb them. This was thus not a defensive sale, as the White House and Pentagon argued, but a "force multiplier" to the 200 F-4, 153 F-5, and 80 F-14 aircraft the US had already sold to Iran over the past decade, not to mention the 160 F-16s that were forthcoming. Senator Frank Church, the Democrat from Idaho, agreed. A "primitive predecessor" to AWACS used in Vietnam had improved the "effective kill rate" of US fighter planes by a ratio of five to one, he claimed.[54]

Adding to the lack of trust was the post-Vietnam perception that national security estimates were inherently political. As Church put it, one of the most damning revelations of his recent Senate hearings on the CIA was that the CIA and other government bureaucracies had "tailored its estimates of enemy strength in such a way as to conform with its perception of what the president wanted to hear." Church described that situation as the ultimate definition of intelligence failure. Nixon had opened up "a blank check arms sales relationship diplomacy" with the shah that Carter seemed bent on continuing, Culver complained. "What the Shah wants the Shah gets."[55]

The Carter administration nonetheless followed the line of reasoning established earlier in the 1970s. In a direct echo of the F-16 hearings, Vance again sent Atherton, now the assistant secretary of state for

[53] Ibid., 5.　[54] Ibid., 41.　[55] Ibid., 22.

Near Eastern affairs, to Capitol Hill to justify the sales. Iran was "a major force for stability in the region," Atherton said. Moreover, the security risk of slippage moved in the opposite direction than the senators seemed to believe. Arms sales did not embolden radicals. Instead, they gave evidence that the United States was a trustworthy ally, which in turn helped to prop up moderates in the Middle East. "I think, because of that, it has helped given encouragement to other moderate regimes in the region to follow moderate policies and to resist more radical pressures," he said, in a nod toward the ongoing debates over the price of oil. Most importantly, he disagreed with their argument that more arms sales would destabilize Iran. To the contrary, Atherton painted a different worst-case scenario. Imagine, he said, if the United States lost Iran because it didn't sell it the arms it needed. A change in the government there would throw into chaos the whole Persian Gulf region and threaten the critical Straits of Hormuz. The shah's government was crucial to "protecting the region's petroleum wealth."[56]

To turn Iran's request down, according to that vision, would cast American credibility into question. Atherton almost repeated verbatim Kissinger's argument to Nixon eight years earlier: the health of the bilateral relationship depended on "our willingness to help them meet what they perceive as threats to their national security." American willingness to arm Iran was linked to American legitimacy, obviously in question worldwide after the fall of Saigon.[57]

Other countries needed evidence that the United States would be steady in its support of its friends. Atherton was joined by Leslie Gelb, the director of the State Department's Office of Politico-Military Affairs. A quick look at the regional map indicated the importance of Iran to American national security, he told the senators. Iran not only controlled the most important sea-lanes of the international oil indus- try; it was also "nestled in between the Soviet Union and Iraq." Given the high stakes, it made sense to yield to the expertise of military

[56] Ibid., 31. Hubert Humphrey could not help interjecting, "It seems like we can hardly resist the temptation to get ahold of the money that he gets from his oil" (37).
[57] Ibid., 30. On the loss of US legitimacy, see Keys, *Reclaiming American Virtue*; Christian G. Appy, *American Reckoning: The Vietnam War and Our National Identity* (New York: Viking, 2015).

planners. An extensive joint study by the Department of Defense and Iranian government had examined forty-one different sites of vulnerability, he told the senators. In this light, the request for only seven AWACs, to be linked to between two and twenty-one "off-the-shelf" ground-based radars and the Iranian air force, wasn't overzealous at all.[58]

One of the few senators who openly supported the sale in the committee hearings was Barry Goldwater, the Republican from Arizona. For him, as for the Carter administration, AWACS was a commitment to the stability of the Middle East. The sale, he said, enhanced US national security by supporting a valuable and vulnerable ally. His analysis of the regional threat also centered on oil and the Cold War. "Iran, with its tremendous oil reserves, is the gateway through which the Soviet Union would have to pass if it decided to take the oil assets of the Middle East," Goldwater said. "The Free World is heavily dependent on this area for oil." Goldwater also advanced the domestic economic argument, emphasizing the nation's balances of payments. "Further engagement of the refusal to sell aircraft, military or civilian, to other countries, will, in my opinion, just continue to destroy this country's ability to meet its balance of payments," he said.[59]

The fact that Goldwater joined forces with the Carter administration on economic and security grounds is revealing. More conditioned by a shared assumption about the unstable Middle East, US national security, oil supply, and the domestic economy than any real political differences in terms of foreign policy, the Carter administration and its unlikely ally turned to the same arguments as its predecessors. But at the same time, the authoritarianism and human rights abuses of the Iranian government had gained greater public scrutiny than previously. In the most well-known instance in the United States, Carter was roundly criticized as a hypocrite for the disjuncture between his administration's emphasis on human rights and his praise of the shah. It

---

[58] *Hearings before the Subcommittee on Foreign Assistance and the Committee on Foreign Relations, Sale of AWACS to Iran*, United States Senate, 95th Congress, 1st Session (U.S. Government Printing Office, 1977), 42–44.

[59] Ibid., 86.

seemed a stroke of justice to some in November 1977 when the Washington, DC, police force's tear gas, meant for protestors, rode the wind over the Rose Garden and ruined a photo session of the two leaders.[60]

The "Loss of Iran" and US-Saudi Relations

The first months of the Iranian Revolution in 1979 seemed to provide support for the more careful approach to arms sales. When the botched rescue attempt of Operation Eagle Claw led to the death of eight soldiers and the resignation of Secretary of State Vance, it seemed to many that restraint was crucial to calm a region that was already reeling from a number of conflicts. At the same time it became more difficult, as National Security Adviser Zbigniew Brzezinski put it in a Special Coordination Committee Meeting, to "differentiate between actions which are escalatory and those which are essentially defensive in nature."[61]

But calls for restraint again were undermined after the revolution, the Soviet invasion of Afghanistan, the renewal of fighting between the Yemen Arab Republic and the People's Democratic Republic of Yemen, the capture of the mosque in Mecca by Saudi dissidents, and the beginning of the Iran-Iraq War. Concerns about regional insecurity and the global economy again played the crucial part in the newly pervasive sense of crisis that enveloped Washington. "Events in Iran have drastically altered power arrangements in the region and make the threat of Soviet encirclement even more immediate," the CIA reported in January 1979.[62] For US Ambassador to Saudi Arabia John West, the Iranian Revolution brought the Saudi leadership a realization of two crucial facts: absolute monarchies were vulnerable and the US and its Western allies were absolutely dependent on oil. West worried that the "U.S.-Saudi relationship, generally defined as oil

---

[60] Javier Gil Guerrero, "Human Rights and Tear Gas: The Question of Carter Administration Officials Opposed to the Shah," *British Journal of Middle Eastern Studies* 43:3 (2016): 285–301.

[61] Summary of Conclusions of a Special Coordination Committee Meeting, September 27, 1980, *FRUS, 1977–1980, Volume XVII, Middle East Region; Arabian Peninsula*, doc. 220.

[62] CIA, Intelligence Memorandum, "The Impact of Iran on Saudi Arabia," January 26, 1979, *FRUS, 1977–1980, Volume XVIII, Middle East Region; Arabian Peninsula*, doc. 181.

for security" had been driven off kilter by Iran. If the United States did not work to prove its worth to Saudi Arabia, it risked losing that nation too.[63]

The Carter administration began to work more closely with the Saudi government to meet their military requests. It also worked to mitigate minor irritants in US-Saudi relations, for example seeking to broker a resolution to the lawsuit brought against OPEC by the International Association of Machinists and Aerospace Workers. As before, much of the public pressure on the White House and against its zero-sum thinking came from the legislative branch. The Senate held its first hearings on Iran and global oil supply in January 1979, just weeks after the revolution began. For Henry "Scoop" Jackson, the Democrat from Washington who chaired the hearings, the combined implications of the most recent OPEC price increase and the revolution were ominous. American imports, at approximately 8.9 million barrels per day, were greater than those of Japan and Germany combined. "Once again we have been warned of the political and economic dangers involved in our heavy dependence on foreign oil," he said dramatically in his opening speech. For Jackson, the example of Iran was now wholly centered on the link between regional security and economic well-being: "Even if OPEC nations continue to be willing to supply us, the possible instability of many of these countries still poses an unacceptable threat to our economy."[64]

One potential solution was at home. As during the 1967 Arab oil embargo and the price increases in 1973 and 1974, a number of actors called for a renewed search for energy in the continental United States, Alaska, and in the continental shelf. They also envisioned limiting the power of environmental groups. For Jackson, a westerner, the most promising sources were in Alaska, the Arctic Wildlife Natural Reserve, and in Prudhoe Bay. For him, the power of "activists" to limit new production, not to mention the stretch of pipelines across the United States, needed to be curbed. "We cannot allow the courts to be used by litigants as a forum to advocate positions on public policy decisions

---

[63] "Report Prepared by the Ambassador to Saudi Arabia, "Saudi Arabia – The Lesson of Iran," National Security Affairs, Brzezinski Materials, Country Files: Saudi Arabia, JCL.

[64] *Iran and World Oil Supply, Hearing before the Committee on Energy and Natural Resources*, United States Senate, 96th Congress, 1st Session, January 17, 1979, part 1 (U.S. Government Printing Office, 1979), 2.

that are political in the classic sense of the term," the senator said. Bipartisan consensus existed on this point. To disallow production where oil lay was "a formula for continued energy instability," according to Senator Mark Hatfield, the ranking minority member on the committee. Government restrictions on production "inevitably produced a straightjacket" that tied the hands of "the productive genius of the American people."[65] He and others criticized, in particular, attempts by environmental groups to block the controversial SOHIO pipeline. Although the ideological and economic rationale for domestic oil production and anti-environmentalism is not the topic of this chapter, it is important to note that the expansion of the commercial exploitation of natural resources on public lands continued under the Reagan administration and its controversial secretary of the interior, James Watt.[66]

The problem of oil scarcity was widely perceived, and influential actors turned to foreign sources even more decidedly than they criticized environmentalists. "We do not know when Iranian production will come back," James Schlesinger, now secretary of energy, warned. He listed a series of events in the past half-decade that the senators probably didn't need reminding of: the 1973–1974 Arab oil embargo, OPEC price control, a domestic national gas shortage in the winter of 1976–1977, a coal strike in 1979. He estimated the Iranian shortfall to the global market as being around 5.5 billion barrels per day. Although the Saudi government had increased its spare capacity production to 3 billion barrels to offset the loss, it was not enough. All of this pointed to US and global vulnerability. Oil from the Persian Gulf was crucial to US national security for Schlesinger. "The Iranian shortfall, of course, underscores the fragility of the logistical and production system on which we depend," he said. "I think that we, in the United States, will have to take steps to shore up the nations around the Gulf that look to the United States for support."[67]

---

[65] Ibid., 5.

[66] On the Department of the Interior, see Megan Black, *The Global Interior: Mineral Frontiers and American Power* (Cambridge, MA: Harvard University Press, 2018), 214–244.

[67] *Iran and World Oil Supply, Hearing before the Committee on Energy and Natural Resources*, United States Senate, 96th Congress, 1st Session, January 17, 1979, part 1 (U.S. Government Printing Office, 1979), 30–31.

The defense-turned-energy secretary meant Saudi Arabia. As luck would have it, the renewal of war in Yemen led the Saudi government to request additional arms deliveries in March 1979. The Carter administration agreed to do so and, as Congressional critics quickly noted, waived the required thirty-day notification period. "Failure to provide adequate munitions will only reinforce the Saudi view that we make decisions about their security needs primarily on political grounds," Secretary of Defense Harold Brown warned Carter.[68] The single best decision the Carter administration made in 1979, Ambassador West believed, was the president's use of his emergency powers to expedite the transfer of F-15 fighter jets and AWACS, to station a military planning team, and to send naval forces to the Indian Ocean. This "restored in the Saudis' minds the credibility and reliability of the U.S. government as a friend and ally in a time of need," he told the State Department.[69]

If questioned by Congress about the waiver and Congressional oversight, Undersecretary of State David Newsom was instructed to respond that US forces were not directly involved.[70] This was not, strictly speaking, true. By October 1, 1980, Secretary of Defense Brown would write jubilantly to President Carter that the deployment of four US-owned AWACS over Saudi Arabia, with supporting equipment and 350 ground personnel, had provided "an entrée to the increased security cooperation with Saudi Arabia so essential in the long run to the viability of our military posture in Southwest Asia." As with Iran previously, arms sales were deemed crucial to the bilateral relationship. Brown added that the United States' willing accommodation of Saudi requests was linked, even if not explicitly, to the Saudi decision to raise oil production by another half-million barrels a day to offset losses from Iran and Iraq. It was in the national interest to further expedite the flow of air defense material to Saudi Arabia. The

[68] Memorandum from Brown to Carter, "Saudi Arabia: Munitions for their F-5 Aircraft," Box 67, National Security Affairs, Brzezinski Materials, Country Files: Saudi Arabia, JCL.

[69] Report Prepared by the Ambassador of Saudi Arabia, n.d. (January 1, 1980), *FRUS, 1977–1980, Volume XVIII, Middle East Region; Arabian Peninsula,* doc. 206.

[70] Summary of Conclusions of a Mini-Special Coordination Committee Meeting, March 7, 1979, *FRUS, 1977–1980, Volume XVII, Middle East Region; Arabian Peninsula,* doc. 275.

Christopher Dietrich

United States needed to be in a position to "respond quickly in the event a similar threat to the oil fields or to AWACS appears to be developing," Brown said.[71]

In June 1979, the secretary of defense called on Carter to follow the recommendations of a military mission led by General Richard Lawrence, which concluded that the United States should work more closely with Saudi Arabia in "central planning and operations assistance" – moving beyond a "Sears, Roebuck" approach to equipment deliveries and training.[72] The same month, NSC expert Gary Sick wrote Brzezinski to support the findings of the Lawrence mission, urging him to support "the genesis of a new military relation" with Saudi Arabia.[73] The men expressed a widely held understanding of US foreign relations. To provide arms and information, including the deployment of AWACS, was "a litmus test of our relationship with the Saudis," CIA Director Admiral Stansfield Turner said on another occasion, "and we should be as forthcoming as possible."[74] "The military supply field was where the U.S. could exercise the most influence over Saudi Arabia," NSC officials Sick and William Quandt told Brzezinski.[75] The Saudi government, like Iran and many other cases before, was aware of this perspective and used it to their advantage in negotiations. "If Congress objected to meeting the defensive needs of the Royal Saudi Air Force," Saudi Minister of Defense Sultan bin Abdul Aziz al-Saud told West on one occasion, "Saudi Arabia would consider itself free to seek other sources."[76]

[71] Memorandum from Secretary of Defense Brown to President Carter, "Assistance to Saudi Arabia," October 1, 1980, *FRUS, 1977–1980, Volume XVII, Middle East Region; Arabian Peninsula*, doc. 221.

[72] Brown to Carter, "Organization of Military Assistance Efforts in Saudi Arabia," June 18, 1979, Brzezinski Materials, Country Files: Saudi Arabia, Box 67, JCL.

[73] Gary Sick and Robert Hunter to Brzezinski, "U.S. Military Relationship with Saudi Arabia," August 8, 1979, *FRUS, 1977–1980, Volume XVII, Middle East Region; Arabian Peninsula*, doc. 197.

[74] Summary of Conclusions of a Special Coordination Committee Meeting, September 27, 1980, *FRUS, 1977–1980, Volume XVII, Middle East Region; Arabian Peninsula*, doc. 220.

[75] Memorandum, William Quandt and Gary Sick to Brzezinski, "Our Influence with Saudi Arabia," May 3, 1979, *FRUS, 1977–1980, Volume XVIII, Middle East Region; Arabian Peninsula*, doc. 191

[76] "Telegram from the Embassy in Saudi Arabia to the Department of State," May 1, 1980, *FRUS, 1977–1980, Volume XVII, Middle East Region; Arabian Peninsula*, doc. 213.

The US deployed those aircraft and, together with the Saudi military, adjusted the locations of ground-based radar systems in the Eastern Province.[77] Supporters of arms sales in 1980 realized that they stood at an important geopolitical and "geoeconomic" moment, to be sure. They were also, however, swept up in that moment. The Carter administration linked its military expansion in Saudi Arabia to regional stability and continued oil flows for the US and global economies, which policymakers believed were both beginning to bounce back from the shocks of the 1970s. Of critical importance was the protection of what US Ambassador West described as "the normal flow of neutral shipping." For Crown Prince Fahd of Saudi Arabia, increased bilateral military cooperation between the United States and Saudi Arabia was of critical importance to "regional defense." He and other leaders from both Saudi Arabia and the United States emphasized "the fundamental nature of the relationship and its benefits to the entire region."[78] After Carter declared the oil of the Persian Gulf a national security interest of the United States in his January 1980 State of the Union address, Brzezinski urged him to be "somewhat more forthcoming" to Saudi Arabian military requests.[79]

When the Soviet Union invaded Afghanistan in December 1979, many leaders in the United States believed that Moscow had embarked on a plan to fill a vacuum of power in the Persian Gulf. This was already a widespread concern before. In a high-level Policy Review Committee Meeting in June 1979, both Schlesinger and Brzezinski warned of "the growing perception of U.S. weakness in the region." It was necessary, according to this view, to preserve the security position of the United States. "Without Middle Eastern oil the Free World as we know it is through," Schlesinger said.[80] Such an

[77] Briefing Memorandum from Saunders to Muskie, "Update on U.S. Security Assistance Efforts in Saudi Arabia," December 18, 1980, *FRUS, 1977–1980, Volume XVII, Middle East Region; Arabian Peninsula*, doc. 228.
[78] "Telegram from the Embassy in Saudi Arabia to the Department of State, 'U.S.-Saudi Military Cooperation,'" October 13, 1980, *FRUS, 1977–1980, Volume XVII, Middle East Region; Arabian Peninsula*, doc. 224. For a definition of geoeconomics, see Deborah Cowen and Neil Smith, "After Geopolitics? From the Geopolitical Social to Geoeconomics," *Antipode* 41:1 (2009): 22–48.
[79] Memorandum, Brzezinski to Carter, February 6, 1980, *FRUS, 1977–1980, Volume XII, Afghanistan*, doc. 197.
[80] Minutes of Policy Review Committee Meeting, June 21, 1979, RAC SAFE39C-17–55–4–7, C03341983, JCL.

explanation, based on the idea that a more assertive Soviet Union sought to take advantage of American weakness and irresolution, had specific policy implications. The threat of a potentially enduring shift to the global balance of power called for a forceful reaction. "I want to assure you that I am prepared to commit the United States to take the necessary steps to enhance security in Southwest Asia and the Middle East, not just because of U.S. interests, but because of the broad stakes the West in general has in this region's stability and the flow of oil," Carter wrote British Prime Minister Margaret Thatcher.[81]

Iran was often raised as an analogy in US meetings. Similar to the shah's regime, Saudi Arabia had begun to show its value as a regional ally, the State Department reported. It had financed Somalian development programs and arms purchases, as recommended by the US Army Corps of Engineers and military survey teams. By October 1979, the Saudi government also had begun to consider US requests that it finance the purchase of F-5 aircraft for the Sudan.[82] Soon after, both Brown and Brzezinski pressed Carter to approve sales of 850 Maverick missiles and 1,000 laser-guided bombs for Saudi Arabia's fleet of F-5s. Failure to do so, Brown said, would "reinforce the Saudi view that we make decisions about their security needs primarily on political grounds."[83] By January 1980, NSC officials were telling Brzezinski that the "weight of Soviet land combat power" needed to be balanced by the expansion of a permanent US military presence in the area. The Carter administration needed to plan for "a more ambitious option of inserting the necessary land, air, and naval forces in Saudi Arabia and the Gulf to protect Gulf oil against direct attack or stoppage of oil flow through political side effects of events elsewhere."[84]

Brown recommended accelerating the delivery of F-15s already approved by Congress in 1978 by diverting deliveries scheduled for the US Air Force. He believed this had the added benefit that it could be done without consulting Congress. In large part, these debates were

---

[81] "Draft Telegram from the Department of State to the Embassy in the United Kingdom," January 10, 1980, *FRUS*, 1977–1980, *Volume XII, Afghanistan*, doc. 156.

[82] Memorandum from Vance to Carter, October 28, 1979, *FRUS*, 1977–1980, *Volume XXVII, Horn of Africa*, doc. 98.

[83] Memorandum from Brown to Carter, November 13, 1979, National Security Affairs, Brzezinski Materials, Country Files: Saudi Arabia, Box 67, JCL.

[84] Memorandum, Ermath to Brzezinski, "NSC on Afghanistan," January 2, 1980, *FRUS*, 1977–1980, *Volume XII, Afghanistan*, doc. 133.

held out of the public eye and were only recently declassified. They also reveal a growing national security consensus around arms sales to the Middle East. In short, decision makers believed that to not acquiesce to Saudi arms requests, in particular AWACS and F-15s, would be to do irreparable damage to the place of the United States in the world.

Carter's Critics

The loss of Iran changed how the Carter administration perceived and responded to the threat of violence and instability in the Persian Gulf, as Brzezinski's famous invocation of the "arc of crisis" made so clear.[85] Brzezinski was not alone in believing that the United States had suffered a series of losses throughout Southwest Asia, and that those losses had emboldened the Soviet Union. "We are probably more vulnerable today to foreign threat than at any time since General Howe landed in New York and set out northward to divide the American colonies," one State Department official wrote. The peril came not from military invasion but "from an attack on our economic wellbeing (and out political cohesion) arising from our extreme dependence on oil imported from politically unreliable and possibly unstable countries."[86]

Not everyone within the Carter administration agreed on the benefits of arms sales. In meetings of the Special Coordination Committee on the question of AWACS for Saudi Arabia, Deputy Secretary of State Warren Christopher warned of the problems of an overly conspicuous US presence in the Persian Gulf. In the context of the Iran-Iraq War, he also argued that any attack on Saudi oil installations would only be symbolic and could not "do much real damage." Brown and Brzezinski hotly rebutted Christopher, reminding him of what he already knew: that Iran had begun to build significant air power in the past decade. "If Iran hits Saudi oil fields, our position is gone," Brzezinski said.[87]

---

[85] See Fain, "Conceiving the 'Arc of Crisis.'"

[86] Memorandum from Cooper to Secretary of State Muskie, "Domestic Economic Policy and Foreign Policy," May 16, 1980, *FRUS, 1977–1980, Volume III, Foreign Economic Policy*, doc. 241.

[87] Summary of Conclusions of a Special Coordination Committee Meeting, September 27, 1980, *FRUS, 1977–1980, Volume XVII, Middle East Region; Arabian Peninsula*, doc. 220.

Christopher remained firm that the expansion of US forces would be provocative and risked expanding regional conflict rather than confining it. But he was in the minority in these and other meetings. Admiral Thomas Hayward of the Joint Chiefs of Staff summarized the consensus at an October 1980 meeting of the Special Coordination Committee: "Every study had shown that access to Saudi Arabia was essential. We should take advantage of the present circumstances to begin developing the kind of relationship with Saudi Arabia on security that will be required if we are to establish an effective military capability in the region."[88] Brown placed the conversation on Saudi arms sales in the broader context of regional political stability and global economic health in a memo to the president. "Without these Saudi facilities," he told Carter, "our whole Persian Gulf/Indian Ocean strategy would be undermined." Moreover, any US influence over Saudi oil production decisions would be lessened.[89]

The loss of Iran provided an opportunity to Carter's political enemies to attack him, and the campaign of former California governor Ronald Reagan cried foul. Leading the charge was campaign director William Casey, a Fordham University and St. John's Law School graduate who had become the chief of intelligence operations for the OSS in Europe during World War II and, afterward, had been a partner at prestigious law firms in New York and Washington, DC. In the Nixon administration, he had been appointed to the Securities and Exchange Commission and then became the undersecretary for economic affairs at the Department of State.[90]

Casey was well-versed in international oil politics and the regional security of the Middle East when he agreed to chair Reagan's campaign. He read the work of State Department consultant and oil expert Walter Levy closely in the 1960s and 1970s, and in October 1973 was selected by Richard Nixon to chair the US delegation to Paris for meetings of the Organization of Economic Cooperation and

[88] Summary of Conclusions of a Special Coordination Committee Meeting, October 3, 1980, *FRUS, 1977–1980, Volume XVII, Middle East Region; Arabian Peninsula*, doc. 222.
[89] Memorandum from Secretary of Defense Brown to President Carter, November 5, 1980, *FRUS, 1977–1980, Volume XVII, Middle East Region; Arabian Peninsula*, doc. 227.
[90] The Johns Hopkins Conference for Corporate Executives, "Casey Bio," September 1973, Box 155, William J. Casey Papers, Hoover Institution Archives, Stanford University, Palo Alto (hereafter, HIA).

Development on the energy crisis. He was responsible then for the decision to revitalize the Foreign Petroleum Supply Committee as a coordinating body within the US government.[91]

Casey had taken a restrained attitude during the 1973–1974 energy crisis. In line with the early policy of the Nixon administration, he had warned his European and Asian counterparts not to yield to their anxiety about high oil prices. "We do not consider it critical or a cause for panic," he said then. "Computer runs" on supply and price revealed that the market would adjust to any shortages, he said, and the United States and its allies could weather supply disruptions without "any serious damage to their economies."[92] In a speech at Johns Hopkins in September 1973, Casey actually argued that high prices would stimulate alternative energy production inside the United States, especially coal mining and oil shale production in Colorado, Utah, and Wyoming. "Everyone needs and everyone gains from more energy," he said. "Much of the talk about the energy crisis, the wringing of hands about the shortages ... has failed to recognize the degree to which we do have destiny in our hands."[93]

He also made economic arguments for US power through oil finance that would continue to be compelling for many well into the next decade. Casey was among those who pressed George Shultz, then treasury secretary, to create policies to encourage the Gulf oil producers to invest heavily in American banks.[94] In a meeting with Henry Kissinger in January 1974, he told the secretary of state that the United States would likely benefit in the long run from high oil prices. The nation would "attract a lot of investment flow" because of the significant technological advantage of the American oil companies. "We have all the oil finding techniques, we have the oil drilling technique, we have the experience, we have the maps," he said.[95]

[91] "DOS, MemCon, Meeting with Oil Company Executives," October 26, 1973, RG 59, Central Files 1970–1973, PET 6, Box 1485, NARA.

[92] "Briefing Book, OECD HLG and Oil Committee Meetings, Paris," October 25, 1973, Box 1482, RG 59, Subject Numeric Files, 1970–73 Economic, NARA.

[93] "The Mounting Energy Crisis and the Middle East," Address before the Johns Hopkins' Conference for Corporation Executives, September 18, 1973, Box 155, Casey Papers, HIA.

[94] "Memorandum for Secretary Shultz," September 19, 1973, Box 155, Casey Papers, HIA.

[95] "Secretary's Staff Meeting," January 8, 1974. Kissinger Transcripts, KT00985. National Security Archive, George Washington University, Washington, DC.

Casey believed in the power of US expertise and linked it to what he and many others described as the unique ingenuity of the American people. But at the same time, he was also prone to more anxious statements when they were politically expedient. When working to convince the Senate to lift environmental regulations on oil production in Alaska earlier that year, for example, he had written in an early draft of his statement that "this was a time fraught with danger for the United States in the world political and economic arena."[96] In the 1980 campaign, the implication of imminent danger was much more useful than the call for calm. Casey developed a strategy meant to hammer Carter for losing Iran and undermining US credibility and power in the Middle East.

Central to that strategy was the argument that Carter lacked the masculine resolve to oppose Soviet adventurism. In an early speech drafted for Reagan, Casey accused Carter of yielding to "McGovernite defense policies" that left the United States in its weakest position vis-à-vis the Soviet Union since the beginning of the Cold War. "We must have a defense build-up or we are in serious danger of seeing a political upheaval, even capture of Persian Gulf nations, that will gravely affect our supplies of petroleum," he wrote.[97]

The Reagan campaign also attacked Carter for bungling Middle East and energy policy more generally. Here they turned to a willing surrogate: Henry Kissinger. The former national security adviser and secretary of state, now a consultant and public intellectual, gave testimony to a Senate Committee on the geopolitics of oil. Carter was right, at least, to proclaim "our strategic stake in the security of the Persian Gulf," he said. Now it was the "bi-partisan obligation" of Congress to fund "the forces needed to give effect to this inescapable commitment." The stakes were too high to not take decisive action; only the military defense of the continental United States was more important to national security. "We cannot tolerate being forced into a state of permanent vulnerability." The statement was so ardent that Casey

---

On financialization, see Greta Krippner, *Capitalizing on Crisis: The Political Origins of the Rise of Finance* (Cambridge, MA: Harvard University Press, 2011).

[96] "Statement by the Honorable William J. Casey to the Senate Committee on Interior and Insular Affairs," May 3, 1973, Box 153, Casey Papers, HIA.

[97] "American Energy, American Minerals: A New Perspective for the 1980's," December 1979, Box 292, Casey Papers, HIA.

distilled it into a five-minute radio advertisement that attacked Carter for not doing enough.[98]

Kissinger was even more emphatic on the popular television show *Meet the Press* three months later, when he was invited to discuss the outbreak of the Iran-Iraq War. The Iraqi invasion threatened to put regional oil reserves "in the hands of the most radical of the OPEC countries, in terms of pricing," he said. Moreover, it was an example in which Soviet arms and treaties had upset the military and political stability in the region. If the Iraqi invasion was placed into a wider perspective that included the collapse of the shah's government, Cuban forces in Ethiopia, the Communist coup in South Yemen, the Soviet invasion of Afghanistan, there now "existed the image in the Persian Gulf ... that the United States is an impotent bystander." This echoed almost word for word his rival Brzezinski's imagery of the arc of crisis. But Kissinger was not satisfied with what he considered the feeble steps the Carter administration had taken toward committing US power to protect the region. A continuation of Carter and his rival Brzezinski's policies toward the Middle East would "lead to the multiplication of crises that we cannot manage," he continued, "and this is the reason I'm supporting Governor Reagan."[99]

It is possible that Kissinger, who seemingly overnight moved from purveyor of détente to war hawk, sensed a shift in the political winds. At any rate he, who along with former treasury secretary and Nixon-Ford "Energy Czar" William Simon consulted the Reagan campaign on energy and foreign policy, represented a consensus about both the importance of foreign oil and the perennial threats to its stability.[100] A related part of that consensus, which landed on the need to recover American power and prestige, was that economic productivity would be a primary concern for the Reagan administration.[101] Once in office,

[98] Statement of the Honorable Henry Kissinger on the Geopolitics of Oil before the Committee on Energy and Natural Resources of the United States Senate, July 31, 1980, Box 291, Casey Papers, HIA.

[99] Transcript, Meet the Press, September 28, 1980, Box 292, Casey Papers, HIA.

[100] William J. Casey to William Simon, April 16, 1980, Box 292, Casey Papers, HIA; William J. Casey to Henry Kissinger, October 29, 1980, Box 292, Casey Papers, HIA.

[101] Casey had copies of several pages of Milton Friedman's *Free to Choose* in his election files. In them, he underlined, "Nothing is more important for the long-run economic welfare of a country than improving productivity." See Box 291, Casey Papers, HIA.

the administration linked national and global economic recovery to oil and thus continued to be sensitive about regional instability and its effect on the steady supply of oil. Relatedly, there was growing interest in the problem of what NSC staffer Gary Sick termed "the advent of Islamic Fascism." Iran and other Middle Eastern states had "a collective tolerance for institutional chaos which is unimaginable in our society," he wrote, predicting that "the present cycle of ever-increasing extremism, paranoia, and repression" would likely continue.[102] For another, there was the belief that military power was the best way "to induce greater Soviet international restraint," as the National Security Council put it early in the Reagan administration when it called for "a new political/military strategy" for the greater region that included Southwest Asia and the Persian Gulf.[103]

The invasion of Iran by Iraq in September 1980 aggravated the sense of insecurity in the United States and emboldened those in the Reagan campaign who called for greater military power in the region. "The Iran-Iraq war gives a crystal-clear, classical, schoolroom, or laboratory case – whatever you want to call it – for what happens to a country when it becomes militarily weak," Republican Senator Jesse Helms wrote James Baker after a discussion with Casey and the conservative patriarch Albert Wohlstetter.[104] For them, the war was another example of instability in the wake of the US decline of power in the 1970s. The view was shared inside the lame duck Carter administration. In an "icy and confrontational meeting" between US Ambassador Thomas Watson and Soviet Minister of Foreign Affairs Andrei Gromyko, the two men accused each other of deception regarding the Iran-Iraq War. "Iran was not a U.S. oil tank," Gromyko said when he criticized US naval activity in the Straits of Hormuz. The United States had "no idea or desire to take oil by force," Watson responded. But it was a fact that "the industrial world" relied on oil that came from the Persian Gulf, Watson telegrammed

[102] Allen to Reagan, "Iran," August 21, 1981, Executive Secretariat, National Security Council Country Files, Near East and South Asia, Box 36, Ronald Reagan Presidential Library, Simi Valley, California (hereafter, RRL).

[103] Allen to Bush, "Checklist on U.S. Responses to Afghanistan Invasion," March 1981, Executive Secretariat, National Security Council Country Files, Near East and South Asia, Box 34, RRL.

[104] Ambassador Helms to James A. Baker III c/o Reagan Tour, October 17, 1980, Box 292, Casey Papers, HIA.

home in frustration. It was in the United States' "vital interest to see that we got the oil out."[105]

"Our best argument in foreign policy comes down simply to the point that weakness invites instability," another Reagan campaign adviser wrote when asked by Casey to reflect on the overall strategy. "Also, hit our country's continuing vulnerability on oil."[106] American weakness was provocative, according to that perspective. Vulnerability, in this case the inability to intervene with greater force when the security of the Persian Gulf faced any threat, further damaged US international credibility.

There was no diplomatic substitute for strength, the Reagan campaign held. Such arguments attested to the fact that an important segment of the United States policymaking elite believed that it was more important to show resolve than to exercise caution, especially after "losing Iran." One means to do so ran through the military sales pipeline, in part, as well as with the growth of a formal US military presence.

AWACS from Tehran to Riyadh

During the 1976 hearings on Iran's F-16 sales, Hubert Humphrey had combined slippery-slope and blowback arguments to justify his opposition to the White House's policy recommendations. "We have in other occasions thought we had national interests someplace and put a good deal of weaponry in there only to find out it went the other way," he said, referring to the "tragic" fact that the Vietnamese Air Force was "made of good American planes." Like others, he found the Middle East inherently volatile and fragile and believed the US government needed to take closer heed to the risk that advanced weapons would fall into the wrong hands. Moreover, Humphrey believed that the new era of arms sales would not stop with Iran. Other oil producers also had massive expendable incomes. He asked, "Isn't it entirely possible that somewhere along the lines the Saudi Arabians, who are very important to us in many ways, are going to say to us, you sold a

---

[105] "Telegram from the Embassy in the Soviet Union to the Department of State," October 14, 1980, *FRUS, 1977–1980, Volume VI, Soviet Union,* doc. 305.

[106] Dave Gergen to Casey, Meese, Wirthlin, and Baker, "Response to Iraq-Iran War," September 24, 1980, Box 292, Casey Papers, HIA.

whole lot of F-16s to Iran, and we are not so sure about the Shah, and we have more oil than Iran?"[107]

Those words would seem prescient five years later, when the newly elected Reagan administration shifted their sights for an AWACS sale southwest from Tehran to Riyadh. For all its critiques of Carter, the Reagan administration approached the global oil problem with policies that mostly continued those set in the 1970s: counterweights to OPEC, support for alternatives to Middle East oil, the use of financial diplomacy to protect private property and capital investments, and the creation of closer cooperative relations with Saudi Arabia. But they were new in scale.

To take just one example, Saudi Arabia was especially important because it had become "the virtual dictator of oil supply conditions," in the words of Brent Scowcroft.[108] Already by the late 1960s, the nation was a global economic power and a crucial ally to the United States. In 1968, repatriated oil profits contributed $500 million to the US balance of payments, Saudi oil provided 80 percent of US military requirements for refined products in Vietnam, and Saudi arms purchases were on the rise. The Near East Division of the State Department wrote then that "a highly favorable climate" in Saudi-American relations was crucial to avoid any erosion of "our tangible interests in the Near East now concentrated in the Arabian Peninsula."[109] In the 1970s, the US government worked to provide sophisticated weapons and an air defense system to Saudi Arabia at the same time as it sold special Treasury issues to the Saudi government. The United States also worked with Saudi leaders to fund and maintain pro-American regimes in North Africa and the Middle East, just as it had done with Iran in the Persian Gulf until the Iranian Revolution. Saudi Arabia also provided funding for the Pakistan military and the Mujahedeen in Afghanistan.

---

[107] *Hearings before the Committee on Foreign Relations and the Subcommittee on Foreign Assistance of the Committee on Foreign Relations, on Proposed Sales of Arms to Iran and Saudi Arabia*, United States Senate, 94th Congress, 2nd Session (U.S. Government Printing Office, 1977), 37.

[108] Scowcroft to Ford, "Meeting with Ambassador William J. Porter," January 10, 1976, Box 28, National Security Adviser's Presidential Country Files for the Middle East and South Asia, GFL.

[109] Joseph Sisco, "Visit of Prince Fahd of Saudi Arabia, Scope Paper," October 7, 1969, RG 59, Central Files 1967–1969, POL 7 SAUD, Box 2471, NARA.

American firms worked with the White House to successfully lobby Congress for increased spending on the controversial AWACS project, this time for Saudi Arabia. For the Bechtel Corporation, which had played a key role in working with Iran on its nuclear power plan during the 1970s, the project was spearheaded by former Saudi ambassador Parker T. Hart, who reported to George Shultz, a former Nixon cabinet member who would soon be appointed as Reagan's secretary of state.[110] That story took place in the context of a new direction for arms sales policy that Reagan made public when he signed a Presidential Directive on July 8, 1981. "The challenges and hostility toward fundamental United States interests, and the interests of its friends and allies, have grown significantly in recent years," Reagan said. "These trends threaten stability in many regions and impede progress toward greater political and economic development." The president continued: The United States could not defend the free world's interests alone. It was true that the nation did need to strengthen its own military. But it also needed to strengthen its allies through "arms transfers." He nodded verbally toward prudence and judiciousness, as Carter had done, but the message was clear. Reagan would make good on his campaign promise of increasing American military might. More specifically, arms sales enhanced preparedness, deterred aggression, and supported friends through "mutual security relationships." Indeed, he said, arms sales fostered both local and international and stability by tamping down disputes. More weapons would thus encourage "peaceful resolution of disputes and evolutionary change."[111]

Reagan's argument for arms sales repeated the justifications made by the Nixon administration for its "blank check" policy toward Iran. The first sales under that policy were F-16s to Pakistan and Venezuela and AWACS to Saudi Arabia. "I have to say that Saudi Arabia, we won't permit to be an Iran," Reagan said in sending the weapons package to Congress.[112] As in the Ford and Carter administrations,

[110] Parker T. Hart to George Shultz, "AWACS Q+A Materials," September 21, 1981, Box 2, Folder 1, Papers of Parker T. Hart, American Heritage Center, University of Wyoming (hereafter, AHC).

[111] Ronald Reagan, Announcement concerning a Presidential Directive on United States Conventional Arms Transfer Policy, July 9, 1981, *The American Presidency Project.*

[112] Gerald F. Seib, "Reagan Asserts U.S. Will Defend Saudi Arabia," *The Wall Street Journal*, October 2, 1981.

the White House expected pushback. Senators indeed were skeptical, and 54 of them, including 20 Republicans, signed a letter to the president in June 1981 stating that the sale "was not in the best interest of the United States." In the House of Representatives, 252 members, 77 of them Republicans, also cosponsored a resolution against the sale.[113] "Neither we nor the nations involved would benefit, and a terrible price would be paid if such a buildup helped bring on renewed conflict," Senator Claiborne Pell said.[114] Senator John Glenn also chided the Reagan administration. He agreed with their threat assessment. The disruption of Saudi oil flow, he said, would have, "to put it mildly, devastating effects on both Saudi Arabia, and the industrialized free world." Nonetheless, Reagan had offered a hasty sales plan that, if not passed, would lead to strains in US-Saudi relations.[115]

Former New York senator and undersecretary of state James L. Buckley explained the underlying rationale of Reagan's policy to a different hearing. Foremost among the areas of preoccupying instability in the world were the "oil-producing nations of the Arabian Peninsula." In particular, Saudi Arabia was in danger of becoming weaker than Soviet-supplied South Yemen. It was natural that the Saudi monarchy felt insecure when, as Buckley painted it, "Iranian fighters can cruise unopposed down the eastern coast of the Arabian Peninsula to underscore a threat to close the Persian Gulf to Western shipping, when Soviet client states flank the entry to the Red Sea, and when Soviet divisions march into Afghanistan, bringing fighters within range of the Straits of Hormuz." The analysis of regional insecurity as a threat to national and global well-being extended beyond the arc of crisis. American allies in North Africa also felt the pinch of insecurity because "oil-rich Libya" had loaded up with an arsenal twice the size of all its neighbors combined and had recently invaded Chad. That quick geopolitical tour of regional crisis was evidence of one central, ugly fact: the Soviet Union was on the march. For Buckley, the communist monolith had used the transfer of sophisticated weaponry to gain an edge in the Cold War. From 1977 to 1980, Soviet arms

---

[113] "Even if He Wins Saudi Arms Sale," *National Journal* (September 12, 1981), Box 2, Folder 1, Papers of Parker T. Hart, AHC.

[114] *Hearings before the Committee on Foreign Relations*, United States Senate, 79th Congress, 1st Session, "On the AWACS and F-15 Enhancements Arms Sales Package to Saudi Arabia" (Washington: GPO, 1981), 4.

[115] Ibid., 7-9.

transfers, he said, had outpaced American ones by more than 20 percent in dollar terms. Although this was clearly false, it fed into the broader belief that the United States had given up the upper hand in the Cold War. The weapons the Soviet Union had sent were also important in this analysis: tanks, armored personnel carriers and reconnaissance vehicles, artillery, combat aircraft, and surface-to-air missiles.[116] "We must not underestimate the range and the severity of the unpredictable threats that arise in this turbulent region," Secretary of State Al Haig told senators.[117]

In 1978, NSC staffer Jessica Tuchman had suggested that the Carter administration "recruit positive supporters" for arms sales to Saudi Arabia by "mounting a major educational effort" on the importance of Saudi Arabia for regional stability and "in the production and pricing of oil."[118] A close examination of the AWACS debate reveals that the Reagan administration took a similar tack. Their emphasis followed the Iranian playbook of the 1970s: the sales were about national vulnerability and the global economy, but also concerned potential profits at home. Reagan also said in his speech announcing the new arms sales policy that the creation of "friendly and cooperative security relationships" would favor American business, described as "United States defense production capabilities and efficiency."[119]

The lobbying of the Bechtel Corporation, led by former US ambassador to Saudi Arabia Hart and future secretary of state Shultz, reveals the intricacy of the politics involved. In Hart's papers, there is a State Department report on the proposed package for Saudi Arabia that indicates how important the sale was for protecting the Saudi oil facilities "critical to the U.S. and its Western allies as well as to the future prosperity of Saudi Arabia itself." The best context in which to understand US arms sales policy was, the report continued, the series

---

[116] *Hearing before the Committee on Foreign Relations*, United States Senate, 77th Congress, 1st Session, "Conventional Arms Sales" (July 28, 1981), 5.

[117] *Hearings before the Committee on Foreign Relations*, United States Senate, 79th Congress, 1st Session, "On the AWACS and F-15 Enhancements Arms Sales Package to Saudi Arabia" (Washington: GPO, 1981), 13.

[118] Memorandum from Jessica Tuchman to Brzezinski, "F-15 for Saudi Arabia," January 27, 1978, *FRUS, 1977–1980, Volume XVII, Middle East Region; Arabian Peninsula*, doc. 166.

[119] Ronald Reagan, Announcement concerning a Presidential Directive on United States Conventional Arms Transfer Policy, July 9, 1981, *The American Presidency Project*.

of recent events that had adversely affected the nation's interests, including the fall of the shah and, subsequently, the Iran-Iraq War, which had demonstrated the willingness of regional adversaries to attack the other's oil facilities.[120]

Upon reading the report, Hart wrote Shultz that the most effective way to rescue the AWACS sale was to target "doubtful" legislators from a list created by Senator Robert Packwood, the main Republican opponent to the sale.[121] Hart drafted letters to forty-five senators in support of the sale. The argument was succinct. Bechtel supported the Reagan administration's position that the sale was vital to the interests of the United States for several reasons: it would bring stability to the region, it directly affected "the continued international flow of oil," and it was not a threat to the security of Israel. "If the proposed sale of this equipment package is not consummated, our strategic military position in the Gulf region and our integrity as a world leader will be severely, and lastingly, damaged," he wrote.[122] Hart also organized a group of former US ambassadors to write a joint public letter urging the Senate not to block the sale.[123] "The AWACS will be a major step in the coordination of American and Saudi defense of the Arabian Peninsula and its vital resources," the four ambassadors said. If the Senate rejected the sale, it was likely that the Saudi government would reconsider its policies on oil prices, which had been "immensely beneficial to the United States and the entire oil consuming world." The credibility of the nation was at stake, they concluded. The sale should proceed.[124]

These efforts complemented what *The Washington Post* described as "the intensified lobbying effort" by President Reagan. Orrin Hatch of Utah and Alan Simpson of Wyoming, both Republicans, were among those who soon declared their support. The Reagan administration, by then, had shifted the thrust of its argument. In the wake of the assassination of Anwar Sadat – "America's closest friend in the Arab

[120] "The Air Defense Enhancement Package for Saudi Arabia," August 1981, Box 2, Parker T. Hart Papers, CAH.
[121] P. T. Hart to G. P. Shultz, "AWACS Q and A Materials," September 21, 1981, Box 2, Parker T. Hart Papers, CAH.
[122] Fred L. Dahl to William V. Roth, Jr., October 5, 1981, Box 2, Parker T. Hart Papers, CAH.
[123] P. T. Hart to G. P. Shultz, "AWACS Q and A Materials," September 21, 1981, Box 2, Parker T. Hart Papers, CAH.
[124] Press Statement, September 22, 1981, Box 2, Parker T. Hart Papers, CAH.

world" – it was all the more necessary to cultivate the cooperation of Saudi Arabia.[125] The White House also released a draft letter to *The New York Times* from the president to the Senate. In it, Reagan echoed almost directly the language of Hart's letters to the senators, mentioning not only "our vital national security interests" but also allaying doubts about the threat to Israel. The weapons sale would improve both the US strategic posture "and the prospects for peace in the region," Reagan said.[126]

The heavy lobbying worked in the end. The Senate passed the sale fifty-two to forty-eight on October 27, 1981. Senators from Washington, Maine, Louisiana, North Dakota, and Nebraska all switched their position upon the roll call vote. Reagan appeared on the front page of national newspapers holding the Senate tally sheet for his victory. "We've seen the upper chamber at its best," he told reporters with a smile.[127]

Conclusion

The debates over arms sales prior to and immediately after the Iranian Revolution reveal much about how policymakers believed that diplomacy should function. Whether Americans proposed, supported, or criticized arms sales, they were arguing about the role of the nation in the world. Even as the arguments about sales to Iran paved the way for sales to Saudi Arabia, the sense of crisis after the loss of Iran narrowed the discussion in the 1980s. The perpetual preparation for a crisis in regional security led to a dramatic change in the nature and scope of American military power.

The United States also began to emphasize more than ever the use of direct US military power in the Middle East. In January 1983, the Reagan administration elevated Carter's Rapid Joint Deployment Task Force, an improvised reaction to the Iranian Revolution and the Afghanistan invasion, to the permanent United States Central Command (CENTCOM). A unified command with the main objective

---

[125] John M. Goshko, "9 More Senators Back Reagan on AWACS," *The Washington Post*, October 8, 1981.

[126] "Text of Draft Letter by Reagan on AWACS," *The New York Times*, October 21, 1981.

[127] Charles Mohr, "Senate, 52-48, Supports Reagan on AWACS Jet Sale to Saudis," *The New York Times*, October 29, 1981.

of safeguarding Persian Gulf oil reserves and oil transport routes, CENTCOM was part of the broader militarization of US oil diplomacy, in which growing arms sales also played an important role. Supported by influential factions at home, the Reagan administration deemed military power the best means to guarantee access to the oil that the United States and its allies needed to sustain their economies. The rationale for this policy was built on the widespread perception of the relative weakness of the United States in the region. Carter had not done enough to prevent the threat to "U.S. interests in the security of the Gulf Arab states and freedom of navigation in the Persian Gulf," Reagan NSC official Charles Hill wrote. The administration needed to be "acutely aware of the limitations on U.S. military activity in the Persian Gulf." Without greater access to facilities – including new airbases, port access, and communications facilities – the American military could not "react quickly or effectively" to challenges to the flow of oil.[128]

Additions to the US military presence in the Arabian Peninsula, typified by the new arms sales to Saudi Arabia, would become a recurring event. Policies that were hotly contested in the public arena and in foreign policymaking in the late 1970s became central to a bipartisan consensus by the 1990s. To look at the contours of debates surrounding arms sales and the use of military power in the Middle East is necessary for a fuller understanding of this important change in the basic assumptions of American power in the first decade of contemporary globalization. Regional security was crucial to the health of the global economy, US officials argued. One way to ensure stability in the Middle East was to arm American allies.

There was some ambiguity in the late 1970s and early 1980s. AWACS, after all, was ostensibly defensive at the same time as it was a force multiplier. Sales were so hotly contested that they almost failed. The same was not the case after the Reagan administration's first battle. That victory, and the school of thought it represented, would have long-lasting effects on the nature of foreign policy. American policymakers in the 1980s and after remain, in some ways, under the influence of a powerful myth about the fundamental role of US military

---

[128] Hill to McFarlane, "Iran-Iraq War: Summary of CPPG Review," March 29, 1984, Executive Secretariat, National Security Council, Records of NSPG, NSPG 0087, RRL.

power as a stabilizing element in the world. The development of that myth in the United States was shaped by the contingent events of the late 1970s, including the Iranian Revolution, but it was also a consequence of political, economic, and ideological forces at home. When it came to the regional security of the Middle East and secure flows of its oil, this was the time when military force became the premier instrument of American diplomacy for the new global age.

PART IV

Circulating Knowledge

9 | The Criminal Is the Patient, the Prison Will Be the Cure:
Building the Carceral Imagination in Pahlavi Iran

GOLNAR NIKPOUR

In the heady days leading up to the 1979 Iranian Revolution, just before the shah's mid-January flight from the country, Iranian revolutionaries stormed central Tehran's Qasr prison and freed numerous political prisoners held there. This was one of several efforts around that time to liberate Iran's political prisoners, many of whom were released in late 1978 and more of whom would be freed throughout that transformative winter.[1] That the Iranian revolutionaries would concern themselves with prisoners was no surprise; by the time of the revolution's success, prisons across Iran had become synonymous with the violence and brutality of the Pahlavi monarchy for Iranians and

---

[1] See the memoir of Abbas Samakar, member of Khosrow Golsorkhi's so-called Group of Twelve, for a narrative by a former leftist political prisoner of these releases. Abbas Samakar, *Man yik shurishi hastam: Khatirat-e zendan va yadbud-e Khosrow Golsorkhi va Keramat Danishian* [I am a rebel: Prison memoirs and reminiscences of Khosrow Golsorkhi and Keramat Danishian] (Los Angeles, CA: Ketab, 2001). A grainy video of the liberation of prisoners has continued to circulate online, reminding contemporary viewers of the highest original aspirations of the revolutionary movement. See "Azadi Zendanian-e Siasi Beh Dast-e Mardom," YouTube video, 1:58, www.youtube.com/watch?v=1uAQhJN2RYI. Before the success of the revolution, the shah's government ceded to some protester demands in the hopes of dulling the revolutionary storm. This included the 1978 release of hundreds of political prisoners. In fall 1978, Ayatollah Mahmoud Taleqani and Ayatollah Hossein Ali Montazeri were released. Those freed also included Kurdish dissident Ghani Bolourian, who after twenty-five years in prison was then Iran's longest held political prisoner. When in 1979 revolutionaries stormed Qasr, they targeted the release of the political prisoners remaining in the prison; some ordinary prisoners also made it out in the chaos that followed. Revolutionaries also stormed SAVAK headquarters in Rasht along with several police stations. For more on these events, see Misagh Parsa, *Social Origins of the Iranian Revolution* (New Brunswick, NJ: Rutgers University Press, 1989).

global onlookers alike.[2] One Iranian leftist intellectual neatly summed up the revolutionaries' position for English-reading audiences in the months after the collapse of the shah's government, writing, "[p]rerevolutionary Teheran was shown to be a sick city dotted with grisly torture chambers."[3]

Yet when Qasr prison first opened its doors fifty years earlier in 1929 on the grounds of a former Qajar castle, those affiliated with the nascent Pahlavi state were proud of the institution they considered the crown jewel of Iran's modernizing prison system. Statesman Ahmad Hooman boasted that with Qasr, Iran had finally built a truly modern prison that would hold prisoners "without any sort of class distinctions."[4] Even before the opening of the prison, the grounds around Qasr were consecrated in the project of Pahlavi state modernism. In 1928, when the first radio mast towers in Iran were built on Qasr's grounds, Reza Shah wrote his hopes for the rest of his reign and for Iran on a piece of paper and buried it in a tin container on-site.[5] It is thus that both the beginning and end of Pahlavi rule would pass through the grounds of its most famous prison.

This chapter tells the story of the making of Iran's modern prison system, but this story is not simply one of Iranian institution- or nation-building. Rather, it reveals transformations in modes of thinking and being that have taken place over the course of the last century in Iran, and it situates those transformations in the global networks in

---

[2] For more on Iran's political prisoners, see Afshin Matin-Asgari, "Twentieth Century Iran's Political Prisoners," *Middle Eastern Studies* 42:5 (September 2006): 689–707. For political prisoners both before and after the revolution, see Ervand Abrahamian, *Tortured Confessions: Prisons and Recantation in Modern Iran* (Los Angeles, CA: University of California Press, 1999). See also Nasir Rubay'i and Ahmad Rahraw Khuajah, *Tarikh-e zendan dar 'asr-e Qajar va Pahlavi* [The history of prison in the Qajar and Pahlavi eras] (Tehran: Entisharat-e Ququnus, 1390/2011). For more on global activists and Pahlavi prisons, see Golnar Nikpour, "Claiming Human Rights: Iranian Political Prisoners and the Making of a Transnational Movement, 1963–1979," *Humanity: An International Journal of Human Rights, Humanitarianism, and Development* 9:3 (Winter 2018): 363–388.

[3] Reza Bareheni, "The SAVAK Documents," *The Nation* (February 23, 1980): 198–202.

[4] Quoted in Rubay'i and Rahraw Khuajah, *Tarikh-e zendan*, 104.

[5] Before these twentieth-century transformations, Qasr was home to a royal castle and garden. The construction of the radio masts was announced in *Ettela'at Monthly*. Quoted in Mohammad Javad Moradiniya, *Hekayat-e Qasr: Az Qajar ta Pahlavi* (Tehran: Entesharat-e Negah, 1397/2018), 39.

which they belong. These historical changes are marked by a turn toward what I, borrowing from the recent tradition of critical prison studies, call the carceral imagination.[6] What I mean to signal with this term is a historical change in ways of imagining the organization of the social. This change reflects transnational processes by which the criminalization and incarceration of large numbers of people has been naturalized as inherent to the project of progress and modernity. In other words, this chapter analyzes the methods by which mass criminalization and mass carceralization came to be seen in Iran as obvious and necessary modern responses to a wide host of social issues, and a needed step toward placing Iran among the "progressive" and "civilized" states of the world. Iran's new modern prisons, meant to

---

[6] My use of the term carceral draws on several generations of scholars working in the field of prison studies, many of whom draw on (but also critique) the work of Michel Foucault. In *Discipline and Punish*, Foucault introduces the notion of the carceral continuum or carceral network, which is linked to institutions including not only prisons but also policing and judicial systems. See Michel Foucault, *Discipline and Punish: The Birth of the Prison*, 2nd ed., trans. Alan Sheridan (New York: Vintage Books, 1995 [1977]). My work is inspired by the growing number of critical studies of US prisons, particularly the pathbreaking work by a number of African American scholars, writers, and activists. Spearheaded by the writing of scholars including Angela Davis and Ruth Wilson Gilmore, this work has been invaluable in understanding and critiquing modern carcerality. Angela Davis, *Abolition, Democracy: Beyond Empire, Prisons, and Torture* (New York: Seven Story Press, 2005); Ruth Wilson Gilmore, *The Golden Gulag: Prisons, Surplus, Crisis, and Opposition to Globalizing California* (Los Angeles, CA: University of California Press, 2007). For work on prisons and US sociopolitical imaginaries, see Caleb Smith, *The Prison and the American Imagination* (New Haven, CT: Yale University Press, 2009). My thinking has also benefited from groundbreaking work on prisons in Global South contexts; for instance, Steven Pierce and Anupama Rao, *Discipline and the Other Body: Correction, Corporeality, Colonialism* (Durham, NC: Duke University Press, 2006). In particular, Rao's work on discipline and coloniality has been foundational for my own thinking. I also draw from the work of Frank Dikötter on modern Chinese prisons. Frank Dikötter, *Crime, Punishment, and the Prison in Modern China* (New York: Columbia University Press, 2002). See also Frank Dikötter and Ian Brown, *Cultures of Confinement: A History of Prison in Africa, Asia, and Latin America* (Ithaca, NY: Cornell University Press, 2007). I further draw from scholars bringing critical analytic tools to the study of policing and punishment in the modern Middle East and North Africa, in particular the work of Laleh Khalili. See Laleh Khalili, *Time in the Shadows: Confinement in Counterinsurgencies* (Stanford, CA: Stanford University Press, 2012). See also Laleh Khalili and Jillian Schwedler, eds., *Policing and Prisons in the Middle East: Formations of Coercion* (New York: Columbia University Press, 2010).

showcase Iran's arrival on the global stage, were integral to this project of imperial nationalism and centralizing sovereignty.

Despite the importance of political prisoners to the story of Iranian carceral modernity, and the outsized part they have played in the historiography of this institution,[7] this chapter concerns itself with Iran's prisons more broadly and with those who in Persian are typically referred to as Iran's "ordinary" prisoners (*zendani-ye 'adi*).[8] It is this latter group that has represented and continues to represent the overwhelming majority of Iran's incarcerated population. But it is not simply because large numbers of prisoners have been held on ostensibly "nonpolitical" charges – drug offenses, sex work, vagrancy, petty theft, brigandage, etc. – that I turn my attention to those prisoners and what has been said about them. Rather, I argue that our collective historical, political, and even *revolutionary* imaginations, in which "political" and "nonpolitical" prisoners are imagined as hermetically sealed categories, elide not only the mixing of these populations in Iran's carceral networks but also the profoundly *political* and constitutively *global* processes by which Iranians were newly classified as socially aberrant, dangerous, criminal, and deserving of carceral "correction."

A driving motivation of this chapter is to consider the historical circumstances that eventually allowed those aforementioned Iranian revolutionaries, while standing on the threshold of a radically new world, to see some prisoners' liberation as intimately linked to their own, while leaving some others locked away in the very institutions

---

[7] Most of the writing on modern Iranian prisons focuses on political prisoners. The most thorough scholarly work in English on Iran's prisons to date is by Ervand Abrahamian, who focuses on forced recantations of political prisoners in both the Pahlavi and Islamic Republic eras. Abrahamian, *Tortured Confessions*. For a theoretically rich Foucauldian study of torture in Iran, see Darius Rejali, *Torture and Modernity: Self, Society, and State in Modern Iran* (Boulder, CO: Westview Press, 1994). See also Matin-Asgari, "Twentieth-Century Iran's Political Prisoners." Among the most insightful monographs on Iran's political prisons in English are those by scholars who were at one point incarcerated for their political work. See Shahla Talebi, *Ghosts of Revolution: Rekindled Memories of Imprisonment in Iran* (Stanford, CA: Stanford University Press, 2011). See also Behrooz Ghamari-Tabrizi, *Remembering Akbar: Inside the Iranian Revolution* (New York: O/R Books, 2016).

[8] In the official parlance of both Pahlavi Iran and the Islamic Republic of Iran, those whom we ordinarily refer to as political prisoners are typically called "security" prisoners (*Zendani-yi amniyati*).

they so powerfully critiqued. This point is meant less as a reproach and more as a historical question: How, in just a few decades, did Iranians – including many of those seeking radical political change – come to take for granted that thousands of people, the overwhelming majority of whom would not have been incarcerated for the same actions before the early twentieth century, could and in fact should be held in cages? In what follows, I outline the global processes through which the modern Iranian carceral system emerged and took root, arguing that even as Iran has undergone political upheavals at the highest levels – the 1921 coup that brought Reza Khan to power, the 1941 Allied invasion that brought his son Mohammad Reza Pahlavi to power, the 1953 coup that kept the latter on the throne, and the 1979 Islamic Revolution that toppled his rule – the carceral institutions and imaginaries inaugurated in the early twentieth century have not only remained in place but also expanded in size and scope.

Early Reforms

Between 1925 and 1979, the Pahlavi government embarked on a dramatic centralization of Iran's legal system as well as a vast expansion of Iran's carceral network, taking European legal and penal systems as its primary source of inspiration. While legal centralization was a centerpiece of Reza Shah's top-down modernizing project, legal reform had been a long-standing concern of Iranian intellectuals trying to combat European colonial encroachment and Qajar corruption. By the end of the nineteenth century, reformists influenced by European ideas of statecraft as well as by events in the Ottoman and Russian empires were arguing that *qanun* – law – was the only way to progress as a nation.[9] During the Constitutional period of 1905–1911, legal reform remained a concern of constitutionalists, reformists, and

---

[9] The focus of Qajar-era reformers like Malkum Khan on legal reform was such that their writing has been referred to as "legal fetishism." Hadi Enayat, *Law, State, and Society in Modern Iran: Constitutionalism, Autocracy, and Legal Reform, 1906–1941* (New York: Palgrave Macmillan, 2013), 52. For more on legal reforms, see Cyrus Schayegh, *Who Is Knowledgeable Is Strong: Science, Class, and the Formation of Modern Iranian Society* (Berkeley, CA: University of California Press, 2009). For the importance of Ottoman and Russian political thought in Iran, see Afshin Matin-Asgari, *Both Eastern and Western: An Intellectual History of Iranian Modernity* (Cambridge: Cambridge University Press, 2018).

revolutionaries alike, although differing notions of law and order, drawing alternately on European models and on various interpretations of Sharia, were advanced by the diverse groups and classes who supported the abstract call for justice.[10] Despite revolutionary efforts, however, the constitutional experiment halted neither European intrusions nor Qajar intransigence, nor did it succeed in establishing the stable constitutional government for which the movement fought. Yet despite the enduring sentiment that the immediate post-Constitutional Revolution era was marked by legal and political chaos, significant (albeit piecemeal) legal reforms along European lines were undertaken in that time, most notably the 1912 Law of the Principles of Criminal Trials, and the temporary Penal Code of 1917.[11]

The late Qajar state also made some efforts toward European-style reform of law enforcement. Like legal reform, policing reform was in part the result of anxieties induced by European territorial and economic encroachment on Persian sovereignty.[12] Europeans traveling through or stationed in turn-of-the-century Persia routinely complained about what they perceived as ineffective Qajar law enforcement and general lawlessness across the country. One Englishman declared, "Our friend the Persian policeman ... will guard you excellently when it is in his interest to do so; he will steal from you when he thinks it is profitable; and, if possible, he will do both at once, and thus obtain a twofold reward for his services."[13] Another British colonial officer insisted that in Persia, "which is full of fanatics over whom the Government has no efficient control, it is evident that British subjects should have some means of defending themselves if attacked. As I have frequently had the honor to report, the starving and ill-clad horde of tatterdemalions, which constitute the so-called Persian Army,

[10] Enayat, *Law, State, and Society*, 51. See also Janet Afary, *The Iranian Constitutional Revolution, 1906–1911: Grassroots Democracy, Social Democracy, and the Origins of Feminism* (New York: Columbia University Press, 1996).
[11] For a chronological table of legal reform between May 1911 and June 1940, see Enayat, *Law, State, and Society*, 193–197.
[12] As Firoozeh Kashani-Sabet notes in her groundbreaking work on Qajar-era nationalism, Qajar reformists "touted legal palliatives for reversing Iran's economic decline. Their attention to legal and economic matters complemented their cultural polemic by addressing the internal maintenance of the country." Firoozeh Kashani-Sabet, *Frontier Fictions: Shaping the Iranian Nation, 1804–1946* (Princeton, NJ: Princeton University Press, 1999), 80.
[13] E. Crawshay Williams, *Across Persia* (London: E. Arnold, 1907), 23.

would, in case of an attack on the Christians, be the first to butcher us, if it were in any way their interest to do so."[14]

In 1878, on the heels of his second voyage to Europe, Nasser al-Din Shah decided to create the nation's first European-style police force, hiring the Italian-born Austrian Conte di Monteforte as an advisor. With the Austrian's arrival, policing in Tehran was partially reorganized, and a police force, at that point called the *nazmiyeh*, was officially formed. The *nazmiyeh* remained relatively small in strength and number, ranging from 250 to 400 members over the next two decades. Still, di Monteforte – who was eventually made Tehran chief of police – took steps toward reorganizing policing in the capital city along European lines, writing the *nazmiyeh*'s first formal police codes and standardizing police uniforms to look like those found in Vienna.[15] In 1912, seeking the further expansion of the capital city's law enforcement capacities, the Qajar government brought in several Swedish officers under the direction of Reserve Lieutenant Gunnar Westdahl. In their ten years in Persia, the Swedish officers helped organize a police force in Tehran of over 1,000 men and introduced some of the basics of then current European evidentiary norms to Persia, including fingerprinting and interrogation tactics. Westdahl also initiated changes to the culture found inside of Persia's penal sites, ending the long-standing practice of putting chains around the necks and blocks around the legs of prisoners. Prisoners were also newly made to wear standard-issue uniforms.[16] Yet these changes, while foundational in shifting norms of law enforcement in the capital city, only hinted at the wholesale changes still on the horizon.

By the time Reza Khan appeared on the national stage in 1921, Iranian reformers were anxious to unify Iran's disparate social and

---

[14] Document no. 241, Mr. E. Grant Duff to the Marquess of Lansdowne. December 6, 1905: India Office Archives, London.

[15] For more details on Qajar-era policing, see Willem M. Floor, "The Police in Qajar Persia," *Zeitschrift der Deutschen Morgenländischen Gesellschaft* 123:2 (1973): 293–315. For a recent look at Qajar-era legal and policing reform in the context of Islamic law, see Nobuaki Kondo, *Islamic Law and Society in Iran: A Social History of Qajar Tehran* (New York: Routledge, 2017).

[16] Rubay'i and Rahraw Khuajah, *Tarikh-e zendan*, 45–46. See also the entry on the Swedish officers in Iran by Mohammad Fazlhashemi in *Encyclopaedia Iranica*, which examines the Swedish sources on the matter: Mohammad Fazlhashemi, "Swedish Officers in Iran 1911–1915," *Encyclopaedia Iranica*, www.iranicaonline.org/articles/sweden-ii.

political forces.[17] For many intellectuals, the soon-to-be first Pahlavi monarch seemed to be just the sort of strong figure capable of restoring Iranian sovereignty. Where once the overriding call among Iranian nationalists was for justice (*'adalat*), the early 1920s saw an amplified demand for a powerful, centralizing figure, a "Mussolini who can break the influence of the traditional authorities, and thus create a modern outlook, a modern people, and a modern nation."[18] Reza Shah understood the value of at least appearing to govern by the rule of law for both the emerging modern middle class and the international community of states. For most Iranian nationalists, Reza Shah represented Iran's last best hope for finally ushering the country into the type of modern system of law and order that had for so long been the desire of reformist political projects. For the shah, international appearances were especially important in the wake of Iran's abrogation of capitulations in 1928, particularly the law that had protected foreign nationals accused of wrongdoing from the Iranian justice system. As historian Hadi Enayat notes, in the wake of the abrogation, "the shah felt it necessary to show the international community that his government was based on sound and predictable legality."[19] New legal codes and prisons were the centerpiece of that outward-looking project.

The centralization of modern Iran's legal system was undertaken almost immediately by the newly crowned king, who in 1927 appointed Minister of Justice Ali Akbar Davar to lead and reform the judiciary. Davar, the son of a Qajar statesman who received his law degree from the University of Geneva in 1920, wholly transformed Iran's legal and judicial structure in short order.[20] Two days after his appointment, Davar dissolved the existing judiciary and

---

[17] See Stephanie Cronin, ed., *The Making of Modern Iran: State and Society Under Reza Shah 1921–1941* (New York: Routledge, 2007). See also the chapters on Reza Shah in Touraj Atabaki and Erik Jan Zürcher, *Men of Order: Authoritarian Modernization under Atatürk and Reza Shah* (New York: I.B. Tauris, 2004).

[18] From an article written by M. Kazemi in the first issue of *Farangestan* journal in 1924. Quoted in Ervand Abrahamian, *Iran between Two Revolutions* (Princeton, NJ: Princeton University Press, 1982), 124.

[19] Enayat, *Law, State, and Society*, 115–116.

[20] For these and further biographical details on Davar, see Baqer 'Aqeli, "Dāvar, 'Alī Akbar," *Encyclopaedia Iranica*, www.iranicaonline.org/articles/davar-ali-akbar.

undertook a complete overhaul of the 1911–1912 organic, civil, commercial, and criminal codes.[21] The wholesale changes in the legal codes of the Davar period, largely undertaken between his appointment and 1931, irrevocably transformed the political and legal landscape in Iran by centralizing law, reducing the power of the Sharia courts, and establishing a completely overhauled judiciary with new personnel and new codes of conduct.

Legal centralization under Davar was coterminous with the initial establishment of an expanding modern prison system. Early in Reza Shah's reign, small penal sites built in earlier decades continued to be used, albeit in more crowded conditions than ever before, including the notorious if generically named Prison Number One and Prison Number Two (both built in the late Qajar era), whose cells were unfavorably compared by one prisoner to coffins.[22] These two facilities were part of a small carceral network located in central Tehran's Tupkhaneh Square across the street from the *Ettela'at* newspaper building.[23] Yet existing facilities were not enough to meet the mushrooming demand for carceral space brought about by a rapidly changing legal and penal order. The same prisoner who decried conditions at Prison Number Two described overcrowding in another facility, writing, "There are four bloody walls into which hundreds of human beings have been poured like animals."[24] In the early 1920s, most prisoners in Tehran were held at the Central Police Jail (*zendan-e markazi-ye shahrbani-ye Tehran*); by the late 1920s, this nominally "temporary" jailing facility housed twice as many prisoners as it was intended to hold.[25] Accordingly, the Iranian government planned to build tens of new prisons in the Reza Shah era to address the need for more space: 5 large prisons of 2,700 square meters for 100 inmates; 50 medium-sized prisons of 1,400 square meters for 50 inmates; 30 small

---

[21] Enayat, *Law, State, and Society*, 113–144.

[22] 'Ali Dashti, *Ayyam-e mahbas* [Prison days] (Essen: Nashr-e Nima, 2003).

[23] Also included in this network was a small interrogation center and temporary holding facility, a small women's prison, a facility called the Public Jail (*mahbas-e umumi*), and the Central Police Jail. Morteza Saifi Tafreshi, *Polis-e Khafih-ye Iran, 1299–1320* (Tehran: Ghafnus Press, 1367/1988), 106–107.

[24] Dashti, *Ayyam-e mahbas*.

[25] The Central Police Jail was known officially as the Temporary Jail (Zendan-e Movaghat), but because it was located on the site of the former royal dungeon, it was colloquially referred to as "Falakeh." Abrahamian, *Tortured Confessions*, 25.

institutions of 1,000 square meters for 30 inmates; and several very small prisons of 200 square meters.[26] Some of these prisons were never built, while others were built in subsequent years. On the whole, the Reza Shah era oversaw the first dramatic expansion of prison space in modern Iran, founding the carceral system with which Iranians have lived until today.

Global Networks, Iranian Prisons

In 1925, members of the Iranian police force including Mirza Abdollah Bahrami and Lieutenant Colonel Abdollah Khan Saif, then Qazvin chief of police, traveled to the International Penal and Penitentiary Conference in London.[27] The 1925 event was the ninth such conference held by the International Prison Commission (IPC), an organization that had first convened in London in 1872. The IPC was initially formed with the mandate to collect international prison statistics and to recommend reforms on prison management and prisoner rehabilitation. The year 1925 was the first time an Iranian delegation participated in an IPC conference, but not the first time an Iranian government had interacted with the organization. In 1876, following a conference in Stockholm, the IPC sent questionnaires on what they called "the penitentiary question" to governments around the world, and received a response from the Qajar government, although evidently nothing meaningful came of this early exchange.[28]

For Sir Evelyn Ruggles-Brise, British prison administrator and president of the IPC, the work of the IPC was no less than an undertaking in the service of civilization and humanity. On the eve of the 1925 conference, Ruggles-Brise boasted that the IPC was a "confederation of most of the civilized States of the world"[29] working "quietly and unostentatiously, to introduce a greater humanity" to punishment

---

[26] These numbers are compiled from Vezarat-e Keshvar Document # – 12062فلا
ش. 4 – .

[27] Tafreshi, *Polis-e Khafih-ye Iran*, 105.

[28] Negley Teeters, *Deliberations of the International Penal and Penitentiary Congresses, Questions and Answers, 1872–1935* (Philadelphia, PA: Temple University Bookstore, 1949), 42.

[29] Sir Evelyn Ruggles-Brise, *Prison Reform at Home and Abroad: A Short History of the International Movement Since the London Conference, 1872* (London: Macmillan and Co., 1924), 1.

systems around the world.[30] Ruggles-Brise claimed the IPC as the torchbearer for "a world-desire for a rational and equitable 'system of punishment.'" For Ruggles-Brise, this "world-desire" was itself "due to the progressive widening of the circle of humanity" in recent years.[31] Ruggles-Brise and the IPC routinely referenced the work of French sociologist Gabriel Tarde, which had grown particularly influential in criminological discourses of the era. Tardian criminology argued that social factors (rather than biological or essential attributes, as in Lombroso's criminological theories) were the foundation both in understanding criminal behavior and for eventually curtailing that behavior. Moreover, arguing against the Durkheimian structuralist functionalism popular in European sociology of the day, Tardian criminologists emphasized the need to understand not only social structures but also the individual personality and psyche of each detainee, opening the door for the rising influence of criminal psychology.[32] For Ruggles-Brise and the IPC, these insights highlighted the interconnected social stakes of their work. Noting recent successes in prison reform in Siam and Japan, Ruggles-Brise credited the IPC for bringing together statesmen and reformists from around the world to promote "the continental system" of prison administration. "Members of different nations breathing in the same civilizing atmosphere come to regard each other as *compatriotes socieux* in the work of humanity," Ruggles-Brise declared, leading to penal reforms that would reduce criminal behavior the world over.[33] For the IPC, the 1925 London conference would be an important step toward bringing new participants, Pahlavi Iran included, into that civilizing atmosphere. The insights gleaned from the conference and from European criminological trends – as well as the civilizational logics buttressing

---

[30] Ibid., 3.   [31] Ibid., 6.

[32] In their own day, Tarde and Durkheim presented rival views in the field of sociology largely owing to the importance Tarde placed on psychological factors for individual behavior in his work. As Andrew Barry and Nigel Thrift note, "Whereas his [Tarde's] contemporary and intellectual opponent Émile Durkheim strenuously sought to demarcate the realm of 'society' from the realm of the psychological and geographical, Tarde's conception of sociology appears more generous in its scope, pointing towards the possibility of connections between the work of sociologists, psychologists and researchers in the natural sciences and humanities." Andrew Barry and Nigel Thrift, "Gabriel Tarde: Imitation, Invention and Economy," *Economy and Society* 36:4 (2007): 509–525.

[33] Ruggles-Brise, *Prison Reform*, 6.

those insights – would influence Iranian criminal justice and carceral trends for decades to come.

The immediate effect of the London conference was to convince the Iranian delegation of the importance of building state-of-the-art carceral sites in Iran. Following Iranian participation in the conference, Reza Shah chose Tblisi-born architect Nikolai Markov to design a new prison on the grounds of the former Qajar palace at Qasr in Tehran. Before establishing himself as an architect, Markov started his professional career as a military man. He served as an officer in the Imperial Russian Army tasked with fighting Bolshevism and was later captain in the Iranian Cossack Brigade, the branch of the Qajar armed forces in which Reza Shah also served.[34] Before his time in the military, Markov studied architecture and Persian literature at St Petersburg University, showing interest and aptitude in both classical Islamic architecture and modern design. In part through the close ties he forged with Reza Shah in their Cossack Brigade years, Markov was granted the task of designing Iran's ministries of finance, defense, and justice, the General Post Office, and a number of schools, factories, embassies, churches, and mosques across the capital. Markov, whose mandate was to design Qasr in such a way that it would be suitable for Iran's climate and culture, brought a mix of Iranian design elements and European architectural frameworks into his design of the prison.[35] His recognizable influence was such that prisoners and statesmen alike would refer to Qasr as "Markov's prison" for years to come.[36]

Qasr was by far the most famous of the prisons built during Reza Shah's reign.[37] Launched under the direction of Tehran Chief of Police

---

[34] For more on Markov's contribution to Iranian architecture, see Victor Daniel, Bijan Shafei, and Sohrab Soroushiani, *Nikolai Markov: Architecture of Changing Times in Iran* (Tehran: Did Publications, 2004). For a brief mention of on Markov's time in the Cossacks, as well as a picture of him serving with Reza Khan, see Stephanie Cronin, "Deserters, Convicts, Cossacks, and Revolutionaries: Russians in Iranian Military Service, 1800–1920," in Stephanie Cronin, ed., *Iranian-Russian Encounters: Empires and Revolutions since 1800* (New York: Routledge, 2013), 173–178.

[35] Tafreshi, *Polis-e Khafih-ye Iran*, 105–107.

[36] In 2008, the grounds and buildings of Qasr prison were turned into a state-run museum. In visiting Qasr museum in 2014, I saw that many signs around the grounds continued to refer to the site as "Zendan-e Markov," or Markov's prison.

[37] Regarding Qasr's notoriety, Abrahamian writes, "A large, tall building perched prominently on the hilltops next to an army barracks, Qasr became a symbol of

Brigadier General Mohammad Dargahi, Qasr opened its doors on December 2, 1929, with 7 cellblocks, 192 rooms, and the initial capacity to hold an estimated 800–1,000 inmates.[38] Qasr alone represented a significant expansion of Tehran's carceral capacity. Just before the Davar-led legal and judicial overhaul, there had been only about 400 total prisoners held in Tehran, but within a few years the need for carceral space had already doubled.[39] The prison would expand further several times over the next decades, though it would remain plagued by complaints of overcrowding until its closing in the mid-2000s. Upon its opening, Qasr included fourteen yards, used ostensibly to categorize prisoners by age and crime type and meant to safeguard against the "corruption of morals," although this separation was not always strictly enforced.[40] Incredibly, just two days after Qasr held its opening ceremony and for reasons that remain contested, Dargahi was dismissed from his post and became the first person to be imprisoned in the new prison. He would be released several months later and, briefly back in the good graces of Reza Shah, given a ranking military post until he again fell foul of the shah and was dismissed in 1937.

Fazlollah Bahrami, then head of the Department of Prisons, claimed that the London conference had convinced the Pahlavi elite that new modern prisons were necessary not just for the good of Iran but for the good of the prisoners themselves.[41] In an essay in the Tehran police journal, Bahrami explained that with the new prisons, Iran's penal system had been "reformed and corrected ... fundamental steps have been taken to improve the situation for prisoners."[42] Yet Qasr was not

both the new Pahlavi state and the modern judicial system." Abrahamian, *Tortured Confessions*, 27.

[38] Rubay'i and Rahraw Khuajah, *Tarikh-e zendan*, 104–130. See also Abrahamian, *Tortured Confessions*. For more on Daraghi, see Baqer 'Aqeli, "Darāghī, Mohammad," *Encyclopaedia Iranica*, www.iranicaonline.org/articles/dargahi.

[39] Fazlollah Bahrami, *Majaleh-ye Polis*, no. 17 (Azar 1306/December 1927).

[40] Tafreshi, *Polis-e Khafih-e Iran*, 105.

[41] For more on Bahrami's life and career, in which he held various official posts in Pahlavi Iran including mayor of Tehran (twice), governor of several provinces, and cabinet member, see Baqer 'Aqeli, *Sharh-e hal-e rajal-e siasi va nezami-ye Mo'aser-e Iran* (Tehran: Nashr Guftar, 1380/2001), 344–345. Interestingly, after retiring from public life in his twilight years, Bahrami traveled to Europe to study law.

[42] Bahrami, *Majaleh-ye Polis*, no. 17.

built solely or even chiefly with Iranian prisoners in mind. Reza Shah intended Qasr to be proof to the entire world that Pahlavi Iran was a civilized modern state. In the late 1920s, Iran's legal system was under international scrutiny due to the shah's abrogation of capitulations to foreign powers in 1928. According to a 1935 message from American diplomat J. Rives Childs to the US secretary of state, Qasr was meant to "provide suitable accommodations for [foreign] prisoners consequent upon the abandonment by the Powers of their capitulary rights."[43] One American held at Qasr, traveler Richard Halliburton, did indeed find the prison suitable. Halliburton described Qasr as "well-lighted, scrupulously clean ... well heated and furnished with a cot, a table and chair, all new and all well made."[44] Other characters of global renown, including T. E. Lawrence (more famously known as Lawrence of Arabia), also found their way to Qasr in these early years; today, a room in Qasr Museum remains dedicated to the famed Brit.[45]

The Prison as Problem

Yet despite the early hopes of reformist statesmen, Qasr quickly became an object of public criticism, as the prison seemed almost immediately to reveal the limits of Pahlavi carceral modernization rather than its successes. In the aftermath of legal centralization, updates appearing in Iranian newspapers more frequently informed readers of happenings in criminal court, particularly in the event of salacious cases.[46] Critiques of Iran's police and prisons also began to

---

[43] 1935 telegram from J. Rives Childs, American *chargé d'affaires* to the United States Secretary of State. From the collection of Firoozeh Kashani-Sabet. My sincere thanks to Dr. Kashani-Sabet for sharing this invaluable source.

[44] Richard Halliburton, *The Flying Carpet: America's Most Dashing 1920s Adventurer Conquers the Air* (n.p.: The Long Rider's Guild Press, 2002), 221.

[45] For a photo of the Lawrence of Arabia room at Qasr, see "A Palace Turned Prison: A Look inside Tehran's Qasr Prison Museum," www.mypersiancorner .com/qasr-prison-museum-tehran.

[46] For instance, literate Iranians were regaled with the exploits of characters like "Sheikh 'Ali the Murderer." "Maktub-e Sheikh 'Ali Ghatil Az Zendan" ["Sheikh 'Ali the Murderer's writings from prison"], *Ettela'at* (Mordad 8, 1309/ July 30, 1930): 1.

emerge. While political communiqués[47] and prison memoirs[48] by political prisoners have gained the most subsequent attention, not all critiques of modern policing or punishment were written by members of opposition parties. In fact, for some modernists, it was not the state that deserved critique but rather its misbehaving *citizens*. As one writer of the era complained, "[I]n our nation there are still people who don't pay enough heed to the importance of the police officer, who is the representative and executor of the law [*qanun*] in the country. Perhaps there are even police officers who do not realize their own worth."[49] For this writer, the modern rule of *qanun* had not yet been achieved in the country in part because of Iran's intransigent and not-yet properly modern citizenry, not because of the failings of Iranian law enforcement officers themselves.

Others critiqued the Pahlavi state's expanding carceral network directly. In 1946, a Tehran-based publisher released *Come with Me to Prison* (*Ba man beh zendan biyaid*) by Hedayatollah Hakim-Elahi, an Oxford-educated journalist, Islamic humanist, and vocal critic of the Pahlavi state.[50] Dedicated to the prisoners of Iran "whose only

---

[47] For one instance of mid-century political communiqués from Qasr, see the 1952 communiqués (*elamiyeh*) from the Fadaiyan-e Islam regarding their imprisoned leader, Sayyid Mojtaba Navab Safavi. One of these, written after Safavi's 1951 arrest, was by members of Fadaiyan-e Islam who went to Qasr to visit their leader and claimed they would stay "until the final hour Hazrat Navab Safavi spends in Qasr Prison." Fadaiyan-e Islam, "Communiqué from a Group of Visitors to Hazrat Navab Safavi Written to the Brave Muslims of Iran and the World." File no. 5-26-256. The Institute for the Study of Contemporary Iranian History Archives, Tehran.

[48] For some exemplary titles from this era, see Bozorg Alavi, *Varagh pareh ha-ye zendan* [Scrap papers from prison] (Tehran: Amir Kabir, 1357/1978); Bozorg Alavi, *Panjah va seh nafar* [The fifty-three] (Tehran: Amir Kabir, 1357/1978). These two memoirs remain the gold standard for prison writing in Persian. For more on Alavi's prison texts as well as their importance, see Abrahamian, *Tortured Confessions*, 48–72.

[49] D. Amini, *Polis Dar Iran* (Tehran: 1325/1946).

[50] Hedayatollah Hakim-Elahi, *Ba man beh zendan biyaid* [Come with me to prison] (Tehran: Sherkat-e Sehami, 1325/1946). Although Hakim-Elahi wrote numerous articles in newspapers and several books from the 1940s to 1960s, there has been almost no scholarly notice of his work. There is one brief reference to his volumes on Tehran's red-light district in Zhand Shakibi's history of Mohammad Reza Shah. See Zhand Shakibi, *Pahlavi Iran and the Politics of Occidentalism: The Shah and the Rastakhiz Party* (New York: Bloomsbury, 2019), 330. His writing on the red-light district also appears passingly in a footnote in Ali Gheissari's work on modern Iranian intellectual history. Ali Ghessari, *Iranian Intellectuals in the 20th Century* (Austin, TX: University of

crime has been poverty and the lack of power," *Come with Me to Prison* is an occasionally salacious work of reformist agitprop written after repeated visits by Hakim-Elahi to Qasr and Tehran's central police jail.[51] The book comprised Hakim-Elahi's serialized newspaper writing and was one of several similar titles, including *Come with Me to the Red-Light District*, *Come with Me to the Asylum*, and *Come with Me to School*, written by the author in this era. *Come with Me to Prison* went through three printings, and the publisher boasted that it couldn't keep up with reader demand.[52] As historian Jairan Gahan notes in her study of Hakim-Elahi's writing on Tehran's red-light district, Hakim-Elahi had ties to Muhammad Baqir Hijazi, who was then editor at the newspaper *Vazifah*. This newspaper, for which Hakim-Elahi also wrote, was "an Islamic opposition publication that advanced a humanitarian idea of Islam" and that "regularly printed articles about the role of compassion in Islam."[53] In the tradition of the Islamic humanist intellectuals with whom he was affiliated, Hakim-Elahi's writing on Iran's prisons attempted to engender sympathy for the woebegone Iranians who found themselves incarcerated in Pahlavi prisons. Like Hakim-Elahi's other writing, *Come with Me to Prison* gestures to the budding sentiment that Tehran, lined with prisons, mental institutions, and brothels, was not only the capital of modern Iran but also the nation's capital of sin. To live in modernizing Pahlavi Iran, Hakim-Elahi's noir Tehran seemed to imply, was to live among criminality and vice. And yet Hakim-Elahi's work was reformist in nature rather than anti-modernist; his prescription for the ills that had befallen innocent Iranians fell along the legalist lines promoted by Iranian reformers for decades, albeit with a moralist bent.

Texas Press, 1998), 155n112. By far the most in-depth engagement with Hakim-Elahi's work, also on his writing on the red-light district, can be found in Jairan Gahan's excellent recent dissertation on prostitution in Iran. See Jairan Gahan, "Red-Light Tehran: Prostitution, Intimately Public Islam, and the Rule of the Sovereign, 1910–1980" (PhD diss., University of Toronto, 2017), 165–177.

[51] The author takes pains to give evidence of his authority and expertise, including photos of him taken with prisoners and prison authorities, such as the head of prison, Pasyar Samii, at Qasr. The publisher's introduction to the text admits that the author is biased but explains that this bias is born from the oppressive conditions the author witnessed in Pahlavi prisons. Hakim-Elahi, *Ba man beh zendan biyaid*, 1–2.

[52] Ibid.   [53] Gahan, "Red-Light Tehran," 165.

Come with Me to Prison followed the experience of what the author called a "typical" Iranian prisoner. Upon capture, Hakim-Elahi explained, the prisoner was first taken to Tehran's Central Police Jail, a facility at that point meant to be a temporary stop for unsentenced arrestees. This is where the accused was meant to remain until sentencing, after which they would be transferred to Qasr. According to Hakim-Elahi, however, this was not the case in practice. Some prisoners were granted their outright release without arraignment because they understood the state's meaning of "freedom": freedom to pay the bribe.[54] This is not the rule of law that constitutionalists and reformists promised, Hakim-Elahi protested, but the "rule of money" (*hukumat-e pul*).[55] Despite the myriad laws put on the books in the two decades prior, the author indicated, legality was merely a suggestion for the Pahlavi government and its law enforcement officials. The notion that law enforcement in Pahlavi Iran was not founded on fairness or legality would be a regular refrain throughout Hakim-Elahi's text.

Hakim-Elahi claimed that corruption was even more rampant at Qasr than at the central jail. Upon arrival, detainees were given one pair of pants and a striped shirt and taken to the "grimiest" section of the prison, cellblock two. The cellblock in which the inmate was eventually housed, Hakim-Elahi wrote, was decided through bribes or social status. Hakim-Elahi was not the only writer to mention differentiated treatment between prisoners; such discrepancies were noted by the era's political prisoners, who were often given preferential treatment due to their higher-class positions and education. Members of the Iranian elite who fell out of favor and were thrown into Qasr also recounted receiving favored treatment. Firuz Nosrat al-Dowleh, who had a hand in the prison's establishment but like Brigadier General Dargahi was himself imprisoned there not long after, marveled at the polite behavior of the guards and the peaceful gardens on Qasr's grounds.[56] For his part, Hakim-Elahi described the prison in quite different terms than did the Pahlavi statesman. Detainees, both male and female, were routinely whipped or punched.[57] Illicit drugs were a

---

[54] Hakim-Elahi, *Ba man beh zendan biyaid*, 4–5.   [55] Ibid., 74.

[56] Nosrat al-Dowleh Firuz, *Majmuah-e makatibat asnad khatirat va asar-e Firzu Mirza Firuz (Nosrat al-Dowleh)* [The complete correspondences, documents, and memoirs of Firza Mirza Firuz Nosrat al-Dowleh] (Tehran: Nashr-e Tarikh-e Iran, 1369/1990).

[57] Hakim-Elahi, *Ba man beh zendan biyaid*, 42.

major problem, among both prisoners and guards, while crime bosses were allowed to move around the facility freely. Another Qasr prisoner from the 1930s confirmed Hakim-Elahi's account, writing, "There were no locks whatsoever on our doors, and we soon found that the guards took no notice of prisoners wandering in and out of their cells."[58] Hakim-Elahi described this freedom of movement sardonically, writing, "The angel of freedom [*ferishteh-ye azadi*] is in flight at Qasr. Long live this democratic government [*zendeh bad hukumat-e demokrasi*]."[59] For Hakim-Elahi, the failure to maintain the rule of law in prisons was tantamount to a larger failure to bring about those political demands – freedom, justice, legality, etc. – that had for so long animated Iranian reformers. Instead, he argued, Pahlavi Iran had produced only a perversion of freedom and legality.

At the time of *Come with Me to Prison*'s writing, there were nine cellblocks at Qasr.[60] Cellblock three housed the infirmary, while a small prison factory was housed in cellblock seven. Each cellblock had a café and grocery staffed by prisoners. Years prior, Brigadier General Dargahi had pushed for a modernized infirmary for Tehran's carceral network.[61] Better health services had been part of the modernist promise of Qasr, but Hakim-Elahi's description of the Qasr infirmary indicated failure in this regard. Meanwhile, Hakim-Elahi explained, the wages paid to prisoners who worked in the small prison factory were often coerced out of the workers' hands by guards and organized crime-linked prisoners.[62] Prisoners of all stripes routinely complained of being held without sentencing, or in some cases even after their sentences had expired.[63] Overcrowding was, as usual, a problem. This issue stemmed in part from the sheer number of new criminal cases in the aftermath of legal centralization, which far exceeded the Iranian judiciary's ability to attend to them in a timely

---

[58] Halliburton, *Flying Carpet*, 221.
[59] Hakim-Elahi, *Ba man beh zendan biyaid*, 7.
[60] Ibid., 9. See also Rubay'i and Rahraw Khuajah, *Tarikh-e zendan*, 104–118.
[61] Dargahi's efforts are recounted in a story first published in *Iran* newspaper in 1922, quoted in Tafreshi, *Polis-e Khafih-ye Iran*, 109.
[62] Hakim-Elahi, *Ba man beh zendan biyaid*, 8–10.
[63] For one late Pahlavi reference to this issue, see Cherikha-ye Fadai-ye Khalq, "Zendanha-ye rezhim va zendanian-e siyasi," *'Asr-e 'Amal* 4: 29. Hakim-Elahi claims, upon his visit to the women's prison, that there were fifty-seven women held there, only five of whom had been sentenced. Hakim-Elahi, *Ba man beh zendan biyaid*, 3.

fashion. This backlog was such an issue that concerned citizens anxiously wrote Iranian newspapers with ideas for relieving the judicial logjam.[64] Remarkably, in the years after the Pahlavi state initiated a prison reform program in the mid-1950s, state literature would admit that many of these issues – drug use, organized crime-run business, overcrowding – were all significant problems in Iran's prisons in years prior.[65]

In the postwar era, Iran's population of incarcerated women increased exponentially, and with it the number of texts condemning the conditions that had seemingly led to the crisis of female criminality.[66] Hakim-Elahi decried conditions at the women's prison in Qasr, along with the fact that many of the women held there had young children in tow or youngsters left behind at home. According to Hakim-Elahi, the conditions at Qasr's juvenile prison, Dar al-Ta'dib, were equally grim, and as such also produced deleterious effects on Iranian family life. Documentary filmmaker Kamran Shirdel, another 1960s critic of Pahlavi state modernism, painted a comparable picture of Tehran's women's prison in his 1965 short film *Women's Penitentiary*. Despite being funded by the Pahlavi Ministry of Culture, Shirdel's 1960s films depict life in Tehran, particularly its prisons, poverty, and sex industry, in gritty, noir-ish detail not unlike that of Hakim-Elahi.[67] Unsurprisingly, Shirdel's films were not well

---

[64] In August 1930, a writer called Abul Fath Irani wrote to *Ettela'at* with ideas for helping Iran's "heroic" but overburdened judges decrease their caseload. The author of this article indicates that there are simply far too many cases for the available number of trained judges. Abul Fath Irani, "Pishnihad Beh Vazir-e 'Adliyeh" ["Suggestions to the head of the judiciary"], *Ettela'at* (Mordad 13, 1309/August 4, 1930).

[65] See Bongah-e Ta'avun va Sanayeh Zendanian, *Fa'aliyat-e seh saleh-ye Bongah-e Ta'avun va Sanayeh Zendanian* [Three years of activity of the Institution for the Cooperation and Industry of Prisoners] (Tehran: 1344/1965), 18–20.

[66] For one example, see Q. Hijazi, *Barrasi-ye jarayim-e zan dar Iran* [A study of female criminality in Iran] (Tehran: Sherkat-e Sahami-ye Enteshar, 1341/1963). For an analysis of Hijazi's text, see Cyrus Schayegh, "Criminal-Women and Mother-Women: Sociocultural Transformations and the Critique of Criminality in Early Post-World War II Iran," *Journal of Middle East Women's Studies* 2:3 (Fall 2006): 1–21.

[67] Kamran Shirdel, dir., *Women's Penitentiary* (1965). For more on Shirdel in the context of state-funded Iranian documentary cinema, see Hamid Naficy, *A Social History of Iranian Cinema, Vol. 2: The Industrializing Years, 1941–1978* (Durham, NC: Duke University Press, 2011), 49–145. For a recent scholarly work on Shirdel's films, see Niki Akhavan, "Nonfiction Form and the

received by the state institutions that had funded them. *Women's Penitentiary* includes footage of imprisoned women raising their young children behind bars and worrying about their families beyond prison walls, as well as interviews with social workers and inmates. One social worker in Shirdel's film admits that having mothers in prison leads to "psychological and emotional problems" for their children. In their emphasis on broken families and damaged children, critiques such as Hakim-Elahi's and Shirdel's offered damning appraisals of the Pahlavi government, in part because they challenged the state using a long-standing discourse of Iranian nationalism: patriotic motherhood.[68] Instead of raising the next generation of healthy patriots and citizens, these critiques indicated, Iranian women were instead raising the next generation of criminals and recidivists.

The concept of female and child criminality, particularly the idea that children were learning to engage in lives of crime rather than going to school, challenged the modernizing state to its core. For their part, Pahlavi state institutions publicized child criminality as a dangerous failing of absentee *parents*, who through negligence let their children fall under the control of corrupting forces. A 1960s radio program broadcast by the national police, for instance, interviewed a twelve-year-old pickpocket who explained that he had been abandoned by his father and left unattended by his mother, leaving him to learn the art of delinquency from street thieves.[69] *Come with Me to Prison* ironically noted that Qasr is a "giant school of ethics" in which one must learn a

---

'Truth' about Muslim Women in Iranian Documentary," *Feminist Media Histories* 1:1 (Winter 2015): 89–111. For essential texts on Iranian cinema more broadly, see Hamid Dabashi, *Close Up: Iranian Cinema, Past, Present, and Future* (New York: Verso Press, 2001); Hamid Dabashi, *Masters and Masterpieces of Iranian Cinema* (Washington, DC: Mage Publishers, 2007).

[68] For more on patriotic motherhood, see "Crafting an Educated Wife and Mother," in Afsaneh Najmabadi, *Women with Mustaches and Men without Beards: Gender and Sexual Anxieties of Iranian Modernity* (Los Angeles, CA: University of California Press, 2005), 181–206. For a discussion of Iran's discourse of nationalist maternalism, see Firoozeh Kashani-Sabet, *Conceiving Citizens: Women and the Politics of Motherhood in Iran* (New York: Oxford University Press, 2011).

[69] This interview, which originally aired May 9, 1968 (Ordibehesht 2, 1347), is reprinted in the literature of the state-run Institute for the Cooperation and Industry of Prisoners [Bongah-e Ta'avun va Sanayeh Zendanian]. See Bongah-e Ta'avun va Sanayeh Zendanian, *Gozaresh-e az zendanha* [A report from the prisons] (Tehran: Edarih-e Kol-e Zendanha va Chapgah-e Bongah-e Ta'avun va Sanayeh Zendanian, 1347/1968), 36–37.

"strange science": the science of criminal behavior.[70] This claim echoed, albeit to different ends, a common refrain by political prisoners of this era who asserted that they received their political educations at Qasr.[71] Hakim-Elahi argued that Pahlavi prisons were pushing Iran's wayward youth to cement their status as recidivists. He noted that one master lockbreaker taught prisoners how to break locks with silk, while another taught them how to slit throats without making a sound.[72] Yet for all these critiques, and for his moralist concern with the lives Iranians were being forced to lead behind bars, Hakim-Elahi believed in the reformist promise of the modern prison. As such, he argued for investment in and expansion of Iran's carceral networks. In particular, Hakim-Elahi argued for the development of Iran's prison factories. Instead of a "factory for pickpockets" and a "university for thieves," Hakim-Elahi insisted, the prison should reform incarcerated persons into useful citizens by making "honest" labor available to all prisoners.[73] It is precisely this expanded carceral project, wherein the carceral system was promoted as a salve for social ills, that both the academic discipline of criminology and the Pahlavi state would take up in subsequent years.

Iranian Criminology and the Science of Prisons

The year 1931 was a watershed moment in the story of Pahlavi modernization. In that year, the University of Tehran first opened its doors, and the Pahlavi monarchy passed a law banning any political organizing with a "communalist" (i.e. communist) outlook, expanding the list of political acts for which Iranians might be incarcerated. In 1946, the first sociology course was offered at Tehran University's Teacher's College, and in 1958 the University established the Institute for Social Science and Research (ISSR).[74] The initial plans

---

[70] Hakim-Elahi, *Ba man beh zendan biyaid*, 5.
[71] In an interview from the 1980s, Tudeh Party cofounder Bozorg Alavi claimed that, "[Qasr] Prison, for us, was truly a school. We learned many things there. Not only about social and political matters, but also ... well, what didn't we learn? For example, I learned Russian in prison. I learned English in prison. In prison ... one read in earnest." Donne Raffat, *The Prison Papers of Bozorg Alavi: A Literary Odyssey* (Syracuse, NY: Syracuse University Press, 1985), 49.
[72] Hakim-Elahi, *Ba man beh zendan biyaid*, 9.   [73] Ibid., 58.
[74] Ali Akbar Mahdi and Abdolali Lahsaeizadeh, *Sociology in Iran* (Bethesda, MD: Jahan Publishers, 1992), 6. For an eye-opening look at the leftist intellectual

for the ISSR were drawn up by the Geneva- and Paris-educated intellectual Ehsan Naraqi, whose connections to the European academy as well as international institutions like the United Nations and UNESCO helped the ISSR secure international funding and draw visiting international scholars.[75] In the aftermath of the ISSR's founding, other universities, including Pahlavi University in Shiraz, Mashhad University, Tabriz University, Isfahan University, and the National University of Iran, also began to offer courses in the social sciences.[76] From its inception, the Iranian academy was linked in complex ways to the project of Pahlavi state modernity. As historian Cyrus Schayegh has argued, the language of the modern sciences (and the positivist logic of this discourse) was first adopted by members of the Pahlavi elite and the new Iranian middle class as part of the Pahlavi government's "modernist urge to hasten Iran's modernization and improve its administration."[77] In the postwar era, the language and logic of the social sciences would also be adopted by members of the Pahlavi elite. Criminology – as well as its offshoots criminal psychology and penology – emerged in the 1940s–1950s as a distinct field in this broader academic and social context. It became crucial to Pahlavi prison reform efforts, which mobilized discourses from the medical and social sciences to legitimize state practices.

Academic writing on prisons in Iran was initially limited. An index of books published in Iran up to 1958 reveals several academic and popular texts on the topic of modern law and legal reform, many published through the University of Tehran law school, but seemingly none solely on prisons and little on crime as such.[78] There was, however, budding interest in *elm-e zendan*, or "prison sciences," in

---

lineage of this research institute, see Matin-Asgari, *Both Eastern and Western*, 194–196.

[75] Kazem Izadi, "Institute of Social Studies and Research," *Encyclopaedia Iranica*, www.iranicaonline.org/articles/institute-of-social-studies-and-research. For more on Naraqi and the institute's intellectual underpinnings and legacy in the context of Iranian leftisms, see Matin-Asgari, *Both Eastern and Western*.

[76] Mahdi and Lahsaeizadeh, *Sociology in Iran*, 6–7. See also Taqi Azad Armiki, *Jam'eh shenasi-ye jam'eh shenasi dar Iran* [The sociology of sociology in Iran] (Tehran: Muasisih-ye Nashr-e Kalameh, 1378/1999).

[77] Schayegh, *Who Is Knowledgeable Is Strong*, 7.

[78] Khanbaba Mushar, ed., *Fehrest-e ketabha-ye chapi-e Farsi* (Tehran: University of Tehran Press, 1337/1958).

Iran's universities. In 1957, a student at the University of Tehran college of law named Abolhasan Behpur completed a doctoral dissertation entitled "Prisons and Prisoners."[79] This text appears to be the first monograph-length treatise on prisons by an Iranian scholar, and as such, it is worth analyzing at length. Behpur, whose thesis borrowed liberally from but never cited classic European criminology, introduced his specific research on prisons in Iran with a general social theory of law. For Behpur, every individual was a cog in a society. In order to maintain the health of society, each individual had to fulfill certain duties. Yet despite this basic principle, there would always be individuals who, due to a lack of moral character and limited "love for humanity" (*bashar dusti*), transgressed social norms.[80] "Just as an individual needs air to breathe in order to live," Behpur argued, "so a society needs laws."[81] Without formally citing either theorists of Islamic jurisprudence or European legal philosophers, Behpur's social theory of law nonetheless drew from both Islamic legal theories of social duties and European natural law theories that understand codified law as derived from the natural emergence of social norms.

Behpur argued that the purpose for punishment is twofold: meting out justice and safeguarding society. Paraphrasing Italian criminologist Cesare Beccaria's argument on punishment and proportionality, the author insisted that a just punishment must be proportionate. That is, the severity of the punishment must match that of the crime. Further, Behpur argued, an effective punishment must be rational, successfully dissuading others from undertaking similar activities.[82] For Behpur, the state had both a moral and practical responsibility to punish correctly and rationally. But what should society's response be "when faced with a thief, a traitor, a swindler ... or those who have committed manslaughter or tens of other crimes of this sort?"[83] For the author, the answer was simple: prison. For Behpur, prison represented the final step in a progressive telos of human punishment. He presented the history of punishment as a progressive march from the inefficient and inhumane toward the socially useful, civilized, and just; none of Shirdel's noir-ish critiques of the dark underbelly of institutional modernization were apparent in his analysis.

---

[79] Abolhasan Behpur, "Zendan va zendanha" ["Prisons and prisoners"] (PhD diss., University of Tehran, 1336/1957).
[80] Ibid., 2.   [81] Ibid., 4.   [82] Ibid., 5–6.   [83] Ibid., 6.

Behpur argued that punishments – in Iran as elsewhere – were once meted out according to the whims of tyrannical rulers rather than by codified law. In this primordial, prelegal era, "no one paid attention to 'criminal law' or 'the reform of the criminal,' issues which are of paramount importance in the laws of (unnamed) progressive [*motaraghi*] nations today."[84] Earlier prisoners, both in Iran and around the world, were thrown into "terrifying, dank, underground dungeons." The life of the prisoner was rendered "worthless" in such spaces, and concepts like "law" and "rights" had no meaning. Behpur argued that Iran was mired in just such a prelegal dark age before the Reza Shah era's efforts at legal centralization. Notably, neither Islamic law nor pre-Islamic Persiannate notions of justice appear in Behpur's schema, simply a before and after Reza Shah's program of legal modernization. Before legal reform, Behpur argued, punishment in Iran was decided by whim; whipping, branding, amputation, and execution were common. He continued, "In prisons of old so much did they torture … that [prisoners] would be forced to confess whether or not the individual had committed crime." According to Behpur, this was no longer the case, as torture in Iran had definitively been put to an end.[85] "[H]uman societies gradually moved toward progress and civilization," Behpur proudly noted, such that "today, punishments must be applied with regard to the law."[86]

Despite Behpur's triumphalist tone, Pahlavi prisons emerged in his work as sites of anxiety at the same time as they were lauded as markers of civilizational progress. He noted, for instance, that Pahlavi prisons lag behind those in other "progressive nations" in securing both the physical and psychological health of prisoners.[87] Prisoner health (both physical and psychological), and the effects of that health on Iranian society more broadly, was a central concern in this era's criminological texts, many of which shared Behpur's concern that Pahlavi Iran was lagging in this regard. An unpublished 1959 dissertation by a scholar named Mahmud Qahremani, for instance, argued that prisoner psychology was not merely a health issue, but

---

[84] Ibid., 8.

[85] Behpur quotes Article 131 of the Pahlavi penal code – the anti-torture article – at length. The text also applauds the Pahlavi reforms in criminal law that grant the accused the right to a speedy trial (the so-called twenty-four-hour rule). Ibid., 10–11.

[86] Ibid., 9.   [87] Ibid., 12.

more critically a broader issue of that ever-elusive reformist desire: "justice." Unfortunately, according to Qahremani, the Iranian criminal justice system of the 1950s rarely took stock of the accused individual's mental health and capacity for healthy reasoning during sentencing. This evident legal lacuna was, for Qahremani, also a *moral* lacuna, insofar as the state had both ethical and legal responsibility for the care of its citizens.[88] Nowhere was this more evident than in the carceral system, which supervised both mentally ill and socially ill elements, as Qahremani reminded readers.

Referring extensively to the work of Tarde, whose work had been championed by the International Prison Commission in the 1920s and had become particularly prominent in American criminology in subsequent decades, Qahremani insisted that the Iranian judicial and penal systems needed to better incorporate lessons from both the fields of sociology and psychology if they were to function justly and optimally.[89] Qahremani's emphasis on individual detainees' mental health was drawn in part from Tarde's insight that criminal justice systems must take both social and individual contexts into account as well as Tarde's emphasis on a sociology that would incorporate the psychological sciences. Qahremani argued that mental health issues complicated the Beccarian principle of proportional punishment (as outlined in Behpur's text, for instance). According to the author, the Iranian criminal justice system still too often looked only at the accused's list of offenses rather than taking stock of their mental health and asking whether they could be held criminally responsible for their actions. Those with mental disorders, the young scholar noted, should not be held responsible for their crimes because they did not have a "unity of personality" (*vahdat-e shakhsiyat*). Criminal justice in Iran needed to incorporate lessons from the modern psychological sciences and sociology, Qahremani argued, because these revealed that mentally ill persons must be cared for differently than healthy persons who know right from wrong.[90] Importantly, for Qahremani, prison was an ideal site of care and of rehabilitation – an answer to the question of how to treat and even cure social pathologies.

---

[88] Mahmud Qahremani, "Barresi-ye ghavanin-e Iran: Masuliyat az lehaz-e ravanpezeshki" ["A study of Iranian laws: Responsibility from the perspective of psychoanalysis"] (PhD diss., University of Tehran, 1338/1959), 1–5.
[89] Ibid., 6.   [90] Ibid.

In the 1960s and 1970s, as criminology further established itself as a regular academic pursuit in Iran, the psycho-medical logics hinted at by these earlier texts became increasingly commonplace. A 1973 monograph written by Taj Zaman Danesh, one of Iran's foremost criminologists both before and after the revolution, represents the culmination of two decades of criminological thought in the country. In Danesh's work, acts deemed criminal were described in pathologized terms: "the criminal is like a patient [*bimar*], and just as a doctor orders various tests on the patient in order to diagnose their disease, the judge must collect information for a file on the individual personality of each offender, in order to discover the reasons and motivations for the crime."[91] The Swiss- and French-educated Danesh, who was a prison reform advocate as well as University of Tehran professor, worked directly with Pahlavi law enforcement institutions to advance reformist aims. The link between the state and the academic field of criminology in the late Pahlavi era is nowhere clearer than in Danesh's relationship with the Tehran Police Academy, where she taught, and which republished some of her writing expressly for use by its cadets.[92] In Danesh's scholarship, the state was cast as a healer-reformer of individual prisoner pathologies, rather than the authority who simply punishes without regard for their health. This preoccupation with prisoners' bodies and psyches represented a new strategy of power that was at once invested in technologies of the body and in management of populations.[93] For criminologists (and the government which employed them), the expanding prison populace represented both a source of latent danger and a site of experimentation with methods of discipline and reform. And for both criminologists and the Pahlavi government, social ills from drug use to vagrancy were increasingly subjected to carceral thinking. In other words, modern prisons were

---

[91] Taj Zaman Danesh, *Usul-e elm-e zendanha* [The fundamentals of prison science] (Tehran: University of Tehran Press, 1353/1973). For more of Danesh's work, see Taj Zaman Danesh, *Keyfarshenasi va huquq-e zendanha* [Criminology and prison law] (Tehran: University of Tehran Press, 1352/1973).

[92] For the police academy publication of Danesh's prison scholarship, see Taj Zaman Danesh, *Kefarshinasi va elm-e zendanha* [Criminology and prison sciences] (Tehran: Entesharat-e Daneshgah-e Polis, Shumareh 21 [Police Academy Publishing, Number 21]), n.d.).

[93] Here, my argument draws on Michel Foucault's theorization of the biopolitical. See Michel Foucault, *Society Must Be Defended: Lectures at the College de France*, trans. David Macey (New York: Picador Press), 2003.

recast as therapeutic institutions that could heal or even cure and thus eradicate these social ailments.

Pahlavi Prison Reform

On October 9, 1954, the Iranian cabinet approved the bylaws for the Institute for the Cooperation and Industry of Prisoners (ICIP) (Bongah-e Ta'avun va Sanayeh Zendanian), a state-run organization mandated with founding prison factories and education facilities and supporting the families of the incarcerated.[94] With financial backing from another state institution, the Organization for the Protection of Prisoners (OPP) (Anjoman-e Hemayat-e Zendanian), the ICIP initiated a prison labor and education program that the Pahlavi elite advertised as an important modernizing victory. It wasn't until 1959 that the ICIP secured funding for the machines and tools necessary to begin its work in Iran's prison factories. That year, the Pahlavi government (through the OPP) gave machines, tools, and capital in excess of 285,000 rials to the ICIP to put toward expanding those factories. The ICIP established new factories in both the men's and women's prisons in Qasr, with workstations for sewing, metalworks, automobile repair, furniture-building, shoe-making, purse-making, embroidery, basket-weaving, belt-making, straw mat-making, rug-making, sock-knitting, frame-building, hair and makeup, handicrafts, and fine arts.[95] By 1965 there were at least 30 skilled experts/technicians in the Qasr prison factory who taught skills classes and worked in a management capacity. There were also an estimated 850 male, 95 female, and 45 youth incarcerated workers in prison work programs throughout Iran.[96]

The ICIP credited its founding to the progressive nature and reformist zeal of Mohammad Reza Pahlavi, who they claimed had reformed Iranian prisons along "civilized" and "humane" principles.[97] After 1963, these successes were situated in the broader context of the shah's White Revolution reforms, a spate of top-down reforms including land reform, infrastructure projects, literacy and health services, and women's enfranchisement.[98] A 1965 speech given at the eighth general

---

[94] Bongah-e Ta'avun, *Fa'aliyat-e seh saleh*, 8.   [95] Ibid., 20.   [96] Ibid., 23.
[97] Ibid., 12.
[98] For more on the White Revolution, see Abrahamian, *Iran between Two Revolutions*, 419–446. For an analysis of the response of some Islamist intellectuals of the era to the White Revolution and the policy's influence on later

conference for the OPP by national chief of police Major General Mohsen Mobassar revealed the extent to which both the language of the social sciences and that of Pahlavi state modernism buttressed the organization's view of Iran's prisons. Highlighting the "humanitarian efforts" (*talashha-ye ensani*) of those working to improve the lives of prisoners in Iran, Mobassar invoked the "language that is common today and is called dialectics" in order to "scientifically explain" the government's reform efforts. "The dialectical method," the chief of police stated, "teaches us that every phenomenon must be studied in a state of flux, transformation, and evolution [*takamol*]."[99] Instead of merely punishing for the sake of punishing, Mobassar told the OPP, enlightened modern nations like Iran under Mohammad Reza Pahlavi now meted out punishment rationally, humanely, and effectively.

According to Mobassar, advances in punishment techniques were not simply technical advances for the state, but rather leaps forward for the betterment of all people. Echoing the Iranian criminologists mentioned above as well as their European influences, the chief of police explained that it was not merely dangerous to punish a detainee disproportionately to their crime, but it would also be dangerous for society if the state were to do so:

> The goal of punishment in earlier society was only retribution [*ghasas*] and revenge ... As a result, punishments were inhumane [*ghayr-e ensani*], using torturous acts without any results in terms of the reality of crime [in society]. Not only was not any positive result achieved but the vengeful atmosphere also led to the committing of worse and more horrific crimes ... Every day, criminality increased in terms of both quality and quantity.[100]

This economy of criminality became a core ideal of late Pahlavi carceral thinking. Drawing from theories first promoted by European criminologists and prison reformers and later promoted by American sociologists and buoyed by the triumphalist telos of Pahlavi state nationalism, Pahlavi prison discourses increasingly promoted the belief that Pahlavi-built prisons would help eradicate (or at least radically reduce) crime in Iran. And, as Mobassar often reminded his

---

revolutionary ideology, see Hamid Dabashi, *Theology of Discontent: The Ideological Foundation of the Islamic Revolution in Iran*, 2nd ed. (Edison, NJ: Transaction Publishers, 2005).

[99] Bongah-e Ta'avun, *Fa'aliyat-e seh saleh*, 5.   [100] Ibid., 6–7.

listeners, credit for instituting these changes belonged to Mohammad Reza Shah.

After the mid-century founding of the ICIP, members of Iran's government and law enforcement agencies increasingly promoted Iranian prisons as therapeutic and curative rather than punitive in nature. In his 1965 speech, Mobassar outlined the by-now familiar metaphor of crime-as-curable-pathology:

Just as the doctor fights against a dangerous disease by before anything learning about its root causes ... a criminologist or judge ... must certainly use this same method in the fight against criminality. Just as a doctor cannot operate on a patient suffering from rheumatism by simply amputating their arm, a judge cannot simply eliminate or imprison one murderer or thief in the fight against murder and theft in general.[101]

According to a 1967 report in *Kayhan* newspaper, Mobassar spread a similar message to Iran's prison wardens that year. The chief of police told prison officials that Iran's prisoners were simply sick people and were to be treated "humanely" so that they could be cured of their criminal impulses.[102] Mobassar was not the only member of the Pahlavi elite to spread this rehabilitative message. No less a personage than Queen Farah Pahlavi remarked in 1968, "Most prisoners are capable of reform and cultivation [*tarbiyat*], and are regretful of their criminal actions."[103] In other words, Pahlavi prisons were spaces where the incarcerated were sent "*as* punishment, not *for* punishment."[104] If prisons did not treat prisoners humanely, then the whole of society would suffer. The empress made this point explicit: "If prisoners see nothing but violence [*khushunat*] inside of prison, and their families outside are in distress and have no refuge, then those prisoners will become cynical toward society and their antisocial aspects will predominate and they will again turn to crime."[105] Prison bore the responsibility for either the recuperation of the incarcerated or their further descent into social pathology. The names of Iran's carceral institutions were changed to reflect this newfound rehabilitative impulse; the Central Prison for Men and Women (Zendan-e Markazi'-ye Mardan va Zanan] was changed to Penitentiary (or Place of Repentance) for Men and Women

---

[101] Ibid., 6.   [102] *Kayhan*, Tehran (October 23, 1967).
[103] Bongah-e Ta'avun, *Gozaresh-e az zendanha*, 1.   [104] Ibid. (emphasis added).
[105] Ibid., 17.

(Nedamatgah-e Mardan va Zanan), while some smaller prisons stopped using the word prison (*zendan*) and instead called themselves a place of counsel (*andarzgah*).[106] This euphemistic sleight of hand mirrored the widespread adoption across the Global South of the "penitentiary" model of mass imprisonment, in which "penitent" prisoners would learn the error of their ways, along the lines first imagined by Euro-American penal reform movements.[107]

The ICIP routinely touted their work as representing great leaps forward for health (physical and mental), hygiene, and dentistry in Iran's prisons, and further boasted that drug abuse and epidemic diseases among prisoners were both nearly eradicated by Mohammad Reza Shah's efforts. Yet evidence from prisons of this era reveals the significant limits of Pahlavi prison reform efforts. Vakil Abad Prison in Mashhad, today referred to as the Central Mashhad Prison, opened its doors in the late 1960s with a ribbon-cutting ceremony headed by Queen Farah, but was within a few years already, "dropping to pieces; the electrics, the plumbing, the showers, the toilets, the locks, the heaters, the fly-screens, the whole place was a mess."[108] At the infirmary at Vakil Abad, a large facility whose incarcerated population has from the beginning held disproportionate numbers of Afghanis and those held on drug-related charges, "most of the medicines had expired [by the mid-1970s], especially the antibiotics, which were rejects or unsold stock sent back by pharmacies and hospitals all over the country."[109] Drug use, violence between prisoners, and organized crime activity also remained issues in prisons despite formal ICIP insistence to the contrary.

Despite these obvious difficulties, Pahlavi law enforcement and prison officials continued to champion the therapeutic and restorative capacity of Pahlavi prisons. In another speech given in 1968, Chief of Police Mobassar again lectured members of the OPP on the necessity of

---

[106] Ibid., 24.
[107] For a study of similar historical processes in Latin America in an earlier era, see the essays in Ricardo D. Salvatore and Carlos Aguirre, eds., *The Birth of the Penitentiary in Latin America: Essays on Criminology, Prison Reform, and Social Control, 1830–1940* (Austin, TX: University of Texas Press, 1996).
[108] Richard Savin, *Vakil Abad Iran: A Survivor's Story* (Edinburgh: Canongate/ Q Press, 1979), 88.
[109] Ibid., 83.

viewing crime as a social disease and boasted that Iranian prisons had been utterly transformed by Pahlavi efforts:

[T]here have been remarkable changes in the science of criminology. The prison system has totally been transformed, such that today the prison is no longer a place meant for the negation of freedom. Instead, the prison is a treatment center in which criminals and lawbreakers are taken into a space ... after which the social illness with which they enter is cured.[110]

But by what mechanism did the state claim to guarantee the transformation of the bad criminal into the good citizen? The primary answer for the Pahlavi government in this era was labor. Prison labor was promoted as being capable of restoring a prisoner's health, honor, social standing, and moral compass. Labor, which was imagined in gendered terms with a strictly defined division of labor for men and women, offered a means through which to remake not only the criminal's body and mind but also his or her subjectivity. Male prisoners were put to work in factories or on farms, while women were taught sewing and embroidery. The ICIP viewed teaching female prisoners sewing, cooking, and home management as integral to its mandate, because women needed to be prepared for future lives as homemakers.[111] The stated goal of Pahlavi prison reformism was the embodied production of normatively gendered citizens. Upon release, the new citizen's body would be healthy, strong, laboring, and gendered, his or her psyche whole.

Labeling its expansion of prison labor "social work," ICIP literature asserted that its goal was not profit-making, despite the organization's close accounting of its bottom line.[112] Rather, it positioned itself as the state's means to "train and educate" those Iranians who had fallen on the deviant path so that they could eventually "live nobly."[113] Yet the

---

[110] Bongah-e Ta'avun, *Gozaresh-e az zendanha*, 2.   [111] Ibid., 9–10.

[112] The state, of course, was interested in its expenditures in its prisons. See, for instance, budgetary reports from the early 1960s, which keep watch on policing and penal budgets. *Qanun-e bujeh-yi sal-e 1345 kul-e kishvar* [The budget laws for 1345] (Tehran: Majles-e Shura-ye Melli, 1345/1961); *Qanun-e bujeh-yi sal-e 1345 kul-e kishvar* [The budget laws for 1346] (Tehran: Majles-e Shura-yi Melli, 1346/1962).

[113] Bongah-e Ta'avun, *Fa'aliyat-e seh saleh*, 10. Despite their insistence that they were uninterested in profits, ICIP materials boasted of raising 4,807,594.23 rials in a decade's time. According to the ICIP, however, prison labor not only benefited state institutions but also aided the prisoners themselves. ICIP literature claimed that 25 percent of prisoner wages would be set aside in bank

Pahlavi government made use of the supply of cheap prison labor, putting the incarcerated to work for the benefit of other state institutions. In 1963, prisoner-workers made new tables, chairs, benches, cabinets, bookshelves, and clothes for police officers all over Iran for "half the cost" of non-prison labor.[114] The Pahlavi state continued to open and promote new prisons throughout the years before the revolution, with many planned specifically to expand the prison labor program. Ghezel Hesar Prison, which was located 11 miles from Tehran in Karaj and opened its doors in 1968, was built with both maximum- and minimum-security wings and outdoor farm facilities for crop management and animal farming.[115] In 1969, the journal of the Tehran police claimed that Ghezel Hesar, which it euphemistically referred to as a "work and training center," was one of the "model" prisons of the world.[116]

Two other new prisons built in this era, 2,000-capacity facilities in Mashhad and Shiraz, were based on blueprints first used at Marion Penitentiary in Illinois in the United States.[117] The relationship between the new Iranian prison facilities and the now-infamous Marion is one upon which it is worth dwelling. Though it is now the smallest prison in the US federal prison system, Marion has long served as an important if troubling blueprint for carceral sites around the world. Opened in 1963, just a few years before its design was transported to Iran, Marion's blueprint was used almost immediately internationally for prisons in locations including New Zealand, Israel, and the United Kingdom.[118] The methods of social control used in Marion, including novel experiments in solitary confinement and "group

---

accounts at Iran National Bank, another 40 percent sent to prisoner families, and 10 percent given to prisoners for daily expenses.

[114] Ibid., 21.   [115] Ibid. 23.

[116] "Ghezel Hesar," *Mahnameh-ye Shahrbani*, Tehran, no. 407 (July–August 1969): 30.

[117] Bongah-e Ta'avun, *Fa'aliyat-e seh saleh*, 11.

[118] As Greg Mewbold writes about Paremoremo, the New Zealand prison based on Marion, "Paremoremo … illustrates how substantially American social trends have become an international phenomenon and how, more particularly, American modes of criminal justice have been adopted in other parts of the world." See Newbold's introduction in Stephen C. Richards, ed., *The Marion Experiment: Long-term Solitary Confinement and the Supermax Movement* (Carbondale, IL: Southern Illinois University Press 2015), vii–ix. See also Stephen C. Richards, "USP Marion: The First Federal Supermax," *The Prison Journal* 88:1 (March 2008): 6–22.

therapy" in which prisoners were made to express penitence for their deviant behavior, were also exported and used in a variety of national contexts (Iran included), all looking for new means to control and transform "trouble" populations.

Conclusion: The Limits of Carceral Modernity

By the eve of the 1979 revolution, the negative consequences of prison expansion in Iran were widely publicized by Iranian dissidents and revolutionaries loudly decrying the brutal treatment of those Iranians incarcerated for "security" reasons – that is, political prisoners. In the years leading up to the revolution, accounts of Pahlavi torture circulated widely both inside Iran and globally among a large group of Iranian dissident students and international human rights activists, Islamist and leftist circles inside of Iran, and the revolutionary clerics who would eventually win the day.[119] Yet even those Iranians who critiqued Pahlavi carceral violence rarely extended their critique to the institution of the modern prison as such. Although the Islamic revolutionaries aligned with Ayatollah Khomeini promised a return to Islamic justice and the eradication of the degeneracy they associated with Pahlavi rule, the nascent Islamic Republic would quickly inhabit many of the same carceral institutions and logics bequeathed to it by its predecessors. While the language of prison management was Islamicized in the postrevolutionary era, the notion that prisons would serve as therapeutic spaces of progress, education, health, and reform has remained a central component of the Islamic Republic imaginary of law and order.[120]

Despite the rhetoric of the Iranian carceral project, which claimed that criminality in Iran would be radically reduced or even eradicated through "progressive" and "humane" carceral methods, the number of incarcerated Iranians has steadily increased in the decades after the centralization of Iranian law. Rather than being "cured" of social contagion of crime, vulnerable members of the Iranian citizenry instead

---

[119] Abrahamian, *Tortured Confessions*; Nikpour, "Claiming Human Rights."
[120] On the official website for the Islamic Republic's Organization of Prisons and Security and Corrective Measures (Sazman-e Zendanha va Eghdamat-e Tamini va Tarbiati-ye Keshvar), there are entire sections dedicated to describing the educational, vocational, and heath measures the Islamic Republic takes toward its prisoners. http://prisons.ir/.

underwent what scholar Lisa Cacho has termed the process of criminalization. In Cacho's theorization, criminalization is not merely the
process by which some individuals or communities get marked as
potentially criminal, but rather the modern processes by which specific
actions are newly categorized as "crimes," thus rendering populations
who have historically undertaken those actions vulnerable to state
intervention and violence.[121] In Pahlavi Iran, drug use, some non-
normative sex acts, border crossing and smuggling, and reading politically radical texts (to give just a few examples) were all criminalized
and carceralized over the course of several decades. In the Islamic
Republic era, many of these same acts have remained objects of state
intervention, and other acts (certain acts of gendered dress, for
instance) have been newly criminalized. In other words, the historical
project of carceral modernity in Iran has not addressed the problem of
an essential criminality; it has produced "criminals" in need of carceral
intervention and discipline by the state.

   In the mid-1920s, there were only about 400 people incarcerated in
Tehran, where most of Iran's prisoners were held. By the 1970s, on the
eve of the revolution, modern prisons and policing were largely taken
for granted as natural components of life in a modern state by Iranians
of most political stripes. Today, close to a century after legal centralization in Iran, there are an officially estimated 240,000 people incarcerated in the Islamic Republic of Iran, in facilities with an official
capacity of only 150,000.[122] But this remarkable historical transformation is not just an Iranian story. The carceralization of Iran mirrors a
global embrace of modern prisons, alongside the prison's concomitant
promises of civilizational progress and citizenship. As I have argued
throughout this chapter, the languages, architectures, economies, and
techniques of modern punishment are transnational and linked. These
connections belie an understanding of contemporary carcerality that
would divide global regimes of punishment along political (or cultural)
fault lines despite shared institutional, material, and conceptual histories. Today's prisons are not natural, stable outgrowths of forms of
governance; that is, we cannot speak coherently of "fascist

---

[121] Lisa Cacho, *Social Death: Racialized Rightlessness and the Criminalization of
      the Unprotected* (New York: New York University Press, 2012).
[122] These statistics are from the World Prison Brief page on Iran. See www.
      prisonstudies.org/country/iran. These match the official numbers often given by
      the Islamic Republic's head of prisons, Asghar Jahangir.

punishment," "liberal punishment," or "Islamic punishment" in an era in which the prison has been naturalized as a necessary tool of social order all over the world. Mass incarceration – an analytical concept that has emerged from the work of critical prison scholarship in the American context – is, I argue, today a *global* phenomenon, even as it takes distinctive local forms. This global history of modern prisons reveals a troubling alternative genealogy of political modernity insofar as modern conceptions of citizenship, social belonging, humanity, progress, mental health, and political emancipation have been imbricated in modern regimes of surveillance, policing, and incarceration.

10 The Cold War and Education in Science and Engineering in Iran, 1953–1979

HOSSEIN KAMALY

During the two and a half decades preceding the 1979 revolution, the ethos of modern science and technology molded the mindset of various agents of social change in Iran. Conceived in the same breath as a corpus of knowledge, a tool, and a weapon, modern learning of mathematics and the natural sciences found equally ardent partisans among radically different parties.[1] Led by Shah Mohammad Reza Pahlavi (r. 1941–1979) himself, top-level policymakers upheld science, medicine, and engineering as the cornerstone of modernization. From the royal court and the ministerial cabinet down to teachers' lounges in schools across the nation, science was valorized everywhere. Even antiestablishment critics and revolutionaries agreed. By arrogating the right to speak in the name of science, different parties wielded it as a weapon against their opponents. Chronologically, these parallel claims to science as a superior corpus of learning, as a key to national progress, and as a weapon occurred in the broader context of the Cold War. The present chapter adds the Iranian case to the expanding literature on global histories of science and technology during the Cold War.[2]

The 1953 coup, which overthrew Prime Minister Mosaddegh's cabinet and gave absolute power to the shah, marks a turning point in modern Iranian history. It also defines a watershed moment in Cold War politics across the Middle East and beyond. Lifting the country's

---

[1] For this threefold of the science of linguistics, see Janet Martin-Nielsen, "'This War for Men's Minds': The Birth of a Human Science in Cold War America," *History of the Human Sciences* 23:5 (2010): 131–155. I thank Reza Kamaly for calling my attention to this article and to Martin-Nielsen's important scholarship in the history of science in relation to the Cold War.

[2] For example, see Elena Aronova and Simone Turchetti, eds., *Science Studies during the Cold War* (New York: Palgrave, 2016); Allan A. Needell, *Science, Cold War and the American State: Lloyd V. Berkner and the Balance of Professional Ideals* (New York: Routledge, 2012); Asif A. Siddiqi, *Sputnik and the Soviet Space Challenge* (Gainesville, FL: University of Florida Press, 2003).

profile amidst the ongoing antagonism between the so-called Western and Eastern blocs, the coup secured Iran's place in the sphere of influence of the former. As an explicit disavowal of the 1953 coup and its legacy, one of the earliest diplomatic gestures in the immediate aftermath of the 1979 revolution was to join the Non-Aligned Movement (NAM). Nevertheless, an unequivocal expression of the shah's long-lasting allegiance to the Western front comes through in his exclusive interview with *Newsweek*, where he averred: "I am the friend of what I call the imperialistic world."[3]

The Cold War delineated international concerns on multiple fronts, including those of ideology, culture, and science. As an offshoot of Cold War dynamics, the coup of 1953, which removed Mosaddegh and re-entrenched the powers of Mohammad Reza Shah, had cultural and educational repercussions as well as political and geostrategic consequences. In what follows, after brief comments on a few examples of cultural developments in postcoup Iran, I provide an outline of the growth of modern scientific and technological education in the country, highlighting the systematic orientation away from older European models and toward the United States in structure and pedagogy, beginning in the 1960s.

Redefining Priorities

Among myriad other consequences, the coup made a priority of the reassessment and revision of the nation's cultural agendas and educational policies. Partly because the shah was conscious of the effective role that the US had played in restoring him to the throne, and for other reasons as well, he set the priorities of his rule in line with requirements on the Western front. No doubt, factors above and beyond personal psychology had weighed in to sustain such a commitment for a quarter of a century. Also, it would be inadequate to reduce the state's efforts at maintaining legitimacy and power to any explanatory schema that disregards the significant role of cultural and educational considerations. Be that as it may, a nationwide battle was launched in the immediate aftermath of the coup, aiming to redirect public sensibilities, primarily through cultural refinement and educational reform in the broad sense. For example, the

---

[3] William E. Schmidt, "I'm Not the Judas," *Newsweek*, January 24, 1977 (US edition), https://bit.ly/2KWtfW5. See also *Rastakhiz* (daily newspaper), Dey 28, 2535S.

(Royal) Institute for Translation and Publication (RITP),[4] Franklin Publications,[5] and the Royal Book Prize all came into being within months after the coup. A programmatic rise in the number of institutions of higher learning, with a focus on technical training, followed soon.

Already in the fall of 1953, the shah decreed that "The [Royal] Institute for Translation and Publication" be founded. Making a direct contribution himself, the shah allocated income from the Crown properties to sustain the RITP's operation. Additional funding followed from the National Iranian Oil Company (NIOC) and the Plan and Budget Organization (PBO). From the beginning, the RITP dedicated itself to producing high-quality translations in Persian. Popular introductions to science, geography, and history for the youth were published. Notably among such translations from the French was the collection that the Presses universitaires de France published under the general title of *Que sais-je?* (*Cheh midanam?* in Persian). More specialized works on literature, philosophy, and history were intended for an advanced readership. The RITP's director, the late Ehsan Yarshater (1919–2018), set translating world classics into Persian as a priority. Besides over 300 titles for children and young adults,[6] a total of 138 volumes on general knowledge were published and translated for adults in addition to 71 works of classical literature and philosophy.[7] Material was carefully vetted. In particular, the RITP

---

[4] Edward Joseph, "Bongāh-e Tarjoma va Našr-e Ketāb," *Encyclopaedia Iranica*, https://iranicaonline.org/articles/bongah-e-tarjoma.

[5] Datus C. Smith, "Franklin Book Program," *Encyclopaedia Iranica*, www.iranicaonline.org/articles/franklin-book-program.

[6] As Edward Joseph summarizes these works. They consisted first of three series, namely, *Majmu'eh kudakan* (for the age group 4–7, 24 vols.), *Majmu'eh nojavanan* (ages 8–11, 27 vols.), and *Majmu'eh javanan* (ages 12–15, 47 vols.). Later included in the literature for the young were four translation series: profile of the nations (*Majmu'eh chehreh melal*, 31 vols.), translated from a series edited by J. B. Lippincott Co., on the geography, history, and culture of various countries, intended primarily for teenagers; stories of the nations (*Dastanha-e melal*, consisting of tales and stories from various countries of the world, 19 vols.); the biographical series (*Sargozasht bozorgan*, 5 vols.); and mirror of Persia series (*Aineh-e Iran*), consisting of original works which purported to provide in fictional or dialogue form accurate information about life in various parts of Persia (3 vols.: *Isfahan* by M. A. Jamalzadeh, *Tehran* by Said Nafisi, and *Gilan* by Karam Keshavarz).

[7] Including, among others, Mohammad Ali Jamalzadeh's translation from German of the Swiss folktales of *Wilhelm Tell*; Parviz Natel-Khanlari's translation from French of Joseph Bédier's recension of *Le roman de Tristan et Iseut*; translations

served as the gatekeeper for the selective translation of Soviet scholarship on Iran. This task was too sensitive to be left to unscrupulous translators, or worse to the sympathizers of the Tudeh Party or other proponents of the Eastern Bloc.

As the following anecdote illustrates, interest in the Russian language could raise eyebrows. Parviz Shahryari (1926–2012) mentioned this in an interview. The leftist schoolteacher and educational reformist recalled that with government crackdown escalating after the 1953 coup, he had decided to leave Tehran. Having spent time in prison as a Tudeh Party sympathizer from 1949 to 1952, he feared being under suspicion. He moved to Shiraz to teach. Together with his mother, he settled in a friend's house. Unbeknownst to him, the fiancé of his landlord's daughter belonged to a group of military officers suspected of connections to the Tudeh Party, and so the house was under surveillance. He continued:

[One day] I had just returned from class when [government officials] raided the house looking for the fiancé. They took me in along with my books, which were in Russian. …. They brought someone who knew Russian to look at the books and determine what they were about. All were on mathematics, except for one, which was a book of history. Then the military commander … called me in. His very first question was, "Why should you want to learn the tongue of Stalin rather than Churchill?" … He then ordered the lieutenant who was there to see that my books were to be put to flames under the lieutenant's direct supervision in my own presence, and to have some snapshots taken. Only then was the prisoner to be set free.[8]

The officer's advising Shahryari to learn the language of Churchill, or Eisenhower for that matter, instead of that of Stalin was in keeping with the official preference of his commanders, as shown by the case of the Franklin Book Project (FBP) or Franklin Publications. The FBP signals a direct convergence between the state's cultural policies and US preferences. The FBP started working in Iran as of 1954. Committing its resources to producing high-quality translations of popular books from the United States, the FBP helped local publishers abide by

---

of Shakespeare's plays by Ala' Din Pazargadi, Abdul-Rahim Ahmadi, and Masoud Farzad; translations of Plato's *Five Dialogues* and his *Republic* by Mahmud Sanai and Foad Rohani, respectively.

[8] Parviz Shahryari, "The Sparrow (Parastoo)," *Chista* 230 (Tir 1385/June–July 2006): 840–843.

international copyright law. Thanks to the FBP's widespread distribution network, these publishers could dispatch copies of thousands of high-quality titles which they published to the farthest corners of the country. This was a major change in book publishing in Iran. Finally, the FBP was shut down in 1977, upon the decision that much of its mission had been accomplished.[9] The organization's corporate records show that a total of $113 million had been received and disbursed to publishers, print houses, translators, editors, and administrators. The cultural role of the FBP and the RITP can hardly be exaggerated in the intellectual history of Iran during the decades leading to the 1979 revolution.

Launched in 1954 and first awarded in March 1955, the Royal Book Prize (RBP) reflected state preferences in no uncertain terms.[10] Again, priorities correlated strongly with the anti-communist priorities of the Western Bloc in the Cold War. Operating under the direct auspices of the shah, the RBP committee displayed a preference for religious books. Two notable early recipients, in this vein, were works from Qum. First, was a rejoinder to Marxist philosophy, written by Allameh Mohammad-Hossein Tabatabai (c. 1904–1981), the uncontested master of Madraseh-style philosophy during the second half of the twentieth century in Iran.[11] Entitled *Foundations of Philosophy and Realist Methodology* (*Osul-e falsafeh va ravesh-e re'alism*), Allameh Tabatabai's work came to be one of the most influential philosophical writings in the Persian language. The second winner of the RBP, Nasser Makarem Shirazi (b. 1927) – a student of Tabatabai and later a grand ayatollah – had penned a fictionalized polemic against Marxism.

Extending accesss to higher education in major cities besides the capital was of paramount necessity. Table 10.1 lists three major

[9] Smith, "Franklin Book Program."

[10] On the Royal Book Prize, see Mohammad-Javad Jazini, "Ketab-ha va entekhab-ha: Bar-rasi faraz o nashib-haye jayezeye behtrarin ketab az gozashteh ta konoon" ["Books and choices: The vicissitudes of book awards from the past to the present"], *Hamshahri Newspaper* (Bahman 11, 1385/February 1, 2007); Fereshteh Sepehr et al., "Ravand Era'eye Java'ez Ketab dar Iran az aghaz to Konoon" ["Procedures for awarding book prizes in Iran from the beginning to the present"], *Fasl-Nameye Motale'at Melliye Ketabdari va Sazemandehiye Etella'at* 27:3 (Fall 1395/2016): 41–56.

[11] See Hamid Algar, "'Allāma Sayyid Muḥammad Ḥusayn Ṭabāṭabāʾī: Philosopher, Exegete, and Gnostic," *Journal of Islamic Studies* 17:3(2006): 326–351; Hossein Kamaly, *God and Man in Tehran: Contending Visions of the Divine from the Qajars to the Islamic Republic* (New York: Columbia University Press, 2018), chapter 5.

Table 10.1 *Universities founded during the 1950s*

Name	Place	Established	Comments
Pahlavi	Shiraz	1954	Integrating schools that dated as far back as 1946[a]
Gondi-Shapur	Ahvaz	1955	
Polytechnic Institute	Tehran	1958	
Melli (National)	Tehran	1959	Privately owned and operated until 1974

[a] The new campus of Shiraz University was designed by the prominent American architect Minoru Yamasaki (1912–1986), who later designed the World Trade Center Towers in New York City.

institutions of higher learning that were inaugurated within a few years after the 1953 coup.

In 1954, with US support the Institute for Business and Administrative Science had started to operate as a new part of the University of Tehran.[12] Also, as early as the same year, ties were established between Pahlavi University in Shiraz and the University of Pennsylvania in the United States.[13] The cooperation with the US Ivy League school helped Pahlavi University to advance academically in strides. In particular, advancement in science and engineering comprised an important objective.

Science, Technology, and the Cold War: The Global Context

Science and technology crucially mattered in the Cold War.[14] The United States, the Soviet Union, and China competed in scientific and

---

[12] Mohammad Reza Shah Pahlavi, "Sokhanan Shahanshah: Farhang o Ayandeye Iran, II" ["The King of Kings' speech on culture and the future of Iran, part II"], *Mahnameye Amuzesh o Parvaresh (Ta'lim o tarbiat)* 35:3 (Khordad 1344/May–June 1965): 6.

[13] See Gaylord Probasco Harnwell, *Educational Voyaging in Iran* (Philadelphia, PA: University of Pennsylvania Press, 1962).

[14] For examples of recent scholarship, see Audra J. Wolfe, *Freedom's Laboratory: The Cold War Struggle for the Soul of Science* (Baltimore, MD: Johns Hopkins University Press, 2018); Aronova and Turchetti, eds., *Science Studies*; Arthur P. Molella and Scott Gabriel Knowles, eds., *World's Fairs in the Cold War: Science, Technology, and the Culture of Progress* (Pittsburgh, PA: University of

technological advancement. The Soviet view closely tied the fundamental redefinition of the "scientific" with the attempts to change the status of science and scientists in the socialist societies.[15] Mao Zedong (1893–1976) weaponized "scientific proofs" in launching his ambitious campaign of rapid industrialization and agricultural collectivization which he dubbed the Great Leap Forward.[16] Major parties involved in this competition monitored each other's policies in science and technology. Expositions around the world, from Brussels to Osaka to Brisbane, provided international grounds for showcasing scientific and technological achievements. As such, they actively shaped Cold War culture.[17]

The launch of the first satellite, the "Prostreishiy Sputnik-1" (Простейший Спутник-1), also known as PS-1, or simply as the Sputnik, placed scientific and technological superiority at the center of Cold War debates.[18] It marked a new milestone for Soviet success in defeating the Western Bloc in science and technology, ever since the secretly conducted nuclear weapon test at the Semipalatinsk Test Site in Kazakhstan, on August 29, 1949. As amateur radio operators around the world picked up an unidentified signal, on the evening of October 4, 1957, Nikita Khrushchev (1894–1971), First Secretary of the Communist Party of the Soviet Union at the time, boasted about this unprecedented achievement in science and technology. Having dinner with Ukrainian leaders, he announced, in a voice that could not quite conceal his elation, that an outstanding event had happened, and a team of Soviet rocket scientists had put an artificial satellite into orbit.[19]

Vigorous competition had already started before the Sputnik. In 1955, the United States and the Soviet Union both had announced their intent to orbit a scientific satellite in time for the International Geophysical Year, in 1957–1958. Now, the Soviet Union had done it and the United States found itself on the defensive. Then, on April 12,

Pittsburgh Press, 2019). See also Zuoyue Wang, *In Sputnik's Shadow: The President's Science Advisory Board and Cold War America* (New Brunswick, NJ: Rutgers University Press, 2008).
[15] See Vítězslav Sommer, "'Scientists of the World, Unite!' Radovan Richta's Theory of Scientific and Technological Revolution," in Aronov and Turchetti, eds., *Science Studies*, 177–204.
[16] Wang, *In Sputnik's Shadow*.
[17] See Molella and Knowles, eds., *World's Fairs*.   [18] Siddiqi, *Sputnik*.
[19] See www.airspacemag.com/space/we-shocked-the-world-19693460/ #IeHROuYQkRaOESgx.99.

1961, news broke out that Yuri A. Gagarin (1934–1968), a Soviet Air Forces pilot and cosmonaut, had orbited the earth. The Space Age had dawned, and with it the Cold War had entered a new phase. Anxieties soared at the highest policymaking centers in the United States that American schools were lagging dangerously behind in science and mathematics. Radical reform in pedagogy in the United States became an immediate objective, with the implicit admission that the Soviet system had excelled. The administration of President Dwight Eisenhower (in office 1953–1961) readily increased national science foundation funding in support of the Physical Science Study Committee (PSSC), an educational advisory group which had taken shape in the United States in 1956. The Eisenhower administration demanded a thorough review of introductory physics education, aimed at designing, implementing, and monitoring improvements at the high school level. The PSSC suggested new physics curricula, textbooks, instructional movies, and classroom laboratory materials during the 1960s and 1970s and beyond.[20] At the college level, two outstanding examples may be seen in the historically brilliant *Feynman Lectures on Physics* (California Institute of Technology, 1963),[21] and the revised *Berkeley Physics Course* (University of California Berkeley, 1963).[22] Both works illustrate how the standard was raised in the teaching of science in elite US universities within a few years after the Soviet Union had launched the Sputnik and orbited a man in outer space.[23] Merely weeks after the latter development, speaking before Congress on May 25, 1961, President John F. Kennedy (in office 1961–1963), who had succeeded Eisenhower into the White House, boldly urged that the United Staes should commit itself to landing a man on the moon and returning him safely to the earth.[24] A strong presidential mandate,

[20] See, for example, Uri Haber-Schaim et al., *Physical Science Study Committee (PSSC) Physics: Teacher's Resource Book and Guide*, 4 vols. (Lexington, MA: Heath & Co., 1961).

[21] Richard Phillips Feynman, Robert B. Leighton, and Rochus E. Vogt, *The Feynman Lectures on Physics*, 3 vols. (Reading, MA: Addison-Wesley Publishing Company, 1964–69).

[22] See Charles Kittel, Walter D. Knight, and Malvin A. Ruderman, *Mechanics* (New York: McGraw Hill Book Company, 1965).

[23] See R. Bruce Lindsay's review of ibid. in "On the Average, Difficult," *Physics Today* 20:1 (1967): 115–117.

[24] See Edgar M. Cortright, ed., *Apollo Expeditions to the Moon* (Washington, DC: Scientific and Technical Information Office, National Aeronautics and Space Administration, 1975); Jim Donovan, *Shoot for the Moon: The Space Race and*

educational reform, along with years of intensive scientific innovation, led by the newly established National Aeronautics and Space Administration (NASA, 1958), paid off. The Apollo 11 Moon Landing Mission in 1969 was the US comeback. In the words of Neil Armstrong (1930–2012), "one small step for man, one giant leap for mankind."[25] And, a definite victory in the ongoing Cold War for the Western Bloc.

The competition between the superpowers reverberated throughout their spheres of influence – countries around the world that had sided with this or the other bloc during the Cold War. This was no less true about scientific and technological rivalries than those in the nuclear arms race or respective claims to economic dominance.[26] The impact on Iran was palpable, directly as well as indirectly. On a superficial level, the Space Age provided an opportunity for the country's public intellectuals to voice their choice, if only implicitly. Marveling at the pioneering role of the Soviet Union, some even doubted the success of the US moon mission altogether, thereby expressing dissent in newspapers, magazines, and casual conversation, toward the state and its pro-US tendencies. Others celebrated the US accomplishment as a human achievement, beyond East and West. The state-run national television covered the launching of Apollo 11 live. Voiceover narration was provided by a popular broadcaster, Iraj Gorgin (1934–2012), who had, after the 1953 coup, abandoned association with the Tudeh Party. Space Age competition ushered in a wave of cultural prioritization and agenda-setting during the 1960s and 1970s.

Cold War and Culture

Cultural and educational policies partly reflect the impact of Cold War rivalries on Iran. For example, the quarterly periodical *Donya*, which

---

the *Extraordinary Voyage of Apollo 11* (New York: Little, Brown and Company, 2019).

[25] www.navytimes.com/news/your-navy/2019/07/13/armstrongs-famous-one-small-step-quote-explained/.

[26] See Sommer, "'Scientists of the World, Unite!'"; and also, for another specific case, see Sándor Hornyik, "Sputnik versus Apollo: Science, Technology, and the Cold War in the Hungarian Visual Arts, 1957-1975," *Acta historiae artium Academiae Scientarium Hungaricae* 56:1 (2015): 165–172. Even the classic work of Thomas Kuhn, *Structure of Scientific Revolutions*, has been referred to as an "exemplary document of the Cold War era." See Hans-Joachim Dahms, "Thomas Kuhn's *Structure*: An 'Exemplary Document of the Cold War Era'?" in Aronova and Turchetti, eds., *Science Studies*, 103–126.

the Tudeh Party published (1960–1973), echoed Soviet triumphalism for its Persian readership. When the first Soviet astronaut, Yuri Gagarin, orbited the earth, the *Dars-ha'-i az Maktab-e Eslam* took notice. Celebrating this as an achievement for humankind, the editorial stated:

As expected, the first space passenger penetrated the atmosphere with a gigantic rocket and entered the mysterious realm *above and beyond*. ... Humankind, this mysterious being, has achieved a marvelous feat, one which a century ago humans could not even predict. ... In any case, this the greatest achievement of natural science throughout history and as such deserves commendation and praise in all respects.[27]

However, the editorialist went on to admonish that

such enormous technological and industrial achievements in the present situation of the world not only fail to mitigate the many difficulties that humanity is struggling with but common practice is that they fuel the Cold War and fan the flames of ideological difference.[28]

Recent academic literature in modern Iranian studies has taken notice of a thrust in cultural policymaking as of the 1960s. Decisions made at the topmost level had far-reaching consequences. As Robert Steele has correctly observed in a recent study, "the imperial court ... was deeply involved in the development of cultural policy in Pahlavi Iran."[29] Also, Afshin Matin-Asgari has noted, in his *Both Eastern and Western*, that from the 1960s the state pursued a "comprehensive cultural policy agenda."[30] Besides the RITP, FBP, and RBP, all from the 1950s, new state-sponsored initiatives were launched. The implementation of cultural policies officially fell under the remit of the Ministry of Culture and Arts, which was founded in 1964. Also, there was the Royal Cultural Council (Shura-e Saltanati-e Farhang, founded in 1962), the Culture Foundation (Bonyad-e Farhang, founded in 1964), and a

---

[27] "Dar Ejtema cheh migozarad?" *Maktab Eslam* (1961), 2 (emphasis in the original).

[28] Ibid., 3.

[29] See Robert Steele, "The Pahlavi National Library Project: Education and Modernization in Late Pahlavi Iran," *Iranian Studies* 52:1–2 (2019): 85–110. On this topic, see also Shojaeddin Shafa's report, as director of the project, *The Pahlavi National Library of Iran: Its Planning, Aims, and Future* (Tehran: 1978).

[30] Afshin Matin-Asgari, *Both Eastern and Western: An Intellectual History of Iranian Modernity* (Cambridge: Cambridge University Press, 2018), 191.

decade later the Royal Academy of Philosophy (Anjoman-e Shahanshahi-e Falsafeh, founded in 1974). Like earlier institutions noted above, the new ones carried explicit or implicit mandates to address and empower national and religious sensibilities; to the detriment of the left, which was presumed to be alien in its origin, outlook, and intent. Besides these cultural institutions, educational policies were revamped – especially educational policies in science and technology.

Among the most wide-ranging and consequential cultural and educational developments of that time one should highlight the state's renewed emphasis on science and engineering. Opening advanced vocational schools and institutions of higher learning with strong programs in engineering and science acquired high priority, more than ever before. So did the expansion of existing institutions. Arguably, this paralleled contemporary emphasis on reforming science education in the United States, which was noted above. Table 10.2 lists twelve major institutions of higher education, universities, as well as vocational technical schools that were established or expanded during the 1960s and 1970s.[31]

As the selective entries in Tables 10.1 and 10.2 indicate together, from the immediate aftermath of the 1953 coup until the mid-1970s, official policy consistently pushed for the expansion of higher education. This period marks an important chapter in the history of modern education in Iran. For some statistics, see the next section.

Educational Reform

Education and educational reform hold the key to understanding the ongoing Iranian experience of modernity. Having deeper roots in modern Iranian history, focusing on education policies sheds light on some aspects developments in the period between the 1953 coup and 1979 revolution. Under the Islamic Republic too, for over four decades until now, such policies have shaped the arena for the manifestation and exercise of the political-cum-cultural power of the state.

Multiple studies that exist on the history of modern education in Iran often begin with the Dar-al-Fonoon (1852), the establishment

---

[31] The fact that well over 30 percent of institutions operated in Tehran or immediately nearby in Karaj reflects the general Tehran-centeredness of development policies at the time.

Table 10.2 *List of some major universities established or expanded,*
1963–1975

Name	Place	Established	Comments
Narmak Higher Vocational School	Tehran	1963	Later Elm-o-Sanaat (1972)
Aryamehr	Tehran	1965	Name changed to Sharif, after the revolution
Rezaiyeh	Urmia	1965	Expanded Westminster Medical School (1878)
Azarabadegan	Tabriz	1967	Founded as Azarbayjan universitesi (1946)
Esfahan	Isfahan	1968	Expanded Clinical College (1946, 1950)
Arak	Arak	1971	
Razi	Kermanshah	1971	
Karaj School of Environmental Studies	Karaj	1972	Going back to Mozaffar al-Din Shah's reign, 1896–1907
Kerman	Kerman	1972	Enrollment began in 1975
Bu-Ali Sina	Hamedan	1974	Started with the French as of 1972
Ferdosi	Mashhad	1974	Expanded (1949, 1955)
Farah Pahlavi	Tehran	1975	Reorganized from Madraseh ʿali-e dokhtaran, 1964

which Mirza Taqi Khan Amir Nezam (1807–1852) had masterminded.
Many then proceed to the opening of the Rosdiyeh schools (first in
Tabriz, 1887), and some trace later developments from the time of the
Constitutional Revolution (1905–1911) to the new wave of educa-
tional overhaul during the reign of Reza Shah (1925–1941).[32] As

---

[32] In English, see, for example, Farzin Vejdani, *Making History in Iran: Education,*
Nationalism, and Print Culture (Stanford, CA: Stanford University Press, 2015);
Reza Arjmand, *Inscription on Stone: Islam, State, and Education in Iran and*
Turkey (Stockholm: Institute of International Education, Stockholm University,
2008); A. Reza Arasteh, *Education and Social Awakening in Iran, 1850–1968,*
2nd ed. rev. and enlarged (Leiden: E. J. Brill, 1969); David Menashri, *Education*

generally informative as such studies have proven to be, finer-grained historical inquiries would be welcome to examine institutional structures as well as pedagogical methods and outcomes in detail. Moreover, the course of education after Reza Shah deserves closer study, especially during the second half of the twentieth century and then up to the present.

Focusing on modernization efforts during the mid-nineteenth to mid-twentieth centuries, most available studies have treated modern education as another example of transitions that unfolded under the general rubric of transition to modernity. Without raising theoretical objections here to commonplace analyses in terms of linear, if only interrupted, transitions from a traditional to a modern system, it is worth pointing out the importance of paying particular attention to science education, in form and content. More substantive examinations of the pedagogy and the curricula are needed – preferably going beyond the restrictions and shortcomings of the hackneyed schema of transition to modernity. Before and after the Constitutional Revolution, Qajar palace intellectuals and their supporters outside the court insisted on the necessity of mastery over nature for the nation's progressive march toward civilization.[33] To them, science and civilization went hand in hand. At the time, changing views on politics, history, and law partly derived from a changing view on nature. All of this drew on a newly emerging appreciation for natural science.[34] The advocacies of influential voices such as Aqa-Khan Kermani (c. 1850–1897), Malkom Khan (1834–1908), and Abdul-Rahim Talebof (1834–1911) in favor of modern science have received some attention in the literature.[35] Still, the more substantive

and the Making of Modern Iran (Ithaca, NY: Cornell University Press, 1992). See also Rudi Matthee, "Transforming Dangerous Nomads into Useful Artisans, Technicians, Agriculturists: Education in the Reza Shah Period," *Iranian Studies* 26:3–4 (1993): 313–336; Soli Shahvar, *The Forgotten Schools: The Baha'is and Modern Education in Iran, 1899–1934* (London: I.B. Tauris, 2009).

[33] Mohit-Tabatabai, ed., *Majmu'eh asar Mirza Malkom Khan* [The collected works of Mirza Malkom Khan] (Tehran: 1327/1948); Abdul-Rahim Talebof-Tabrizi, *Masalek-al-Mohsenin* [Righteous trajectories] (n.p.: 1323/1905).

[34] For a brief discussion of the transformation in philosophical outlook as well as such practical matters as writing science textbooks, see chapter 1 in Kamaly, *God and Man.*

[35] Two important studies that focus on some aspects of modern medical science in nineteenth- and early twentieth-century Iran are Mohamad Tavakoli-Targhi, *Refashioning Iran: Orientalism, Occidentalism, and Historiography* (New

contributions of important but oft-neglected pioneers such as Abdul-Ghaffar Najm al-Doleh (c. 1843–1908) and Dr. Mohammad Kermanshahi (c. 1827–1908)[36] to the theoretical and practical advancement of modern science in Iran remain to be explored in detail.

Modern education rapidly struck roots in Iran during the late 1910s and the 1920s with the establishment of such institutions as the School of Law (Madraseh-e 'ali-e hoquq, 1918), the Teacher's Training College (Dar al-mo'allemin-e markazi, 1919; later Danesh-sara-e 'ali), and the transformation of Tehran's American-accredited Modern College (Kalej-e Emrika'i, later the Alborz high school, see below).

Not counting institutions of specifically religious training here, in 1921, no less than 43,000 students were enrolled in some 440 primary schools nationwide.[37] The number of high schools was limited to 46, with a total enrollment of below 10,000. The Dār al-Fonūn produced merely 15 graduates in 1922.[38] Fewer than 100 men, only men, had the privilege of attending the Teacher's Training College, the country's sole institution of higher education. That changed quickly. Designing the modern Military Academy (Daneshkadeh-e afsari), in 1922, modeled on the French École spéciale militaire de Saint-Cyr, marked a milestone.[39] By 1932, the number of primary and high schools, and presumably the number of students enrolled in them, grew sixfold. A momentous era dawned in 1935, with the inauguration of the

---

York: Palgrave, 2001); and Cyrus Schayegh, *Who Is Knowledgeable Is Strong: Science, Class, and the Formation of Modern Iranian Society, 1900–1950* (Berkeley, CA: University of California Press, 2009). For a good discussion of debates on modern mathematical astronomy, see also Kamran Arjomand, "The Emergence of Scientific Modernity in Iran: Controversies Surrounding Astrology and Modern Astronomy in the Mid-nineteenth Century," *Iranian Studies* 30:1–2 (1997): 5–24.

[36] Shireen Mahdavi, "KOFRI, Moḥammad Kermānšāhi," *Encyclopaedia Iranica*, www.iranicaonline.org/articles/kofri-mohammad-kermansahi-physician. See also Willem M. Floor, *Public Health in Qajar Iran* (Washington, DC: Mage Publishers, 2004).

[37] Pahlavi, "Soḵanān-e Shāhanshāh II," 1.

[38] Matthee, "Transforming Dangerous Nomads," 315, citing Amin Banani, *The Modernization of Iran, 1921–1941* (Stanford, CA: Stanford University Press, 1961), 108.

[39] For a brief discussion of Iran's Military Academy at this time, see Yann Richard, "La fondation d'une armée nationale," in Jean Calmard, ed., *Entre l'Iran et l'occident: Adaptation et assimilation des idées et techniques occidentales en Iran* (Paris: 1989), 54.

colleges (or faculties) of science, medicine, and engineering[40] as three of the six original divisions of the University of Tehran.

Beyond the walls of schools and colleges, the ideals of adopting a scientific worldview and abiding by the scientific method permeated the discourse of the educated public. By the 1930s, there existed a critical mass of potential participants in that discourse. Instructors and students, from high school to the university, shared the language and the values it conveyed. Periodicals such as Taqi Arani's *Donya* and *Majalleh-e musiqi* gave voice to them. In a series of highly popular weekly broadcasts on the radio (1942–1959), the learned orator Hossein-Ali Rashed (1905–1980) advocated that perfect harmony held between the teachings of Islam and the findings of modern science.[41] The ethos of modern learning, especially science learning, played increasingly significant social, political, and ideological roles in shaping Iranian society.[42] It fed into complex cultural and economic processes that culminated in the unprecedented expansion of Iran's modern urban middle class from the mid-1920s to the early 1950s.

By the early 1950s, hundreds of graduates, students, and instructors from Tehran University's colleges of medicine, science, and engineering sang the praise of science. From among the graduates of the Military Academy several hundred had joined the choir as well. They too had received training in certain areas of mathematics and engineering, such as artillery calculations and applied physics. Members of the legion of informed promoters of modern learning hailed from different social and ideological backgrounds, but they all shared a strong commitment to the cause of science. Mehdi Bazargan (1907–1995), a French-educated engineer who ran the university's College of Engineering from 1945 to 1951, was a leading Muslim modernist. Convinced of the foundational harmony between the true teachings of religion and

[40] On the history of Tehran University's College of Engineering, see Maqsud Farasatkhah, *Tarikh hashtad saleh Daneshkadeh Fanni – Daneshgah Tehran: Dastan yek khaneh, dastan yek sarzamin* [The eighty-year history of the College of Engineering at the University of Tehran: The story of a house, the story of a land] (Tehran: Nashr Ney, 1393/2015).

[41] See Jafar Pajoom, *Yadnameh Hossein-Ali Rashed, ba Maqalati az Bozorgan-e Adabiyat o Tarikh* [Commemorating Hossein-Ali Rashed with papers by the grandees of literature and history] (Tehran: Entesharat-e Sokhan, 1387/2008).

[42] For historical background and theoretical observations on science and the formation of the Iranian modern middle class during the first half of the twentieth century, see Schayegh, *Who Is Knowledgeable Is Strong*, 13–38.

modern science, he exercised enormous influence on two generations of reform-minded Muslims. Years later, he served as the prime minister of the Transitionary Cabinet of the 1979 revolution, with many of his former students and followers providing rank and file of the government during the first couple of years after that. Captain Khosrow Ruzbeh (1915–1958), a graduate of the Military Academy who went on to become a popular instructor there, having several pamphlets on mathematics to his name, was an ardent communist and the de facto head of the military organization of the Tudeh Party.[43] Khalil Arjomand (1910–1944), a respected academic, editor of technical gazetteers, and pioneering industrialist, was Baha'i.[44] Several others were Jewish or Armenian; a significant percentage were women.

For years, a diverse body of academics could align their objectives with government policy, for the most part. As of 1942, they even had elected their chancellor themselves. In Ali-Akbar Siyasi (1895–1990) they had found a fellow academic as well as a seasoned statesman and a capable administrator. The coup changed all that.

On December 27, 1953, twelve days shy of four months after the coup, military forces raided the campus of the University of Tehran. They fatally shot three students outside the College of Engineering. Mostafa Bozorgnia (c. 1931–1953), Ahmad Qandchi (c. 1931–1953), and Mehdi (Azar) Shariat-Razavi (1932–1953) had been protesting the state visit by US Vice President Richard Nixon (1913–1994). This was the first visit by a senior US official since the coup. The three students came from different backgrounds: Bozorgnia had ties to the Tudeh Party and Qandchi was a card-carrying member of the pro-Mosaddegh National Front. Shariat-Razavi's membership in neither party is substantiated. After a tumultuous year that followed the tragic killing of these students, Siyasi left on January 8, 1955. The shah appointed Dr. Manuchehr Eqbal (1909–1977) to succeed him as chancellor of the University of Tehran. Bringing universities under full control constituted a major concern for the state.

Eqbal ran a tight ship, from 1955 to 1957, aiming to depoliticize the university. He insisted on raising academic standards, especially in the

---

[43] On Ruzbeh, see Ervand Abrahamian, *Tortured Confessions: Prisons and Recantation in Modern Iran* (Los Angeles, CA: University of California Press, 1999), 81, 94–95.
[44] See Rava Azeredo da Silveira, "ARJOMAND, Ḵalil," *Encyclopaedia Iranica*, https://iranicaonline.org/articles/arjomand-kalil-1910-1944.

three faculties of medicine, science, and engineering. Training professionally knowledgeable and politically loyal graduates defined a clear
priority, not least in science, engineering, and related vocational fields.
The secret police had prepared a long list of banned books; finding any
of those listed titles in a student's belongings could result in temporary
suspension or permanent expulsion from university. Looking up to the
nation's most important institution of higher learning, academic institutions outside the capital followed suit – in Mashhad, Tabriz, Shiraz,
Isfahan, Ahvaz, and elsewhere.

After the coup, academia hardly ever realigned itself with the state as
before. Even though education, especially higher education, continued
to loom large in planning the nation's future,[45] views diverged on
priorities, preferred pedagogy, and ideals.

In what may be called a manifesto on "Culture and the Future of
Iran" (1965), the shah emphasized the unification of learning, ethics,
and service, centered around himself.[46] He outlined a history of education in Iran. Following a broad-brush historical chronology, he
referred to the ancient Sassanian center of learning (which he called a
daneshkadeh, college) at Gondi-Shapur, embraced the ethical and
educational values of Islam, welcomed the developments that the
Qajar monarch Nasser al-Din Shah (r. 1848–1896) had undertaken,
and especially highlighted the achievements of his own father, Reza
Shah. He added:

As of 1941 when my reign began, I too pursued the same general principles
that my father had embraced on the matter of education. ... Ever since, our
educational system has developed and currently one-fifth of the country's
annual budget is spent on it.[47]

The statement is quite informative as it highlights some major historical developments:

The number of students in elementary schools has surpassed one million, and
the number of students in high schools, agricultural and other vocational

---

[45] See Roham Alvandi, ed., *The Age of Aryamehr: Late Pahlavi Iran and Its Global
Entanglements* (London: Gingko Library, 2018).

[46] Mohammad Reza Shah Pahlavi, "Sokhanan Shahanshah: Farhang o ayandeh
Iran, I)" ["The King of Kings' speech on culture and the future of Iran, part I"],
Mahnameh Amuzesh o Parvaresh (Ta'lim o tarbiat) 35:2 (Ordibehesht 1344/
April–May 1965): 1–7; Pahlavi, "Sokhanan Shahanshah II."

[47] Pahlavi, "Sokhanan Shahanshah II," 5.

institutions in crafts, music, and administrative skills has reached 22,500, with as many as 45,000 teachers, a third of which are women.[48]

An update later appeared in the shah's book *Toward the Great Civilization*, reemphasizing the idea that he regarded education as the principal vehicle on the nation's journey under his leadership.[49] Turning toward an American model of pedagogy comprised an implicit but highly significant element in the shah's vision for the future path of education, especially in science and engineering. Until the early 1960s, European – particularly French – pedagogy prevailed, if only because the majority of the faculty had received their training in Europe, especially in France. The American turn in higher education came with the revamping of the educational system at the Abadan Institute of Technology, renamed Petroleum College of Abadan (Daneshkadeh-e Naft-e Abadan), as of 1962, and more importantly with the establishment of the Aryamehr University in Tehran (1965). Modeled after the Massachusetts Institute of Technology (MIT) in the United States, this bastion of science and engineering was planned to be replicated in Isfahan, within a few years.[50]

The shah took the title of the president (or rector) of Aryamehr University for himself. He placed the seasoned educator Mohammad-Ali Mojtahedi (1908–1997) at the helm of operating the institution day to day. Mojtahedi, a French-educated engineer himself, had an impeccable track record of a disciplinarian educator as well. He had run the Alborz high school (see below) since 1944 and had a stellar record in training academically overachieving youth, especially in science and technical education.

The Americanization of the nation's systems of higher education was deemed too important to take lightly or indeed to be left out of direct government supervision. The Ministry of Higher Education (Vezarat-e 'Olum o amuzesh-e 'ali) was created in February 1968, and a year or so

---

[48] Ibid., 6.
[49] Mohammad Reza Shah Pahlavi, *Beh sooye Tamaddon-e Bozorg* [Leading the way toward the Great Civilization] (Tehran: Ketabkhaneh Pahlavi, 2536R/ 1977).
[50] Zarghamee presents an account of the founding of the Aryamehr University of Technology in 1965, emphasizing the instrumental role played by Dr. Mohammad Ali Mojtahedi. See Mehdi Zarghamee, "Mojtahedi and the Founding of the Arya-Mehr University of Technology," *Iranian Studies* 44:5 (September 2011): 767–775.

later, as of 1969, the Central Council of Universities (Shura-e markazi-e daneshgah-ha) took shape. The policy was also pursued in medical training. As Ali Sheikholeslam (1920–2009), founder of the National University (Daneshgah-e Melli), recalled in his memoirs,

We completely reformed the curriculum in the new School of Medicine, basing it on the American model, with some notable modifications.[51]

As a student at New York University, Sheikholeslam had felt inspired to establish a similar, private, and respectable institution of higher learning back home. The fruit of his dreams and actions, the National University of Iran, had opened its doors with high hopes in 1959 as the nation's only private institution of higher learning during the 1960s. It gave advanced degrees in architecture, science, and medicine.[52]

Drawing inspiration from Americanization acquired momentum during the 1960s and 1970s. From the Plan and Budget Organization, the powerhouse of the nation's technocrats, to television programming and clothing – among the middle class – all things American were preferred. The new phenomenon went beyond mere Westernization, internationalization, or modernization. To implement the policy of Americanization of higher education, a US-educated and culturally well-rounded scientist-engineer was invited from abroad to take over as the new chancellor of the University of Tehran. Fazlollah Reza (1914–2019), an early graduate of the College of Engineering at the University of Tehran, had traveled to the United States in his twenties, completed his studies at Columbia University and at the New York Polytechnic Institute, continued to work at MIT, and taught at Syracuse University. He seemed to be a perfect fit. Revered as Professor Reza, he presided over the University of Tehran for a short term (1968–1969). Before long, the shah decided that running his American-style temple of science and engineering at Aryamehr University was better left to an American-educated overseer. So, he summarily had Mojtahedi transferred to another post and replaced him at Aryamehr University with Professor Reza.

---

[51] Ali Sheikholeslam, *Ronesans Iran: Daneshgah Melli Iran o Shah* [The Iranian renaissance: The National University and the shah] (n.p.: 1369/1990), 234.
[52] Ibid., 1–19.

The pace of expansion of Americanizing institutions of higher education accelerated nationwide. From 1962 to 1972, the number of university students rose with an average annual rate of over 15 percent.[53] According to an official government report from 1972:

During the last decade Iran has experienced a considerable increase in enrolment at the universities and institutions of higher education. The enrolment leaped from 24,456 in 1962–3 to 97,338 in 1971–2, an increase of about four times. The female enrolment has increased from 4,183 in 1962–3 to 28,869 in 1971–2, an increase of about seven times, and the male enrolment has more than tripled, from 20,273 to 68,469 during the same period.[54]

Two years after this report, in March 1974, the daily newspaper *Ettela'at* projected that of the 100,000 contestants as many as 25,000 new students would be admitted to the nation's institutions of higher learning.[55] Of those 25,000, 8,300 students entered public universities by competing in the National Contest (*konkur-e sarasari*) and 1,700 students were admitted to Pahlavi University in Shiraz and Aryamehr University in Tehran. These two first-tier public institutions held their own entrance examinations independently. Moreover, room was made for another 10,000 students in nongovernmental private or semiprivate institutions of vocational training that usually conferred terminal associate degrees.

In addition to universities inside Iran, a sizeable number of students went abroad to pursue higher education. An unofficial estimate claims that as many as 18,000 to 20,000 Iranian students were studying abroad in 1963.[56] By the mid-1970s and on the eve of the revolution this number had grown manyfold. Of course, going to the Soviet Union was out of question. So were other countries of the Eastern Bloc, those referred to be "Behind the Iron Curtain." Instead, going to the United States was often the first choice.

Tens of thousands of Iranian students went to the United States, from the 1950s to the 1970s. A majority found their way into accredited schools. Some failed to graduate or matriculated in

---

[53] Average based on data presented in table 1, Institute for Research and Planning in Science and Education, *The System of Higher Education in Iran* (Tehran: 1972), 15.
[54] Ibid., 9.   [55] *Ettela'at* daily newspaper (Farvardin 19, 1353/April 8, 1974).
[56] Mahmoud Sanaie, "Tarbiat va eqtesad" ["Education and the economy"], *Masa'el Iran*, nos. 28–29 (Khordad–Tir 1344/May–June 1965): 101.

nonaccredited programs. Still, several hundred individuals acquired advanced degrees from top-tier universities and many of them returned home to participate in the nation's progress. For example, as many as forty Iranian nationals received PhDs from MIT between 1953 and 1979.[57] Similar estimates hold for the number of Iranian graduates from other leading universities, including Columbia University, the University of California, the University of Michigan, and a handful of other schools that were popular with Iranian students.

Despite systematic policies to expand higher education opportunities inside the country, and the relative ease of acquiring educational subsidies to study abroad, universities and other institutions of higher learning stood as centers of dissent nationwide. Complex reasons were at work. For one, not enough seats were available inside the country. Secondly, entrance examinations were deemed too difficult. So, year after year, many applicants remained behind the wall of competition (*posht-e sadd-e konkur*). Moreover, the rapid social mobility that higher education promised was not always delivered by the tardier labor market, and many graduates failed to find ideal jobs. Legitimately or not, state policies stirred resentment with a sizeable portion of the rapidly growing student body during the 1960s and 1970s.

In particular, colleges of science and engineering hosted the red embers of anti-shah, anti-government, and anti-American activism. A telling example is provided by the case of the founders of guerrilla organizations. Mohammad Hanifnejad (1939–1972), Ali-Asghar Badizadegan (1939–1972), and Said Mohsen (1940–1972) – the three founders of the Islam-oriented Sazeman-e Mojahedin-e Khalq-e Iran (The Iranian People's Mujahedin, founded in 1965) – had studied agricultural machinery, chemical engineering, and HVAC engineering, respectively. Also, two of the three founders of the Marxist group Sazeman-e Cherik-ha-e Fada'i-e Khalq-e Iran (The Iranian People's Sacrificial Guerrillas, founded in 1971), namely, Hamid Ashraf (1946–1976) and Masoud Ahmadzadeh (1946–1971), had studied mechanical engineering and mathematics as undergraduates, respectively. Many of the members and sympathizers of these groups had also

---

[57] The author of the present paper culled this conclusion from a large list (provided by Dissertation Abstracts, PROQUEST) of 7,912 doctoral degrees MIT conferred from 1953 to 1979.

enrolled in similar programs. All five men named here, and many other male and female students and graduates of science and engineering, were killed by government security forces. The turbulent context of the processes involved in the perceptions of science and engineering by the state and the public is better understood by considering the unfolding of the Cold War on ideological fronts.

Besides universities and higher vocational training institutes, the nation's high schools also provided grounds for ideological initiation and experimentation. Two high schools in Tehran provide good examples: Alborz and Alavi.

Alborz had inherited the legacy of several generations. The grade school which American Presbyterian missionaries had founded in 1873 had grown into a junior college in 1924, and an accredited liberal arts college by 1928 under the leadership of Dr. Samuel Martin Jordan (1871–1952).[58] It was called the American College until 1941 when the Iranian government purchased its properties and shut it down. Renamed as Alborz, it continued to operate as a high school. A legion of well-trained men graduated from the school, many of them becoming scientists and engineers, and its achievement was in many ways unique. As Homa Katouzian (b. 1942), a former student, has observed:

A number of factors accounted for this uniqueness of Alborz ... First was the legacy of the Americans, in general, and Dr. Jordan and his wife in particular.[59]

Historically, Alborz students and teachers had had their hand on the pulse of social and political developments. As Hamid Enayat (1932–1982), who was a student there in 1951, later recalled in an interview, at the peak of oil-related national protests, the Alborz high school had closed for some ten days.[60] Nevertheless, the headmaster, the same Dr. Mohammad-Ali Mojtahedi who later led Aryamehr University into excellence, committed himself to keeping the students,

[58] Y. Armajani, "Alborz College," *Encyclopaedia Iranica*, www.iranicaonline.org/articles/alborz-college; Michael Zirinksy, "Jordan, Samuel Martin," *Encyclopaedia Iranica*, www.iranicaonline.org/articles/jordan-samuel-martin.
[59] Homa Katouzian, "Alborz and Its Teachers," *Iranian Studies* 44:5 (September 2011): 743.
[60] Mahmoud Enayat and Bijan Asadipoor, "Goft-o-goo ba Mahmud Enayat," *Kelk* 51–52 (Khordad–Tir 1373/May–June 1994): 177.

and the instructors, out of trouble. He maintained tight discipline, creating a densely competitive atmosphere in schoolwork, and making sure that anti-shah protests never occurred under his watch. That is not until 1978, in the heat of uprisings that culminated in the 1979 revolution.

The case of Alavi was different. Ali-Asghar Karbaschian (1914–2003) and his friend Reza Ruzbeh (1921–1973) had founded the school in 1955.[61] The former had emigrated to Tehran from Qom, and drawing on his reputation as a man of religious learning had convinced some *bazaaris* to invest in a high school for training the youth up to the highest academic standards of the day but also to bring them up with what they considered to be properly religious character. To that end, every day at the Alavi high school started with a twenty-minute recitation from the Qur'an and weekly lessons were given on ethics. As Karbaschian later reminisced,

It saddened me to see that once our kids completed primary education and went to high school, they become devoid of faith [*la-mazhab*]. We were not going to tell the kids simply go recite the Qur'an, or go attend religious functions [*rozeh*], or go beat their chests. But our goal was not to produce doctors and engineers like Alborz did.[62]

Perhaps equally intent on steering pupils away from political agitation, Karbaschian was not as successful as Mojtahedi in doing so. Mojtahedi stressed loyalty to the king and the nation, and Karbaschian seems to have agreed. Both educators shared the shah's envisioned role for education in the nation's march toward the Great Civilization. Nevertheless, quite a number of Alavi students and graduates joined the ranks of political activists and even armed guerrilla fighters – some as ardent Muslims and some as outright Marxists.

Several other academically competitive high schools existed. The leftist Parviz Sharyari, mentioned above, had founded Kharazmi and Marjan in 1960 and 1961, one for boys and the other for girls, respectively.[63] Within years, branches under these franchised names opened their doors across Tehran. By 1972, the flagship Kharazmi

---

[61] https://bit.ly/3s52Fto.

[62] Eqbal Qasemi-Pooya, "Tabyin va tahlil madares-e movaffaq dar amoozesh o parvaresh Iran mo'aser" ["Analysis and explanation of successful schools in contemporary Iranian education"], *Ta'lim o tarbiat* 96 (Winter 1387/2009): 201–239.

[63] Parviz Malekpur, "Geramidasht ostad Parviz Shahryari" ["Celebrating Parviz Sharyari"], *Chista* 202–203 (Aban–Azar 1382/October–December 2003): 155.

high school #1, standing within a stone's throw from the western gate of the University of Tehran, enrolled 5,000 students, 3,200 students during the day and 1,800 for nightly classes.[64] In the words of the principal of that high school, the educator and publisher Abdul-Hossein Al Rasool (b. c. 1921), "The objective of high school education ... was to train good, useful, and conforming [*sazegar*] citizens."[65] Both girls and boys came under this umbrella. There were other schools besides the Alborz, Alavi, Kharazmi, and Marjan. Anushiravan-e Dadgar, Hadaf, Andisheh, Khaza'eli, and Hashtroodi high schools drew students in Tehran, and the Hakim-Nezami high school in Qom, the Golbahar high school in Isfahan, Shah-Reza in Mashhad, and several others in all major cities of Iran. These schools set the standard – in form, content, and ethos. Deciding on priorities in training "good, useful, and conforming citizens" varied somewhat. In general, students were encouraged to make presentations on various literary, historical, and scientific topics. A survey of library usage at Kharazmi high school reported student interest in the social sciences in 1971.[66] Interest in social science, religion, and other disciplines was not mutually exclusive, but often overlapped. Above all good schools supplemented the regular state-mandated curriculum by placing extra emphasis on problem-solving skills in science and mathematics. Such skills came to be particularly essential in scoring high on university entrance examinations.

So, competitive students actively sought after difficult problems and solution manuals to improve their aptitude in science, and especially in mathematics.[67] Abol-Qasem Qorbani (1911–2001) and Hasan Saffari (1916–2002), who had taught in Alborz and authored high school mathematics textbooks, pioneered the production of highly popular problem solutions manuals (*hall-al-masa'el*). Both men contributed to the promotion of mathematical science by making translations into

[64] Abdul-Hossein Al Rasool, "Goft-o-goo'i azad ba Abdul-Hossein Al Rasool, Ra'is Dabirestan Shomareh Yek-Kharazmi I" [A conversation with Abdul-Hossein Al Rasool, Part I], *Ta'lim o tarbiat* 61 (Mehr 1351/September–October 1972): 17.

[65] Ibid., 23.

[66] Abdul-Hossein Al Rasool, "Donbaleh Goft-o-gooi'i azad ba Abdul-Hossein Al Rasool, Ra'is Dabirestan Shomareh Yek-Kharazmi II" [A continuation of the conversation with Abdul-Hossen Al Rasool, Part II], *Ta'lim o tarbiat* 62 (Aban 1351/October–November 1972): 111.

[67] Ibid., 113.

Persian as well. Following their example, Parviz Shahryari, who had become a successful educational entrepreneur, ventured to publish his translations of problems and solutions. Drawing on his earlier interest in Russian, when he had been detained for learning the language of Stalin (as cited above), he published *Problems from Math Competitions together with Solutions (Soviet Math Contests)*, in 1968.[68] This was a great success, and within a year three reprints of it sold out. Similar translations followed.

While linking interest in translations from Russian to Cold War sympathies directly lacks a firm foundation, circumstantial evidence exists to substantiate an indirect and implicit connection. No doubt, during the Cold War Western and Eastern blocs competed – among other things – over demonstrating the superiority of their respective educational systems. Iran stood out as a coveted sphere of influence. All parties involved invested in education, especially in modern science and technology, in the same breath as a system of knowledge, an instrument for progress, but also a weapon to fight political and ideological adversaries. Falling short of penetrating the structurally US-oriented educational system of Iran from above, the Soviet Union cultivated indirect and implicit ways of shaping opinion. One of its most effective conduits for doing so was showcasing the best examples of scientific and mathematical achievements in translation. For years before the revolution, Mir Publishers, founded in 1946, distributed English translations of such works in Iran, in high-quality but low-priced editions. Like many other forms of political action in Iran during the 1960s and 1970s, dissent was often expressed implicitly and indirectly. Interviews conducted with former Iranian students and instructors who attended high school, vocational schools, or universities indicate that such translations often functioned as a means for advocating the superiority of Russian mathematics and mathematicians, which was sometimes meant to imply the superiority of the Soviet system in general.[69] At least implicitly and at least sometimes.

---

[68] Parviz Shahryari, *Masa'el-e mosabeqat riyazi "ba hall" (Konkoor-ha riyazi Shuravi)* [Problems and solutions from Russian mathematics competitions] (Tehran: Amir Kabir, 1347/1968).

[69] A most helpful interview was with Professor Behrooz Parhami, former professor of computer science and engineering at Aryamehr and later Sharif University in Tehran, a prolific author, and founder of the Informatics Society of Iran (1979).

Conclusion

The impact of the postcoup educational expansion, especially education in science and technology, on the long fermentation of the 1979 revolution cannot be overstated. On the eve of the revolution, diverse groups agreed that a better future awaited the nation and held it as a self-evident truth that modern science and technology had an instrumental role to play in building that future. The relatively high number of former students and graduates of engineering and technical schools among the revolutionaries paved the way for imagining it primarily in terms of construction and control. Therefore, one of the earliest institutions that emerged after the 1979 revolution was called Jahad-e Sazandegi (Construction Jihad). It was also hoped that once empowered by the global message of the revolution, the ethos of science and technology would transcend divisions between the East and the West. Reality proved otherwise.

PART V

Aspirational Universalisms

11 Between Illusion and Aspiration: Morteza Avini's Cinema and Theory of Global Revolution

HAMED YOUSEFI *

"There is no doubt that for today's man a '*jahani* revolution' is unavoidable," wrote Iranian filmmaker and theorist Morteza Avini, "because today's civilization has inevitably acquired a *jahani* expanse."[1] In English, the Persian word *jahani* is commonly translated as "global." For example, *enqelab-e jahani* is global revolution, *amperialism-e jahani* is global imperialism, and *hakemiiat-e jahani-e eslam* is Islam's global rule. Yet, the term is more complicated than its simple translation as "global" conveys. From the same root, *in-jahani* means worldly, which associates *jahani* with material values and ordinary life rather than a spiritual existence. *Jahani* also means "world," as in world war (*jang-e jahani*), World Bank (*bank-e jahani*), and world literature (*adabiiat-e jahani*). Additionally, jahani is one of the common words used in Persian for the notion of universal: *Elamiieh-ie Jahani-e Hoghough-e Bashar* (The Universal Declaration of Human Rights), *shomoul-e jahani* (universal validity), *jahani boodan-e eslam* (Islam's universality). Finally, in the artistic community and among the intelligentsia, cosmopolitanism is *jahan-vatani*: to have the entire world as one's homeland. *Honar-e jahani* (*jahani* art), a recurring theme in intellectual debates since the 1960s, concerned artists' negotiation between local rootedness and global belonging, which gives *jahani*, in phrases like *honar-e jahani*, a further association

* Thanks are due to Naghmeh Sohrabi, Arang Keshavarzian, and Arash Davari, my patient and generous interlocutors during the writing of this chapter. To them, my debt of gratitude remains beyond acknowledgments. Rebecca Johnson and Maya Dukmasova also read drafts and offered invaluable comments. I thank them, as well as the participants of the Global 1979 Workshop at Columbia University (December 2019), for their instructive observations.

[1] Morteza Avini, "The Beginning to an End: The Islamic Revolution and the End of Awaiting," in *Aghazi bar yek pyan: Enqelab-e eslami va payan-e entezar* [The beginning to an end: The Islamic Revolution and the end of awaiting] (Tehran: Vaheh, 1397/2018), 157.

with cosmopolitanism. Considering this complicated linguistic dynamic can lead us to a fuller understanding of the mentality of some Iranian revolutionaries when they thought of their revolution as *jahani*. For them, the revolution's globality was inseparable from the universality of its Islamic ideology, the worldliness of its political cause, and the cosmopolitan network of its players. They conveyed all of these with just one word.

In the 1980s, the Iranian writer and filmmaker Morteza Avini (1947–1993) articulated the discursive multiplicity of *jahani*, revealing its political significance for the revolution and for the postrevolutionary government. More than any other artist or intellectual of the period, Avini captured the overlapping semantics of the global, worldly, cosmopolitan, and universal in the process of producing films and television series that have often been dismissed as little more than state propaganda. Avini was theoretically minded (obsessively engaged with distilling philosophical and religious truths from language) and politically engaged (deeply committed to Ayatollah Khomeini as a governmental leader and a religious guide), but his practice advanced in sustained relationship with uprisings of the disenfranchised poor throughout the country.

Avini developed his idea of *enqelab-e jahani* (global revolution) by negotiating a seemingly contradictory position. On the one hand, he had roots in the artistic discourse of cosmopolitan modernism in pre-revolutionary Iran. On the other hand, after the revolution, he became a committed supporter of Khomeini's political Islam. His films appropriated the aesthetic form of avant-garde cinema for his political activism as a member of Hezbollah.[2] These contradictions in his personal biography were mirrored in the complexities of articulating *enqelab-e jahani* in Avini's practice. I trace the genealogy of this revolutionary concept at the intersection of four seemingly divergent tendencies in Iran's intellectual and political history:

---

[2] In the context of the Iranian Revolution, Hezbollah (not to be confused with the Lebanese political and military group of the same name) can be distinguished from their rival revolutionary groups based on their unique devotion to Khomeini both as a guide and as a modernizer of Islam. See Farhad Khosrokhavar, "Attitude of Teenage Girls to the Iranian Revolution," in Elizabeth Warnock Fernea, ed., *Children in the Muslim Middle East* (Austin, TX: University of Texas Press 1995), 394–395. In this chapter, I use Hezbollah, Islamism, and political Islam in connection with each other.

(1) religious belief in the *universality* of Islam's message (the assumption of convertibility according to which the entire world can, and eventually will, convert to Islam);
(2) revolutionary commitment to the *worldly* cause of the disenfranchised poor;
(3) philosophical (specifically Heideggerian) critique of modern civilization's *global* expanse over the world; and
(4) a *cosmopolitan* network of modernist artistic practice.

Together, these trends form the juncture of *jahani* in Iran's revolutionary thought, grounding the word's linguistic fluidity in concurrent historical discourses. They also shape Avini's attempts to articulate the revolution as *jahani* and reflect the mindset of an entire generation of Islamist activists. In his films and writings, Avini unites divergent histories of modern art and political Islam in Iran. In analyzing his work, I argue that the artistic modernisms of the 1960s and 1970s are relevant to understanding the Islamist movement that assumed state power in the 1980s. Analyzing Avini's theory of *enqelab-e jahani* reveals a shared mentality amongst those in his generation who were educated in prerevolutionary academic and intellectual circles, but, to the surprise of many, joined Hezbollah after 1979.

Today, Avini is celebrated by the Iranian government for his documentaries about the Iran-Iraq War (1980–1988), particularly the TV series *Chronicles of Victory* (*Ravaayat-e Fath*), which ran from 1985 until April 1993 when Avini stepped on a landmine and died while filming in the former battlefields. The conservative elite of the Islamic Republic consider their rule legitimized through the Iran-Iraq War and Avini is the preeminent narrator of their victory.[3] Avini has been lionized by the government as no other artist, writer, or filmmaker. Supreme Leader Ayatollah Ali Khamenei attended his funeral procession in person and honored Avini with a title that can be loosely translated into English as "the ultimate literary martyr" (*sayyed-e shahidan-e ahl-e ghalam.*) Avini's films and writings have since been widely distributed across the country, throughout mosques and school libraries. It may be safe to speculate that today there is virtually no urban center in Iran without a movie theater or lecture hall bearing

---

[3] On the significance of the Iran-Iraq War for the establishment of the Islamic Republic, see Shahram Chubin and Charles Tripp, *Iran and Iraq at War* (Boulder, CO: Westview Press, 1988).

Avini's name. In recent years, international curators and film scholars have revisited Avini's work, but their focus, much like the government's, has remained on his war films in the context of "the Iranian cinema of the sacred defense" (*sinema-ye defa'e moghaddas*).[4]

In this chapter, I deal with a less-acknowledged, early period of Avini's work. These early films reflect the filmmaker developing his own ideas in parallel with the revolution, whereas the later, better-known films, produced after the full establishment of the Islamic Republic, demonstrate a solidified worldview that has fused with the hegemonic order. Before he fully engaged with the war, Avini had a prolific output and it was through those films that he articulated a dynamic between specifically local issues and an abstract theory of the global revolution.

The Disenfranchised Poor: A Revolutionary Subject

In just two years, from 1980 to 1981, Avini produced three short documentaries and four documentary series in which he engaged with core issues shared among various groups of the revolution: economic and social destitution in rural areas, ethnic uprisings, class struggles, and infightings of the revolutionary forces. These films included *The Khoozestan Flood* (1980), about a deluge that killed nearly thirty people and damaged the old Gatvand dam and the Masjed Soleyman oil pipe between February 11 and 17, 1980, immediately after the

---

[4] Among scholarly works on Avini's war documentaries, see Agnès Devictor, *Images, combattants et martyrs: La guerre Iran-Irak vue par le cinéma iranien* (Paris: Karthala, 2015); Hamid Naficy, *A Social History of Iranian Cinema, Vol. 4: The Globalizing Era, 1984–2010* (Durham, NC: Duke University Press, 2012), 12–21; and Mehrzad Karimabadi, "Manifesto of Martyrdom: Similarities and Differences between Avini's Ravaayat-e Fath [Chronicles of Victory] and More Traditional Manifestoes," *Iranian Studies* 44:3 (May 2001): 381–386. I have also previously written about Avini's war documentaries in the context of a survey exhibition of modern and contemporary Iranian art held in Paris and Rome: Hamed Yousefi, "Morteza Avini's Avant-garde Populism," in Catherine David et al., eds., *Iran: Unedited History* (Paris and Rome: Paris Musée d'Art Moderne & MAXXI Roma, 2014), 219–225. There is also a body of literature concerning Avini's role as a "propagandist" for the Islamic Republic. For example, see Esha Momeni, "Red Death and Black Life: Media, Martyrdom and Shame," *Middle East Critique* 28:2 (2019): 177–195.

celebrations of the first anniversary of the revolution;[5] *Six Days in Turkmen-Sahra* (1980), about armed conflicts between supporters of the People's Fedai Guerrillas, a Marxist group, and Islamist forces organized through Revolutionary Committees and the Revolutionary Guards;[6] *Bitten by Landowners* (1980, six episodes), about conflict with *khan*s in Fars;[7] *The Triumph of Blood* (1980, three episodes), about urban wars between Iranian and Iraqi forces before the fall of Khorramshahr;[8] *Lost in Forgotten Land* (1981, six episodes), about the wretched state of penury near the southeast borders in Hormozgan;[9] and *Seven Stories from Baluchestan* (1981), about the Zarabad village on the peripheries of Iranshahr in southern Baluchestan.[10] Although most of these early works were lost in the frenzy of the revolutionary years or survived only in parts, what we know about them indicates that Avini's original "chronicles of victory" was not his account of the Iran-Iraq War (Figure 11.1). Rather, it was his cinematic documentation, all across the country, of the triumph of the Islamist Hezbollah over competing forces (including secular leftist and nationalist groups) in the postrevolutionary struggles over alternative imaginings of the nation's future. This was not only a military and political victory, but also a discursive one concerning who has the right to represent the people (*mardom*) in undoing the damage caused by the Pahlavi monarchy.

Mapping his journeys throughout the country while producing these films takes us to the borderlines of the nation, both geographically and in terms of the degrees of social and political inclusion. From the flood-stricken Arabs of Khoozestan in the southwest to Torkman small-farmers in the north, from the Baluch villagers in the east to the Qashqai tribes of Fars in the south, Avini's protagonists do not necessarily speak Persian as their first language, and they also live outside metropolitan centers in areas marked by precapitalist modes of production and lack of modern infrastructures. Despite his interest in

[5] *Seil-e Khoozestan* (1358). Less than a year later, the locations filmed by Avini during the flood became frontlines of the Iran-Iraq War, where he would spend most of the rest of his career as a filmmaker.
[6] *Shesh Rooz Dar Turkmen-Sahra* (1358).
[7] *Khan-Gazide-Ha* (1358–1359). Of this series only one full episode and a few other sequences survive.
[8] *Fath-e Khoon* (1359). [9] *Haft Ghesseh az Baluchestan* (1360).
[10] Morteza Avini, *Ayne-ie jadoo* [The magic mirror], vol. 3 (Tehran: Vaheh, 1396/ 2017), 245.

Figure 11.1 Morteza Avini (standing, third from right) and his Hezbollah crew in the 1980s.

revolutionary infightings, Avini ignored politically defining events in Tehran such as clashing demonstrations in 1980–1981 between the Hezbollah forces of the Islamic Republic Party and other groups such as the People's Mujahedin (Mojahedeen-e Khalq), the People's Fedai Guerrillas (Cherik-ha-ie Fada'i-e Khalq), and the National Front (Jebheh-ie Melli) – a series of events that left lasting impact on the arrangement of power after the revolution and otherwise received widespread media coverage both inside and outside the country. Yet, Avini was not alone in identifying the revolution with uprisings of poor and marginalized people. As sociologist Asef Bayat has argued, by the late 1970s, the urban poor were generally seen as villains by policy-makers and as victims by the opposition to the Pahlavi state.[11] Reclaiming the lost dignity of the poor and the marginalized in urban and rural areas (in Ali Shariati's Islamic-Marxist terminology also

---

[11] Asef Bayat, *Street Politics: The Poor People's Movements in Iran* (New York: Columbia University Press, 1997), 23.

adopted by Ayatollah Khomeini, the *mostazafin*) was a point at which most revolutionary groups converged. After the fall of the shah, in the absence of state suppression, the marginalized poor acquired new political agency and began spontaneous local mobilizations. By virtue of their exclusion from politics under the Pahlavi government, the poor villagers effectively became the name of the political subject – a conceptualization upon which nearly all revolutionary groups agreed.[12] Avini's early films follow a number of these uprisings and offer Hezbollah's perspective about them.

This is particularly apparent in a sequence from his six-episode documentary series *Bitten by Landowners* (*Khan Gazideh-ha*, 1358–1359/1980), in which a large group of impoverished villagers from Abu Tarbeh in the southern province of Fars share accounts of their abuse by the region's landed gentry. People in the crowd take turns telling the camera that the *khan*s unleashed a reign of terror, appropriated property, beat the men, assaulted the women, and responded to protest by breaking bones and threatening murder. A man implicates the *khan*s in the death of a number of children and young adults. As he names the dead, we hear women cry in the background. From behind the camera the interviewer asks for specifics, but another man and a woman express shame in detailing what the landowners have done to them: "If we tell you, this would bring disgrace on us. How can we tell you?" The camera pans over crying faces and zooms in on a gun-carrying soldier who wipes his tears. Three women say that their men sought refuge in the mountains and when the *khan*s blackmailed the women, one of them threatened to set herself on fire in front of the *khan*'s family. A man whose elocution indicates urban education speaks about the unjust distribution of harvest between the peasants and landlords that left families starving, to which the crowd respond by chanting "that is right."

The alleged crimes remain ambiguous and unsubstantiated, but the immediacy of the relationship between the camera and its varying subjects sidelines the question of bad intention or manipulation. The sequence appears truthful to the eruption of defiance by a people empowered after the revolution. "Why do they beat us?" one man

---

[12] My language here is inspired by Sherene Seikaly, "Egypt's Bread Intifada: On the Subject of the People," filmed February 2015 at Stanford University, Stanford, CA, video, https://cddrl.fsi.stanford.edu/arabreform/events/egypt's-bread-intifada-subject-people.

asks, "because people write Islamic slogans, 'Long live Khomeini.'"
Another man expands the political context and accuses the shah's land
reform of having failed to end peasants' subjugation while also leaving
landowners increasingly unchecked. The mood of the gathering
conveys intellectual conviction and political determination. The
makers of the film also see themselves as part of the event, rather than
its impartial observers. "We have performed a ceremonial washing
[*ghosl*] in preparation for martyrdom and are ready to be martyred,"
the director's commentary tells us. Despite the aesthetics of realism, the
film means to intervene in the unfolding of its own story. The next
sequence follows a mass demonstration of peasants who hold photographs of Ayatollah Khomeini and demand the execution of the *khan*s.

Two years after *Bitten by Landowners* was broadcast on national
television, long-standing armed struggles between local supporters
of the *khan*s and the forces associated with the Islamic Republic's
Revolutionary Guards reached their final conclusion: in October
1982 Khosrow Sowlat Qashqai, the grand-chief of the Qashqai tribe
and a well-known anti-shah nationalist who spent twenty-five years
before the revolution in exile in Europe because of his association with
Mossadegh, faced a firing squad in Shiraz. The execution of the Qashqai
chief was one of many incidents in 1982 that marked the final triumph
of Hezbollah over socialist and nationalist revolutionary groups who
had once fought the shah alongside them. For Hezbollah, who mobilized
its Revolutionary Guards around Khomeini's flag and his idea of political Islam, Avini's cinema was part of the ammunition.

To a large extent, postrevolutionary infighting between revolutionary
elites concerned conflicting views on how to respond to the demand for
dignity on behalf of those left out of the process of state modernization
during the Pahlavi era. For example, the Qashaqai *khan*s in Fars tried to
renew a traditional mode of decentralized power around the age-old
structure of nomadic tribes. Meanwhile, the Fedais followed a Marxist
model to mobilize Turkmen-Sahra peasants in the north. The Islamists,
on the other hand, tapped into religious sentiments of tribesmen and
peasants, and, behind the undisputedly charismatic leadership of
Ayatollah Khomeini, marshaled militia organizations such as the
Revolutionary Guards and Revolutionary Committees.

By focusing on the marginalized poor in his early documentaries,
Avini zoomed in on a point of revolutionary convergence that became
a site of contestation after the revolution. He followed the Islamists'

point of view throughout the country's ethnic and economic margins, and recorded the Islamists establishing a legitimate claim over the leadership of the dispossessed (*mostazafin*). By 1982, when Avini stopped making films about ethnic and economic margins and began to fully concentrate his efforts on the Iran-Iraq War, the Islamists had a clear monopoly to speak in the name of the people (*mardom*) against the former regime's authoritarian modernization. As the transition between Avini's early and late films demonstrates, by merging the revolution into the war, Islamists also succeeded in keeping *mardom* and *mostazafin* constantly mobilized, while making continued mobilization governable.

But where did the figure of marginalized poor, central to Avini's practice, acquired its revolutionary impetus? One short answer is the land reforms of the early 1960s. The Pahlavi land reforms massively benefited parts of the population, but also led to the emergence of a new category, "poor," not simply as an economic one, but also as a cultural identity with a political charge.[13] As a result of the reforms, big landowners who ruled over large swaths of land for generations lost their villages to smaller owners. However, not every villager ended up owning a piece of land, and new landlords also enjoyed unprecedented, forceful backing from the newly empowered and expansive central state, with its gendarmerie planting a branch in every town and village to suppress dissent. Anthropologist Mary Elaine Hegland resided in a Fars village during and after the revolution in the same area that Avini traversed in *Bitten by Landowners*. According to her, before land reforms the Qavam landlords of the region typically remained nonpartisan toward the two *taifeh*s or kinship-based factions of the village, giving communities no ownership but a degree of autonomy at the local administrative level. The *taifeh*s interchangeably took over the position of *kadkhoda* or village headman, and the country's weak and small central government had little interest in such local matters. As a result of the Pahlavi land reforms, one influential *taifeh* became the village's main landowner while the other *taifeh* gained nothing: "After several violent struggles to improve the situation in their village, people realized they could no longer influence local politics. In fact, local politics was no longer controlled locally. Resentment and dissatisfaction against the local political elite continued to build

---

[13] Bayat, *Street Politics*, 23.

up, but people could do nothing about it; they were no match for the armed gendarmes."[14] Eventually, the revolution dismantled the coercive alliance between the *khan*s and the Pahlavi government, resulting in mass revolts in the villages.

The villagers that we see in Avini's *Bitten by Landowners* are emerging out of this land reform experiment. The reforms divided their communities into haves and have-nots, while the Pahlavi government, operating solely as an agent of force more powerful and enlarged than any previous government, stood on the former's side. Avini documented these villagers' uprisings after the revolution as a new force to be reckoned with in Iran's political sphere. However, instead of a socioeconomic approach to the villagers' political plight, which would be a Marxist position, Avini translated material conditions into mythological narratives of eternal battle between the good and the evil. This was in no small part sanctioned by the villagers' actual point of view: familiar binary structures were reenacted in the age-old opposition of the two *taifeh*s. Hegland observes that "because of lack of political modernization and therefore lack of knowledge about alternative ways of approaching political process, villagers returned to their local *taifeh-keshi* (political competition and conflict among kinship-based factions), applying this political paradigm to the 1978–1979 revolutionary process."[15] But Avini commonly employed religious and literary metaphors to blur the boundary between political events and ontological fiction, therefore elevating *taifeh-keshi* beyond village triviality: "The flesh of the pain-stricken people is the kebab of their master and their blood is his wine," Avini's emotive commentary tells us over close-up faces of sun-burned peasants protesting in *Bitten by Landowners*. Avini narrated the failure of land reforms in terms of a "fairytale story" of a *khan* who "sought happiness in the deprived's torment: From behind the walls of his monstrous castle, the *khan* enslaved the toiling poor. He saw his life in their death and his happiness in their misery." This language epitomizes the framework through which Islamists acknowledged marginalized poor as *the* political subject of the revolution, while also framing this subjectivity through an undemocratic model of mythological binaries. The fact

[14] Mary Elaine Hegland, *Days of Revolution: Political Unrest in an Iranian Village* (Stanford, CA: Stanford University Press, 2014), 17.
[15] Ibid., 3.

that this model made sense in Iran because the Pahlavi government had previously blocked the emergence of alternative models for democratic politics demonstrates a continuity in political discourse before and after the revolution.

There were, of course, alternative imaginations, but they were overpowered by Hezbollah and pushed out of the political stage. Apart from Avini, numerous artists and filmmakers reflected on the infightings after the fall of the shah. Avini's films can be productively contrasted with works made in opposition to Khomeini's Hezbollah; for example, *Iran: A Revolution Betrayed* (1983).[16] This film follows events in Tehran that Avini decided to ignore, including a march of unemployed industrial workers whose leaders are eventually arrested by the Revolutionary Guards, or the disruption of liberal demonstrations by "mobs of Hezbollahis." Focusing on political confrontations between hostile camps in the ruling elite, the film provides a grand narrative of the revolution and the final victory of Hezbollah for an assumed impartial viewer. It is not that the filmmakers avoid political judgment, but the bigger picture in their inquiry emerges from a rationalized compilation of detailed evidence, contrasting with Avini's aesthetic use of mythological structures.

Avini's films pursue a far less mediated kind of politics. For example, although *Bitten by Landowners* is a six-episode TV series, it essentially consists of only three types of sequences. One set of footage follows tribespeople and the urban poor as they march against the *khans* and declare their support for the Revolutionary Guards who fight them. The second set of images consists of the same group of people gathering in front of the camera and voicing their grievances, holding the central government responsible and demanding action. Finally, there is actual footage of tribesmen and Revolutionary Guards in the battlefields. We see them move across the hilltops of Fars, taking cover behind the rocks, and at times exchanging fire with the supporters of the *khans*. While *Iran: A Revolution Betrayed* followed a quick pace and used music for additional excitement, Avini's shots are

---

[16] *Iran: A Revolution Betrayed* was filmed in Tehran during the course of the revolution from early 1977 to late 1979 by Ahsan Adib, almost certainly a pseudonym. The film's commentary was written by British author Edward Mortimer, and, as the title's reference to Trotsky's 1936 book indicates, offered a left-leaning perspective on the cause and failures of the revolution. The film was produced and broadcast by the BBC.

disproportionately long with little editing intervention. In one case, a man speaks to the camera for an entire eight minutes, five minutes of that without a cut. In another moment, the camera stays zoomed in on a chanting crowd's march, their tightly cropped faces and clinched fists enter and leave the focal point one after another. This claustrophobic shot provides little visual and mental space for the viewer outside of the mood of the demonstration. Avini seeks to immerse his audience in the sensory fullness of rural revolt, its evocation of precapitalist community, and the slow pace of village life, all of which he presents in opposition to middle-class, urban subjectivity. We face a similar immersive experience in footage of hillside battles: Avini's camera generally stays very close to armed men, and we join them as they discuss attack strategies and exchange fire. There is little sense of a safe shelter or heavy machinery support. The fighters appear as part of the natural landscape. As a result of Avini's cinematic style, viewers find themselves dragged into the scene, losing the ability to stay impartial. Rather than looking at events from a god's-eye view and engaging in an inductive reasoning process based on evidence and argument, Avini puts his viewers right at the center of events, forcing them to be on one side.

It is this particular cinematic technique, combined with his interest in the marginalized poor, that links Avini's local politics to the cosmopolitan heritage of avant-garde cinema. In order to better understand this dynamic, we have to consider the transnational network through which artistic modernism and avant-garde ideas traveled to and through Iran's intellectual community before the revolution.

Film-Truth: The Poor as Image and the Poor as Subject

That cinematic immediacy and realist camerawork were artistic devices that could confront colonial and capitalist modernity had already been theorized before the revolution. During the 1960s and 1970s, in the context of a cosmopolitan and transnational space for intellectual exchange, documentarist Kamran Shirdel translated into Persian a seminal article about anti-capitalist realism and the work of Soviet revolutionary filmmaker Dziga Vertov, who coined the term *kino-pravda* (literally meaning film-truth and translated into French as *cinéma vérité* and into Persian as *cinema haghighat*). In his attempt to rip through the increasing abstractions of reality, Vertov developed a method of filming "based on truth" that he called "life caught unaware," that is, "filming people and other living things without them being consciously aware of, or prepared for, the presence of the cameraman and equipment, because such awareness would result in certain changes in the behavior and reaction of the subject."[17] This description of *kino-pravda* corresponds with Avini's account of how he approached his subjects in *Bitten by Landowners*. In an essay called "Reality in Documentary Cinema," written in 1990, a decade after the film was released, Avini recalls that "for *Bitten by Landowners* we had to spend a few days with our camera among villagers so that they would get used to the camera and not change their *natural* state."[18] Then,

[f]or hours we spoke with people without recording anything. Only when they forgot the presence of the camera, we started filming. I remember a scene when men and women gathered around us and began recounting their misery at the hands of *khans*. They stepped forward one by one, speaking to the camera, shouting, crying. The camera would turn around and approach another person. He or she would also scream his or her suffering. Tears of the cameraman were falling from behind the viewfinder. The sound recordist was sobbing but still holding his microphone toward the people . . . I was also crying. And the scene continued.[19]

Here Avini takes pride in the fact that the filmmaking crew lose themselves in the force of the reality that they witness. Like Vertov, he is interested in a truth behind the surface level of life's modern abstractions. Cinematic immediacy becomes the technique through which his films penetrate abstraction and reach what he believes to be truth in its concrete purity: the spontaneity of revolutionary life. The ultimate goal of Avini's revolutionary cinema is to give a cinematic form to the new kind of political subject that emerges through the revolution and whose name is *mostazaf* (pl. *mostazafin*). By losing their own subjectivity in the revolutionary reality of peasants' uprising, Avini's crew dissolve their authorial position (their role as authors of the film) and transfer authorship from filmmakers to the

[17] Georges Sadoul, "Az Dziga Vertov ta Jean Rouch: Cinéma Vérité va Doorbin-Chashm" ["From Dziga Vertov to Jean Rouch: Cinéma Vérité and Kino-Eye"], trans. Kamran Shirdel, *Negin 75* (Mordad 1345/July 1966): 35.

[18] Avini, "Reality in Documentary Cinema," in *Ayne-ie jadoo*, 3:233 (emphasis added).

[19] Avini, "A Lasting Experience," in *Ayne-ie jadoo*, 3:250.

disenfranchised poor who are understood as the ultimate subjects/
makers of both the film and the revolution.

Avini's cinematic representation of *mostazafin* signified a departure
from Iranian political cinema before the revolution. In 1966, the same
year that Shirdel translated and published the essay on *kino-pravda*, he
also filmed three short documentaries that opened new grounds in
Iran's documentary cinema. *Women's Prison (Nedamatgah*, 1966),
Tehran Is the Capital of Iran (Tehran, Paietakht-e Iran Ast, 1966),
and *Women's Quarter (Qal'eh*, 1967–1980) each offer alarming depictions of poverty and destitution in Tehran, challenging official discourse on modernization. In fact, the gap between reality and its
ideological representation by the Pahlavi state constitutes the core of
Shirdel's cinematic method. The most damning of these films, *Tehran
Is the Capital of Iran*, opens with an elongated shot of the camera
peeping into a winding, cavernous ruin. The filmmaking crew's
blinding flashlight illuminates rows of forlorn men sleeping on the
ground. We approach the individuals one after the other and focus
on their coarse faces, soiled feet, and tattered clothing. This act of
revealing has a jarring effect: the sleeping homeless remain immobile
with their eyes closed, oblivious to their observers, as if lifeless, unconscious, drugged, or all three. In Shirdel's montage, the voice of an
official from a charity organization tasked with eradicating poverty
in south Tehran exegetically accompanies the unsettling images.
What Shirdel shows as spiritless and inhuman becomes, in the official's
account, "effective measures" taken "in order to bring the
Shahanshah's revolution into fruition."

Film historian Hamid Naficy describes Shirdel's technique as the
"critical structure of juxtaposing official ideology with lived experience."[20] What is particularly intriguing about *Tehran* is that in
Shirdel's juxtaposition, ideology and lived experience are not reduced
to opposing poles of a binary. In the film, the voice of official modernization comes from representatives of a charity. This is not the patriarchal and militaristic voice of the state nor capitalist figures
advocating industrialization and exploitative schemes. The social
workers whose voices run against the grain of people's lived experience
are educated female volunteers at a nonprofit organization which has

---

[20] Hamid Naficy, *A Social History of Iranian Cinema, Vol. 2: The Industrializing
Years, 1941–1978* (Durham, NC: Duke University Press, 2011), 121.

also commissioned Shirdel to make this film as part of a campaign for the betterment of women and the disenfranchised.[21] Though voices of ideology, theirs is an unsettled and gendered voice, emphasizing care and the political economy of gift-giving: "In the first days when we arrived here, they welcomed us with stones and melon peels. Since then, we have familiarized ourselves with their pains and sufferings." The gap that separates these "saviors" from the poor remains unbridgeable, but there is no questioning of their intention. We find the filmmaker himself, commissioned by the same organization, to be implicated in their ideological position. This further complicates a straightforward dichotomy between critique and ideology. Yet, at the end of the day, value rests with poor, abandoned, and marginalized people who function, to use Shirdel's own term, as "counterpoints" to the idea of modernization.[22] Rather than approving attempts to save them, by merely being there, the poor negate modernist teleology. Despite seeming similarities, the difference between Avini's interpretation of film-truth (*cinema-haghighat*) and Shirdel's work is clear: Shirdel critically implicates himself in the Pahlavi state's apparatus, while Avini dissolves art's critical function into the Islamic Republic's ideology of political Islam.

This turn toward hegemony is characteristic of the generation of young Hezbollahis who appeared on the political scene after the 1979 revolution. As interviews conducted by sociologist Farhad Khosrokhavar in 1980 show, the young Hezbollahis' memory was "unencumbered by the failure and, ultimately, by the overthrow of the Mossadeghist movement in the fifties." In contrast to the previous generation, who understood the country's inner politics in terms of heteronomy ("superpowers make the major political decisions about Iran"), young Hezbollahis believed that "a very large autonomous political scene exists in Iran."[23] The presumed autonomy of the

---

[21] The Women's Organization of Iran, a semiofficial NGO headed by Princess Ashraf Pahlavi (the shah's twin) and directed by Mahnaz Afkhami, who later became the first minister of women's affairs, was established in 1966. In the same year, the organization sponsored the production of Shirdel's three documentaries. Yet the films were too critical to pass through censorship. *Women's Prison* was given limited screening and *Tehran* was banned and left incomplete. Shirdel only managed to edit his *Women's Quarter* footage after the revolution.

[22] Naficy, *A Social History*, 2:121.

[23] Khosrokhavar, "Attitude of Teenage Girls," 395.

Islamic state mirrored the autonomy of the *mostazafin* on whose behalf
the state spoke, and this combination legitimized Avini's collapsing of
the distinction between critique and ideology in an exactly opposite
way to Shirdel's: Shirdel put ideology at the service of critique and
Avini put critique at the service of ideology. Moreover, belief in poor
people's autonomy and agency distinguished Avini's approach to his
subjects from the prerevolutionary tradition of film-truth. Despite its
complicated form, in his film Shirdel struggles to attribute any agency
to the poor. If they serve as a "counterpoint" to the progressive
temporality of modernization, it is through their inability to act and
move forward. They are merely there, and they are being looked at.
Note the voyeuristic structure of Shirdel's opening scene: The crew
projects light on immobile figures for the handheld camera to roam
and closely look at them from a high angle. The imbalance of agency
between the makers of the film and its subject matters finds perfect
cinematic articulation in this scene. Although Shirdel does not affirm
the middle classes who seek solace in charitable acts, his film does not
show the degraded poor as political subject either. In contrast, as Avini
describes in his account of making *Bitten by Landowners*, his film
involves an emotional encounter between the film crew and the peasants. The real-world interactions between the politicized poor and the
filmmakers ultimately allow the film to become a powerful challenge to
middle-class subjectivity.[24]

The Tension of Cosmopolitanism and Universalism

Avini persistently engaged in criticizing Iranian intellectuals and avant-
garde artists. His close engagement with this scene situates his films in
the broader context of Iran's avant-garde cinema. Before the revolution, he studied architecture at the University of Tehran. He also wrote
modernist poems and published a collection of short stories. But in the
context of the 1979 revolution he experienced a spiritual turn, "burned
all previous writings" and embarked on a new journey in the path of
Ayatollah Khomeini. In an autobiographical note from the early
1990s, he reflects on this personal reinvention:

[24] That avant-garde artists have always considered their art to attack (and, ideally,
destroy) bourgeois, middle-class subjectivity is theorized by many artist and
critics, including Peter Burger, *The Theory of the Avant-Garde* (Minnesota:
University of Minnesota Press, 1984).

For many years I studied at an art school, went to poetry nights and art galleries, listened to Western classical music, wasted my time in pointless debates over what I did not have a clue about, and, in order to present myself as an intellectual, I grew a goatee beard and a Nietzschean mustache. I even used to carry around a copy of Herbert Marcuse's *One-Dimensional Man*, without having actually read it, so that everyone could see the title and think that I am very clever. But then life took me down a path which forced me to face myself and others, and to admit that "knowledge" is not the same as "philosophical studies," let alone pretentious intellectualism. Been there, done that.[25]

Underneath this condescending language, a complicated dynamic is at play in Avini's text: his support for Khomeini's political Islam is not a mere matter of religious belief; it is also a response to his sense of dissatisfaction with Tehran's prerevolutionary intellectual scene. It should therefore not be surprising that in his postrevolutionary work, Avini remains in constant dialogue with intellectual debates from before the revolution. As a filmmaker and a theorist, his practice owes more to prerevolutionary intellectual thought than earlier Islamic texts. Instead of mosques and hussainiyas, it was within the cosmopolitan environment of modernist thought before the revolution – a milieu of poetry nights, art galleries, and Continental philosophy – that Avini reached intellectual maturity. In the above-cited reflection, he capitalizes on this background only to then attack Iranian intellectuals with charges of shallow performativity and pretentiousness: obsessed about their appearance in the public space but lacking real knowledge and honest critical thinking. The revolution, for him, comes as the moment in which he breaks through this web of appearance and approaches the essence of an examined life.

For Avini, Khomeini's political Islam provided an exit from certain impasses that prerevolutionary artists who opposed the Pahlavi state left unresolved. Generally speaking, by the time of the revolution, we can identify two major understandings of the country's malaise among Iranian avant-garde artists and filmmakers: Those on the left, like Kamran Shirdel or his collaborator, photographer Kaveh Golestan, highlight class division and structural exploitation but, as we saw, fail

---

[25] "Zendegi-nameh-ie Shahid Avini" ["Martyr Avini's autobiography"], Shahid Avini General Cultural and Religious Website, www.aviny.com/Aviny/Autobiography.aspx.

in their work to mobilize the disenfranchised poor as a force with revolutionary impetus. A second group, mostly nativist and concerned with Iran's Persian-Islamic cultural authenticity, resent Pahlavi modernization for corrupting national identity, language, and art with materialism, commercialization, and bad Western influence. Parviz Kimiavi's satirical fiction, *O.K. Mister* (1978), produced months before the revolution, epitomizes this second lineage: After the discovery of oil and the arrival of British figures, the idyllic life of a remote village succumbs to the alienating seduction by Western commodities, to such an extent that the villagers eventually forget their own language and become grotesque hybrids of neither-this-nor-that culture. Before *O.K. Mister*, Kimiavi, who was a key figure in Iranian "New-Wave" cinema, made a number of films, including documentaries such as *O Deer Savior* (*Ya Zamen-e Ahu*, 1971), which advocated nativist ideas by celebrating religious rituals and Persian-Islamic mysticism (*erfan*) as cornerstones of Iran's authentic identity. Like most other artists in the second group, Kimiavi's avant-garde nativism had a romantic undertone. His *modernist* form was at odds with his celebration of Islamic culture as *traditional* culture.[26] It was in contrast to both these leftist and nativist groups that Avini found political Islam to be an empowering alternative. As Khosrokhavar's previously mentioned interviews with young Hezbollahis in 1980 demonstrate, Khomeini's supporters considered him a modern figure who revolted against the traditional institution of clergy. His political Islam, for them, was a new kind of Islam which advocated revolution, and was, therefore, "related to freedom and not to community and tradition."[27] This was what enabled Avini to account for the agency of the poor, on the one hand, and to disentangle Islam from the obsolete logic of tradition, on the other. Unlike the localized, bucolic, and inert Islam of the nativists, Khomeini's Islam was an equal match for the dynamic modernism of Avini's form.

---

[26] Understanding prerevolutionary malaise in terms of a dichotomy between (good) tradition and (invasive/illegitimate) modernity was a ubiquitous trope among Iranian intellectuals during the 1960s and 1970s. Ali Mirsepassi has dealt with this trope and its contradictions extensively. See Ali Mirsepassi, *Iran's Quiet Revolution: The Downfall of the Pahlavi State* (Cambridge: Cambridge University Press, 2019).

[27] Khosrokhavar, "Attitude of Teenage Girls," 397.

The fusion between Khomeini's modern understanding of Islam and the prerevolutionary discourse that criticized Western modernity as alienating, materialist, and godless led Avini to reformulate the dichotomy between tradition and modernity in a decisively new manner. Instead of an opposition between *particular* native culture that was threatened by *universal* modernity, he argued that the opposition between Islam and modern civilization was nothing less than a new manifestation of the eternal opposition between good and evil, between prophet and devil: "it was God's wisdom to create both."[28] This, according to Avini, was an opposition of two parallel universals, which were in productive clash with each other. In his films and writings, Avini methodically associates Islam with war and political mobilization, which is different from prerevolutionary filmmakers' imaging of Islam as an element of Iran's national culture. For him, Islam is not a historically intact reservoir of meaning, which would always already be available to assuage modern alienation. Nor does he suppose Islam to give disenchanted modern life a new sense of meaning – Avini doesn't believe that modernity's ailments could be cured by Islam. The clash between the two is eternal, and it is thanks to this clash that Islam remains relevant and alive.

Comparing the young Hezbollah activists with previous generations who experienced Mossadegh's fall through an Anglo-American coup, Khosrokhavar observes that "[t]his youth does not feel humiliated by Western or any other hegemonic power." In the 1960s and 1970s, Iranian artists and intellectuals were in constant dialogue (virtual, via print media, and actual, through travels) with their European and Third-Worldist counterparts. They understood modern art as a universal quest and positioned themselves within its cosmopolitan network. Yet, a degree of provincialism constantly overshadowed their cosmopolitan aspirations: their subject matter remained either objectified (Shirdel et al.) or restricted to locality (Kimiavi et al.). Sanctioned by

---

[28] Avini, *Aghazi bar yek pyan*, 163. As Talal Asad has argued, "In medieval theology, the overriding antinomy was between 'the divine' and 'the satanic' (both of them transcendent powers) or 'the spiritual' and 'the temporal' (both of them worldly institutions), not between a supernatural sacred and a natural profane." Talal Asad, *Formations of the Secular: Christianity, Islam, Modernity* (Stanford, CA: Stanford University Press, 2003), 32. Avini's universalism entails reformulating anti-colonial politics in terms of a medieval understanding of theology.

political Islam, Avini took the cosmopolitan debates of the 1960s and 1970s one step further and turned the cultural dialogue into a battle-field. For him, if modern technological cinema was a universally valid medium, so was the human divine nature. The relationship between these two, according to Avini, was not that of form and content, rather the clash of two forms.[29] As we will see, his understanding of Islam as a universal revolutionary form (rather than a cultural particularity or a content) transferred the cosmopolitan legacy of modern art to the universalist cause of the global jihad.

Political Revolution and the Awakening of Nature

Since 9/11 and the Global War on Terror, scholars such as Faisal Devji and Darryl Li have spoken of jihad in terms of universalism.[30] Avini's work and, by extension, the rest of the Hezbollahis of his generation, are different from the twenty-first-century jihadists that Devji and Li study, insofar as the historical context of the 1979 revolution differs from that of al-Qaeda. Recent jihadist movements developed in the globalized post-Soviet political and economic landscape, and responded to a new transnational dynamic of exchange and migration. Khomeini's political Islam, by contrast, emerged out of the anti-colonial nationalisms of the post-WWII era. In this context, Avini's articulation of Islamist universalism unfolded through his inquiry into the nature of modernization and the national project of economic justice. His notion of jihad was global but organically intertwined with the politics of national development and the disenfranchised poor's uprisings. The philosophical mediation that made the organic inter-twinement of a global scope and a national project possible was not necessarily Islamic, rather inspired by Heideggerian existentialism.

One of his early works, *With Jihad's Doctor in Bashagard* (*Ba Doctor-e Jahad dar Bashagard*), an episode from the series *Lost in Forgotten Land* (*Gomghashteh-haye Diar-e Faramoushi*), set in one of the most deprived and isolated areas near Iran's southeast border in

---

[29] Morteza Avini, "Hekmat-e sinema" ["Philosophy of cinema"], *Farabi* 18 (Bahar 1372/Spring 1993): 6–19.

[30] Faisal Devji, *Landscapes of the Jihad: Militancy, Morality, Modernity* (Ithaca, NY: Cornell University Press, 2005); and Darryl Li, *The Universal Enemy: Jihad, Empire, and the Challenge of Solidarity* (Stanford, CA: Stanford University Press, 2019).

Figure 11.2 Stills from the opening sequence of Morteza Avini's *Lost in Forgotten Land*. Frame enlargement.

Hormozgan, is an illustrative example (Figure 11.2). The film begins with a close shot of a gravedigger, an old man in a white scruffy shirt who toils through the stony soil with what appears to be a crowbar. On the horizon, a group of younger men approach. They carry the body of a fellow-villager over a flat, make-shift coffin. As the camera zooms in and the group fills up the frame, the image freezes and the title emerges in Nasta'liq writing: *Lost in Forgotten Land*. The villagers are burying the man, while the cameraman asks who will be providing for his wife now that he is dead.

"Provide for his wife?" one of the men ponders. "God?" He hesitantly continues.

"Does she have a family?"

"They have nothing, no country, no possession, no money, the poor wretched have nothing."

The camera pans to the right and we see a lone woman, presumably the wife, entirely wrapped in black chador, weeping over the fresh grave.

Highlighting the conditions of life in an area neglected by the central government, Avini's film can be read as revolutionary propaganda against the previous regime and its uneven distribution of wealth and infrastructures. This is confirmed by the film's narrative structure, which rotates around the figure of a young medical student working for Jahad-e Sazandegi (literally: "jihad for development" or "construction jihad").[31] Avini's doctor embarks on a journey throughout the villages of eastern Hormozgan, where small and disjointed communities live in rudimentary wicker tents and survive on date seed flour. He listens to them, examines their illnesses, and offers medicine and health advice. However, while Avini does not hesitate to applaud the doctor's (and the revolutionary government's) service, his main protagonists remain the villagers: it is they who offer an alternative to modern civilization's alienation from divine truth. They have no belonging to this earthly life. Time, so valued by the middle classes in Tehran who are obsessed with progress, means nothing to them except, in Avini's words, "hand-grinding date seeds to make a bread of sickness and hoariness for children."

Like Shirdel, Avini is an educated savior who is disillusioned about educated saviors: there is no amount of medical care by Jahad's doctor that can hoist these people out of the circle of illness and death. "This man who is speaking with the doctor died," Avini's voice narrates, interrupting a conversation between the doctor and a villager. Yet, unlike Shirdel, Avini sees an unprecedented opening for a new worldview in the failure of Jahad's doctor – that is, the failure of modernization. That failure twists the film's plot in an unanticipated direction. Acknowledging the futility of Jahad against injustice, starvation, and poverty, Avini welcomes death: "What a kind and amiable friend death is," his narrative commentary continues, taking the form of an internal monologue, "but *you* have forgotten this." Cut to the gravedigger of the opening sequence, now working deep inside a grave as deep as his entire height. At this moment in Avini's film, economic underdevelopment finds existential salvage and becomes the condition for a new universalism; a perceptive that, as we will see, was inspired by Avini's Islamist reading of Heidegger.

The marginalized poor, in Avini's account, are the ultimate political subjects not merely because of their fight against injustice, but also because they experience life as a constant encounter with death. That is how Avini sees them confronting modern civilization at an existential level. By invoking the finality of earthly life and eventual unification

---

[31] Jahad-e Sazandegi was an Islamic revolutionary organization of volunteer doctors, engineers, and teachers established immediately after the revolution in response to Khomeini's call for a jihad/mobilization to improve conditions of poverty, illiteracy, and destitution in rural areas.

with God, Avini underscores the existentialist significance of their status as outsiders to the progressive temporality of development. For these people, unlike for the middle-class urbanites, there is no peaceful habitation in the world: "The poor wretched have nothing," Avini tells us, and therein lies the secret of overcoming the anxieties of modernity. From their standpoint, crises of modernity are not to be overcome; crisis *is* life and life is being death-aware, *marg-agah* – a term inspired by Heidegger's being-toward-death that Avini frequently used.[32]

With Jihad's Doctor has two endings, or, to be precise, an ending and a coda. First, the crew leave the doctor to continue his journey through isolated villages on a donkey's back. Over still photographs of ill people and their pitiful conditions Avini bids farewell to this place: "We left ourselves in Bashagard while we moved on. We found what was lost in a forgotten land, as if a little fire that was still running at the heart of our soul's darkness was waiting for us to wake up and remember it. Now we were awakened ..." The film ends here. And then it begins again with a very different kind of image: a colorful shot of a Tehrani woman walking in front of a row of larger-than-life prints of prerevolutionary film celebrities: icons of urban leisure. This is followed by a jewelry shop's window display, and a clean-shaven man in sunglasses taking a long drag on his cigarette. Spaces of middle-class pleasure and consumption are mixed with images of young revolutionaries mounting political statements on city walls.[33] And finally Avini chimes in again:

We return to Tehran ... and fear overcomes us. Did all that we saw take place in a dream? And is this [Tehran] what it means to be awake? No! When we set our eyes on the billboard of a greedy man eating a sausage sandwich, we see beyond it Zeinab, the girl whose bowl contains nothing more than a dough of date seed flour. This means that we have been *awakened* and our

---

[32] Avini's investment in combining Heideggerian phenomenology of death with Islam finds parallel in the work of Egyptian philosopher Abd al-Rahman Badawi (1917–2002). As Yoav Di-Capua has argued, philosophers like Heidegger taught Badawi that "death is not simply an event that happens by the end of one's life, but an experience that shapes one's entire way of being and, especially, illuminates the condition of authenticity upon the eventual encounter with death itself." Yoav Di-Capua, *No Exit: Arab Existentialism, Jean-Paul Sartre and Decolonization* (Chicago, IL: University of Chicago Press, 2018).

[33] The film was made in 1981, before the final suppression of Mujahedin and other political groups in Tehran, yet this brief visual, edited alongside images of urban "neglectful" life, is enough to indicate Avini's contempt for political confrontations in the capital.

witness is the image of Imam [Khomeini], the only light in the dark hovel of
the Bashagard old woman, shining like a wakeful consciousness [*vejdan*].
No, Bashagard is no longer a land for forgetting.

Through Avini's cinematic editing and linguistic maneuvering,
Bashagard turns from a passive, forgotten land (the perspective of those
concerned with economic development) to a source of awakening and
spiritual enlightenment. The gravedigger who opens the film and the
sausage-greedy jewelry shoppers of Tehran represent for Avini the two
poles of awareness and neglect (*gheflat*): religious unity and modern
alienation. In the film's coda, the two pillars of Avini's political thought
(Khomeini's unification of political and spiritual leadership, and the
death-awareness of the marginalized poor) find cinematic representation
in the Bashagard woman's hovel. At the same time, while elements of
prerevolutionary urban lifestyles can still be found in the streets of
Tehran in 1980, Avini makes a rare use of them in his film to visualize
his philosophical view of modern civilization as urban leisure and
alienation from God. In so doing, he superimposes his attack against
the ancien régime onto a general critique of modern materialism.

Avini was inspired by an Islamist-Heideggerian lineage in Iran's philosophical and political thought, handed down to him by Ahmad Fardid
(1910–1993) and his intellectual disciple Reza Davari Ardekani (b. 1933).
These thinkers argued that today's world is entirely unified under the
dominance of a modern, technological civilization, and its unity is internally undivided: You cannot pick and choose from Western modernity; it
comes at you in its totality. Their Heideggerian notion of oneworldedness
rejected a common approach among Iranian intellectuals of the 1960s and
1970s who believed in a practical divide between a Western material world
and an Eastern spiritual one. Fardid and his followers argued that today
there exists only one world, and that world is dominated by the substitution
of God with an autonomous humanist subject (*suje-ie khod-boniad-e
Omanisti*). Those in search of an authentic life, according to Islamist-
Heideggerians, had to first accept the fact that the world they inhabit is
entirely under the banner of idolatry (*taghoot*). If it is to be vanquished, this
globalized idolatry requires an equally global revolution.[34]

---

[34] For a direct Fardidian take on the Islamic Revolution, the oneworldedness of the
globe, and Fardidian critique of Eastern spirituality, see Reza Davari Ardekani,
Enqelab-e eslami va vaz'e konooni-e aalam [The Islamic Revolution and the
current state of the world] (Tehran: Mehr-e Newsha, 1388/2009 [1982]).

Fardid creatively translated the modern notion of subject (Kant's transcendental "I") into the Islamic notion of *nafs* (self-centered and sinful ego), who tempts man to deny subservience to God. Avini wants us to read images of urban middle-class leisure in prerevolutionary Tehran as evidence of *nafs*/modern subjectivity dominating human relations. According to him, the Islamic Revolution departs from other political events of modern history precisely because of the break it offers from the sovereignty of the modern subject. In an article called "Islam or Republicanism," he writes:

Other revolutions in today's world took place based on the political form of humanism. Or, like the Chinese and the Russian revolutions, had a socialist identity. Or originated from the ideology of nationalism. Theoretically speaking, these revolutions were caused by political forms of humanism so, completely naturally, after their victory, they resulted in one of the few familiar governance systems of today's world ... But what was at the origin of the Islamic Revolution of Iran?[35]

Avini's response to this question is crucial for understanding both the singularity *and* the global significance of the Iranian Revolution in his view. The originator of the Islamic Revolution, Avini insists, cannot be located in people's economic or political discontent (although that is an initiating factor), but in a much deeper event of religious awakening: the people's revolt against their own *nafs* (subjectivity), and in their return to *nafs*'s antidote, *fetrat*, or human divine nature. This is another concept that Avini inherits from prerevolutionary intellectual debates.

In the context of rapid social and scientific transformations of the 1960s and 1970s, *fetrat* was conceptualized in Iran by religious intellectuals as a source of stability (*sabet*), in a world otherwise determined by constant change (*motoghayyer*). In the late 1960s, Seyyed Hossein Nasr, a scientist and scholar of Islamic thought, articulated *fetrat* as follows:

Some people who find everything in transformation have lost touch with stable values ... This is strange, because ... nature, over thousands of years of human history, has not changed. ... Humans have also not changed fundamentally ... No matter how much their conception of themselves and their environment changes, their position in the world remains the same: blocked between two infinites and two unknowns that are their beginning

---

[35] Avini, "Islam or Republicanism?" in *Aghazi*, 81–82.

and end. Their deep nature is also the same nature that [at the dawn of creation] responded to God's question, "Am I not your Lord?" by saying: "Yes! We testify to that."[36]

In this passage, Nasr invokes the Qur'anic narrative of creation to posit a constantly stable "deep nature" in all humans, one that always already testifies to the Lord. According to Nasr, this human divine nature (*fetrat*) is obscured in today's world, because "man, who used to always maintain a connection with the world of spiritual meanings … is now preoccupied with passing shadows of the world, with material and earthly life." Nonetheless, Nasr is convinced that, despite man's false preoccupations, "the message of religion will always make sense to him/her" in accordance to the divinity of his/her nature.[37]

By framing modern anxieties of change and disenchantment in terms of "passing shadows," Nasr is able to offer his reader a solid ground of stability through spiritual connection. Set against the backdrop of Pahlavi modernization in Iran, his discourse provides a counterbalance to social and political discontent. He helps individuals ward off the external world, merely by not engaging it. If the poor, in Shirdel's film, are unable to act in a socially meaningful way to change their condition, the middle classes, according to Nasr, have only to resign from the world of action in order to reach God-given inner peace. In contrast to Avini, Nasr assumes a divorce between Islam and modernity. His "traditional" Islam is impervious to "modern" civilization, insulating *fetrat* from modern subjectivity.[38]

While Nasr remains a quintessentially conservative thinker and a supporter of the Pahlavi monarchy, Avini argues that *fetrat* would not be accessible without serious engagement with the material world through a political revolution. The revolution is *jahani*, not only in the sense of being global (because it opposes the globality of modern civilization) and universal (because it is Islamic), but the revolution is also *jahani* because it is worldly (*in-jahani*). Without a revolutionary

[36] Seyyed Hossein Nasr, *Ma'aref-e eslami dar jahan-e mo'aser* [Islamic sciences in the contemporary world] (Tehran: Elmi Farhangi, 1388/2009 [1969, repr. 1974]), 241–242.

[37] Ibid., 243–244. Nasr's conception of nature is similar to nineteenth-century liberal thought, but depoliticized. See Asad, *Formations of the Secular*, 57.

[38] I put tradition and modernity in scare quotes to indicate Nasr's own terminology. See Seyyed Hossein Nasr, *Traditional Islam in the Modern World* (London and New York: Kegan Paul International, 1987).

engagement with the material world, Avini believes, *fetrat* would not be available to us. Only an awakened *fetrat* can clash with modern subjectivity. Avini's conceptualization of the dialectic between change and stability from an Islamic point of view clarifies his departure from Nasr's model:

> Man's historical transformation is not possible unless through a revolution. Those who refuse to accept this theory have investment in the status quo. Inside every man, there is a desire for habitation/stability [*mandan*] and another desire for going/departure/death [*raftan*], and the latter is stronger. Yet, man is susceptible to his/her habits [*aadaat*] and gets used to habitation/ stability, therefore, historical transformation is impossible without a revolution. Revolution is a sudden and unexpected change that overthrows all past habits ... The deeper and more expansive the sphere of habits, the bigger the revolution that is needed to free man's soul from its shackles. And the deeper and more expansive the habit of habitation and stability, the stronger the pain of departure and revolution.[39]

The opposition, for Avini, is not between tradition (stability) and modernity (change), but between belonging and movement, between habitation and departure. More importantly – and this dimension of Avini's thinking is both representative of Hezbollah *and* truly revolutionary in Iran's intellectual history – he pins Islam not to habitation and stability, but to revolution and movement, radically subverting common association of modernity with change. Substituting the modernity-tradition dichotomy with an opposition of revolution vs. habitation (*enqelab o esteghrar*), Avini argues that behind the ever-changing appearance of modern civilization, there is a false promise of worldly belonging, which fails *fetrat*'s desire to leave this world and unify with God. "For man, habitation is in lack of habitation, because for human [divine] nature 'the habitat' [*dar ol-gharar*] is only in a heaven external to this world," Avini writes. "No matter how deceptive this world can briefly be, it cannot stop human nature from its eventual spiritual departure."[40]

---

[39] Avini interchangeably uses *mandan*, *gharar*, and *esteghrar*, all of which I translate here as habitation/stability, hoping that something of the nature of Avini's Heideggerian language transfers through the word choice. Avini, "The Beginning to an End," 157.

[40] Ibid.

Both Nasr and Avini suggest returning to nature as a way to God, but Nasr defines nature as the site of stable laws, while Avini's vision of nature is essentially violent and riddled with conflict: "creation and revolution refer to the same meaning: the truth of divine nature is rupture. Just as a seed ruptures so that a sprout emerges from its inside ... revolution and burst are also concomitant: a shell breaks so that it blooms. Burst, bloom, and blossom. It is as such that the world renews/modernizes [*tajdeed*] itself, and so does man."[41] Yet again, we encounter a linguistic twist in Avini's writing, playing with two synonymous words, *tajdeed* and *tajaddod*, the latter of which has been traditionally employed in Persian as an equivalent for modernity. Thus, Avini interprets the rupture-inducing experience of modernity as an equivalent of natural renewal, and reclaims this experience for Islam.

In doing so, Avini also manages to maintain the duality between good and evil without denying modernity its universal omnipotence. "Habits [*aadaat*] corrupt every practice, including worship [*ebadat*]," Avini asserts. "The wisdom behind the creation of Satan in the world is that [thanks to Satan seducing believers], the believer constantly renews his/her practice in relation to the true meaning of that practice, and therefore avoids entrapment in habits. The Devil is tasked with instigating doubt, and although doubts disturb the foundation of belief, they also strengthen conviction. Without doubts, how can conviction be achieved? Without the night, how can the truth of light be reached?"[42] As the naturalizing metaphor of day vs. night affirms, for Avini good and evil are opposing poles, but they are also dialectically interdependent. One cannot manifest itself without the other. God created both. Table 11.1 summarizes the dialectic of two universals in Avini's theory.

Defining the universality of modern civilization as "satanic," Avini seeks a universal revolution against it, which returns us to the quotation in the beginning of this chapter: "A global revolution (*enqelab-e jahani*) is unavoidable for today's man, because today's civilization has inevitably acquired global expansion."[43] The Islamic Revolution, for him, indicates a beginning to that end.

---

[41] Avini, "Renewal and Modernization," in *Aghazi*, 164.   [42] Ibid., 163–164.
[43] Avini, "The Begining to an End," 157–158.

Table 11.1 *Morteza Avini's theorization of the Islamic Revolution in key binary concepts*

Good	Evil
Islam	Modernity
Change	Stability
Revolution	Status quo
Human divine nature (*fetrat*)	Autonomous subject (*nafs*)
Culture	Civilization
Departure	Habitation
Worship (*ebadat*)	Habit (*aadat*)
Conviction	Doubt
Day/light	Night/darkness
Spiritual enlightenment	Humanist enlightenment
Death	Life

Conclusion: Ambition and Frustration

In her final judgment about Pahlavi land reform, Hegland asserts that during the revolution Iranian people "were reacting not so much against modernization as against insufficient or uneven modernization. Why should other, richer Iranians have so much more of it than they did? Inequitable modernization kindled resentment."[44] Similarly, Ervand Abrahamian has argued that the Pahlavis pursued a flawed project in which modernization was deprived of its political dimensions including democratic institutions and social justice, and therefore it was susceptible to collapse.[45] In contradistinction to these thinkers, Avini strongly believes that the problem with the Pahlavi project does *not* lie in it being insufficiently modern for a sufficient number of people but in the modern idea of development itself – in technological modernity's secular, progressive temporality, which reduces life to a denial of death and a neglect of God. His anti-developmentalist streak put Avini at odds with the mainstream of anti-colonial nationalist thought, and ultimately created friction between him and the Islamic Republic's administration.

[44] Hegland, *Days of Revolution*, 1.
[45] Ervand Abrahamian, "Structural Causes of the Iranian Revolution," *MERIP Reports* 87 (May 1980): 21–26.

As early as 1986, in response to plans for postwar reconstruction, Avini wrote a series of articles in Jahad-e Sazandegi's monthly magazine that conveyed a biting critique. Collectively titled "An Islamic Inquiry into Development and the Foundations of Western Civilization," the articles questioned the idea of the developmentalist state as a model for Islamic governance: "The goal of the Islamic government in fighting poverty is to achieve social justice, but does that equate economic development?" For Avini, the idea of economic development reduced humans to a labor force, rendering human divine nature socially and politically irrelevant.[46] Avini's ideas were so controversial that even the editors of *Jahad* distanced themselves from him, emphasizing the personal nature of Avini's opinions. Yet, Avini deserves credit for dealing with a key contradiction in the revolutionary project from inside the Hezbollah ideology, and his voice is representative of a broader disillusionment that defined the Hezbollah movement after the war. This contradiction can be summarized as follows: Like liberal, socialist, and anti-colonial revolutions the world over, Khomeinism, as the ideology of Hezbollah, also made a claim to universality. However, its universal claim refused the two existing modern political forms of universality – the nationalist state and the idea of citizen-subject; and the developmentalist state and the model of proletarianization. In distinguishing itself from other revolutions of the modern period, Khomeinism's claim to universality was based on a religious conviction: that all humans are universally convertible to Shia Islam and that, deep inside them, there is a human divine nature which can respond to the revolution's call as long as they overcome modernity's alienation. In other words, for Avini and other Khomeinists, the revolution was global not because it followed an already existing global model of governance, but precisely because of the singularity of the politics it perused in a world otherwise determined by capitalist modernity. This universalism was "a question of aspiration, not a claim of empirical reality."[47] It was a universalism without universality. The question, then,

---

[46] Morteza Haghgoo, "Tose'e va mabani-e tamaddon-e gharb" ["Development and the foundations of Western civilization"], *Jahad* 104 (Azar and Dey 1366/November–December 1987), 28 and 31. Morteza Haghgoo was one of Avini's numerous pen names. This series of articles were posthumously collected into a book: *Tose'e va mabani-e tamaddon-e gharb* [Development and the foundations of Western civilization] (Tehran: Vaheh, 1387/2008).

[47] Li, *The Universal Enemy*, 12. I owe the distinction between universalism and universality to Li.

remained: How was one supposed to eradicate poverty and restore social justice for the marginalized poor without recourse to a degree of capitalist integration? After writing twenty articles on this score, Avini still failed to provide a convincing answer. The twentieth part of his series of articles in *Jahad* magazine ends with the promise of further explication in the next issues, but the series stops there without further explanation.

"Revolution is a sudden and unexpected change that overthrows all past habits," Avini wrote in 1992, "therefore, it cannot find a permanent form. 'Permanent revolution' is a sweet dream, but unattainable. Life in itself entails habitation, peace, security, and foresight. Man's life entails habits that invite habitation/stability [*mandan*], whereas revolution is passage/migration [*kooch*]."[48] These sentences read tragically in Avini's oeuvre. After the Iran-Iraq War and the coinciding death of Ayatollah Khomeini in 1989, many Hezbollahis were disenchanted about the political limits of their project. It was no longer possible for the revolutionary government to postpone its integration in capitalism's global order without significant loss of legitimacy. "The war that was imposed on us overwhelmingly," Avini lamented, "prevented the ideal horizon of our movement from being blocked by 'the utopia of development.'"[49] With the war ending, the battle over the claim to representing the people, which he once considered won, was open to contestation once again. Moreover, Avini had managed to articulate an alternative universalism to modernity at the expense of a constant mobilization of the disenfranchised. That formula was also no longer sustainable as war mobilizations ended and the state turned to a developmentalist plan (*tose'e*) for economic reconstruction (*sazandegi*).

Yet, as an alchemist of political Islam and avant-garde modernism, Avini brought to the fore some of the most pressing questions of Iran's intellectual history since the 1960s and carried them over to the revolutionary years of the 1980s. Through Khomeini's political Islam, Avini found a way to overcome the polarized debate between universal modernity and particular cultural identity (so-called tradition). He left a prolific body of work that is a window to the mentality of his Hezbollah generation. For him and for other Hezbollahis, Khomeini liberated Islam from the framework of tradition, and transferred

[48] Avini, "The Begining to an End," 157.
[49] Avini, "Gerdab-e Sheitan" ["Satan's whirlpool"], in *Aghazi*, 37.

political categories of particularization such as nativism, traditionalism, and nationalism into a new model of universalist aspiration.
Avini's idea of *enqelab-e jahani* (global revolution) combined the
legacy of prerevolutionary political, artistic, and philosophical debates
and culminated in what he considered to be the revolution's radical
critique of modern civilization – that is, the decentering of the urban,
middle-class subject through the disenfranchised poor's proximity to
death. This critique was, of course, inseparable from a mythologization
of poverty and thus ultimately thwarted its own attempt to center the
disenfranchised as the political subject of the revolution. Yet it is only
by emphasizing his critical significance that we can recognize the
magnitude of Avini's ideological function in state power after the
revolution and understand the extent to which his voice was representative of the hopes and aspirations, as well as the ultimate frustration
and disillusionment, of an entire generation who believed in
Khomeini's promise of an authentic liberated life.

12 | Planetarity:
The Anti-disciplinary Object of Iranian Studies

NEGAR MOTTAHEDEH *

For the fields in which my work intervenes, among them, cinema studies, Iranian studies, and comparative literature, the category of "translation" seems best suited to evoke the notion of "the world," and its corresponding senses, *monde*, *Welt*, *dunya*, in the titular Global 1979. I am, in part, thinking here of the centrality of translation in the wide circulation of reinterpreted and adapted international revolutionary songs and chants in the course of the 1978–1979 Iranian Revolution (e.g. *The International*, *El Pueblo Unido* (translated as *Bar Pa Khiz*)); the translation of Leninist and Maoist literature and of the handbooks that mapped stages of the socialist revolution and those of guerrilla warfare for agitators; the dubbing and subtitling of revolutionary films (*The Battle of Algiers*); the dubbing of interviews in news clips and reports from the streets and squares of the Iranian mass uprising for television; and the coming together of collectives to prepare and translate talks by prominent visitors, such as Kate Millett, and the newspaper articles and thought pieces written by her and others, in particular the French philosopher Michel Foucault, who would initially publish his writings on the Iranian Revolution in the Italian newspaper *Corriere della serra*, before having these translated into his native French. In all of these, a form of translation, one could say "an activist translation" of sorts, articulates the perforated threshold between the self and the other in the rich encounter of the Iranian Revolution with the world. In all these instances, too, it is translation that is "a vital clue to where the self loses its boundaries" as literary theorist Gayatri Chakravorty Spivak

* I am grateful to Maryam Alemzadeh, Arash Azizi, Arash Davari, Jane Gaines, Jason Goldfarb, Arang Keshavarzian, Ranjana Khanna, Ali Mirsepassi, Manijeh Moradian, Bita Mousavi, Golbarg Rekabtalaie, Austin Sarfan, Naghmeh Sohrabi, Hamed Yousefi, and my fellow Global 1979 workshoppers for nudging me in ever-new directions in my attempt to understand the work of the French feminists and their film on the March 1979 women's protests in Iran.

reflects, and in this act of fluidity transgresses from the traces of the other in "the closest places of the self."[1]

Yet, so much of the encounter between Iran and the world has been fixed and sedimented over time by the two overarching theoretical concepts arising from within my disciplines: "Orientalism," on the one hand, and "Westoxification," on the other, which though admittedly imaginative, compose a wholesale rejection of the lessons of that encounter with the world, as one that is at once sweeping, exoticizing, and ill-informed. Is this hallucinatory toxicity the only potentiality that is unleashed in the encounter with the world in the revolutionary years? Or have these terms, "Orientalism" and "Westoxification," once useful, become reified and lazy shorthands for a critical engagement with an encompassing planetary history in which all three disciplines have a stake?

While Ali Shariati's translation of the Martiniquan psychoanalyst Franz Fanon into Persian and the translation of Italian journalist Oriana Fallaci's 1970s interviews with the shah and ayatollah into a myriad of languages, along with the reflections of Foucault on the Iranian Revolution, may be among the most prominent instances of such acts of translation in the course of the revolutionary years, my own thinking turns to an almost forgotten, small band of French journalists and filmmakers who joined the iconic American feminist Kate Millett in Tehran – a group much overshadowed by her presence, but one that left one of the most remarkable historical documents of Iran's encounter with the world in the period immediately after the fall of the Iranian monarchy and the return from exile of Mohammad Reza Shah's bête noire, the ayatollah, Ruhollah Khomeini.

Known as the Psych et Po (from Psychanalyse et Politique), a radical feminist research group, and publishing venue within the nascent women's liberation movement in France (MLF),[2] the group came to Iran between March 8 and 18, 1979, to join in solidarity with the Iranian women's movement. French feminist and psychoanalyst Antoinette Fouque, who was at the helm of the movement, was a friend of Millett, and a comrade. She had initially promised to meet the American feminist in Tehran on March 8 for the celebration of

---

[1] Gayatri Chakravorty Spivak, *Outside the Teaching Machine* (New York: Routledge, 1993), 179.

[2] Antoinette Fouque, *There Are Two Sexes: Essays in Feminology*, trans. David Macey and Catherine Porter (New York: Columbia University Press, 2016), 202.

"Freedom is neither western nor eastern but universal."

Figure 12.1 "I will say it in every moment / I'll say it under torture / Either death or freedom! / Freedom is neither Eastern nor Western. It is planetary!"

International Women's Day, but would instead send as proxies, the journalist Claudine Mulard, who was also the person responsible for the publishing branch of the movement, Des Femmes, and Sylvina Boissonnas, the heiress of the Schlumberger family under whose patronage the movement ran their independent bookstore, a feminist journal, and a minor feminist film unit.

On the afternoon of March 11, 1979, faced with a roomful of journalists gathered at the InterContinental Hotel at the only press conference in which the French feminists appeared in Tehran, Boissonnas would move to introduce the international group of feminists to the journalists in French, and after inquiring about the need for translation, would continue in English to issue the group's declaration of solidarity in a gesture of impromptu interpretation for the international press corps: "We are here concretely," she declared, "with our voices, our ears, our bodies – given to the Iranian women." Emphasizing the international character of women's struggles, Boissonnas underscored that: "When Iranian women break their chains, women of the whole world can advance."

This declaration, in its French original, overlays the sound track in the opening sequence of the film produced by the French feminists, as Iranian women are captured by the camera marching, veiled and unveiled, and declaring their freedom with the following chant in Persian (Figure 12.1): "Lahze be lahze goftam / zire shekanje goftam / ya marg ya azadi" ("I will say it in every moment / I'll say it under torture / Either death or freedom!"). The film proceeds from here to document a mass mobilization of Iranian women and girls who

assembled as a force of thousands in the city of Tehran to protect the
freedoms for which they had fought. In interviews with Claudine
Mulard on camera, the film takes stock of Iranian women's
vision for the future and the hopes and experiences that motivated
their struggle.

Drawing on the work of Fouque and the French feminists' remarkable historical record of the protests that took shape around the
International Women's Day celebrations of 1979 in the short film
Mouvement de Libération des Femmes Iraniennes, Année Zéro
(*Liberation Movement of Iranian Women, Year Zero*), my aim in this
chapter is to grapple with the foundations of the embodied solidarity
informing Psych et Po's Tehran visit as Iranian women of every class
came together to claim their freedom in the throes of an anti-imperialist
revolution. While Fouque would reflect on May '68 as her own "birth
into history," recalling this unrest in France as the context in which the
women's liberation process emerged,[3] Boissonnas's declaration, which
opened the press conference in Tehran in French, underscored importantly that women's unfettered participation in the Iranian Revolution
was not the first Third World uprising to inspire the "women of
struggle" who made up her own French feminist corps, "Des luttes
de femmes sont d'emblée international" ("Women's struggles are international from the outset"). For the Psych et Po, the genealogy of the
women's liberation movement was always already international in
scope and planetary in outlook. As we shall see, the movement's very
notion of solidarity could be said to be founded on the interstitial – the
threshold ecology of translation.

Looking to historical sources, it is of course irrefutable that the
Vietnamese Revolution was the expansive foundation for the possibilities that sustained May '68. Vietnam was the translated blueprint for
the May '68 student uprising. It was its undercurrent and inspiration.
This was the French existentialist Jean Paul Sartre's take on the French
scene as well. For, as he argued, if a class of peasants in Vietnam
"could defeat the most powerful military machine in human history,
then anything was possible."[4] While many radicals attempted to capture the articulation of the Vietnamese struggle in the particulars of

[3] Ibid., 201.
[4] Salar Mohandesi, "Bringing Vietnam Home: The Vietnam War,
Internationalism, and May '68," *French Historical Studies* 41:2 (April
2018): 238.

local conditions, inventing expressions like "The university is our Vietnam," committed feminists in France looked to the Vietnamese women as standard-bearers. For they had shed their traditional roles as mothers and caregivers to support the "gentle" revolution in Vietnam.[5] The promise and possibilities of planetary transformation could be gleaned, if we were to believe the French feminists, from the ways in which the Vietnamese women participated in the historical struggle. As one Mouvement de Libération des Femmes flyer explained:

In Vietnam, women do not stay confined to their maternal and domestic role .... They take on, in their own right, constant reconstruction, the defense of villages, or they enlist in the liberation army. They therefore wholeheartedly take part in the fight, whether that means picking up the rifle or taking on responsibilities.
In actively struggling, in the same way as the men, for the liberation of the Vietnamese people, they move toward their own liberation, breaking with the image and the role that until now has been assigned to them: passivity, domestic tasks, the exclusive functions of mother and spouse.

"There is ruin, death, suffering in Vietnam," the flier concluded, but also the seeds of something new: "the laying of the foundations of a new world, liberating women and men."[6] In sum, women had pushed gender boundaries in the revolutionary struggle in Vietnam and it was *this* aspect of their courage, more precisely, that had inspired French feminists who, in due course, translated the triumphs of the Vietnamese women into their own context.[7]

While the uprising of the intellectual and activist circles of May '68 was motivated by the global anti-imperialist revolt set in motion in Vietnam, it was the stance of the men in the May '68 cohort that would ultimately appall the emergent feminist cell. Fouque was, of course, among them. May '68 was transformative, but the uprising on the French scene represented, for her, "a male-dominated revolution." While "[y]oung men threw paving stones ... launched actions and organizations," women, Fouque writes, "were restricted to the mimeograph machine, or even to the bedroom, and could not speak out in

[5] Ibid., 242.
[6] Des groupes du M.L.F., "20 janvier: Journée internationale pour le Vietnam: Des groupes de femmes y participent, voilà pourquoi" (1972?), F Delta Res 151, BDIC; Mohandesi, "Bringing Vietnam Home," 243.
[7] On the question of translating the Vietnamese struggle to local conditions and idioms, see Mohandesi, "Bringing Vietnam Home," 244–245.

meetings. They were not there as sexed persons but as derivative revolutionary subjects, the second sex."[8] It was in this setting that the Vietnamese Revolution provided not only the blueprint but an expansive sense of vision and possibility for the French female activists. Frustrated with this state of affairs at home, Fouque claims to have formed, with Wittig and Josiane Chanel, the Mouvement de Libération des Femmes (MLF) in 1970, a movement consisting of numerous feminist groups and French collectives. "Between May at the Sorbonne and the MLF in October, we went from culture to a fleshly materialism," Fouque recalls, liberating both "pleasure and maternity from enslavement."[9]

A little over a decade after May '68, in the autumn of 1979, and just a few short months after Psyche et Po's Tehran visit, Fouque would register the acronym "MLF" as the trademarked property of her own feminist collective, a gesture of demarcation that would signal her group's radical difference from all other feminist groups in France. There were hints of this distinction as early as that spring in Tehran, when Mulard would remark to the North American feminists in her company that the French feminist group en route to Tehran under Simone de Beauvoir's leadership was not made up of "women of struggle." Eschewing French solidarity, she drew a line in the sand distancing her own group and the late arrivals to Tehran.

The legal takeover of the acronym "MLF," which, until that autumn was the umbrella term used more generally for the feminist movement in France, created a controversy that would visibly splinter the French feminist movement as such. Beauvoir, who had, like Fouque, supported Millett's efforts in Tehran in 1979, and had spoken vehemently on behalf of the Iranian women on several occasions that year,[10] would in response to Fouque's move, publicly denounce Fouque for her acquisition of MLF as the nomenclature of her own feminist organization, horrified that a single group such as Fouque's could claim to speak on behalf of all feminists in France. As one feminist observed, in 1982, in the aftermath of this bloodbath, "If you leave Paris for a couple of months, you need to be briefed on who is on the

---

[8] Fouque, *There Are Two Sexes*, 201.   [9] Ibid., 202 and 204.
[10] See, in particular, Behrooz Ghamari-Tabrizi, *Foucault in Iran: Islamic Revolution after the Enlightenment* (Minneapolis, MN: University of Minnesota Press, 2016); Nima Naghibi, *Rethinking Global Sisterhood: Western Feminism and Iran* (Minneapolis, MN: University of Minnesota Press, 2007).

outs with whom." Freud had a vivid term for these harsh divisions: "a narcissism of minor differences." But what is also foregrounded for me in this breakdown of solidarity amongst the French is the failure of translation.

I mean by this that the uneasy portrait of feminist solidarity in France shows the concept of solidarity for the French movement as crucially entwined with the act of translation. One could even go so far as to say that, historically speaking, the movement was underived from it. Articulated as a movement in contact with the Vietnamese and Algerian revolutions, this originary threshold memory (a memory of contact and exchange with otherness) was reactivated in March 1979 by the courage and passion of the Iranian women, only weeks after the return to Iran of the "undisputed leader of the revolution," Ayatollah Ruhollah Khomeini, from his exile in Neauphle-le-Château. This is evident in the scenes that open the film *Mouvement de Libération des Femmes Iraniennes, Année Zéro* in which the French voiceover enumerates feminist activities in Paris, Bordeaux, Lyon, and Marseilles in conversation with the women's uprising in Iran, highlighting French demonstrations, sit-ins, meetings, and discussions in solidarity. In interview with the only foreign talking-head in the film, Millett, the film also positions the Iranian women as exemplary of what she will consistently refer to as "the most polished feminists in the world," feminists who, moreover, having organized themselves in the midst of a revolution, were facing down the guns and tanks of the most capable military force in the region. Returning home to France with five reels of film from the Iranian women's protests, the Psych et Po was haunted by the ghosts of its originary context, a habitus of translation that was the French movement's own first encounter with the world; its moment of birth. This haunting, which is apparent throughout the film, appears unadorned in the untranslated and therefore unconscious refrain in the Persian *ya marg ya azadi*, in a soundscape of voices that reverberate throughout in the opening sequence of the film. It shows up explicitly in the most powerful chant of the Iranian women's march, *Azadi na sharghist na gharbist, jahanist,* translated by the voiceover with the following: "Freedom is neither Eastern nor Western, it is universal." Cultivated within a gendered landscape and recorded in the film as a clarion call for a planetary liberation, the chant alights French feminist solidarity on its foundations, namely, the threshold of translation.

   This cry, the cry for an unfettered experience of freedom, evolved from a lifetime of compulsion. Khomeini had, from his exile outside of Paris, encouraged Iranian women to take to the streets with their male comrades in anti-shah demonstrations inside Iran. The hope was the overhaul of a repressive regime and a long anticipated emancipation. Khomeini's return home after the shah's departure, however, heralded the vanishing of freedoms for which women had struggled hand-in-hand with men during the course of the revolution. With Khomeini's return, the 1967 Family Protection Act, which made abortion legal and divorce accessible to both men and women in the civil courts, was summarily retracted. Judgments on such matters were strategically transferred to the clerics, whose hunger for booty from the ruins of the monarchy Khomeini was forced to feed. In these early days of revolutionary zeal, the interim government pronounced women "too emotional" to be judges, removing them from the Iranian court system. Khomeini's declaration on March 6, specifying mandatory veiling for all women working in the nation's ministries, came on the heels of this wholesale effacement of women's bodies from the secular public sphere. Khomeini's declaration, which began circulating in the hours that led up to the celebration of International Women's Day, motivated in his supporters the harassment of any and all women who appeared without a head cover on the streets of Tehran. Thus, barely five weeks into Khomeini's return from his political exile in France, women had had enough. Seeing their liberties waning, they flocked to the streets in collective outrage. The planned International Women's Day celebrations of 1979 turned into six days of demonstrations in which Millett and the Psych et Po feminists also participated.

   Beauvoir, who had defended Algerian women in their fight for national liberation a decade earlier, now turned her sights on Iranian women. Iranian women had courageously fought for liberation shoulder to shoulder with their Iranian brothers, but it was now clear that their rights were to take second place. "I have seen many revolutions," Beauvoir maintained, reflecting on the unfolding situation in Iran, "and each time the question of defending women's rights came up, I was told it wasn't the time." "[T]he condition of women as such is in question," she insisted, "and that is what motivates our emotion."[11]

---

[11] Quoted in Marie-Jo Bonnet, "Foucault en Iran: 'Il ne voyait pas les femmes,'" BibliObs, February 16, 2018, https://bibliobs.nouvelobs.com/idees/20180216 .OBS2318/foucault-en- iran-il-ne-voyait-pas-les-femmes.html.

In Tehran, Iranian women eagerly anticipated Beauvoir's arrival in the midst of their protests. The esteemed feminist's rights discourse would add fuel to many of the interviews conducted by the French feminists with the educated among the protestors, students, nurses, teachers, women who would zealously respond to questions the French asked of them, questions about the nature of their demands; about their outrage over the demise of their situation in both English and French. Beauvoir again:

So far, all the revolutions have required women to sacrifice their demands for the success of the action carried out essentially or solely by men. I join Kate Millett's wish. And of all my comrades who are at present in Teheran: let this revolution be an exception; that the voice of this half of the human race, women, be heard. The new regime will also be a tyranny if it ignores their desires and does not respect their rights.[12]

Like her contemporary Fouque, Beauvoir was firm in her conviction regarding the need for an international mobilization in support of the Iranian women. Fouque's psychoanalytic approach, which articulated itself as an "embodied solidarity" represented by her feminist group on the ground in Tehran, struck a deeper, more radical, cord, however.

While Beauvoir had been the voice of feminism for decades before the establishment of the MLF, Fouque would, by the late 1970s, declare the aging feminist passé. Beauvoirian feminism, Fouque maintained, had to be surpassed by a notion of liberation that would take into account a fleshy, materialist, and political stance, one that was rooted in another threshold habitus, the uterus. The Austrian British psychoanalyst Melanie Klein had in the 1950s articulated the uterine as the origionary site of subjectivity. Indeed, she argued, the violence of birth was the threshold experience that necessitated the translation of that orginary scene into the new experience of life. The French psychoanalyst Jacques Lacan, too, having expounded on the Freudian unconscious, had described the pre-subjective drives, those imperceptible energies formative of our conscious subjectivity, as falling upon the "anatomical trace of a margin or border," a threshold habitus, one could say , of the "lips," the "rim of the anus, penile fissure, vagina, fissure of eyelid, indeed hollow of the ear."[13] One could surmise from

---

[12] Ibid.

[13] Jacques Lacan, "The Subversion of the Subject and the Dialectics of Desire in the Freudian Unconscious," in *Écrit*, trans. Bruce Fink (New York: Norton, 2007), 692.

this vantage point, that, as the Bengali linguist and literary theorist Gayatri Chakravorty Spivak argues, "border thinking" or translation is a primary constituent of our conscious perception of reality. Reason, too, is formed on the ground of this undecided threshold element that genealogically precedes it.

It is out of this foundational understanding of the formation of the psyche that Fouque would posit the uterine, indeed, the "hospitality of the flesh," that is, pregnancy and gestation, against the idea of a singular, and emphatically phallic, libido in psychoanalytic theory. Rejecting this latter and largely Lacanian dogma in analytical theory as one that excluded women from the symbolic (an exclusion that would consign the feminine to psychosis in the work of her analyst and teacher, Lacan), Fouque formulated a fleshy materialism that she saw as "the very paradigm of ethics."[14] This stand for the liberation of a fertile female body – a threshold anatomy if there ever were one – one, indeed, that stood as the source for the thinking of an ethical politics, would reach beyond Beauvoirian rights discourse, to correspond in *some* measure to the Third Worldism and anti-imperialism of the women's movement encountered by the Psych et Po in Iran. As Fouque recalled:

In a period when the battles for liberation were taking place through decolonization, my first hypothesis was that women were in a situation analogous to that of colonized peoples, colonized because they possessed wealth ... The appropriation of women's fecundity very quickly struck me as the first cause of their servitude, their exploitation, their enslavement. This colonized dark continent contained a tremendous spiritual, psychic, ethical, and sexual resource, which I called the libido creandi or dark energy, something that cannot be found in the workings of phallocentrism.[15]

It is essentially this, the pronounced Third Worldism (*tiers-mondisme*), that Fouque projected onto the fertile female body that is expressive of the kind of border thinking that I have translated here and elsewhere as "planetarity."[16]

Tiers-mondisme proper was articulated at a time when most European communist movements were stagnating and discredited, a

---

[14] Fouque, *There Are Two Sexes*, 205.   [15] Ibid., 208–209.

[16] Planetarity, as I understand it, drawing on the work of Spivak, is a threshold consciousness which, in its encounter with the world, and underived from it, *translates* the prelinguistic impulses it receives into the formation of the self.

time in which the Third World seemed to offer a renewed hope for the revolutionary project. Third Worldism was, in that regard, the belief in the generative and revolutionary aspirations of the Third World masses. It was, for many Europeans, the utopian hope for the fulfillment of these visionary goals. The Third World's revolutionary fervor stood for many Europeans for that alterity that we each provide as the mark of our (prelinguistic) origin – "mother, nation, god, nature"– a point from which we admittedly emerge, and which we also ultimately disavow.[17] As Fouque would later argue, the dark continent of the fecund female body had, like the Third World, been "colonized by an economy of reproduction," an economy that was both patriarchal and phallocentric. The uterus was the "first colony" of Western domination Fouque proclaimed, and indeed, "the last historically known."[18] Having been a witness to Vietnam, and before that, affected by the anti-colonial struggles in Algeria, Fouque would insist that Third World women were essentially "slaves among slaves, over which the hypercapitalist, rich, and sterile West continue[d] to exert ... domination."[19] Seen in this same originary light, if Iranian women were "breaking their chains" and liberating themselves from slavery to a barren capitalism, they represented a significant advance for women everywhere.

One could, of course, read my reexamination of Fouque's flesh-bound feminist liberation and reclamation from patriarchy in terms of a better understood Third Worldism, one epitomized by Fanon in *Black Skin, White Masks*. In that discussion of the body, Fanon argues that the perception of blackness within the language of the colonizer prevents the black man from being a fellow human: "Ontology ... does not permit us to understand the being of the Black man [*le Noire*]. For not only must the Black man be black; he must be so in opposition to the White man [*en face du Blanc*]." Responding to this self-understanding, Fanon would, as a black Martiniquan in colonial France, "advance a vision of liberation predicated upon embodiment – the immediate presence of the physical bodies that had otherwise been limited by colonial discourse." As Arash Davari explains regarding

---

[17] See Gayatri Chakravorty Spivak, *Death of a Discipline* (New York: Columbia University Press, 2003), 73.
[18] Fouque, *There Are Two Sexes*, 205.   [19] Ibid., 210.

Fanon's return to the body as the site for the engagement with the world as such, that is, its transformation and translation:

> Where the history of language and perception have determined the signifi-
> cance of the colonized's body, restricting and distorting it, the metaphors of
> "life" and "movement" proposed by the notion of a "return" [to the self]
> necessarily take on a corporeal valence for Fanon. The future of the new man
> promises to be grounded in a body that feels – and that can freely move – as
> the basis of its engagement with the world.[20]

Just as "corporeality provided the seeds for a new conception of human recognition and selfhood" in Fanon's *Black Skin, White Masks*, the return to the self in Fouque's work conceived a corporeal turn. In hers it was toward the fecundity of the liberated uterus.[21] "It is the alpha and the omega, the beginning and the end of the humanity," writes Fouque. The uterus "transmits, transforms and evolves." The liberation of the uterus in Fouque, echoing the corporeal in Fanon, was a liberation that was at once a *yes* to life and to the generosity of the flesh and a *no* to the exploitation and the extraction of that which one considers most fundamentally human.[22] "Each gestation returns us back to the origins of life and in that sense, a reinvention of life," Fouque underscores. And this experience "is eminently poetic, creative and ethical." Uterine liberation, as I understand it in Fouque, is gen-erative; generative of not only art, literature, and thought, but of political theory and praxis, as well.

In Fouque's work, a woman's capacity to create a "living-speaking" being (*le vivant-parlant*) positioned her as "creator." The fecund female body was the origin of all humanity. The uterus was not the dark hole of a dark continent as it had been construed in the context of patriarchy, but the originary ground for a new emancipatory ethics which would allow us to think alterity (that of the mother for the child or the child for the mother's body) as underived from the self. For Fouque the uterine libido stood as, at once, the origin and the ground, for a new and emancipatory ethics.

---

[20] Arash Davari, "A Return to Which Self? Ali Shari'ati and Frantz Fanon on the Political Ethics of Insurrectionary Violence," *Comparative Studies of South Asia, Africa and the Middle East* 34:1 (2014): 94.

[21] Ibid., 89.

[22] Frantz Fanon, *Black Skin, White Masks*, trans. Charles Lam Markmann (New York: Grove Press, 1967), 222.

Uterine ethics was an ethics of accompaniment conceived on the threshold habitus both binding and demarcating the self from other, an ethics, that in my reading of Fouque's work would highlight translation as primary to subject formation; translation, indeed, as part and parcel of the pre-subjective drive, that is, before conscious thought, and fundamental to the act of receiving, accepting, and the giving over of oneself to the foreign body of the other. In the process of gestation, the relationship to the other is invented and reinvented over and over in the course of nine months without interruption, Fouque observes.[23] A relationship invented and reinvented, I would like to emphasize, in that doorway between self and other, the threshold topography of translation as such.

This may be why the *libido creandi*, the creative libido, had to be "restored to free, not enslaved, production" in Fouque's decolonizing vision.[24] Arguing against the exclusion of the feminine in psychoanalysis, Fouque would assert that the focus on the phallus and the attribution of penis envy to girls were incongruous with the creative power of the uterus. Indeed for Fouque, in contradistinction of Lacan's theorization of feminine lack in the Symbolic Order, there are two sexes, and neither sex is reducible to the other. This recognition of fundamental irreducibility resolves for Fouque an exclusionary human history, in which women are absent, and in doing so, ultimately leads to a fertile, that is, a creative and just heterosexuality. In my reading of Fouque, then, the liberation and reclamation of fertility and, fundamentally, its cycles are the foundation of a feminist revolution on a planetary scale.

As I have suggested in my reading of the feminist's scattered writings above, Fouque's uterine ethics would not only reinscribe the bordered relationship between the self and the other, but in its attention to the cycle of gestation, would also necessarily establish a different relationship to temporality and transformation. Even as the revolution and rotation of the earth are said to inscribe the sidereal day, and in that sense, the earthbound transformation of day into night, so the fertility cycle of the uterus and the incubation of the human baby in the womb could be said to inscribe the time of civilizational renewal and, in that sense too, the revolutionary transformation of the planet.[25]

---

[23] Antoinette Fouque, "Every Gestation as Reinvention of Humanity," 2012 (afterword to Folio pocket edition of *There Are Two Sexes*, www. antoinettefouque.com/concepts/).
[24] Fouque, *There Are Two Sexes*, 205.   [25] Ibid., 213.

Foundational, this understanding of the cycle of fertility and its temporality could indeed reconcile, in my rereading of Fouque's theoretical frameworks, the oft-opposing poles of nature and nurture, of gentle hospitality and revolutionary insurrection.[26] This spells for me an advancement in our understanding of the individual as one who is underived from its originary origin, and thus closer, at once, to both ecology and planetarity.

The gestation and birth of every child represents a revolutionary transformation of both nature and culture, in that this encounter with the womb and world is an act of translation that is formative of the self and other. The child translates the world and also transforms the world in its encounter with it. Drawing on the work of Fouque, I understand this transformative impulse, which arises from the ground of translation, as the revolutionary impulse that is cultivated in the prelinguistic, namely, the threshold habitus and temporality of the uterine.

These reflections on the planetary consequences of a feminist revolution in Fouque's work situate an entry point for my reading of a particularly rich sequence in the documentary film that her Psych et Po comrades made on the Iranian women's movement immediately after the film crew's return to Paris.

Lasting for a little under a minute, the sequence that best captures the "paradigm of ethics," particular to the Psych et Po, begins at 2 minutes and 47 seconds of screen time. In my reading, this sequence inscribes on celluloid, the fully embodied hospitality of the maternal, one that is given over to the defense and the freedom of the other. As such, this sequence which strikes many audiences as the most mesmerizing sequence of the film *Libération des Femmes Iraniennes, Année Zéro* delivers too, in my reading, the kind of truly revolutionary practice that is inscribed by the logic of the *libido creandi*. It is to this

---

[26] As Fouque insists, "Whereas the time that takes us from childhood to death is a time without generation, women ensure regeneration." To truly understand civilizational change and to conceive of a revolutionary transformation for the planet, a different temporality had to be envisioned. Women, she writes, ensure "the linking of generations in the life drive." This foundational realization of the fertile body's regenerative potency, in Fouque's schematic, revolutionizes our relation to time through the temporality of gestation and reconnects us directly by its means to the ecological and planetary space that we inhabit. Civilizational change is inscribed in the temporality of the *libido creandi* – "the time of fertility." Ibid.

brief sequence that I now turn to understand the ways that the Iranian women's protests articulated themselves for the French feminists who came to Iran in a gesture of "embodied solidarity."[27]

Brief, the sequence consists of four shots. It opens to a shot (Figure 12.2) of a white-veiled woman standing next to two other veiled figures. They stand on a rooftop, presumably high above ground, overlooking the crowd of protesting men and women who are marching from Tehran University toward Azadi Square on the fourth day of the women's protests, March 12, 1979.

The three figures on the rooftop are framed by the snow-clad Alborz mountain range which looms in the background of the shot. The mountain is a "living symbol," as Millett reflects in her book *Going to Iran*, from which many have taken comfort and courage. A symbol of Iran's resistance against despotic and foreign rule, this mountain and the Damavand peek in particular has been significant in Iran's literary tradition and, too, in Persian mythology. Zahak, a mythic three-headed dragon, is said to be chained within the magical mountain, as its protector, depicted as such by the Persian poet Abu'l Qasim Ferdowsi in the *Shahnameh*.

While the image of the three women against the mountain range could be said to reanimate the three-headed dragon's magical presence and its powers of resistance by way of equivalence (or transference, if

---

[27] The short thirteen-minute documentary produced by Des Femmes, *Mouvement de Libération des Femmes Iraniennes, Année Zéro* (*Liberation Movement of Iranian Women, Year Zero*), was filmed on the streets of Tehran by the French feminists Sylvina Boissonnas, an heiress, accomplished filmmaker, and the current head of MLF, Claudine Mulard, Michelle Muller, and Sylviane Rey. Boissonnas, Muller, and Rey joined Kate Millett and Mulard in Iran on March 11 for the press conference on the planned women's march from Tehran University to Azadi Square. The group filmed the march on March 12 as well as the protests at the National Iranian radio and television station on March 13. Boissonnas and Muller left Iran on March 16 immediately after the announcement of Millett's expulsion (presumably on charges of espionage) at Deputy Prime Minister Abbas Amir-Entezam's press conference on the morning of March 15. Boissonnas and Muller left Iran with four rolls of 16 mm film, each about twelve minutes in length. Mulard and Rey stayed in Iran, conducting two further interviews (one of which is set outside of the InterContinental Hotel with Millett). They left on March 18, 1979, with an additional reel of film, consisting of a rare interview with Millett's lesbian Persian-speaking interpreter, Taraneh.

The edited film along with Mulard's voiceover was first screened at La Mutualité shortly after the feminists' return to Paris. A four-minute clip was broadcast on Antenne 2 (French television) a few weeks later.

Figure 12.2 Shot 1.

Figure 12.3 Shot 2.

Figure 12.4 Shot 3.

Figure 12.5 Shot 4.

you prefer), what is most pronounced about the staging of shot 1 is the visually arresting way that the wind perforates the woman's white veil in this cinematographically striking scene. Harboring the wind's powers and underived from its flurries, the veil opens and closes, responsive to the rapid gusts of wind on the rooftop. It is this, admittedly orientalized and indeed nativist, three-headed figure of a perforated veiled organism in the foreground of the mountain range that is cast visually by the film as that body that receives, toward the end of shot 1, the voice of another veiled figure, the voice of Mahboubeh. The white veiled figure is thus situated by the film as opening itself not only to the wind, the "voice of nature," but also to the voice of the other (woman), a voice in staunch demand of freedom.

Dressed in black, this second veiled figure whose voice we hear in shot 1 appears visually in shot 2 (Figure 12.3). Typical of continuity editing, the aural bridge between shots 1 and 2 places the two shots in conversation with one another and, crucially, conveys the meanings and messages of the latter to the former (and vice versa). Mahboubeh's anguished voice is, in this way, embraced and accompanied by the three-headed figure staged in front of the mountain range even before this other appears in the full embodiment of her own voice in shot 2.

The cut to shot 2 shows the viewer that the Mahboubeh is speaking to Mulard about her own fight for freedom (here Mahboubeh's eyeline match anticipates shot 3 (Figure 12.4) in which Mulard appears sitting in the midst of a group of women from various social and economic backgrounds): "We fought for the people's freedom, and our own freedom with and without the veil," Mahboubeh underscores gesticulating vigorously. "We fought shoulder to shoulder with men. We [women] gave martyrs [during the insurrection against the shah] and we are now here for our freedom. If Khomeini continues like this," referring to the leader's recent pronouncements on mandatory veiling, "I, who am a believer, will leave my religion."

In underscoring her embodied participation in the struggle for the freedom of the people, in other words, her gesture of accompaniment and her acceptance of the other's wants as her own, Mahboubeh emphasizes a repeated refrain from the protestors' slogan in the shots that lead up to this four-shot sequence. Her words reiterate the chant (Figure 12.1) that is left untranslated in the film's subtitles and thus remains unconscious to the French film, "Lahze be lahze goftam / zire shekanje goftam / ya marg ya azadi" ("I will say it in every moment/ I'll say it under torture / Either death or freedom!"). Her words, though different in articulation, bring to consciousness a repeated refrain in the language of the other, and inscribe onto the filmic narrative the choice that is voiced by other Iranian women in the demonstrations. In the choice between death or freedom, Mahboubeh sees herself willing to sacrifice the woman she knows herself to be, a religious woman, for a collective freedom deserved by all who have struggled on its behalf: "We fought, with and without the veil, for our freedom. And if Khomeini continues like this, me, a true Muslim, I will quit my religion." As a mother of six daughters, all educated women, she continues her fierce declaration in shot 4 (Figure 12.5), that it is *their* freedom she is here for. "I did not come to the demonstration because I want to stop wearing the chador. I have six daughters, and I came because I do not want them to be forced to wear the chador. I came to defend my daughters against the chador." The sequence of four shots positions Mahboubeh as a figure that willingly sacrifices herself for the freedoms desired by all, underscoring the ethics of hospitality present in Fouque's work on the mother's body. It is this allegorical figure of the mother's body (Figure 12.5), and importantly not the educated, French-speaking rights activists, that the film situates as having the ethical and revolutionary capacity to renew civilization on behalf of all.

The eyeline match to shot 3 establishes Mulard and the Psych et Po as the receivers of the mother's voice (Figure 12.4). As such, the eyeline match corresponds to the sound bridge that connects the three-headed figure on the rooftop in shot 1 (Figure 12.2) to Mahboubeh in shot 2 (Figure 12.3). By focusing the camera on yet another veiled woman (Soghra), in the continuation of shot 3 (Mulard's shot), as Soghra speaks of her willingness to become a *kafir* and also leave her religion, the film reiterates the Iranian women's emancipatory ethics as its own (Figure 12.6). The repeated cutaways to other veiled figures in the midst of the protesting crowd, following this sequence, though at first glance, extradiegetic insertions of a rabid French Orientalist aesthetic into the film, function to remind us as viewers of the Psych et Po's foundational stance on the hospitality of the flesh and the revolutionary potential arising from the ethics of the uterine. These veiled figures, in my reading of the film, in other words, embody a position that stands in stark contrast to the rights discourse espoused by other French feminists and, too, a whole generation of university-educated, English- and French-speaking Iranian woman interviewed throughout

Figure 12.6 "When Iranian women break their chains, women of the whole world can advance."

the film. This latter point is repeated visually and aurally in the allegorical mother's willingness to forgo "the religion of the ancestors" in an embodied defense of the revolution's dream of freedom for all.

The film's emphasis on the Iranian women's rejection of any form of compulsion is reframed in Mulard's interview with Mojgan. At eight minutes of screen time Mojgan, a fourteen-year-old school girl who we come to understand has skipped her classes to join the women's protests (against the instructions of her school's headmistress), beams at Mulard: "I want to be free, I want to speak when I want to, do whatever I want to do ... I want to write what I want to write. My mother agrees with me."

The evocation of Mojgan's revolutionary "mother" who has also joined the women's protests in response to the compulsions against her freedoms by the interim government and now, too, by the violence of Khomeini's ardent supporters situates the demonstrable bravery of the Iranian women. It would seem, indeed, that for the film it is precisely this instance of unfettered resistance to all forms of injustice and compulsion that bears witness to Millett's observations about the characteristics of the Iranian women as "the most polished feminists she has ever seen."[28]

Sitting under a weeping willow, in the garden outside the InterContinental Hotel in Tehran on March 14, Millett holds one of the tree's hanging tresses in her hands (Figure 12.7). Speaking to Mulard, she reflects on the Iranian women she has met in the street demonstrations since her arrival on March 5: "they participated in the

[28] Quote from her press conference in New York City on March 26.

Figure 12.7 Kate Millett (right) sitting under a weeping willow in interview with Claudine Mulard (left): "These are the most polished feminists I have ever seen."

revolution, they took to the streets, they were brave enough to face the army tanks, they know how to confront real danger and many women told me that they *are ready to die for their rights* ... I've never heard feminists speak this way!" Millett, the American feminist and the spearhead of the women's liberation movement, is posited by the film as the translator of the women's cry for freedom. In the film the interview with Millett leads up to and is followed by the two-shot sequence that includes the interview with Mojgan. As the latter sequence closes, it is edited to and once again bridged by the voices of Iranian women chanting the film's unconscious and untranslated refrain: "Lahze be lahze gooyam / zire shekanje gooyam / ya marg ya azadi" ("I will say it in every moment / I'll say it under torture / Either death or freedom!"). The Iranian women's literal gasp for freedom is translated by Millett as a demand for "their rights" – leaving me to wonder if this interpretive move in the name of solidarity is not more aligned with the Global Sisterhood, namely, Millett's own emergent feminist brand in the 1970s.

Whatever the case may be here, the a priori reception of these women's words by Millett, framed as she is by a tree, repeats the film's earlier gesture by which the three-headed figure of the women framed by Damavand mountains receives Mahboubeh's anguished voice, and aurally bridges the threshold to the universality that is evoked by the women's demands for freedom. The freedom conjured as "neither Eastern nor Western" in the opening chant resists in this nature-framed reception of Iranian women's voices on the visual track the logic that is Capital's claim on the term "global," and emphatically evades the boundaried logic of the 1970s *inter*nationalist discourse. The chant's evocation of a *"jahani"* freedom, a freedom worth dying for in these untranslated aural bridges, conjures instead, in my reading, a different mode of collectivity and (e)cohabitation grounded in the radical alterity of the planetary.

Framed as that which is "above and beyond our own reach," *jahani* or the "planetary," as I have translated it here, "is not continuous with us" just "as it is not, indeed, specifically discontinuous."[29] For as Spivak observes, if we can "imagine ourselves as planetary creatures rather than global entities, alterity remains underived from us; it is not our dialectical negation, it contains us as much as it flings us away." It is the planetary, indeed, that accompanies and accommodates us as that "species of alterity" that we inhabit, albeit "on loan." The Iranian women's revolutionary evocation of a "freedom" that is *"jahani,"* wed as it is at once to and by the unconscious grammar of the film (which one could also call a prelinguistic media ecology) to the ecological (namely, to that un-boundaried element that is both natural and underived from the human species), gives way to Millett's words, awaiting the translation of a generation yet to be born.

For, as I have argued here, translation as a concept, particularly in the context of the revolution, presents a dimension of radical openness to the other that the insistence on both nativism and the proprietary and such tropes as Orientalism and Westoxification in Iranian studies miss. This dimension, I would argue, accounts for the worldly or "universal" status of the Iranian Revolution in which a multiplicity of foreign constituents and also a variety of national feminist liberation movements in the 1970s envisioned the possibility of their birth/rebirth. For the French feminist filmmakers who immortalized this moment in *Mouvement de Libération des Femmes Iraniennes, Année Zéro*, the revolution achieves this universality by speaking to Fouque's notion of the uterine, that is, to speak more precisely, by locating the revolution's radical ethics in that openness to the other which Spivak terms the planetary. The evocation of *jahani* by the Iranian women in protest retrieves in this originary threshold encounter with the world, that is, in the moment of translation, a scale-bending framework, which critically responds to the effects of capitalism's globalization

[29] Gayatri Chakravorty Spivak, *An Aesthetic Education in the Era of Globalization* (Boston, MA: Harvard University Press, 2013), 339.

discourse by evoking this notion of the planetary. Distancing itself from the siloed and unruly discourse of recognition and rights, that language wielded by identity politics and the neoliberal logic of globalization governing area and gender studies today, the elicitation of *jahani* in these chants calls instead for a transformative, collective, indeed, a redistributive struggle on a planetary scale.

The Iranian Revolution contains a planetary dimension, in other words. And it is this planetarity, preceisely, that is made palpable in *Mouvement de Libération des Femmes Iraniennes, Année Zéro*. I have suggested that the revolution's planetary dimension is most evident in the evocation of a natural and embodied hospitality which the feminist film conceives as a politics. *Mouvement*'s attention to this politics unearths a radical openness to the world, an openness that upends the discipline-bound language with which this revolutionary moment's political ethics has typically been read. The challenge for Iranian studies as a discipline largely engaged with anti-disciplinary objects, like this documentary, is to retool its deep knowledge of languages and cross-cultural research. It can do this by working from within the anti-disciplinary ecology of objects such as this film to evolve reading and translation practices that may move the field beyond the veneration of nativism and an easy turn toward a siloed rights discourse, and conjure a disciplinary transformation that could – indeed, *must* – reimagine the humanities by leading a planetary collective toward the creation of a just world.

Select Bibliography

Abazari, Abdorrahim. *Dar vadi-ye eshgh: khaterat-e hojjat-ol-eslam seyyed Taqi Musavi Dorche'i* (Tehran: Oruj, 1389/2010).

Abdi, Abbas. *Jonbesh-e daneshju-yi-e politeknik-e Tehran (daneshgah-e Amir Kabir), 1338–1357* (London: Nashr-e Ney, 2013).

Abrahamian, Ervand. "Iran in Revolution: The Opposition Forces," *MERIP Reports* 75/76 (March–April 1979): 3–8.

"The Guerrilla Movement in Iran, 1963–1977," *MERIP Reports* 86 (1980): 3–15.

"Structural Causes of the Iranian Revolution," *MERIP Reports* 87 (May 1980): 21–26.

Iran between Two Revolutions (Princeton, NJ: Princeton University Press, 1982).

Radical Islam: The Iranian Mojahedin (London: I.B. Tauris, 1989).

Khomeinism: Essays on the Islamic Republic (Berkeley, CA: University of California Press, 1993).

Tortured Confessions: Prisons and Recantation in Modern Iran (Los Angeles, CA: University of California Press, 1999).

Adelkhah, Fariba. *Being Modern in Iran*, trans. Jonathan Derrick (New York: Columbia University Press, 2000).

The Thousand and One Borders of Iran: Travel and Identity, trans. Andrew Brown (New York: Routledge, 2016).

Adib-Moghaddam, Arshin. *The International Politics of the Persian Gulf: A Cultural Genealogy* (London: Routledge, 2006).

Afary, Janet, and Kevin Anderson. *Foucault and the Iranian Revolution: Gender and the Seductions of Islamism* (Chicago, IL: University of Chicago Press, 2010).

Afshar, Iraj. "Keaab-shenasi-e Mirza 'Abd al-Ghaffar Najm al-Doleh," *Farhang-e Iranzamin*, no. 20 (1353/1974).

Ahmadzadeh, M. *Mobareze-ye mosallahaneh. Ham esteratezhi, ham taktik* (n.p.: 1970; republished by the Fada'is on Bahman 19, 1359/February 8, 1981; www.iran-archive.com).

Ahvazi, Abdorrazagh. *Emam Khomeini be ravayat-e ayatollah Hashemi Rafsanjani* (Tehran: Oruj, 1385/2006).

Akhavan, Niki. "Nonfiction Form and the 'Truth' about Muslim Women in Iranian Documentary," *Feminist Media Histories* 1:1 (Winter 2015): 89–111.

Akhavi, Shahrough. *Religion and Politics in Contemporary Iran: Clergy-State Relations in the Pahlavi Period* (Albany, NY: SUNY Press, 1980).

Alavi, Bozorg. *Chashmhayash* (Tehran: Amir Kabir, 1357/1978).

Panjah va seh nafar (Tehran: Amir Kabir, 1357/1978).

Varagh pareh ha-ye zendan (Tehran: Amir Kabir, 1357/1978).

Her Eyes, trans. John O'Kane (Lanham, MD: University Press of America, 1989).

Alemzadeh, Maryam. "Institutionalization of a Revolutionary Army: The Islamic Revolutionary Guards Corps (1979–82)" (PhD diss., University of Chicago, 2018).

Algar, Hamid. "'Allāma Sayyid Muḥammad Ḥusayn Ṭabāṭabā'ī: Philosopher, Exegete, and Gnostic," *Journal of Islamic Studies* 17:3 (2006): 326–351.

Al Rasool, Abdul-Hossein. "Goft-o-goo'i azad ba Abdul-Hossein Al Rasul, Ra'is Dabirestan Shomareh Yek-Kharazmi I," *Ta'lim o tarbiat* 61 (Mehr 1351/September–October 1972): 17–25.

"Donbaleh Goft-o-gooi'i azad ba Abdul-Hossein Al Rasul, Ra'is Dabirestan Shomareh Yek-Kharazmi II," *Ta'lim o tarbiat* 62 (Aban 1351/October–November 1972): 111–113.

Altbach, Philip G. "The International Student Movement," *Journal of Contemporary History* 5:1 (1970): 156–174.

Alvandi, Roham. *Nixon, Kissinger, and the Shah: The United States and Iran in the Cold War* (New York: Oxford University Press, 2016).

Alvandi, Roham, ed. *The Age of Aryamehr: Late Pahlavi Iran and Its Global Entanglements* (London: Gingko Library, 2018).

Amini, D. *Polis Dar Iran* (Tehran: 1325/1946).

Amir Arjomand, Said. "Iran's Islamic Revolution in Comparative Perspective," *World Politics* 38:3 (April 1986): 383–414.

Amjadi, Jalil. *Tarikh-e shafahi-ye goruh-ha-ye mobarez-e haftganeh-ye mosalman* (Tehran: Markaz-e Asnad-e Enqelab-e Eslami, 1383/2004).

Ansari, Ali. *The Politics of Nationalism in Modern Iran* (New York: Cambridge University Press, 2012).

Appy, Christian G. *American Reckoning: The Vietnam War and Our National Identity* (New York: Viking, 2015).

Apter, Emily. "Philosophical Translation and Untranslatability: Translation as Critical Pedagogy," *Profession* (2010): 50–63.

'Aqeli, Baqer. *Sharh-e hal-e rajal-e siasi va nezami-ye Mo'aser-e Iran* (Tehran: Nashr Guftar, 1380/2001).

Ruzshomar-e tarikh-e Iran: Az mashruteh ta enqelab-e eslami, vol. 2 (Tehran: Nashr-e Goftar, 1384/2005).

Araghchi, Ali. *Partov-e aftab: Khaterat-e hazrat-e ayatollah haj sheykh Ali Araghchi* (Tehran: Oruj, 1389/2010).

Arasterh, A. Reza. *Education and Social Awakening in Iran, 1850–1968,* 2nd ed. revised and enlarged (Leiden: E. J. Brill, 1969).

Ardestani, Hoseyn. *Rah: Tarikh-e shafahi-ye Doktor Mohsen Reza'i* (Tehran: Markaz-e Asnad va Tahghighat-e Defa'-e Moghaddas, 1394/ 2015).

Arjmand, Reza. *Inscription on Stone: Islam, State, and Education in Iran and Turkey* (Stockholm: Institute of International Education, Stockholm University, 2008).

Arjomand, Kamran. "The Emergence of Scientific Modernity in Iran: Controversies Surrounding Astrology and Modern Astronomy in the Mid-nineteenth Century," *Iranian Studies* 30:1–2 (1997): 5–24.

Armiki, Taqi Azad. *Jam'eh shenasi-ye jam'eh shenasi dar Iran* (Tehran: Muasisih-ye Nashr-e Kalameh, 1378/1999).

Armitage, David, and Sanjay Subrahmanyam, eds. *The Age of Revolutions in Global Context, c. 1760–1840* (Basingstoke: Palgrave Macmillan, 2010).

Armstrong, Elizabeth. "Before Bandung: The Anti-imperialist Women's Movement in Asia and the Women's International Democratic Federation," *Signs: Journal of Women in Culture and Society* 41:2 (Winter 2016): 305–332.

Aronova, Elena, and Simone Turchetti, eds. *Science Studies during the Cold War and Beyond* (New York: Palgrave, 2016).

Asad, Talal. *Formations of the Secular: Christianity, Islam, Modernity* (Stanford, CA: Stanford University Press, 2003).

Ashraf, H. *Jam'bandi-ye se-saleh* (Tehran: Entesharat-e Negah, 1358/1979).

Asnadi az jonbesh-e daneshju-yi dar Iran, vol. 1 (Tehran: Sazman-e Chap va Entesharat, Vezarat-e Farhang va Ershad-e Eslami, 1380/2001).

Atabaki, Touraj, and Erik Jan Zürcher. *Men of Order: Authoritarian Modernization under Atatürk and Reza Shah* (New York: I.B. Tauris, 2004).

Atabaki, T., and N. Mohajer, eds. *Rahi digar: Ravayet-ha'i dar bud-o-bash-e charik-ha-ye fada'i-ye khalq-e iran,* 2 vols. (Cedex, France: Noghteh, 2018).

Avini, Morteza. "Hekmat-e sinema," *Farabi* 18 (Bahar 1372/Spring 1993): 6–19.

Tose'e va mabani-e tamaddon-e gharb (Tehran: Vaheh, 1387/2008).

Ayne-ie jadoo, vol. 3 (Tehran: Vaheh, 1396/2017).

Aghazi bar yek pyan: Enqelab-e eslami va payan-e entezar (Tehran: Vaheh, 1397/2018).

"Zendegi-nameh-ie Shahid Avini," Shahid Avini General Cultural and Religious Website, www.aviny.com/Aviny/Autobiography.aspx.

Axworthy, Michael. *Revolutionary Iran: A History of the Islamic Republic* (Oxford: Oxford University Press, 2013).

Ayatollahi Tabaar, Mohammad. *Religious Statecraft: The Politics of Islam in Iran* (New York: Columbia University Press, 2018).

Bakhash, Shaul. "Iran," *The American Historical Review* 96:5 (December 1991): 1479–1496.

Banani, Amin. *The Modernization of Iran, 1921–1941* (Stanford, CA: Stanford University Press, 1961).

Banuazizi, A. "Alunak-neshinan-e khiyaban-e profesor Brown," *Ketab-e Alefba*, no. 3 (July 1983): 53–64.

Bareheni, Reza. "The SAVAK Documents," *The Nation* (February 23, 1980): 198–202.

Barry, Andrew, and Nigel Thrift. "Gabriel Tarde: Imitation, Invention and Economy," *Economy and Society* 36:4 (2007): 509–525.

Bashiriyeh, Hossein. *The State and Revolution in Iran, 1962–1982* (New York: St. Martin's Press, 1984).

Basosi, Duccio, Giuliano Garavini, and Massimiliano Trentin, eds. *Counter-shock: The Oil Counter-revolution of the 1980s* (London: Bloomsbury, 2018).

Bayat, Asef. *Street Politics: The Poor People's Movements in Iran* (New York: Columbia University Press, 1997).

   "Revolution without Movement, Movement without Revolution: Comparing Islamic Activism in Iran and Egypt," *Comparative Studies in Society and History* 40:1 (1998): 136–169.

   Making Islam Democratic: Social Movements and the Post-Islamist Turn (Stanford, CA: Stanford University Press, 2007).

   Revolution without Revolutionaries: Making Sense of the Arab Spring (Stanford, CA: Stanford University Press, 2017).

Bayly, C. A., Sven Beckert, Matthew Connelly, et al. "*AHR* Conversation: On Transnational History," *The American Historical Review* 111:5 (December 2006): 1441–1464.

Behpur, Abolhasan. "Zendan va zendanha" (PhD diss., University of Tehran, 1336/1957).

Behrooz, Maziar. *Rebels with a Cause: The Failure of the Left in Iran* (New York: I.B. Tauris, 1999).

   "The Iranian Revolution and the Legacy of the Guerrilla Movement," in Stephanie Cronin, ed., *Reformers and Revolutionaries in Modern Iran: New Perspectives on the Iranian Left* (London: Routledge, 2004), 189–205.

Berberian, Houri. *Roving Revolutionaries: Armenians and the Connected Revolutions in the Russian, Iranian, and Ottoman Worlds* (Berkeley, CA: University of California Press, 2019).

Biao, Lin. "Long Live the Victory of People's War! In Commemoration of the 20th Anniversary of Victory in the Chinese People's War of Resistance against Japan," pamphlet written September 3, 1965; republished online: www.marxists.org/reference/archive/lin-biao/1965/09/peoples_war/index.htm.

Bill, James A. *The Eagle and the Lion: The Tragedy of American Iranian Relations* (New Haven, CT: Yale University Press, 1988).

Binder, Leonard. *Iran: Political Development in a Changing Society* (Berkeley, CA: University of California Press, 1964).

Bini, Elisabetta, Giuliano Garavini, and Federico Romero, eds. *Oil Shock: The 1973 Crisis and Its Economic Legacy* (London: Bloomsbury, 2016).

Bird, Jon, Barry Curtis, Tim Putnam, George Robertson, and Lisa Tickner, eds. *Mapping Futures: Local Cultures, Global Change* (London: Routledge 1993).

Black, Megan. *The Global Interior: Mineral Frontiers and American Power* (Cambridge, MA: Harvard University Press, 2018).

Bongah-e Taʻavun va Sanayeh Zendanian. *Faʻaliyat-e seh saleh-ye Bongah-e Taʻavun va Sanayeh Zendanian* (Tehran: 1344/1965).
Gozaresh-e az zendanha (Tehran: Edarih-e Kol-e Zendanha va Chapgah-e Bongah-e Taʻavun va Sanayeh Zendanian, 1347/1968).

Boodrookas, Alex, and Arang Keshavarzian. "The Forever Frontier of Urbanism: Historicizing Persian Gulf Cities," *International Journal of Urban and Regional Research* 43:1 (2019): 14–29.

Booth, Heather, Day Creamer, Susan Davis, et al. "Socialist Feminism: A Strategy for the Women's Movement," Hyde Park Chapter, Chicago Women's Liberation Union, 1972, www.historyisaweapon.org/defcon1/chisocfem.html.

Borges, Jorge Luis. *The Aleph and Other Stories: 1933–1969*, trans. and ed. Norman Thomas Di Giovanni (New York: Bantam Books, 1970).

Borstelmann, Thomas. *The 1970s: A New Global History from Civil Rights to Economic Inequality* (Princeton, NJ: Princeton University Press, 2011).

Brenes, Michael. *For Might and Right: Cold War Defense Spending and the Remaking of American Democracy* (Amherst, MA: University of Massachusetts Press, 2020).

Brenner, Neil. "Beyond State-Centerism? Space, Territoriality, and Geographical Scale in Globalization Studies," *Theory and Society* 28:1 (February 1999): 39–78.

Brenner, Neil, and Christian Schmid. "Towards a New Epistemology of the Urban?" *City: Analysis of Urban Trends, Culture, Theory, Policy, Action* 19 (2015): 151–182.

Brew, Gregory. "'What They Need Is Management': American NGOs, the Second Seven-Year Plan and Economic Development in Iran, 1954–1963," *The International History Review* 41:1 (2019): 1–22.

Brown, Timothy S. "'1968' East and West: Divided Germany as a Case Study in Transnational History," *American Historical Review* 114:1 (2009): 69–96.

Burger, Peter. *The Theory of the Avant-Garde* (Minneapolis, MN: University of Minnesota Press, 1984).

Burke III, Edmund, and Paul Lubeck. "Explaining Social Movements in Two Oil-Exporting States: Divergent Outcomes in Nigeria and Iran," *Comparative Studies in Society and History* 29(October 1987): 643–665.

Byrne, Jeffrey J. *Mecca of Revolutions: Algeria, Decolonization, and the Third World Order* (Oxford: Oxford University Press, 2016).

Cacho, Lisa. *Social Death: Racialized Rightlessness and the Criminalization of the Unprotected* (New York: New York University Press, 2012).

Castiglioni, Claudia. "No Longer a Client, Not Yet a Partner: The US-Iranian Alliance in the Johnson Years," *Cold War History* 15:4 (2015): 491–509.

CENTO Conference on Engineering Education. "Isfahan, Iran; Ankara: Office of United States Economic Coordinator for CENTO Affairs," 1967.

Chamberlin, Paul T. *The Global Offensive: The United States, the Palestine Liberation Organization, and the Making of the Post-Cold War Order* (Oxford: Oxford University Press, 2012).

The Cold War's Killing Fields: Rethinking the Long Peace (New York: Harper, 2018).

Chambers, Samuel. "Jacques Rancière and the Problem of Pure Politics," *European Journal of Political Theory* 10:3 (2011): 303–326.

Chamran, Mostafa. *Lobnan* (Tehran: Bonyad-e Shahid Chamran, 1362/ 1983).

Chap dar Iran beh ravayat-e SAVAK (Tehran: Markaz-e Barresi-ye Asnad-i Tarikhi-ye Vezarat-e Ettela'at, 1378/1999).

Chehabi, Houchang E. *Iranian Politics and Religious Modernism: The Liberation Movement of Iran under the Shah and Khomeini* (Ithaca, NY: Cornell University Press, 1990).

"Sport and Politics in Iran: The Legend of Gholamreza Takhti," *The International Journal of the History of Sport* 12:3 (1995): 48–60.

Cherikha-ye Fadai-ye Khalq-e Iran. "Zendanha-ye rezhim va zendanian-e siyasi," *'Asr-e 'Amal* 4: 29.

Chubin, Shahram, and Charles Tripp. *Iran and Iraq at War* (Boulder, CO: Westview Press, 1988).

Cohen, Lizbeth. *Saving America's Cities: Ed Logue and the Struggle to Renew Urban America in the Suburban Age* (New York: Farrar, Straus and Giroux, 2019).

Cooper, Frederick. *Colonialism in Question: Theory, Knowledge, History* (Berkeley, CA: University of California Press, 2005).

Corboz, Elvire. *Guardians of Shi'ism: Sacred Authority and Transnational Family Networks* (Edinburgh: Edinburgh University Press, 2015).

Cortright, Edgar M., ed. *Apollo Expeditions to the Moon* (Washington, DC: Scientific and Technical Information Office, National Aeronautics and Space Administration, 1975).

Cowen, Deborah, and Neil Smith. "After Geopolitics? From the Geopolitical Social to Geoeconomics," *Antipode* 41:1 (2009): 22–48.

Cronin, Stephanie. "The Left in Iran: Illusion and Disillusion," *Middle Eastern Studies* 36:3 (July 2000): 231–243.

"Deserters, Convicts, Cossacks, and Revolutionaries: Russians in Iranian Military Service, 1800–1920," in Stephanie Cronin, ed., *Iranian-Russian Encounters: Empires and Revolutions since 1800* (New York: Routledge, 2013), 143–185.

Cronin, Stephanie, ed. *The Making of Modern Iran: State and Society under Reza Shah 1921–1941* (New York: Routledge, 2007).

Dabashi, Hamid. *Close Up: Iranian Cinema, Past, Present, and Future* (New York: Verso Press, 2001).

Theology of Discontent: The Ideological Foundation of the Islamic Revolution in Iran, 2nd ed. (Edison, NJ: Transaction Publishers, 2005).

Masters and Masterpieces of Iranian Cinema (Washington, DC: Mage Publishers, 2007).

Dahms, Hans-Joachim. "Thomas Kuhn's *Structure*: An 'Exemplary Document of the Cold War Era'?" in Elena Aronova and Simone Turchetti, eds., *Science Studies during the Cold War and Beyond* (New York: Palgrave, 2016), 103–126.

Danesh, Taj Zaman. *Keyfarshenasi va huquq-e zendanha* (Tehran: University of Tehran Press, 1352/1973).

Usul-e elm-e zendanha (Tehran: University of Tehran Press, 1353/1973).

Daniel, Victor, Bijan Shafei, and Sohrab Soroushiani. *Nikolai Markov: Architecture of Changing Times in Iran* (Tehran: Did Publications, 2004).

Dashti, 'Ali. *Ayyam-e mahbas* (Essen: Nashr-e Nima, 2003).

Davani, Ali. *Nehzat-e ruhaniyun-e Iran*, vol. 4 (n.p.: Bonyad-e Farhang-e Imam Reza, n.d.).

Davari Ardekani, Reza. *Enqelab-e eslami va vaz'e konooni-e aalam* (Tehran: Mehr-e Newsha, 1388/2009 [1982]).

Davari, Arash. "A Return to Which Self? Ali Shari'ati and Frantz Fanon on the Political Ethics of Insurrectionary Violence," *Comparative Studies of South Asia, Africa and the Middle East* 34:1 (2014): 86–105.

"Indeterminate Governmentality: Neoliberal Politics in Revolutionary Iran, 1968–1979" (PhD diss., University of California, 2016).

"On Inexactitude in Decolonization," *Comparative Studies of South Asia, Africa and the Middle East* 40:3 (2020): 627–635.

Davis, Angela. *Abolition, Democracy: Beyond Empire, Prisons, and Torture* (New York: Seven Story Press, 2005).

Dehbashi, Ali. "Didari dustaneh ba ostad Zein al-'Abedin Mu'tamin va gofto-gu'i dustaneh-tar," *Bokhara*, no. 38 (1383/2004): 24–63.

Des groupes du M.L.F. "20 janvier: Journée internationale pour le Vietnam: Des groupes de femmes y participent, voilà pourquoi" (1972?), F Delta Res 151, BDIC.

Devictor, Agnès. *Images, combattants et martyrs: La guerre Iran-Irak vue par le cinéma iranien* (Paris: Karthala, 2015).

Devji, Faisal. *Landscapes of the Jihad: Militancy, Morality, Modernity* (Ithaca, NY: Cornell University Press, 2005).

DeVore, Marc. "The United Kingdom's Last Hot War of the Cold War: Oman, 1963–1975," *Cold War History* 11:3 (2011): 441–471.

Di-Capua, Yoav. *No Exit: Arab Existentialism, Jean-Paul Sartre and Decolonization* (Chicago, IL: University of Chicago Press, 2018).

Dietrich, Christopher. *Oil Revolution: Anticolonial Elites, Sovereign Rights, and the Economic Culture of Decolonization* (Cambridge: Cambridge University Press, 2017).

Dikötter, Frank. *Crime, Punishment, and the Prison in Modern China* (New York: Columbia University Press, 2002).

Dikötter, Frank, and Ian Brown. *Cultures of Confinement: A History of Prison in Africa, Asia, and Latin America* (Ithaca, NY: Cornell University Press, 2007).

Donovan, Jim. *Shoot for the Moon: The Space Race and the Extraordinary Voyage of Apollo 11* (New York: Little, Brown and Company, 2019).

Doustdar, Aramesh. *Emtena' e Tafakkor dar Farhang Dini* (Paris: Kharavan Publication, 1982).

Derakhshesh Hay-e Tire (Cologne: Andishe Azad Publication, 1993).

Edelstein, Dan, and Keith Baker, eds. *Scripting Revolution: A Historical Approach to the Comparative Study of Revolutions* (Stanford, CA: Stanford University Press, 2015).

Ehteshami, Manuchehr. "Geramidasht-e yek ostad-e bozorg, doktor Mohammad-'Ali Mojtahedi," *Hafez* 5 (Mehr 1387/September–October 2008): 17–20.

Elbaum, Max. *Revolution in the Air: Sixties Radicals Turn to Lenin, Mao and Che* (New York: Verso Books, 2002).

El-Ghobashy, Mona. *Bread and Freedom: Egypt's Revolutionary Situation* (Stanford, CA: Stanford University Press, 2021).

Enayat, Hadi. *Law, State, and Society in Modern Iran: Constitutionalism, Autocracy, and Legal Reform, 1906–1941* (New York: Palgrave Macmillan, 2013).

Enayat, Mahmoud, and Bijan Asadipoor. "Goft-o-goo ba Mahmud Enayat," *Kelk* 51–52 (Khordad–Tir 1373/May–June 1994): 176–186.

Eng, David, and David Kazanjian. "Introduction: Mourning Remains," in David Eng and David Kazanjian, eds., *Loss: The Politics of Mourning* (Durham, NC: Duke University Press, 2003), 1–26.

Engels, Frederick. *The Origin of the Family, Private Property and the State* (New York: International Publishers, 1972).

Esposito, John, ed. *The Iranian Revolution: Its Global Impact* (Miami, FL: University of Florida, 1990).

Evans, Sara Margaret. *Personal Politics: The Roots of Women's Liberation in the Civil Rights Movement* (New York: Knopf, 1979).

Fain, W. Taylor. "Conceiving the 'Arc of Crisis' in the Indian Ocean Region," *Diplomatic History* 42:4 (2017): 694–719.

Fakhrzadeh, Sa'id. *Khaterat-e Ali Jannati* (Tehran: Markaz-e Asnad-e Enqelab-e Eslami, 1381/2002).

Fanon, Frantz. *Black Skin, White Masks*, trans. Charles Lam Markmann (New York: Grove Press, 1967).

Farasatkhah, Maqsud. *Tarikh hashtad saleh Daneshkadeh Fanni – Daneshgah Tehran: Dastan yek khaneh, dastan yek sarzamin* (Tehran: Nashr-e Ney, 1393/2015).

Farhi, Farideh. *States and Urban-Based Revolutions: Iran and Nicaragua* (Urbana, IL: University of Illinois Press, 1990).

Fatemi Nevisi, Seyyed Abbas. *Zendegi va marg-e Jahan Pahlavan Takhti dar ayeneh-ye asnad* (Tehran: Entesharat-e Jahan-e Ketab, 1377/1998).

Ferguson, James. *Global Shadows* (Durham, NC: Duke University Press, 2006).

Fernée, Tadd. *Enlightenment and Violence: Modernity and Nation-Making* (New Delhi: Sage, 2014).

Feynman, Richard Phillips, Robert B. Leighton, and Rochus E. Vogt. *The Feynman Lectures on Physics*, 3 vols. (Reading: MA: Addison-Wesley Publishing Company, 1964–1969).

Firuz, Nosrat al-Dowleh. *Majmuah-e makatibat asnad khatirat va asar-e Firzu Mirza Firuz (Nosrat al-Dowleh)* (Tehran: Nashr-e Tarikh-e Iran, 1369/1990).

Fischer, Michael M. J. *Iran: From Religious Dispute to Revolution* (Cambridge, MA: Harvard University Press, 1980).

Floor, Willem M. "The Police in Qajar Persia," *Zeitschrift der Deutschen Morgenländischen Gesellschaft* 123:2 (1973): 293–315.

"The Revolutionary Character of the Ulama: Wishful Thinking or Reality?" in Nikki R. Keddie, ed., *Religion and Politics in Iran: Shiʻism from Quietism to Revolution* (New Haven, CT: Yale University Press, 1983), 73–100.

Public Health in Qajar Iran (Washington, DC: Mage Publishers, 2004).

Foran, John. *Fragile Resistance: Social Transformation in Iran from 1500 to the Revolution* (Boulder, CO: Westview Press, 1993).

"The Iranian Revolution of 1977–79: A Challenge for Social Theory," in John Foran, ed., *A Century of Revolution: Social Movements in Iran* (Minneapolis, MN: University of Minnesota Press, 1994), 160–188.

Taking Power: On the Origins of Third World Revolutions (Cambridge: Cambridge University Press, 2005).

Forozan, Hesam, and Afshin Shahi. "The Military and the State in Iran: The Economic Rise of the Revolutionary Guards," *The Middle East Journal* 71:1 (2017): 67–86.

Foucault, Michel. *Discipline and Punish: The Birth of the Prison*, 2nd ed., trans. Alan Sheridan (New York: Vintage Books, 1995 [1977]).

Society Must Be Defended: Lectures at the College de France, trans. David Macey (New York: Picador Press, 2003).

Fouque, Antoinette. *There Are Two Sexes: Essays in Feminology*, trans. David Macey and Catherine Porter (New York: Columbia University Press 2016).

Frank, Jason. "Logical Revolts: Jacques Rancière and Political Subjectivization," *Political Theory* 43:2 (2015): 249–261.

Fraser, Nancy. "Feminism, Capitalism and the Cunning of History," *NLR* 56 (March–April 2009), https://bit.ly/3qXDWXy.

Freeman, Jo. *The Politics of Women's Liberation: A Case Study of an Emerging Movement and Its Relation to the Policy Process* (Lincoln, NE: iUniverse.com Inc., 2000).

Furet, François. *Interpreting the French Revolution* (Cambridge: Cambridge University Press, 1981).

Gahan, Jairan. "Red-Light Tehran: Prostitution, Intimately Public Islam, and the Rule of the Sovereign, 1910–1980" (PhD dis., University of Toronto, 2017).

Gamson, William A., and David S. Meyer. "Framing Political Opportunity," in Doug McAdam, John D. McCarthy, and Mayer N. Zald, eds., *Comparative Perspectives on Social Movements: Opportunities, Mobilizing Structures, and Cultural Framings* (New York: Cambridge University Press, 1996), 275–290.

Gasiorowski, Mark, *U.S. Foreign Policy and the Shah: Building a Client State in Iran* (Ithaca, NY: Cornell University Press, 1991).

Gavin, Francis J. "Politics, Power, and U.S. Policy in Iran, 1950–1953," *Journal of Cold War Studies* 1:1 (Winter 1999): 56–89.

Gellner, Ernest. *Muslim Society* (Cambridge: Cambridge University Press, 1981).

Getachew, Adom. *Worldmaking after Empire: The Rise and Fall of Self-determination* (Princeton, NJ: Princeton University Press, 2019).

Ghamari-Tabrizi, Behrooz. *Foucault in Iran: Islamic Revolution after Enlightenment* (Minneapolis, MN: University of Minnesota Press, 2016).
Remembering Akbar: Inside the Iranian Revolution (New York: O/R Books, 2016).

Ghaznavian, Mohammad. *Ta'amolati darbare-ye kharej az mahdudeh* (n.p.: Praxies, 2016).

Ghessari, Ali. *Iranian Intellectuals in the 20th Century* (Austin, TX: University of Texas Press, 1998).

Gil Guerrero, Javier. *The Carter Administration and the Fall of Iran's Pahlavi Dynasty: US-Iran Relations on the Brink of the 1979 Revolution* (New York: Palgrave Macmillan, 2016).
"Human Rights and Tear Gas: The Question of Carter Administration Officials Opposed to the Shah," *British Journal of Middle Eastern Studies* 43:3 (2016): 285–301.

Gilmore, Ruth Wilson. *The Golden Gulag: Prisons, Surplus, Crisis, and Opposition to Globalizing California* (Los Angeles, CA: University of California Press, 2007).

Goldstone, Jack A. "Theories of Revolution: the Third Generation," *World Politics* 32 (1980): 425–453.
"Toward a Fourth Generation of Revolutionary Theory," *Annual Review of Political Science* 4 (2001): 139–187.

Göndogdu, Ayten. "Disagreeing with Rancière: Speech, Violence, and the Ambiguous Subjects of Politics," *Polity* 49:2 (2017): 188–219.

Goodell, Grace E. *The Elementary Structures of Political Life: Rural Development in Pahlavi Iran* (New York: Oxford University Press, 1986).

Gopinath, Gayatri. "Archive, Affect, and the Everyday: Queer Diasporic Re-visions," in Janet Staiger, Ann Cvetkovich, and Ann Reynolds, eds., *Political Emotions: New Agendas in Communication* (New York: Routledge, 2010), 165–192.

Graf, Rüdiger. "Between 'National' and 'Human Security': Energy Security in the United States and Western Europe in the 1970s," *Historical Social Research/Historische Sozialforschung* 35:4 (2010): 329–348.

Granovetter, Mark. "Strength of Weak Ties," *American Journal of Sociology* 78:6 (1973): 1360–1380.

Grigor, Talinn. *Building Iran: Modernism, Architecture, and National Heritage under the Pahlavi Monarchs* (New York: Periscope, 2009).

Guarnizo, Luis Eduardo, and Michael Peter Smith, "Locations of Transnationalism," in Michael Peter Smith and Luis Eduardo Guarnizo, eds., *Transnationalism from Below* (New Brunswick, NJ: Transaction Publishers, 1998), 3–34.

Haber-Schaim, Uri, John H. Dodge, Robert Gardner, Edward A. Shore, and Felicie Walter. *Physical Science Study Committee (PSSC) Physics: Teacher's Resource Book and Guide*, 4 vols. (Lexington, MA: Heath & Co., 1961).

Hadjebi-Tabrizi, V. *Dad-e bidad: Femmes politiques emprisonées 1971–1979*, vol. 1 (Cologne: BM-Druckservice, 2003).

Dad-e bidad: Femmes politiques emprisonées 1971–1979, vol. 2 (Cologne: BM-Druckservice, 2004).

Haghgoo [Avini], Morteza. "Tose'e va mabani-e tamaddon-e gharb," *Jahad* 104 (Azar and Dey 1366/November–December 1987): 28–31.

Hakim-Elahi, Hedayatollah. *Ba man beh zendan biyaid* (Tehran: Sherkat-e Sehami, 1325/1946).

Hall, Stuart. *Theorizing Diaspora: A Reader*, ed. Jana Evans Braziel and Anita Mannur (Malden, MA: Blackwell Publishing, 2003).

Halliburton, Richard. *The Flying Carpet: America's Most Dashing 1920s Adventurer Conquers the Air* (n.p.: The Long Rider's Guild Press, 2002).

Halliday, Fred. *Iran: Dictator and Development* (Harmondsworth: Penguin, 1979).

"Testimonies of Revolution," *MERIP Reports* 87(May 1980): 27.

Arabia without Sultans (London: Saqi Books, 2020 [1974]).

Hamidian, N. *Safar bar bal-ha-ye arezu* (Stockholm: self-published, 2010).

Hanieh, Adam. *Money, Markets, and Monarchies: The Gulf Cooperation Council and the Political Economy of the Contemporary Middle East* (Cambridge: Cambridge University Press, 2018).

Hanson, Brad. "The 'Westoxification' of Iran: Depictions and Reactions of Behrangi, Āl-e Ahmad, and Shari'ati," *International Journal of Middle East Studies* 15:1 (1983): 1–23.

Haqshenas, Mehdi, and Zahra Zar'ei, eds. *Bacheh-ye Khani Abad (Zendegi va zamaneh-ye marhum Jahan Pahlavan Gholamreza Takhti)* (Tehran: Markaz-e Asnad-e Enqelab-e Eslami, 1390/2011).

Harnwell, Gaylord Probasco. *Educational Voyaging in Iran* (Philadelphia, PA: University of Pennsylvania Press, 1962).

Hartmann, Heidi. "The Unhappy Marriage of Marxism and Feminism: Toward a More Progressive Union," *Capital and Class* 3:2 (Summer 1979): 1–33.

Harvey, David. *The Urbanization of Capital: Studies in the History and Theory of Capitalist Urbanization* (Baltimore, MD: Johns Hopkins University Press, 1985).

"Space as a Key Word," in Noel Castree and Derek Gregory, eds., *David Harvey: A Critical Reader* (Oxford: Blackwell Publishing, 2006), 270–293.

Hashemi-Rafsanjani, Ali Akbar, et al. *Hashemi-Rafsanjani: Karnameh va khaterat-e sal-ha-ye 1357 va 1358, enqelab va piruzi* (Tehran: Dafter-e Nashr-e Ma'aref-e Enqelab, 1383/2004).

Haykal, Mohammad. *Iran: The Untold Story – An Insider's Account of America's Iranian Adventure and Its Consequences for the Future* (New York: Pantheon Books, 1982).

Hazbun, Waleed, and Arang Keshavarzian. "Re-mapping Transnational Connections in the Middle East," *Geopolitics* 15:2 (2010): 203–209.

Hedayat, Sadeq. *Zendeh be gur* (Tehran: Ferusi Publisher, 1309/1930).

Seh ghatreh khun (Tehran: Amir Kabir, 1311/1932).

Buf-e kur (Bombay: 1315/1936).

Hegland, Mary Elaine. *Days of Revolution: Political Unrest in an Iranian Village* (Stanford, CA: Stanford University Press, 2014).

Hendrickson, Burleigh. "March 1968: Practicing Transnational Activism from Tunis to Paris," *International Journal of Middle East Studies* 44:4 (2012): 755–774.

Hijazi, Q. *Barrasi-ye jarayim-e zan dar Iran* (Tehran: Sherkat-e Sahami-ye Enteshar, 1341/1963).

Hirschman, Albert O. "The Search for Paradigms as a Hindrance to Understanding," *World Politics* 22:3 (1970): 329–343.

Ho, Engseng. "Inter-Asian Concepts for Mobile Societies," *The Journal of Asian Studies* 76:4 (November 2017): 907–928.

Hobsbawm, Eric. *Age of Revolution: 1875–1914* (New York: Vintage Books, 1989).

Hojjati-Kermani, Ali. *Lobnan be revayat-e emam Musa Sadr va doktor Chamran* (Tehran: Ghalam, 1364/1985).

Hong, Grace Kyungwon, and Roderick Ferguson. "Introduction," in Grace Kyungwon Hong and Roderick Ferguson, eds., *Strange Affinities: The Gender and Sexual Politics of Comparative Racialization* (Durham, NC: Duke University Press, 2011), 1–22.

Horn, Gerd-Rainer. *The Spirit of '68: Rebellion in Western Europe and North America, 1956–1976* (Oxford: Oxford University Press, 2007).

Hornyik, Sándor. "Sputnik versus Apollo: Science, Technology, and the Cold War in the Hungarian Visual Arts, 1957–1975," *Acta historiae artium Academiae Scientarium Hungaricae* 56:1 (2015): 165–172.

Huber, Matthew. *Lifeblood: Oil, Freedom, and the Forces of Capital* (Minneapolis, MN: University of Minnesota, 2013).

Hughes, Geraint. "A 'Model Campaign' Reappraised: The Counter-insurgency War in Dhofar, Oman, 1965–1975," *Journal of Strategic Studies* 32:2 (2009): 271–305.

Hushyar Shirazi, Mohammad-Bagher. "Tarbiat va sarnevesht-e bashar, I," *Ta'lim o tarbiat* 26:8 (Mordad 1332/August–September 1953): 449–456.

"Tarbiat va sarnevesht-e bashar, II," *Ta'lim o tarbiat* 26:9 (Shahrivar 1332/September–October 1953): 522–525.

Institute for Research and Planning in Science and Education. *The System of Higher Education in Iran* (Tehran: 1972).

Iranian Students Association, Northern California Women's Committee. "University Women Are Getting Organized" (Shokat Collection, Hoover Archives, Stanford University, c. 1968).

Jacobs, Meg. *Panic at the Pump: The Energy Crisis and the Transformation of American Politics in the 1970s* (New York: Macmillan, 2016).

Jafarian, Rasul. *Jaryanha va jonbeshha-ye mazhabi siyasi-ye Iran: Az ru-ye kar amadan-e Mohammad Reza Shah ta piruzi-ye enqelab-e eslami, salha-ye 1320–1357* (Tehran: Pazhuheshgah-e Farhang va Andisheh-ye Eslami, 1381/2002).

Jazani, B. *Cheguneh mobareze-ye mosallahaneh tudeh'i mi-shavad* (n.p.: 1973; republished in *19-e Bahman Te'orik*, no. 2 (Tir 1355/July 1976)).

Vaqaye'-e si-saleh-ye akhir-e Iran (n.p.: 1976; https://iran-archive.com/sites/default/files/sanad/jazanifvaghayee-si-saale.pdf).

Che kesani be marksism-leninism khiyanat mi-konand? (n.p.: Entesharat-e 19-e Bahman, n.d.).

Jazani, B., and H. Zarifi. *Masa'el-e jonbesh-e zedd-e este'mari va azadi-bakhsh-e khalq-e Iran va 'omdeh-tarin vazayef-e komunist-ha-ye Iran dar sharayet-e konuni* (n.p.: 1346/1967; online version republished by The Organization for the Unity of the People's Fada'iyan of Iran, 1382/2003).

Jazini, Mohammad-Javad. "Ketab-ha va entekhab-ha: Bar-rasi faraz o nashib-haye jayezeye behtrarin ketab az gozashteh ta konoon," *Hamshahri Newspaper* (Bahman 11, 1385/February 1, 2007).

Jazani-Zarifi Group. "Tez-e goruh-e Jazani," *19-e Bahman* (Farvardin 1355/March 1976; originally compiled in fall 1967).

Jebheh melli beh ravayat-e asnad-e SAVAK, vol. 1 (Tehran: Markaz-e Barresi-ye Asnad-e Tarikhi-ye Vezarat-e Ettela'at, 1379/2000).

Johns, Andrew L. "The Johnson Administration, the Shah of Iran, and the Changing Pattern of U.S.-Iranian Relations, 1965–1967: 'Tired of Being Treated like a Schoolboy,'" *Journal of Cold War Studies* 9:2 (2007): 78–79.

Jurdem, Laurence. *Paving the Way for Reagan: The Influence of Conservative Media on U.S. Foreign Policy* (Ithaca, NY: Cornell University Press, 2018).

Kamaly, Hossein. *God and Man in Tehran: Contending Visions of the Divine from the Qajars to the Islamic Republic* (New York: Columbia University Press, 2018).

Kamola, Isaac. "Why Global? Diagnosing the Globalization Literature within a Political Economy of Higher Education," *International Political Sociology* 7:1 (2013): 41–58.

Kapuscinski, Ryszard. *The Shah of Shahs*, trans. William R. Brand and Katarzyna Mroczkowska-Brand (New York: Vintage, 1992 [1985]).

Karimabadi, Mehrzad. "Manifesto of Martyrdom: Similarities and Differences between Avini's Ravaayat-e Fath [Chronicles of Victory] and More Traditional Manifestoes," *Iranian Studies* 44:3 (May 2001): 381–386.

Kashani-Sabet, Firoozeh. *Frontier Fictions: Shaping the Iranian Nation, 1804–1946* (Princeton, NJ: Princeton University Press, 1999).

Conceiving Citizens: Women and the Politics of Motherhood in Iran (New York: Oxford University Press, 2011).

Katouzian, Homa. "Alborz and Its Teachers." *Iranian Studies* 44:5 (September 2011): 743–754.

Kazemi, Farhad. "Urban Migrants and the Revolution," *Iranian Studies* 10 (1980): 257–277.

Kazemi, Mohsen. *Khaterat-e Marzieh Hadidchi (Dabbagh)* (Tehran: Sureh Mehr, 1393/2014).

Keddie, Nikki R. *Iran: Roots of Revolution* (New Haven, CT: Yale University Press, 1981).

"Iranian Revolutions in Comparative Perspective," *The American Historical Review* 88:3 (June 1983): 379–398.

Keeley, Theresa. "Reagan's Real Catholics vs. Tip O'Neill's Maryknoll Nuns: Gender, Intra-Catholic Conflict, and the Contras," *Diplomatic History* 40:3 (2015): 530–558.

Keshavarzian, Arang. "Regime Loyalty and Bazari Representations under the Islamic Republic of Iran: Dilemmas of the Society of Islamic Coalition," *International Journal of Middle East Studies* 41 (2009): 225–246.

"Geopolitics and the Genealogy of Free Trade Zones in the Persian Gulf," *Geopolitics* 15:2 (2010): 263–289.

Keys, Barbara J. *Reclaiming American Virtue: The Human Rights Revolution of the 1970s* (Cambridge, MA: Harvard University Press, 2014).

Khadkhudazadeh, Esma'il. *Saramadan-e varzesh-i Iran: Moruri bar tarikh-e varzesh-e qahremani-ye Iran: Zendegi nameh-ye saheban-e neshan-hayeh Olampik va jahan* (Tehran: Negareh Pardaz Sabah, 1386/2008).

Khalili, Laleh. *Time in the Shadows: Confinement in Counterinsurgencies* (Stanford, CA: Stanford University Press, 2012).

"The Infrastructural Power of the Military: The Geoeconomic Role of the U.S. Army Corps of Engineers in the Arabian Peninsula," *European Journal of International Relations* 24:4 (2018): 911–933.

Khalili, Laleh, and Jillian Schwedler, eds. *Policing and Prisons in the Middle East: Formations of Coercion* (New York: Columbia University Press, 2010).

Khosrokhavar, Farhad. "Attitude of Teenage Girls to the Iranian Revolution," in Elizabeth Warnock Fernea, ed., *Children in the Muslim Middle East* (Austin, TX: University of Texas Press, 1995), 392–309.

Kimball, Jeffrey. "The Nixon Doctrine: A Saga of Misunderstanding," *Presidential Studies Quarterly* 36:1 (2006): 59–74.

Kimiafar, Seyyed Mohammad. *Khaterat-e Habibollah Askarowladi* (Tehran: Markaz-e Asnad-e Enqelab-e Eslami, 1391/2012).

Kittel, Charles, Walter D. Knight, and Malvin A. Ruderman. *Mechanics* (New York: McGraw Hill Book Company, 1965).

Kondo, Nobuaki. *Islamic Law and Society in Iran: A Social History of Qajar Tehran* (New York: Routledge, 2017).

Krippner, Greta. *Capitalizing on Crisis: The Political Origins of the Rise of Finance* (Cambridge, MA: Harvard University Press, 2011).

Kurzman, Charles. "Historiography of the Iranian Revolutionary Movement, 1977–79," *Iranian Studies* 28:1–2 (Winter–Spring 1995): 25–38.

"Structural Opportunities and Perceived Opportunities in Social Movement Theory: Evidence from the Iranian Revolution of 1979," *American Sociological Review* 61 (1996): 153–170.

The Unthinkable Revolution in Iran (Cambridge, MA: Harvard University Press, 2005).

Democracy Denied, 1905–1915: Intellectuals and the Fate of Democracy (Cambridge, MA: Harvard University Press, 2008).

Labban, Mazen. "Oil in Parallax: Scarcity, Markets, and the Financialization of Accumulation," *Geoforum* 41:4 (2010): 541–552.

Lacan, Jacques. *Écrit*, trans. Bruce Fink (New York: Norton, 2007).

Lajevardi, Habib, ed. *Memoirs of Mohammad-Ali Mojtahedi: Headmaster of the Alborz High School (Khaterat-e Mohammad-Ali Mojtahedi: Ra'is-e Dabirestan-e Alborz (1324-1357) va Mo'sses-e Daneshgah-e Aryamehr (1344))* (Cambridge, MA: Center of Middle East Studies, Harvard University, 2000).

Lapidus, Ira, and Edmund Burke III, eds. *Islam, Politics, and Social Movements* (Berkeley, CA: University of California Press, 1988).

Lawrence, Bruce. *Defenders of God: The Fundamentalist Revolt against the Modern Age* (Columbia, SC: University of South Carolina Press, 1995).

Lawson, George. "A Global Historical Sociology of Revolution", in Julian Go and George Lawson, eds., *Global Historical Sociology* (Cambridge: Cambridge University Press, 2017), 76–98.

Leake, Elisabeth. "Spooks, Tribes, and Holy Men: The Central Intelligence Agency and the Soviet Invasion of Afghanistan," *Journal of Contemporary History* 53:1 (2018): 240–262.

Lefebvre, Henri. *Production of Space* (Oxford: Blackwell, 1991).

Lenczowski, George, ed. *Iran under the Pahlavis* (Stanford, CA: Hoover Institution Press, 1978).

Lesch, David W. *1979: The Year That Shaped the Modern Middle East* (Boulder, CO: Westview Press, 2001).

Lewis, Bernard. *Political Language of Political Islam* (Chicago, IL: University of Chicago Press, 1988).

Li, Darryl. *The Universal Enemy: Jihad, Empire, and the Challenge of Solidarity* (Stanford, CA: Stanford University Press, 2020).

Lindsay, R. Bruce. "On the Average, Difficult," *Physics Today* 20:1 (1967): 115–117.

Louër, Laurence. *Transnational Shia Politics: Religious and Political Networks in the Gulf* (New York: Columbia University Press, 2008).

Mahdi, Ali Akbar, and Abdolali Lahsaeizadeh. *Sociology in Iran* (Bethesda, MD: Jahan Publishers, 1992).

Maktab Eslam. "Dar Ejtema cheh migozarad?" vol. 3 (Khordad 1340/May–June 1961): 2–7.

Malekpur, Parviz. "Geramidasht ostad Parviz Shahryari," *Chista* 202–203 (Aban–Azar 1382/October–December 2003): 154–160.

Mansuri, Javad. *Tarikh-e shafahi-ye ta'sis-e sepah-e pasdaran-e enqelab-e eslami* (Tehran: Markaz-e Asnad-e Enqelab-e Eslami, 1393/2014).

Manuchehri, Shapur. "Zendegi-nameh-e kutah-e doktor Nur al-Din Farhikhteh," *Chista* 222–223 (Aban–Azar 1384/October–December 2005): 149–156.

Markaz-e Barrasi-ye Asnad-e Tarikhi. *Shahid-e sarafraz doktor Mostafa Chamran, yaran-e emam be revayat-e asnad-e SAVAK, jeld-e 11* (Tehran: Markaz-e Barrasi-ye Asnad-e Tarikhi-ye Vezarat-e Ettela'at, 1378/1999).

Shahid hojjat-ol-eslam Mohammad Montazeri, yaran-e Emam be revayat-e asnad-e SAVAK, jeld-e 37 (Tehran: Markaz-e Barrasi-ye Asnad-e Tarikhi-ye Vezarat-e Ettela'at, 1385/2006).

Marotti, William. "Japan 1968: The Performance of Violence and the Theater of Protest," *The American Historical Review* 114:1 (2009): 97–135.

Martin-Nielsen, Janet. "'This War for Men's Minds': The Birth of a Human Science in Cold War America," *History of the Human Sciences* 23:5 (2010): 131–155.

Massey, Doreen. *For Space* (London: Sage, 2005).

Matin-Asgari, Afshin. *Iranian Student Opposition to the Shah* (Costa Mesa, CA: Mazda Publishers, 2002).

"Twentieth-Century Iran's Political Prisoners," *Middle Eastern Studies* 42:5 (September 2006): 689–707.

Both Eastern and Western: An Intellectual History of Iranian Modernity (Cambridge: Cambridge University Press, 2018).

Matthee, Rudi. "Transforming Dangerous Nomads into Useful Artisans, Technicians, Agriculturists: Education in the Reza Shah Period," *Iranian Studies* 26:3–4 (1993): 313–336.

McAlister, Melani. *Epic Encounters: Culture, Media, and U.S. Interests in the Middle East since 1945* (Berkeley, CA: University of California Press, 2005).

McFarland, Victor. *Oil Powers: A History of the U.S.-Saudi Alliance* (New York: Columbia University Press, 2020).

McGlinchey, Stephen. *US Arms Policies towards the Shah's Iran* (New York: Routledge, 2014).

McGlinchey, Stephen, and Robert W. Murray. "Jimmy Carter and the Sale of the AWACS to Iran in 1977," *Diplomacy & Statecraft* 28:2 (2017): 254–276.

Members of the Group. "Goruh-e Jazani-Zarifi, pishtaz-e jonbesh-e mosallahaneh-ye Iran," pamphlet published in *19-e Bahman Te'orik*, no. 4 (Tir 1374/June–July 1975).

Menashri, David. *Education and the Making of Modern Iran* (Ithaca, NY: Cornell University Press, 1992).

Mirsepassi, Ali. *Intellectual Discourse and the Politics of Modernization: Negotiating Modernity in Iran* (Cambridge: Cambridge University Press, 2000).

Transnationalism in Iranian Political Thought: The Life and Thought of Ahmad Fardid (Cambridge: Cambridge University Press, 2017).

The Quiet Revolution: Downfall of the Pahlavi State (Cambridge: Cambridge University Press, 2019).

Mitchell, Nancy. *Jimmy Carter in Africa: Race and the Cold War* (Stanford, CA: Stanford University Press, 2016).

Mittelstadt, Jennifer. *The Rise of the Military Welfare State* (Cambridge, MA: Harvard University Press, 2016).

Moaddel, Mansoor. *Class, Politics, and Ideology in the Iranian Revolution* (New York: Columbia University Press, 1992).

"Ideology as Episodic Discourse: The Case of the Iranian Revolution," *American Sociological Review* 57:3 (June 1992): 353–379.

Moallem, Minoo. *Between Warrior Brother and Veiled Sister: Islamic Fundamentalism and the Politics of Patriarchy in Iran* (Berkeley, CA: University of California Press, 2005).

Mo'asseseh-ye Tanzim va Nashr-e Asar-e Emam Khomeini. *Gushe'i az khaterat-e hojjat-ol-eslam seyyed Mahmud Doa'i* (Tehran: Oruj, 1387/2008).

Khaterat-e hojjat-ol-eslam Esma'il Ferdowsipur (Tehran: Oruj, 1389/2010).

Khaterat-e hojjat-ol-eslam Mohammad Hasan Akhtari (Tehran: Oruj, 1392/2013).

Mobasher, Mohsen. *Iranians in Texas* (Austin, TX: University of Texas Press, 2012).

Moghissi, Haideh. *Populism and Feminism in Iran: Women's Struggle in a Male-Defined Revolutionary Movement* (New York: St. Martin's Press, 1996).

Mohajer, Nasser, and Mehrdad Baba Ali. *Beh zaban-e qanun: Bizhan Jazani va Hassan Zia Zarifi dar dadgah-e nezami* (Creteil, France: Noghteh, 1395/2016).

Mohandesi, Salar. "Bringing Vietnam Home: The Vietnam War, Internationalism, and May '68," *French Historical Studies* 41:2 (April 2018): 219–251.

Mohanty, Chandra Talpade. "'Under Western Eyes' Revisited: Feminist Solidarity through Anticapitalist Struggles," *Signs* 28:2 (Winter 2003): 499–535.

Mohit-Tabatabai, ed. *Majmu'eh asar Mirza Malkom Khan* (Tehran: 1327/1948).

Mojtahedi, Mohammad-Ali. "Sokhani darbareh-e Alborz va Bonyad-e Alborz," *Kanun* 10:3 (Shanrivar 1345/1966): 126–131.

Molella, Arthur P., and Scott Ganriel Knowles, eds. *World's Fairs in the Cold War: Science, Technology, and the Culture of Progress* (Pittsburgh, PA: University of Pittsburgh Press, 2019).

Momeni, Esha. "Red Death and Black Life: Media, Martyrdom and Shame," *Middle East Critique* 28:2 (2019): 177–195.

Monroe, Elizabeth. *Britain's Moment in the Middle East, 1914–1971* (New York: Vintage, 1981).

Moradian, Manijeh. *Neither Washington, Nor Tehran: Iranian Internationalism in the United States* (Durham, NC: Duke University Press, forthcoming).

Moradiniya, Mohammad Javad. *Hekayat-e Qasr: Az Qajar ta Pahlavi* (Tehran: Entesharat-e Negah, 1397/2018).

Mottahedeh, Negar. *Whisper Tapes: Kate Millet in Iran* (Stanford, CA: Stanford University Press, 2019).

Mottahedeh, Roy. *The Mantle of the Prophet: Religion and Politics in Iran* (New York: Simon and Schuster, 1985).

Mouvement de Libération des Femmes Iraniennes, Année Zéro. Filmed by Sylvina Boissonnas, Michelle Muller, Sylviane Rey, Claudine Mulard, and Iranian women in Iran and Paris, 1979.

Moyn, Samuel, and Andrew Sartori, eds. *Global Intellectual History* (New York: Columbia University Press, 2013).

Muñoz, José. *Cruising Utopia: The Then and There of Queer Futurity* (New York: New York University Press, 2009).

Muñoz, José, and Lisa Duggan. "Hope and Hopelessness: A Dialogue," *Women & Performance: A Journal of Feminist Theory* 19:2 (2009): 275–283.

Mushar, Khanbaba, ed. *Fehrest-e ketabha-ye chapi-e Farsi* (Tehran: University of Tehran Press, 1337/1958).

Myers, Ella. "Presupposing Equality: The Trouble with Rancière's Axiomatic Approach," *Philosophy and Social Criticism* 42:1 (2016): 45–69.

Naficy, Hamid. *A Social History of Iranian Cinema, Vol. 2: The Industrializing Years, 1941–1978* (Durham, NC: Duke University Press, 2011).

A Social History of Iranian Cinema, Vol. 4: The Globalizing Era, 1984–2010 (Durham, NC: Duke University Press, 2012).

Naghibi, Nima. *Rethinking Global Sisterhood: Western Feminism and Iran* (Minneapolis, MN: University of Minnesota Press, 2007).

Najafpur, Majid. *Az jonub-e Lobnan ta jonub-e Iran: Khaterat-e sardar seyyed Rahim Safavi* (Tehran: Markaz-e Asnad-e Enqelab-e Eslami, 1383/2004).

Najmabadi, Afsaneh. "'Is Our Name Remembered?' Writing the History of Iranian Constitutionalism as if Women and Gender Mattered," *Iranian Studies* 29:1–2 (1996): 85–109.

Women with Mustaches and Men without Beards: Gender and Sexual Anxieties of Iranian Modernity (Los Angeles, CA: University of California Press, 2005).

Nasr, Seyyed Hossein. *Ma'aref-e Eslami Dar Jahan-e Mo'aser* (Tehran: Elmi Farhangi, 1388/2009 [1969]).

Traditional Islam in the Modern World (London and New York: Kegan Paul International, 1987).

Nasrabadi, Manijeh. "'Women Can Do Anything Men Can Do': Gender and the Affects of Solidarity in the U.S. Iranian Student Movement, 1961–1979," *Women's Studies Quarterly* 42:3–4 (Fall–Winter 2014): 127–145.

"Letter from Tehran," www.jadaliyya.com/Details/24067/Letter-from-Tehran.

Needell, Allan A. *Science, Cold War and the American State: Lloyd V. Berkner and the Balance of Professional Ideas* (New York: Routledge, 2012).

Nightingale, Carl. "The Global Urban History Project," *Planning Perspectives* 33 (2018): 135–138.

Nikbakht, Rahim. *Jonbesh-e daneshju-yi-e Tabriz beh revayat-e asnad va khaterat* (Tehran: Sureh, 1381/2002).

Nikpour, Golnar. "Claiming Human Rights: Iranian Political Prisoners and the Making of a Transnational Movement, 1963–1979," *Humanity: An International Journal of Human Rights, Humanitarianism, and Development* 9:3 (Winter 2018): 363–388.

Nunan, Timothy. "'Neither East Nor West,' Neither Liberal Nor Illiberal? Iranian Islamist Internationalism in the 1980s," *Journal of World History* 31:1 (2020): 43–77.

Offiler, Ben. *US Foreign Policy and the Modernization of Iran: Kennedy, Johnson, Nixon and the Shah* (New York: Palgrave Macmillan, 2015).

Organization of the Iranian People's Fada'i Guerrillas (OIPFG). *Pare'i az tajrobiyat-e jang-e chariki-ye shahri dar iran* (n.p.: 1973; republished by Payam-e Fada'i: Organ of the People's Fada'i Guerrillas of Iran (n.p.: 2017)).

Amuzesh-ha'i bara-ye jang-e chariki dar shahr (n.p.: 1974).

Gozareshati az mobareze-ye dalirane-ye mardom-e kharej az mahdudeh! (n.p.: 1978).

Ostovar, Afshon. *Vanguards of the Imam: Religion, Politics, and Iran's Revolutionary Guards* (New York: Oxford University Press, 2016).

Pahlavi, Mohammad Reza Shah. "Sokhanan Shahanshah Farhang o Ayandeye Iran, I," *Mahnameye Amuzesh o Parvaresh (Ta'lim o tarbiat)* 35:2 (Ordibehesht 1344/April–May 1965): 1–7.

"Sokhanan Shahanshah Farhang o Ayandeye Iran, II," *Mahnameye Amuzesh o Parvaresh (Ta'lim o tarbiat)* 35:3 (Khordad 1344/May–June 1965): 1–8.

Beh sooye Tamaddon-e Bozorg (Tehran: Ketabkhaneh Pahlavi, 2536R/1977).

"Mosahebeh-e A'la-Hazarat Shahanshah," *Rastakhiz* (Dey 28, 2535R/January 18, 1977).

"Notq-e Eftetahiyeh-e Shahanshah dar Doreh-e 1354 Majles-e Shura-e Melli va Majles-e Sena: Surat-e Mozakerat-e Majles-e Shara-e Melli," https://bit.ly/2ZiXeuI.

Paidar, Parvin. *Women and the Political Process in Twentieth-Century Iran* (Cambridge: Cambridge University Press, 1995).

Pajoom, Jafar. *Yadnameh Hossein-Ali Rashed, ba Maqalati az Bozorgan-e Adabiyat o Tarikh* (Tehran: Entesharat-e Sokhan, 1387/2008).

Parsa, Misagh. "Theories of Collective Action and the Iranian Revolution," *Sociological Forum* 3:1 (Winter 1988): 44–71.

Social Origins of the Iranian Revolution (New Brunswick, NJ: Rutgers University Press, 1989).

States, Ideologies, and Social Revolutions: Comparative Analysis of Iran, Nicaragua, and the Philippines (Cambridge: Cambridge University Press, 2000).

Phillips-Fein, Kim. *Fear City: New York's Fiscal Crisis and the Rise of Austerity Politics* (New York: Metropolitan Books, 2017).

Pierce, Steven, and Anupama Rao. *Discipline and the Other Body: Correction, Corporeality, Colonialism* (Durham, NC: Duke University Press, 2006).

Qahremani, Mahmud. "Barresi-ye ghavanin-e Iran: Masuliyat az lehaz-e ravanpezeshki" (PhD diss., University of Tehran, 1338/1959).

Qanun-e bujeh-yi sal-e 1345 kul-e kishvar (Tehran: Majles-e Shura-ye Melli, 1345/1961).

Qanun-e bujeh-yi sal-e 1346 kul-e kishvar (Tehran: Majles-e Shura-yi Melli, 1346/1962).

Qasemi-e Pooya, Eqbal. "Tabyin va Tahlil Madares-e Movaffaq dar Amoozesh o Parvaresh Ira Mo'aser," *Ta'lim o tarbiat* 96 (Winter 1387/2009): 201–239.

Rahnema, Ali. *An Islamic Utopian: A Political Biography of Ali Shari'ati* (London: I.B. Tauris, 2014).

Call to Arms: Iran's Marxist Revolutionaries (London: Oneworld Publications, 2021).

Ra'isi, Reza. *Khahar Tahereh: Khaterat-e khanom-e Marzieh Hadidchi (Dabbagh)* (Tehran: Oruj, 1392/2013).

Raffat, Donne. *The Prison Papers of Bozorg Alavi: A Literary Odyssey.* (Syracuse, NY: Syracuse University Press, 1985).

Rafighdust, Mohsen. *Baray-e tarikh miguyam: Khaterat-e Mohsen Rafighdust*, 2 vols. (Tehran: Sureh-ye Mehr, 1393/2014).

Ramazani, R. K. *Revolutionary Iran: Challenge and Response in the Middle East* (Baltimore, MD: Johns Hopkins University Press, 1986).

Rancière, Jacques. *Staging the People: The Proletarian and His Double*, trans. David Fernbach (London: Verso, 2010).

Rashidi, Ahmad. *Obur az shatt-e shab: Khaterat-e Alimohammad Besharati* (Tehran: Markaz-e Asnad-e Enqelab-e Eslami, 1383/2004).

Rejali, Darius. *Torture and Modernity: Self, Society, and State in Modern Iran* (Boulder, CO: Westview Press, 1994).

Richard, Yann. "La fondation d'une armée nationale en Iran," in Jean Calmard, ed., *Entre l'Iran et l'occident: Adaptation et assimilation des idées et techniques occidentales en Iran* (Paris: 1989), 43–60.

Richards, Stephen C. "USP Marion: The First Federal Supermax," *The Prison Journal* 88:1 (March 2008): 6–22.

Richards, Stephen C., ed. *The Marion Experiment: Long-term Solitary Confinement and the Supermax Movement* (Carbondale, IL: Southern Illinois University Press 2015).

Ricks, Thomas M. "Letters to the Editor," *Iranian Studies* 51:6 (2018): 987–990.

Rodgers, Daniel T. *Age of Fracture* (Cambridge, MA: Harvard University Press, 2011).

Rosenberg, John. "The Quest against Détente: Eugene Rostow, the October War, and the Origins of the Anti-Détente Movement, 1969–1976," *Diplomatic History* 39:4 (2015): 720–744.

Ross, Kristin. *May '68 and Its Afterlives* (Chicago, IL: University of Chicago Press, 2002).

Communal Luxury: The Political Imaginary of the Paris Commune (London: Verso, 2015).

Roy, Ananya, and Aihwa Ong, eds. *Worlding Cities: Asian Experiments and the Art of Being Global* (Malden, MA: Wiley-Blackwell, 2011).

Roy, Oliver. *The Failure of Political Islam* (Cambridge, MA: Harvard University Press, 1994).

Rubay'i, Nasir, and Ahmad Rahraw Khuajah. *Tarikh-e zendan dar 'asr-e Qajar va Pahlavi* (Tehran: Entisharat-e Ququns, 1390/2011).

Ruggles-Brise, Sir Evelyn. *Prison Reform at Home and Abroad: A Short History of the International Movement since the London Conference, 1872* (London: Macmillan and Co., 1924).

Sabel, Charles, and Jonathan Zeitlin. "Stories, Strategies, Structures: Rethinking Historical Alternatives to Mass Production," in Charles Sabel and Jonathan Zeitlin, eds., *World of Possibilities: Flexibility and Mass Production in Western Industrialization* (Cambridge: Cambridge University Press, 1997), 1–33.

Sachs, Albie. "Towards a Bill of Rights for a Democratic South Africa," *Journal of African Law* 35 (1991): 21–43.

Sadat-Musavi, Seyed Amir. "Yadnameh-ha: Mirza 'Abd al-Ghaffar Najm al-Doleh az Pishgaman-e Vorud-e 'Olum-e Jadid beh Iran," *Miras-e 'Elmi-e Eslam o Iran* 8 (Fall–Winter 1394/2015–2016): 95–117.

Sadeghi-Boroujerdi, Eskandar. "The Origins of Communist Unity: Anticolonialism and Revolution in Iran's Tri-continental Moment," *British Journal of Middle Eastern Studies* 45 (2017): 796–822.

Sadoul, Georges. "Az Dziga Vertov ta Jean Rouch: Cinéma Vérité va Doorbin-Chashm," trans. Kamran Shirdel, *Negin* 75 (Mordad 1345/ July 1966): 34–37.

Safai-Farahani, A.-A. *An che yek enqelabi bayad bedanad* (n.p.: 1349/1970; online version republished by The Organization for the Unity of the People's Fada'iyan of Iran, Mordad 1381/July–August 2004).

Said, Edward. *Orientalism* (New York: Vintage Books, 1978).

    Covering Islam: How the Media and the Experts Determine How We See the Rest of the World (New York: Pantheon Books, 1981).

Salehi, A. *Esm-e shab: Siahkal (Jonbesh-e Cherik-ha-ye Fada'i-ye Khalq az aghaz ta esfand 1349)* (Spånga, Sweden: Baran, 2016).

Salvatore, Ricardo D., and Carlos Aguirre, eds. *The Birth of the Penitentiary in Latin America: Essays on Criminology, Prison Reform, and Social Control, 1830–1940* (Austin, TX: University of Texas Press, 1996).

Samakar, Abbas. *Man yik shurishi hastam: Khatirat-e zendan va yadbud-e Khosrow Golsorkhi va Keramat Danishian* (Los Angeles, CA: Ketab, 2001).

Sanaie, Mahmoud. "Tarbiat va eqtesad," *Masa'el Iran* 14 (Khordad–Tir 1344/November–December 1965): 91–102.

Sanasarian, Eliz. *Women's Rights Movement in Iran: Mutiny, Appeasement, and Repression from 1900 to Khomeini* (New York: Praeger, 1982).

Sargent, Daniel J. *A Superpower Transformed: The Remaking of American Foreign Relations in the 1970s* (New York: Oxford University Press, 2014).

Sato, Shohei. *Britain and the Formation of the Gulf States: Embers of Empire* (Manchester: Manchester University Press, 2016).

Savin, Richard. *Vakil Abad Iran: A Survivor's Story* (Edinburgh: Canongate/Q Press, 1979).

Schayegh, Cyrus. "Criminal-Women and Mother-Women: Sociocultural Transformations and the Critique of Criminality in Early Post-World War II Iran," *Journal of Middle East Women's Studies* 2:3 (Fall 2006): 1–21.

    Who Is Knowledgeable Is Strong: Science, Class, and the Formation of Modern Iranian Society, 1900–1950 (Berkeley, CA: University of California Press, 2009).

    "Iran's Karaj Dam Affair: Emerging Mass Consumerism, the Politics of Promise and the Cold War in the Early Post-war Third World," *Comparative Studies in Society and History* 54:3 (2012): 612–643.

    "Iran's Global Long 1970s: An Empire Project, Civilisational Developmentalism, and the Crisis of the Global North," in Roham Alvandi, ed., *The Age of Aryamehr: Late Pahlavi Iran and Its Global Entanglements* (London: Gingko, 2018), 262–291.

Schlesinger, Jr., Arthur. *The Imperial Presidency* (New York: Houghton Mifflin, 1973).

Schraeder, Stuart. "Henri Lefebvre, Mao Zedong, and the Global Urban Concept," *Global Urban History Blog* (May 1, 2018): https://globalurbanhistory.com/2018/05/01/henri-lefebvre-mao-zedong-and-the-global-urban-concept.

Seikaly, Sherene. "Egypt's Bread Intifada: On the Subject of the People," filmed February 2015 at Stanford University, Stanford, CA, video, https://cddrl.fsi.stanford.edu/arabreform/events/egypt's-bread-intifada-subject-people.

Sepah-e Pasdaran-e Enqelab-e Eslami. *Ruzshomar-e jang-e Iran va Iraq: Peydayesh-e nezam-e jadid* (Tehran: Markaz-e Motale'at va Tahqiqat-e Jang, 1373/1994).

Sepah dar gozar-e enqelab, 11 vols. (Tehran: IRGC Publications, 1389/2010).

Sepehr, Fereshteh, et al. "Ravand Era'eye Java'ez Ketab dar Iran az aghaz to Konoon," *Fasl-Nameye Motale'at Melliye Ketabdari va Sazemandehiye Etella'at* 27:3 (Fall 1395/2016): 41–56.

Sewell, Jr., William. *Logics of History* (Chicago, IL: University of Chicago Press, 2010).

Shafa, Shojaeddin. *The Pahlavi National Library of Iran: Its Planning, Aims, and Future* (Tehran: 1978).

Shafi'i, Alieh. *Parvaz ba noor: Do revayat az zendegi-ye khanom-e Marzieh Hadidchi (Dabbagh)* (Tehran: Oruj, 1385/2006).

Shahidian, Hammed. "The Iranian Left and the 'Woman Question' in the Revolution of 1978–79," *International Journal of Middle East Studies* 26 (1994): 223–247.

"Women and Clandestine Politics in Iran, 1970–1985," *Feminist Studies* 23 (1997): 7–42.

Shahryari, Parviz. *Masa'el-e mosabeqat riyazi "ba hall" (Konkoor-ha riyazi Shuravi)* (Tehran: Amir-Kabir, 1347/1968).

"The Sparrow (Parastoo)," *Chista* 230 (Tir 1385/June–July 2006): 840–843.

Shahvar, Soli. *The Forgotten Schools: The Baha'is and Modern Education in Iran, 1899–1934* (London: I.B. Tauris, 2009).

Shakibi, Zhand. *Pahlavi Iran and the Politics of Occidentalism: The Shah and the Rastakhiz Party* (New York: Bloomsbury, 2019).

Shannon, Matthew K. *Losing Hearts and Minds: American-Iranian Relations and International Education during the Cold War* (Ithaca, NY: Cornell University Press, 2017).

"Reading Iran: American Academics and the Last Shah," *Iranian Studies* 51:2 (2018): 289–316.

Shawcross, William. *The Shah's Last Ride* (New York: Simon and Schuster, 1989).

Shayegan, Daryush. *Le regard mutilé, Schizophrénie culturelle: pays traditionnels face à la modernité* (Paris: Albin Michel, 1982).

Qu'est-ce qu'une révolution religieuse? (Paris: Albin Michel, 1991).

Cultural Schizophrenia: Islamic Societies Confronting the West (Syracuse, NY: Syracuse University Press, 1997).

Sheikholeslam, Ali. *Ronesans Iran: Daneshgah Melli Iran o Shah* (n.p.: 1369/1990).

Shirdel, Kamran, dir. *Women's Penitentiary* (1965).

Siyasi, Ali-Akbar. *Gozaresh-e yek zendegi* (London: 1987).

Skocpol, Theda. *States and Social Revolutions: A Comparative Analysis of France, Russia, and China* (Cambridge: Cambridge University Press, 1979).

"Rentier State and Shi'a Islam in the Iranian Revolution," *Theory and Society* 11:3 (May 1982): 265–283.

Slobodian, Quinn. *Foreign Front: Third World Politics in Sixties West Germany* (Durham, NC: Duke University Press, 2013).

Smith, Caleb. *The Prison and the American Imagination* (New Haven, CT: Yale University Press, 2009).

Smith, Simon C. *Ending Empire in the Middle East: Britain, the United States, and Post-war Decolonization* (New York: Routledge, 2013).

Snyder, Sarah. *From Selma to Moscow: How Human Rights Activists Transformed U.S. Foreign Policy* (New York: Columbia University Press, 2018).

Sohrabi, Nader. "Historicizing Revolutions: Constitutional Revolutions in the Ottoman Empire, Iran, and Russia, 1905–1908," *The American Journal of Sociology* 100:6 (1995): 1383–1447.

Sohrabi, Naghmeh. "The 'Problem Space' of the Historiography of the 1979 Iranian Revolution," *History Compass* 16 (2018): 1–10.

"Remembering the Palestine Group: Global Activism, Friendship, and the Iranian Revolution," *International Journal of Middle East Studies* 51:2 (2019): 281–300.

Soja, Edward W. "The Socio-spatial Dialectic," *Annals of the Association of American Geographers* 70:2 (1980): 207–225.

Sommer, Vitězslav. "'Scientists of the World, Unite!' Radovan Richta's Theory of Scientific and Technological Revolution," in Elena Aronova and Simone Turchetti, eds., *Science Studies during the Cold War and Beyond* (New York: Palgrave, 2016), 177–204.

Spivak, Gayatri Chakravorty. *Outside the Teaching Machine* (New York: Routledge, 1993).

Death of a Discipline (New York: Columbia University Press, 2003).

An Aesthetic Education in the Era of Globalization (Boston, MA: Harvard University Press, 2013).

Springer, Kimberley. *Living for the Revolution: Black Feminist Organizations, 1968–1980* (Durham, NC: Duke University Press, 2005).

Steele, Robert. "The Pahlavi National Library Project: Education and Modernization in Late Pahlavi Iran," *Iranian Studies* 52:1–2 (2019): 85–110.

Stein, Judith. *Pivotal Decade: How the United States Traded Factories for Finance in the Seventies* (New Haven, CT: Yale University Press, 2010).

Stern, Roger J. "Oil Scarcity Ideology in US Foreign Policy, 1908–97," *Security Studies* 25:2 (2016): 214–257.

Sweig, Julia E. *Inside the Cuban Revolution: Fidel Castro and the Urban Underground* (Cambridge, MA: Harvard University Press, 2002).

Tabari, Azar. "Islam and the Struggle for Emancipation of Iranian Women," in Azar Tabari and Nahid Yeganeh, eds., *In the Shadow of Islam: The Women's Movement in Iran* (London: Zed Press, 1982), 5–25.

Tabatabai, Sadeq. *Khaterat-e siyasi-ejtema'i-ye doktor Sadeq Tabatabai*, 3 vols. (Tehran: Oruj, 1387/2008).

Tafreshi, Morteza Saifi. *Polis-e Khafih-ye Iran, 1299–1320* (Tehran: Ghafnus Press, 1367/1988).

Talebi, Shahla. *Ghosts of Revolution: Rekindled Memories of Imprisonment in Iran* (Stanford, CA: Stanford University Press, 2011).

Talebof-Tabrizi, Abdul-Rahim. *Masalek al-Mohsenin* (n.p.: 1323/1905).

Tavakoli-Targhi, Mohamad. *Refashioning Iran: Orientalism, Occidentalism, and Historiography* (New York: Palgrave, 2001).

Taylor, Keeanga-Yamahtta. *How We Get Free: Black Feminism and the Combahee River Collective* (Chicago, IL: Haymarket Books, 2017).

Teeters, Negley. *Deliberations of the International Penal and Penitentiary Congresses, Questions and Answers, 1872–1935* (Philadelphia, PA: Temple University Bookstore, 1949).

Trioullot, Michel-Rolf. *Silencing the Past: Power and the Production of History* (Boston, MA: Beacon Press, 1995).

Tsing, Anna. "The Global Situation," *Cultural Anthropology* 15:3 (August 2000): 327–360.

Vahabzadeh, Peyman. *A Guerrilla Odyssey: Modernization, Secularism, Democracy, and the Fadai Period of National Liberation in Iran, 1971–1979* (Syracuse, NY: Syracuse University Press, 2010).

A Rebel's Journey: Mostafa Sho'aiyan and Revolutionary Theory in Iran (London: Oneworld Publications, 2019).

Vance, Cyrus R. "Striking the Balance: Congress and the President under the War Powers Resolution," *University of Pennsylvania Law Review* 133 (1984): 79–96.

Vejdani, Farzin. *Making History in Iran: Education, Nationalism, and Print Culture* (Stanford, CA: Stanford University Press, 2015).

Wang, Zuoyue. *In Sputnik's Shadow: The President's Science Advisory Board and Cold War America* (New Brunswick, NJ: Rutgers University Press, 2008).

Wickham-Crowley, Timothy P. *Guerrillas and Revolution in Latin America: A Comparative Study of Insurgents and Regimes since 1956* (Princeton, NJ: Princeton University Press, 1992).

Williams, E. Crawshay. *Across Persia* (London: E. Arnold, 1907).

Williams, Raymond. *Marxism and Literature* (Oxford: Oxford University Press, 1977).

Wimmer, Andreas, and Nina Glick Schiller. "Methodological Nationalism and Beyond," *Global Networks* 2:4 (2002): 301–334.

Wolfe, Audra J. *Freedom's Laboratory: The Cold War Struggle for the Soul of Science* (Baltimore, MD: Johns Hopkins University Press, 2018).

Wu, Judy Tzu-Chun. *Radicals on the Road: Internationalism, Orientalism, and Feminism during the Vietnam Era* (Ithaca, NY: Cornell University Press, 2013).

Yaqub, Salim. *Imperfect Strangers: Americans, Arabs, and U.S.-Middle East Relations* (Ithaca, NY: Cornell University Press, 2016).

Yousefi, Hamed. "Morteza Avini's Avant-garde Populism," in Catherine David et. al., eds., *Iran: Unedited History* (Paris and Rome: Paris Musée d'Art Moderne & MAXXI Roma, 2014), 219–225.

Zarghamee, Mehdi. "Mojtahedi and the Founding of the Arya-Mehr University of Technology," *Iranian Studies* 44:5 (September 2011): 767–775.

Zonis, Marzin. *The Political Elite of Iran* (Princeton, NJ: Princeton University Press, 1971).

Zubaida, Sami. *Islam, the People and the State: Essays on Political Ideas and Movements in the Middle East* (London: Routledge, 1989).

Index

Abrahamian, Ervand, 27–28, 296, 385
activism. *See* diasporic activism
Afghanistan, Soviet Union invasion of, 273–274
Age of Revolution, 43–44
  Islamic Revolutionary Guard Corps after, 207–209
Aghazamani, Abbas (Abusharif), 196
Ahmadzadeh, Masoud, 148–150, 348–349. *See also* Fada'i Guerrillas
  on urban guerrillas, purpose and goals of, 150–155
  on urban toiler, political struggles of, 165–174
Ala'i, Hoseyn, 178–179
Alavi, Bozorg, 77
  Chashmhayash, 69, 73–89
  aesthetic dimensions of, 83–84
  as political novel, 81–83
  themes in, 78–79
  in group of fifty-three, 77
  literary works of, 77–78
  in Tudeh Party, 77, 313
Al-e Ahmad, Jalal, 86
Algerian War of Independence, 181
Allameh Tabatabai, 332
Anjoman-e Hojjatieh, 101–103. *See also* hojjatieh
anti-imperialism, 19
anti-intellectualism. *See bifarhangi*
Antonioni, Michelangelo, 22
Arab nationalism, 181–183
Arab uprisings, 40
Arani, Taqi, 77, 238, 342
archaic, residual concept compared to, 15
Arctic Wildlife Natural Reserve, 269–270

Ardekani, Reza Davari, 380
Arendt, Hannah, 74–103. *See also* banality of evil
Arjomand, Khalil, 342–343
Arjomand, Said Amir, 26
Armed Struggle (Ahmadzadeh), 148
Arms Control Export Act, US (1976), 256
arms sales. *See also* F-16 jets
  of AWACS, 281–287
  Bechtel Corporation and, 283, 285–286
  during Carter administration, 264–265
  during Reagan administration, 282–287
  to Saudi Arabia, 282–284
  US Congressional response to, 283–284
  during Vietnam War, 281–282
  during Carter administration, 261–268
  of AWACS, 264–265
  of F-16 jets, 263–264
  F-15 jets, 274–275
  oil and, links between, 260–261
  between US and Saudi Arabia, 247–248
  of AWACS, 282–284
  Vinnell Corporation, 252–256
Asad, Talal, 375
Ashraf, Hamid, 348–349
assassinations
  by Fada'i Guerrillas, 155–156
  of Sadat, 286–287
Atherton, Alfred, 258–259, 265–266
authoritarianism
  in Golpayegan, 67
  under Pahlavi modernity, 67

439

9 781108 969741